IMAGES of the
NEW JERUSALEM

IMAGES *of the* NEW JERUSALEM

Latter Day Saint Faction Interpretations of Independence, Missouri

CRAIG S. CAMPBELL

THE UNIVERSITY OF TENNESSEE PRESS
Knoxville

"Prayer for a New Name," in chapter 7, reprinted with permission of Danny A. Belrose and the Community of Christ.

First Edition.

This book is printed on acid-free paper.

Library of Congress Cataloging-in-Publication Data

Campbell, Craig S., 1959–
Images of the New Jerusalem: Latter Day Saint faction interpretations of Independence, Missouri / Craig S. Campbell.— 1st ed.
p. cm.

Includes bibliographical references and index.

ISBN 1-57233-312-X (cl.: alk. paper)

1. Independence (Mo.) Region—Church history.
2. Zion (Mormon Church)—History of doctrines.
3. New Jerusalem (Mormon theology)—History of doctrines.
4. Mormon Church—Doctrines—History.
5. Community of Christ—Doctrines—History.
6. Church of Christ (Temple Lot)—Doctrines—History.
7. Church of Jesus Christ of Latter-day Saints—Doctrines—History.
I. Title.

BX8643.Z55C36 2004
289.3'77841—dc22 2004010580

To my academic and intellectual mentors

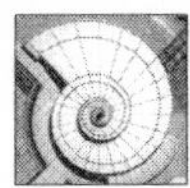

Frederick L. "Rick" Bein
James A. Baldwin
Stanley D. Brunn
Karl B. Raitz
and
James R. "Pete" Shortridge,
who first read this work

Contents

Illustrations

Tables

Preface

The Paradoxes of Independence, Missouri

> Miss Gertrude Stein may have been perfectly right when she said that a dawn can be very beautiful depending on which end of the day you see it from. But surely she was speaking of . . . summer Parisian dawns. A November dawn in Independence was not beautiful, never ever.
>
> —Merle Miller, *Plain Speaking: An Oral Biography of Harry S. Truman*

Merle Miller's quotation above refers to a bad day in the later life of President Harry Truman, the most famous son of Independence, Missouri. Both parts of the quotation can apply to his hometown, where Truman's library and home are located. Much of Independence is unremarkable; it is not marvelously planned or preserved. Typical scenes of this greater Kansas City suburb of over one hundred thousand residents are the deteriorated used car thoroughfare of Truman Road, the many parking lots of the sleepy downtown, the commercial repetition of the Noland Road strip, and the haphazard development along Twenty-third Street. By contrast, part of the city's cultural-historical memory is rooted in a vibrant religious hope related to Truman. The fact that Israel became an independent nation while he was in office has great religious significance to some. That he was the only American president to use atomic weapons in warfare has apocalyptic significance for others. If America has a popular image of Independence, it is the one related to Truman.

Apart from the presidential trappings, another religious heritage exists in Independence—one that transcends the prosaic and is very beautiful, fantastic in fact, depending on "which end of the day you see it from." The most visible clue that Independence holds something out of the ordinary is the seashell-shaped two-hundred-foot spiral rising from the hillcrest just west of Courthouse Square. Cattycornered from the spire is another imposing structure with a large green turtle-shell copper dome. Adjacent is a square building with several dozen delicate columns. These buildings surround a grassy area conspicuous for its openness. Farther southward is another expanse of grass used for a variety of religious and civic activities. To the north of the green is a notable stone church. The look of the most massive building is rather governmental, with that imposing dome. Is the one with the slender columns a library or perhaps a performing arts center? And what of that otherworldly spiral? Something extramundane is afoot here at the intersection of River and Walnut Streets.

This odd landscape comprises several historically related churches, some headquartered here. Their names are mouthfuls: The Reorganized Church of Jesus Christ of Latter Day Saints (now officially called The Community of Christ); and The Church of Jesus Christ of Latter-day Saints; The Church of Christ (Temple Lot). With some exploring, the religious details in Independence become more conspicuous. The Thrift Store of the Reorganized Church on barren Truman Road, pioneer Mound Grove cemetery, and the LDS "Mormon" Mission Home and Stake Center all give hints of a unique and complex religious landscape. Scattered around the town, a variety of other churches can be found that are historically related to, but independent from, the three mentioned above.

This area is regarded as sacred space by hundreds of thousands, if not millions. Joseph Smith Jr., the founder of the Latter Day Saint movement, declared Independence the site of the New Jerusalem in 1831, where a sacred city, the center of Zion, would be built.[1] To be the American counterpart to old-world Jerusalem, Smith prophesied that Jesus Christ would someday return in millennial and glorious advent to Independence, Jackson County, Missouri. This book is a historical interpretation of the millennial geography of Independence and its surroundings as seen by the Latter Day Saint churches.[2]

All Latter Day Saint groups derive from Joseph Smith's original teachings, interpreting to varying degrees his revelations declaring that Independence was to be the center place of Zion. Groups have tried to arrange landscape according to each unique interpretation of doctrine. David Sopher wrote that the importance of religious geography is in "how land provides a record of religious systems, their associated institutions, and the patterns of religiously conditioned behavior" (Sopher 1967:24). Considering Sopher's emphasis, this work is an examination of related but overlapping religious views of millennial place. Perceptions molding the entirety of religious behavior are not uniform in source, nor are they of simple provenance. Brooke, in the introduction to his hermetic interpretation of Latter Day Saint origins (1994:xvi), mentions the importance of understanding that the totality of religion is a combination of leadership directives with the interpretation of those directives by believers. The hinge linking the two levels is usually the interpretation of scripture, biblical or otherwise.

Evolving leadership directives reveal the first tier of official views toward sacred space. For example, Joseph Smith's own architectural drawings for the proposed New Jerusalem city demonstrated evolving, otherworldly scenery. Later leaders of the different groups have interpreted Smith's sacred space in myriad ways, but leadership directives alone are only part of the religious landscape. This work contrasts the official scenery with the more elusive second tier of the perceptions of the common members. The journey on which you are about to embark shows a vernacular geography of the New Jerusalem, where individuals desire to hold their millenarian vision in addition to, or in spite of, official proclamation. The interaction between church directive and common perception brings a greater understanding of the ecology of place belief. Ecology in this sense implies the merging of plural beliefs whether within one group, among members of different groups, or even contrasting with attitudes of the non–Latter Day Saints.

This book focuses on insiders' views, but it is also necessary to balance the different Latter Day Saint experiences with the perceptions of outside groups. Viewpoints of early Missouri Southerners as well as more recent community feeling toward the Latter Day Saint phenomena are investigated. For example, early church leaders created plans on paper and in their minds for a heavenly city with no regard for how the Missourians were using the land in reality. Apparently, meshing an otherworldly plan with the real landscape was not considered a problem—the existing plan for Independence was completely ignored. Views of place exist at the same time as, but at odds with, the reality of others. This lesson was taught in Kollmorgen's (1969) study of the woodsmen's imaginative actions in mistakenly perceiving the dry Great Plains lands as potentially wet and fertile. Like ancient peoples who designed communities as celestial archetypes

(Duncan 1990; Wheatley 1971), the Saints drew up "common geometric forms, [and] discerned the lineaments of a grander pattern corresponding to the heavenly sphere above" (Lane 1988:37). Placing those heavenly patterns on the real ground in the face of westward settlement and burgeoning technology was a task fraught with difficulty.

Many members of today's Latter Day Saint groups visualize an earthly establishment of a divinely planned city, regardless of how Independence or Kansas City are presently laid out. The Latter Day Saint New Jerusalem, as Lane has stated in one of his axioms for sacred place, is an "ordinary" place that is set apart as "extraordinary" (1988:21). The common and profane are transformed into the sacred by historical proclamation by leadership as well as by otherworldly interpretation by the membership (Eliade 1959). The difference with Independence is that varied schisms over the decades have created multiple views of "extraordinary" millennial experience. The pith of this examination is in the overlay of multiple viewpoints toward one site. These perceptual visions exist simultaneously, like many layers of transparencies on an overhead projector that complete the view of the subject.

Cultural geographers devote much time and feeling toward the interpretation of place as a collective mental construct of local or regional surroundings. Kenneth Foote has written that the key to the establishment of a successful place image depends on how well the players (whether individual believers or their collective institutions) make an "interpretive scaffolding" so their vision appears on the landscape in some similar way to how it exists in their minds (Foote 1997:293). Many elements of the Latter Day Saint struggle for millennial utopia were common ideas in the cultural and political formative years of America that still exist as a subset somewhere in our historical identity or national subpsyche, whichever analogy fits. My emphasis is on competing millennial perceptions of different Latter Day Saint groups toward a single site and how their mental scenery has evolved over the last century and a half. More generally, this theme is an overarching example of how different groups of people view the same place in different ways and then act on those beliefs. For present purposes, if acceptance of a place for settlement or survival requires portraying it as mystical, otherworldly, or wondrous, then so be it, but as Porter and Lukerman have stated, images of utopia depend on such elements as "change, equilibrium, time, boundaries, size location, nature, resources, technology, and work" (Porter and Lukerman 1975:205). One cannot separate otherworldly utopia from the material landscape, and how these practical elements of the imagined result in the visible and tangible is a central focus of this study.

Varied interpretations of the local scene range from those of the uninformed outsider to the biased insider, similar to how Lowenthal (1968:72) describes one tourist's view of Twain's Mississippi as a silvery wonder while the local sees in the same scene unrepentant waters of catastrophe and death. Both sides lack needed information to complete the picture. The outsider knows not the danger; the insider knows not the beauty. I have approached this study hoping to be, as best I can, an informed outsider who can see different viewpoints and describe and contrast as objectively as possible. Perfect objectivity eludes the best scholar, however, and vernacular sources of information, whether popular or archival, may precondition the view of place (Lemon 1966; Brown 1943). I have tried, however, to see each scene somewhat like the camera sees: it simply takes a picture, which then has to be interpreted compared to other photos in the series.

The researcher then carefully enters the realm of internal perception, where place is discerned either as a combination of personal feelings and social relations (Tuan 1975), individual psychology and physiology (Lowenthal 1961), or cumulative history (Whittlesey 1929). As David Harvey has summarized, place is viewed with varying levels of "experience," "perception," and "imagination" within specific space contexts (Harvey 1989:220–21). No observer is completely bias-free, but a goal here is to report perceptions from many angles, as objectively as possible, since the different Latter Day Saint groups cannot view each other without bias. The attempt is made to breach the unseen world of Independence for one group. Then the perception of the next group is breached. And then the next. The resulting landscape is arguably postmodern, as "radically different realities may coexist, collide, and interpenetrate" (41). Such multiple perceptions, however, date from the beginnings of modernism in the 1840s, when the original Saints split into factions, and not from the early 1970s, a time often proposed as the end of modernism (39–41).

Also instrumental to the couching of this book is John K. Wright's concepts of how environmental ideas impact thought and action—the term *environmental* here being understood in the loosest fashion (see Lowenthal and Bowden 1976:6; Wright 1966). Latter Day Saint Independence is a play composed of many imagined religious stages, supposed actors, and envisioned props. Some of the envisioned becomes permanently marked on the land, but nothing is marked in a crystal clear manner, be it symbol or structure, to members of other groups of Saints, and the scene may be totally undecipherable to many observers.

In concept, this book has few rivals, perhaps none. Independence manifests a plural dynamic that has not been identified previously, and relating this plurality of views in itself is sufficient. Good description creates the need for more fieldwork and prompts further scholarship. I am hopeful that this work is worthy of acceptance in a small but extraordinary paradigm established by the geographers John K. Wright, David Lowenthal, Walter Kollmorgen, James R. Shortridge, Patrick McGreevy, and Kenneth Foote, who emphasized the influence of collective perception, attitudes, and subjective values in establishing landscapes—and in interpreting imagined ones. Before such works, geography often championed unilateral description in defining a landscape in detail and not necessarily as the result of a multiplicity of viewpoints. Formerly, the basis of our discipline was empirical—landscape *as it is*—in depth where these works uphold varied landscape forms according to the beholder. Simultaneous perceptions are thus held for any particular place at different collective levels. As a result, this work is in part positivist and in part humanist, but here the phenomenological pervades. It deals with the intuitive views of the different groups of participants in the New Jerusalem scene (Johnston 1983:57–58).

Particularly valuable have been the continuum of landscape values laid out by Kenneth Foote in *Shadowed Ground* (1997). According to Foote, stages of sanctification, designation, rectification, and obliteration form landscapes from a genesis of violence or tragedy. These stages were useful in conceptualizing several aspects of Latter Day Saint space and reinforce that the space represents an odd transition from modern to postmodern. For example, how have Latter Day Saints today reconciled the original Missouri expulsion of the 1830s, where Saint land ownership was obliterated, with the modern desire to sanctify territory to differing degrees? Depending upon the group, much irony exists and the Saints' impact on the land is frank and reticent simultaneously. However useful, Foote's themes are more appropriate to landscapes of violence and tragedy in the shorter term. In chapter 9, a broader framework is undertaken; that landscapes of the sacred on a global scale develop according to the stages of validation, delimitation and form, politicization, and conflict mitigation, depending on the world regional contexts of culture.

Shortridge's view (1984, 1985) of the Middle West as a perceptually dynamic and ever shifting collective regional label in the United States was an important foundation to this study, but his work outlined regional perception and values at a broad and innate consciousness, while here prophetic pronouncement has made views of Independence geographically and demographically more limited, though relatively near the perceptual surface of the believers. Belief here is not a motivator hiding somewhere beneath the outer layers of consciousness; it is obvious and nearly tangible, though variable from individual to individual, group to group, and church to church. Yet little of the Latter Day Saint experience has leaked into the surrounding American culture except perhaps in parts of the intermountain West. Perhaps this decided place emphasis is a unique subset of the American exceptionalism that Wilbur Zelinsky (1994:32) and others have discussed. Americans think America has to be different, and Mormons have a place attitude that exaggerates the concept. Instead of an overall perceptual attitude that sweeps the country and varies with location through time, as does Shortridge's Midwest label, the New Jerusalem idea fluxes and wanes, pulsates, if you will, in the center among many different local believers—perhaps only 3 percent of Kansas City's sprawl but about 35 percent of the inhabitants of Independence proper.

The views of Latter Day Saint groups toward Independence also brings to mind studies of the persistence of error in times of exploration, such as the belief in the Open Polar Sea (Wright 1953), a Northwest Passage (Kramer 1964:21–28), or the exaggerated possibilities of waterpower at Niagara Falls (McGreevy 1987). In these examples, error and exaggeration were rife, but the power of such collective mental constructs dictated explorers' paths, routed ocean fleets, and even directed national policies. Similarly, images of the future New Jerusalem over time have persisted, altered, and diverged, always uneasily coexisting with the material world of the Kansas City area. The difference is that the multiple beliefs in Independence are perpetually ahead and have acquired a permanence (if a fluid permanence) *among the believers*—unlike fancied routes proved false by exploration or booster's towns whose lack of growth disappointed expectation. The Saints' religious expectations are less practical. In an economic world, proposed millennial events can always be postponed.

In the field of Mormon Studies other accounts dealing with place, such as Flanders's book on Nauvoo or LeSueur's study of the Mormon War in Missouri, are geographically narrow historical treatises rather than scrutinies of place attitude. For example, Tuveson's *Redeemer Nation* focuses on millennial America as a whole, and Norris's *Dakota: A Spiritual Geography* looks at a place in a purely theological sense. This book is somewhat a subset of Tuveson's work—at an extreme from the national to the central, and from the general to the specific. There are few studies of the Latter Day Saint Missouri experience; this one focuses intently on examining a case from a thorough review of sources, both official and vernacular.[3] A discourse on Mormon history or theology in Independence, Missouri, is not enough—place must be understood from several overlooks. The combination of all views completes a rich perceptual landscape, and, as a powerful and elaborate description of diverse perceptual geographies of a single place, this is a lonely work.

A few themes of religious inquiry recur throughout this book. What follows is informed by the thesis of Jan Shipps that the Latter Day Saint movement is a fundamentally new religious tradition branching out of Christianity. Shipps's focus, however, was on the western LDS Church. Since Independence maintains multiple Latter Day Saint discourses in tantalizing layers, Shipps's thesis is found to lack uniformity throughout the Latter Day Saint families of independent churches, though she does discuss some differences between LDS and RLDS interpretations (Shipps 1985:59). Her views on the LDS experience following trends of recapitulating biblical experience were particularly useful, however, as this tendency appeared much earlier than Shipps proposed (55–59). Also, different smaller Latter Day Saint churches have established their own traditions within the larger doctrinal and historical framework. These traditions are little known and little studied.

Though most of this work was completed over a decade ago as a doctoral dissertation in geography at the University of Kansas, it is sufficiently informed by Grant Underwood's book as to almost be a spin-off (Underwood 1993). In many ways his ideas on the confirmation of the Latter Day Saint movement as premillennial (or millenarian) are extended. A divergence of millenarian beliefs has come about gradually over nearly sixteen decades since Joseph Smith's death in 1844. Though most of the groups involved are still premillennial overall, some have de-emphasized literal millennial events more than others, and the leadership/membership dichotomy becomes a widening gulf. For example, LDS members of the Utah church hold to traditional teachings of the New Jerusalem and wait expectantly as multitudes of temples are built worldwide, but the leadership does not often discuss the subject of millenarian Missouri. The leadership of the RLDS Church has liberalized to a postmillennial or, better stated, a nonmillennial stance. More fundamentalist RLDS members have more or less delicately broken away, claiming that a satanic tide of secularism has gripped the main body of the church. Some of the smaller groups, like the Church of Christ (Temple Lot) have gone the other direction, at times exhibiting supermillenarian traits, even in throwbacks (in Millerite reference) to date-guessing and discussion of imminent unfolding of events that are less common in the larger groups. Though most Latter Day Saint churches focus their millenarian eschatologies on the Americas as divine, most are not as prone to wild apocalyptic speculation as more fundamentalist Christian groups in the country (see Boyer 1992). The smaller groups, however, come closer in this regard. More to the point, the divergence of the splinter millenarian beliefs makes for a needed elaboration on Underwood's thesis that is accomplished here in geographical form, an approach lacking in most modern religious studies.

Since the 1830s, such varied Latter Day Saint millenarian understandings of Independence have naturally altered in geographical scale according to different scriptural interpretations. The Temple Lot Church has taken a lesser stand, for example, seeing the concept of the city of Zion as growing out of a very small area. The LDS group takes a much larger and amplified view of the geography of their millennial space. The spatial view of the RLDS group has become somewhat vague over the last quarter century. The study area is, therefore, not rigidly fixed. The perception of sacred space, depending on the group, ranges from two revered acres in Independence, to adjacent Kansas City, and even to a sizable portion of western Missouri and eastern Kansas. Occasionally, Oklahoma and Iowa enter the mix. Usually the groups get along, but at times they see the other's landholdings as profane. These perceptions correlate rather neatly with the extent and location of each groups' real estate holdings, which have been mapped.

The different groups have developed and applied a variety of symbols to the western Missouri area as a sacred place, both in written literature and in the design of edifices. The Native American, for example, has been an important symbol to all splinter groups since the beginnings of Latter Day Saint history. *The Book of Mormon*, a religious history of the Americas used by most Latter Day Saint groups,[4] is addressed to Native Americans, who are seen as descendants from ancient Hebrews. *The Book of Mormon* refers to them as "Lamanites" and mentions their eventual participation in the building of the New Jerusalem. The Saints originally had an "expansive, almost romantic vision of what lay ahead for the Native American," an idea not at all popular with most European settlers (Underwood 1993:79–81). The symbol of the Native American has since become a crucial element in the many-layered perceptions of the Missouri Zion by all of the major Latter Day Saint groups. It is a recurring theme throughout the book.

Within the city of the New Jerusalem, according to Smith, a temple was to be constructed. This was to be a special structure that Christ would visit and claim at His Second Coming. The original plan evolved into a temple complex with multiple structures. Its final size and function has been widely interpreted by the different Latter Day Saint groups; some see it as one single structure, while others still envision a future complex of temples. Precisely what that temple will be used for is debated. For example, the RLDS Church has recently developed particularly intriguing symbols related to increasingly liberal and democratic directions involving new roles for women in the priesthood and a startling new imagery for Joseph Smith's temple. The symbol of the temple is extremely important to understanding the varied images of the New Jerusalem and is treated accordingly. Other symbols developed by each group are examined in turn.

The organization of the book is generally chronological, with a couple of exceptions. Chapter 1 investigates the origin of New Jerusalem belief. As Brooke wrote, "We have to ask from where these ideas come" (Brooke 1994:xvi), and belief in a physical Zion was a process of millennial ideas that preceded Joseph Smith by several hundred years. Such an approach should in no way be seen as an attempt to undermine faith, as believers can assume God combined preexisting bits and pieces into a combined whole of truth anyway. Chapter 1 also seeks to understand the position of the Saints within the milieu of contemporary American culture.

To best understand the complete picture of Missouri at the time, chapter 2 opens describing the view of the average Missourian contrasted with that of the Latter Day Saint, since the mixture of the two groups provided explosive results. The chapter continues with investigation of Joseph Smith Jr.'s earliest proclamations of the New Jerusalem and the Latter Day Saints' original attempt to establish Zion in Missouri in the early 1830s.

After expulsion from Missouri, the Saints settled in Nauvoo. Many longed for the Missouri Zion and hoped to return. How the Saints interpreted the inability to reestablish their Zion in Missouri is the subject of chapter 3. Chapter 4 details the splintering so important to understanding how later groups of Latter Day Saints began to perceive the establishment of the New Jerusalem in myriad ways. The chapter also details the earliest returns of Latter Day Saint groups to Independence starting in the late 1860s.

Chapter 5 outlines the early perceptions of the Utah Saints toward millenarian Jackson County, Missouri. The early LDS view occurs in a time subsequent to great chafing with the U.S. government over polygamy when millenarian trends became subdued. It also charts the western group's interest anew in things Missourian. The increasing interest in Zion as a historical site and in terms of the acquisition of landholdings is presented in chapter 6. This chapter investigates the typical LDS trend from about 1900 forward where New Jerusalem discussion lessens—while, simultaneously, plans seem to be made for its eventuality.

Chapter 7 examines the modern RLDS movement and schism resulting from a more liberal direction. New ideas and attitudes for Joseph Smith's temple have sprung forth, surprising the most progressive of observers and resulting in the widest variety of schism. Chapter 8 reviews images associated with smaller Latter Day Saint groups who variously see Zion as diminutive, deductive, or profane and lost—only to be saved by God Himself in his own time. The chapter includes modern views of the Church of Christ (Temple Lot), its family of churches, smaller independent groups, and the new churches and associations founded through RLDS dissent.

Since few places in North America hold such vivid images for the believers, chapter 9 compares Independence with the world's sacred places, ancient and modern. Though lacking the depth of history of a Jerusalem, a Cordoba, a Varanasi, or an Ayodhya, Independence is informed by the examples of the premier sacred places of the world. Finally, the last chapter brings together many strands of inquiry in interpreting the simultaneous perceptions of Independence, Missouri, as a rather primitive idea of sacred place brought forth within the milieu of developed, industrialized, secular, and legalistic America.

Wherever in the world John K. Wright is, I hope he enjoys it.

Acknowledgments

I am grateful to a number of people for their contributions to, and support of, this project. In particular, I would like to thank my original dissertation adviser Pete Shortridge for honing my ideas and helping me to think and write with more clarity.

Many thanks to all at the LDS Library and Archives in the Church Office Building in Salt Lake City and to Ron Romig and Patricia Struble at the RLDS Library and Archives in Independence. Many thanks to the University of Kansas System of Libraries, especially the workers in the Kansas Collection. I am in debt to several individuals whose personal contribution I wish to note. Special thanks to William Sheldon of the Temple Lot Church; James Sorgen of the Elijah Message Church; Brad Evans of the Elijah Message Church; Jared Smith of the Elijah Message Church; Richard W. Lawson of the Church of Jesus Christ (Monongahela, Pennsylvania); Ben R. Madison of the Restoration Church of Jesus Christ of Latter Day Saints; Joseph F. Smith, president of the Unity of Restoration Saints; Richard Price of Price Publishing; Nancy Kluth and employees at the Jackson County, Missouri, Courthouse; and the employees of the Map Department at the Clay County, Missouri, Courthouse. Many others shared feelings and ideas, which I considered special or sacred. Herein, I protect their identities, but to a great degree this book is a reflection of their minds and spirits.

Origins of the New Jerusalem

From Edenic to Industrial

And the city had no need of the sun, neither of the moon, to shine in it; for the glory of God did lighten it, and the Lamb is the light thereof.

—Rev. 21:23

Among believers there has always been a dichotomy of symbolic versus literal interpretation of the Bible. As Protestant ways decreased dogmatic trends, individual interpretation of scripture increased. This transformation led to an inevitable split in millennial belief: those who saw Jesus' return as a gradual process that would take place after a millennium (postmillennialism) and those who saw his return as an imminent event that would occur previous to a millennium of peace (premillennialism or millenarianism). Underwood has shown that the Latter Day Saints clearly fall into the latter, millenarian category, despite beliefs and doctrines that have been difficult to classify (Underwood 1993). The millenarian milieu conditioned the views the Saints had of America, which were literal views of Zion and the New Jerusalem. The destiny of America for Latter Day Saints was rarely symbolic.

The concept of America, specifically the United States, as a chosen place of God, dates back to the beginning of European settlement in New England, a time when, as Tuveson observed, the Protestant millenarian paradigm sought to designate biblical places "on maps" (1968:139). The standing of the new continent in God's eyes was the subject of intense scriptural speculation both in England and in early America, where the new continent was often placed "at the center of redemptive history" (Hatch 1977:156). Though members of Latter Day Saint groups are typically religiocentric, believing that the New Jerusalem as an American sacred place originated with Joseph Smith, the idea predates him by two hundred years or more. Early New England was built on a rich heritage of millennial interpretation on America.

America as Chosen

The early Latter Day Saints saw America as a land chosen by God for His elect, just as Judea was chosen for the Israelites. For most Latter Day Saint groups this concept has altered little with time, though perhaps the concept has faded slightly. The Saints did not invent the concept of America as chosen; it surrounded America's Puritan beginnings.

At the turn of the seventeenth century, the Puritan clash with Anglican orthodoxy was well under way in England. In exodus, many of the Puritans in undeveloped America had goals that were ostensibly aimed at duplicating the old cultural system in order to appease the English. In reality, the settlers carved their own niche and reformed religion to their own liking (Miller 1965:100). Though it has been argued that the Puritan experience was not overtly millennial (Brooke 1994:35–36), the ideas of several writers on the Puritan fringe can be seen in early Latter Day Saint thought. Extraordinary events described in Revelation were felt by many early settlers to be unfolding at an unprecedented pace; the question was how they fit into America and how America fit into the chiliasm.

Early writers, in Old as well as New England placed America low on the ladder of millennial importance. The English religious philosopher, Joseph Mede, for example, thought most of the events in the Book of Revelation would pertain to Europe, specifically Rome (Tuveson 1949: 76–79). Through the 1600s, as a vast land of unrefined savages, America's millennial role was at times even cast as devil's advocate. When the final decisive battle of Gog and Magog would take place, Mede conjectured that American Indians "might do" as a source for the forces of Satan's last gasp (Davidson 1977:53–54). The unsettled forest appeared, to Mede and his peers, a "Devil's Den" where the Indians were "not merely heathens but . . . horrid sorcerers and hellish conjurers" (Smith 1970:4; Nash 1982:36). The Puritan Increase Mather did not generally hold much millennial hope for the recent settlers. As the prophecies unfolded, America would "be Hell . . . and New England the wofullest place in all America" (Davidson 1977:65).

In the early part of the seventeenth century, untamed New England was not much of a haven, but with more than a foothold on American shores, not everyone agreed with Mede's speculations. Some began to see America in a more positive light, supporting the belief that even though they had been "under the control of the Devil," Native Americans were "of the stock of the lost tribes of Israel," a hopeful credence originating with Spanish missionary beliefs in the 1500s. The view would not be mainstream in nascent America (Glacken 1967:361, 367; Underwood 1993:78–81). In 1633, Roger Williams rejected the idea that the settlers had received their New England "by pattent from the King" and stated the rebellious idea that "natives are the true owners of it," probably more to offend the British than to glorify the native (Miller 1965:214–15). In some cases, millennial accounts appeared supposedly written by Native Americans themselves. One document was titled *Apocalypse of Chiokoyhikoy, Chief of the Iroquois* (Tuveson 1968:113–16). In it, a vision describes a people who would rise up on American soil, be an agent for blessed revolution, after which "the supreme god" will return, subsequently bringing "good times." Speculation exists as to the real author, but certainly the clairvoyance proposed for the Native American here is remarkable. This view was unpopular on the American scene, but the Native American would play a crucial and positive role in the millennial world of Latter Day Saint groups.

Scholar of the Puritan movement Perry Miller further emphasized the effect of tendencies to view American circumstances positively—and with a prophetic bent—as the elders had "some anxious moments as they turned the pages of their Bibles to find parallels between the Israelites' occupation of Canaan and the Massachusetts settlement" (1965:214–15). America, in terms of both people and land, was steadily gaining favor as a special and independent entity and not simply a Puritan extension of England.

Around the turn of the eighteenth century, prophetic attitudes toward North America were further altered. William Stoughton, known for taking a lead in a number of witchcraft trials, wrote the oft-quoted "God sifted a whole nation that he might send choice grain over into this wilderness" (Miller and Johnson 1938:246). Cotton Mather differed with his father, Increase, and believed that America would not be cast off and, particularly meaningful to later followers of Joseph Smith, might even become a "refuge for the saints" where "His divine providence hath irradiated an Indian wilderness" (Davidson 1977:61; Miller and Johnson 1938:163). The previous dark attitudes toward the new land eventually gave way to a glowing view of the wilderness and its native inhabitants. New England minister Nicholas Noyes followed the belief that the American Indians were descended from Noah and thought Mede's negative interpretation was far-fetched. Samuel Sewall wondered whether America might be the "New Jerusalem, or part of it." This was the most providential view yet on America's millennial destiny (Davidson 1977:65). Around 1740, Jonathan Edwards taught that the preparatory work toward the Second Coming of Jesus would begin in America (Weber 1983:13–14).

Whereas Mede had thought of America as the repository for Satan's forces in the 1620s, by 1700 Cotton Mather favored the positive spiritual aspects of America and Samuel Sewall was describing the decline of "Antichristian" forces there. The turnabout in attitude was complete by the time of the Revolutionary War. Salem minister Samuel West, for example, described America as the leader in an attack on the Antichrist, which was assumed (naturally) to be England (Davidson 1977:66–67, 245–50). In 1777, West preached that in America

> pure religion will revive and flourish among us in a greater degree than ever it has done before: that this country will become the seat of civil and religious liberty; the place from which Christian light and knowledge shall be dispersed to the rest of the world; so that our Zion shall become the delight and praise of the whole earth, and foreign nations shall suck of the breasts of her consolations, and be satisfied with the abundant light and knowledge of Gospel truth which they shall derive from her. (Davidson 1977:250)

This basic philosophy is applicable to Latter Day Saint beliefs even to the present day. LDS leaders particularly have often taught of America as a repository of worthiness and therefore an example for the entire globe. America's "sins" of crime, murder, drug use, etc. are ironic to the place-as-purity stance and are usually interpreted as the results of divine free agency. That the United States contains the "most righteous" as well as the "most evil" of all people is a thread commonly heard in LDS circles.

From Celestial to Material

The origin of the term *New Jerusalem* comes from the New Testament book of Revelation: "Him that overcometh will I make a pillar in the temple of my God, and he shall go no more out: and I will write upon him the name of my God, and the name of the city of my God, which is new Jerusalem, which cometh down out of heaven from my God: and I will write upon him my new name" (3:12). A variety of rich interpretations exist for this verse and also for Revelation, chapter 21, where the heavenly city is described in some detail. Early interpretations saw the New Jerusalem as symbolic of God's gradually expanding work on earth, not as an actual place. For example, a group of Englishmen, called the Seekers, believed in the coming of a new dispensation and a New Jerusalem but saw that advent in more abstract, even mystical, form (Brooke 1994:22). Millenarian trends, however, gradually lent solidity to the place, as scripture was interpreted more literally and biblical prophecies seen as generally concrete (Underwood 1993:63–64).

The earliest manifestation of the New Jerusalem as a real place, and not a symbolic one, was exhibited as early as the late second century with the followers of Montanus, who awaited the coming of a literal New Jerusalem to western Asia Minor, but by contemporary standard such beliefs were too worldly (Weber 1999:43; Underwood 1993:16). Since the time of the Crusades, many thought the New Jerusalem that would "come out of heaven" would be a reinvention of the Old Jerusalem at the same place (Boyer 1992:51; Brooke 1994:97). In the 1500s, Englishman Thomas Brightman taught of the coming of a New Jerusalem that was more than metaphorical (Underwood 1993:18), but for Joseph Mede, the millennial New Jerusalem was undoubtedly to be separate from the Old Jerusalem and located in Europe; he even described it as having "some kind of equivalent of organized government," a strange concept to postmillennial views, which saw earthly government as useless in the heavenly realm. "All formal order would be unnecessary" in that great future city (Tuveson 1949:87–89). Some Protestant groups naturally interpreted their own towns as New Jerusalems. One particular Anabaptist group wished to transform the German city of Münster into a New Jerusalem in the early 1500s, a rather different task than that of the Latter Day Saints, who wished to make a literal heavenly city out of one barely established, rough, American frontier town (Brooke 1994:14).

Mede mentioned that the nations of the earth would walk in the light of the New Jerusalem, but he did not postulate its place. Similarly, John Cotton in 1647 did not designate a site when writing of the "visible state of a new Hierusalem, which shall flourish many years on earth before the end of the world" (Vogel 1988:192). Later, Samuel Sewall asked only vaguely if America might not be part of the New Jerusalem.

Adding to the confusion is the description in Revelation, chapter 21, that the city would measure 12,000 furlongs (1,500 miles), which leaves plenty of room for speculation. That the measure could be interpreted as relating to the distance along the total circumference of the city or along one of its sides (375 miles) is a moot issue. By any interpretation, a huge entity is described, perhaps one where immense size was only symbolic of spiritual strength, yet Increase Mather's "New Jerusalem," written in 1687, emphasized that since the city is described as coming out of heaven, the implication was a real earthly place (Zamora 1982:103–4). Most writers even today see this as a heavenly state coming to earth at the location of Old Jerusalem.

Still, New England Puritan clergy circa 1700 were reluctant to assign a location to the New Jerusalem any more precise than America in general. The term *New Jerusalem* was used symbolically. It represented a heavenly condition and was not usually seen as an actual city. Rather, it was to be a gathering place of the righteous, the "visible" Kingdom of God, and a state of mind or being (Tuveson 1968:53–59; Vogel 1988:191–92). For example, Emanuel Swedenborg's eighteenth-century New Jerusalem Church lacked specificity. Here the New Jerusalem was a spiritual state of being lacking physical attributes (Swedenborg 1857:9–16), yet his ideas of a spiritual world paralleling this real one may have had later fruition in the Latter Day Saint beliefs of a primary spiritual creation and spirit world where people go after they die but before a resurrection (Brooke 1994:96).

In terms of location, the purpose of the Puritan's "errand in the wilderness" on behalf of God was also generally obscure. Emphasized was the covenant, a two-way pact with God, kept by observing the proper Puritan life. In return, God was "under obligation to supply grace" to those who kept the contract (Miller 1956:10, 85). In America, the Puritans saw themselves in biblical terms as a light shining in the wilderness, or in Jesus' words, "a city set on a hill" (Matt. 5:14; Miller, 1956:11). The "city" may simply have signified a proper Christian attitude, but some preferred to interpret it as an actual location, so a characteristic Puritan town plan was created. Stilgoe (1976) discussed the geography of a village composed of concentric circles that placed the church meetinghouse in the center of Puritan community life (Figure 1). The innermost circles of the plan were residential, followed by common fields for industry and livestock management. The middle rings were divided between families of greater estate and other free-standing farms. The outermost ring of the town pattern was profane space used for swamps, rubbish, and waste, and, beyond this, the dreaded wilderness. No roads were mentioned in the model, thus the isolation of such pastoral settlements was prominent, even while standing as a model for settlements westward—symbolic New Jerusalems across the inhospitable wilderness (Zamora 1982:102). In hindsight, the Puritan model lent little to the Latter Day Saint experience, though the view of a religious place as both a pastoral garden and an urban center is a guiding concept that reoccurs in Puritan, Shaker, and Latter Day Saint religious landscapes (Wood 1991).

In a region as free in thought as America, some interpreted the meaning of "new Jerusalem" symbolically, others, literally. As will be seen,

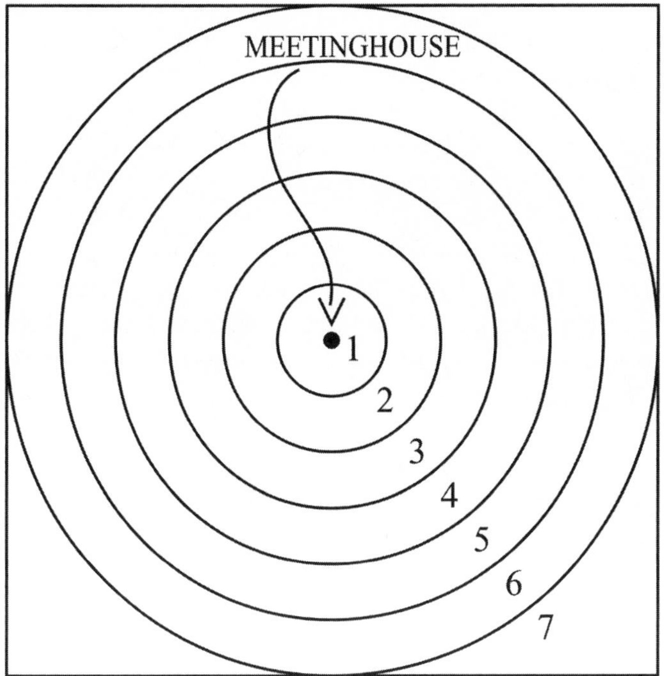

1. Central residences
2. Common fields for industry
3. Livestock management
4. Estates of the wealthy (400 acre lots)
5. Larger farms
6. Swamps and rubbish; waste grounds
7. Wilderness

FIG. 1 | *The idealized Puritan town plan.*

the Latter Day Saint movement preferred specifics, as did other utopian groups, and the appearance of God's kingdom in Isaiah 2:3, where "out of Zion shall go forth the law, and the word of the Lord from Jerusalem" was not seen as "Hebrew poetic parallelism"; rather, it was seen as two distinct locations (Underwood 1993:63; see also Zamora 1982:98). The rise of the view of America as a chosen place, the New Jerusalem (now capitalized, whereas in Revelation the "new" is not), also corresponds in time with the emergence of New England's growing economic and political clout. Ambitions for the New World were great, and, in general, discussions regarding the holy millennial place gradually turned more tangible and specific. They also were urban and distinctly non-Jeffersonian. Samuel Sewall posited the theory that America could be the "Seat of the Divine Metropolis"; he supposed its location might be in Mexico. Sewall's theory caused considerable consternation and, for a time, drew the millennial gaze of a number of prominent New Englanders southward and away from problems associated with independence from England. In troubled times, as will be seen in Latter Day Saint experience, forecast spiritual events are conveniently projected to distant times—and to distant places. When confronted with the idea that the New Jerusalem might be in Europe, Sewall expressed natural American bias. While describing the grand yet humble nature of the holy city, he stated that "God will as readily tabernacle in our Indian wigwams" as enter into spacious European buildings (Davidson 1977:66–70). Considering the Revolution, such views for this side of the Atlantic were to be expected.

Cotton Mather had speculated on the establishment of the New Jerusalem in America, also thinking it might be located outside of New England, or possibly farther west. Mather wrote that in "the brave Countries and Gardens which fill the American Hemesphere our Glorious Lord will have an Holy City in America; a City, the Street thereof will be Pure Gold" (Vogel 1988:193). Note that Mather used the terms *garden* and *city* in concert. The blending of urban and paradisiacal realms is evident, and this irony would tinge Latter Day Saints and other groups perceptually split between the importance of the balance between the urban East Coast and the Anglo penetration of the West (Wood 1991:32, 41–42). In 1785, a pamphlet of unknown authorship and origin entitled *The Golden Age* ("Celadon" is the author's fictitious name) described a vision of America from a high place centrally located in North America (Marx 1964:105–7). The beauties and grandness of the new American republic were described, as were its chiliastic qualities. In the pamphlet, western America is a land to where the persecuted will flee. Jews are described as gathering to America, the New Canaan, to establish a New Jerusalem (Vogel 1988:193). The abstract promise of the glory of a newly settled area was sufficient for most readers, but surely others imagined that if the old Jerusalem was material, the new one should be as well.

During colonial times, the New Jerusalem, true to the verse in Revelation, was almost always seen as "coming down" from heaven, which gave credence to specific locale. New Englanders rarely thought of it as being built on earth by people, but with the birth of a new American nation, more emphasis was given to building up the new country, so ideas of a tangible millennial construction became popular. The concept of a New Jerusalem as an American millennial form was speculated upon at least two centuries before the time of Joseph Smith. As a new American civilization emerged, such speculation increased, and the term *New Jerusalem* became a handy banner to express the country's ambitions and sense of Manifest Destiny, especially among fringe religious groups.

The New Jerusalem in Upstate New York

The early leaders of the Latter Day Saints were New Englanders who found themselves in the midst of this New Jerusalem speculation. Specific religious information that Joseph Smith could have utilized in the restoration of all things came from two general sources. First, there was a substrate of radicalized religious credence in New England and, in particular, southern Vermont, where Smith, Brigham Young, and many other original Saints were born, which contributed many ideas to the foundation of the Latter Day Saint movement. As we have seen, such ideas included teachings on the establishment of an American Zion, on a possible New Jerusalem, and on the lost ten tribes of Israel, among other increasingly millenarian themes. These were in the culture and mindset of the people long before Smith's birth in Sharon, Vermont, in 1805. Second, many events and movements contemporary to Joseph Smith influenced doctrinal development.

An example of substrate influence contemporary to Joseph Smith's family in Vermont was one group led by Nathaniel Wood in Middletown circa 1790. Wood's group was called the New Israelites, whose doctrine included ideas that God's chosen land was America, where a New Jerusalem would be established. A temple was constructed and the group, which may have included Joseph Smith Sr. and family members and friends of future Latter Day Saints, finally looked forward to January 14, 1802, a day of reckoning when a "Destroying Angel" would bring devastation (Brooke 1994:57–58). Followers were advised to give of their wealth "to pave the streets of the New Jerusalem," but, predictably, the group broke up after the advent failed (Marini 1982:54–55).

Other events in western New York contributed, directly or indirectly, to the New Jerusalem theme of the Saints. In 1825, Mordecai M. Noah, a well-known Jewish writer/politician dedicated the city of Ararat on Grand Island just north of Niagara Falls as "A City of Refuge for the Jews" (Jewish Virtual Library 2003). Noah's purpose was to heighten prospects for the restoration of the Jewish nation, so America had become a Zion in the traditional, not solely the Christian, sense. He taught that Native Americans were descendants of the lost tribes of Israel, making his location even more a culmination as a Jewish haven. Additionally, the Niagara Falls region with its promise of saving power, whether natural or electrical, has been documented as a place where grandiose dreams were propagated by a multitude of boosters. It is not coincidence that Niagara would anchor the western edge of "the burned-over district" (see McGreevy 1987).

Joseph Smith officially organized a church in upstate New York just southeast of Rochester in 1830. From the late 1700s up until about 1850, this region was the center of extreme religious competition and communitarian creativity (Cross 1950). Here, utopian experiments were common and often couched in a millenarian tone. So were discussions of how the New Jerusalem might be established by the faithful. Many of these ideas were carried on by Joseph Smith and the Latter Day Saint experience.

In particular, Joseph Smith encountered Quaker-derived utopian groups for whom the idea of a New Jerusalem was quite concrete. Some early converts came in from Quaker and Shaker backgrounds, so Smith and his followers undoubtedly had heard varied views on the subject (*Doctrine* 1981:49). Jemima Wilkinson established one group in 1787, a community called Jerusalem located on the central western side of Seneca Lake (Cross 1950:33, 328). Later, Wilkinson's experimental community moved to Keuka Lake, only forty miles from Palmyra, Joseph Smith Jr.'s home. Wilkinson's Jerusalem, or New Jerusalem, as it was often called, was established as a communal "new Zion" and was among the earliest of upstate New York's social group experiments (Bloch 1985:167; Cross 1950:143, 328; Hudson 1974:9).

A second major contribution to the New Jerusalem theme of the Latter Day Saints came from the Shaking Quakers of Mother Ann Lee, who established their New Lebanon settlement in eastern New York just across the state line from Pittsfield, Massachusetts. To the Shakers, the Messiah's Second Coming had occurred in the form of Mother Ann, and her presence signified the beginning of the millennium on earth and the union of earth with heaven (Kephart 1976:159–61). This settlement was begun about the same time as Wilkinson's Jerusalem, and the Shakers were mentioned specifically in Latter Day Saint scripture (*Doctrine* 1981:49). Soon after Joseph Smith Jr. moved the headquarters of the church to Kirtland, Ohio, the Saints eventually sent a revelation to the Shaker group not far away in Cleveland (the neighborhood is still called Shaker Heights), warning that Smith would yet assemble Zion at a specific place, but the Shakers appear to have been unmoved by the Latter Day Saint urgings (*Doctrine* 1981:49:25). Since the Shakers thought that the millennium was already in force, they designed their communities and conducted their ceremonies as if heavenly patterns were inevitably blending with the earthly realm. Lane's words (1988:132) that "they lived in two worlds with equal vigor" are apropos.

The Shakers tried to produce the New Jerusalem in their very midst by tirelessly adhering to an orderly plan. An emulation of the Holy City of Jerusalem was required, and the layout of Shaker towns, fields, and gardens was kept rectangular, conforming to a design perceived as heavenly (Fletcher 1977:38; Lane 1988:134). The people tried to live in such efficiency as to usher along the millennium; any tool or invention that saved time was readily accepted. Community members danced energetically in patterns thought to conform to the symmetry of the heavens, and sometimes even normal physical movements were abbreviated to increase efficiency and enhance simplicity. For example, Shakers avoided the nonorthogonal act of reaching diagonally across the meal table.

Shakers' views of a New Jerusalem were more often experienced in dreams and visions than in drawn plans. The Shakers were not planners in the graphic sense of the word, but one member of the New Lebanon community drew a map of the "Holy City with Its Various Parts" in 1843 that consisted of an intriguing geometry of circles and squares in a pastoral Puritan-like setting (Lane 1988:145; Figure 2). "There were buildings on either side of the street, all white as snow, flanked by rows of tall maple trees." For this particular believer, the pleasures of the vegetable gardens

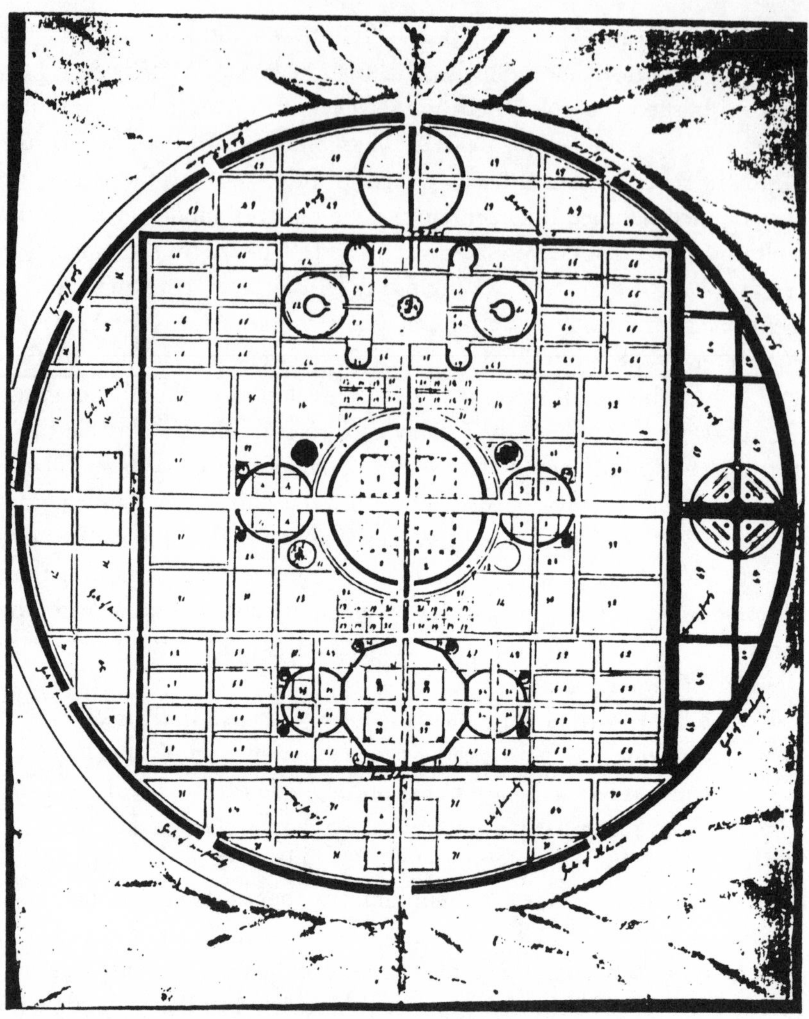

FIG. 2 | *"Explanation of the Holy City" of the Shakers, dated March 1843. Concrete interpretations of heaven literally designed on earth were sometimes seen before Joseph Smith Jr.'s day. Reprinted, by permission, from* Philadelphia Museum Bulletin *57, no. 273 (spring 1962):95.*

"ripe with herbs in early spring," linked heaven with a lush Edenic setting (Lane 1988:139). De Pillis's (1960) thesis stresses the importance of Shaker influence on Latter Day Saint beginnings, but since this particular Shaker plan appeared a decade subsequent to Joseph Smith's 1833 "plat of Zion," a reverse influence from Latter Day Saints to Shakers could also be asserted.

From Edenic to Pastoral

Geographers Porter and Lukerman wrote that all utopian experiments could be placed on a continuum between the Garden of Eden in the book of Genesis and the New Jerusalem of Revelation (Porter and Lukerman 1975:199). The Latter Day Saint experience, then, can be seen as the epitome of a utopian ideal. They tried to pack both extremes into one place in Missouri, which did not work in the 1830s but has created since an extremely satisfying, for the scholar at least, combination of juxtaposition and competition among related groups.

The Shaker contrast between a "city plan" for the New Jerusalem versus the concept of New Jerusalem as a "dream garden" exhibits this dichotomy and merits more attention. Here lies both a union and conflict of ideals that is compelling, since later groups of Latter Day Saints would have difficulty imagining the mesh of an otherworldly millenarian plan with the established real world layouts of Independence, Missouri, and greater Kansas City. The themes of an American wilderness, pastoral setting, and garden are all important for the Saints' New Jerusalem. Equally important were the burgeoning images of urban/industrial life. In the rhetorical, how much park or wilderness would be planned into a millennial New Jerusalem? How much industrial land? How would such a celestial city function economically? To answer these questions, the Saints drew from varied landscape images.

Studies of early attitudes toward the American landscape have been popular in a broad range of disciplines since World War II. Leo Marx (1964) described the pervasive American pastoral image as continually interrupted by noisy contraptions in the eighteenth and nineteenth centuries, and his book is appropriately entitled *The Machine in the Garden*. Roderick Nash (1982) described changing views of American attitudes toward wilderness, from feared and hated in Puritan times to highly valued later. The attitude shift is intricately interwoven with new patterns of industry, urbanization, and transportation. Henry Nash Smith closely followed the theme of the "garden of American agrarianism" with a "new calculus" of urban intrusion into the frontier. According to Smith, urban influences were already altering life in the West "by the 1830s" (1970: 155–56) when the Latter Day Saint movement was gaining steam.

Cincinnati was John Jakle's (1977) prime example of urban encroachment into the pastoral garden, and his work used traveler's accounts to reconstruct urban images intruding on the pastoral scene. Yi-Fu Tuan

(1986:25–78) presented a variety of cross-cultural views of what constitutes a "good life," whether from rural and pastoral perception or from bourgeois urban lifestyles. He does not attempt to interpret or search for clues of the good life of industrial, blue-collar factory workers, but such lifestyles have often been romanticized.

These scholars have all interpreted American culture as a contrast between the garden/pastoral setting and the urban/industrial one. All portray technology invading the garden, distorting the Arcadian attitude, and making the interpretation of landscape an ambiguous challenge. Frontier people were caught off-guard by the rapidly changing mixture of ideals. The contrast is important among garden, pastoral, and urban/industrial modes because all three compete for expression in the development of Joseph Smith's New Jerusalem.

The Garden in the Wilderness

Though not written as an official revelation, Joseph Smith declared Jackson County, Missouri, as the original location of the Garden of Eden. During his first visit there, he generously described Jackson County's gardenlike attributes (Roberts 1978:197–98). Later, when the Saints were driven from the county, an analogy with the expulsion of Adam and Eve from the biblical Eden was prompted. Both removals were interpreted as the result of disobedience. Different Latter Day Saint groups even today have maintained this tendency to view aspects of early history as "imprinting" scripture on the landscape.

The image of the earth as a garden place is an ancient theme. Its earliest expressions are obscure, but Glacken has written of the evolution of some of the meanings of the Judeo-Christian "garden." In Genesis, chapter 2, man (Adam) is placed as a caretaker to tend the Garden of Eden. Glacken (1967:153) explained, "the vocabulary of the myth is that of a peasant farmer; the plants are domesticated and the gardener of Eden tends them, perhaps removing the weeds, but he is a caretaker, not a farmer."

Tuan has discussed how in the Garden of Eden time stopped; since Adam and Eve were immortal, there was no decay. It was not until long after their dismissal from Eden that illness was gradually introduced to the body. With regard to life in Eden and in the subsequent wilderness, "Adam and Eve . . . would not have known death, Methuselah lived to be 969 years old, but thereafter life spans declined until the normal expectation was only three score and ten" (Tuan 1986:31–32). Such halting of time is symbolically sought in any garden re-creation, and the Latter Day Saint Jackson County is no exception.

Chapter 2 of Genesis contains a vague account of the location of the garden and of the four rivers that flowed out from it. This description has caused much geographical speculation by people anxious to locate the Garden of Eden in or near native soil (Glacken 1967:164). With the proximity of the Kansas and Missouri Rivers, the Saints in Independence imagined their Eden within a prediluvian biblical reinterpretation of the Mississippi River Valley. Noah's arc in the Latter Day Saint scenario departed from somewhere in western Missouri and came to rest somewhere in the "old" world, Ararat or otherwise.

During the Middle Ages the Garden of Eden was reported as a perfect and ideal location. According to Isidore, "paradise" was at such a height that the floods of Noah's time failed to reach it. Thus, the preserved garden had an eternally temperate climate—latitude and adiabatic rates aside. Paradise was "conspicuous for health, fertility, [and] lushness of vegetation" (Glacken 1967:273). St. Thomas Aquinas stated that the location of the Garden of Eden was probably eastward, "the most excellent part of the earth," since the east is "the right hand on the heavens" in some isolated place. The care of pleasure gardens at home became popular in the Middle Ages, simulating the tending of the Garden of Eden; it recapitulated the beginning myth of human origins (348). The founding of monasteries in remote locations was also symbolic of having tamed wilderness and carved out paradise (306–7). The New Jerusalem in Missouri was to be such a haven garden forged amid wilderness, yet the view was also different from that of early Christian writers. Early views had remnants of paradise existing in isolated highland locales. For the Latter Day Saints, the flood had destroyed the garden, but the vegetation and climate of western Missouri was still imagined with Edenic qualities.

Though always in close proximity, garden and wilderness were seen as mutually exclusive; Eden was "the antipode of wilderness" (Nash 1982:15). The discovery of the New World made it possible for Europeans to dream of a new paradise to the west. At the beginning of European settlement on North America's coasts, the continent was still largely an uninterrupted wilderness. The Creator's will was to be accomplished "by conquering the heathen savage to evolve a garden in the wilderness," but even in early times explorers and writers were loath to apply any adverse values to the great expanse (Jakle 1977:120; Nash 1982:25). On a 1584 voyage to Virginia, Capt. Arthur Barlowe typically constructed an image of the land as a plentiful garden, full of all the necessities for the good life (Marx 1964:36–39). Thus, the new continent became a repository for English, if not greater European, hopes and ambitions. It was in this context that utopian experiments and American New Jerusalems could most effectively be imagined.

In the Revolutionary War era literary views of the land as a garden continued to predominate. John Filson wrote of Kentucky as "like the land of promise, flowing with milk and honey, a land of brooks of water . . . a land of wheat and barley and all kinds of fruits" (Smith 1970:129). With such biblical terminology, the interior of the continent became "the garden of the world" in the imagination of the American people (123, 129). The center of what was to become the United States developed a mythical aura that surely *someone* would eventually take literally. It is no surprise that such descriptions are similar to those of 1830s Missouri by the first Latter Day Saint settlers in Jackson County.

Throughout the nineteenth century, primitivism was an important element of the vast American garden. Time seemed to stop in this Eden, and settlers often reverted to simpler technologies. Joseph Smith in early 1831 lamented the backward and uncivilized character of the non–Latter Day Saint Missourians (Roberts 1978:189). The contrast explains much of the clash between Mormon and Missourian. In a more positive view, Henry Nash Smith (1970:75) pointed out that life on the Texas Great Plains was once described as "a New Eden of unsophisticated life where the antelope are so tame they walk up to sniff the saddles . . . thrown upon the grass." Whether viewed positively or negatively, the issue of primitivism is prevalent in the American garden.

In his five-panel 1836 landscape painting *The Course of Empire*, Thomas Cole depicted a cycle moving from wilderness, to a pastoral setting, to a glorious civilization, which then is invaded by savages and taken back to a wilderness stage (Nash 1982:81–82). The painting reflects the uncertainty of values that existed toward rural land use in the early 1800s. It was contemporary with Latter Day Saint persecutions in frontier Missouri and accurately reflected the divided nature of settlement there. If frontier America was in the pastoral section of the cycle, then was the approach of urban civilization a good thing? Wilderness was the beginning and ending theme, yet the return of wilderness would indicate either that civilization was in retreat or that the wilderness state was the norm.

In a summary of contemporary thought in the early 1800s, Nash wrote that "anticipations of a second Eden quickly shattered against the reality of North America," yet there is no mistaking that the theme of millennial hope and religious "mission" were consistently apparent (Nash 1982:25; see also Merk 1963:266). Wilbur Zelinsky explained that the theme of mission, or, in his words, "messianic perfectionism," has been common in American life:

> From the very beginning of serious settlement along the Atlantic Seaboard, potent strains of a visionary perfectionism were mingled with more mundane economic and political considerations, and not only in the New England colonies. In this errand into the wilderness, there was a quite conscious attempt to seek out or build a New Zion—later the New Athens or New Rome—the City upon the Hill, or quite literally, an earthly Eden with a Manifest Destiny. (1973:62)

This is particularly apropos to the Latter Day Saint experience, though compared to others the Latter Day Saints tended to define their visionary perfectionism more concretely. Marx (1964:74) wrote that the American continent "has been capable of carrying an immense burden of hope." The hope of the early Latter Day Saints became more fixed as the Old Testament was read. Isaiah (51:3) declared that God would comfort Zion "and make her wilderness like Eden, her desert like the Garden of the Lord." It was inevitable that a variety of interpretations regarding America as a Garden of Eden would surface. Those views were almost always set within a context of wilderness or decay. Such thinking was ingrained in the western, Christian civilization. The Latter Day Saints were only slightly unusual in taking such promises literally. They were among the most ardent at applying the theme to a particular place, with rich biblical imagery intact.

Jackson County, Missouri, was the most prominent but not the only site to be seen as the Garden of Eden in early America. A Methodist Episcopal minister named D. O. Van Slyke in the mid- to late 1800s saw the Mississippi Valley in the environs of Galesville, Wisconsin, as the site of paradise (Lane 1988:125–31). His description seemed more than just frontier boosterism, which was rampant at the time. High bluffs at a particular bend in the river made for a rather enclosed and isolated valley. Even today Van Slyke's *Found at Last: The Veritable Garden of Eden* is still distributed to tourists. No evidence exists, however, that anyone besides Van Slyke took seriously this location's mythical qualities.

Subsequent to Latter Day Saint history and lore, some have still located their Gardens of Eden westward. An eccentric named Samuel Perry Dinsmoor built one out of cement on a property in Lucas, Kansas, over a twenty-two-year period (from 1907 to 1929). Sculptures on the property have an antigovernment anticorporate theme as much as a religious one (Manning 2000). The property is only about 50 miles from the geographical center of the conterminous United States in Smith County and only 20 miles from Meade's Ranch, the original datum for horizontal survey in the country, in all about 240 miles west of Jackson County. In the visionary perfection of America, central location produces utopia.

The Garden Turned Farmland

Because of Adam's partaking of the forbidden fruit the premier couple were sent from the garden to "till the ground from whence [they were] taken" and to eat bread "in the sweat of [his] face" (Gen. 3:19, 23). Thorns and thistles came forth and the ground became cursed for "Adam and Eve's sake." The goal of the Puritans and their successors, including a major portion of the earlier Latter Day Saint experimentation and success with settlement westward, was to "carve a garden from the wilds" of America, not simply to conquer the wilderness for its own sake (Nash 1982:35). The words of one early Ohio settler, Caleb Atwater, followed this sentiment. This garden of America had "been given to [the American] by God, who has commanded him to cultivate and enjoy it" (Jakle 1977:120).

Early on, trees instead of grassy plains were associated with the quality of the garden's soil, but in the American perspective, toiling over the soil was a worthier life compared to wilderness survival as a primitive hunter-gatherer (Jakle 1977:55). Clearing the land became a charge as agrarian frontier life represented the qualities of self-reliance and stalwart independence (103). As America's pioneers held increasing dominion over the land, a right that was usually upheld by the Bible, the "rural became the fruitful" and the pastoral life of cultivation "seemed closest to paradise and the life of ease and contentment" (Kay 1989; Nash 1982:30–31). In the nineteenth century, a constantly growing agricultural society was a dominant symbol of "the real genuine America" (Smith 1970:123–24).

Marx (1964:71, 87, 105) described the American literary development of a "middle landscape" that was a semiprimitive retreat to a middle ground of reconciliation between the savage and the refined. This landscape is a wholly agrarian one. By the late 1700s, this dream of the agrarian middle condition had taken on a new credibility. The predominant view of the Latter Day Saint membership in Independence was this pastoral one. The Saints, however, were somewhat more accustomed to a broader range of mercantile activities than the native Missourians. By the time of Joseph Smith, Thomas Jefferson's call to cultivate was unconsciously etched in the minds of most frontier people, including the majority of early Latter Day Saints: "Those who labor in the earth are the chosen people of God, if ever He had a chosen people, whose breasts He has made His peculiar deposit for substantial and genuine virtue. It is the focus in which he keeps alive that sacred fire, which otherwise might escape from the face of the earth. Corruption of morals in the mass of cultivators is a phenomenon of which no age nor nation has furnished an example" (157). In further support of agrarian values, Jefferson blamed the corruption in any society on industry (157–58). Most early Latter Day Saints in Jackson County received "an inheritance in Zion" to farm in typical Jeffersonian tradition, while waiting for the establishment of the New Jerusalem, Eden expounded (*Doctrine*, 1981:38:19–20, see also *Doctrine*, 52).

Today, by great contrast, mechanized agriculture has diminished the American labor force to about 5 percent and the pastoral "middle border" is large in area but small in persons (Sauer 1963:32–41). Most Latter Day Saints, of whatever group or splinter, have been reared in urban/suburban homes. Their yards exist as remnants of pastoral life (Jackson 1977), but employment for them, as with most other Americans, is industrial or service related. Though believers, the thought of cultivating a given plot of land in the New Jerusalem is a strange idea. If not agrarian, then what kinds of jobs can be offered in the millennial city? In my experience, western Mormons see themselves participating in building, artwork, crafts, and maintenance.

The Machine in the Saints' Garden

The garden and pastoral views of the American landscape are necessarily intertwined with the growing influence of urban civilization westward. As early as the Revolutionary War period, problems of urban growth existed on the eastern seaboard of the Americas (Nash 1979). Many writers were already describing this industrial ascendancy west of the Appalachian Mountains in the early nineteenth century.

In a vision over the American continent, one anonymous author of *The Golden Age* saw spacious cities and thriving towns in the East as well as a millennial future for the West (Marx 1964:107). The French observer, Alexis de Tocqueville, during his trip to the United States in 1831, the same year the Saints began their New Jerusalem venture, wrote that agriculture tends to improve slowly in democratic nations, while "on the other hand, almost all the tastes and habits which the equality of condition produces naturally lead men to commercial and industrial occupations" (1956:213). Tocqueville's view was that the urban industrial way of life was inevitable in America and such was the norm for the Saints as well. The question arises, how does any group, if so inclined, try to mesh otherworldly millennial goals with existing "urban industrial America"?

Jakle wrote that at the turn of the nineteenth century urban seeds were bearing the early fruit of the industrial age within the pastoral garden (1977:122). At close view, paved streets with their orderly foliage provided a clean pastoral look, but "after 1830, . . . less care was taken to plant [and] many streets lost their trees to street widening, sewer construction, and other improvements" (125–26). The predominant pattern of contemporary writers was to try to view urban development from a positive angle, even as the myth of the garden waned with the intrusion of technology (Smith 1970:124). Thus, Cincinnati was consistently named the "Rose city" and the "Queen city" in the 1820s and 1830s, at the same time that pigs filled the streets, blood of slaughterhouses permeated local streams, and fires were a constant hazard. Even the later air pollution of Pittsburgh was seen as providential, even chiliastic, the hopeful smoke "that must enrich America" (Jakle 1977:136–37). Much of frontier America was caught in this zone of cultural uncertainty between pastoral morality and the "golden age" dreams of the industrial era. This is reflected in the work of Zamora, who wrote that "America continued to represent Europe as it had for two centuries." After all, "the New Jerusalem was a city, no matter how divine its architect" (Zamora 1982:107–8). The pastoral garden dream was an ideal interlude largely overlain by the industrial ethic, though that garden substrate is still evident in American attitudes and landscape.

Henry Nash Smith referred to these entirely new urban industrial symbols as a "New Calculus" in frontier America. In the Mississippi Valley by the 1830s, nature and technology combined to solidify America as a unique entity (Smith 1970:155–56, 162). Independence, Missouri, in this era was not immune to the theme of millennial industrialism. The booster William Gilpin in the mid-1800s saw the area as the cradle of "the greatest civilization of them all" and tried to establish "Centropolis" as its chief city. Centropolis, again at the mythical center of America, was to be sited between Kansas City and Independence and was proposed to be the railroad tie between the eastern seaboard and the westward Passage to India (39). No Saints were left in Missouri, so this image was a gentile view of progress rooted in industrialism. Boosters could create otherworldly images of great central cities as well as Saints. The two views of the future city were simultaneously similar and opposed.

Considerable public awe surrounded industrial developments even in the 1830s. Marx wrote, "The invention of the steamboat had been exciting, but it was nothing compared to the railroad. In the 1830s the locomotive, an iron horse or fire-Titan, is becoming a kind of national obsession. It is the embodiment of the age, an instrument of power, speed, noise, fire, iron, smoke . . . confined by its iron rails to a predetermined path, it suggests a new sort of fate" (1964:191). The Latter Day Saints were seemingly swept westward on the cowcatcher. The church was officially established April 6, 1830, in Fayette, New York. By June 1831, the church had moved to Ohio and had been commanded to establish itself in Missouri, the "center place." By 1833 the church was established in Independence. Later, most of the believers went farther into the wilderness to carve out another garden in Utah. Those staying behind were more influenced by urban America. The Saints always lingered on the outer boundaries of civilization yet were not prone to lapse into a primitive state. The early leaders and missionaries of the Latter Day Saints were largely from educated New England society, and their values permeated the religious culture. Hatch succinctly summed up the dual contrast among the early Latter Day Saints who "knew intense alienation from mainstream culture . . . [and] withdrew from society but did not retreat to modest aims and private ambitions. They were fired with a sense of national, even international, mission: God's kingdom would yet rise in America, they believed, and their endeavors would serve as decisive leaven. Like Puritans, they set themselves to accomplish great and mighty things" (1989:188).

The millenarian, Yankee Latter Day Saints were forced toward the wilderness as a site to carve out their New Jerusalem garden at the same time that the industrial revolution was about to shift into high gear in America. The New Jerusalem of the 1830s was to be a "Holy City," and

Joseph Smith set out on an incremental path to urbanize it in a manner that may have been inconceivable to many members. Many Saints were farmers, yet somehow they were going to be incorporated into a heavenly city. Others had experience with development along the eastern seaboard, yet they were expected to take up farms in the millennial Zion. The contrast between the values of the pastoral garden against millennial industry was often confusing. Often, landholdings to be farmed were drawn up and subsequently overlain by Smith's later more urban plans. Zamora has stated that if it seems that Eden and the New Jerusalem are terms at odds, it should be remembered, "the two are nevertheless cognates in their visions of timeless perfection" (Zamora 1982:108). Also, since the Bible starts with Eden and ends with the New Jerusalem, it was natural for the Latter Day Saints to place both at the same site—Jackson County, Missouri (Boyer 1992:321)—yet irony is implicit in the concept.

The New Jerusalem was the same as the Garden of Eden, from opposed ends of the timeline—the holiest of places. Yet even today members of the different Latter Day Saint groups have a hard time interpreting the duality of Jackson County as a garden when Kansas City and its suburbs sprawl over most of the area. This contrast of ideas is a major reason for the downfall of the 1830s' New Jerusalem of Independence, Missouri, and yet also is the reason for the survival of the New Jerusalem theme in the same place to this day. The idea was too lofty to be established yet tied tightly enough into the substrate American ideal of garden to have maintained strength over the decades. And if it were not the Mormon Independence, Missouri, perhaps an ideal central location in the United States would have been established in the vicinity by some other place-minded religious people.

The effort, originally, was to fit the pastoral image into a middle ground between the archetypal garden and a real peopled place. With the broach of the frontier by American culture, a continuum from garden, to the pastoral, to the urban/industrial was seen as settlement thickened. In early Independence the three ideas coexisted uneasily, and with the American context unfolded, the next chapter treats the early history of the Saints and their abortive attempt to establish the literal dualistic New Jerusalem.

2

The Missourians and the Saints

> Turn, O backsliding children, saith the LORD; for I am married unto you: and I will take you one of a city, and two of a family, and I will bring you to Zion.
>
> —Jer. 3:14

Joseph Smith did not reveal in one sudden pronouncement that Jackson County, Missouri, was of utmost millennial importance for Latter Day Saints. The initial development of the New Jerusalem occurred over a five-year span from 1829 to 1834. For clarity on the Saints' perspective, and the ensuing conflict with the Missourians, however, the backdrop of frontier Missouri culture must be examined. The Latter Day Saint Zion was far from a tabula rasa.

The Missourians

Missouri was made a state in 1821, and by 1830 it had a population of over 140,000 (Gerlach 1986:15). The Missouri-Kansas border, however, was still the edge of the frontier, the first settlers arriving there in the early to mid-1820s. Jackson County was organized in 1826 and included the present counties of Cass and Bates until 1835, along the boundary with Kansas (Atkeson 1918:133; Conard 1901:3:404; *History* 1881:117). Early settlers of the county were overwhelmingly southern in origin and, in descending order, came from Kentucky, Virginia, Tennessee, and North Carolina (Conoyer 1973:65; Gerlach 1986:13, 62; Hudson 1988:399–402; McCurdy 1969:4). Such immigrants, as part of a greater influx, soon created a region known as Little Dixie along the tributaries of the Missouri River in the

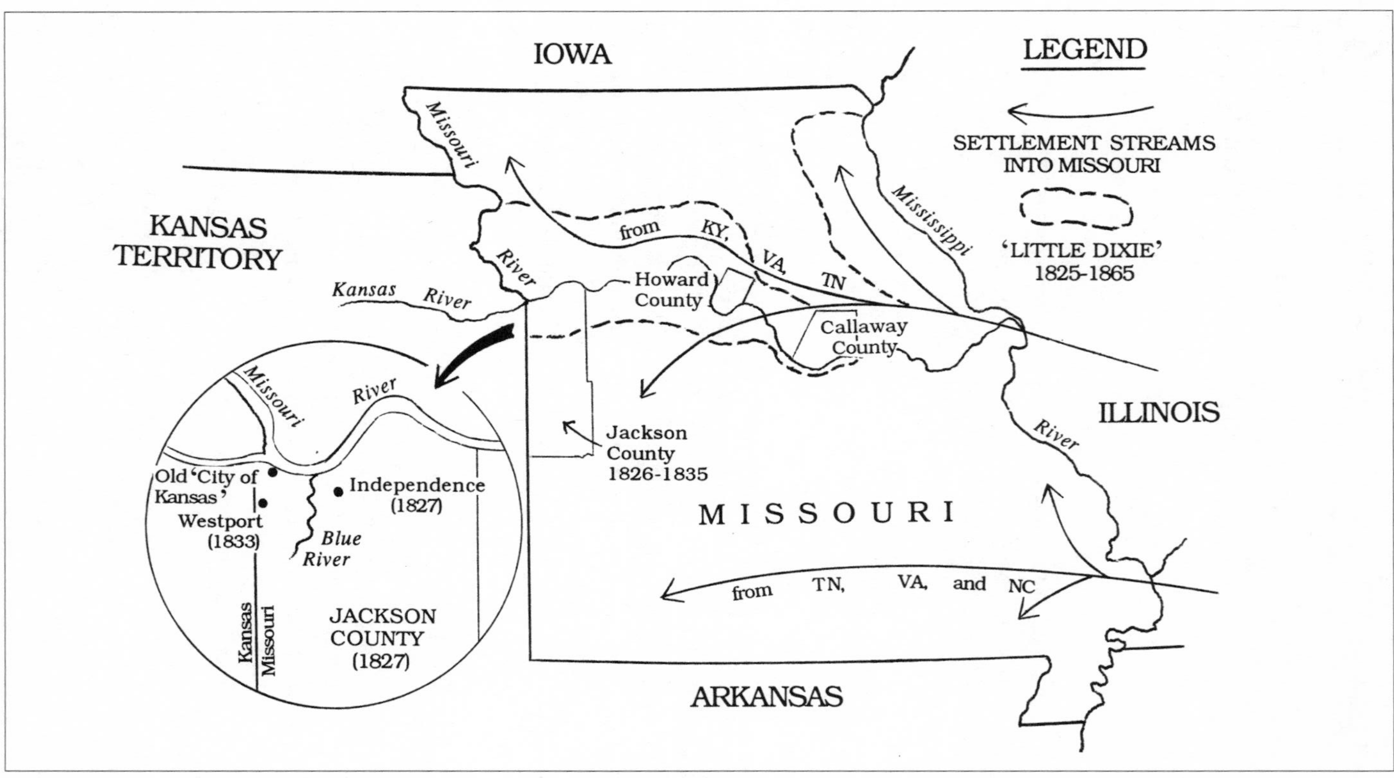

FIG. 3 | *Early settlement of Southerners in Missouri. Data from Conoyer (1973), Hudson (1988), and Gerlach (1986).*

western part of the state (Figure 3). Many of the wealthier of these pioneers were high Scotch-Irish or Ulstermen in derivation (see Gerlach 1986:15–17). For Saint and Southerner alike, these sites provided good springs, easy access to the main river system, and protection from floods (Rafferty 1983:57; Figure 3). Platted in 1827, Independence was such a settlement about five miles south of the Missouri River, near the Blue River tributary (Writers' Program 1941:378). The site soon became a departure point for trade across the Santa Fe Trail (Harris 1933a, 1933b; Nagle 1977:61–62).

Frontier Missouri settlers came for a variety of reasons. Many were people previously disappointed in political or professional hopes, veterans who received land grants from the government, younger sons without inheritances, adventurers, or lawless desperados (McCurdy 1969:4). Many descriptions of pioneer life in the Upper South portray an unmistakable element of "frontier crudity" (Jordan and Kaups 1989:1–18). The early Missourians were no exception; they "built rough cabins and made rude beds by throwing piles of deerskins over poles laid across forked sticks driven into the ground" (McCurdy 1969:5). When Joseph Smith and others first arrived in Independence in 1830, they described three stores and twenty houses, mostly of log construction. The scattered houses the Missourians lived in had dirt floors, mud-plastered chimneys, and paneless windows (Barrett 1973:186–87).

Missourians considered themselves as educated in "the school of experience"; illiteracy ran high and life expectancy was low (McCurdy 1969:13–15). Despite their unrefined nature, the settlers were stalwart, "hoping to prosper with the advance of civilization" (5). One itinerant preacher, Nicholas Patterson, found the folk of Howard County in central Missouri "kind, hospitable, and, though ignorant of the outside world—not stupid" (155). Civilization meant different things to Missourians and Latter Day Saints. The Latter Day Saints arriving in Jackson County were from an area extending from Vermont through Ohio's Western Reserve. Though most were farmers, they were of a more erudite tradition of public meetings set in organized town greens. This was the swath of territory across which the township and range system developed, and the Genesee Country of western New York, where the church was organized, had been an agricultural region of major importance at least thirty years before the establishment of Independence (Meinig 1966:144–48). Furthermore, the transport corridor of the Erie Canal through western New York was established a decade before.

Religion only gradually became important on the frontier. The revivalist zeal that had swept Kentucky around the turn of the nineteenth century was somewhat less emotional when it passed through Missouri in the 1820s and 1830s (Cleveland 1959; Writers' Program 1941:119–20). Baptist and Methodist itinerant preachers were the most successful on the frontier fringe, but many Scotch-Irish settlers were Presbyterian (Gerlach 1986:16–17; Writers' Program 1941:120). Most ministers initially had difficulty in Missouri. The earlier Missourians were friendly but generally unwilling to contribute to the preachers' support (McCurdy 1969:16, 164; Writers' Program 1941:122). Still, approaching 1830, revivals were popular and emotional, if rather capricious. One account told of the dismissal of a camp meeting so members could watch their dogs "tree a catamount" (Writers' Program 1941:121). "Indecent conduct" sometimes passed for the influence of the Holy Spirit and "epidemics of pregnancies" followed some revival meetings (McCurdy 1969:158). The Latter Day Saints who moved to the area were generally from the Northeast, where religious custom, if extremely diverse, was approached with more decorum.

The issue of slavery in Missouri was complex and was just as often a symbolic political device as it was economic practice (Nagle 1977:45–46). Most Missourians had been born in areas of the Upland South where slavery was less firmly entrenched (Hudson 1988:402; Gerlach 1986:19), but significant numbers of slaves existed especially in the plantocracy culture along the Missouri River and its tributaries (Gerlach 1986:wall map; McCurdy 1969:11–12). Slaves made up 18.6 percent of Missouri's total population in 1830 (Gerlach 1986:19), but 31.2 percent in Jackson County (Barrett 1973:187; Conoyer 1973:52), so the issue may have carried more weight there. As a broader issue, Missouri's rights as a state in the Union muted the slavery issue after the Missouri Compromise, but "on the western border owners of slaves were a significant group" (Nagle 1977:126).

The Saints were generally antislavery, but, as the editor of their Independence newspaper, William W. Phelps did, they often appeared to meander from one side of the issue to the other. The Saints would preach to African Americans, but an ethnic focus on the welfare of the Indians was more dominant in their ideology. The Saints often said little or nothing on the subject. This indecisiveness regarding a matter of utmost importance to the locals generated suspicions that ultimately entirely altered the culture of western Missouri. Being from the northeast, Latter Day Saints, while not openly prohibitionist, were at odds with the Missourians on the issue.

The view that Missouri was a second Eden, an extension of Kentucky paradise, was in the minds of most of the southern settlers (McCurdy 1969:138–39; Nagle 1977:49–50). Frontier orators spoke of Missouri as being as "rich in resources as the original Eden" and saw her eternal nature as the "garden of America" (McCurdy 1969:57; Nagle 1977:51, 54–55). This view, however, was symbolic and not overtly literal, as was the view of the Saints. Missourians were not likely to have seen western Missouri as the actual location of Eden. These garden images were transmitted back to Europe in such writings as Duden's *Report on a Journey to the Western States of America and a Stay of Several Years along the Missouri*, which later contributed to the immigration of Germans in particular (Nagle 1977:51–52; Writers' Program 1941:141).

Jackson County was likewise symbolically Edenic to many of its settlers. Josiah Gregg (1845:1:33, 314), the western adventurer, explorer, and writer, wrote in 1831 that "the rich and beautiful uplands in the vicinity of Independence might well be denominated the 'garden spot' of the Far West." The county could serve as a market for a group of "half-civilized emigrant Indians close [by] . . . and [for] the wants of the half-starved tribe of Kansas Indians, who reside farther out" (Brown 1963:1:17). In an 1832 sojourn, author Washington Irving enthusiastically extolled the surroundings of Independence:

> Many parts of these prairies of the Missouri are extremely beautiful, resembling cultivated countries, embellished with parks and groves, rather than the savage rudeness of the wilderness. Yesterday I was out on a deer hunt in the vicinity of this place, which led me through some scenery that only wanted a castle, or a gentleman's seat here and there interspersed, to have equaled some of the most celebrated park scenery of England. The fertility of all this western country is truly astonishing. The soil is like that of a garden, and the luxuriance and beauty of the forests exceed any that I have seen. (Anderson 1971:287)

Missouri settlers were farmers from the beginning. Mirroring Jeffersonian ideals, virtue, for them, lay in the "increase of property" and the "cultivation of the earth" (McCurdy 1969:4, 23). Missouri politician Thomas Hart Benton exuded the pastoral element in nineteenth-century culture when he defended the "sturdy farming life" of low land prices and traditional "hard" currency (Nagle 1977:106–12). "Old Bullion's" entire career in Missouri (1815–58) revolved around the preservation of old-fashioned pastoral society. Benton's landscape prescription was "for a democracy of small farmers rejoicing in free and cautious government amid natural abundance" (112–13, 118).

The Latter Day Saints converging upon western Missouri spoke and acted differently than the majority of Missourians. Mutual suspicions arose. Slavery was one source of Saint-Missourian trouble in Jackson County (Bush 1973:11–13), but more friction came when the Saints purchased massive plots of Jackson County land. There ensued a fear of regional cultural and political domination by a new people of different religious persuasion (Bushman 1960:15). A prominent Latter Day Saint leader in the 1830s, John Corrill summed up the sentiments of the frontier people of the time, who "saw their country filling up with emigrants. . . . They disliked their religion, and saw, also, that if left alone, they would in a short time become a majority, and of course, rule the country. The church grew . . . and the old citizens became more and more dissatisfied" (Corrill 1839).

One distraught newspaper editorial hinted that the millenarian Saints would eventually control all aspects of government, probably at the expense of the traditional Missourian:

> The day is not far distant when the sheriff, the justices, and county judges will be Mormons, or persons who wish to court their favor from motives of interest or ambition. What would be the fate of our lives and property in the hands of jurors and witnesses, who do not blush to declare, and would not upon occasion hesitate to swear, that they have wrought miracles, and have been the subjects of miraculous supernatural cures, have conversed with angels, and possess and exercise the gifts of divination and of unknown tongues, and fired with the prospect of obtaining inheritances without money and without price—may better be imagined than described. (*Western* 1833)

The similar goals of the two sides overlapped in very different ways, and the two approaches fed mutual animosity that eventually doomed the Saints' venture. The Missouri farmers were fiercely individualistic and independent regarding property rights; in contrast, the Latter Day Saints attempted integration into a collective group experiment, though many traits of individuality remained. Whereas itinerant preachers took the

Baptist and Methodist gospel to individual settlers on the Missouri frontier, the Latter Day Saints ostensibly brought to the frontier a unified group of people already imbued with it.

Beginning the New Jerusalem

For the early Latter Day Saints, the term *New Jerusalem* is first encountered in the period when Joseph Smith was translating the *Book of Mormon* in upstate New York. A reference to a special new city of gathering occurs about halfway through the *Book of Mormon* in a speech by Jesus Christ Himself. The main body of that reference is: "And behold, this people will I establish in this land [that is, the Americas], unto the fulfilling of the covenant which I made with your father Jacob; and it shall be a New Jerusalem. And the powers of heaven shall be in the midst of this people; yea, even I will be in the midst of you" (*Book of Mormon*, 3 Nephi 20:22). One chapter later, the speech continues:

> And they [gentiles] shall assist my people, the remnant of Jacob, and also as many of the house of Israel as shall come, that they may build a city, which shall be called the New Jerusalem.
>
> And then shall they assist my people that they may be gathered in, who are scattered upon all the face of the land, in unto the New Jerusalem.
>
> And then shall the power of heaven come down among them; and I also will be in the midst.
>
> Yea, and then shall the work commence, with the Father among all nations in preparing the way whereby his people may be gathered home to the land of their inheritance. (*Book of Mormon*, 3 Nephi 21:23–25, 28)

Smith's translation of the *Book of Mormon* was begun in April of 1828 and completed, with one major interruption, late in 1829 (Berrett 1977:38; Roberts 1978:1:20, 52–55, 71–75). Whether Joseph Smith really translated the *Book of Mormon* or wrote it himself is a moot question here; he undoubtedly had read Revelation 3:12 and 21:2 and was familiar with vernacular usages of New Jerusalem. In any case, these citations were the first Latter Day Saint expressions of the phrase and were recorded during the last few months of the year, and since the *Book of Mormon* is a religious record of the Americas, the idea of a New World location for a millennial city was subtly introduced.

The usage in the *Book of Mormon* was the first inkling of what was to become an incremental plan for Smith's New Jerusalem. The plan consisted of three major parallels with frontier America in a Latter Day Saint microcosm. An ideal of saving the Indian in the wilderness was prominent, initially, and then came a stage of establishing, in that wilderness, the pastoral garden by agricultural Saints. Lastly, came a stage of strong urban millennial symbolism.

Lamanites Saved in the Wilderness

Joseph Smith's vision for building Zion involved a complex scriptural interpretation where the Native American was a critical player. To this day, the Indian has remained an important focus of the doctrines of the various Latter Day Saint groups. To preface this development, a short explanation of the peoples of the *Book of Mormon* narrative is necessary.

In general, the *Book of Mormon* gives an account of two peoples: the Nephites and the Lamanites. In the history, these two groups developed from a single family that fled Jerusalem about 600 B.C. They built ships and, in time, came to the Americas. The Nephites and Lamanites grow and wane in righteousness throughout the thousand-year history of the book. The Nephites were usually the more upright and obedient of the two, but they nevertheless were ultimately destroyed in warfare with the Lamanites because of wickedness. The Lamanites remained, and since circa 400 A.D., when the book ends, these people were left to wander the face of the Americas in a decrepit state. Accordingly, the belief follows that many, if not all, Native Americans are Lamanite descendants.[1]

The title page of the *Book of Mormon*, as Joseph Smith dictated it, tells that the book is "written to the Lamanites, who are a remnant of the House of Israel; and also to Jew and Gentile." Consequently, the early Latter Day Saints offered a promise to the Lamanites, because the *Book of Mormon* was their own history that needed to be retaught to them. Early Latter Day Saint teachings emphasized the importance of the role of the Native American, as "pedigreed from the Jews," in building up the city of the New Jerusalem (Underwood 1993:66).

The major Indian tribe in Missouri on the eve of Anglo settlement was the Osage. These people had ceded most of their lands to the U.S.

government in 1808 but retained a six-mile-wide strip of land south of the Missouri River in what was to become Jackson County until complete cession in 1825 (Rafferty 1983:60). Even before the Latter Day Saints had moved their infant church out of New York, Joseph Smith saw the Indian Removal Act of 1830 as providential (Underwood 1993:31; Vogel 1988:198). This act relegated settlement of numerous Indian tribes to the Kansas Territory at the very edge of the frontier (Miller 1881:18–19). Thus situated, Smith felt that the Native Americans in Kansas were ripe for the *Book of Mormon* gospel. Joseph Smith wrote a revelation in September of 1830 that discussed Zion in more concrete terms for the first time. One early member, Hiram Page, had been receiving messages with the help of a small stone, which he used to discuss the whereabouts of Zion (Brooke 1994:189). Putting this dissent to an end, Smith rebuked Page. Smith's revelation implied that teaching the Lamanites and establishing the millennial New Jerusalem would go hand in hand:

> And now, behold, I say unto you that you shall go unto the Lamanites and preach my gospel unto them; and inasmuch as they receive my teachings, thou shalt cause my church to be established among them; and thou shalt have revelations, but write them not by way of commandment.
>
> And now, behold, I say unto you that it is not revealed, and no man knoweth where the city of Zion shall be built, but it shall be given hereafter. Behold, I say unto you that it shall be on the borders by the Lamanites. (*Doctrine* 1981:28:8–9)

With first-person narrative in these revelations generally understood to be the Savior, this pronouncement was the first written indication that the "city of Zion" would actually be placed farther west. Action soon followed the pronouncement, and four men were called by revelation to go among the Lamanites (Roberts 1978:1:111–19). The leader of this group, Oliver Cowdery, apparently had a dual mission: to preach to the tribes and to find a prime location for the establishment of the "holy city" (Bushman 1984:168–69). The group first visited a Seneca tribe on the Catteraugas reservation near Buffalo, New York, and then traveled to the vicinity of Kirtland, Ohio (Church Educational System 1989: 80–83). They visited the Wyandot tribe near Sandusky, Ohio, and then journeyed to Jackson County, where they preached to the Delawares and others in Kansas Territory. The effort was well received but short lived (Jennings 1971:295–96).

In May of 1831, Oliver Cowdery reported to the church that Kansas showed great promise as a site for the New Jerusalem. Later LDS writers overlook a once-possible location for the holy city in the Kansas Territories (Lund 1971:99); after all, only one place was eventually named by revelation. The greater "Lamanite" world loomed in millenarian possibility as Cowdery started emphasizing reports received about the "Navashoes" farther to the southwest (Roberts 1978:1:182). Within a couple of weeks, however, the Mormons were prohibited from preaching by the Indian agent Maj. Richard W. Cummins, who grew suspicious of Mormon-Indian cooperation and wrote negatively to William Clark, lead agent for the tribes of the entire Louisiana Territory (Davis 1989:95–96; Jennings 1971:297–98). Oliver Cowdery likewise wrote to Clark, asking him to permit missionaries among the Native Americans (Church Educational System 1989:86–88). It is not known if Clark ever responded to this request, but without much emotion, Parley P. Pratt, one of the missionaries, noted, "We accordingly departed from the Indian country and came over the line, and commenced laboring in Jackson County, Missouri, among the whites" (Roberts 1978:1:185).

The Mormons preached to the Native Americans for only a matter of weeks but remained strongly sympathetic afterward. Because of the forced westward migration of the various tribes, starvation, disease, and conflict increased among them. In a letter to Clark from the Indian agent John Dougherty, an epidemic of "distemper" was described among the Pawnee: "They were dying so fast, and taken down at once in such large numbers, that they had ceased to bury their dead, whose bodies were to be seen in every direction, laying about in the rivers, lodged on the sand bars, in the weeds around their villages, and in their old corn fields, others again were dragged off by their hungry dogs . . . . their misery was so great that the survivors seem to be unconscious of it" (Schusky 1971:253–54). Alleviation of such suffering was important to the Saints. William W. Phelps (1832a) wrote of the "tolerably good" prospect for crops in this region of the country but cautioned that "calls for provisions will undoubtedly be considerable . . . for the United States is settling the Indians . . . immediately to the west, and they must be fed." Perhaps a reflection of their immersion in broader American culture, the Saints never questioned the ethics of the U.S. government on the issue of Indian removal; they only asked how they could help. This attitude of support of the government would soon change.

In this manner the plan for the New Jerusalem went through its first major alteration, passing from a brief focus on Indian lands in Kansas

Territory to Anglo Missouri eastward. The principle of gathering to the garden continued, but the importance of the Native American in the gathering process became a latent element of church policy through external government influence. A sign of the new religious movement in its infancy, the theme of saving Native Americans in the wilderness did not receive emphasis from any of the Latter Day Saint groups through the remainder of the 1800s. With time, preaching to the "Lamanites" resurged, and through the 1900s all of the major churches of the Saints would faithfully return to their roots on the issue.

Establishing the Garden in Jackson County

Throughout the extremely harsh winter of 1830–31 and into the spring,[2] a great amount of new information regarding the establishment and location of the New Jerusalem was disclosed to the Saints. First came the announcement of the short-lived missionary effort to the Indian Territory. It appeared that the New Jerusalem was to be sited within Kansas Territory, although the exact location was to "be given hereafter" (*Doctrine* 1981:28:8–9). The early importance of this region is totally lost on contemporary Latter Day Saints, and Kansas today is rarely mentioned in any millenarian capacity, though talk of the importance of the Native American remains prominent.

What followed in November and December of 1830 were some strongly millennial writings given as revelations. Edward Partridge, the first Bishop in Independence, received the following chiliastic statement from Smith: "I am Jesus Christ, the Son of God; wherefore, gird up your loins and I will suddenly come to my temple" (*Doctrine* 1981:36:8). This is the earliest reference in the revelations of Joseph Smith to a "temple." Little did Partridge know the depth that the word *temple* would shortly acquire, nor could he foresee the future breadth of temple planning and building among the different future Latter Day Saint churches. The usage and development of this term in early Latter Day Saint culture will be examined shortly.

In December of 1830, the church was commanded to move to "the Ohio" (*Doctrine* 1981:37). From this, it is likely that some Latter Day Saints inferred that the New Jerusalem would be at Kirtland, Ohio, itself (de Pillis 1960:145–46; O'Dea 1957:41–42). At the same time, Joseph Smith enticed the members further by providing vague place information in garden/pastoral trappings. In January of 1831, a revelation promised the

Saints an inheritance forever in "a land of promise . . . flowing with milk and honey" (*Doctrine* 1981:38:18–20). The phrase, of course, is reminiscent of Old Testament Israel as well as many subsequent utopias, including John Filson's description of "Kentucke" in the late 1700s (Smith 1970:129).

Another of Smith's revelations, written in February 1831, detailed groundwork for the New Jerusalem, though still not the actual place. This revelation indicated that the site would be revealed if the people asked in prayer. It also described the basic workings of "consecration"—how members were to give lands and goods to the church—in exchange for an appropriate new parcel of land, or an "inheritance," in Zion (Arrington, Feramorz, and May 1976:15). The revelation also indicated that the people of the New Jerusalem would be involved in a covenant with the Lord keeping commandments, and He would respond in kind with blessings and protection (*Doctrine* 1981:42:8–10, 34–36, 62–68). Much of the responsibility for the earthly establishment of the New Jerusalem was given to a newly called bishop, Edward Partridge, who had settled in Independence, by far the busiest settlement in the area. Over the next few years Partridge was responsible for virtually all consecration exchanges of families' assets and the assignation of land parcels for settlement in Jackson County.

By March of 1831 the Saints were especially anxious as expectations surged, though little detail had yet been revealed regarding what or where Zion was to be precisely. Many had moved from New York to Ohio and were unsure if they should purchase lands in the Western Reserve or wait for a move elsewhere. Instructed to stay in Ohio, they were to purchase lands where possible and to be patient because the location had "yet to be revealed; but . . . it shall be given to know the place, . . . it shall be revealed" (*Doctrine* 1981:48:4–6). The instructions went on to state that then—and only then—could families begin to gather.

A revelation reported in June of 1831 commanded many of the priesthood elders of the church to travel to Missouri, where the "land of their inheritance" would be made known (*Doctrine* 1981:52:2–5, 42–43). This revelation was the first to mention Missouri, a state pronounced in the writings to be a land held by "enemies." Nearly a premonition, such words surely did not smooth Missourian–Saint relations, especially if the locals interpreted "land of inheritance" to mean permanent settlement, which is what the Saints had in mind. The first congregation of the church to move to Missouri was the New York Colesville Branch, one that had previously moved to Thompson, Ohio. Commanded to move to Jackson County in

June, they arrived at Independence in July—in remarkable time. They settled at the site of a natural spring approximately twelve miles west of Independence, in Kaw Township. The place in Kansas City today is Troost Lake and Spring Valley Park adjacent to the north-south Paseo corridor about three miles from the Missouri–Kansas border.

With a jaundiced eye, E. D. Howe, Ohioan editor of the *Painesville Telegraph*, recorded the westward movement of the Saints, writing: "After all the good followers of Jo Smith from York state had got fairly settled down in this vicinity, which [Sidney] Rigdon had declared to be their 'eternal inheritance,' Jo must needs invent another 'command of God.' At a meeting of the tribe . . . 28 Elders were ordered to start immediately for Missouri . . . where they contemplate building the New Jerusalem . . . and they have expressed doubts whether they will ever return to this 'land of promise'" (Howe 1831). Despite Howe's uncertainty regarding the revelations, the evidence of the Lamanite mission strongly indicates rather public knowledge that Smith had always aimed for a more westerly New Jerusalem location, one that involved preaching to, and the conversion of, Native Americans. The plans and the move were not done at all incognito.

As the Colesville congregation began to settle just west of Independence and Joseph Smith and other church leaders came in July 1831 to investigate the chosen Missouri for the first time, the differences between Latter Day Saints and Missouri frontiersmen became immediately apparent. William W. Phelps, Independence "voice of the Saints," indicated that some of the material goods of the transplanted, educated Yankees seemed unbelievable to Missourians, whose "customs, manners, [and] modes of living . . . [are] entirely different from the northerners, and they hate yankees worse than snakes, because they have cheated them or speculated on their credulity, with so many Connecticut wooden clocks, and New England notions" (Anderson 1971:276). Conversely, Joseph Smith noted the backward nature of Missouri frontier culture:

> But our reflections were many, coming as we had from a highly cultivated state of society in the east, and standing now upon the confines or western limits of the United States, and looking into the vast wilderness of those that sat in darkness; how natural it was to observe the degradation, leanness of intellect, ferocity, and jealousy of a people that were nearly a century behind the times, and to feel for those who roamed without the benefit of civilization, refinement, or religion. (Roberts 1978:1:189)

The perceived cultural depravity of the frontier folk was enough of a burden on Joseph Smith that he yearned for a garden to flourish in the desolation. He wrote, "When will the wilderness blossom as the rose? When will Zion be built up in her glory, and where will Thy temple stand, unto which all nations shall come in the last days" (Roberts 1978:1:189). For Smith the plea was not rhetorical, and an answer was recorded in July 1831 in the following revelation:

> Hearken, O ye Elders of my church, saith the Lord your God, who have assembled yourselves together, according to my commandments, in this land, which is the land of Missouri, which is the land which I have appointed and consecrated for the gathering of the Saints.
>
> Wherefore, this is the land of promise, and the place for the city of Zion.
>
> And thus saith the Lord your God, if you will receive wisdom here is wisdom. Behold, the place which is now called Independence is the center place; and the spot for the temple is lying westward, upon a lot which is not far from the court-house.
>
> Wherefore, it is wisdom that the land should be purchased by the Saints, and also every tract lying westward, even unto the line running directly between Jew and Gentile [the Kansas-Missouri border].
>
> And also every tract bordering by the prairies, inasmuch as my disciples are enabled to buy lands. Behold, this is wisdom, that they may obtain it for an inheritance. (*Doctrine* 1981:57:1–5)

Since Smith was seen as a prophet, his declarations served to heighten fervor and action and were unique to the concrete millenarian stance of the Saints. These instructions were the first to name Independence, Missouri, as the specific center place, the site for the city of Zion. Though Underwood states that the Latter Day Saints, overall were less communitarian than most have been led to believe (Underwood 1993:103), it is certain that the attempts of the early Saints in building the New Jerusalem were associated more with material purchase and preparation than by any spiritual rapture. The instruction was to purchase as much of Jackson County as possible, even the "whole region" (*Doctrine* 1981: 58:53). In addition, land was to be bought as close to Indian Territory as possible, indicating the desire to resume associations contiguously with the

Lamanites. Since Jackson County in 1831 included present-day Cass and Bates Counties to the south, at least seventy miles of border with the Lamanites was pondered (Atkeson 1918:133; *History* 1881:117).

The Dedication Spot

On August 2, 1831, the Colesville Saints placed the first log for a Latter Day Saint home in Jackson County. Twelve men set it, symbolic of the twelve tribes of Israel (Roberts 1978:1:196). Immediately afterward, Sidney Rigdon led a ceremony of consecration and dedication of the Jackson County area to the Saints.[3] He asked those gathered if they were willing to accept the land as an inheritance from the Lord, if they would keep the law of God from this time forward, and to see to it that future gatherers would also keep the law. The congregation responded in the affirmative. Rigdon then pronounced the land consecrated and dedicated to the Lord for an inheritance and possession "for the Saints, and for all the faithful servants of the Lord to the remotest ages of time" (Roberts 1978:1:196).

In 1831, William W. Phelps wrote back to New York an extensive description of Missouri's land and resources. Though positive, the description did not seem overly millenarian. Summer weather was described as harsh. It was "warmer than in New York State, and when it grows cold at night with the wind from an easterly direction, depend upon a deluging rain before morning, and then it clears off hot enough to roast eggs" (Anderson 1971:276).

Wildlife and soils were praised:

> Prairie pluvers [plovers], prairie hens, wild turkies, rabbits, gray squirrels, prairie dogs, wolves, rattlesnakes (the big breed), prairie rattlesnakes [massaugas], copperheads, panthers [possibly mountain lions], deer, etc., go when they have a mind to and come when they please . . . [the soil is] a rich black mould, bedded on clay from 3 to 8 feet deep [where] . . . corn, in good seasons, does well; wheat, tolerable, but nothing like York state. Cotton, sweet potatoes, wild honey, wild grapes, wild roses, strawberries, dewberries, black berries and raspberries are common. (275–76)

A yearning for the Yankee region and climate was apparent. Joseph Smith echoed Phelps's assessment and referred to Jackson County at this time as the "goodly land," a phrase often still heard in local Latter Day Saint vocabulary. In a revelation later in 1831, Joseph Smith wrote the following:

> Blessed, blessed, saith the Lord, are they who have come up unto this land with an eye single to my glory, according to my commandments. Verily I say that . . . the fulness of the earth is yours, the beasts of the field and the fowls of the air, and that which climbeth upon the trees and walketh upon the earth; yea and the herb, and the good things which come of the earth, whether for food or for raiment, or for houses, or for barns, or for orchards, or for gardens, or for vinyards; yea, all things which come of the earth, in the season thereof, are made for the benefit and use of man, both to please the eye and to gladden the heart. (*Doctrine* 1981:59:1, 16–18)

Such words reinforce the idea that, for the Saints, spiritual matters were thickly intertwined with the good things of the solid earth. These scenes were gardenlike, and Joseph Smith eventually told the Saints that Jackson County was literally the site of the original Garden of Eden "from which Adam was driven" (Barrett 1973:373, 377), but at this time the comparison with Eden remained largely symbolic, similar to how other contemporary non-Saint writers had presented it. As reported in the church's official newspaper, the *Evening and Morning Star,* the Saints apparently were to return the area to its gardenlike state. "Zion, according to the prophets, is to become like Eden, or the garden of the Lord." There was much work to do, though, for as Phelps continued, "yet, at present it is as it were a wilderness and desert, and the disadvantages of settling in a new country, you know, are many and great" (Phelps 1832a).

The Saints Purchase Land

A strong pastoral element can be discerned as the Saints began to purchase land in Jackson County. The millennial inheritances were seen by many, if not most, of the Saints as eternal and to be farmed (de Pillis 1960:112). Land consecrated was mainly acreage from Kirtland, Ohio, given by Saints to be sold in order to purchase new territory in Jackson County, Missouri. Goods consecrated were usually returned to the same family and included tools, farm implements, and livestock (Arrington 1972:45; Arrington, Feramorz, and May 1976:373).

Other economic activities also began to grow in the area. William Wine Phelps was to publish a religious newspaper at Independence, and Oliver Cowdery, originally called to preach to the Indians, was encouraged to aid Phelps. The Saints settled with a presumption and enthusiasm that was difficult for the local county residents to understand. Later in August, the first Saints in Jackson County were instructed in detail, through another revelation given by Joseph Smith, on how to purchase lands:

> Wherefore, I the Lord will that you should purchase the lands, that you may have advantage of the world, that you may have claim on the world, that they may not be stirred up unto anger.
>
> For Satan putteth it into their hearts to anger against you, and to the shedding of blood.
>
> Wherefore, the land of Zion shall not be obtained but by purchase or by blood, otherwise there is none inheritance for you.
>
> And if by purchase, behold you are blessed;
>
> And if by blood, as you are forbidden to shed blood, lo, your enemies are upon you, and ye shall be scourged from city to city, and from synagogue to synagogue, and but few shall stand to receive an inheritance. (*Doctrine* 1981:63:27–31)

This decree, given one month after the sacred site of the New Jerusalem was revealed, was an eerie premonition. The Saints viewed the revelation as an admonition to purchase Jackson County lands without violence, since bloodshed was prohibited. The words were seen by non–Latter Day Saints as a threat, and eventually blood was shed on both Saint and gentile sides. The revelation also shows the purchase of sacred land as divine injunction. Holy land in Jackson County had to be bought before the Saints could realize their prophetic city—God would not simply give it to them.

In 1831, Partridge began to purchase large acreages in Jackson County. In fact, at the time of the above revelation, he had already purchased three hundred acres (Eakin and Eakin 1985:112). These purchases emphasized building a material Zion as well as a spiritual one, an eternal millennial possession. The Saints had always given an earthly interpretation to bringing about God's work, and this emphasis endowed the physical landscape with millennial importance. According to Mormon tradition, at a sacred grove near Palmyra, New York, Joseph Smith had seen his first vision of God the father and Jesus Christ. Smith found the sacred record of the *Book of Mormon* on a wooded glacial drumlin near Palmyra. Subsequently, Joseph Smith and Oliver Cowdery were baptized in the Susquehanna River, and then the

Saints were commanded to gather to Ohio's Western Reserve. Independence and Jackson County were to be the culmination of sacred spots, the location for the holy city of Zion, where the Lord would appear a second and final time. In step after step of early church geography and doctrinal development, specific places were made sacred. There is little mystery in the purchase of Jackson County lands. Preparation by purchase and farming easily fit into the cosmology of the early Saints (Lifchez 1976:33). The Second Coming was something to be prepared for through strenuous work, and a physical transformation of the landscape as directed by God through Joseph Smith. Ultimately, Edward Partridge bought about two thousand acres for the church in Jackson County (Eakin and Eakin 1985:4–5, 112). His purchases have been thoroughly documented (Britton 1922:147; Eakin and Eakin 1985), and are mapped here (Figure 4). This map does not portray landholdings of Latter Day Saints who may have bought tracts apart from church consecration procedures.

The initial survey of northern Jackson County was done during 1827, and land entries began in November 1828 (*History* 1881:102). The price was $1.25 an acre, with some lands held in reserve at $2.00 an acre (Brown 1963:21; Eakin and Eakin 1985:22; *History* 1881:102; *Illustrated* 1976:14). A few townships were reserved for educational institutions, as was the land grant custom, in the eastern portion of the county and along the Blue River (*Illustrated* 1976:14). Missourians had acquired many parcels by the time of the Saints' arrival, but since the population in the county at this time was around 1,500 inhabitants, there was plenty of land to go around (Britton 1922:146–47; *Political* 1902:27; Romig and Siebert 1988:102). Land purchased in Independence was state land deeded by the United States government (Price and Price 1982:28–31), but most of the Saints' purchases were original entries at the federal land office in Lexington. Since prices for these abundant public lands did not vary throughout the county, the sites selected were chosen for a variety of reasons.

In light of the revelations given by Joseph Smith and the nature of government land sales at the time, the pattern of the Saints' purchases made sense. Land was purchased in Independence proper, but not as much as might be expected for a heavenly city. The proximity of the Saints' land to that of other Missouri landowners may have precluded the Saints from buying more in town. Most Missourians at the time were concentrated in three major spots: around Independence, in the vicinity of the area near the Missouri-Kansas border that was to be platted as Westport in 1834, and also at Chouteau's landing to the north on the Missouri

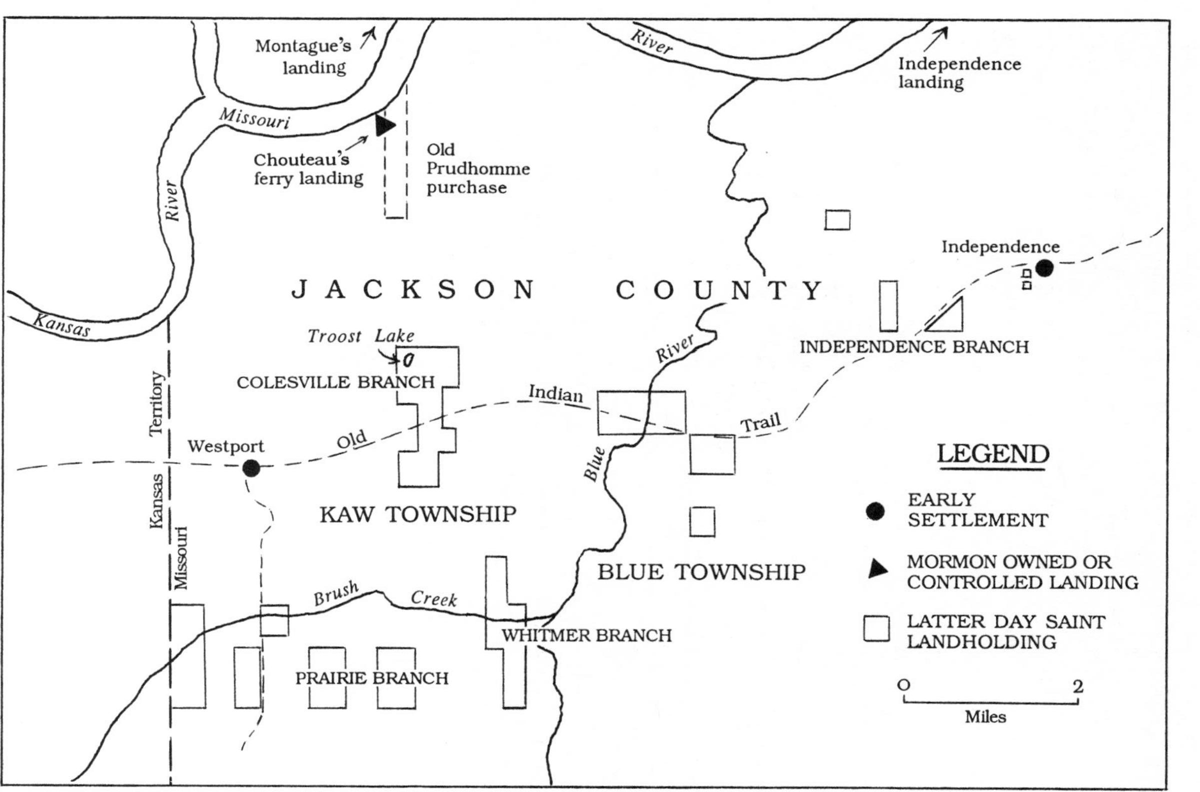

FIG. 4 | *Latter Day Saint landholdings in Jackson County, 1833.*

River. The Saints' predispositions directed their purchases farther westward, away from Independence, Jackson County's center of population, toward Lamanite settlement but south of the Missourian dominated area that was to become Westport (Figure 4).

Smith had commanded Partridge to purchase "every tract lying westward, even unto the line running directly between Jew and Gentile"— the Missouri–Kansas border (*Doctrine* 1981:57:4). Partridge attempted to comply with the revelation to the best of his ability; the first lands purchased in July 1831 were directly along the border with the Kansas Territories (Figure 4; Eakin and Eakin 1985:112). The land dedicated for the temple and center of the New Jerusalem was not purchased until December 1832, a year and a half later. The immediate need for land for settlement of incoming Saints took precedence over the millennial goals around Independence.

Church property purchased at Troost Lake for the Colesville Branch lay close to land directly north near the Missouri River purchased in 1831 by Gabrielle Prudhomme, one of the earliest non-Mormon settlers in the area to become Kansas City (Chamber 1938:3). The Saints apparently wished to capitalize on prime commercial and transportation zones as well as on good upland agricultural areas. Tracts were bought along the corridor of road leading to the Kansas Territory (later the road to Westport) obviously to enhance trade possibilities. Another factor was access to water along Brush Creek, Blue River, and at springs (again see Figure 4). Three small sections of land along the Missouri River were purchased as landings for general commerce and transportation. Furthermore, lands were purchased along what is today Brush Creek south to Fifty-fifth Street and westward to the Kansas border, just as Smith's revelation had directed (*Doctrine* 1981:57:4). Given time, even more land would have been accumulated by the Saints since they were instructed to "purchase this whole region of country" (*Doctrine* 1981:58:51–52). Since Jackson County, from 1826 to 1835, was more than three times its present size (a fact lost on modern Saints), there were great hopes for new acquisitions.

From 1831 through 1833 almost 1,200 Latter Day Saints settled in Jackson County, though early on they had been instructed to "assemble not in haste, lest there be confusion, which bringeth pestilence" (*Doctrine* 1981: 63:24–25). This instruction was intended to keep Missourians from alarm and also to keep Edward Partridge from being overwhelmed with land transactions. Of the 1,200 Saints, about 700 of them were new converts from various locations (Arrington, Feramorz, and May 1976:22). Lands in Jackson County were purchased through the consecrations given to the church by members coming mostly from the region of Kirtland, Ohio. These lands were then divided up, more or less equally, into plots for individual families to work each according to its own ingenuity. Apparently, no hard and fast rules existed for how individual land allotments to members should be farmed or otherwise worked, reflecting a respect for agricultural independence typical in wider American culture (17).

De Pillis (1960:168) has aptly stated that if Independence was the proposed "center" of the church in the early 1830s, then Kirtland, Ohio, was the "epicenter." The building effort required eastern energy and eastern money, so, except for a few relatively short visits, Joseph Smith resided in Kirtland (163). This separation of leadership from New Jerusalem development caused a number of problems in the consecration plan. Edward Partridge found his calling to apportion lands extremely difficult. First there was the issue of property rights. If a person left the church or was excommunicated, his or her original properties or goods given to the church were not returned. This policy was in conflict with Jeffersonian tradition, of course, which held that property was the raison d'être of the American agriculturist. For the church to retain lands because of a member's dissatisfaction with the organization meant that the individual was without means to support him or herself. It was a practice that could not endure. After several outcast members sued successfully for the return of their properties, Joseph Smith changed the policy. In the future, members who sued the church would receive their original donation, but the church would retain any surplus gifts of property or goods that had already been given to the church (Arrington, Feramorz, and May 1976:24–26). This practice may have prevented a complete solidarity of land ownership by the Saints, but, on the other hand, dissatisfaction among some new settlers was unavoidable.

Additional problems arose regarding the size of the plots given to settling Saints (Arrington, Feramorz, and May 1976:23). Many land parcels, averaging between 15 and 20 acres, were allotted as inheritances before the introduction of the design of the proposed city of the New Jerusalem (Harris 1933b). How these inheritances were to be reallotted, or reckoned with later in the subsequent New Jerusalem plans, is unknown, since the early Saints did not stay in Missouri long enough for such problems to be confronted. It would have been a serious predicament. For example, a farmer named Titus Billings received a large inheritance of 27.5 acres of property in Independence that was later to be included in the first plat of the New Jerusalem (Barrett 1973:235; Romig and Siebert 1986: 289–94).

In the proposed city plan, a change of house lots of one-half acre each was to be instituted.

In addition, the value of the consecrations was evidently insufficient to provide appropriate inheritances to all who were entitled to them (Arrington, Feramorz, and May 1976:31–32). Some members therefore came to Jackson County and squatted on land, as did the first Saint settlers in the county (see Launius 1984:21), or purchased their own without consecrating their possessions to the church by working through Bishop Partridge. These actions indicate that members of the church, at best, leaned toward aloofness with regard to land ownership. Agrarian attitudes and prevailing settlement patterns clashed with Joseph Smith's increasingly urban interpretation of millennial events, and Smith indicated that those who did not follow the divine instructions would not "have their names enrolled with the people of God; neither is their genealogy to be kept, or . . . found on any of the records or history of the church" (Roberts 1978:1:297–99).

Smith also became upset that some mail-carrying Saints traveling to Jackson County kept Kirtland leadership letters from reaching Bishop Partridge, indicating less than total dedication to the building of Zion. Evidence also exists that the function of the new office of bishop was not altogether clear to the people. An 1833 statement of Smith's indicates that friction was developing between local authority and the individual church member:

> The matter of consecration must be done by the mutual consent of both parties; for to give the Bishop power to say how much every man shall have, and he be obliged to comply with the Bishop's judgement, is giving to the Bishop more power than a king has; and, upon the other hand, to let every man say how much he needs, and the Bishop be obliged to comply with his judgment, is to throw Zion into confusion, and make a slave of the Bishop. The fact is, there must be a balance or equilibrium of power, between the Bishop and the people; and thus harmony and good-will may be preserved among you. (Smith 1977:23)

In modern analysis, Arrington says that there is no reason to think that Partridge was anything but sincere and diligent in his role as middleman between the idealist Smith and the agricultural Latter Day Saints in settling the New Jerusalem. Partridge took Smith's abstract idea and tried to realize it in concrete form, with written proof of consecration and deeds of new inheritances. Problems were inevitable because "the essence of the system did not translate easily into legal forms" (Arrington, Feramorz, and May 1976:365–66). Furthermore, agrarian values of the more rural Saints did not always correspond to Smith's urban plans.

Urban Millennialism in Jackson County

As discussed earlier, Joseph Smith's first expression of the New Jerusalem was in late 1829 when translating the *Book of Mormon*. Between June 1830 and February 1831, when Smith was also writing a new translation of the Bible, he wrote a revelation called "The Book of Moses." In this writing, information was given not only about the building up of the New Jerusalem but also about a city from the time of Enoch—a character of scanty account in Genesis. According to the revelation, this ancient city was so righteous that it was taken up into heaven. The application of this celestial urbanization became clear when Joseph Smith wrote that after the New Jerusalem was to be built, this "City of Enoch" would be reunited on earth to "meet" it (Selections 1981:7:62–69). Thus, Revelation 3:12 (also 21:2), describing the "new Jerusalem . . . which cometh down out of heaven" was externally supported. This early use of imagery from both the Old and New Testaments added substance to Smith's New Jerusalem program but started a duality of thought that would persist to this day. It has always been difficult for later groups of Saints to figure which part of the New Jerusalem would be built in Jackson County and which part would descend from heaven and at what time.

When Joseph Smith visited Jackson County in August 1831 and described the gardenlike qualities of the area, he also revealed a kernel of thought that was later to grow to impressive proportions: "The disadvantages here, as in all new countries, are self-evident—lack of mills and schools; together with the natural privations and inconveniences which the hand of industry, the refinement of society, and the polish of science, overcome" (Roberts 1978:1:198).

On August 3, 1831, Smith and six other men left the Colesville settlement toward Independence to dedicate the actual site for the temple of the New Jerusalem. The Saints did not own the site at the time, and the mood was subdued. The Eighty-seventh Psalm was read, which discusses "holy mountains," the Lord's love for "the gates of Zion," and "the city of God." Other than the Old Testament flavor of the ceremony, little detail is given in Smith's own account (Roberts 1978:1:198–99). Although the original Saints never constructed anything on this dedication spot, a stone marker may have been placed there.

Western Missouri was to be the site of the Saints' first temple and it was to be a millenarian structure. It is striking that this chiliastic geography was focused smack in the center of today's United States while, at the time, the Missouri-Kansas border was not politically central for most U.S. citizens. Smith's desire to build a central temple held communitarian focus for the Saints. Surely the promise of organized utopia was an attempt at social unification.

The Saints were not the first to purchase this temple spot. Four months after the dedication, on December 12, 1831, Jones H. Flournoy, a non–Latter Day Saint, purchased the site from the state of Missouri (Price and Price 1982:28–31). It is not known if the purchase by a gentile was of great concern to the Saints. The purchase comprised the entire southeast quarter of section 3 of township 49 north and range 32 west away from the 5th principal meridian (Figure 5, sec. A). One year after Flournoy's purchase, on December 19, 1832, Bishop Edward Partridge purchased a triangular 63.43 acre parcel out of Flournoy's original 160-acre quarter-section of land (Figure 5, sec. B; Davis 1989:152–53; Dyer, 1976:40–43; Eakin and Eakin 1985:41).[4] The price was $2 per acre, about $0.75 higher than the average price of government land, for a total of $130. Flournoy profited about $48.

That parcel included the spot that Joseph Smith dedicated for the temple, and the entire triangular tract henceforth was known as the Temple Lot, a place that at the time was "destined to become the center of the universe" for the Saints (de Pillis 1960:155). It may seem odd that Partridge waited so long to purchase this sacred site, and the Saints definitely paid a premium, but in all likelihood the settlement of the members on their own farmlands was of more practical importance than the possession of the Temple Lot. Additionally, the Temple Lot was not government property to be homesteaded. Partridge needed time to negotiate with Flournoy the price and the size, which included the designated sacred site. Soon after the purchase, Partridge made his residence on the northeastern corner of this parcel, at the intersection of Union and Lexington Streets.

The curving northwest face of the Temple Lot (Figure 5, sec. B) seems unorthodox when compared to the regularity of the survey, but the line corresponded with the path of an old road connecting the Indian territories in Kansas with Independence and with Lexington, where the land

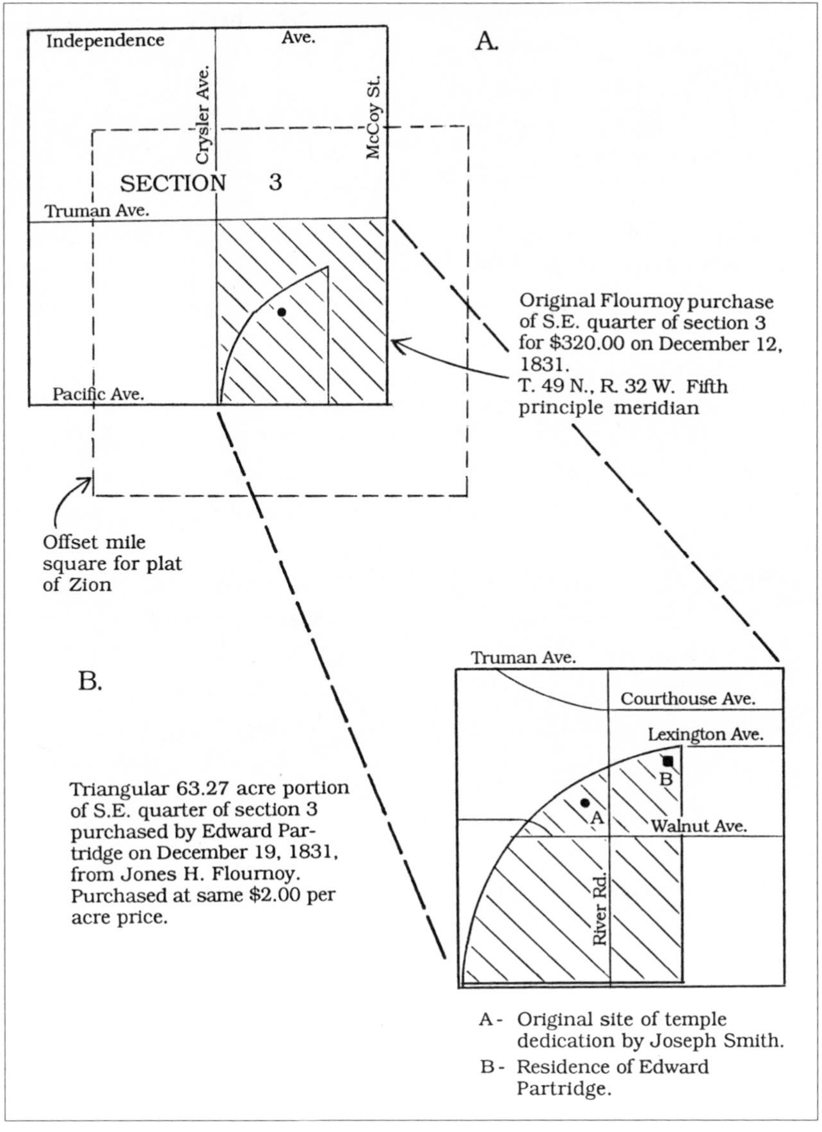

FIG. 5 | *The sixty-three-acre parcel purchased by Edward Partridge. Data from USGS, Independence, Missouri, 7.5 minute quadrangle.*

office was located. This road later became known as Westport Road and is still prominent on the landscape today as Lexington Avenue. According to RLDS archivist Ronald Romig (1990), the eastern boundary of the

Temple Lot parcel does not reach to the section line because Jones H. Flournoy apparently lived in this portion of his purchase and decided to keep the acreage there for himself.

The First Layout

In October 1832, while lands were being purchased and allotted in Missouri, Smith traveled from Kirtland to New York City. What he saw there may have influenced the design for his plan of the New Jerusalem. In a letter to his wife, Emma, Smith wrote the following:

> This day I have been walking through the most splendid part of the city of New York. The Buildings are truly great and wonderful to the astonishing of every beholder and the language of my heart is like this: Can the Great God of all the earth, maker of all things magnificent and splendid, be displeased with man for all these great inventions sought out by them? My answer is no, it cannot be, seeing these works are calculated to make men comfortable, wise, and happy. Therefore not for the works can the Lord be displeased, only against man is the anger of the Lord kindled because they give Him not the glory (Smith 1832; spelling corrected and punctuation added).

Smith became increasingly drawn to symbols of an urban/industrial theme. Lands in Kirtland, Ohio, were purchased and an organized city plan developed. The Ohio plan was based on a standard grid pattern with three temples or "sacred houses" at its core: one for instruction (the only one in Kirtland actually constructed), one for the presidency of the church, and one for a printing and translation center (Romig and Siebert 1988: 107–9). A similar pattern of three structures was apparently to be copied in Independence, but their number was soon multiplied.

On the June 25, 1833, Joseph Smith sent from Kirtland a plan for the layout of the city of Zion to the Saints in Missouri. This design, the "plat of Zion," was organized around a basic one-mile square piece of land with focal points of church, government, welfare, and commerce to be located at center (Figure 6). This one-mile square plat did not coincide with previously surveyed section lines. Its center was the original temple site dedicated by Joseph Smith, about one mile west of Independence proper, in the southeast quarter of section 3 (Figure 5). According to the instructions

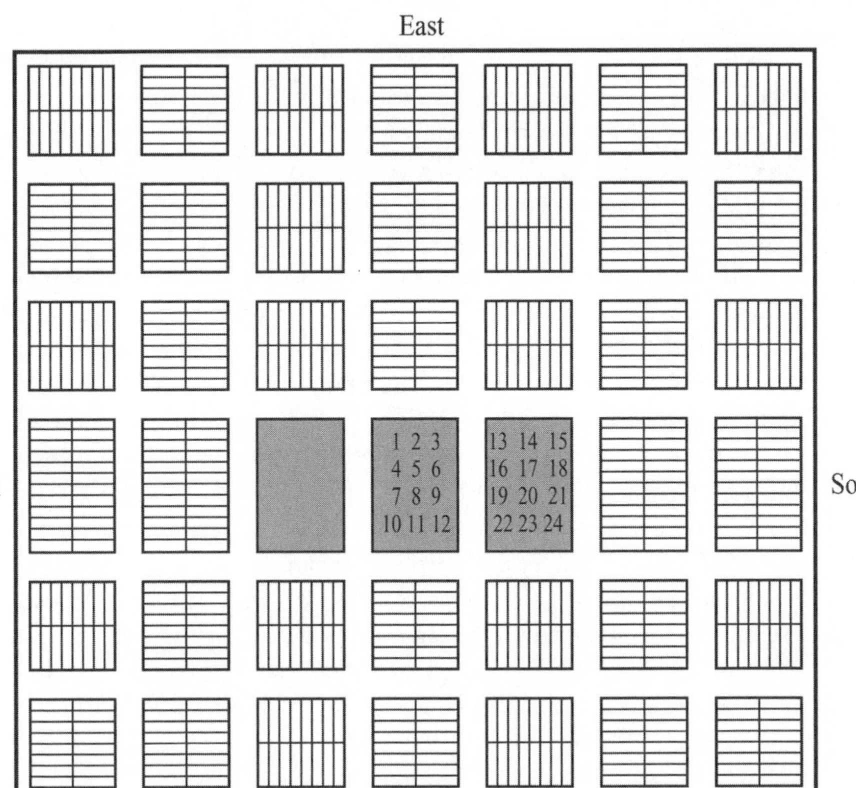

FIG. 6 | *The first plat for the City of Zion. Reprinted, by permission, from Church Educational System (1989:129). Courtesy of the Church of Jesus Christ of Latter-day Saints.*

accompanying the plat design, land north and south of the plat was to be used for agricultural pursuits. It is possible that this statement emphasized leadership perceptions that, since Kansas Territory was closed westward and Missourians were more prominent eastward, logical directions for agricultural advance would be latitudinal. The plat itself was to be divided into lots and settled. In the description accompanying the plat, Smith wrote of his vision to "Zionize" the world: "when this square is thus laid off and supplied, lay off another in the same way, and so fill up the world in these last days; and let every man live in the city, for this is the city of Zion" (Roberts 1978:1:358–59). In this design, farms would be relegated to areas between the mile square cities, similar, as de Pillis (1960:214) has noted, to what eventually developed on the Great Plains generally anyway.

The layout of the Zion plat was fairly detailed, but the plan soon would be altered according to the needs of the incoming Saints. Inconsistencies in the Zion plat were apparently ironed out as time passed. One of the main problems was that Joseph Smith either was not familiar with the original layout of the city of Independence or in the long run did not think the existing city was important in light of the millennial New Jerusalem. The one-mile square plat did not correspond with either existing survey section boundaries or the established city of Independence (Romig and Siebert 1986:296–98). A possible explanation for this inattention might be the Missouri Saints' previous experience in New York and in Ohio's Western Reserve, where rigors of the 1785 land survey did not apply (102), though large manageable squares were often the case. Another example of the lack of precision in the original plan concerns its settlement capacity. The city was to contain 960 lots, which were stated to be room enough for 15,000 to 20,000 people. Closer examination of the plat shows that even if you consider a generous household number of 6 people per lot, a total of only 5,760 people for the entire city would be the result (Billeter 1946:54–56). Obviously the details had not been examined thoroughly and revisions were needed.

Two of the three center blocks of the plat were to hold not just one temple, as earlier supposed, nor three temples following the Kirtland model, but rather a temple complex of twenty-four structures, each of equal size (Figure 6). The plat was drawn oriented toward the east. The temples marked 1–12 in the middle square were said in the plat description to be for the use of the presidency. They seem oriented toward the functions of a higher, or Melchizedek, priesthood that has subsequently developed in most Latter Day Saint groups. The structures labeled 13–24 were apparently to be used by offices of the lower, or Aaronic, priesthood.[5] In any case, the terms used in the description indicate that the priesthood was being developed in a similar incremental manner to the city plat. The functions and purposes of these temples beyond these facts were described in only the most general of terms:

> The names of the temples to be built on the painted squares as represented on the plot of the city of Zion . . . :—numbers 10, 11, and 12 are to be called House of the Lord, for the Presidency of the High and most Holy Priesthood, after the order of Melchizedek, which was after the order of the Son of God, upon Mount Zion, City of the New Jerusalem. Numbers 7, 8, and 9, the sacred Apostolic Repository, for the use of the Bishop. Numbers 4, 5, and 6, the Holy Evangelical House, for the High Priesthood of the Holy Order of God. Numbers 1, 2, and 3, the House of the Lord for the Elders of Zion, an Ensign to the Nations. Numbers 22, 23, and 24, House of the Lord for the Presidency of the High Priesthood, after the Order of Aaron, a Standard for the People. Numbers 19, 20, and 21, House of the Lord, the Law of the Kingdom of Heaven, and Messenger to the People; for the Highest Priesthood after the Order of Aaron. Numbers 16, 17, and 18, House of the Lord for the Teachers in Zion, Messenger to the Church. Numbers 13, 14, and 15, House of the Lord for the Deacons in Zion, Helps in Government. Underneath must be written on each house—HOLINESS TO THE LORD. (Roberts 1978:1:359)

An architectural plan for the first structure to be built on the Temple Lot was drawn up apparently by church leader Frederick G. Williams and later revised by Oliver Cowdery under the supervision of Joseph Smith. Figure 7 shows a modern-day rendition of how the early version of this temple would have looked. It is similar to the Kirtland, Ohio, temple, which was also in the planning stages at this time—and later completed. The original plat of the city of Zion marked the location of this first of the twenty-four planned structures with a cross over a circle marked with the number 5.[6] Temples 4, 5, and 6 were described as being for "the Holy Evangelical House, for the High Priesthood of the Holy Order of God." The division of spiritual labor among these three primary structures was unclear, but the location of this main temple, the first proposed to be constructed, is usually assumed to be on the precise spot dedicated under the direction of Joseph Smith two years earlier. Since the original dimensions of each temple had been given as eighty-seven by sixty-one feet (Roberts 1978:1:359–60), it is possible to draft a map (Romig and Siebert 1988: 106) depicting the alignment of the twenty-four temples overlaying present-day features of Independence (Figure 8). This assumes, of course, that the original spot of dedication has been accurately carried down through time. A

FIG. 7 | *Rendering of the first Independence Temple. Reprinted, by permission, from Harlacher (1989). © by Nancy Harlacher.*

certainty is that the Saints had continual difficulties fitting themselves in structures, and all twenty-four buildings may have been intended simply to seat levels of the priesthood quorums completely in their Sunday meetings (Luce 1990:34–36).

The Second Plat

In June and July of 1833 the first mob violence against the Latter Day Saints took place. These actions seem to have been spurred by certain articles in the church's Independence newspaper, the *Evening and Morning Star*, which increased friction between Latter Day Saints and nonmembers by referring to slaves as "free people of color." Eventually, angry Missourians destroyed the press located in the center of Independence and severely damaged the home of editor William W. Phelps. Bishop Edward Partridge was tarred and feathered, as was an assistant.

Despite the increased tensions, the leadership of the church in Kirtland, Ohio, continued to revise the city of Zion, and a second plan for the New Jerusalem was conceived (Figure 9). Joseph Smith and Oliver

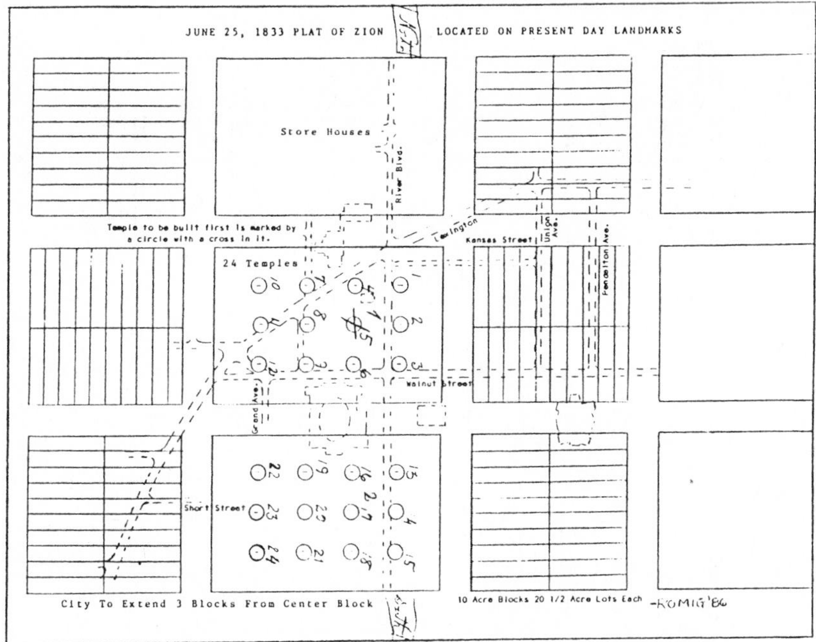

FIG. 8 | *Temple layout for the first plat. Reprinted, by permission, from Romig and Siebert (1988:106).*

Cowdery put the new plan together, but Bishop Partridge refined the details. Romig and Seibert have estimated that this plan was also hastily drafted right after the first plat design was delivered to Independence. It was sent sometime in August 1833 (Romig and Seibert 1986:295–301). This second plat was somewhat larger than the first, appearing to cover about two square miles, but since no description accompanies the second plat, we cannot be absolutely sure of its dimensions. Instead of 49 blocks it shows 132 blocks, all of equal size. Two center blocks were reserved for temples and the others were to be subdivided into 20 lots apiece, for a total of 2,600 lots. Again assuming 6 members per family unit, the new city layout now might hold some 15,600 people, on a par with the original estimate of between 15,000 and 20,000 people for the whole of the city.

Alterations in the placement of the twenty-four temples also occur on the new plat. The temples were now laid out in an eastward instead of a southward direction (compare Figures 8 and 10). Oliver Cowdery, undoubtedly with the approval of Joseph Smith, had also slightly updated to

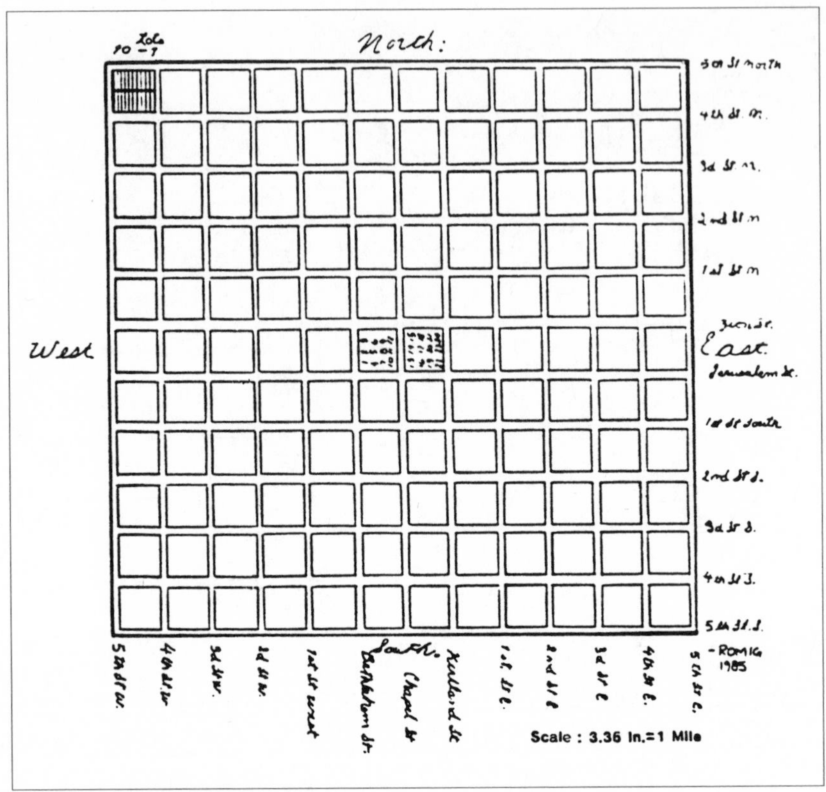

FIG. 9 | *The second plan for the City of Zion. Reprinted, by permission, from Romig and Siebert (1986:296–97).*

97 feet by 61 feet the size "within the walls" of each individual structure to be built, slightly elongating each temple (Dyer 1976:104–5). Edward Partridge, combining elements of both plat designs, experimented further with the layout of the twenty-four temples. This plan was particularly presumptuous because six of the temple structures eastward, it seems, were outside of land owned by the church.

Since the city New Jerusalem clearly had become an ever-changing design, its precise form was not seen as direct revelation. Rather, the city of Zion was likely considered generally approved by God. In this view, the specifics were left to the members of the church. Edward Partridge alluded to such a stance: "I have arranged them [the temples] so as to leave the spaces between them more equal, and according to the natural judgement

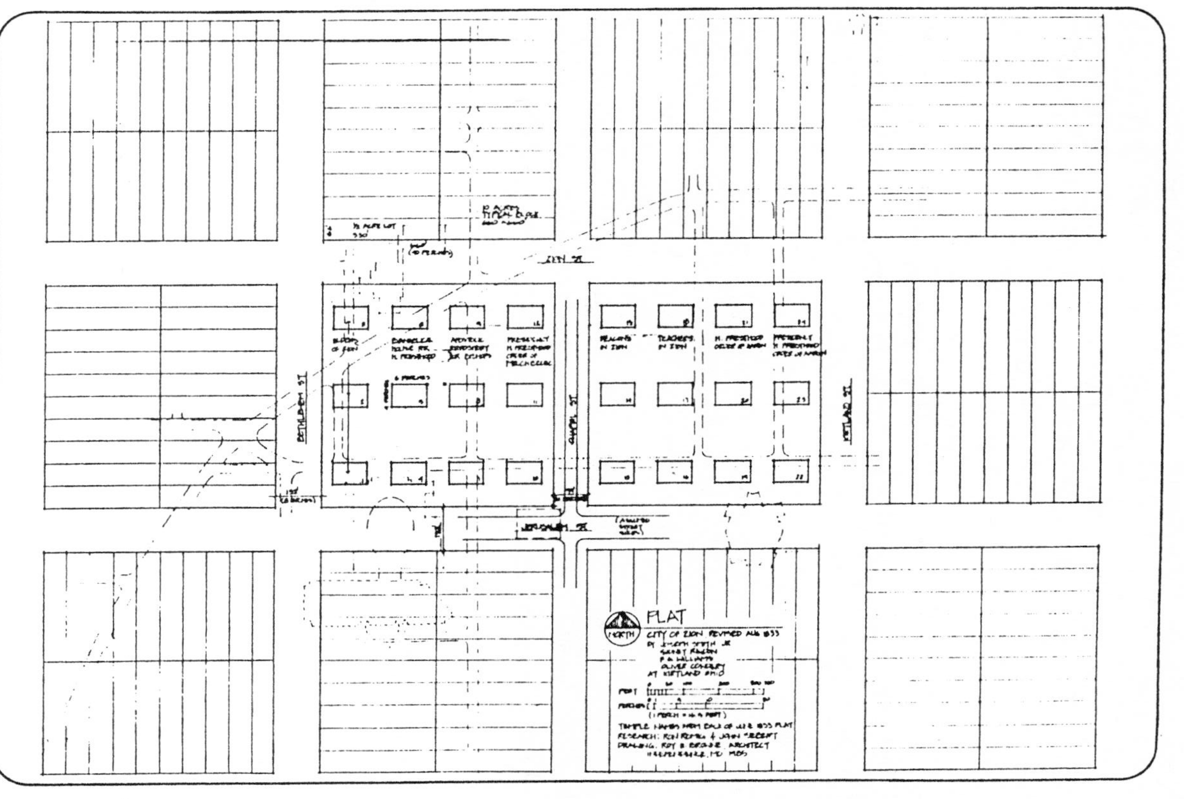

FIG. 10 | *Temple layout for the second plat. Reprinted, by permission, from Romig and Siebert (1986:301).*

of man would be preferable to the arrangement on the plat you sent [referring to the revised plat]—Thinking perhaps that the arrangement was not by revelation, and also that you had not seen them platted out has induced me to plat them this way for you to view & reflect upon" (Romig and Siebert 1988:111–13).

The relationship between revelation and individual judgment described here by Partridge seems to have been the rule for the New Jerusalem. Joseph Smith usually began with basic revelatory instructions that started the process. He then delegated the detailing and revision to other leaders such as Frederick G. Williams, Oliver Cowdery, and Edward Partridge. The problems of meshing the existing city of Independence with the New Jerusalem were of secondary importance to Joseph Smith, if of any importance at all.

A Review of Biblical Re-experience

Smith commonly borrowed millennial imagery for his city of Zion from prophetic writings of the Bible. He often paraphrased or quoted passages from Isaiah and other Old Testament authors and placed these in new and imaginative American contexts. Interspersed through his revelations were millennial pronouncements that emphasized the glory and strength of the New Jerusalem:

> And with one heart and with one mind, gather up your riches that ye may purchase an inheritance which shall hereafter be appointed unto you,
>
> And it shall be called the New Jerusalem, a land of peace, a city of refuge, a place of safety for the saints of the Most High God;
>
> And the glory of the Lord shall be there, insomuch that the wicked will not come unto it, and it shall be called Zion.
>
> And it shall come to pass among the wicked, that every man that will not take his sword against his neighbor must needs flee unto Zion for safety.
>
> And there shall be gathered unto it out of every nation under heaven; and it shall be the only people not at war one with another.
>
> And it shall be said among the wicked: Let us not go up to battle against Zion, for the inhabitants of Zion are terrible; wherefore we cannot stand.

And it shall come to pass that the righteous shall be gathered out from among all nations, and shall come to Zion, singing with songs of everlasting joy (*Doctrine* 1981:45:65–71).

These words indicate that the New Jerusalem would be an impervious dwelling place where the spirit of the Lord would be powerfully present. Other writings emphasized the importance of gathering to the New Jerusalem or the millennial and postmortal aspects of Zion.

Saints were to gather to Zion so that "the borders of my people may be enlarged, and that her stakes may be strengthened and that Zion may go forth unto the regions round about" (*Doctrine* 1981:133:9). The image of Zion as a large tent covering the land would come to have great significance over a century and a half later to the descendants of those Saints who went west. "Rising generations shall grow up on the land of Zion, to possess it from generation to generation" (69:8). The Lamb would "utter his voice out of Zion" and everyone everywhere would hear it (133:21). Furthermore, those living were not the only ones who were going to dwell in the New Jerusalem since the dead "shall rise . . . and shall not die after, and shall receive an inheritance before the Lord, in the holy city" (63:49). Of a postmortal city another revelation further stated, "And the graves of the saints shall be opened; and they shall come forth and stand on the right hand of the Lamb, when he shall stand upon Mount Zion, and upon the holy city, the New Jerusalem, and they shall sing the song of the Lamb day and night, forever and forever" (133:56).

Shipps (1985:59–65, 122–25) has discussed how Israelite history was seen to be recapitulated or "re-experienced" by the Saints. The pioneer trek from Nauvoo, Illinois, across the plains into the Rocky Mountains, starting in 1847, is a primary example, a modern exodus. Shipps wrote that this "re-experience" of Old Testament Israel extended up to Wilford Woodruff's 1890 manifesto that halted the practice of polygamy in the LDS Church in Utah. After this, Israelite recapitulation ceased in the LDS Church as it attempted to mold itself more in the mainstream of American experience. Shipps was reluctant to discuss the idea of Israelite recapitulation any earlier than the commencement of the Mormon trek westward in 1847. In reality, recapitulation murmurings can be observed much earlier, mixed with the chiliastic sentiments of establishing the New Jerusalem. Activities drawn from Old Testament scripture are seen over and over again during the Missouri phase of early church history, though the doctrine, church hierarchy, and organization were in constant flux.

Smith said that as early as 1820 an angel appearing to him had extensively quoted Isaiah, Malachi, Joel, and other prophets. From 1830 to 1833, Smith continually borrowed from prophetic biblical writings, specifically Isaiah, to enhance the themes of the place, nature, and majesty of Zion, as well as the gathering process. Smith's attempts to build the New Jerusalem around the idea that Jackson County was the actual Garden of Eden illustrate these recapitulations of scripture in early Latter Day Saint history. The importance of Jackson County as a crucial future place was also emphasized. Tremendous changes in the physical landscape were to take place; the area would eventually become both garden and a holy city. The construction of temples as edifices of special functions became an issue in 1833 and also hearkened back to temples of biblical times.

Mario de Pillis (1960:14) wrote that by 1837 the ideas of the church were already "set." Although this may be an exaggeration, certainly the beginnings of standard doctrinal patterns were observed earlier than many have claimed. The element of Old Testament recapitulation that Shipps sees as so important in later LDS history was in force even in these early years of millennial development and yearning. In later Independence, the process, as will be seen, becomes complex as multifaceted interpretations color the area with a variety of millennial views and as individual groups often invent their own recapitulations.

A Model for Latter Day Saint Dominance in Missouri

To better understand the Latter Day Saint position in 1830s Jackson County, some speculation based on the established facts seems in order. If one assumes that friction would continue in Jackson County between Saints and Missourians (but in a restrained manner with no expulsion of the Saints from the county), that the Saints would purchase no more land, and that immigration by the Saints would continue, then a model for Latter Day Saint influence in the region into the early 1840s can be proposed.

The fundamental mechanics of this generalized model are summed up in Figure 11 (compare Figure 4). The church headquarters would almost surely have been established in Independence, but the majority of church strength would have straddled the Blue River and extended westward to the Kansas border. Here the church center and society would have

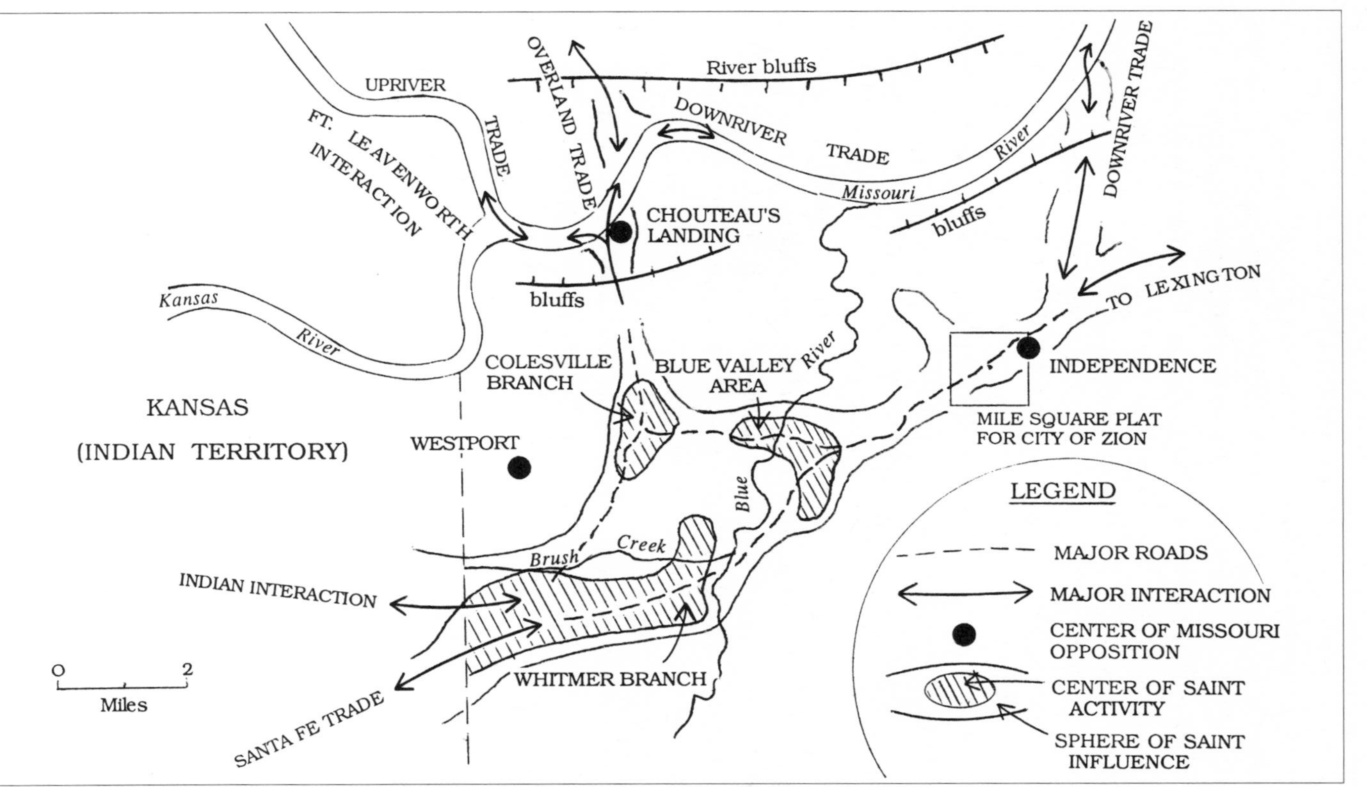

FIG. 11 | *A model for Latter Day Saint dominance in Missouri.*

burgeoned, initially based on agrarian pursuits that gradually would have given way to other commercial ventures as a result of Missouri River commerce, the Santa Fe Trail trade, and Indian interaction. As de Pillis (1960:240–41) has observed, "until persecution destroyed their settlement in the summer of 1833, the [Saints] were on their way to the mastery of the trans-Mississippi trade." Problems would have developed at choke points in trade corridors due to the dominance of Missourians in the Independence area and at Chouteau's Landing. The growth of non-Mormon Westport might also have provided a zone of friction against the Latter Day Saint region. Immigrant flow into the central areas of Saint dominance would have undoubtedly continued while their sphere of influence expanded.

In light of the above assumptions, it would have taken some time for the church to develop much strength eastward in the Independence area—delaying the full implementation of the New Jerusalem plans. The Saints would have been preoccupied in their agrarian and trade pursuits between the Blue River and the Kansas line, waiting still for the day when they could occupy their New Jerusalem location. This observation, of course, precludes any further revelation changing the location of the New Jerusalem.

Missourian fears of Latter Day Saint dominance in the region had a solid foundation in that the newcomers would have been in a position to control urban development, the local vote, the Santa Fe trade, and a substantial amount of Indian contact (Brown and Dorsett 1978:4–5). The Saints introduced an urban scheme in contrast to the actual landscape, and were possibly "too capable as city builders" (1978:4–5). Though unrefined, their planning succeeded. They stuck with their ventures, and with each move they improved in cultural sophistication and political influence. The majority of Missourians were not prepared to move so swiftly in the "Mormon" way.

The Contradictions of the Plan

Joseph Smith described living conditions in the New Jerusalem in terms of garden, pastoral, and urban millennial ideals. All approaches accurately reflected images of early 1800s America. The problem was that the Latter Day Saint plan was incomplete. Original immigrants to these shores saw stages of "original creation, then chaos, now garden . . . a land that simultaneously attracted and repelled," but which "in the end had to be brought to terms" (Lowenthal 1968:71–72). The Latter Day Saints never "brought to terms" their millenarian concept, and the plan has since evolved into fractured panoply.

Smith's views of the New Jerusalem were continually revised from a sacred mission to the Native Americans, to a literal Garden of Eden in the wilderness, to a positive pastoral scene, to a variety of urban plans involving complexes of temples in different layouts. Smith and other church leaders were constantly altering the development of the city of the New Jerusalem as the church had to confront a number of inconsistencies and contrasts.

It is unclear whether the Saints' general membership ever really knew where they stood in Smith's rapidly changing realm of images, even though his changes paralleled the encroaching values of urban society into mainstream frontier America. Smith's designs did not foresee much industry or technology, and yet they were clearly removed from traditional agrarian values. His urban images were neither wilderness nor garden, but the city of New Jerusalem was somewhat pastoral, a place devoid of mechanized industry, poverty, and the stench of disease. It was Joseph Smith's version of paradise.

It is not certain how the early Saints would have withstood the transformation of rural land inheritances—some of which were quite large—into the much smaller lots that the city of Zion plans would have required. Furthermore, it never seems to have mattered to Joseph Smith how the plan would mesh with Independence as a city, or with the established land survey system. Perhaps it was believed that the problems of obtaining all the land in the "region round about" would be divinely resolved with time. Neither did the church ever seriously confront problems with nonmembers. Even after the Saints had been forcibly removed from Jackson County, plans for the development of the city of Zion continued, with the disillusioned Saints again reinterpreting the meaning of "Zion," with lessened use of the phrase "New Jerusalem."

The geography shows each plan a revision of a previous stage. Sometimes a step was undertaken because of a roadblock, but change progressed through Smith's revelations regardless. Instructions were subsequently delegated to other leaders in a spirit of "here is what we need to do, go about it the best that you can." For their part, the Saints always felt that the Second Coming of Jesus Christ was imminent. For example, Phelps stated, "the Saints are gathering home to the land Zion, that they may be ready to meet the Lord when he comes suddenly to his temple" (Phelps 1833:63). This division of leadership directive from the interpretation of the individual member is largely missing in Grant Underwood's description of the early Latter Day Saints as millenarian. That the Saints were millenarian is not in doubt. What is more intriguing is the level of practical millenarianism within the ranks.

Despite the emphasis given by church leaders to constant diligence in labor and building, Arrington, Feramorz, and May (1976:22) mention that some of the Latter Day Saint settlers in Jackson County may have been so filled with the wonder of a millenarian spirit that they may not have understood the concept of working to build a concrete New Jerusalem. To some settlers, the practicality of labor may have become overshadowed by such activities as attempts to calculate the exact date of the rapture by means of examining biblical clues. This tendency does not seem to have been all-pervasive, yet William W. Phelps, editor of the *Evening and Morning Star*, attempted some of these traditional millennial calculations tongue-in-cheek. He concluded that the world was nine years from the beginning of the seven thousandth year, which could have been a reference to the seventh seal, which John the Revelator had spoken of in Revelation (8:1). Phelps summed up this line of thought in a manner that demonstrates that preparation and gathering to the chosen place were stressed over any particular date: "But as all have the privilege of ascertaining such facts for themselves, we ask no man to take our word for the age of the world; the word of the Lord is enough, and whether it be 160, or only 9 years to the coming of the great day, is not so much matter as the solemn reality—Are we ready?" (Phelps 1832b:22).

How much faith did the Saints put in the revelations and descriptions given to them? Certainly some settlers who came to Jackson County did not follow the guidelines and were not viewed as productive in an approved Latter Day Saint way. These people often seem to have been the rural converts, who could not easily grasp Smith's constant changes. Others did their best to adjust and to build for when Christ would come to the New Jerusalem. Overall, irony and contrast were notable at each turn and have played a part in each era of millenarian Jackson County ever since.

The Displacement of Zion

> When you flee to Zion . . . prepare all things, that you may be ready to labor for a living, for the Lord has promised to take the curse off the land of Zion in His own due time.
>
> —Joseph Smith Jr.

DURING LATE 1833 INTO 1834, THE IDEA OF ZION BEGAN TO CHANGE. THE SAINTS LOST THEIR MOST SACRED OF PLACES, THE NEW JERUSALEM. FOR MOST OF THE NEXT DECADE, REFERENCE TO IT GRADUALLY ebbed. At the same time, they vastly amplified the meaning of the term *Zion* as the church struggled in other sites in northwestern Missouri and then in its new city of Nauvoo in Illinois. Finally, in the mid-1840s, the original Latter Day Saints factionalized, with a major migration stream going west. Diverse pockets of Saints, however, were left in the western Great Lakes states.

The Loss of Jackson County

As more Saints gathered in Jackson County, Missourians strongly feared their growing political and economic influence. By 1833, nearly 1,200 Saints were settled there, roughly one-third of the county's total population (Lyon 1972:17). A statement in the July 1833 issue of the church's newspaper brought tensions to a head. It referred to "free people of color, who may think of coming to the western boundaries of Missouri." The Missourians interpreted this as an open invitation to free Negroes to come to Jackson County and settle under "Mormon" protection. There were few, if any, free Negroes in Jackson County, but the statement by a people who had already proposed a suspicious association with the Indians was viewed as tantamount to promoting insurrection among the established slaves (Bush 1973:12).

The slavery issue, though not the main problem between the Saints and Missourians, served as the trigger to violence. Shortly afterward, the non-Mormon citizens of Independence gathered at a public meeting and demanded that the Saints sell their lands and businesses and leave (Lyon 1972:18). On July 23, the church leadership agreed to go the following year. Tension abated for a time, but attacks began three months later when the Saints announced that they would allow the courts to decide the issue. According to Davis, some Saints took refuge on the Temple Lot, possibly hoping for divine protection. Missourians took advantage of the convenient grouping and drove other, homeless Saints to the Temple Lot in an expulsion roundup (Davis 1989:180). The Saints began to move out of Jackson County north into Clay County by November 1833 (Lyon 1972:18–19).

As troubles brewed, Joseph Smith had already laid out a partial rationale for the forced evacuation of Jackson County. Leadership and pastoral problems inherent in land allotments became obvious even in distant Kirtland, Ohio. In a letter to William W. Phelps, editor of the *Evening and Morning Star,* Smith expressed concern that many in Zion were being disobedient:

> I say to you . . . hear the warning voice of God, lest Zion fall, and the Lord swear in His wrath the inhabitants of Zion shall not enter into His rest.
>
> He [the Lord] has promised us great things, yea, even a visit from the heavens to honor us with His own presence. . . . Our hearts are greatly grieved at the spirit which is breathed both in your letter and that of Brother Gilbert's, the very spirit which is wasting the strength of Zion like a pestilence; if it is not detected and driven from you, it will ripen Zion for the threatened judgments of God (Smith 1977:19)

These words spawned a legacy for the interpretation of the Jackson County expulsion. In the minds of many types of Saints then and now, Jackson County was lost because of the uncooperative disobedience of the early Saints. In June 1834, one of Smith's revelations clarified this point of view. This excerpt suggests its collective harshness:

> Behold, I say unto you, were it not for the transgression of my people, speaking concerning the Church and not individuals, they might have been redeemed even now; But behold, they have not learned to be obedient to the things which I required at their hands, but are full of all manner of evil, and do not impart of their substance as becometh Saints, to the poor and afflicted among them,
>
> And are not united according to the union required by the law of the celestial kingdom;
>
> And Zion [New Jerusalem] cannot be built up unless it is by the principles of the law of the celestial kingdom, otherwise I cannot receive her unto myself;
>
> And my people must needs be chastened until they learn obedience, if it must needs be, by the things which they suffer.
>
> [God] will deliver [the church] in time of trouble, otherwise we will not go up unto Zion, and will keep our moneys.
>
> Therefore, in consequence of the transgressions of my people, it is expedient in me that mine Elders should wait for a little season for the redemption of Zion. (*Doctrine* 1981:105:2–6, 8–9)

The common view, accepted by factions of Saints to the present, was that the church, as a whole, had been self-centered, disobedient, and in need of rebuke. The New Jerusalem could not be established under such a burden. The last section of the quotation states that the "redemption" of Zion, supposedly the time it would again be ready, would have to wait "for a little season" so that the Saints could prepare more thoroughly. The duration of that little season has been a subject of speculation to the present.

The image of early Jackson County as sacred among today's Latter Day Saint factions is ironic because they have had to come to terms with the violent act of expulsion. Each of Kenneth Foote's traits of landscape development of tragic events: sanctification, designation, rectification, and obliteration are incongruously evident (see Foote 1997:179). Similar to how the site of the Salem witch hangings—and other sites of public tragedy—have been completely expunged from the landscape (1–4, 175–79), the Saints have de-emphasized old landholdings now possessed by Missourians. For the most part, the substantial acreage of Jackson County land once owned—and never sold—by the Saints has not been marked or memorialized. The Missourians obliterated most of that geography, and the Saints have been reluctant to re-mark it openly. At the same time however, the desire exists to rectify the situation by establishing Latter Day Saint religious markers where possible, usually in Independence proper. The groups are attempting gradual levels of landscape sanctification in physical terms, trying to match the surroundings of Independence to millenarian mental images, but the complexity of the situation among the different groups often has only permitted reticence limited to designation but not full sanctification of the landscape. Tragedy still tempers action, but not as much as the prevailing plurality of religious attitude.

Upon their forced removal from Jackson County, the Saints scattered throughout Clay County to the immediate north. Despite the stigma of disobedience, Joseph Smith nevertheless told the Missouri Saints that it was "your privilege to use every lawful means . . . to seek redress for your grievances from your enemies, and prosecute them to the extent of the law," working on local, state, and national political levels (Smith 1977:32). Laws of the land were seen as divine, as portrayed in a letter from Oliver Cowdery in Kirtland to one of the Clay County refugees: "we are pleased to hear that the governor is likely to give you aid; for we pray continually that the Lord will stir up the hearts of the rulers of men in authority, to avenge his children. The law is sufficient, the constitution was established according to the will of heaven, and all (we?) lack is for those whose duty it is to see that they are kept inviolable, . . . for God is able to turn the hearts of all men sufficiently to bring his purposes to pass" (Cowdery 1834a).

The prospect was that Missouri's Governor Dunklin would intercede on behalf of the Saints. Faith in government, despite their plight, was common among early church members (Cowdery 1834b). The prospects then were positive, and Joseph Smith had told the Saints that it was not the will of the Lord to sell their lands in Jackson County since it was "the place appointed of the Lord for your inheritance, and it is right in the sight of God that you contend for it to the last" (Smith 1977:33). Smith was confident God would open the way for a return and wrote much about lands in Jackson County being restored and redeemed. In another divine statement, it was promised that the "brethren which have been scattered shall return to the lands of their inheritances, and shall build up the waste places of Zion" (*Doctrine* 1981:103:11). When this return was to happen was not revealed.

Naturally, feelings kindled between Missourian and Saint. The Missourians claimed the ouster was justified by the "law of nature, as by the law of self-preservation," in saving the whole structure of their society from the domination of the Saints (de Pillis 1960:232). Conversely, in January 1834, Cowdery wrote that the Missourians ousted the Saints because they were jealous of the ability to acquire land seemingly at will. With bitter hindsight of the winter's events in a letter to his brother, Cowdery wrote the following:

> I must say with propriety that one of the most disgraceful scenes has transpired that has ever been the painful duty of any American citizen to record or relate since these colonies were organized into free states. Peaceful inhabitants have been vilely and inhumanly treated, and one killed; helpless women and children have been compelled to seek an asylum among strangers and some to wander in the open prairies without food, or anything but the open canopy to shelter them. These unlawful proceedings will no doubt be accounted for, though not made to appear justifiable, when I inform you that those men were principally immigrants from the Southern states, and settled in that county before the land came into market and the probability is that few were able to purchase and if they are not the offscourings of the United States, the society from whence they came is equally to be pitied with themselves. (Cowdery 1834c; see also Arrington 1974:38)

At the outset of this unfortunate affair, Governor Dunklin sanctioned the return of the Saints to Jackson County. This is obvious in the following excerpt from a letter written to church leadership in Missouri, dated February 4, 1834: "I . . . should consider myself very remiss in the discharge of my duties were I not to do everything in my power consistent with the legal exercise of them, to afford your society the redress to which they seem entitled. One of your requests needs no evidence to support the right to have it granted; it is that your people be put in possession of their homes from which they have been expelled" (Roberts 1978:1:476). As the months passed, however, Dunklin gradually reduced his support (Launius 1984: 109–10). Attorneys for the Saints proposed to divide Jackson County into a "Mormon sector" and a "Gentile sector" (Parrish 1961:11). Each side was to take "separate territory, and confine their members within their respective limits, with the exception of the public right of ingress and egress upon the highway" (Launius 1984:111; Roberts 1978:2:86). This plan, however, failed to get beyond discussion between the attorneys and Governor Dunklin (Crawley and Anderson 1974:418). One of Smith's revelations in late 1833 had instructed the Saints to purchase "all of the land which can be purchased" in Jackson County "and the counties round about," so the new proposal was unacceptable to the church from the outset even if it did come from its own legal counsel. Though Jackson County was only mentioned directly a few times in the revelations of Smith (*Doctrine* 1981:101:71, 105:28, 124:51), the area clearly had become sacred space to the Saints.

The Saints viewed any plans to control or limit settlement with suspicion (Roberts 1978:2:75–76). Likewise, Missourians did not wish to share the county and saw any possibility of Mormon influence with disdain and distress. The Missouri River and Independence were guarded to prevent the Saints' return (Crawley and Anderson 1974:418). As the problem persisted, Dunklin still skeptically defended the rights of the Saints, but the issue of returning to Jackson County was now more in doubt. In a letter to Col. John Thornton of Clay County, Dunklin wrote:

> They [the Saints] have the right constitutionally guaranteed to them, and it is indefeasible, to worship Joe Smith as a man, an angel, or even as the only true and living God, and to call their habitation Zion, the Holy Land, or even heaven itself . . . so [long as] they do not interfere with the rights of others.
>
> It is not long since an imposter assumed the character of Jesus Christ and attempted to minister as such; but I never heard of any combination to deprive him of his rights.
>
> I consider it the duty of every good citizen of Jackson County and the adjoining counties to exert himself to effect a compromise to these difficulties. . . . My first advice would be to the Mormons, to sell out their lands in Jackson County, and to settle somewhere else, where they could live in peace, if they could get a fair price for them, and reasonable damages for injuries received. (Roberts 1978:2:85–86)

Dunklin refused to reinstate the Saints on their Jackson County lands, advised them to sell, and instructed them to take their grievances to the local county courts. In so doing he effectively distanced himself from unstable political ground (Launius 1984:111–13).

The Missouri situation became bleaker. Most of the 170 buildings that the Saints had constructed in Jackson County were burned. The Saints also had to post lookouts for those church members still in the process of immigrating to Jackson County (Roberts 1978:2:61–62, 99). Jackson County, though revered, was becoming an obliterated landscape with as many images associated with destruction and loss as with millenarian success.

In early May, Joseph Smith prepared to march with an "army" to Missouri in a grandiose effort to help the Saints return to their lands with the support of Governor Dunklin (Launius 1984:68, 108). He made a call for 500 men and donations of $2,000 to aid in the march of "Zion's Camp," but he left on May 8 from New Portage, Ohio, with only some 130 men and less than $200 (Barrett 1973:277–79; Launius 1984:38, 45–46). More donations, and men were received en route (Roberts 1978:2:77), but the group encountered an epidemic of cholera upon arrival in western Missouri. They disbanded shortly thereafter when Governor Dunklin failed to provide expected support (LeSueur 1987:16; Roberts 1978:2:106). This period was one of great loss and despair for the Saints. At the end of the Zion's Camp march, one of its members, Charles C. Rich, wrote this melancholy description when finally reaching the planned Zion: "I went to the Missouri River. Looked at it. Looked over to Jackson County" (Arrington 1974:42).

Although the Saints had been initially welcomed into Clay County as persecuted refugees, most Missourians still felt threatened by the incompatible religious presence. By mid-1834 the continued presence of the Saints in Clay County was in doubt (Roberts 1978:2:97). Even such powerful nonmember allies as Alexander Doniphan, David Atchison (both had previously served as attorneys for the Saints), and, later, James S. Rollins could not convince the masses of the Saints' cause (Parrish 1961:6–28).[1]

In August 1834, Joseph Smith wrote to the church leaders that an aggressive stance should be continued in Missouri. The expulsion was yet fresh memory and, though painful, hope was maintained. Sanctification of the land was still possible. If harassment persisted, Smith said the Saints should "gather up [their] little army and be set over immediately into Jackson County, and trust in God, and do the best [they] can in maintaining the ground." Furthermore, the Saints should continue to gather to the area, "in readiness to move into Jackson County in two years from the eleventh of September next, which is the appointed time for the redemption of Zion" (Roberts 1978:2:145). That would have been September 11, 1837.

Jackson Countians had destroyed the Saints' printing press in Independence preceding their expulsion from the area, but the church prepared to publish another newspaper, this time out of Kirtland (Ham 1970: 82–83). The editorials of this *Messenger and Advocate* further incited the Missourians' tempers. The newspaper claimed that, by divine intervention, the Saints would soon be returned to Jackson County. The January 1835 edition, for example, declared that the Saints would "literally tread upon the ashes of the wicked after they are destroyed from off the face of the earth" (LeSueur 1987:18). Compared with the newspaper's editor, Smith's tone in the September 1835 edition was less harsh, but his statement that "all who build thereon [in Jackson County], are to worship the true and living God" was further evidence to the Missourians that the Saints desired regional domination (Ham 1970:91–92).

During 1835 and 1836 the church continued to be geographically divided, with an ever-increasing membership in western Missouri—mostly in Clay County. With the main body and leadership in Kirtland, Ohio, however, Joseph Smith hedged his bets. With the dedication in Kirtland of the first temple in March 1836, and also with the establishment of the Saints' own bank, the Kirtland Safety Society, a greater sense of permanence was established in Ohio. At the same time, though, talk of Zion persisted and the move of the entire leadership of the church to Missouri was contemplated. Things changed quickly for the worse in Kirtland. One year later, with the failure of the Kirtland bank (Allen and Leonard 1976: 111–14), Smith thought such a move, en masse, would coincide with when Jackson County lands would be retaken.

Because sanctification of land had been delayed during these years, both the leadership and the general membership of the church were forced to broaden their view of Zion. In March 1835, Smith gave specific instructions to church bishops. They were to be "judge[s] among the inhabitants of Zion, or in a Stake of Zion," anticipating the time when "the borders of Zion are enlarged" (*Doctrine* 1981:107:74). In June of the same year, Joseph Smith referred to the "Elders in Zion or *in her immediate region*" (Roberts 1978:2:228; italics added). Smith's use of a feminine pronoun to describe this modest expansion of Zion is intriguing, though symbolic and customary. The female theme in the New Jerusalem is one that surfaces again in the contemporary discussion of the RLDS Church.

More important was Smith's reinterpretation of scale. Zion, which once had meant Jackson County specifically, was now being redefined to include Clay County and other portions of northwestern Missouri. By September 1835, Smith wrote of members traveling to "Missouri, the place designated for Zion" (Roberts 1978:2:281). He did not specifically mention Independence or Jackson County. This expansion of meaning for Zion was perhaps necessary to maintain the cohesiveness of the religious body of the Saints, but Smith and other leaders nevertheless still envisioned a return to Jackson County. In October 1835, it was anticipated that the Saints might be dining together within one year "around a table on the land of Zion" (294).

As mentioned above, Smith and other leaders encouraged migration anew to Missouri for the spring of 1837 in expectation of divine aid in the reoccupation of Jackson County sometime late in October of that year. The leadership also solidified its plan to move to Missouri as financial troubles mounted in Kirtland. Joseph Smith summarized results of a meeting held in March 1836:

> Met with the Presidency [Smith and his two counselors] and some of the Twelve [apostles] and counseled with them on the subject of removing to Zion this spring. We conversed freely upon the importance of her redemption, and the necessity of the Presidency removing to that place, that their influence might be more effectually used in gathering the Saints to that country; and we finally resolved to emigrate on or before the 15th of May next. (Roberts 1978:2:406–7)

The Saints Move to Caldwell County

Ironically, as the leadership of the church prepared to move to Missouri for the reestablishment of landholdings in Jackson County, plans were made in Clay County to locate the growing church immigration farther north. The idea was to create a new county as an exclusive destination for the Saints. During the minutes of a public meeting held at Liberty, Missouri, in June 1836, the Saints were given an admonition. It described the apparent actions and desires of the Saints and made suggestions for ameliorating local tensions:

> we urge on the Mormons to use every means to put an immediate stop to the emigration of their people to this [Clay] county. We earnestly urge them to seek some other abiding place, where the manners, the habits, and the customs of the people will be more consonant with their own.
>
> For this purpose we would advise them to explore the territory of Wisconsin. This country is peculiarly suited to their conditions and their wants. It is almost entirely unsettled; they can there procure large bodies of land together, where there are no settlements, and none to interfere with them. It is a territory in which slavery is prohibited, and it is settled entirely with emigrants from the North and East.

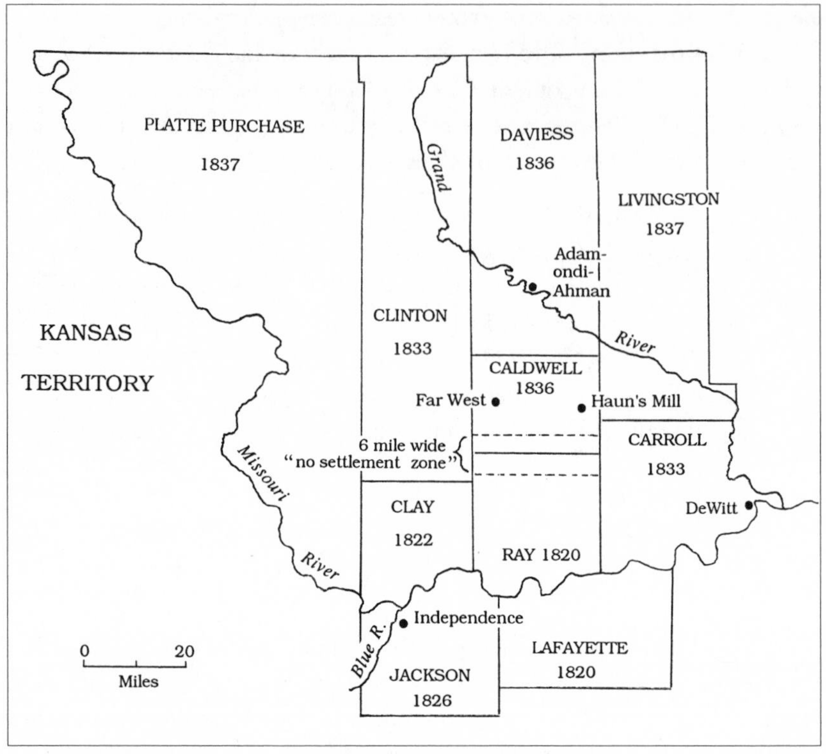

FIG. 12 | *Northwestern Missouri in 1837.*

> We, therefore, in a spirit of frank and friendly kindness, do advise them to seek a home where they may obtain large and separate bodies of land, and have a community of their own. (Roberts 1978:2:450–51)

The Saints were not about to give up so easily on Missouri. William Phelps and other local leaders extolled the virtues of Missouri land farther north to the church leadership in Kirtland (Church Educational System 1989:183). A few good mill sites were located about thirty-five miles northeast of Liberty, Missouri, and shortly thereafter, "several half-quarter and quarter sections were entered in the names of Joseph Smith, Hyrum Smith, and Oliver Cowdery" (Cannon and Cook 1983:105). On this border to the Bluestem grasslands, Phelps was uneasy "out of sight of timber," but generally ecstatic about the prospects of prairie settlement:

> I have to exclaim—What are man and his works, compared with the Almighty and His creations? Who hath viewed His everlasting fields? Who hath counted His buffaloes? Who hath seen all His deer on a thousand prairies? . . . the bees of a thousand groves banquet on the flowers, unobserved, and sip the honeydews of heaven. The backsettlers are generally very honorable, and more hospitable than any people I ever saw, you are in most instances, welcome to the best they have. (Roberts 1978:2:445)

Reconnaissance by Phelps culminated in a settlement for the Saints in northern Ray County. This site was called Far West and was located on a section of land purchased August 8, 1836 (Cannon and Cook 1983: 105–6). In an attempt to resolve Saint/Missourian friction, the lawyer Alexander Doniphan presented legislation to the Missouri government to create an entirely new county, reserved solely for the Saints. Sliced off from northern Ray County, it would contain the Far West site. The Missourians raised few objections (Barrett 1973:362), and the Saints, too, were content. After some quibbling over size, the new county, named Caldwell, after a Kentucky-born friend of Doniphan's father, was organized when newly elected governor Lilburn W. Boggs signed the bill in December 1836 (Church Educational System 1989:183; LeSueur 1987:19–24). A proposal also was accepted for a buffer zone three miles wide on either side of the Caldwell/Ray County line. Here neither Saint nor Missourian could settle (Church Educational System 1989:183). Missourians to the north did not want to be included in the new "Mormon" county, so an additional county, named Daviess, was also proposed by Doniphan and established.

The northwestern Platte purchase was added to Missouri in 1837 (Rafferty 1983:40–41), and the Saints may have viewed it as a good area for new settlements (see Figure 12). Since the region had been so recently shifted from Indian Territory to the state of Missouri, the Saints, in fact, may have seen it as providential. For their part, the Missourians may have been more prone to give the Saints land northward knowing of the addition of this sizable parcel to the state.

Even before Caldwell County was officially formed, the Saints had been gathering there, and settlement after the formal organization could be considered zealous even by the standards of Joseph Smith. Far West was designed and platted by local leaders without Joseph Smith's formal approval. Likewise, plans for a temple were made by local stake presidents William W. Phelps and John Whitmer without first having received such instruction through revelation by Smith, as was standard procedure (Roberts 1978:2:481–84). Upon his arrival in Missouri,[2] Smith declared Far West a sacred site according to the usual revelation. Smith wrote, "Let the city Far West, be a holy and consecrated land unto me, for the ground upon which thou standest is holy; . . . and one year from this day let them re-commence laying the foundation of my house" (*Doctrine* 1981:115:7, 11). One year from the day Smith indicated would have been April 26, 1838, and belief would dictate that preplanning a temple site without Smith's approval indicated that the will of the Saints was in tune with what would eventually be revealed anyhow. Yet the one-year delay could have been instituted to avoid dwelling on the idea that the force of popular will might guide revelation. At any rate, the Saints were to "re-commence" construction of the temple at Far West now with divine approval. Cornerstones were laid to mark the site, but rapidly changing events prevented construction.[3] No specific reason was given for the holiness of the Far West site, so at the time no biblical event was recapitulated.

Most of the land in Caldwell County was government territory when the Saints arrived, and claims were soon made (Roberts 1978:2:475). Funds for new purchases were scarce. With a few exceptions, no money was gained from Jackson County lands, since the Saints had been forced to leave without remuneration. Funds came from Kirtland or were borrowed from sympathetic Missourians. An additional problem ensued when Phelps and Whitmer sold acquired property in Far West to Saints at a profit. These two leaders were removed from their positions by majority vote of the local members, but Smith soon reinstated them (Church Educational System 1989:184–87; Roberts 1978:2:521–24). Church leaders Oliver Cowdery and David Whitmer were later excommunicated for having sold "the lands of their inheritance" in Jackson County. The question of assigning culpability for selling of lands may be moot. Friction already existed between church members and Missourians, but more was added among the Saints themselves in the bickering over the acquisition, parceling, and sale of landholdings. Apparently, Edward Partridge's original system of apportioning lots failed as confusion arose when the Saints were uprooted. Still, the church did not view favorably decisions to sell sacred holdings in Jackson County, even when permitted to by Missourians.

Far West emerged in a time of chaos but nevertheless was planned according to the original 1833 Independence "plat of Zion." The Far West plat has survived in a number of different versions,[4] but all of them portray a one-mile-square pattern that contains 121 blocks with 8 lots to a block.

The square in the center was to be reserved for the temple. Why this plat did not copy the two-mile-square Independence plat is curious since leaders were certainly aware of the ever-increasing influx of Saints. Why hadn't the lesson been learned the first time around? Perhaps the establishment of the township and range system in Ohio had by this time influenced some surveyors among the Saints to think in terms of one-mile squares, but the Far West plan was soon enlarged to the two-mile-square format, anyway (Church Educational System 1989:184).

Letters written to family members during 1837 indicate that the Saints now viewed a substantial portion of western Missouri as somehow sanctified. For example, Charles C. Rich wrote of "going up to Zion" and "tarrying in Zion" when referring to Caldwell County (Arrington 1974:56). Caldwell County apparently was close enough to Jackson County to cause continued hope that the Saints would indeed be reinstated there. Far West therefore came to be viewed as an extension of the future New Jerusalem. For many in the Latter Day Saint experience today it remains an important, though vacant, site.

Adam-ondi-Ahman in Daviess County

The hyphenated term *Adam-ondi-Ahman* was first seen in an 1832 revelation of Joseph Smith. It attributed to the biblical Adam an important role as a major ruler and prince (*Doctrine* 1981:79:15–16), "the father of all, the prince of all, the ancient of days" (27:11). Smith may have derived the phrase from his Hebrew studies, but he never gave a translation of its meaning (Roberts 1957:1:421).[5] In March 1835, Smith identified Adam-ondi-Ahman as a specific valley where Adam anciently lived with his remarkably extended family toward the end of his mortal life (*Doctrine* 1981: 107:53–56). At this time, however, the location of this hallowed valley remained unrevealed (Matthews 1972:28–29). About the same time, William Phelps wrote a song entitled "Adam-ondi-Ahman," which was sung on various occasions, including at the dedication of the Kirtland temple in 1836 (Roberts 1978:2:364–65, 417).

In May of 1838, an expedition with Joseph Smith, Sidney Rigdon, Edward Partridge, and others proceeded north of Caldwell County to search for additional prime settlement sites for the burgeoning influx of Saints. One of Smith's apostles, Lyman Wight, settled on a sharp bend of the Grand River in central Daviess County (Figure 13; Gentry 1986:46–47).

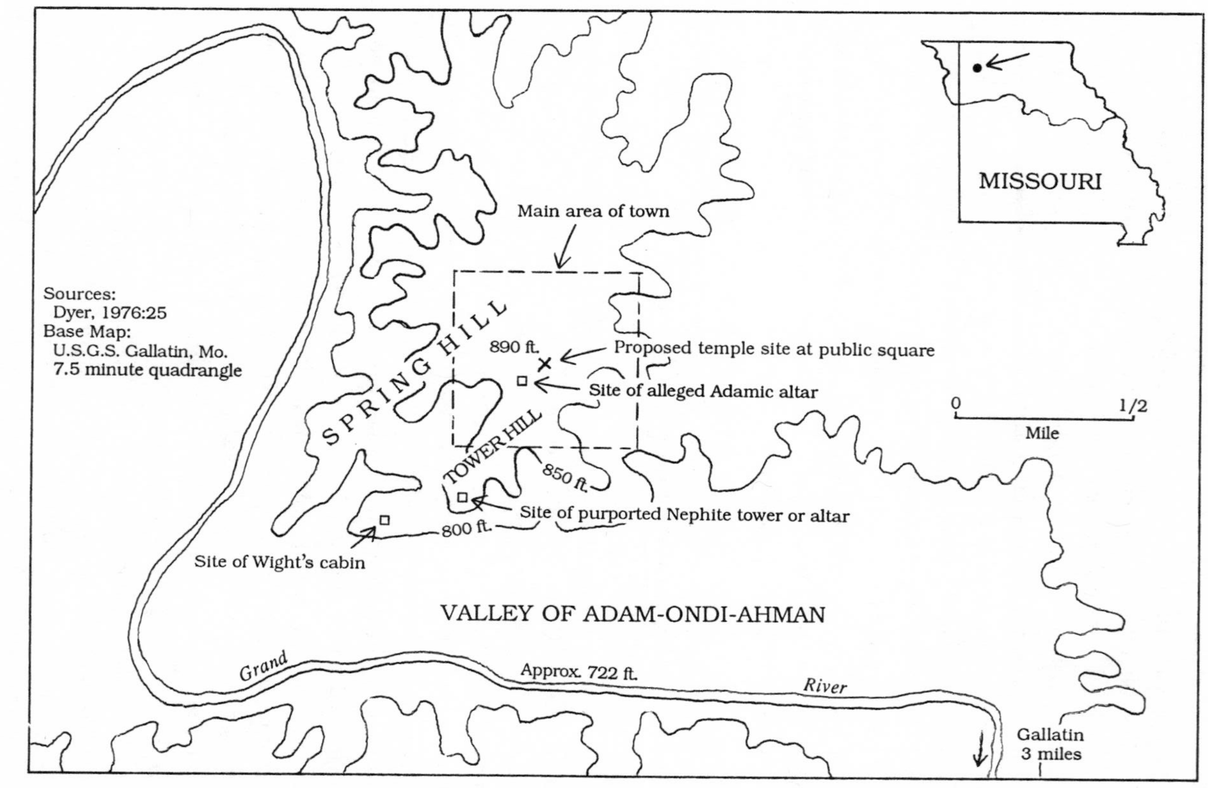

FIG. 13 | *Vicinity of Adam-ondi-Ahman, Daviess County, Missouri, 1837. Data from Dyer (1976:25). Base map from USGS, Gallatin, Missouri, 7.5 minute quadrangle.*

When the party arrived at Wight's cabin, Smith named one physical feature "Tower Hill . . . in consequence of the remains of an old Nephite altar" that he identified, ostensibly from *Book of Mormon* times (Roberts 1978:3:35). He also identified other Adamic remnants (altars or towers) to church members, but the sources for these accounts differ greatly one from another, often having been recorded in interviews years after 1838 (Gentry 1973:564–76; Kenney 1983:8:172). Early LDS Church history (the LDS Church later made this scripture as a section of the *Doctrine and Covenants*) says that Smith revealed the future importance of the area, specifically the larger Spring Hill, which was called "Adam-ondi-Ahman, because, said He, it is the place where Adam shall come to visit his people, or the Ancient of Days shall sit, as spoken of by Daniel the Prophet" (*Doctrine* 1981:116).

The earlier revelation gave emphasis to a valley, but this one emphasized adjacent Spring Hill. Generally, the whole area was viewed as sacred because of the past and future presence of Adam. This was also the time when Joseph Smith told the Saints that Jackson County was literally the site of the original Garden of Eden "from which Adam was driven" (Barrett 1973:373). The implication was that after expulsion from the Garden of Eden (in Jackson County), Adam gradually moved northward to this spot where his family grew to great numbers. This information is absent from Smith's history of the church but was recorded in a number of Saints' diaries from the period (Barrett 1973:377; Gentry 1973:566). Smith's aim was apparently to make a number of sites in northwestern Missouri sacred not only by emphasizing their links to past sacred scriptural events but also by implying their future importance. Especially in a time of despair after having been ousted from Jackson County, their New Jerusalem, other sacred biblical-historical sites were designated to help maintain the faith of the Saints.

Nestled in the curve of the Grand River, a town plat for Adam-ondi-Ahman was based on a two-mile square nucleus within a twelve-mile square grid (Gentry 1973:560–63). Both Adam-ondi-Ahman and Far West seem to have been envisioned as cities of Zion according to the original Independence plan of laying out settlements to cover all the earth (557–61). The Saints could envision millennial cities patterned evenly all across the plains, though for a time without the center place intact at Independence. At Adam-ondi-Ahman, however, the designers began with a two-mile-square grid, having learned to plan for larger numbers of migrating Saints. "Diahman" (a popular contraction of the longer name) was never officially registered as a town, and only a few streets were actually laid out; certainly none of them extended southward into the major valley as had been drafted on the plat. A two-block public square was the focus of the town's activity. A temple on Spring Hill near the square was anticipated but was never built (Figure 13; Matthews 1972:34).

Though land in Caldwell County had been purchased from the government, the early church settlers in the vicinity of Adam-ondi-Ahman never received title to their properties. Furthermore, this was Daviess County established for Missourians northward who did not want association with the Saints. That the Saints would settle there was a particularly piercing affront. At $1.25 an acre, the Saints had made claims by preemption right of first settlement and by the improvement of squatted tracts, but they were forcibly removed from Missouri before the acreage officially came up for sale on November 12, 1838 (Gentry 1973:558; 1986:47–49). Missourians were quite aware of this date, which added incentive to quickly remove the Saints from the region (LeSueur 1987:237–38).

Throughout the summer of 1838, Adam-ondi-Ahman grew rapidly and houses were raised at a rate of "two or three a day" (Gentry 1986:48). In June a new "stake" of the church was organized at Adam-ondi-Ahman (Britton 1920:7–8). With a number of new converts from Canada and elsewhere within a matter of a few months, it grew to be the largest town in Daviess County (Barrett 1973:371–73).

It was important to church members to make Adam-ondi-Ahman function as a center of a Latter Day Saint economic region. To this end, two prominent church leaders in Far West, George M. Hinkle and John Murdock, were sent to found a settlement of the Saints at the confluence of the Grand and the Missouri Rivers in Carroll County (Figure 12). The town, previously named DeWitt, was to serve as a steamboat landing for Latter Day Saint immigrants coming up the Missouri (Church Educational System 1989:189). Traders had used the Grand River to transport goods by flatboat (Britton 1920:2–3), and new settlers on the tributary hoped that navigation could be further exploited. At DeWitt, people and goods had to be transferred from steamboat to flatboat, hence the town's locational raison d'être as a port for Adam-ondi-Ahman fifty miles upstream (Roberts 1957:1:419–20). On June 23, 1838, Hinkle and Murdock purchased half of the town plat of DeWitt and families began to gather there in July (Cannon and Cook 1983:197). This lifeline to Adam-ondi-Ahman grew to about six hundred people (McGlumphy 1923:235), but three months later in October, the Saints were forced to leave DeWitt, presaging their complete expulsion from Missouri.

For a brief period, Adam-ondi-Ahman (and DeWitt as well) functioned as a useful safety valve for the rapidly growing settlement of Far West (Gentry 1973:559). Over one thousand Saints gathered in Adam-ondi-Ahman before being forced out of the state. Since Smith announced Jackson County as the location of the Garden of Eden, the Saints could place greater northwestern Missouri into a broad religious context. Adam and Eve were forced out of paradise (Jackson County) and moved seventy miles to the north into the dreary workaday world. The Saints, perceiving themselves as God's chosen people, had the opportunity to re-experience these sacred places and even the expulsion process. Their view was that they were necessarily forced out of Jackson County by disobedience, as was Adam, and into other historic Biblical sites as God directed them. Just as there was purpose in Adam's expulsion—to begin the endless generations of humanity—the Saints also saw purpose in their travails—to prepare themselves and the land for the second return of Christ.

The Loss of Missouri

Serious friction with Missourians in Caldwell and Daviess Counties began on Independence Day, July 4, 1838. It was a day of special jubilation in Far West, for the cornerstones were laid for a temple "one hundred and ten feet long and eighty feet broad," in the basic style of the model for Kirtland and Independence (Roberts 1978:2:41–42). Sidney Rigdon initiated trouble with a long speech containing strong language regarding the treatment of the Saints. The speech was meant for local ears, but its highlights were published in a Liberty newspaper, which once again set embers of distrust aglow (Barrett 1973:373–75). A riot broke out the next month at Gallatin, Daviess County, when locals tried to prevent Saints from voting at a state election (LeSueur 1987:58–64).

Both Saints and Missourians, from this time forth, prepared for battle, and lawlessness prevailed. State militia forced the evacuation of the Latter Day Saint settlement at DeWitt in Carroll County and then bands of militant Saints plundered Gallatin and Millport in Daviess County and Grindstone Forks in Clinton County. In the eyes of many Saints, civil war was now a necessity. By this time, many believed God would help them to place the foundation of Zion in Missouri through military force (LeSueur 1987: 83–89, 107–21, 126). Continued persecution begat violent reaction.

There followed a brief but extremely violent skirmish between an expedition of Saints and a Missouri militia unit just east of Far West (Cannon and Cook 1983:214–16). The military commander, the Saints' old attorney David R. Atchison, wrote to Gov. Lilburn Boggs, commenting that he was disgraced that the state "was acting the part of a mob" (Parrish 1961:25; see also Anderson 1986). Boggs, himself a Jackson Countian, not only removed Atchison from command but also refused to visit the scene of tensions, as many of the militia leaders had requested. Rather, Boggs arbitrarily favored the reports against the Saints and issued the famous "extermination order," declaring that the Saints "must be treated as enemies, and must be exterminated or driven from the state if necessary for the public peace." Boggs commented further that the Saints' "outrages are beyond all description" (LeSueur 1987:152).

The state militia besieged Far West, and after the murder of eighteen Saints at Haun's Mill in eastern Caldwell County (Cannon and Cook 1983:215), the crestfallen leaders at Far West surrendered. Fifty-two Saints were initially taken prisoner, but only Joseph Smith, Hyrum Smith, Sidney Rigdon, Lyman Wight, and two others were placed in permanent custody. They were taken to Independence and then to Richmond, where a preliminary hearing was held (LeSueur 1986). The six captives were finally taken to a jail in Liberty, Missouri, where they were held for four months. It was a time of deep and poignant reflection for leadership as well as membership. When security lapsed, perhaps intentionally, the captives finally escaped. For church members the event of imprisoning revered church leaders sealed forever the sacredness of Liberty.

Many of the Saints stayed for a few months on their Caldwell County farms but soon lost all hope of a return to Jackson County through litigation in state and local courts. They were forced to abandon their lands in Daviess County and to sell the acreage at Far West for practically nothing. The majority of the more than seven thousand Saints fled east. Most traveled through Missouri, crossing the Mississippi into Quincy, Illinois, but some Saints took a northward route through the Iowa territory exiting Missouri as quick as possible (Allen and Leonard 1976: 108–9). Residents of Illinois and Iowa were generally appalled by the treatment the Saints had received. Most refugees began to settle in the vicinity of Quincy, Illinois, and also Montrose, Iowa. In both locations, local citizens gave considerable sympathy and aid (Roberts 1978:3:265–67). The trek was accomplished without revelatory instruction, though able leaders and apostles, particularly Brigham Young, helped to organize the Missouri exodus. Joseph Smith designated no specific settlement place for some months. Only a few hundred Saints stayed in Missouri, and most of these left the church permanently (LeSueur 1987:223).

From then on, the Saints viewed Missouri with a certain pall as sacred space was de-emphasized. To use Kenneth Foote's (1997) terminology, to a remarkable degree, the tragedy of the Missouri experience has been largely obliterated from the landscape. Missouri was even considered cursed. The thousands of acres once owned by the Saints and the lands of sacred inheritance in Missouri even today have been largely wiped from the collective memory of most Saints, whatever their splinter affiliation, and from the minds of most Missourians as well. Very few Saints today have any idea that thousands of acres comprising many of the wealthiest old neighborhoods of Kansas City today were once theirs; they only know that Missouri is the land of the New Jerusalem and that Independence is the center place.

Jackson County and Zion in the Nauvoo Era

After recuperation in Quincy, Illinois, the Saints purchased large tracts of land in Lee County, Iowa. They also targeted the previously platted twin towns of Commerce and Commerce City on the Mississippi, in Hancock County, Illinois (Kimball 1978). Sympathetic citizens of Illinois and Iowa allowed loans with generous credit, which enabled the Saints to buy considerable acreage in these states (Church Educational System 1989:216). Nearly twenty thousand acres had been purchased in Iowa territory, but the Saints soon discovered that they had been sold false titles and within two years lost much of the Iowa land, so some Iowans were not as friendly as they first had seemed. Before the Saints' arrival, growth was stunted in the area of Commerce and Commerce City, where marshy lowlands made an unhealthy swamp. Originally a greater settlement area on both sides of the Mississippi was envisioned, but church leaders then focused on Commerce and the surrounding area in Illinois. The town site was purchased and subsequently renamed Nauvoo, which according to Smith meant in Hebrew, "a beautiful situation, or place, carrying with it the idea of rest" (Roberts 1978:4:268). The place was not "beautiful" yet, but surely the idea of "rest" gave comfort to the beleaguered Saints.

During late 1839 and early 1840 the swamp of the westward trending "Nauvoo peninsula" was gradually drained as the Saints hoped to match the implication of the purported Old World name. Other than the given etymology, Smith did not link Nauvoo to any Old Testament place or event. Nauvoo eventually grew to roughly ten times the size of Commerce and Commerce City combined, being platted in a grid similar to previous town plans at Independence and Far West, yet truncated on its western side because of the Mississippi. The town of Montrose, across the river in Iowa, also became an area of settlement, though the Saints only retained a small portion of land there.

By the end of 1839, when the Saints were well settled in Nauvoo, Joseph Smith and other church leaders traveled to Washington, D.C., to petition Congress for reinstatement to their Jackson County lands, or at least for redress for losses and damages while in Missouri (Roberts 1978: 4:39–42). Additionally, letters from a variety of parties were written to President Martin Van Buren supporting the Saints' cause (Lucas 1839; Rigdon 1839; Wight 1839), but there is no official record of any action or response by the president (see Library of Congress 1910). Territorial Gov. Robert Lucas of Iowa solicited an investigation in 1839, but it is unlikely that one was ever undertaken. A hint of the problem, however, may be seen in Van Buren's Fourth Annual Message to Congress one year after Smith's visit: "A series of questions of long standing . . . in which the rights of our citizens and the honor of the country were deeply involved, have in the course of a few years . . . been brought to a satisfactory conclusion; and the most important of those remaining are, I am happy to believe, in a fair way of being speedily and satisfactorily adjusted" (Sloan 1969:95–96).

In fear of losing the support of Missouri in the 1840 election against the Whig candidate, William Henry Harrison, Van Buren apparently ignored the Mormon issue. Joseph Smith reported that in their meeting with the president, Van Buren told the Saints that he could do nothing for them, because "If I do anything, I shall come in contact with the whole state of Missouri" (Roberts 1978:4:40). This lack of federal support was disheartening, as the Saints could not take their complaints back to the Missouri state government (Hansen 1970:80). The encounter set the church more firmly on a course of isolation from the American mainstream, greater autonomy for Nauvoo and once again for greater political involvement in the establishment of an organized autonomous Zion (Flanders 1970:29).

The Saints could have controlled local Hancock County government by 1842, but instead Nauvoo sought separation and independence from county as well as state government and law enforcement (Flanders 1970:34). The difficulties of the Saints in Missouri were seen as a "prelude to a far more glorious display of the power of truth, and of the religion [they] . . . espoused" (Roberts 1978:4:271). That glory was, in part, manifested under the Nauvoo Charter of 1841. This document, written by Joseph Smith and John C. Bennett, was based upon the charter of Springfield, Illinois, and many of its sections were identical. The charter, however, authorized a local government "largely free from outside interference, even by the state that authorized it" (Flanders 1965:92–93, 98). In the Illinois state legislature's haste to approve many city charters amidst a financial crisis and a depression, and perhaps also to show fairness to the Mormons, only a clause for an "extraordinary militia" (the Nauvoo Legion) was briefly questioned. After passing quickly through the state Senate and the House of Representatives, the charter was approved without change on December 18, 1841, by a review body that included Illinois Gov. Thomas Carlin (96–97).

Smith "conceived Nauvoo to be federated with Illinois somewhat as Illinois was federated to the United States, with strong legal and patriotic ties to be sure, but also with guaranteed immunities and rights of its own" (Flanders 1965:104). The sovereign nature of Nauvoo was stretched to extreme proportions, but a theocratic city-state can be seen as the natural progression of the urban millennial elements originally seen in the city of Zion plans for Independence, Missouri. These elements were subsequently mixed with practically militaristic tendencies of self-preservation as a result of a decade of continuous persecution (Bushman 1970:57). Nauvoo was not Independence, and neither was it the new New Jerusalem. Rather, it was an abode for the strengthening of the Saints prior to a return to the true Zion, which was "not to be removed" from Jackson County (*Doctrine* 1981:90:37; Hampshire 1985:22). The Nauvoo Legion military unit reportedly drilled in preparation for this reclamation of Missouri (Lee 1877:112).

In the minds of the Saints of the early 1840s, the Missouri years developed a dreamlike aura. The western Missouri setting became exaggerated and ultra-pastoral. In 1831 William W. Phelps had written an objective description of the Missouri landscape. He wrote another, more nostalgic one in 1834 (Anderson 1974; *Messenger and Advocate* 1834). Several years later, in Nauvoo, Joseph Smith approved still another more exaggerated and millennial account based upon the earlier one of Phelps. This sequence seems to have been typical, for other writings from Nauvoo about Missouri also have a decidedly exaggerated flavor, and the descriptions were written with the surety that God would eventually return their Missouri lands (Anderson 1974; Ham 1970:209). It is instructive to compare Phelps's earliest rendering with Smith's 1840s version of Missouri now published in Roberts's *History of the Church.*[6]

Whereas some early observers had denigrated the agricultural productivity of Jackson County, Smith extolled the pastoral prairie "spread out like a sea of meadows." The flowers were painted as "so gorgeous and grand as to exceed description," and Jackson County's bottomland was described as covered with "luxuriant forests." Smith saw soil there two feet deeper than Phelps originally had and, correspondingly, made more of its potential productivity. He wrote that the soil "yields in abundance, wheat, corn, sweet potatoes, cotton and many other common agricultural products" (Roberts 1978:1:197).

Smith's descriptions of animal life, both domestic and wild were more varied than Phelps had reported. His words reverberated with millennial, if not Edenic, promise:

> Horses, cattle, and hogs, though of an inferior breed, are tolerably plentiful and seem nearly to raise themselves by grazing in the vast prairie range in summer, and feeding upon the bottoms in winter. . . . The wild game is . . . plentiful . . . in the wild prairies. Buffalo, elk, deer, bear, wolves, beaver and many smaller animals here roam at pleasure. Turkeys, geese, swans, ducks, yea a variety of the feathered tribe, are among the rich abundance that grace [these] delightful regions—the heritage of the children of God. (Roberts 1978:1:197)

Missouri's climate was now seen as "mild and delightful three quarters of the year" despite Phelp's blunt earlier description of summers "hot enough to roast eggs" (Anderson 1971:276). For Smith, the land bid fair "to become one of the most blessed places on the globe" (Roberts 1978: 1:198). Modern-day Missourians might argue with the assertion that the winters of the region were "milder than the Atlantic states of the same parallel of latitude, and the weather is more agreeable," yet Smith persisted in the pastoral garden mode, finally comparing the area to the biblical image of the forested and productive Lebanon of old (Barrett 1973:186; Mikesell 1969; Roberts 1978:1:198).

While descriptions made Missouri paradisiacal, interpretations of the term *Zion* also underwent a forced alteration during the Illinois period. *Zion* became diffused to mean more where the Saints happened to be located and less a specific site in Missouri. Thus Missouri simultaneously became more yearned for and more distant in the minds of Smith's followers. Converts from successful missionary efforts in England were commanded to "gather to Zion" but naturally were directed to Illinois, not to Missouri (Roberts 1978:4:268). Another example of broadening of meaning comes from terminology in church organization. Geographical groupings of believers were called "Stakes of Zion," the analogy being Zion as a tent held up by "stakes" or groupings of the membership. By the end of 1840, at least seven stakes of the church existed in Illinois and Iowa besides the main membership in Nauvoo and in the old Kirtland Stake (Roberts 1978:4:233, 236, 361–62). Zion was thus increasing in size, but its precise form remained uncertain since the center place that God had chosen remained unoccupied and presumably would remain so until the church had somehow repented and changed. For many Saints such change was rapidly approaching. Brigham Young and some of the other apostles wrote in October 1841 that "the set time to favor Zion" had come and its "redemption" was discussed (436–37).

Insight into the broadening image of Zion can be found in the church's newspaper published in England, the *Millennial Star* (begun mid-1840). Consider, for example, the following quotations of English converts preparing to traverse the Atlantic. They would "purchase provisions by the quantity, and duty free, and the moment they bid farewell to their native shores they hoist the FLAG OF LIBERTY—the Ensign of Zion—the stars and stripes of the American Union; and under its protection they completely . . . nullify the bread tax." One paragraph later was a promise that the emigrants would: "add to the strength of Zion, and help her rear her cities and temples—'to make her wilderness like Eden and her desert like the garden of the Lord'" (Roberts 1978:4:512). These words clearly imply that Zion meant all of America as a sacred place. As such, the flag of the United States was the "Ensign of Zion," a place where "cities and temples" would be built.

The images were typical of the time. For the Saints, immigrants or otherwise, Zion had somehow absorbed many national properties in just a few short years. The term *New Jerusalem* was virtually abandoned and Jackson County was rarely referred to. That the future position of Jackson County, Missouri, was vague even in the mind of Joseph Smith is evident in the well-known letter that Smith wrote to editor John Wentworth of the *Chicago Democrat* probably in February 1842. This letter, a brief history of the church from its New York beginnings (Roberts 1978:4:535–41), ended in a list of beliefs that have been canonized by the Utah LDS Church as the "Articles of Faith" (*Pearl* 1981:60–61). One of these statements reads as follows, without mention of Missouri or of any other place of lesser scale than America: "We believe in the literal gathering of Israel and in the restoration of the ten tribes; that Zion will be built upon this [the American] continent; that Christ will rein personally upon the earth" (Roberts 1978:4:541; brackets subsequently added by LDS Church).

In a March 1844 "friendly hint to Missouri," Smith pronounced what may have been a last plea to Missourians for the Jackson County lands: "like the woman in Scripture who had lost one of her ten pieces of silver, arise, search diligently till you find the lost piece, and then make a feast, and call in your friends for joy" (Roberts 1978:6:247). To Smith, "friends" obviously meant "Saints." In the same letter, Smith also condemned the Missourians, writing that they should wash themselves clean. The whole essay carries a spirit of resignation, with a feeling that the Saints would not return to western Missouri any time soon. One month after this—and two before his assassination—Joseph Smith aligned himself more forcefully with the new enlarged meaning of Zion:

> You know there has been a great discussion in relation to Zion—where it is, and where the gathering of the dispensation is, and which I am now going to tell you. The whole of America is Zion itself from north to south, and is described by the Prophets, who declare that it is the Zion where the mountain of the Lord should be, and that it should be in the center of the land.
>
> I have received instructions from the Lord that from henceforth wherever the Elders of Israel shall build up churches and branches unto the Lord throughout the States, there shall be a stake of Zion. (Roberts 1978:6:318–19)

The statement lacked the old specificity but did match *Book of Mormon* teachings generally. Brigham Young, Hyrum Smith, and Heber C. Kimball all supported Smith's statement. In the admission of a greater area for Zion, Kimball's remarks were especially curious, since he even denied having ever taught about any gathering place. He stated: "I never teached anything else but the [basic] principles. When first we went to England, we preached nothing else, and never even touched on the gathering, the Church having been driven from Jackson county and also from Kirtland . . . and prophesied of coming to this land, as being the land of Zion. . . . Yet we never taught the doctrine of gathering" (Roberts 1978:6:324).

To Kimball's credit he was probably defending an innate desire in many of the European converts to come to America—not discussing the meaning of Missouri as the earlier gathering place. Joseph Smith never denied the previous importance of the "center of the land" but did now reinterpret a "center" as being more importantly focused on work done in temples instead of at the specific gathering site of Independence, Missouri. Nauvoo, for example, had been a place of rich doctrinal addenda for the fourteen-year-old church. Baptisms for the dead, instructional endowments, teachings on intelligence and the creation, polygamy, and eternal marriages all began in Nauvoo and all were directly related to temple activities. None of these doctrines were clear during the consecration years in Jackson County. The center of all things was now to be the temple "and that [the temple] should be the center of the land."

The Saints held an ultra-pastoral view toward Jackson County in the 1840s because a return was impractical. During 1841, the state of Missouri tried to extradite Smith for retrial for treason as a result of the Mormon War of 1838. In May 1842, an unknown assailant shot former governor Lilburn W. Boggs, author of the extermination order.[7] Naturally, many Missourians suspected the Latter Day Saints, and further attempts were made to extradite Smith to stand trial.[8] Smith was arrested and taken to a municipal court in Nauvoo where the unique city charter set him free under a writ of habeas corpus (Flanders, 1965:233–234; Gayler 1955: 10–11). The citizens of both Missouri and Illinois were surprised at the bold powers of the Nauvoo charter and sought to abolish it (Flanders 1965:104–5).

By 1844, the church and Nauvoo were rapidly changing. In an attempt to counteract mounting pressures against the church, Smith announced his candidacy for president of the United States in June. The strong block vote of the church and the autonomy of Nauvoo made the people of Illinois uneasy. Also, bold new doctrines such as temple rites, baptisms for the dead, and polygamy vexed some Saints. An antagonistic newspaper, the *Nauvoo Expositor,* was planned by bitter ex-members who had rebelled against these new directions in the church, particularly polygamy (Gayler 1961:5–6; O'Dea 1957:60–67). The paper was deemed injurious to the well-being of Nauvoo and on June 10 was ordered destroyed by Joseph Smith, mayor of the city, after only one issue had been published (Gayler 1961:8–10). A writ for the arrest of Smith was made, and he, his brother Hyrum, and fellow leaders Willard Richards and John Taylor voluntarily went into custody at Carthage, Illinois. On June 27, a mob that included ex-members of the church, rushed the two-story jail and Joseph

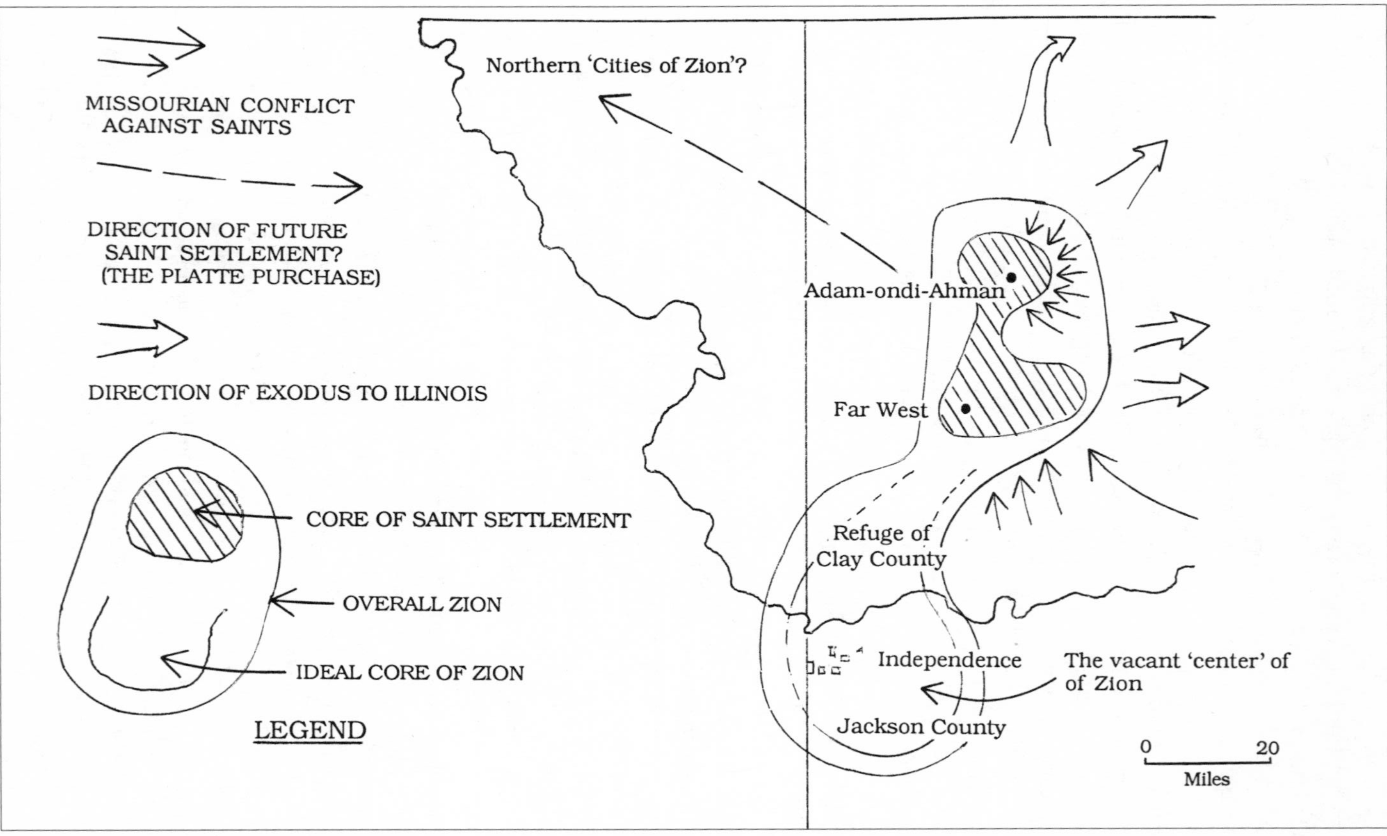

FIG. 14 | *The Saints' view of Zion, 1837–38.*

and Hyrum Smith were shot to death. Taylor was shot four times but later recovered and became the third president of the LDS Church. Richards escaped injury. The Nauvoo charter was completely repealed seven months later on January 29, 1845 (Flanders 1965:324).

Zion Generalized

Jackson County, Missouri, became less commonly referred to as a sacred place as the Saints were forced to move farther away from it. Clay County was a temporary, haphazard refuge, and while there the Saints expected to return shortly to Jackson County. Both Far West in Caldwell County and Adam-ondi-Ahman in Daviess County were platted as cities of Zion, in close proximity to Independence, which was still revered as the center. These towns were considered the beginning of a westward spread of new cities of Zion, a spread that, with time, may have focused on the new lands of the Platte purchase in the northwestern corner of Missouri (Figure 14).

Nauvoo was a city that was not easily inserted into the existing view of a Missouri-centered Zion. The Saints were forced to move to Illinois against their wishes and in an unexpected easterly direction. As a return to Missouri became more and more in doubt into the mid-1840s, Smith began to overemphasize the pastoral properties of Missouri, while Zion became a wider geographic concept. Simultaneously, the term *New Jerusalem* fell into disuse, as did references to Missouri. This phase also represented a distancing of the Saints' leadership and membership from millennial end-times. For them, the plan was no longer so imminent; more changes were obviously in store as further preparation awaited the believers. Missouri's residents were viewed as cursed for persecuting the Saints as the Saints viewed themselves as cursed for disobedience.

A Splintering and a Return

> We found . . . at Independence . . . some of the Hedrickite, Brighamite, Whitmerite, Framptonite, Morrisite, and Strangite brethren, all with the Josephites [RLDS] indulging a hope that the time for favoring Zion, the land of Zion, had fully come.
>
> —Joseph Smith III

Overwhelmingly, scholars treating the Latter Day Saints have focused on the larger Utah group, but another dimension of Zion exists, that which concentrates on the minority of Saints left behind. Most of these were scattered in small groups east of the Mississippi. As time passed, these peoples coalesced into new religious entities, each emphasizing different concepts of the original Latter Day Saint organization started by Joseph Smith (Shields 1991). Variations in the understanding of "original" church teachings resulted in geographic and doctrinal isolation among the groups. During the mid-1800s, some of these groups were determined to reoccupy the sacred core prophesied as the future New Jerusalem, and from this time forward, perceptions of Independence and its surroundings became truly diverse.

As these smaller independent churches of Saints emerged, the stage was set for a variety of interpretations of Jackson County as a sacred place of gathering. After some initial momentum, the LDS, RLDS, and Temple Lot Churches became the most recognized players on the Independence scene (see appendix 1). All of these groups retained and solidified distinct images of the New Jerusalem that they began to act upon in the latter half of the nineteenth century. These views are examined in this chapter.

The Missourians and the Temple Lot

After the fragmentation of the original Saints, the Missourians took possession of Jackson County lands. A seventeen-year interim existed between expulsion and reoccupation, of sorts, by believers, and with the evacuation and virtual abandonment of Missouri lands sacred to the Saints after 1838, those landholdings were divided and claimed by local residents. Most of the lands in western Jackson County, near the Kansas border, were swallowed up in the growth of the city of Kansas, the emerging metropolis of the central Great Plains (Spalding 1858:10, 14). Development around Independence took a backseat. The locals used the now vacated Temple Lot as a woodlot, and as the regional population grew it was gradually cleared for fuel. After his visit to Independence in 1878, LDS apostle Orson Pratt said that he found "not so much as a stump" on the Temple Lot (*Journal of Discourses* 1966:24:24). At least three deeds for the lot appeared and a

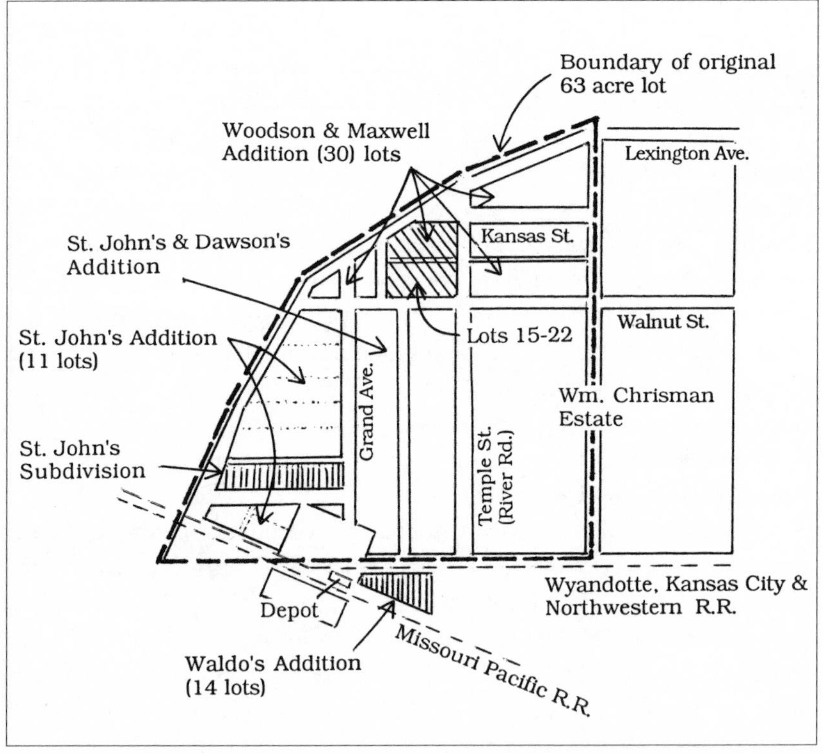

Fig. 15 | *Subdivision of the sixty-three-acre temple parcel, 1850–80.*

FIG. 16 | *The William Chrisman estate about 1875, viewed from the southeast. A portion of the land Partridge purchased became part of the estate and was located beyond the house. Reprinted from* Illustrated Historical Atlas Map of Jackson County *(1877:65).*

struggle for its possession disrupted the quiet existence it had experienced since the expulsion of the Saints in 1834.[1] Two of the deed holders, John Maxwell and Samuel Woodson, eventually reconciled their differences and together in 1851 divided the northern portion of the sixty-three-acre temple land into thirty lots. This portion was called the Woodson and Maxwell Addition, which reputedly contained the original site that Joseph Smith dedicated for a temple. Local citizens gradually purchased most of these individual lots, but a few, as will be discussed later, were eventually purchased by Granville Hedrick for the small Church of Christ (Figure 15; Flint 1953:111).

By 1877, about three-fourths of the greater Temple Lot land of sixty-three acres had been incorporated into three main additions to Independence: the Woodson and Maxwell Addition, St. John's Addition to the west, and the St. John's and Dawson's Addition east of River Boulevard (Figure 15; *Illustrated* 1976:73). By the turn of the century, St. John's addition had been substantially subdivided and many residences constructed, but the housing divisions of the rest of the Temple Lot changed little (*Platt Book* 1911:42).

The southeast portion of the Temple Lot remained undivided into the early 1900s, as it was the western portion of the large William Chrisman estate (*Illustrated* 1976:45, 65; *Platt Book* 1911:42). Chrisman, an Independence leader in banking and education, kept the property well tended and lightly wooded (Figure 16; Wilcox 1975:417–18, 467–69). Present-day River Boulevard, which passes the Temple Lot north-south on the crest of the hill, marked the western boundary of the Chrisman estate. It was referred to as Temple Street even by the Missourians of the time (Figure 15; *Illustrated* 1976:73).

The Kansas City area grew steadily during the 1850s, and by about 1860 the Temple Lot in Independence was surrounded by transportation and industrial pursuits aimed at mere commercial glory. Construction of the Missouri Pacific railroad advanced westward from St. Louis (Brown and Dorsett 1978:33; Spalding 1858:58–61) and passed immediately to the south of the Temple Lot in Independence (Figure 15). In fact, the railroad chopped off about an acre of the southwestern corner of the original temple property, which became a depot site (O'Brien 1982:7). The Wyandotte, Kansas City & North Western Railroad also was constructed along the southern boundary of the Temple Lot (the southern line of section 3; see Figure 5) in 1877. Later, during the streetcar era, Lexington Avenue, the angled thoroughfare bounding the Temple Lot on the northwest, was called Electric Street. Here the Metropolitan Street Railway ran its trolley cars on two separate tracks (*Platt Book* 1911:42). The Temple Lot was not the isolated dedication spot it once was, and as time passed it became more a part of the urban scene of Independence. Industry loomed, as the urban east infiltrated the western frontier. For the first Saints returning to Independence this posed an altogether new situation. After extended periods of isolation and conflict, a new era of mixing with the Missourians was now at hand.

With the rise in economic prosperity, gradual changes can be detected in the attitude of Missourians toward the Mormons. The overall tone remained decidedly negative until well after the turn of the century, in part because of the general American rejection of Utah polygamy. *The History of Jackson County*, published in 1881, was typical, referring to Mormons as "people of ignorant and superstitious minds" (252). In one post–Civil War atlas of Jackson County, the Saints were portrayed in less than glowing terms: "As their [the Saints'] numbers and strength increased they became arrogant and insulting, and daily proclaimed to the old settlers that the Lord had given them the whole land of Missouri. . . . They were a moral blot and a constant menace and could not be endured" (*Illustrated* 1976:14).

The tenor of statements was more evenhanded by the turn of the century, though understandably pro-Missourian. One reported that "[the Saints] put forth such extravagant claims as that the Lord had given them Missouri, and that the other people would either be destroyed or become their slaves. They were increasing so rapidly in 1833 that the old citizens feared that they would control the fall elections, and organized steps were taken to expel them" (Conard 1901:3:405–6). Another description said Joseph Smith's intention was to build a great structure "in imitation of King Solomon's temple," an analogy that the Saints never made but might have approved. This book made the claim that the Saints were attempting to possess the land "by purchase or by blood," indicating the common interpretation of Smith's revelations as threats (*Doctrine* 1981:58:52–53; 63:27–31). The book stated that by 1833 the "Christian settlers had become alarmed and aroused over the incendiary teachings and arrogant acts of the Mormons who preached and wrote in their newspaper declaring that the land was given to them as a spoil, and that no Gentile should inhabit it" (*Political History* 1902:34–35).

The terse statements of these writers were tempered, though, by the recognition of the growth of the Reorganized Church in Independence as will be discussed later in this chapter. Two churches of these Latter Day Saints who "practice and teach monogamy" were reported (Conard 1901: 3:406). It was hoped that this midwestern variety of Saint might prosper, at least at the expense of the disfavored Utah branch, though in the 1960s, Harry Truman said that the old Missourians "hate them just as much now as they did then" (Miller 1973, 450). The RLDS Church, it was reported, kept "missionaries actively at work in Utah, seeking to convert Brigham Young Mormons from that doctrine [of polygamy]" (*Political History* 1902:43). Generally, they had little success.

Fragmentations

After Joseph Smith was shot to death in June 1844, church leaders and members alike were confused as to who might follow him as prophet and president. Though many individuals claimed to have Joseph's blessing or authority as the new leader, most of the Saints eventually followed Brigham Young, the senior member of the twelve apostles, to the Rocky Mountains (Figure 17). The late-nineteenth-century views of the Utah group toward Missouri are covered in the following chapter.

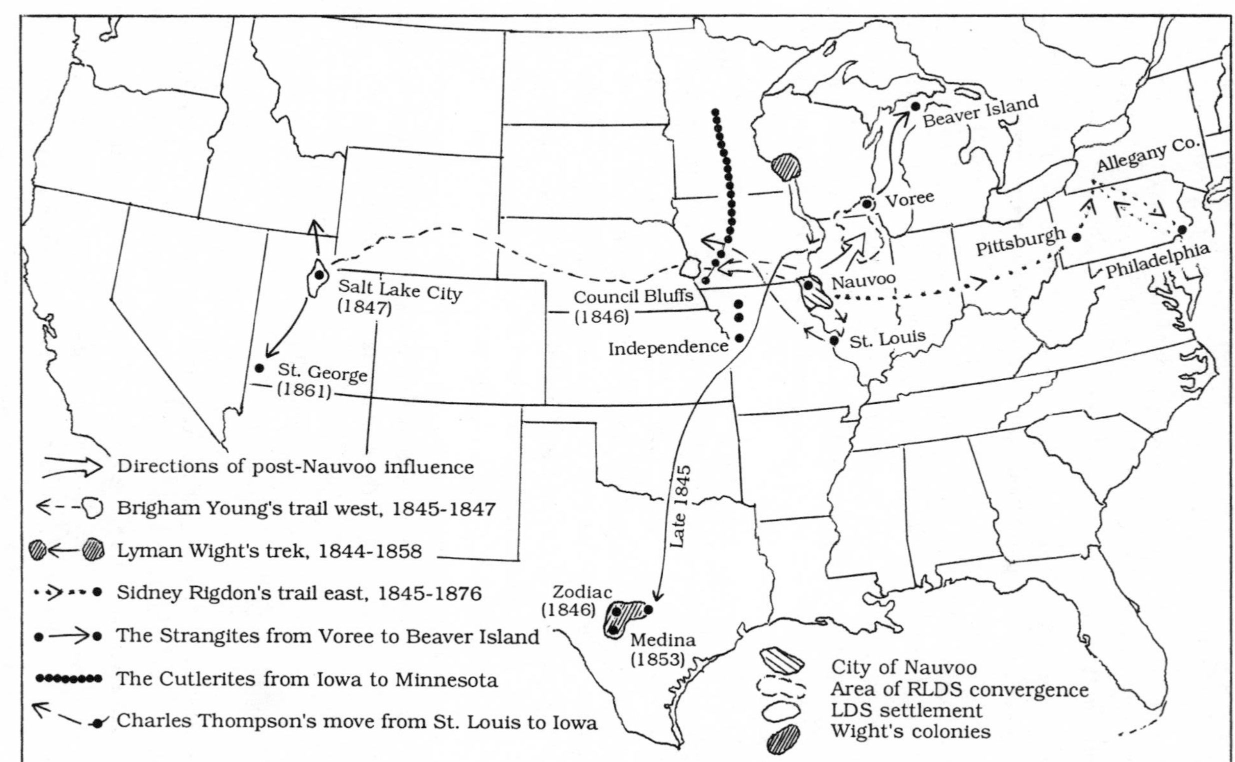

FIG. 17 | *Latter Day Saint splinter groups from the late 1840s.*

Notwithstanding the dominance of Young's movement, divisions had already occurred among the Saints. Many congregations were already scattered in other places beyond Nauvoo, particularly in Wisconsin, Illinois, Ohio, Pennsylvania, and New York. These were areas where the members lived and were converted, but most held dear to the sacred primacy of Independence, Missouri (Howard 1970:63). These people decided against moving west, reasoning that to migrate to the Utah territory would be abandoning Zion and rejecting the return to Jackson County prophesied by Joseph Smith Jr. (Anderson 1981:63). This scenario was particularly true for the Reorganization (RLDS) movement that eventually attracted Joseph Smith III—and for the Church of Christ (Temple Lot). These two groups today hold lands of historical and theological importance in Independence. Because of their belief in a millenarian place, one would expect these churches to hold more imminent millenarian beliefs, but this is not quite the way it has worked out—the development and interaction of these two organizations is treated in detail later. The fate of several small, early splinter groups first needs reviewing to show how the concept of a gathering place held the potential for fragmentation almost from the start (see appendices 1 and 2).

The Texas Mission of Lyman Wight

When Joseph Smith was killed, one group of the Saints was preparing to settle in Texas, and Lyman Wight, an outspoken apostle of the early church, led them (Roberts 1978:6:255–60; Davis 1989:376–77, 380). Wight had been in the area of the Black River in southwestern Wisconsin "pine country" in charge of a small lumbering operation of the Saints (Bitton 1970:ii). Wood and supplies from this area had been used for the construction of a variety of buildings, most importantly for the Nauvoo temple (Roberts 1978:4:608–9, 6:255). Wight suggested a southwestern movement for his group, and Smith backed Wight's endeavors, an indication that the waters of exodus were being tested. Wight saw the call to colonize Texas as divinely inspired and as a base to convert Native Americans who would eventually help to build the temple in Jackson County (Davis 1989: 376–77, 380; Roberts 1978:6:255–60).

After Smith's death, this peripheral group of Saints was left in a prophetless vacuum. Wight snubbed overtures from Brigham Young, Sidney Rigdon, and leaders of other smaller Latter Day Saint groups, and pioneered settlement in five different counties of central southern Texas (Figure 17;

Davis 1989:379–82). The colony lasted until the death of Wight in 1858 (Bitton 1970:iii), and he seemed to have always believed that "God in his infinite wisdom will most assuredly build upon that spot which he has pointed out with his own finger" (Davis 1989:385). Later, his son, Levi Lamoni Wight, joined the RLDS Church (Bitton 1970:viii).

The Kingdom Goes to Beaver Island

Another splinter group was also oriented toward a belief in magical and angelic apparitions similar to those that Joseph Smith claimed to have received. After the death of Joseph Smith, James Jesse Strang, a heretofore-obscure Saint, produced a letter supposedly written by the prophet. The letter proclaimed Strang as the next church leader (Fitzpatrick 1970:xxv, 148, 266; Van Noord 1988:7–11). Strang established his church at Voree, Wisconsin (present-day Burlington), and proposed a temple consisting of a central structure surrounded by twelve smaller ones and covered by a canvas. The entire structure was to be about 200 by 200 feet (Plan of the Temple 2001). Strang produced new writings that he claimed were divinely translated from plates dug up near the White River in 1845 (Fitzpatrick 1970:34–40). Strang later took a small group to Beaver Island in northern Lake Michigan (see Figure 17), where he crowned himself king. It is significant that Voree (Burlington) was in the RLDS core and that many Strangites eventually joined the Reorganization movement. Many early Saints who did not go to the Rocky Mountains were at some point associated with Strang. He died July 9, 1856, shot by assassins (Van Noord 1988:248–50, 264–65).

A small group of perhaps two hundred "Strangites" remains around Burlington. They call themselves "the original" Church of Jesus Christ of Latter Day Saints (Shields 1991:67–68; Original Church 2001), but members believe the "true church" has been in "a shattered and disorganized state" since the assassination of Strang (Hajicek 2000). They claim original ownership of the Nauvoo site and of the Kirtland temple and claim that the sacred temple grounds in Voree are "like the ones . . . started in Independence and Far West" (Original Church 2001). The Voree temple site is found in a grassy field similar to what one sees today at Far West. Strangites give millennial and gathering importance to the usual historical sites but also include Wisconsin and the Great Lakes islands as central gathering places. As Strangites see the true church in a disorganized state, the time of a millennial gathering is uncertain. Since the LDS Church does not generally recognize the smaller splinters of historical Saints, the Strangites see the larger western church as an organization too large, bold, and arrogant for its own good.

Rigdon's Eastern Influence

At the death of Smith, one important leader of the Latter Day Saints sought to renew the earlier Ohio experience of the church. Sydney Rigdon, who had been an important influence as one of two counselors to Joseph Smith,[2] thought that no prophet would succeed Smith and tried to appoint himself "guardian" of the church in 1844. Brigham Young, as president of the twelve apostles, asserted control and offered Rigdon a continued position of prominence in the church. Rigdon refused and was excommunicated by Young (McKiernan 1971:115). Rigdon retained a following, however, and returned east to Pittsburgh, Pennsylvania, where he had already moved his family. There, not far from Kirtland, he established a separate "Church of Christ" in 1845, claiming that Joseph Smith had been a fallen prophet and Nauvoo, a fallen city (136).

In Pittsburgh, Rigdon taught a gospel patterned after the Kirtland period of earlier church history when he had been more influential among the Saints (136–37). Rigdon made plans for the establishment of a New Jerusalem in Allegheny County, New York (not Pennsylvania), apparently believing that if Smith had "fallen," the sacredness of the Independence location should also be reconsidered. Rigdon's plan thus exhibited little of the element of American centrality as sacred. He moved his group of about 150 believers to New York in April of 1845 (McKiernan 1971: s142–43). Here they purchased a farm, but payments became difficult and Rigdon's Church of Christ disbanded late in 1847. Rigdon later went to Philadelphia and in May 1863 formed another organization called the Church of Jesus Christ of the Children of Zion (Gregory 1981:52–55). By the 1880s few members were left in any of his millennial groups (see Figure 17).

One of the converts of Rigdon, William Bickerton, started a small but successful movement based in Monongahela, Pennsylvania, that today has about six thousand adherents (Whalen 1964:280; Shields 1991:7 4–75). More will be discussed on this group in chapter 8, but this church also maintains branches in Ohio and Detroit, Michigan, in particular (see appendix 2).

An Experiment in Iowa

In 1848, Charles B. Thompson, a successful missionary for the early Latter Day Saints, went to St. Louis, Missouri, and began to publish a series of religious pamphlets independent of any of the other Latter Day Saint groups. In one of them he wrote that "the Lord will have no more church organization until after the redemption of Zion," which seemed to indicate that no church could be organized until some sort of gathering to Jackson County took place (Davis 1989:387–89). In 1854, Thompson, who claimed to speak for a spiritual being named Baneemy, took his group of some two hundred people to western Iowa and preempted "several thousand acres of the best land to be found in that community" (Davis 1989:388). By 1860, the experiment had fallen apart, the lands sold, and Thompson had fled back to St. Louis. How Thompson's Zion would fit with Independence eschatology is uncertain.

William Smith

A brother of Joseph Smith, William, who held the calling of patriarch in the church (usually a calling to give special blessings to members) saw himself as the rightful heir to the presidency of the church as a relative of the deceased prophet (Howard 1970:64). He established a following, which diminished in importance after he advocated polygamy at a conference at Covington, Kentucky, in 1850. After this, William Smith never directly associated himself with any of the Saint organizations, though he did, on occasion, speak to congregations of the RLDS Church. A similarity with the later Midwesterner Joseph F. Smith (not the LDS president) is striking. This Temple Lot Church member is also advocating "unity" among the Saints today.

The Temple-Oriented Cutlerites

Some of the new groups that formed during this period of Latter Day Saint reformation were intent on building the New Jerusalem temple as Joseph Smith had described, but much variation existed in the doctrines that the new splinters borrowed from the early church. Alpheus Cutler, a mason who had worked on the Nauvoo temple, led one of the groups that broke ranks with the Brighamites. Nine years after Smith's death he rejected Young's leadership and convinced about forty families to break from the westward movement at Winter Quarters (Dewey 1986:152). He took his "True Church of Christ" to a settlement called Fisher Grove in Fremont County, Iowa, where he established the town of Manti (Dewey 1986:-152; Cannon and Cook 1983:257). Like the followers of Lyman Wight, this group apparently had aspirations to erect the prophesied temple in Independence and, during the early 1860s they made ready wagons, tents, and "other appurtenances of nomadic life" for a return (Anderson 1952: 207–8). Cutler died in 1864 but not before receiving a vision that "described a land between two beautiful lakes," and the group moved to Minnesota and established the village of Clitherall in 1865 (Figure 17; see Dewey 1986:152). There the group remained until the 1930s when a branch of the Cutlerite Church was also established in Independence (Davis 1989:360–61). Their meetinghouses in Minnesota and Independence were considered "temples," and their top floors are reserved for private ceremonies that date to the endowment rites originally performed in Nauvoo (Shields 1991:70–71).

Membership in the various groups described above was surprisingly fluid. Leaders spoke to one another and many individuals passed from one group of Saints to the next. Many who followed William Smith later followed Strang. Many who followed Strang later aligned themselves with the RLDS movement. Others kept in contact with Rigdon. Later, Rigdon tried to contact Lyman Wight. Wight's son became a member of the RLDS Church. There was a coherence in belief that caused most of the Saints who chose not to go to Utah to seek linkages to other groups of Saints rather than revert to mainstream Protestant practices (McKiernan 1971: 136–37). "Eastern" Saints later went to Utah, however, and likewise, some in Utah eventually joined the RLDS Church and returned eastward.

Today, the survivors of the early splinter groups of Cutler, Strang, Rigdon, and Wight can almost be counted on fingers and toes. If the quilted patterns of geography had unfolded differently, substantial centers of the Saints might exist today in Wisconsin, northern Michigan, Pennsylvania, and Texas. These initial splinter groups each had unique, though brief, views of gathering places and meanings of Zion. For most of them Independence as sacred American space remained paramount. Reflecting on an 1877 visit to Independence, Joseph Smith III remarked on the variety of different Saints found there, a demonstration of the considerable interest already mounting in Jackson County: "We found Brethren . . . from Canada, at Independence, together with some of the Hedrickite, Brighamite, Whitmerite, Framptonite, Morrisite, and Strangite brethren, all with the Josephites [RLDS] indulging a hope that the time for favoring Zion, the land of Zion, had fully come" (RLDS 1967:4:190). These organizations were diminutive and most slowly died out or have left very few followers in the twentieth century. The mention of Framptonites and the Morrisites is still vague, and of these two little is known. Of these varied eastern groups of Saints, the two most important in control of sacred territories in Independence were the Church of Christ (Temple Lot) and the Reorganized Church of Jesus Christ of Latter Day Saints.

At the Precise Spot: The Church of Christ (Temple Lot)

About 1850, several of the eastern branches of the original church were located in central Illinois, isolated in Woodford County just north of Bloomington. In the early 1850s they began their own religious self-determination and under the leadership of Granville Hedrick a new brand of Latter Day Saintism emerged (see Figure 18; Flint 1953:98). In 1853 these local Saints, in reaction to news of polygamy being openly practiced in Utah, declared themselves "free from all wicked factions and united upon the pure principles of the Church of Jesus Christ (of Latter Day Saints)" (Flint 1953:99). In 1857 Granville Hedrick was chosen to lead the group in the office of "first Presidency of the Church . . . and to be a prophet, seer, revelator, and translator." In 1863, he was ordained president of the Church of Christ (102, 104). Later, this nomenclature was dropped, the head of the church being a "presiding elder" among—and not in addition to—twelve apostles (Shields 1991:75).

This church followed tenets from the earlier period of the Saints. Hedrick's group believed in most of the early church's practices founded by Joseph Smith Jr. up to the 1830s when Independence was declared the site of the future New Jerusalem. The Hedrickites' interpretation, however, was that Smith had begun to incorporate ideas into the church, which were not inspired by God. These ideas included various temple rites such as baptisms for the dead, eternal marriages, and polygamy. They also rejected the idea that the prophet had to be a lineal descendant of Joseph Smith, thus breaking with the Reorganization movement's point of view despite several years of friendly relations during the late 1850s (Flint 1953:101, 104). The Hedrickites were so distraught by the actions of other Saint churches that they even rejected the concept of a first presidency (a prophet and two counselors) that both the LDS group in Utah and the RLDS Church

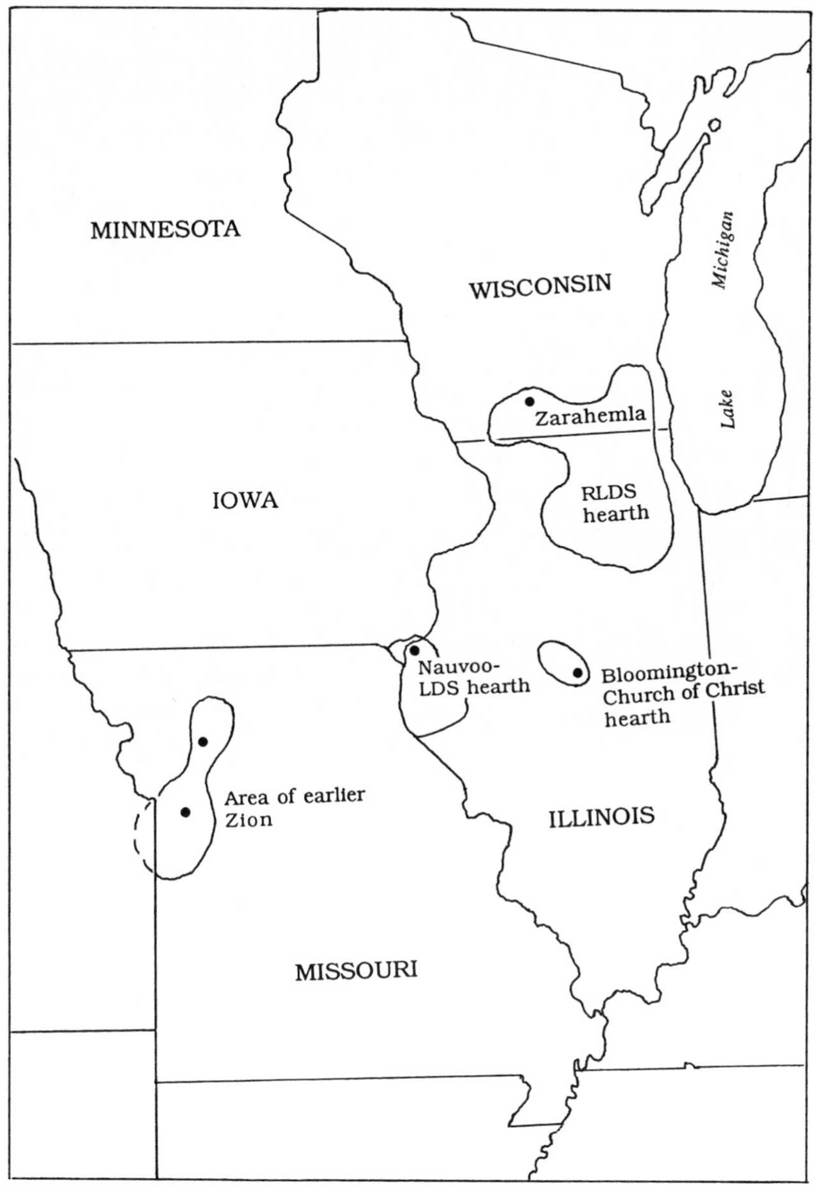

FIG. 18 | *New agglomerations of Saint activity, 1855*

adopted and use to the present. The idea of a first presidency was seen as another later development of Smith, one not inspired by God. The Church of Christ eventually recognized the need for twelve apostles, one of them being a "president of the high priesthood," but no person of prophet status or leading group of three men have ever been chosen (105). Joseph Smith Jr., for all his perceived human failings, was seen as the only prophet God had needed.

As the Civil War was winding down in 1864, Hedrick, though not considered a prophet, received millenarian revelations to prepare for the little church's imminent return to the consecrated land of Jackson County. One document, written in the divine first person, stated: "Prepare yourselves and be ready against the appointed time which I have set and prepared for you, that you may return in the year A.D. 1867, which time the Lord . . . [will] prepare a way before you that you may begin to gather" (Flint 1953:107). Some sixty followers of Hedrick went according to the instruction and arrived at the Missouri River adjacent to Jackson County in February 1867. Slush-topped ice covered the river, but the cautious caravan safely crossed "into Zion" (108).

Upon their return, the small Church of Christ worked to purchase specific lots of the Woodson and Maxwell addition. They especially desired those lots seen as the most sacred, numbers 15 through 22, lot 15 being, according to all available evidence, Smith's temple dedication site. All these were purchased between 1867 and 1874 (Figure 19); the group apparently never being interested in the larger sixty-three-acre parcel originally bought by Edward Partridge (Flint 1953:111). This larger land area was seen by the Church of Christ as simply a convenient acquisition by Partridge in order to obtain the temple dedication spot, a convenient belief considering the group's meager finances. The group rejected Joseph Smith's extended plans for the New Jerusalem, particularly those for a layout of twenty-four temples. They argued that this plan was his own idea and that it was not received by revelation from God (RLDS 1967:5:118). By contrast, in later decades the larger RLDS and LDS groups have not limited their acquisition aims to this smaller spot, though the possession of it has become a struggle of some interest, particularly to the RLDS Church.

Between 1867 and the early 1870s a small house was built on the Temple Lot as a headquarters for the Hedrickite Church. The site at the muddy crossroads of River and Lexington Streets was far from idyllic. Hedrick himself settled in Gardner, Johnson County, Kansas, and continued as the head of the organization's apostles (Flint 1953:114). Because of

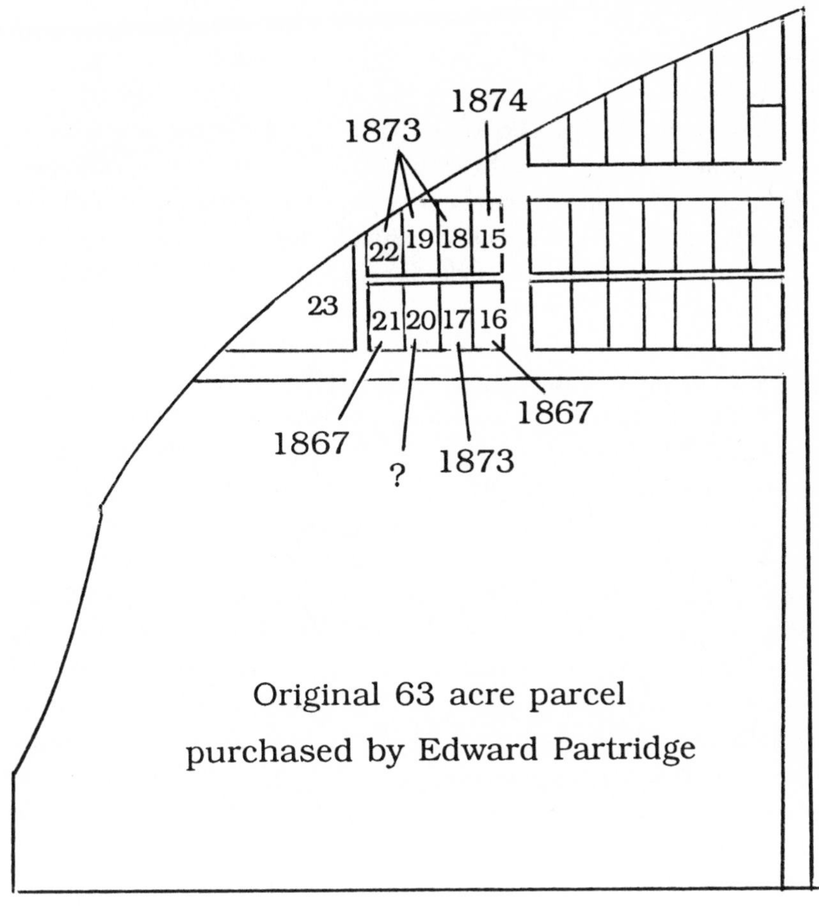

FIG. 19 | *Lots purchased by Hedrick's group, 1867–74. Data from Flint (1953:11).*

a lack of funds, the church did not approve construction of a meetinghouse on the Temple Lot until April 1887. This construction was likely spurred by RLDS discussions to build a church just to the north of the Temple Lot, known as the Stone Church. The Church of Christ wood frame structure was a one-room schoolhouse-sized building that could hold only about fifty people. In the fall of 1898, one W. D. C. Pattyson apparently saw himself called by God to keep the Temple Lot free from occupation and burned the small Church of Christ building. Pattyson had some history of vandalism, as he had previously attempted to destroy fencing around the lot (116). Thus began a thread of belief through the decades that the site was in need of purging and purification.

In 1891 troubles began over the ownership of the Temple Lot when the RLDS Church took the Church of Christ to court. The two groups had met earlier to see if differences could be settled and unification achieved, but the efforts failed (RLDS 1967:5:118). Because of the uniqueness of doctrine and isolation from the general populace, members of the various Latter Day Saint churches have always tended to stream from splinter to splinter, though interpretations of Smith and the original teachings have solidified an immunity to ecumenicalism. Latter Day Saint churches splinter but rarely merge or unify.

The RLDS Church decided on legal action, the details of which are presented in the RLDS discussion below. By 1895 the Church of Christ still retained the land against the legal intent of a much larger organization. The little church had to raise approximately five thousand dollars in this first defense of their property, solidifying their view of its value, if not its sanctity. In hindsight perhaps the small group should have purchased more lots.

After the burning of the small headquarters building, in the fall of 1898, discussions began on the construction of a new Church of Christ headquarters on the Temple Lot. A new two-story structure, built at approximately the same site as the old building, was completed and dedicated for the church's April conference in 1902. West of this building a line of trees, perhaps a small apple orchard, was evident in an early postcard of the lot (Kansas City Public Library 2002). This building stood for eighty-eight years until it, too, was burned by a troubled, dancing man on January 1, 1990. At the April 1901 conference, a plan was also discussed to build a bishop's storehouse on the Temple Lot to supply needed goods to members of the church. This plan was never realized.

W. D. C. Pattyson, the man who burned the Church of Christ's first church building, was released from an insane asylum in St. Joseph, Missouri, in 1906. He proceeded once again to set fire to the church's newer building on the Temple Lot; he was stopped this time and again committed to the asylum. To Mr. Pattyson can be given the honor (or dishonor) of starting a negative perception of New Jerusalem space that has appeared intermittently to the present. This view, discussed further in chapter 8, usually involves Saints who feel left out of the revelatory process or those who are disgruntled with the current landowners in Zion, whether they are of the LDS, RLDS, or Temple Lot Churches. These negative beliefs in the New Jerusalem usually revolve around the perceived need for some sort of "cleansing" of the sacred property. The beliefs range from simple "dark clouds over Zion" to the need for the area's total destruction.

The Reorganization Movement

The Church of Christ (Temple Lot) is one of the more enduring churches developed out of the scattered eastern Saints. It was not, however, the largest group. That distinction belonged to one known for a "reorganization" and another coinciding reinterpretation of early church doctrine. This movement began along the Wisconsin-Illinois border, around which many of the isolated midwestern Saints coalesced.

In the 1850s, one Jason W. Briggs, from Beloit, Wisconsin, became disillusioned with the organizations of James J. Strang and William Smith. Along with another Saint named Zenas H. Gurley, Briggs began to unify remnants of Saints in southern Wisconsin and northern Illinois (Figure 20). Gurley and Briggs argued that a new organization, a "reorganization" of the church was needed, since, in their view, the Lord had rejected the church during the time of the "Nauvoo experiment." Doubts arose regarding several doctrines and practices instituted in Nauvoo, including baptisms for the dead, temple marriages, and the beginnings of polygamy. Though still held dear by Saints following Brigham Young, many viewed these beliefs as extreme and fallacious, especially the disconnected Saints in the settlements peripheral to Nauvoo (Howard 1970:72).

From Wisconsin to Illinois

Briggs and Gurley insisted that the Reorganized Church should be led by a direct descendant of Joseph Smith and set about convincing Joseph Smith's oldest living son, Joseph Smith III, to accept a place with their group as prophet (RLDS 1967:3:207, 247–52).[3] Having never gone west, he finally agreed to this position in April 1860 at a conference in Amboy, Illinois (Howard 1970:67). Joseph III lived at Nauvoo at this time but moved to Plano, Illinois, in 1866 to become chief editor of the Reorganization's publication, the *Saints' Herald* (Anderson 1952:118, 210–11). Plano was centrally located among the Illinois and Wisconsin Saints and thus became the first, though temporary, headquarters of the church.

Previous to Joseph Smith III's acceptance of leadership in the reorganization, the tenuous grouping of Saints in southern Wisconsin and northern Illinois had begun to have conferences in 1852, following the same biannual schedule as the early church. The first conference was held in Beloit, Wisconsin, in June. From 1852 until 1858, conferences were held in Wisconsin, usually in Zarahemla,[4] in Lafayette County, a now defunct town

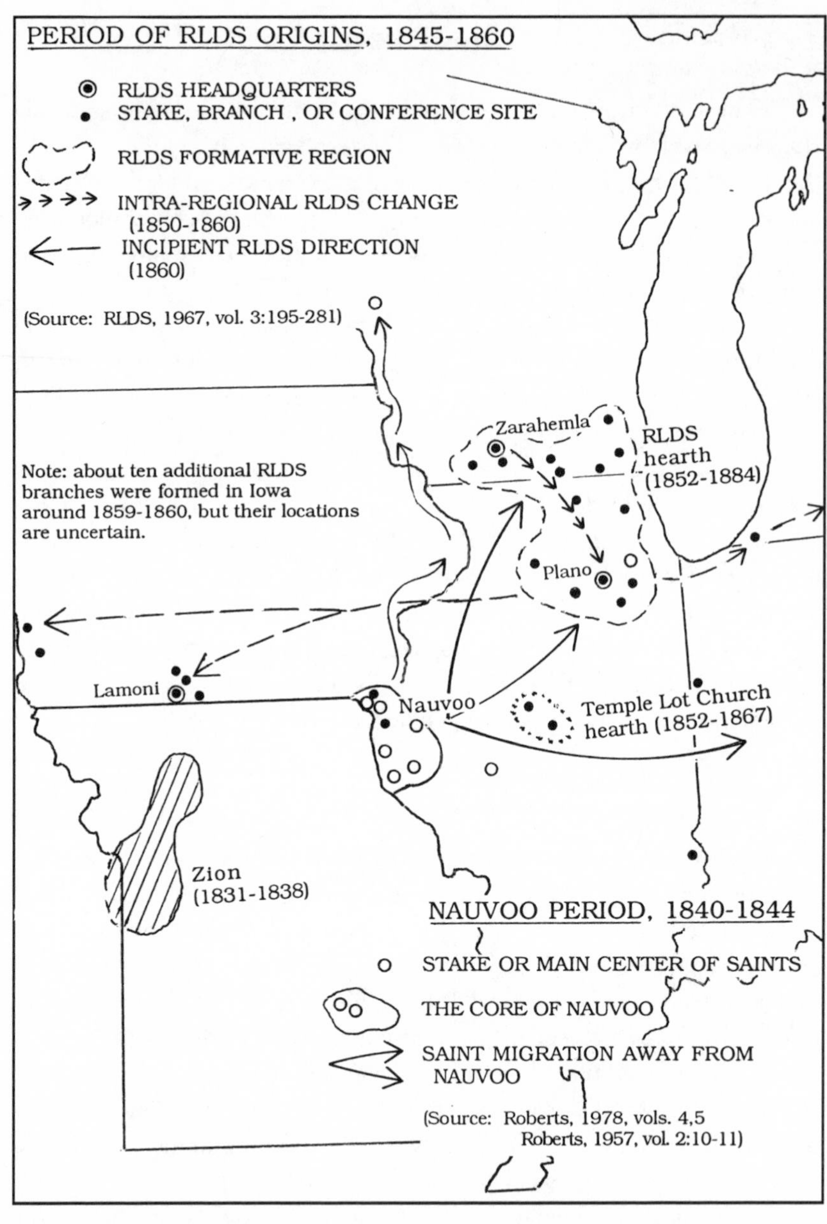

FIG. 20 | *Post-Nauvoo origins of the Reorganization. Southern Wisconsin and northern Illinois were a post-Nauvoo focus generally not discussed in Latter Day Saint diffusions. Data from RLDS (1967:3:195–281) and Roberts (1957:2:10–11; 1978:4, 5).*

close to Argyle (*Early* 1959:iii). Even at this early stage of the reorganization, church leaders instituted a democratic and businesslike atmosphere in meetings, which was to become emblematic of the RLDS Church. Church members passed resolutions regarding doctrinal positions of the fledgling church in parliamentary-style procedure. In early years, not more than one hundred people usually attended (RLDS 1967:3:218). This manner of decision making was quite foreign to the western Latter Day Saints where a top-down organizational style predominated. One of these resolutions portrayed an interest in a return to Independence even before Smith III joined the group. It read:

> Resolved that in the opinion of this Conference there is no Stake to which the Saints on this Continent are commanded to gather at the present time, but that the Saints on all other lands, are commanded to gather to this land preparatory to the reestablishment of the Church in Zion, when the scattered Saints on this land will also be commanded to gather & return to Zion & to their inheritances, in fulfillment of the promises of God. And it is the duty of the Saints to turn their hearts & their faces towards Zion and supplicate the Lord their God for such deliverance. (*Early Minutes* 1959:4; RLDS 1967:3:210)

Though some of the geographic vagueness with regard to western Missouri was still evident from the Nauvoo period, the point of the resolution was clear. Shortly after the conference, two members of the group, David Powell and John Harrington, were sent on a mission southward through Illinois and to western Missouri to check on the situation there and to visit the prominent Whitmer family who had remained in Ray County.[5] Afterward, they traveled to Arkansas (RLDS 1967:3:212–13).

The admonition not to gather at any particular stake was practical and kept "their" Saints from uniting with other offshoot groups, and particularly from following Brigham Young to Utah. Nevertheless, Jason Briggs labeled Zarahemla, Wisconsin, a "preparatory stake" two years later, in 1854. Zarahemla, portrayed as "a mining, as well as grain, and stock-raising region," was described in much the same hopeful terms as was Utah for Young's followers. It seems that Briggs hoped that the Saints who were affiliating with the reorganization would consider gathering there temporarily since "considerable unclaimed government land" remained in the vicinity

(Briggs 1854b: 14). Or perhaps Briggs himself did not want to move. Although some of the Saints of the reorganization may have begun to move to Zarahemla, its peripheral location led to failure as a church center.

Starting in 1859, Joseph Smith III gained a greater interest in the church's development and conferences began to be held farther southward in the Illinois towns of Amboy and Plano. Plano, Illinois, as the home of Smith III, was made the administrative center of the church by 1866. Throughout the 1850s, Briggs and Gurley held constant the belief of the return of the reorganized movement of Saints to Zion. Missouri was usually, but not always, implicated. Briggs and others, to show that the Saints would eventually return redeemed, heavily backed their stance with Old Testament scriptures. Usually these writings referred strictly to Zion and mentioned Jackson County and Missouri less frequently than did the documents of the Saints who had gone to Utah. Still, belief in an eventual migration was unmistakable. When the Illinois Saints had repented sufficiently, they believed that their faces would be turned toward Zion and one "like Moses," a "successor of Joseph," would be raised up to lead them back (Briggs 1854a:13). At the 1854 conference, Briggs insisted that "Zion cannot be built up unless it is by the principles of the law of the celestial kingdom" and referred to the New Jerusalem described in Revelation that was to be "fifteen hundred miles square" (Briggs 1854b:12–13), though other Latter Day Saint groups have interpreted this scripture as a celestialized heavenly city to come to the earth postmillennium. Though the emphasis seems to have been on Independence, hesitation existed in openly proclaiming the location of Zion. Perhaps Briggs and Gurley still pondered a center being established in northern Illinois, southern Wisconsin, or elsewhere. In addition to western Missouri, missionaries were also sent to Nauvoo and to Council Bluffs, Iowa, in 1859 (RLDS 1967:3:237). A variety of locations were investigated for Zionic settlement.

Many letters of invitation were written to Joseph Smith III in order to solicit his acceptance of the position as prophet of the Reorganized movement. In one of these, Jason W. Briggs wrote that the church was awaiting "the true successor of Joseph the Prophet" so that the restoration of "the exiled sons and daughters of Zion to their inheritances" might be brought to pass. Despite the search for temporary places of gathering, any mention of "inheritances" meant Jackson County, and Joseph Smith III, as son of Joseph Smith Jr., was seen as a key to the return of the Saints to that chosen land of Missouri (RLDS 1967:3:261–62).

Looking for Missouri and Finding Iowa

When Joseph Smith III finally accepted the position as prophet of the Reorganized Church in 1860, he cautiously sought land to purchase for settlement. As tensions built toward the Civil War, Smith III may have also been preparing a haven for members of the church. Jackson County was one of the first places he looked. He sent a Quincy, Illinois, lawyer named Godfrey to Independence to gather information on land records (Launius 1988:170–71) and then dispatched his stepfather, Lewis Bidamon, to investigate the possibility of the return of some of the early church's lands. Smith said that Bidamon "made no discoveries of value touching our claims to Missouri lands" (RLDS 1967:3:266). Bidamon also went north through Missouri and into Iowa, continuing to look for a good site for settlement.

Upon Bidamon's return to Plano, Smith seemed polarized. He chided Bidamon for "looking for land outside of Jackson County," all while assuring him that the Reorganization had "no concrete plans" for any communitarian venture (Launius 1988:171). Smith III was cautious and continually tried to balance the radical doctrinal declarations of his father with his tendency to be practical and unhurried in selecting a site for Zion. In his memoirs, in reaction to seeing the Cutlerites' desire to return to Jackson County from southern Iowa in 1863, he wrote of the need for the Saints to be fully prepared: "it was folly for men to anticipate going to Zion to build a great and beautiful city and a great and beautiful Temple, who would be absolutely poverty stricken when they reached there, with no money to help themselves or any body else, or to further any great project" (Anderson 1952:208–9). He had told Saints then living in Iowa that within a few years their land would be blessed in preparation for settlement in Independence, but this was quite different from what the Saints were admonished to do in the early 1830s. At that time the Saints were to gather or be destroyed, as the millennium was imminent, so this leisurely gathering was millenarianism somewhat postponed (Underwood 1993: 26–27). Smith III also foresaw a new railroad that would aid the Saints in Iowa. Smith, however, wrote these observations with hindsight in his memoirs during the first decade of the 1900s (Anderson 1952:209).

Joseph Smith III clearly accepted the idea of a utopian Zion, though he did not take the concept as literally or millennially as had his father. Smith III placed more emphasis on personal morality and a gradual reformation of American values and less on geographic specificity (Launius 1988:170).

Nevertheless, in the winter of 1869–70, a joint stock company by the name of the Order of Enoch (the name was reminiscent of the 1830s experiment of the early church in Independence) was established through the instrumentality of one Israel L. Rodgers and with the approval of Smith. This organization was legally empowered to "buy and sell land and securities, construct buildings, manufacture machinery, lease assets, and make contracts" (176). Preparations were made to find a physical base for this semi-communal endeavor. By late 1870, the order's primary field operative, Elijah Banta, had located good land in Decatur County, Iowa, near an already established settlement of reorganized Saints in the town of Pleasanton. Here, a member of the church from the Missouri era, Ebenezer Robinson, had received a vision that Latter Day Saints would gather in large numbers on both sides of the Missouri-Iowa state line. Robinson said that he heard the angels of God singing the following verse (Launius 1988:177):

Give us room that we may dwell!
Zion's children cry aloud:
See their numbers—how they swell!
How they gather, like a cloud!

With spiritual confirmation in hand, Banta proceeded to purchase land for eight dollars an acre in Fayette Township, Decatur County, with approval of the order's board of directors. The possibility that a railroad would be built through the immediate area provided additional incentive for purchase. By April 1871, 2,680 acres had been acquired in one large tract and the small RLDS settlement there, called the Lamoni Branch, flourished (Launius 1988:178–79).

Joseph Smith III at first let the Order of Enoch develop independently of direct church intervention, but as early as June 1875 he conferred with members of the church first presidency and directors of the Order of Enoch about moving the headquarters of the church to Decatur County, Iowa. In 1879, RLDS citizens convinced the Chicago and Burlington Railroad to locate its line a bit farther southward than planned, and subsequently the town of Lamoni was officially platted along the tracks (Launius 1988:181–82). The railroad's presence induced greater numbers of Reorganized Saints to move, and by late 1879 Smith specifically advised members to go to Lamoni. Prompted by worsening economic conditions in Plano, Joseph Smith III himself joined the migration on October 7, 1881, as did the church's publishing concern shortly afterward. Southern Iowa had become the center for the Reorganized Church.

RLDS interest in Jackson County was subdued during the 1860s and 1870s. Part of the reason for this was the focus of the RLDS Church on missionary work among the Mormons of Utah (Launius 1988:218–46). By the 1870s, a split had begun within the leadership of the RLDS Church. The two founding apostles of the reorganization movement, Jason Briggs and Zenas Gurley, began to preach for the acceptance of a more liberal, rational, and democratic church administration, against the more conservative grain of Joseph Smith III. Briggs, in particular, began to teach against literal interpretation and acceptance of scripture and prophetic revelation. Briggs even contradicted his own previous interpretation and challenged "Joseph Smith, Jr.'s conception of the gathering of the Saints into a close-knit community for the building of Zion" (Launius 1988:274). The attempt to gather and locate Zion had been a failure and the doctrine should have been discarded, according to Briggs. The general membership, however, could not let go of the gathering ideal.

The circumstances surrounding the selection of Iowa as a new headquarters for the RLDS Church reflected a general tendency toward an informal, "bottom up" percolation of millennial sentiment in the church. Ideas started by individual members were often important in influencing later church decisions. Though Smith approved the Order of Enoch, it operated initially at a grassroots level with Smith initially reluctant to push for its improvement. Similarly, Smith was slow to advocate a move of church headquarters to Lamoni. The prophet's words were certainly influential, but he let the RLDS Church take on a more democratic flavor in this era. He purposefully steered it away from the more theocratic and enthusiastic mode of the Mormon hierarchy in Utah. The result has perhaps been that the RLDS Church has been shaped and molded more by its membership than by its leadership.

Parliamentary order might well be expected of a Latter Day Saint group formed closer to the mainstream of America. For example, the RLDS Church leadership took a more reserved, less millennial view of the concept of a gathering than did the Utah Saints. On one occasion, however, when visiting in Utah with Orson Pratt, Smith III seemed surprised when Pratt indicated his belief that not all of the Utah Saints would return to Missouri to build the New Jerusalem. Though not taking into account the size of the LDS body even then, Smith reaffirmed his own intent to return worthily one day to Independence (Anderson 1952:65–66). Smith may have envisioned an all-or-nothing venture, but he was hesitant to begin that return, even though many members saw millennial expectations being fulfilled. Joseph Smith III's brother, Alexander Hale Smith, said: "I could not help thinking that God in his own time and way was preparing for the return from exile those who are faithful, to their land of promise, and my heart was soft, my trust strengthened in the work" (Davis 1989:553).

Independence and "Regions Round About"

Jackson County acted as a magnet of increasing strength throughout the 1870s. Many members, holding more millennial expectations than did the RLDS Church leadership, chose to settle in Independence (Davis 1989:552). On January 1, 1877, Smith advised the Saints who chose to settle there "to pay strict heed to a popular maxim of the old prosperous days, 'mind your own business,' observing the rule laid down, 'talk not of judgement, boast not of mighty faith.'" He taught to purchase the land in an orderly manner so as not to incite violence. With the experience of the 1830s in mind, Smith counseled the Saints of the reorganization to live peacefully among the Missourians and if ever compelled to leave their lands again to "refuse to sell a foot" of it and to hide or carry away title deeds. For the most part, Smith considered it safe to begin a cautious rehabitation of the Jackson County area. Smith's counsel was not to immigrate to the area "in a mass," nor to resume any litigation for a return of lands. He left it for the members to trickle to Jackson County at their own leisure (RLDS 1967:4:166–68).

As the RLDS Church's membership in Independence gradually increased, more and more church emphasis focused upon Jackson County as well. Joseph Smith III quietly visited Jackson County in the fall of 1877 and referred to Independence in hopeful terms

> as handsomely situated, and sits not like Rome on seven hills, but on hundreds of hills, surrounded by hundreds more. A constant succession of vale, hill, farm, valley, villa, dell, grove, plain, meadow, spring, wood, reaches every way from this Jerusalem of modern Israel [where] wood, water, and stone are everywhere to be had and beauty of prospects lies in every direction. We slept one night in the city, walked over the Temple Lot, sang and prayed with earnest souls there, and left them anxious, waiting, and willing. (RLDS 1967:4:187)

In 1877, Smith III also traveled to Decatur County, Iowa, and described the situation there. Its location with respect to Jackson County must have been important to him—he referred to it several times. Members talked of Lamoni's location in Zion, since Smith mentions that Decatur County was located outside of the sacred Missouri of the 1830s "whatever may be said of it now." The general membership was anxious to include south-central Iowa within the area of a greater Zion and to perhaps not have to move, but Smith seemed to discourage the idea despite it being an RLDS center. Smith implied that Lamoni could not be compared with Jackson County as a sacred place, yet, conversely, Smith considered the millenarian attributes of the lands in Missouri between Decatur County, Iowa, and Jackson County, Missouri. After traveling to Decatur County and visiting a number of reorganized Saints' homesteads in northern Missouri, Smith favorably described "the better portions of land passed over" in Harrison County (across the Iowa border into Missouri), and in De Kalb and Clinton Counties just to the west of historic Daviess and Caldwell Counties. Smith pragmatically reviewed the quality of timber and soil in these areas, as well as their water supplies and markets. "Prices for farms range from five to thirty dollars per acre; now and then improved farms being offered for twelve dollars and fifty cents." De Kalb County was given special consideration. Smith mentioned the presence of German Saints in De Kalb County who assumed themselves to be in "the regions round about" Zion and who proposed to help build it up (see fig. 22). Such was the typical polarized view of membership to leadership. The members saw an increasing spiritual gradient from Lamoni to Jackson County. Smith's millenarian side saw it—his cautious side did not (RLDS 1967:4:187–88, 189–90).

De Kalb County's position "fifty miles overland from Independence" was emphasized in this ongoing discussion, but it is curious that no mention was made of the early settlements of the Saints in Caldwell or Daviess Counties, perhaps out of a historical mix of reverence and fear. Smith investigated the practical advantages of the general region and emphasized those areas of northwestern Missouri that to him seemed to offer the most productivity, yet the collective memories of the early expulsion may have still been too ominous to consider those counties as possible sites for resettlement. Perhaps a fear of Missourian retribution in those counties lingered as Smith disguised his new location formula in a sort of socioeconomic mix of factors. It was difficult to overcome the effects of obliteration.

The almost total lack of reference by the RLDS leadership to Far West and Adam-ondi-Ahman remains something of a mystery, but it is also possible that they knew of the importance of these sites to the Mormons in Utah and, to avoid being compared with their arch rival, the RLDS leaders dismissed them. There *was* a supplementary conference at

Far West on March 30, 1879, which was addressed by Joseph Smith Jr.'s brother, William B. Smith. William did not adhere to any particular splinter of Saints but was respected for being a Smith. So the meeting was a fluke of nostalgia. If the speaker were any contemporary RLDS leader of the 1870s, the meeting probably would not have been held in Far West, and its occurrence is given only brief coverage in the standard RLDS history. The membership, however, passed a resolution that encouraged Reorganized Saints to investigate "splendid locations near the city of Far West that are now for sale" (RLDS 1967:4:253–54). How much unease this caused the leadership is uncertain, but it seems that the sacred perceptions of the membership were more influential in moving the RLDS Church closer to Independence.

When RLDS Church headquarters were moved to Lamoni from Plano, solid transportation and business qualities were given as reasons for the change in location. Leaders had investigated relocating church headquarters in Nauvoo, but they rejected that town because it lacked major rail connections. The move to Lamoni, though, clearly did not diminish the importance of Independence. On the contrary, it was closer to Independence, which remained the more sacred site, and the church's newspaper in June 1881 said that it was considered "something more than a dream that the waste place will be rebuilt" (RLDS 1967:4:358–59). Not wanting to move too hastily, however, church leaders temporarily located in Lamoni as "an outpost of Zion" (5:600). The selection of Lamoni as a center for the church shows a geographical compromise between the hesitancy of RLDS leadership to act and the willingness of the RLDS membership to return to the New Jerusalem.

The Possession of Sacred Space

By July 1884, the RLDS Church in Independence had about 350 members, a number that rivaled the total in Lamoni, and by 1887, at least 500 members lived there (Davis 1989:560). Marking the area's growing significance, RLDS General Conferences for April 1882 and 1885 were held in Independence. The selected site was near a brick chapel that the group had constructed in 1881 on East Lexington Street. Growth soon dictated the need for a larger structure. Some members thought that a new structure should be built adjacent to the old one, but local leader Joseph Luff chose a site available immediately north of the Temple Lot (Davis 1989:560;

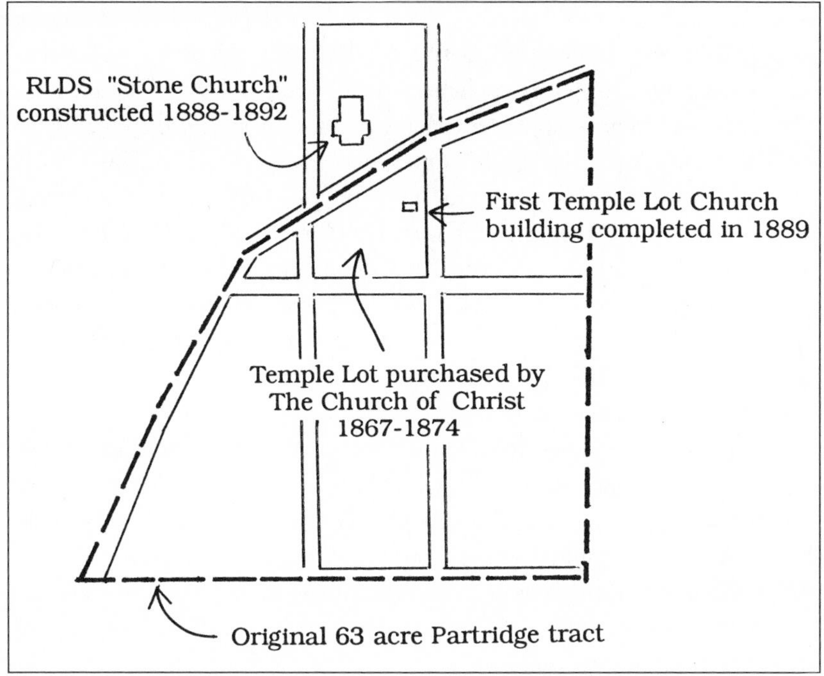

FIG. 21 | *"Location of the RLDS Stone Church facing the Temple Lot. This structure is the earliest example of a visible statement of the RLDS Church toward the lot.*

Wilcox 1959a:14–16). All discussion over proper location of the building then ceased.

The basement for the new building, known as the Stone Church, was completed by April 1888; an upper auditorium, with a seating capacity of 1,200, was finished four years later (Anderson 1952:410–11; Davis 1989:560; RLDS 1967:4:554; Wilcox 1959b:14). Wilcox reported that while the Stone Church was being roofed, a celebration took place on the grounds. When a storm suddenly drenched surrounding Independence residents but somehow avoided the festival participants, the church members considered it a miracle (Wilcox 1959a:15–16). Most Latter Day Saints see divine provenance in weather, good and bad.

Naturally, the Stone Church was constructed to face southward toward the Temple Lot, the two-and-one-half-acre piece of land owned by the Church of Christ (Temple Lot). This orientation showed the RLDS

Church's respect for the sacred property and its suggested intent on possession of the spot (Figure 21). Between 1885 and 1890, RLDS leaders had met on a regular basis with people from the Church of Christ (Temple Lot), but doctrinal differences prevented any merger. In an aggressive, but not surprising, move, the RLDS Church attempted to acquire the Temple Lot through a lawsuit against the Church of Christ in 1890. In 1892, an article in the *Saints' Herald* accused the Church of Christ of planning to mortgage the Temple Lot with the intent of obtaining money to print an edition of the *Book of Mormon*. The RLDS Church feared that the Temple Lot Church might turn the property over to the Utah church, "a consummation not desirable" (RLDS 1967:5:177). For the Temple Lot Group it was a consummation unimaginable.

Circuit Court Judge John F. Phillips began to hear the case in February 1894 (Launius 1988:307). An earlier lawsuit revolving around the Kirtland temple in Ohio had recognized the RLDS Church as the "legal successor" to the original church of Joseph Smith Jr., and in 1887 the RLDS Church had purchased a deed that made up the bulk of their case to gain possession of the Temple Lot. The church did not recognize any other deeds (including the one that resulted in the Maxwell and Woodson addition) and was convinced that all of the Temple Lot should be awarded since the RLDS Church was the "legal" successor to the original church (RLDS 1967:5:53; see pages 92–94 for deed histories).

Joseph Smith III, with a confidence uncharacteristic of earlier decades, thought the court would rule in his favor. In April 1894, he claimed to have received a revelation stating that a "storehouse and the temple and the salvation of my people" was as paramount now as for the early church. Moreover, the duties of "purchasing lands, building houses of worship, building up the New Jerusalem, and the gathering of the people" were priorities of the church (*Book of Doctrine* 1989:122:6). For Smith, this was strong talk. Apparently anticipation of winning the case inspired speculation on the use of the Temple Lot under RLDS possession. One day before the judgment, Smith stated that he heard a voice that said "the decision of the Court will be in favor of the Reorganized Church on every point" (Anderson 1952:478; Launius 1988:308).

Judge Phillips awarded the territory to the RLDS Church in March 1894, but the decision was later reversed upon appeal (Launius 1988:307; Reimann 1961:149). It was noted that neither of the churches actually held original title to the territory, and the reversal was based on the Temple Lot Church's quarter-century possession of the property, improvements made to the land, and property taxes paid. The question of the real successor to the original Latter Day Saint church was not a factor in the appeal. Although the RLDS Church tried to appeal further in 1895, the Supreme Court refused to hear it (Launius 1988:309; RLDS 1967:5:287). The Church of Christ (Temple Lot) has retained this crucial spot of land ever since.

Possibly in anticipation of its possession of the Temple Lot location, the RLDS Church started a donation fund "for the Independence temple" in 1893 or 1894 (RLDS 1967:5:248, 295). By April 1894, $1,045.07 had been put in the fund, but one year later, after the judgment in favor of the Temple Lot Church, no new donations had been received. By 1896, the temple fund was not even mentioned in the annual statistical review; apparently ambitions had cooled on any RLDS New Jerusalem temple construction (337–38). Since the Temple Lot case, an important change in nomenclature has been apparent in church documents. While Independence continues to be referred to as "Zion" or the "central place," references to a "New Jerusalem" have become rare. Since the mid-1890s, the church has developed a "social-welfare" image within more secular, urban surroundings. If the RLDS Church were to have won the case, more millennial overtones would likely have followed and the Temple Lot would have developed much earlier. Later liberal trends would have been delayed or avoided, perhaps lessening the current dissent in the RLDS Church. It seems the combination of litigious defeat mixed with parliamentary procedure and a practical approach to Zion, even at this early time, aimed the church on a less millenarian path that would become magnified several times by the year 2000.

Subsequent to the events related to the Temple Lot case, the RLDS Church continued to show interest in the Temple Lot and to continue discussions with the Temple Lot Church to draw the two closer together on the question of sacred land. In 1897 a meeting was proposed for the three main groups who had interests in the Temple Lot, but the Utah church, always cordial but nonecumenical, declined to participate. The RLDS and Temple Lot Churches met, ostensibly to discuss doctrinal similarities but in reality to possess symbolic sacred territory. The two groups agreed that "the City of Zion will be built at Independence, Missouri, and that the saints of God will gather there" (RLDS 1967:5:385), but differences ran deep. Each group saw itself as the one chosen to develop God's tract.

During these meetings Alexander H. Smith, the RLDS chairman of the joint council between the two churches and a son of Joseph Smith Jr., received a revelation. It stated in part:

> My children of the Church of Christ are not sufficiently humble or willing to submit to my will; . . . Behold, it is my will that you [of the Church of Christ] become reconciled to thy brethren of the Reorganization of my church, and join with them in the work of building up Zion, and the gathering of my people, and the building of my Temple, which I will command in mine own time to be built. Be not overly anxious; thy sacrifices and sufferings I have witnessed, and am well pleased; yet in many things ye have been deceived. It is my will now that my children no longer stand in the way of the progress of my work, neither make thy brother an offender for a word. (Anderson 1952:487–88)

This entreaty in deified voice had little effect upon the smaller church, which only offered to "lay it before the Church of Christ in conference assembled" (489). In due time, the condescending "communication" was rejected, and the RLDS and Temple Lot Churches never reconciled their differences.

During the writing of his memoirs, Joseph Smith III expressed his dismay that the Church of Christ remained in possession of the Temple Lot. That the RLDS Church could not acquire that sacred parcel to build the prophesied temple pained him much:

> The Church of Christ has continued to hold the land and has erected a small frame building . . . as a meetinghouse. The lot has been enclosed by a good fence, and the premise is carefully guarded against intrusion. So far, they are absolutely too few in numbers and too entirely in confusion through division of sentiment among themselves to do anything toward either a settlement of the trust or an attempt to build a temple upon the spot. I have wondered if their attitude does not come within the scope the old, old adage of the "dog in the manger" who could not eat the hay upon which he was lying nor permit those for whom it was provided to have it. They will not, cannot, themselves build the temple, and they will not permit others to do so. (484–85)

This is the only time in the history of the Temple Lot that a fence surrounded it. It is difficult to imagine what consternations might arise if the Temple Lot Church were to construct a barrier there today. In 1901, *Zion's Ensign*, a pro-RLDS newspaper in Independence, took special pride in improvements made to the Temple Lot, namely a new sidewalk along the north side, which was charged by the city to George A. Blakeslee, bishop of the RLDS Church. The paper exulted, "This looks well! The Reorganized Church acknowledged as the proper pay master for Temple Lot improvements" (RLDS 1967:5:72–73). This was typical of the RLDS attitude where any improvement or move regarding the Temple Lot was seen as being influenced by the RLDS Church itself, which perceived it was the rightful owner of the land. Later, circa 1990, the RLDS organization would completely reject the Temple Lot, even with three prominent structures facing it.

By 1900 the RLDS Church was baptizing many new members in Missouri. Though encouraging the gathering ideal, the church's leadership was still cautious and its headquarters still remained in Lamoni, Iowa (RLDS 1967:5:431, 6:173). The prophesied center place was not to be resettled by the Saints in the same rapid manner attempted by the first

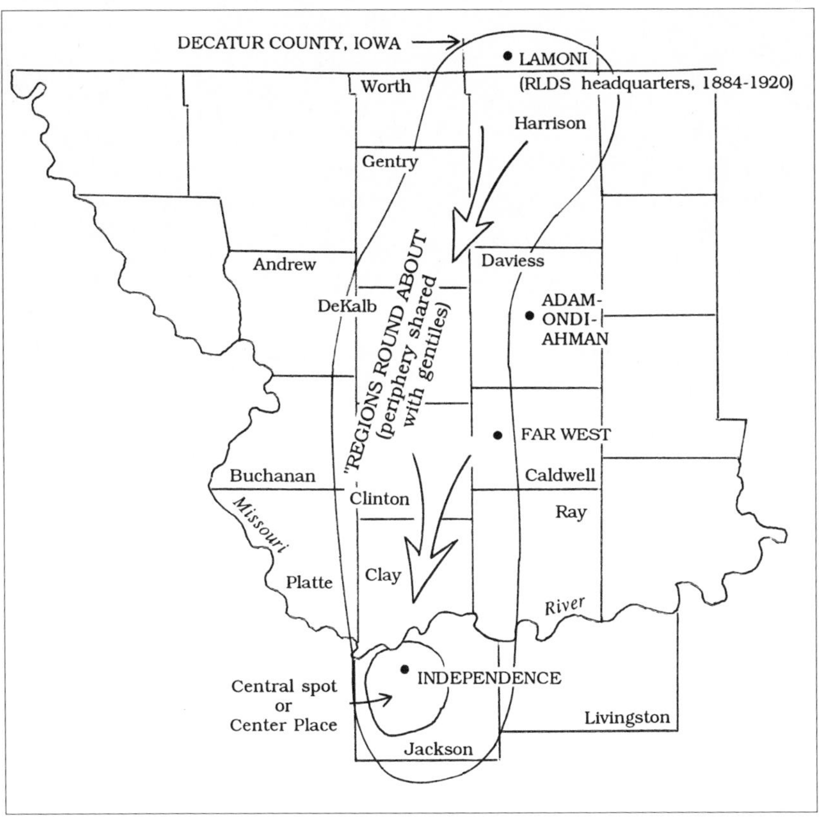

FIG. 22 | *RLDS Lamoni-Independence axis of Zion, 1880–1910.*

Saints (Figure 22). The frontier isolation of the 1830s had disappeared and, naturally, a much greater proportion of non-RLDS people lived in the area (5:600). The RLDS leadership took a pragmatic view of their situation with Kansas City developing rapidly, and they saw possibilities for Independence as an industrial Zion (6:119–20).

Independence was increasingly the focal point of RLDS activity. Frederick M. Smith, the son of Joseph Smith III, but as yet not leader of the church, declared on a visit to Salt Lake City in 1904 that the "great temple of God" would be built in Independence, but he diplomatically sidestepped the issue of which group would do it. More practically, in April 1906 Joseph Smith III instructed that a "sanitarium or hospital" be built in Independence as "a place of refuge and help for the sick and afflicted" (RLDS 1967:6:111, 207; *Book of Doctrine* 1989:127:1). President Smith said that he saw the sanitarium in a vision and he hoped "these Independence people will not go wild over it, because I saw it, and it was presented to me" (RLDS 1967:6:207). In the usually reserved style of the RLDS leadership, Smith was trying to foster a "social reformation" view of Zion, in a vein similar to other eastern contemporary religious movements in the United States that had to deal with urban poverty, labor, and physical and mental illness (White and Hopkins 1976). The hospital was completed late 1909. Also functioning by this year in Independence were two separate RLDS homes for the care of the aged (RLDS 1967:6:341).

The revelation that spoke of the hospital also encouraged a steady, prepared gathering to Zion without the "spirit of speculation" or the "exhibition of greed" (*Book of Doctrine* 1989:127:7). Now in failing health, Joseph Smith III nevertheless saw fit to join the movement to Independence personally and moved in August of 1906 to "an unpretentious cottage" less than one block from the Temple Lot (Anderson 1952: 562–64). Smith said that the choice of Independence as a new home was logical and that it was his "religious duty to become a resident of the place designated of old as Zion" and to "die in the goodly land" (RLDS 1967: 6:169; Launius 1988:347). It took him forty-six years to make the decision.

The prevalent church position toward Zion at this time is nicely expressed by the apostle Joseph Luff, in what he called a divine "communication," written as in the first person of deity: "Once I have spoken!—yea, twice have I declared that the set time to favor Zion has come; but my army is not yet very great, and their weapons, many of them, are yet carnal. Nevertheless my word shall not fail, neither shall my purpose be changed, notwithstanding my people are slow to perceive and the confidence of some has failed" (RLDS 1967:6:200).

The RLDS push to gather was leisurely, and the scale of Zion was vague, though certainly not diminutive. Two more revelations were reported in 1909. One was an answer to an inquiry from the church's bishopric on how to help members come to Zion. Somewhat defining the periphery of Zion, the region was described as "*more* than a small area of country round about the central spot" (*Book of Doctrine* 1989:128:5; italics added). The fuzzy periphery of the revelation seems an attempt to include Lamoni, still the official headquarters of the church, in the area of gathering, thus avoiding a rapid evacuation of that town. The importance of the periphery of Zion was also emphasized when a *Book of Mormon* verse discussing "gentiles" assisting in rebuilding Zion was interpreted as nonmembers who would aid and mix with the Saints in the semi-sacred periphery. According to Smith's revelation, members "pure in heart" would occupy Zion's center, while "gentiles" would be relegated to a peripheral position.[6] This talk emphasized a perceived dominance of Latter Day Saints, but in reality the Saints were more mixed with nonmembers in adjacent Kansas City than in the outlying areas of northern Missouri.

As many Saints as possible were to settle carefully "in one region as may be practicable and profitable," but it was obvious that members could not all live "in near proximity to each other" (*Book of Doctrine* 1989: 128:5–6). As the RLDS Church matured within a non-Saint controlled urban/industrial culture, the members interpreted their Zion accordingly, though this gradual gathering was certainly at odds with the plans of imminent growth inherent in Joseph Smith Jr.'s original town layout. In an article in the *Saints' Herald* in 1909, fifty-nine RLDS-owned businesses were proudly listed (RLDS 1967:6:344). Interest in maintaining urban cleanliness in a Zionic environment was also at a peak during this period. Frederick M. Smith, Joseph Smith III's son and successor as prophet, with a master's degree from the University of Kansas in sociology, gave a public lecture on sanitation conditions in Independence and described how they might be greatly improved (RLDS 1967:6:349).

The second revelation given during the April 1909 General Conference reinforced the first stating that the church had to abide by inspiration, warning, and instruction or its people could not receive and enjoy "the blessings which have been looked for when Zion should be fully redeemed" (*Book of Doctrine* 1989:129:8). Millennial events were apparently not close at hand for the RLDS leadership, and as time passed they would become more distant. In 1911, a statement approved by President Smith encouraged members to gather to Lamoni as much as to Independence and called the Iowa site still "central" to the church (RLDS 1967:6:416–17, 428–29). Clearly, charismatic Independence had more potential for development than did Lamoni.

In October 1903, a twenty-acre tract between central Independence and the Missouri River to the north had been purchased as a church burial site. Joseph Smith III was buried here in Mound Grove Cemetery in December 1914 (Wilcox 1979:87–89). The RLDS Church, now in the able hands of Smith's son, Frederick, embarked upon a Zionic experiment noticeably influenced by its leader's academic background of sociology and psychology (RLDS 1967:6:555).[7] At the dawn of a new period, the church, with typical RLDS hesitation and distancing from millenarian views, functioned with Independence as de facto headquarters. It was not officially declared such until 1920.

Views of Jackson County from Utah

1845–1900

> It is said the Saints look back to Jackson County with the same devotion as the Mahomedan to his Mecca, with the same undying faith as the Israelite to the Holy Land . . . , and it is one of their traditions that they shall return to "Zion."
>
> —*Illustrated Atlas of Jackson County, Missouri*

As difficulties had increased for the Saints in Nauvoo, Illinois, and little hope remained for a return to Missouri, Joseph Smith Jr. discussed moving the church to a more remote political and social environment. Missourians had suggested Wisconsin, and Smith had established a lumbering settlement there at Black River Falls. Smith also explored moves to Texas and to the Rocky Mountains, where Brigham Young eventually led the majority of Saints in 1847 (Jackson 1978). The place of the eventual New Jerusalem, for the western Saints, was still Jackson County, Missouri, and, like the RLDS and Temple Lot groups, the LDS Church maintained fascinating ideas regarding it.

As shown earlier, the ambitious tendency of all the Latter Day Saint groups to gather caused volatile political debacles wherever they settled. Increasing upheaval was their lot as they moved westward. Friction in New York and Ohio was limited to the local level, while a mixture of local animosity and action by the state was encountered in Missouri. In Illinois, conflict was generated between autonomous Nauvoo and the state. Similar conflict was carried through to the LDS Church in Utah, which was nearly undone by the federal government over the polygamy issue. As pressures mounted, the feelings of church members were projected to Jackson County. Missouri became an escape hatch for emotion during these hard times. Once again, the New Jerusalem became their future haven.

The View from the West

Approximately two months after the death of Joseph Smith in Illinois, Brigham Young reiterated Smith's words of a broad view of Zion extending across North and South America. Young's intent seemed focused on keeping the Saints temporarily nucleated at Nauvoo while also maintaining a hope not only for future peace but for future expansion as well: "To those who want to go away from this place, I would say wait until the time comes . . . do not be in haste, wait until the Lord says go. You may go all over North and South America and build up stakes when the time comes. The whole continent of America must be organized into districts and presiding elders appointed over each district; the time has come when all things must be set in order" (Roberts 1978:7:258). An LDS member today would see these words as particularly prophetic considering the steady growth of the church, particularly in the Americas.

In 1845, shortly after the death of Smith, the quorum of the Twelve apostles, under the leadership of Young (not formally sustained as president of the church until 1847), issued a written proclamation to world leaders. In it the doctrine of a New Jerusalem was reemphasized, and the American continent was referred to seven times. The word *Zion* was written five times and *temple* three times, but neither Independence nor Missouri were mentioned. In keeping with a trend seen in Nauvoo, especially as civil life for the Saints in Illinois was disintegrating—references to millennial location were kept generic. "Come let us go up to Mount Zion and to the temple of the Lord," the proclamation emphasized, even as the leadership was contemplating moving out of Illinois, abandoning the Nauvoo temple. That the Lord had commanded "us to build up holy cities and sanctuaries" (Matthews 1992:1154) was written, but, for the Brighamites, where and how many were issues yet to be decided in the West.

Much of what was written during Brigham Young's leadership was naturally oriented toward the problems of building Zion in the West—the exodus to territory in transition from Mexican to U.S. hands delayed talk of Jackson County. Soon enough, however, Young began to mention it again and often in Sunday meetings and at General Conferences twice a year (Larson and Larson 1980:76 n). His line of thought was influenced and echoed by other LDS apostles, including Heber C. Kimball, George Q. Cannon, Wilford Woodruff, and, in particular, Orson Pratt, who spoke profusely about returning to Jackson County and about associated millennial themes.

It is common knowledge that the first settlement in the intermountain valleys, Salt Lake City, was patterned after the "City of Zion," its platting familiar from the Mormon "square" system already seen in Far West, in Adam-ondi-Ahman, and, less rigidly, in Nauvoo. Many other towns in the valleys of Utah were planned with the same uniformity, with simple numbering systems for street addresses (Arrington 1966:24; Sopher 1967:32). The Saints envisioned this pattern across the landscape as a natural progression of that begun in Independence, where a grid of sacred cities was to extend outward across the globe.

In 1867, apostle George Q. Cannon gave a concise summary of what appears to have generally been the average Saint's view of Utah as a place of preparation before a return to Missouri: "We are, as it were, in a school where we are to be taught of God, and prepared for the great events that are coming on the earth. We do not wish to leave this land because it is not fertile, or because it is not a favoured land. We appreciate the home that God has given us here . . . but we look forward to that land [Jackson County] with indescribable feelings, because it is the place where God has said his city shall be built" (*Journal of Discourses* 1966:11:336–37).

Originally, Utah, the "resting place in the rich valleys . . . and Everlasting Hills" (Kenney 1983:3:520), was never meant to be the New Jerusalem for the Saints despite repeated misunderstandings by outsiders over the years. The Great Salt Lake Valley was only a temporary haven yet an important center of a greater Zion. For example, according to apostle Orson Pratt:

> It is there [Utah] that they [the Saints] intend gathering from the various nations of the earth, until the Lord, by revelation or his providence, shall direct otherwise.
>
> But where is the spot where the city of Zion or the New Jerusalem shall stand? We answer, in Jackson County, State of Missouri, on the western frontiers of the United States. (Pratt 1851:18)

In 1870, George Albert Smith, LDS apostle and later president of the church, sure of a return to western Missouri, said, "our hearts do not cling in the least to any spot in the world any longer than is necessary to stay there to do our duty" (*Journal of Discourses* 1966:13:298). In the late 1800s, LDS Church leadership was obviously convinced of the temporary nature of their intermountain dwelling, even though members saw the Salt Lake Valley as sacred and prophetically assigned territory as headquarters of the church (Kenney 1983:4:193).[1]

Brigham Young always insisted that he was still the "rightful owner" of his own lands and farms in Missouri and Illinois, which he was never able to occupy (*Journal of Discourses* 1966:8:224–25). He said he knew how the Saints in Jackson County felt in the 1830s. "All their desire," he said, "was to get into . . . Jackson County, where they expected to find all sin and iniquity dried up, heaven begun on earth, and an end to all their mortal griefs" (1:313). A place of justice and tolerance, Young said that not only Mormons would occupy the New Jerusalem, but good people of all faiths:

> Zion will extend, eventually, all over this earth. There will be no nook or corner upon the earth but what will be in Zion. It will all be Zion.
>
> You cannot imagine anything that will not be in Zion, except sin and iniquity . . . . All classes of people will come to Zion. Will there be Methodists there? Yes; and they will have the privilege to worship a God without body, parts, and passions, just as they do now, if they choose to. (9:138)

As time passed, however, a sense of permanence set in. The Saints realized that Utah as a "temporary abode" probably meant at least several decades of occupation.

On Building the Salt Lake Valley

Church leadership in Utah emphasized building up the new Latter-day Saint society through hard work. Many settlers thought their residence along the Wasatch Mountains would last only a few years. Thus the image of Jackson County as an almost folkloric destiny was employed to spur the Saints to make the Salt Lake Valley a lovely place. It was obvious to church leaders that their Utah dwelling would be permanent enough.

In a push to beautify the stark and often harsh surroundings, Young told the people, "I do not see the first fruit or shade tree in this city. Come . . . and get some Fruit trees and . . . have some fruit growing" (Kenney

1983:4:369). Young seemed frustrated with the lack of development and asked how, if Salt Lake City were not fervently built up, could an even greater city ever be constructed? If a single person had the sum total of all earthly knowledge, he said, that person would not know enough to build even "a kitchen in [nor] lay the first stone in the wall around the New Jerusalem to say nothing about building the city & Temple" (4:368). For motivation, Young often referenced Jackson County's future importance. In late 1864, for example, Young argued that acreage should be used intensively and not wasted, since, as Smith's original plan entailed: "When we go to the Centre Stake of Zion [that is, Jackson County] we shall not have 600 acres of land each to run over. No, we shall have a small spot. There will not be a Chicken, Pig, Cow, horse, or any animal in the City" (6:189; punctuation added). Perceptually, Young appears to have adhered fairly closely to the original plat designed for the New Jerusalem and to have pondered somewhat the conflict between the pastoral and urban pursuits there.

During the 1850s, Heber C. Kimball occasionally used a similar carrot-before-the-horse teaching technique to motivate development. In 1857 he instructed the Saints to "put out peach trees, apple trees, apricots, and currants. . . . We were told that we were going into the woods before we came here; and then when we got here, there were no woods. But you need not be afraid; you go and graft and inoculate your trees, and build houses, that you may know how to build when you get to Jackson County" (*Journal of Discourses* 1966:5:165). Two years later, he urged members to raise crops, mend fences, and live right, "as tho we were going to live here forever. For I tell you in the name of the Lord God that we shall stay here until we go back to Jackson County, that is the righteous I mean." In the LDS realm, just as only the righteous are allowed entry in sacred temples—then being constructed in Utah—only those worthy would return to Missouri.

In the 1870s both Orson Pratt and Lorenzo Snow, another later president of the church, encouraged the Saints to persevere with their farms despite problems of maintenance and irrigation in the semiarid environment. Pratt compared the local agricultural conditions with an idealized and blessed Jackson County, notwithstanding the fact that the Saints had only lived in Missouri for three years. He said, "We can not work here as we could in Jackson County, Mo. In that country we did not have to irrigate. We could settle on a piece of rising ground there, and the rains of heaven watered it" (*Journal of Discourses* 1966:17:34). Perceptually, Missouri stood out though the Saints had been more rooted in both Kirtland and Nauvoo.

The usage of Jackson County as an incentive to progress continued into the 1870s and was even occasionally heard in the early 1900s. For example, Orson F. Whitney in 1916 said that the mission of the church would not end in Utah. He rhetorically asked, "Is the state of Utah the proper monument of the Mormon people? No, the monument to Mormonism will stand in Jackson County, Missouri. There the great city will be built: There Zion will arise and shine," but such comments from the leadership were becoming more rare (Smith and Sjodahl 1967:147). At this time, to advance the church's mission, now verging on the national, a carrot was still occasionally held out. Church growth and the push for national acceptance, however, would later squelch much millenarian talk.

Back in the 1870s, Snow emphasized how easy work in Missouri would someday "be accomplished after we have learned to build up cities and temples here . . . Our present experience is a very needful one. Without it, we should be totally unfitted for the performance of such a work" (*Journal of Discourses* 1966:18:374). Underwood's theme that the Saints' beliefs were millenarian is valid but simplistic—the reasons and context for millenarian discussion varied over the decades. Vernacular consideration of prophetic timelines occurred in the early church, though discouraged by Smith Jr. and other leaders. In the Missouri years the millennium was about to commence and the New Jerusalem just about to be established (Underwood 1993:124–25). Among the later Utah Saints, however, the tables turned as leaders used the New Jerusalem as a call to practical improvement. This is one way premillennial attitudes of the Saints started to vary both through time and according to doctrinal interpretation and social needs within the related, but now separate, factions. For the LDS Church and usually at the incentive of the leadership, absence made the heart grow fonder—for a time. By contrast, the RLDS Church, closer to the mainstream diversity of American culture, saw Zion more as a social gospel call, gradually distancing itself from otherworldly millennial attitudes.

New Jerusalem Chronology

From the mid-1800s through the Civil War, Brigham Young and other LDS leaders believed the time to return to Missouri was fairly close, perhaps a couple of decades away at most. When war was imminent, Young was sure the establishment of the New Jerusalem was at hand. Orson Pratt expressed millennial immediacy in 1855, stating that he thought the original Saints in the 1830s must have expected to be "speedily restored" to Jackson County, but "[now] the people think of almost everything else but the redemption of Zion, . . . individuals put it off a great distance ahead. I will give you my opinion . . . I think that this event is nearer than this people are aware of" (*Journal of Discourses* 1966:3:17).

During this time, the membership of the church commonly located millennial events farther in the future than did the leadership. One might speculate that when the leadership perceived the need to urge members to work harder, this pulled the establishment of the New Jerusalem closer. When results were positive, millennial talk subsided. From the leadership point of view, the membership generally was slow to hear the word, but not always. In the early 1850s, Saints remaining in midwestern stations such as Kanesville, Iowa (now Council Bluffs), knew they would have "but a short way to go" to return to Jackson County (Kenney 1983:4:370). The admonition from church authorities, however, was to proceed to the Salt Lake Valley, since the quickest way to Jackson County was thought by leadership to be by "way of the Rocky Mountains," where the church could develop in refuge. George Albert Smith, cousin of Joseph Smith, said, "the longest way around will be the shortest way there" (Kenney 1983:4:370). Among the Saints, preparation through living, and not distance, seems to have been the primary factor in calculating a return to Jackson County. That is how permanence and stability was fostered among the western Mormon populace.

Around 1860, bitterness from the Missouri and Illinois years was still evident in the public discourses of church leadership. As tensions increased toward the Civil War, so did talk of returning to Jackson County. Stegner (1981:92) stated a view that the church saw divine provenance returning the sacred Missouri lands "after the states had destroyed each other," but reality was not so simplistic. The acts of both the North and South were viewed as the futile efforts of immeasurably wicked peoples who would try to get the aid of the Saints perhaps by some offer of land in Missouri. Suspicious, Brigham Young preached:

> if the men who have driven us—the counties, States, and the General Government of the United States, proffer to take me back to the land of my inheritance, I shall refuse to go by their hands. I think I shall say, "You can go to hell: I came here without any of your assistance, and I shall return again on the bounty of God, asking no assistance from you." I do not intend to be brought

> under obligations to or any alliances with the wicked, nor to have any affinity with them in heaven or on earth, nor to go to hell to have any with them there. I expect to individually own enough horses, wagons, carriages, oxen, cows, sheep, and everything this people will need in going back to Jackson County, Missouri, and ask no assistance of those who have driven and persecuted us. (*Journal of Discourses* 1966:8:222–23; quotation marks added)

The Saints were not to be allied with either side. Any return to Jackson County was to be orchestrated by the Saints—with no outside help.

In the postwar years, Brigham Young thought the Saints would be better off than other U.S. citizens. During any exodus from the West to Missouri, the Saints would be well clothed, while other, more unfortunate souls would go naked and hungry (*Journal of Discourses* 1966:8:223). This much at least was owed to the Saints. Of this speech, Charles L. Walker wrote in his diary that Young "showed how we should return to Jackson Co Mo. The Lord would open up the way before us. Said that he asked no odds of our enemies or their riches and expected to see the time when we should ride in our carriages while they were naked and barefoot" (Larson and Larson 1980:1:143).[2] The Missouri and Illinois Trials were not quickly forgotten.

Whereas New Jerusalem talk before the war had been spurred by the practicality of improving land and life, the Civil War motivated most millennial talk in the early 1860s. Because of polygamy, easterners increasingly criticized the LDS Church. The response of the church was understandably terse; easterners weren't married to all their women, so the perceived root of war was the wickedness of America, especially in its treatment of the Saints, and the culmination of secular iniquity would be millennial glory. At the beginning of 1861, Heber C. Kimball, like Young, expressed distaste toward specific U.S. leaders. Referring to the hardships of the Saints in migrating to the West, Kimball said with sarcasm:

> the Kings and Queens of the Gentiles will never gather the Saints. I want to know how many of the Latter-day Saints were gathered to these mountains by king James Buchanan? How many did [Missouri Senator] Tom Benton gather? The most of us: that is to say, he was the means of driving us from our homes to this place, which was then a wilderness; but he never helped us. James Buchanan never put forth his hands to aid this people. Will he ever strive to restore this people and make right that which he has

made wrong? I don't suppose he ever will . . . but he will have to pay the debt he has contracted with this people. If you wait for him or for any of the wicked, to take you back to Jackson County, Missouri, you will have to wait some millions of years. (*Journal of Discourses* 1966:8:348–49)

Despite the earlier interpretation of the loss of Jackson County as the result of the disobedience of the Saints, which likely was still believed, Kimball now also blamed both the Missouri and the federal governments for past injustices. A return to sacred Missouri territory was to be instigated by God, and accomplished in austere self-sufficiency, though it must be clarified that James Buchanan and Tom Benton here were proxies for government injustice; neither was in office during the Saints' early Missouri years.

In 1862, as the Civil War broke out in full, Brigham Young saw prophecy in the chaos and said that the Saints would return to Jackson County within seven years (Vogel 1988:204). The war was going "to cleanse the land, and prepare the way for the return" of the Saints. Fire would burn periodically for seasons, "and it will spread and continue until the land is emptied" (*Journal of Discourses* 1966:9:137, 142–43). In possible preparation for the return, Young proposed in 1863 that missionaries be sent to Missouri (Campbell 1988:291).

Charles Walker also saw the Civil War evidently as a cleansing, in preparation for a return to Missouri. On November 9, 1864, he wrote from St. George, Utah:

> The war is still going on as fearful as ever. Every mail brings intelligence of Strife between the contending parties and neither of them have gained the victory yet, nor will they until the decree of the Lord has been fullfilled and the way prepared for the return of the People of God to the center Stake of Zion. . . . Missouri has been scourged and almost laid waste by the ravages of war. [They're] meeting out to them that which they meted unto us. Great is thy justice, oh King of Kings. (Larson and Larson 1980:1:245)

Though Civil War violence was moderate in Missouri it was still seen as God's revenge for the Saints' previous sufferings there. Bitterness still ran deep, and the Missourians were also blamed for the expulsion from Illinois. Walker had migrated from England in 1850 and had not seen Missouri firsthand, yet he was as vengeful in his commentary as those who experienced the early calamities. Also in 1864, George Q. Cannon reiterated that the day was near when a temple would be "reared in the Center Stake of Zion" (*Journal of Discourses* 1966:10:344).

Insight into the Civil War era can also be culled from an important non-Mormon observer of the period. Stephen S. Harding, who was appointed territorial governor of Utah in 1862, was astonished at the Mormon attitudes toward the United States and Missouri in Tabernacle preaching. Young and his apostles taught that the United States lay in ruins, Harding said, and was a nation to be destroyed. He said the Mormons taught

> That the Gentiles, as they call all persons outside of their church, will continue to fight with each other until they perish and then the Saints are to step in and quietly enjoy the possession of the land and also what is left of the ruined cities and desolated places. And that Zion is to be built up, not only in the valleys and the mountains but the great center of their power and glory is to be in Missouri where the Saints under the lead of their prophet were expelled many years ago. (Campbell 1988:291–92)

The Civil War fervor also apparently enticed Englishman John Taylor, who followed Brigham Young as president of the LDS Church, also to wax millennial in his April 1863 description of Mormon life in the future. Taylor, however, tried to emphasize the positive and productive sides of a return to Jackson County, which certainly was a change of pace from Young, Kimball, and Cannon. The Saints eventually would have

> the most magnificent buildings, the most pleasant and beautiful gardens, the richest and most costly clothing, and be the most healthy and the most intellectual people that will reside upon the earth.
>
> This is only a faint outline of some of our views . . . hence we talk of returning to Jackson County to build the most magnificent temple . . . and the most splendid city that was ever erected; yea, cities if you please. . . . from the president down will all be under the guidance and direction of the Lord in all the pursuits of human life. (*Journal of Discourses* 1966:10:147)

As a result of new federal laws designed to inhibit polygamy (Shipps 1985:164–65), Young in the 1860s thought that continued oppression by the U.S. government would offend God and actually hasten the return to Jackson County. He said that the expulsion of the Saints from Jackson County had served "to bring us to our senses" but that the Lord still wanted to "pour upon this people" the blessing of a return there: "If our enemies do not cease their oppression upon this people, as sure as the Lord lives it will not be many days before we will occupy that land and there build up a Temple to the Lord. If they would keep us from accomplishing this work very soon, they had better let us alone. 'I will purge the land,' saith the Lord, 'cut off the evil doer, and prepare a way for the return of my people to their inheritance'" (*Journal of Discourses* 1966:9:270). Just as internal disobedience of the Saints inspired Jackson County talk, external oppression had a similar effect. Though Young's words regarding divine cause and effect were bold, he was struck by reports of violence in Missouri. From their intermountain dwelling, the Saints saw the war as fulfilling prophecy, but they did not enjoy the news of suffering that had taken place. Young heard that one "may ride through the large districts of the country and see one vast desolation. A gentleman said here that one hundred families were burned alive in their own houses in the county of Jackson, Missouri. Whether this is true or not it is not for me to say, but the thought of it is painful" (Campbell 1988:296).

Using a millennial tone in 1869, Young associated the growth of the Saints with biblical events. Clearly, many of these had specific Missouri origins:

> It was the opinion of the Prophet Joseph [Smith] that the City of Enoch had been in the Gulf of Mexico, and that Adam offered his sacrifice & built his first altar in Adam-Ondi-Ahman, & the stones of his altar are there now to be seen. The City of Enoch was taken up, but the City of Zion which we shall build will remain and not be taken away as his city was. Noah was 110 years in building an Ark. We have not been 40 years yet in building up Zion in our day. (Kenney 1983:6:482; spelling added and punctuation corrected)

The "City of Enoch" refers to a city in the *Book of Mormon* that was taken directly into the heavens because of its righteousness. With the passing of the war, the emphasis of *only* "40 years" of growth indicates that Young thought the time to return to Missouri was now not so close. "Gentlemen, don't be startled," Young later exhorted, "for if we don't go back there, our sons and daughters will; and a great temple will be built upon the consecrated spot, and a great many more besides that" (*Journal of Discourses* 1966:6:296). All of a sudden sons and daughters might have the blessing, not necessarily those now living. It was evident that Young was now not in such a hurry. Giving progeny thirty years or so to grow up would have placed Young's time of return roughly around 1900. The return to Jackson County originally was to have taken place in the aftermath of war; when such a return was not achieved, it was projected a short generation into the future.

Also interesting was Young's projection of a "great temple" apparently being first, followed by "a great many more besides." Young was not speaking of the Salt Lake Temple, then under construction. This is the reverse of the Latter-day Saint view circa 2003 when many temples large and small dot the continent and beyond while a rather conspicuous space exists at Jackson County, the center place.

Heber C. Kimball and others generally echoed Young's sentiments. Kimball stated that "the kingdom would roll on and we should go back to Jackson County before many years and all Hell could not stop us" (Larson and Larson 1980:1:65, 91). Of course, the phrase "before many years" was not specific, but Orson Pratt, in 1871, was certain that the return to Jackson County would occur within the lifetime of the generation who personally experienced the Missouri expulsion. He said, "The generation has not passed away; all the people that were living thirty-nine years ago have not passed away; but before they do pass away this will be fulfilled" (*Journal of Discourses* 1966:14:275). This would have meant either that the return was imminent or that the people of Salt Lake City at that time were again becoming slothful in building the Utah Zion.

Obviously, perspectives on the return varied from speaker to speaker, according to the theme of the preaching. For example, George Q. Cannon feared that, as in the Missouri days of church history, the Saints might "not be permitted to go back and build up the Centre Stake of Zion" because of disobedience. Orson Pratt later imagined the return to Jackson County as further distant in the future than previous LDS leaders had viewed it. In 1879, he foresaw the time when the youth of the church "in those days" would return to Jackson County (*Journal of Discourses* 1966:21:149). Varying from imminent, to a decade, to several decades, the chronology of events regarding the millennial New Jerusalem were not uniformly agreed upon by all LDS people. The leadership held disparate views of the order of monumental events in the "last days," and their views were usually based on the interpretation of scripture mixed with contemporary instructional need. On such millennial matters no specific details were normally given. The membership, usually not as versed in Mormon scripture and belief, often borrowed their beliefs from the leadership—but into the next century the reverse would occur.

Belief in how the New Jerusalem was to be physically established also varied from speaker to speaker. Wilford Woodruff's view was that Jackson County would eventually be desolated, empty, and ready for the Saints to enter and rebuild the city of God (Kenney 1983:7:422–23). Others, however, were in doubt about whether the city would be built by the Saints or if the majority would return to a city that had come down out of heaven as was described in Revelation (Ellsworth 1990:240–41). A uniform frame of time reference for LDS millennial thought has never been truly set out, but some tendencies did begin to take hold in the 1900s and will be discussed in chapter 6.

In an attempt to control the intrusion of outside forces that might dilute Mormon hegemony, the Utah church eventually cooperated with eastern companies in railroad construction, established its own commercial stores, and renewed communitarian cooperative ventures (see Arrington 1966:chaps. 9, 10, 11). With newly found economic and emotional attachments to Utah, it would seem to have been more difficult for members to conceptualize a return to Missouri. When no return to Jackson County came, as Young and others prophesied, little consternation was apparent. The Saints were busy instead expanding the Mormon kingdom while simultaneously combating the increasing non-Mormon business influence in Utah. The Jackson County event was pushed farther into the future, though some millennial images were still vivid. After the death of Brigham Young, the new president, John Taylor, said less of Jackson County, but the theme remained popular with some of the apostles until the 1890s.

The Size of the Holy City

LDS leaders during the late 1800s gave enough information to sketch the perceived size and sphere of influence of the New Jerusalem yet to be established. The framework, as always, was historical and biblical, and many sites in northwestern Missouri continued to be important. George Q. Cannon made this clear:

> It is the land where Adam, the Ancient of Days, will gather his posterity again, and where the blessings of God will descend upon them. It is the land for which the wise and learned have travelled and sought in vain. Asia has been ransacked in endeavoring to locate the Garden of Eden. Men have supposed that

FIG. 23 | *The vernacular Jackson County of the LDS Church leadership, circa 1860–90.*

> because the ark rested on Ararat that the flood commenced there, or rather that it was from thence the ark started to sail. But God in his revelations has informed us that it was on this choice land . . . where Adam was placed and the Garden of Eden was laid out. (*Journal of Discourses* 1966:11:337)

That the Garden of Eden was in Jackson County was never actually laid out in writing in LDS scripture, but the prominence of such recapitulation sites in LDS belief is overwhelming, especially when contrasted with the RLDS manner of downplaying the millennial significance of any particular place, with the possible exception of the Temple Lot itself.

New Jerusalem was a fairly extensive region as promulgated by the LDS leadership, and "Jackson County" was the common phrase signifying it. Specificity lost, the Jackson County generic label was applied overall—it meant a large portion of northwestern Missouri (Figure 23). This greater perceptual millenarian region included central Daviess County where Adam-ondi-Ahman was believed to have been the place where Adam and at least eight of his generations dwelt (*Journal of Discourses* 1966:18:342–44). It also included the future temple spot at Far West and likely the town of Liberty in Clay County where Joseph Smith and other church leaders were imprisoned during the winter of 1838–39. Joseph Smith III, the first RLDS president, gave a rare view of Liberty. He wrote that Liberty's environs presented "a view surpassed for beauty by none that we ever saw; south, east, and west, the undulating landscape gave rise to the thought that it was one of the fairest portions of God's heritage to man" (RLDS 1967:4:560–61). No doubt the western Saints agreed with this even more than RLDS adherents.

The "eastern counties" of the state of Kansas were also included within the New Jerusalem, according to Orson Pratt (Figure 23). Other leaders neither supported nor refuted the idea. According to Pratt, this large "region round about" would one day be thickly populated with productive Latter-day Saints (*Journal of Discourses* 1966:21:135; see also 21:149, 24:23–24). With at least three LDS stakes in the region today (about twelve thousand members), certainly Pratt would have been impressed, yet the LDS presence overall is negligible compared to total population.

Considering the importance of the Kansas "Indian" Territory to the early church, it is surprising that Pratt seems to have been the only LDS leader to talk of eastern Kansas as part of the New Jerusalem. Perhaps the idea was lost because of the distraction of the Civil War and the slavery issue, but one would think that Kansas, as a new free state, would have attracted Mormon millennial attention sooner and more often than it did.

An idea of the New Jerusalem's size can be grasped through discourses on how the future city would attract multitudes of people seeking shelter. The leadership and membership alike viewed the New Jerusalem as a magnet for a gathering that would include the lost ten tribes of Israel who had dwelt in unknown territory since Old Testament times. Heber C. Kimball, for example, in the midst of the desperate arrival of the handcart companies in 1856, made a reference to a future time of even more smitten refugees on their way to Missouri: "Two [handcart] companies have come through safe and sound. Is this the end of it? No; there will be millions that will come much in the same way, only they will not have hand carts, for they will take their bundles under their arms, and their children on their backs, and under their arms, and flee; and Zion's people will have to send out relief to them, for they will come when the judgments come on the nations" (*Journal of Discourses* 1966:4:106). As will be seen, a return in deprivation is a recurring theme, but not a consistent one. Regarding quantity, Brigham Young asked rhetorically in 1861, "Will they come merely by one or two shiploads? No; it will require many more ships than we have heretofore employed. . . . Millions of people that now sit in darkness . . . will come to Zion." Immigrants, apparently, were to come from all over the world. In response to a question as to whether Jackson County would be large enough to hold them all, Young ambiguously pointed to worthiness and preparation as paramount. He replied that Zion, based in Independence, "will be just large enough to receive all that will be prepared to possess it" (9:138).

The Views of Orson Pratt

After the death of Brigham Young in 1877, some of the Mormon apostles, specifically Wilford Woodruff and Orson Pratt, helped to maintain New Jerusalem discussion in the church. Pratt, a responsible and scholarly individual who was made an apostle in 1835, was by far the most prolific writer, particularly from the early 1870s to his death in 1881. His Mormon experience was vast; he knew Joseph Smith and outlived Brigham Young. Because of his lifelong contributions to the church, and his calling as an apostle, most LDS members seriously received his views.

Pratt said that the Utah settlement of Saints was a fulfillment of several Old Testament prophesies and that it was a preparatory period guided by God. He argued that the Saints could not have built the New Jerusalem in Missouri in 1830 because prophecy stated that Native Americans were to have had a part in its construction, but the early church was prohibited from teaching to them. In the future, however,

> many of the Indian nations will become a civilized and christian people, . . . [and] will build the city called the New Jerusalem or Zion, being assisted by the Gentile Saints.
>
> If the Gentile Saints had built up the city of Zion in Jackson county, Missouri . . . before many of the Indian nations became converted, it would have falsified the prediction of Jesus [made in the *Book of Mormon*].

> The converted remnants of Joseph [Indians] are to be the principal actors in the great work . . . after which the Indian nations will be gathered in one to the city of Zion and the surrounding country; then the powers of heaven will be revealed, and Jesus will descend in his glory and dwell in the midst. (Pratt 1851:19)

The reference to Indians as "remnants of Joseph" comes from the *Book of Mormon*, which teaches that American Indians are descendants of ancient migrating Jews. The use of the term *gentile* as applied to the Saints ostensibly refers to the European, non-Jewish heritage of most Mormons. Pratt emphasized that the dominant participation of Native American peoples in building the New Jerusalem was a prediction taken from the *Book of Mormon* (3 Nephi 21:23–24) and as such was infallible doctrine, to take place as described. The majority of Mormons, being of European background, would only be "helpers . . . who co-operate" with the Native Americans, whom God would favor (*Journal of Discourses* 1966: 17:300–301).

Whereas most religious scholars associated biblical references of Zion to the Old Jerusalem in Palestine, Pratt, of course, was "constrained to believe them to be two different places and cities" (Pratt 1851:20). Imagined separately, the American Zion even becomes a rescuer of Old Jerusalem. In 1870, Pratt insisted that Zion, in Independence, would be the center of the LDS Church, "the place where the Prophets, Apostles and inspired men of god will have their headquarters." Accordingly, the faith of the Saint was even stronger than that of the Jew regarding their returns to the respective Jerusalems, an idea that has not necessarily held true circa 2000 (*Journal of Discourses* 1966:13:138). In his 1851 discourse, Pratt wrote that the city would be built up "before the Lord appears in his glory" and that there would "assuredly be more revelation given to accomplish so important a work," since

> no uninspired man would know when to commence such a work; neither would he know the place where the Most High would have such a city; neither would he know any thing of the order of architecture which would be most pleasing . . . neither . . . the size or pattern of the sanctuary and tabernacle which, according to the scriptures, must be built in Zion. An uninspired man would be in total ignorance in regard to every thing connected with this preparatory city for the coming of the Lord. Hence the [need] for more revelation and inspired prophets in the last days. (Pratt 1851:20)

Pratt's assertion that an uninspired man would not "know the place where the Most High would have such a city" is curious, especially considering his own admission, four years later, that "the temple must be built upon the consecrated spot" in Independence (*Journal of Discourses* 1966: 3:18). Pratt's original statement implies that though Independence was generally the right place, the Lord might approve eventual construction elsewhere in Jackson County; a slim possibility but convenient if the sacred site was unavailable in the future. Or perhaps his speech was just symbolic of how oblivious the gentiles were to God's work. At any rate, his statement gives emphasis to LDS belief in ongoing revelation, that heavenly communication would take precedence over the importance of place.

Pratt seems to have had a genuine interest in his subject, and he was extremely creative in his "Golden Age" interpretations. His detailed descriptions of the New Jerusalem were compelling and meant to inspire confidence and motivation. It seems that Pratt was highly trusted, but his elaborate descriptions occasionally clashed with the more pragmatic views of Brigham Young and other leaders.[3] The leadership, however, did not publicly contradict Pratt's views, no matter how extra-scriptural they might have been. The church membership probably received his New Jerusalem preaching with interest; undoubtedly, common Mormons saw Pratt as the foremost authority on the subject. Brigham Young may have wished Pratt had remained silent, but Pratt's ruminations, as will be seen, became even more imaginative after Young's death.

The Exodus from Utah

In the 1870s, millennial speculation reached a peak among the Saints as more stringent attempts were made by the federal government to weaken the church in order to curtail polygamy. LDS leaders and members alike imagined some wild and somber scenes. The Civil War had been of national importance and spurred millenarian talk, but that era could not compare with the perceived direct threat that the church faced from the U.S. government two decades later. Orson Pratt continued his descriptions of a return to Missouri and the nature of the city to be built. Wilford Woodruff also described images memorably apocalyptic.

In a speech given four months before his death, Brigham Young still affirmed that the Saints would return to Jackson County as well as spread to a variety of other places:

> It has been asked if we intend to settle more valleys. Why certainly we expect to fill the next valley and then the next, and the next, and so on. . . . Are we going back to Jackson County? Yes. When? As soon as the way opens up. Are we all going? O no! of course not. When we do return will there be any less remaining in these mountains than we number today? No, there may be a hundred then for every single one that there is now. It is folly in men to suppose that we are going to break up these our hard earned homes to make others in a new country. We intend to hold our own here, and also penetrate the north and the south, the east and the west. (*Journal of Discourses* 1966:18:355–56)

Young, pragmatic and quite prophetic to the end, saw that a complete abandonment of Utah was not logical. To vacate the Utah territory would not be necessary, as Young accurately predicted a tremendous population growth supplying more than enough people to remain at the feet of the Wasatch Mountains. The total LDS Church population at the time of Young's comments was about 160,000 (Shipps 1985:165). Though often clairvoyant on future growth, Young foresaw the possibility of a Utah with sixteen million people—a Texas-sized population more than ample to feed migration back to Missouri!

A theme of Saints returning to Missouri in wealth, opposite some of the apostles' earlier views, became important. In 1868, Orson Pratt encouraged members to build the kingdom of God "and extend its borders, that when the time shall come for that Great Central City . . . this people may have wealth in their possession to perform the work of god. We have to build that city; we have to furnish riches to do it. We must prepare ourselves for it" (*Journal of Discourses* 1966:12:321).

In order to go back, Pratt thought, the Saints must keep the law of consecration (Pratt called it "the celestial law") similar to the one that the Saints were introduced to when in Missouri. At the time of the return, the Saints would have "property and means sufficient to accomplish this work." Once under way, the return of the Saints to Missouri would produce terror in the "nations of the earth" since the "supernatural power" of God would be made manifest in spectacular manner just as the "cloud by day" and "flaming fire by night" accompanied Moses as he led Israel back to the promised land. A special prophet would lead the church back and nations would know of this event "when telegraphic dispatches are sent forth to the most distant parts of the earth" (*Journal of Discourses* 1966:17:306). Of course

Pratt was ignorant of satellites, fiber optics, the Internet, and cell phones, but the return to Jackson County was inevitable, and the return would consist of a "very large organization of thousands and tens of thousands," and the majority of the Saints would thus "walk forth into Jackson County," a view strikingly opposite that of Young (*Journal of Discourses* 1966:15: 364–65, 17:305–6).

Pratt said it would probably be necessary to "purchase that whole region of country" according to the earlier instruction of Joseph Smith. Settled again in Jackson County, the Saints would apportion lots among themselves according to divine equanimity. They would eventually control the region, but Pratt assured his listeners that prior occupants would receive fair treatment in the redistribution of lands. Pratt also discussed how the Saints would make their living in the New Jerusalem. "A great many" of the Saints would be farmers there, and mills would be built. "All kinds of machinery and manufactures" would be introduced to the region, not a very impressive statement considering Kansas City's industrial might today, though the church does lease a portion of the temple grounds property to Deutz-Allis Gleaners, makers of agricultural equipment. In the contemporary perspective, perhaps the church would be open to operating General Motors' Fairfax and Ford's Claycomo automobile production plants as well.

The architecture, layout of the streets, pavement, gates and walls, adornment, and other aspects of the city would all be revealed by the Lord, and construction begun. "Many hundreds" of meetinghouses and schools would be built. Academies and universities would be established throughout the region. The statement that the city would be "illuminated" by God's divine power and be more densely populated than any in Utah carries little weight today, considering there are nearly as many people in greater Kansas City as in the entirety of Utah. Furthermore, Pratt said the city would stand through the millennium. It eventually would be taken up into the skies (along with the Old Jerusalem) while the world endured a final fiery purification. These two cities would then be returned to a glorified earth (*Journal of Discourses* 1966:15:365; 17:304–6; 18:348; 21:149, 152–54; 24:23–24).

Pratt was not completely consistent in his views on Missouri's future reoccupation. He restated the problem that disobedience might still impede a return. If the Saints were to return in 1874, for example, "after the order we have been living in during the last forty years, we should be cast out again, the Lord would not acknowledge us as his people, neither would he acknowledge the works of our hands in the building of a city" (*Journal of Discourses* 1966:17:112). In 1880, a year before his death, Pratt, surprisingly, could not conceive how lands might ever be returned to the Saints. While insisting that the Saints would eventually receive the Missouri lands due them, he said that if it was not to happen "this year, or ten years hence, we will ask our Father to give us that land after the resurrection, at any rate" (*Journal of Discourses* 1966:21:330). In his final years, Pratt may have begun to tire of the wait. He seemed resigned and doubted that migrating to Missouri again was possible within a realistic time period.

The view that the return to Missouri would be in the midst of desolation, first heard in the Civil War years, remained an important theme in the 1880s. Notwithstanding earlier comments that the Saints would return with wealth, a juxtaposed idea suggested that circumstances would be difficult and the trek back to Missouri anything but easy. Memories of hardships along the pioneer trek to Utah did not easily fade. Scottish immigrant John MacNeil, in a letter written home, included a description of an anonymous woman's vision. The return was to be harsh: "the time was nigh at hand for the lost ten tribes to come from the north and live amongst us & also for some of the saints to go back to Jackson County & that many of them would die by the road and some would be changed in the twinkle of an eye" (Buchanan 1988:106).[4]

After Brigham Young's death, in December 1877, Wilford Woodruff wrote in his journal a similar gruesome vision.[5] Woodruff appears sincere, since he did not write to a contemporary audience with any discernible purpose. Neither did Woodruff claim it to be a revelation, rather a personal experience, which lends authenticity. He wrote that he saw many cities laid desolate (Figure 24), apparently by disease, including Salt Lake City. Washington, D.C., was destroyed, "the White House Empty, the Halls of Congress the same, everything in ruins." In Baltimore, the dead filled the city square. Philadelphia was totally vacant, and Woodruff saw New York consumed by fire. Omaha, Nebraska, was the object of detailed attention. There he saw "the roads full of people, principally women with just what they could carry in bundles on their backs travelling to the mountains on foot" (Kenney 1983:7:420–22). Woodruff finally wrote of the central object of the vision:

> Missouri and Illinois were in turmoil and Strife, Men killing each other and women joining the fight, family against family Cutting each other to pieces in the most horrid manner.

. . . I was here given to understand that the same horror was being enacted all over the Country, North South East and West, that few were left alive. Still, there were some.

Immediately after, I seemed to be standing on the west bank of the Missouri River opposite the City of Independance, but I saw no City. I saw the whole States of Missouri & Illinois and part of Iowa were a Complete wilderness with no living human being in them. I then saw, a short distance from the river, Twelve men dressed in the robes of the Temple Standing in a square, or nearly so.[6] I understood it represented the Twelve gates of the New Jerrusalem, and they were with hands uplifted Consecrating the ground and laying the Corner Stones. I saw myriads of Angels hovering over them and around about them and also an immens pillar of a cloud over them and I heard the singing of the most beautiful music, the words, "Now is esstablished the Kingdom of our god and his Christ and He shall reign forever and Ever, and the Kingdom shall never be Thrown down for the Saints have overcome." And I saw people coming from the river and different places a long way off to help build the Temple, and it seemed that the Hosts of the angels also helped to get the material to build the Temple. (Kenney 1983:7:422–23)

The description is consistent with the general LDS attitude that sacred space in Missouri (or rather profane space obliterated to be made sacred) is general and spread over a wide area. Woodruff mentions where Independence should have been but dwells on no real places in the vision, which superimposes, postcalamity, the millennial municipality over the Kansas City area. Woodruff's words exemplify the view of an increasingly besieged church with increased antipolygamy pressures by the U.S. government. In any case, the feelings of Woodruff, the senior apostle, may have initiated new interest in the spiritual welfare of Jackson County, and in September 1878 Orson Pratt and Joseph F. Smith were called to go there and obtain an early history of the church and an original manuscript of the *Book of Mormon*, both of which David Whitmer reportedly possessed.[7] The missionaries were apparently unsuccessful (Kenney 1983:7:431; RLDS 1967:4:244–45).

Considering the events of September 11, 2001, and subsequent fears of terrorist activity, war in Iraq, confusion among NATO members, and threats, real or imagined, from North Korea, most LDS adherents would

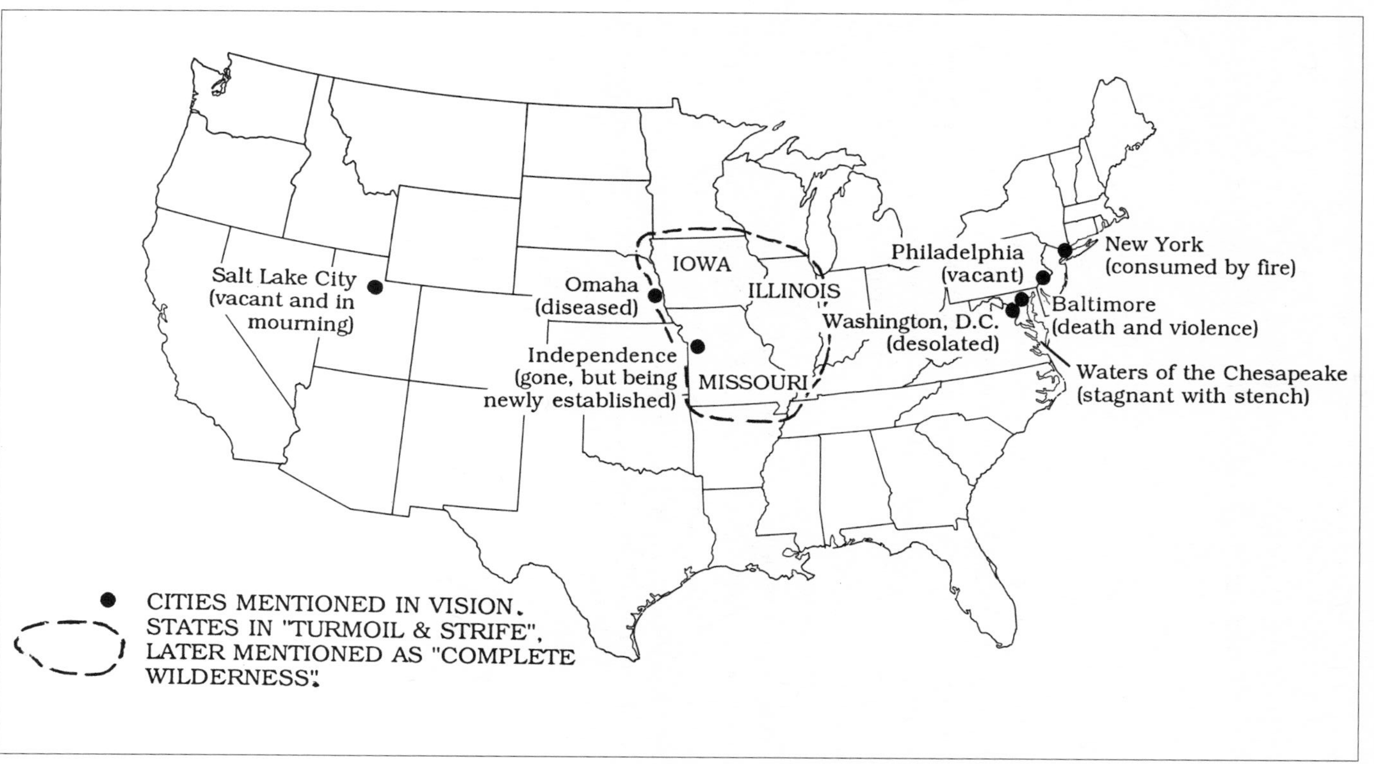

FIG. 24 | *The geography of desolation in Wilford Woodruff's 1877 vision.*

find Woodruff's vision quite frightening. Even if events had been different, the LDS view has perpetually been to prepare and "know the signs." Unfortunately, the vagueness of scriptural account has always left the Saints loosely interpreting every different ominous world event in a very personal way.

Descriptions of the Temple

While in Independence, the two apostles Orson Pratt and Joseph F. Smith visited the Temple Lot. The experience inspired Pratt to describe certain details of the future temple. The structure would be of "a design very different from the little temples we now build"—which were actually not little (*Journal of Discourses* 1966:19:19, 24:24). Though based on Smith's original pattern, God would newly reveal the exact configuration to a servant whom he would raise up. Pratt envisioned a very large single structure with twenty-four "compartments," or "rooms, in a circular form" instead of twenty-four separate buildings (24:24–25). Besides the temple, "tabernacles and meeting houses" would exist for other assemblies such as Sunday meetings. The temple, as well as public buildings there, would be abundantly ornamented with all types of gems and precious stones "sufficiently pure and crystallized" (24:27).

The temple would be protected from the ravages of storms and time (21:153, 24:25–27). It would contain the throne of the Lord Jesus Christ, where "he will, at times, personally sit," and it would also contain twelve other thrones for the original twelve apostles of Jesus, who would sit as judges over the tribes of Israel. His description emphasized his belief that the temple of the New Jerusalem would be the epitome of connection between earth and the heavens, very likely having "an apartment, with a table, on which food and drink will be prepared such as are suitable to the taste and happiness of immortal resurrected beings" (19:19–20).

Despite firm millennial beliefs, such a level of otherworldly talk was far from the norm for the practical-minded western Saints. Besides the visit to the Temple Lot, a variety of circumstances led Pratt to such a premillennial high. First of all, Orson Pratt had seen the 1830s Missouri experience firsthand. In 1877, the St. George temple was dedicated while ground was broken for similar structures in Manti and Logan the same year. The Salt Lake Temple would not be completed until 1892, so these former were the first temples constructed in the west. The celebrations surrounding these events had to be tinged with what could have been, and what yet might be, in Independence. Brigham Young died in 1877, and John Taylor had not as yet been sustained as the next president of the church. The combination of the first temples in the West with the death of the man who had led the church for more than thirty years had to have been some cause for more anticipation than usual as to what the Lord had planned for the Saints. At least for Orson Pratt in particular.

Practicality at the Turn of the Century

During the 1880s, LDS leaders' views became more pragmatic in tone, though the circumstances of a return were seen as likely to be fraught with difficulty. In 1882, apostle and later president of the church Joseph F. Smith said that although "two or three hundred thousand people" would wend their way "across the great plain" toward Missouri, these Utah emigrants might not see much of divinity in their course. The image of a quarter of a million people wending their way to Missouri today is striking even considering if they could use automobiles, but no such technology could be envisioned. They would endure

> the nameless hardships of the journey, herding and guarding their cattle by day and by night, and defending themselves and little ones from foes on the right hand and on the left, as when they came here. They will find the journey back to Jackson County will be as real as when they came out here. . . . And though you may be led by the power of God "with a stretched out arm," it will not be more manifest than the leading the people out here to those that participate in it. (*Journal of Discourses* 1966:24:156–57).

In a similar style as Wilford Woodruff, Joseph F. Smith said that a great many hardships would be endured, and "perhaps it would be left to the children to see the glory of their deliverance." According to Smith's view, the Saints could not use railroads in the return, since, in this mode of travel, "the sifting process would be insufficient." Traveling in the lap of luxury, the Saints would not be full participants in the necessary molding process that would precede arrival in New Jerusalem territory. God forbid the Saints travel in too much comfort: the trek might be regarded "commonplace" (*Journal of Discourses* 1966:24:157). Walking, then, was divine, which means minivans and SUVs were definitely out.

Several comments by Joseph Smith Jr. in the early years of the church had implied that the Second Coming would occur in the late 1800s, perhaps in the year 1891.[8] By 1890, however, the kinds of external pressures that before had spurred church leaders into millennial talk had begun to decline. After Wilford Woodruff prohibited new polygamous marriages (*Doctrine* 1981:291–93), the Saints had renewed hope for Utah statehood, and by 1891 there was no reason for an immediate return to Missouri. The monumental Salt Lake Temple was completed in 1892, and the Saints were not planning to abandon it after forty years of construction.

The aging Woodruff, along with the Tabernacle Choir, made a trip to the Chicago World's Fair in August 1893. Along the way, they stopped in Jackson County. Perhaps Woodruff expected a harsh reception there, but the choir was surprised by the "striking incident" that "even the Mayor & Citizens of Jackson County entertained us . . . & made us welcome" (Kenney 1983:9:258–59, 278). The occasion provided renewed hope for the visiting church officials. With Utah statehood now hanging in the balance, the warm receptions in both Chicago and Independence must have seemed millennial to some degree. Or perhaps they were confusing; weren't the Midwesterners supposed to mistreat the Saints?

At the turn of the new century, Woodruff's successor, Lorenzo Snow, also taught that the trek back across the plains was inevitable, but direct references to Missouri were now less frequent. In an exception to common discussion, Snow announced that some then living would go back to Missouri to help build the temple. Supposing that the youngest person to hear this statement was about twenty years old, and assuming a life span of seventy years, this would put a return to Missouri at 1950. Though the talk subsided, an ember of hope was kept alive regarding Missouri.

In 1890, the apostle James E. Talmage published a five-hundred-page rendering of basic LDS tenets titled the *Articles of Faith* (1925). The book is still popular today and provides a good turn-of-the-century overview of a vague Latter-day Saint Zion and a remote New Jerusalem (Talmage often used the two terms interchangeably). Talmage adheres to the doctrine of a return to Independence but gives emphasis on the return occurring according to the faithfulness of the Saints, since "wickedness causes the Lord to tarry" (Talmage 1925:353–54). Around 1900, more prosperity for, and national acceptance of, the Utah church made a return to Missouri unlikely. In such an environment, Talmage renewed a focus on the theme of disobedience of the people, which ostensibly caused the Lord to push the promised establishment of the New Jerusalem further into the future.

Shifting Toward Taciturnity

The millennial leanings of the LDS leadership throughout the mid- to late 1800s were pronounced, but discussion of the establishment of the New Jerusalem waned at the end of the century. Through the 1850s, Jackson County was often used as a spur to encourage the Saints to build up the Salt Lake Valley. During the Civil War, the destruction reported was viewed as fulfilling prophecy, and imaginative scenes of New Jerusalem establishment were envisioned. For most of his life, Brigham Young thought the time of the return to Missouri to be relatively close.

Another increase in interest in the New Jerusalem occurred in the 1870s and 1880s as increased pressures were placed on the LDS Church to abolish polygamy. Orson Pratt became the unofficial spokesman on the theme of the New Jerusalem. During this time, events involving desolation and a return to Jackson County were emphasized over the actual nature of the city to be established. After 1890, millennial fervor lessened and Missouri was mentioned less frequently; the supernatural essence of the New Jerusalem in talks by the LDS leadership also diminished. The church sought acceptance in greater American society, and the attitude toward Independence changed from the idea of an imminent return to a concept of a gradual purchasing of sacred plots and establishing a mission presence there. The belief in a return to Jackson County remained, but the time of the event began to be pushed further away.

LDS Views since 1900

Millenarian Taciturnity

"I suppose most Mormons have thought sometime or other that there'd come a time when they had to make their way to Utah."

"Or Jackson County," said Analee.

"Somewhere," said Tina.

—Orson Scott Card, *The Folk of the Fringe*

The quotation above from novelist Orson Scott Card shows the ambiguity of the Utah Mormon Church today toward Jackson County as a future gathering place. Most individual Mormons, especially in the central United States, believe in an eventual gathering to Jackson County, but one is hard pressed to find much millennial talk on the subject by the church leadership. While Independence and Jackson County were prevalent in church talk in the 1800s, the LDS Church today has softened on millennial matters because of phenomenal growth and activity on many simultaneous fronts. Still, talk among the general membership, overall temple building, the purchase of large acreage in the Kansas City area, and the upgrading of certain properties there indicate a definite LDS interest in western Missouri.

The church has never rejected any of Joseph Smith's doctrines regarding western Missouri, but it is officially hesitant toward Independence, for a variety of reasons. This taciturnity is contrasted with the imaginative views of members who tend to think more millennially, often envisioning mental New Jerusalems of their own.

A Purchase Instead of a Return

The LDS Church never attempted to reestablish a presence in the Jackson County area throughout the 1800s. Although the Reorganized and Temple Lot Churches were both well established in Independence by 1880, the LDS Church was busy trying to get out of debt and had distanced itself even from the legal fight over the Temple Lot. In 1897, a small LDS "branch" (congregation) was organized in Independence. The Utah church did not attempt a greater presence until 1900, when its Southwestern Mission headquarters were moved to Kansas City from the town of St. John in Stafford County, Kansas (Billeter 1946:116–17).

A greater LDS impact in the Independence area took place after Joseph F. Smith, Joseph Smith Jr.'s nephew, was made president of the church in October 1901. This was a time when the church was trying to demonstrate patriotic fervor in order to be accepted in the American mainstream and to leave the polygamy issue behind (Church Educational System 1989:467). Bonds were issued and all church debt was paid off between 1899 and 1907 (Arrington 1966:403), and, for the first time, extra funds were available (Rich 1972:471, 476). Starting an important trend, the LDS Church began to use the monies to purchase properties of historical interest.

In 1904, James G. Duffin, head of a small LDS mission school in Kansas City, purchased an L-shaped twenty-five-acre portion of land in Independence for the church from Maggie Swope ("Mormons Rebuying" 1904; Billeter 1946:116; RLDS 1967:6:111). Eleven acres of this parcel had been the southeastern corner of Edward Partridge's original sixty-three-acre triangle of "Temple" property. This rectangular part of the LDS purchase, often called the "meadow" or "pasture" (Figure 25; Dyer 1976:69), had once been part of the estate of William Chrisman, an influential educator and banker in Independence during the 1800s. The northwest corner of the parcel was diagonally adjacent to the Temple Lot. At the time, the *Kansas City Star* reported that "intentions with regard to the property could not be definitely learned" ("Mormons Rebuying" 1904), and apparently the LDS Church had no immediate plan other than to obtain a portion of the historic Independence site. Nine smaller land purchases in Independence, including a few small lots elsewhere within the "Partridge triangle" were also made at this time, amounting to a total expenditure, meadow and all, of $64,450 (Rich 1972:477–78). One two-acre portion of land was located south of Pacific Street and has since been on long-term lease to the Deutz-Allis Gleaner combine factory (Duesterhaus 1992; Gunnerson 1992).

Also in 1904, the LDS mission headquarters was relocated from Kansas City to Independence, and the mission name was changed from the "Southwestern Mission" to the "Central States Mission" (Billeter 1946: 116). This signaled the need for a "central" connotation, and Independence was a natural historical and spiritual hub for missionary work. This focus was solidified in 1907, when Independence became a continentwide publishing center for all United States missions of the LDS Church. It is possible that some millennial expectations could have been attached to the publishing house, which remained there until 1945, but little was written about it (Billeter 1946:116–17).

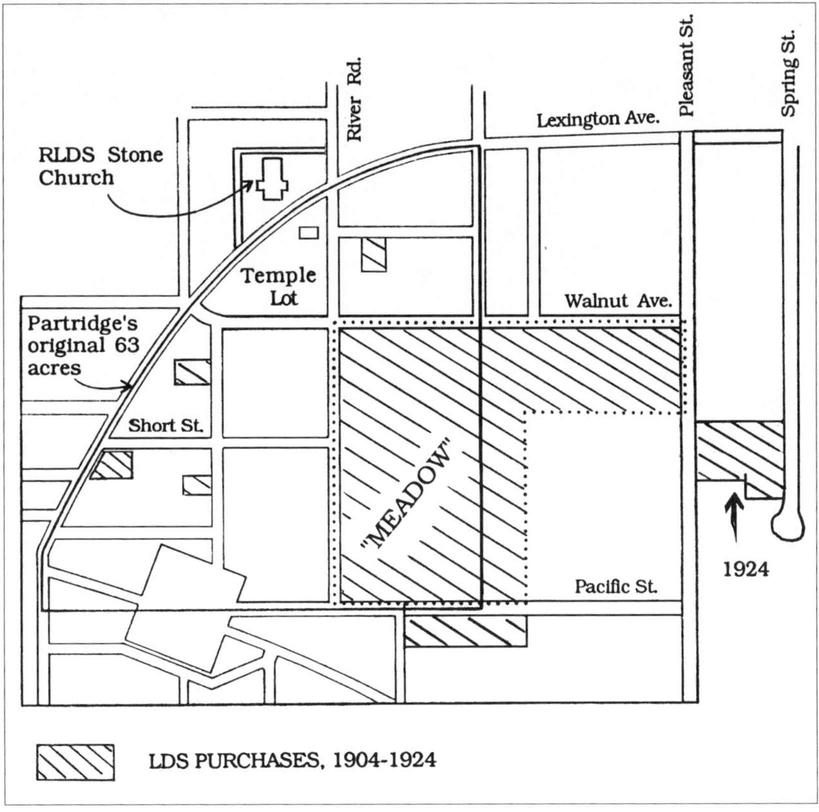

FIG. 25 | *LDS land acquisitions in Independence through the 1920s.*

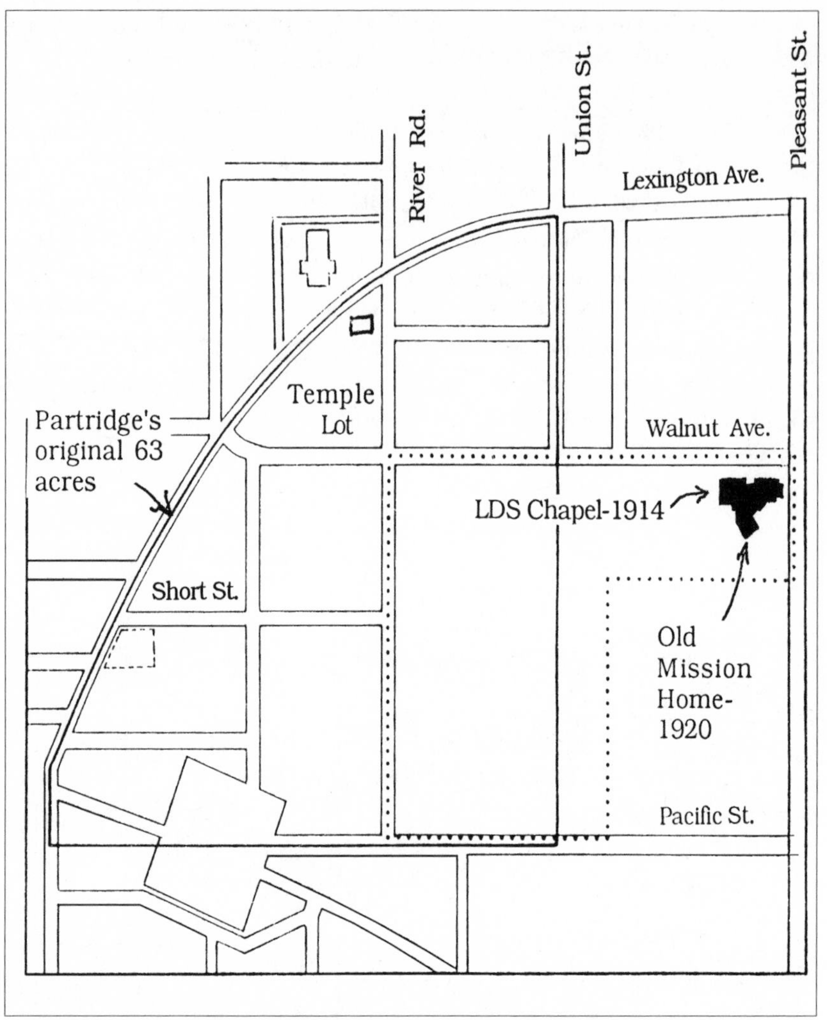

FIG. 26 | *The first LDS chapel in Independence with mission home.*

Independence, however, was not the only place to attract the acquisitive interests of the LDS Church. Important historical sites in Vermont, New York, and Ohio were also purchased at nearly the same time. Other sites in northwestern Missouri were acquired as well. In 1909, the LDS Church purchased a forty-acre tract at the heart of what was Far West, Missouri, the short-lived headquarters site of the church in Caldwell County. This purchase included the site that had been dedicated for a temple, located in the center of that now defunct town (Rich 1972:498).

Compared to other groups, it took some years before the LDS Church built its first structure in Independence. A chapel was built in 1914, constructed on the LDS land purchased by Duffin, at the corner of Pleasant and Walnut. The new building was two blocks east from, but within sight of, the Temple Lot property that the church did not own (Figure 26; Nebeker 1990). Though the leadership of the church may have imagined an eventual return to Jackson County, it did not claim that the recent purchases were signs of imminent millennial events, and the location of the new chapel demonstrated a reserved attitude toward historical sacred land. The chapel did "not stand on the sacred 'Temple Lot,' which is a quarter of a mile further west," wrote the *Kansas City Times* referring to the Church of Christ's important spot ("Rival Prophets Friends" 1914). In fact, the building was not even constructed on Partridge's original sixty-three acres, diagonal from the Temple Lot, but was placed as far away from it as possible, yet still on LDS-owned land (note Figure 26). In delimiting territory, the LDS approach was peripheral. As time passed, as will be seen, land closer to the Temple Lot was used more boldly, but the church during the 1900s has had difficulty even using the phrase "Temple Lot" in general discourse, preferring to talk of "Zion" or, more specifically, the "New Jerusalem."

The new chapel was roughly a block, with windows arched in a semi-Italianate style. Biblical, specifically Jewish, symbols were incorporated into the chapel's architecture. A prominent stone on the top gable of the eastern facade (away from the Temple Lot) portrayed two tablets: one represented the Bible; the other, the *Book of Mormon*. More intriguing were dual Stars of David on the same side, denoting a shared heritage with the ancient Jews as God's chosen people. Besides its function as a chapel and social center, the building also contained a small post office to handle mail for missionaries throughout the Central States Mission. For a congregation of only about seventy adherents, the $25,000 building was imposing, though no particular millennial meaning seemed attached to it ("Mormon Church Is Ready" 1914; "Rival Prophets Friends" 1914). The church was cautiously starting to make its mark again east of the Rocky Mountains and the building's shy placement, away from the Temple Lot, revealed the church's trepidation in marking traditional sacred territory as its own.

President Joseph F. Smith personally saw to the dedication of the new chapel on Sunday, November 22, 1914 ("Head of Mormons" 1914). The afternoon dedicatory session was crowded, with citizens of Independence, including curious RLDS members, attending in addition to the LDS entourage. Even Ada Clark Smith, the wife of ailing RLDS President Joseph Smith III, was present. Almost 150 of the Central States Mission's Mormon missionaries served as ushers and hosts. In terms of the Mormon presence in Missouri, it was a reserved but auspicious beginning.

The Muted Years

A mission home was added behind the chapel in 1920, and a parcel of land was bought across Pleasant Street in 1924 (Jackson County Deed Office 1924), but the LDS Church made no strong statements in Independence for the next forty years. At the most, the official LDS view toward sacred space in Independence was peripheral; at the least it was indifferent. Unlike the Civil War, neither world war evoked much millennial talk from church leaders. They focused instead on the safety and care of LDS members in ravaged Germany, France, and England.

Still, an interested observer could find scattered comments in LDS literature of the time that reflected vernacular New Jerusalem views. In one of the church's early magazines, the *Juvenile Instructor*, one author reminisced that "the fondest dream of many an old Utah pioneer" was to return and establish the "great work" in Jackson County. The author went on to note that at present, however, the Saints were only trickling into the area "in a quiet way" (Driggs 1920:539). Apparently, the fervor of the early church toward gathering in Jackson County was not soon to be replicated.

The LDS view of Independence often ignored other factions. The author quoted above said that in 1920 the "temple grounds" were empty except for the Hedrickite Church (Driggs 1920:542). If this statement referred only to the Temple Lot, then it was factual, but no RLDS presence is mentioned, not even the dominant Stone Church (Figure 26). It is evident in this quotation that the members' feelings at this time were more intense toward the smaller Temple Lot, created through lot divisions in the 1850s, than toward the greater sixty-three-acre tract, even though the LDS Church had purchased a substantial chunk of the latter's acreage.

Be Millennial or Lose Your Land

Renewed LDS interest in Jackson County occurred in 1950 when the city of Independence expressed a desire to acquire church property for the construction of a high school (Reimann 1981). Sometime during the summer of 1950 the mayor of Independence, as well as the city's school board president, traveled to Salt Lake City to address President George A. Smith on the matter (Pusey 1981:349). Considering the perceived sacredness of the meadow, Smith wrote in his journal the understatement that "we did not feel that we wished to sell the property" (Smith 1950:12:836–38).

Fearing eminent domain proceedings over the "Swope lands," the LDS Church offered the city of Independence a contribution of $25,000 toward the development of an educational facility—elsewhere (Reimann 1981:13–14). The offer was graciously accepted, and the church retained the lands in the environs of the Temple Lot. With the help of the donation, the city chose an alternate spot for the school about a mile to the northeast. If the city had had its way, today's William Chrisman High School would have been located on the one-time William Chrisman estate (Wilson 1992). Apparently, the city's goal was to develop for the "meadow" a secular Missourian historical legacy through the use of the Chrisman name, an understandable, though ironic, view considering the

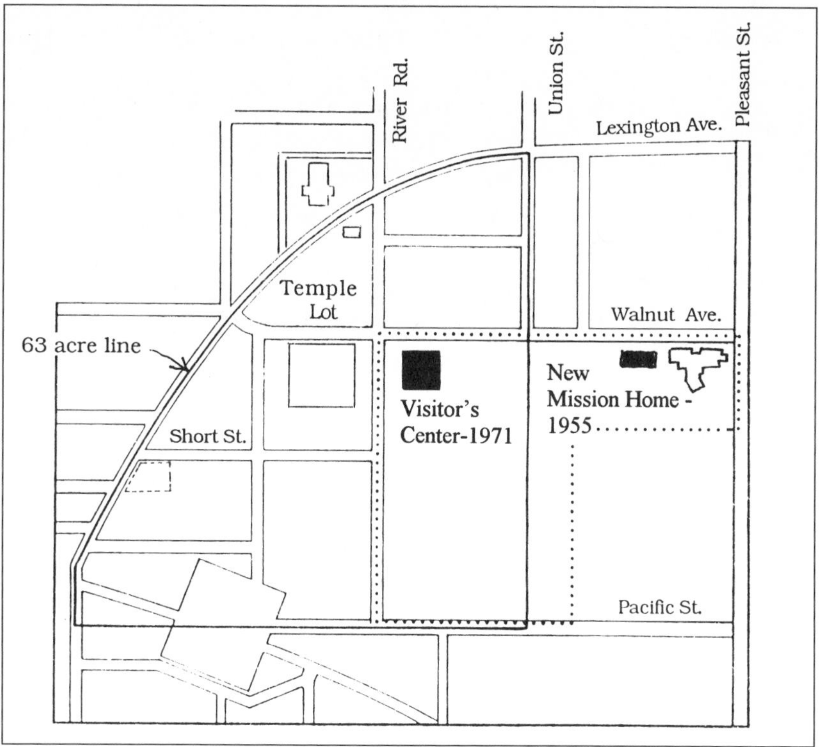

FIG. 27 | *Locations of the LDS chapel, new mission home, and Visitor's Center.*

LDS perceptions of sanctity. In this instance the religious view won out, but the contrast between secular and religious land use competition is notable and sometimes reminiscent of such tensions in other countries. For example, secular authority and Hindu fundamentalists often clash in the struggle to decipher what kind of country India should be ("How Hindu an India?" 2001). Arguably, secular authority has more influence in America.

In 1952 rumors spread in local circles that the LDS Church was attempting to acquire the Church of Christ's sacred Temple Lot. An article in the *Kansas City Times* ("Church History Surrounds" 1952) claimed that the lot was worth as much as a million dollars to the Westerners and that the LDS Church was in the midst of offering extravagant sums to the Temple Lot Church. Since this time, rumors of LDS offers have become common but cannot be substantiated, though leaders of the Temple Lot Church on occasion have fun at the expense of the larger organization. Temple Lot Church apostle William Sheldon told the author that the LDS Church at one time "offered us a blank check" for the property (Sheldon 1990f). On another occasion Sheldon said that someone "probably" in the LDS presidency "offered a million dollars for this spot" (Wolfson 2002). Sheldon's vagueness on specifics shows a tongue-in-cheek attitude with regard to the rumor. In 2002, the only thing LDS Church spokesman Dale Bills would say on the matter was that the Temple Lot "is only part of a larger area believed by Latter-day Saints to be the site of several future temples" (Wolfson 2002).

The 1952 newspaper article also discussed the possibility that the LDS Church might build a temple on their portion of sacred territory adjacent to the Temple Lot that would serve "to complicate further an already complicated situation" ("Church History Surrounds" 1952). Rumor spread that the Utah group had made architectural plans for their temple (Reimann 1981:25–26), but during the 1950s the only structure that the LDS Church built was a flat, prairie-style mission home on Walnut Street next to the older, more upright chapel, but still some distance away from the Temple Lot (Figure 27).

Native Americans and the LDS New Jerusalem

One thread of the traditional LDS New Jerusalem story evolved significantly in the 1950s and 1960s: missionary work among the American Indians. As discussed in the previous chapter, there has always been some question as to exactly who would construct the New Jerusalem and its temple. Traditionally, according to interpretation of *Book of Mormon* verses, both the American Indian and LDS members of European descent would participate, yet the proportion of work to be allotted to each has been a question discussed throughout the 1900s.

LDS leaders Joseph Fielding Smith (not to be confused with his father, President Joseph F. Smith) and Spencer W. Kimball wrote the most important words on the role of the Indians during the 1950s and 1960s. Both men would eventually become presidents of the church, but at the time were members of the Quorum of the Twelve Apostles. Joseph Fielding Smith, especially, had written quite a bit about millenarian scenarios, so many probably saw his ascendance to prophet as truly divine, but he was only president for a year and a half and died at the age of ninety-six.

Many members had construed *Book of Mormon* passages to indicate that the Lamanites (that is, American Indians) would eventually take the lead in building the temple in Missouri. In a manner that might have been surprising in some circles, Smith had written, "I fail to find any single passage which indicates that this is to be the order of things when these great events are to be fulfilled" (1955:2:247). He argued that responsibility for the construction of the New Jerusalem temple rested with the "House of Israel," meaning the LDS Church. That Indians would be major participants in Jackson County "is certainly consistent," but the church "will stand at the head and direct the work" (251).

Spencer W. Kimball was church president from 1973 to 1985. Previously he was widely known in the church as the "Lamanite apostle," because of his dedication to American Indian causes. At services dedicating an Indian mission home in Arizona in 1963, Kimball spoke directly about the importance of Native American participation in the future New Jerusalem. He told those present:

> You must flourish, and you must become a great people so that you can go back to Jackson County with us and we with you, and we will build there the magnificent temple which Orson Pratt said will be the most beautiful building that ever was built or that ever will be built. It will be the culmination of everything that is beautiful and within its walls [will be] the sealing power.
>
> They [Indians] must be leaders in their communities, because not too far away there is going to be a great migration to Jackson County, Missouri, and there we are going to build the great temple. And, you Indian people must be educated. The

> Indian boys and girls [must] learn the arts and the sciences as these prophets have said.
>
> Why? Because with all their artistic ability—and they are superior in art—perhaps they will be the ones to decorate the temple and to help build it. Accordingly, they must know the building trades. I hope our Indian boys will seek and to learn about materials and how to put them together and lend their art in building beautiful edifices, because the Lamanites and we, the other children of Jacob, will work together in the building of the great temple in Jackson County. (Church Educational System 1979:426–27)

Kimball's discourse is poignant in that a greater New Jerusalem goal is used to urge an embattled, isolated, and reservation-bound Indian people to better themselves. The attempt to raise hopes is similar to that of Kimball's predecessors in the Salt Lake Valley who tried to inspire settlers downcast by the difficult environment. His teaching, however, is unique and inconsistent considering the usual reticent views on the New Jerusalem expressed by the twentieth-century leadership. When Kimball became president of the LDS Church, however, he spoke nothing more on the subject.

It must be kept in mind that since the Kansas Indian Territory was adjacent to Missouri, in the 1830s Joseph Smith Jr. saw their border as an ideal millennial setting. Kansas was eventually opened for European settlement. Today there are only a couple of small reservations, a shadow of Kansas's frontier Native American self. The closest parallel now would be the stronger Native American presence in northeastern Oklahoma, and there are indications that many of the church groups feel that the Native American work on the New Jerusalem may somehow originate there.

Images in the 1960s

In contrast to the official views of the church, a definite surge of millennial belief on the part of the membership can be detected in a number of personalized views of the New Jerusalem published during the 1960s. Speculation is widespread in these accounts partly because of the reluctance of LDS Church leadership (The president, his two counselors, and the twelve apostles) to say much on such matters, especially in view of cold war fears or the growing alarm over the Vietnam War. Such millennial works included Kenneth Porter and Hermann Ruf's *Chosen Missouri and the Question of Zion* (1960), Alvin Dyer's *The Refiner's Fire* (1976, originally published in 1960),

Ruf's *Three Days in the Holy City Zion* (1964), Roy Doxey's *Zion in the Last Days* (1965), and Bruce R. McConkie's influential *Mormon Doctrine* (1966). A well-respected latecomer to the pre-millenarian enthusiasm was Gerald N. Lund, who wrote *The Coming of the Lord* (1971).

Few church leaders have participated in the end-of-times guesswork. The Doxey name has a rich heritage of LDS activity, and Roy Doxey was former dean of religious education at Brigham Young University. Alvin Dyer temporarily became an assistant to President David O. McKay (Todd 1968), and McConkie was one of the Twelve Apostles. Their works were never published by the LDS Church and have been accepted in varying degrees. Despite Dyer's influential position, his works were seen as somewhat controversial and are not often discussed today. Doxey's work is still quoted in higher ranks but not generally known among average churchgoers. Most of Gerald N. Lund's career was spent in the LDS Church Educational System (CES) until he was called as a Seventy in April 2002. McConkie, on the other hand, was highly influential especially in the 1970s and 1980s. As one of the Twelve Apostles, Bruce McConkie's works are seen by the membership along a continuum from "approximately" to "absolutely" doctrine and are still cited in LDS Sunday school and sacrament meetings. Taken together the words of these authors on the New Jerusalem are intriguing and fanciful descriptions that show how *influential* members have contemplated the future scene.

Doxey's *Zion in the Last Days* relied on a number of diverse sources to describe the future New Jerusalem. He often quoted from Orson Pratt and Brigham Young, who contemplated an exodus from Utah. Doxey envisioned a return to Jackson County without the marvels of 1960s "space age" technology, just as earlier millennial teachings had foreseen returning without the luxury of the railroad. The automobile, so ubiquitous in today's society, was not mentioned. Whereas the earlier leaders saw the Civil War as a harbinger of the millennium, America in the 1960s faced the threat of civil rights unrest, political turmoil, and nuclear weapons. Doxey (1965:55) could imagine a pre-millennial holocaust like no other: "If some disaster, wrought by the forces of nature or war, is thus going to befall the [Jackson County] area, it is entirely likely that it may be part of some general and widespread calamity, which incidentally would add to the difficulties of the returning Saints."

Porter and Ruf, in a personal view opposed to the low profile of general church leadership, offered some of the most striking statements regarding a modern-day establishment of the New Jerusalem. Whereas Doxey eschewed technology, Porter and Ruf, who were not as elevated in church hierarchy, saw such as integral to the building of the New Jerusalem. Technology was a divine gift of Godly knowledge. They wrote:

> It seems probable that the original plan for the city of Zion may be greatly altered due to changed living conditions and scientific advancement.
>
> We can rest assured, in any event, that the Lord will reveal minute details for His holy city. . . . Civic and community planners have learned much about the most desirable ways of building cities; but when the Lord speaks . . . the plans will be far, far superior to anything now contemplated by the unaided mind of man. (Porter and Ruf 1960:216–17)

This quotation echoes Orson Pratt's words nearly a century earlier that "no uninspired" man could know how to create the New Jerusalem. New technologies would abound there since God "will be the designer" (Porter and Ruf 1960:218). Modern vehicles of transportation would be developed, and the city would have a much greater population than the limit of twenty thousand people originally imposed by Joseph Smith. Perhaps in light of the contemporary Kansas City metropolitan population, that restriction, said Porter and Ruf, "will probably be lifted" (216). Though monotony of design "would not be wisdom," Porter and Ruf believed that, since it would be the Lord's city, He will "give instructions even concerning the nature of the residences to be built" (225–26).

Rather contrary to the normal energetic Mormon work ethic, much leisure time would be enjoyed in the New Jerusalem. The city would abound in "fascinating and restful parks," and a spirit of peace and good would prevail:

> The most beautiful shrubs, trees, flowers and other vegetation of all the world shall abound at New Jerusalem. Here will be ample opportunity for the development and display of one's artistic talents. Americans generally have been too much intent on pursuit of temporal and fleeting pleasures. Here at last will be a chance for greater appreciation of beauty than most have heretofore taken or enjoyed. Artists in various fields of endeavor will find singular pleasure in helping to embellish their surroundings. (226)

Porter and Ruf do not tell what activities "temporal and fleeting pleasures" might signify, but apparently the New Jerusalem would be built in a manner of permanence and artistic appreciation that would even make Temple Square in Salt Lake City pale in comparison. A wall with twelve gates would likely surround the future city. In it a great temple would glisten, adorned by precious stones and completely radiating heavenly light (232–33). Of the form of the temple, Doxey (1965:63–66) gave emphasis to Pratt's interpretation of a single large structure with "24 compartments" instead of Joseph Smith's original plan for twenty-four separate temples. In an age when the LDS Church was constructing new and relatively large temples in Utah, a large structure like Pratt described sounded more feasible than the 1834 plan of twenty-four smallish buildings.

In 1964, Ruf expanded upon the imagery that he had begun with Porter in 1960. A newer description of the New Jerusalem was given in the form of a fictional novel filled with stunning imagery. Ruf describes the visit of LDS members from New Zealand to a New Jerusalem still under construction (Ruf 1964). No time period is indicated, and no reference is made to Independence, Kansas City, or to any of the other Latter Day Saint groups.

In the story, those entering the city are required to obtain recommendations of worthiness similar to those required of members entering real LDS temples (Ruf 1964:16–17). Selected arriving visitors at the New Jerusalem are surprised to discover the presence of a silvery cloud hovering over the temple by day and a pillar of fire by night, a millennial interpretation of an image taken from Isaiah (4:5–6). It is a sign of protection; enemies of the church apparently would not be able to enter or harm the city in any way (Ruf 1964:57–60). Even attempts to drop "atom bombs" on the city (scavenged by hooligans from nearby Whiteman Air Force Base?) will be miraculously thwarted (129). Such miracles abound in the New Jerusalem. Here birds "of paradise" speak plainly to humans and heavenly choruses are occasionally heard. Formulas for construction materials such as asphalt, and the location of quarried rock, deemed "secrets" presently, will be revealed (71, 74–76, 82–83).

The "quarried rock" statement is interesting since many subsurface limestone shelves are found in the Kansas City area, with attending monumental artificial caverns. Such make Kansas City "the most significant pioneer in the development and use of commercial and underground space in the world" with "90 percent of the world's developed and leased underground space" (Woodward 1998). Local LDS Church members mention these in apocalyptic scenarios, and they have at least two primary reasons to do so. First of all, they could be used to shelter the Saints in time of apocalyptic destruction. In fact, the Kansas City tunnels were the basis for the sealed underground "ark" portrayed in the 1998 movie *Deep Impact*, where individuals were to live protected from a comet "strike" (Review of *Deep Impact* 1998). Secondly, the tunnels are most often used for storage, including for records of the Social Security Administration (Banks 1999). With the world's largest genealogical records facility cut out of granite in the Wasatch Mountains, it is easy for Latter-day Saints to see how the Lord has richly endowed and prepared the Kansas City area, even on the geological level. Despite such occasional imaginings, Mormons are not generally as preoccupied with wild eschatological scenarios of apocalyptic predicaments common elsewhere in fundamentalist Christian America (see Boyer 1992). Beliefs parallel dispensational premillennialism, but in the Mormon view there is no rapture before calamity, and the church adheres to the practical missions of teaching the gospel, fortifying the family, and "building the kingdom"—which means to strengthen church organization.

Overall, Ruf portrayed a pristine New Jerusalem as the ultimate representation of the LDS-built kingdom—another major difference with non-restoration dispensational premillennialism. He projected it as a place where nothing commonly conceived of as dirty, foul, or filthy would exist. The industry of Zion is described as purely tertiary; no factories are located in the city proper, and underground trains take trash out of the city to be burned (Ruf 1964:100, 106). Of course this would add pollutants to the atmosphere, but western Saints have rarely been known for environmentalist bias. Weather is described as highly altered; the western Missouri climate is now moderate and no winter season exists (70). No bugs exist to eat the roots of entirely new plant species, which have miraculously appeared (65, 121). No weeds crowd the paradisiacal plant life. In Ruf's world it is surprising that we find vegetation arising from something as base as soil. Though cleanliness is a strict priority in the New Jerusalem, for Ruf ecosystem chains obviously are not.

With few exceptions, the views of Dyer and McConkie of sacred space in Missouri were less imaginative than those of Doxey and of Porter and Ruf, but Dyer and McConkie held much more important positions in the church and were bound to a conservative approach. The latter threesome had attempted to describe the New Jerusalem in a cumulative, creative, and evocative manner, accepting and integrating the images of many others. Alvin R. Dyer's discussions, by contrast, did not usually stray far from Joseph Smith's early plans (Dyer 1970, 1971). He supported the original twenty-four-temple premise, for example, which was quite different from the extravagant single-temple structure views of Pratt during the 1870s or of Doxey in 1965, which might gratify RLDS/Community of Christ believers, as it could lend support to their modern temple interpretation as a single structure. Dyer also considered the entire sixty-three-acre Partridge parcel as sacred, not just the small Temple Lot. Since the LDS Church already had acquired twenty-five acres of that property, his interpretation represented a spiritual and natural extension of space from the LDS viewpoint. In other words, if only the Temple Lot Church possessed sacred land, the LDS and RLDS Churches were left out in the cold.

McConkie wrote a great deal on millennial events in his encyclopedic *Mormon Doctrine*, a work found in nearly every devout Latter-day Saint home, especially during the 1970s and 1980s. He emphasized that the New Jerusalem would be built by the LDS Church in Jackson County, an idea echoed by Doxey, who wrote that building the New Jerusalem would be a result of a "call" coming "only when the revelation is received by the prophet" (Doxey 1973:58). The building of the Holy City, wrote McConkie, would fulfill the scripture in Isaiah (2:3), where "out of Zion shall go forth the law, and the word of the Lord from Jerusalem." The world would then have two capitals, Jerusalem of old, in an educational and spiritual sense, and the New Jerusalem, for political and legal functions. The "ecclesiastical kingdom" would thus expand into a "political kingdom also," and through the framework of the LDS Church "the full government of God will eventually operate" (McConkie 1966:338, 532, 855). Though not generally known outside the LDS Church, his ideas on the separate functions of the two leading millennial "capitals" are pervasive. Surprisingly, the idea was thrown back at Latter-day Saints by the former major of Jerusalem Teddy Kollek. During the 1979 dedication of the LDS-sponsored Orson Hyde Memorial Garden on the Mount of Olives, Kollek quipped that Israelis were "very grateful that all of you made the effort to come to the *other* Jerusalem" ("President Kimball Dedicates" 1979:68). Whether Kollek was referring specifically to Missouri is doubtful, but in LDS parlance "New Jerusalem" has never meant Salt Lake City. LDS members were pleasantly surprised at the recognition and accepted it as evidence of a spiritual union between God's ancient and modern peoples.

McConkie accepted a dual meaning for the New Jerusalem in North America. The Saints would construct a portion of the city, with another portion coming down from heaven as described in the book of Revelation, but McConkie perhaps made less than other LDS writers of the distinction between the premillennial Missouri city prepared by the Saints and the postmillennial New Jerusalem that will be a union of Independence, Missouri, with the heavenly "City of Enoch." For example, Hugh Nibley, former professor of ancient scripture at Brigham Young University, wrote an impressive essay on the removal of the City of Enoch from the earth in ancient times and its future astonishing return, using conventional scripture references mixed with less-well-known apocryphal writings (Nibley 1977). McConkie's teachings, being more well known, were reiterated in a 1979 LDS Institute manual for LDS college religion classes that is still used today. In it four separate Jerusalems are described: one in Israel; one built in America; Enoch's city to be joined to the American New Jerusalem; and an even later joining of heaven and earth postmillennium when the earth becomes celestialized and pure (*Life and Teachings* 1979:469). Neither Independence, nor Missouri, however, are specified in the manual—both McConkie's and Nibley's earlier writings are much more specific.

McConkie interpreted the verse in Malachi (3:1) that "the Lord, whom ye seek, shall suddenly come to his temple," to mean that the Lord may visit a number of his LDS temples, "more particularly that which will be erected in Jackson County, Missouri" (McConkie 1966:693–94). In this sense McConkie shaped all LDS temples as somewhat millennial, not just the one to be built in Independence. The belief that Christ visits LDS Temples wherever they are located, every single one, at least at dedication time, is widespread in the church. As will be reviewed shortly, McConkie contributed even more to Adam-ondi-Ahman as a sacred place.

In 1971, perhaps inspired by new LDS activities at Independence, Gerald N. Lund wrote one of the most complete compilations of the church leadership on the subject of the New Jerusalem. Most of the book's contents are from the words of Brigham Young or Orson Pratt, but some twentieth-century interpretation slips through.

Meanwhile, in serving as church presidents, David O. McKay, Joseph Fielding Smith, Harold B. Lee, Spencer W. Kimball, Ezra Taft Benson, and Howard W. Hunter have said very little, if anything, on the status of Independence, Missouri, as the center of Zion. The official taciturnity of the LDS Church toward matters of the New Jerusalem seems to have spurred a great deal of millennial speculation on the part of the general membership, though some of the speculation seems on the decline. The examples above represent a share of this speculation, but since the leadership says little, there may be a gradual erosion of "New Jerusalem knowledge" for the general membership as well. New converts to the church learn of the New Jerusalem concept much later in their introductory period than was the case two or three decades ago. Also, there is the problem of history changing course and negating pronouncements. For example, one apostle during the 1950s, George Q. Morris, spoke of "the rise of an evil power," which was interpreted as communism. Ezra Taft Benson sometimes touched on this subject, which was revisited in 1971 by Lund (1971:19). With the fall of the Soviet Union and commercialization of China post-1993, such interpretations have become obsolete, so, unless the Lord reveals his will directly and specifically, mum's the word. The writings of Dyer and McConkie, because of their important offices in the church, were the closest thing to official LDS positions, since the First Presidency (the president and his two counselors) have said virtually nothing on the subject. The situation was directly opposed to that of the early days of Utah settlement when the leadership commonly motivated members by projecting a grand New Jerusalem goal.

The Reluctant Taking of Center Stage

When new doctrines are initiated in the LDS Church, the First Presidency announces or reemphasizes them. Few edicts have come forth regarding Missouri, and the church has been reluctant to make special developments there. By the 1960s, the official establishment of the New Jerusalem seemed put off indefinitely, though the church has become active in land acquisition around the greater urban area.

Through the influence of Alvin R. Dyer, a previous mission president in Independence, the church purchased additional land in the vicinity of Adam-ondi-Ahman in 1966 (Dyer 1976:6–23). This purchase prompted church president David O. McKay to visit important millennial sites in Missouri, apparently at the urging of Dyer, who went on the trip as narrator of historical events. The aging McKay apparently enjoyed the trip, but he appended nothing new to the LDS New Jerusalem legacy. Since a prophet was involved, the membership of the church, however, saw the visit as millennial and wondered at its significance. A local rumor that an angel cleared a path for President McKay down into the valley of Adam-ondi-Ahman is a good example of the membership's desire to see millennial promises fulfilled.[1]

Oddly enough, stronger LDS stances in the vicinity of the Temple Lot were bolstered when the city of Independence again tried to obtain the "meadow" in the mid-1960s, this time for park development (Wilson 1992). The move apparently initiated two church responses. Lots bought in 1904 were consolidated and reregistered at the Jackson County Deed Office during a personal visit of apostle Joseph Fielding Smith in late 1965 (Jackson County Deed Office 1965). Soon thereafter, the church announced plans for a museum to be built on the property. This announce ment was enough to deter the city from passing a bond issue for the site (Wilson 1992). Representing a notable change in the local LDS stance, the new building was to be called the Mormon Visitor's Center (Figure 27). It would be boldly located adjacent to the RLDS auditorium and diagonally southeast from the Temple Lot (Figure 28; Dyer 1976:26–27). At the groundbreaking, Harold B. Lee, then president of the twelve apostles, said:

> It is not difficult for me . . . to think of this as the Garden of Eden. It is in truth today a beautiful and verdant place. It may not be known to you people, but to us it is the Center Place because it is here where the commencement of the inhabitation of human beings upon the earth began. . . . So we come back here to a place that to us is not just Kansas City and Independence, but a place we call the center place, a place where a great temple will be built. We do not know the time when that great temple will be built, but it will be built because the time will come when it will be the New Jerusalem spoken of in scripture. (Lee 1968)

During the twentieth century, few LDS leaders have made a stronger affirmation of the importance of the New Jerusalem. The directness of the statement is rare indeed, and no LDS president since has ever repeated it.

The Visitor's Center was dedicated in May 1971 (Van Orden 1971: 3–5). Rumbling thunderclouds held their rain until after the completion of speeches by the new LDS church president, Joseph Fielding Smith, and by Alvin R. Dyer. The environment of the occasion remains a powerful memory for the LDS faithful present, and the scene is oddly reminiscent of the stormy RLDS roofing celebration of the Stone Church some eighty years before.

With the construction of the LDS Visitor's Center, though not a temple, the Mormons had finally made a more impressive and visible statement about the Temple Lot area (Figure 28). The site was indubitably important to the LDS Church, though official words were muted. The purpose of the Visitor's Center was to tell Mormon and Independence history through the use of displays and audiovisual technology of a type started at the 1964–65 LDS Pavilion at the New York World's Fair (Top 1989). The center would also warn all to be watchful of premillennial

FIG. 28 | *Architectural rendering of the Visitor's Center. Reprinted, by permission, from Dyer (1976:26).*

events—a huge mural depicting Jesus Christ returning in glory is the first image seen by visitors. At the dedication, Dyer said that the temple of the New Jerusalem will be "here in this very area, on the very ground" where the crowd was then gathered (Dyer 1971:4), but, of course, no schedule for its placement could be presented without divine revelation to President Smith ("City Is of Great Significance" 1971:5). The building's purpose was conciliatory, offering instruction on LDS themes, but it was not a sign of an imminent LDS end-times event ("Mormon Visitor's Center" 1971; Dyer 1971:2). The stance emphasized an early version of a "common ground" approach, one that has appeared occasionally in church publications, where good relations with the RLDS and the Temple Lot Churches were stressed, especially since the 1990s (see "Bridge Building" 1993; also Baugh 2001:47).

By contrast, the membership on occasion has been known to speculate whether the Visitor's Center could easily be converted into a temple, after all it is a multilevel structure with grounds decorated in templelike manner. One member expressed to me that the Visitor's Center's twelve columns were like those stated in the prophesy in Revelation. The Bible verse refers to twelve gates of "the holy Jerusalem, descending out of heaven from God" (Rev. 21:11–12). In reality, the Visitor's Center has thirty-eight slender pillars covering all four sides of the building, so quite a bit of millennial imagination was employed in converting a museum into a temple. Powers of observation often diminish as believers envision what they will.

Skeptics see little of millennial reach in the establishment of the LDS Visitor's Center. On two occasions in the twentieth century, the church only acted after the city attempted to established secular civil projects. What of divinity is found in fending off civil land grabs? The LDS Church might counter that its defenses need not appear divine; no direct revelation was claimed for either helping the city of Independence find an alternate site for William Chrisman High School or for the location and construction of the Visitor's Center. In the church's view, the Lord will make specific instructions about the site later.

One line of thinking bolsters a need for LDS millenarian talk for the 1970s. Lund gives the account of apostle Orson Pratt in 1877, saying that people present then would yet live to see the temple of Zion constructed. Lund said that today many would dismiss such because infants at that time would be nearly one hundred years old now—and still no temple (1971:32). Lund mentions earlier *Book of Mormon* and Bible prophecies where people also doubted until fulfillment at the very last, unexpected moment. Though not a Millerite people, this may have given the year 1977 or shortly thereafter more significance.

Bicentennial Fervor

In 1976, as the United States celebrated the bicentennial of its independence from Great Britain, the LDS Church saw an opportunity to forge a stronger association with the "American" ideals of God-fearing strength and purity. In this push there was some reinforcement of a spiritual geographic centrality. With a premillennial flavor much influenced by the writings of the patriotic apostle Mark E. Peterson, the church prepared publications explaining the "prophetic history and destiny of America" (Peterson 1975; *Great Prologue* 1976). The church taught that America was "foreordained" to be the land of the reestablishment of the Lord's gospel. A number of historical figures from Martin Luther to Thomas Jefferson, it was said, had expressed their disdain for contemporary religion and hoped that Christ's church would be founded once again. The United States was the site of that church, of course, a land with a divine mission (*Great Prologue* 1976:1–6). The culmination of America's divine calling, in the LDS view, would be the establishment of the New Jerusalem in Jackson County. In the words of Peterson (1975:106–7), this site would be

> equidistant from coast to coast and from border to border in the United States. It is the center of the land, and there the city of Zion, or the New Jerusalem, will be built, a place of refuge and peace for the latter days.
>
> How important this is! What a great destiny! How wonderful is the future of America!

Peterson's statement was a powerful and direct assertion of the importance of the future of Jackson County. For many LDS members it was truly a millennial bicentennial, but in terms of overall pronouncement, Peterson's proclamation was still fairly rare and isolated, particularly for an authority of the church, but his words and fervor were echoed for several years by less prominent LDS writers. One exception was Jeffrey R. Holland, former president of Brigham Young University and an LDS apostle since 1994, who emphasized that the New Jerusalem will be built on the land that is only to be temporarily called America (Holland 1976:23). In this view the United States will be, approaching the return of Christ, more popularly associated with the religious scenarios of millennial Zion than with Euro-Anglo settlement.

The LDS Church continued to make its presence more apparent in Independence after the construction of the Visitor's Center. By 1980, a new turtle-shaped Stake Center had been constructed between the Visitor's Center and the prairie-style mission home (Figure 29). This large meetinghouse replaced the old Italianate chapel, which was torn down in the fall of 1981. Thus, within only a few years the LDS focus in constructions jumped markedly westward and toward the Temple Lot.

By 2001, three LDS congregations ("wards" in LDS-speak) were housed in the Stake Center while three others were housed in a newer building in the Independence suburbs. Previously, four congregations had met in the central Stake Center, so LDS Church growth in Independence has been steady. One interesting article printed in the LDS magazine for children in 1993 highlighted the life of one young member, Julianne Burkhardt, in Independence. She expressed how she was happy to worship at this sacred place and see the Temple Lot, but the article mistakenly locates her Stake Center "on part of the original 63 acres" (Clayton 1993). The Visitor's Center is on the sixty-three-acre plot, but the Stake Center

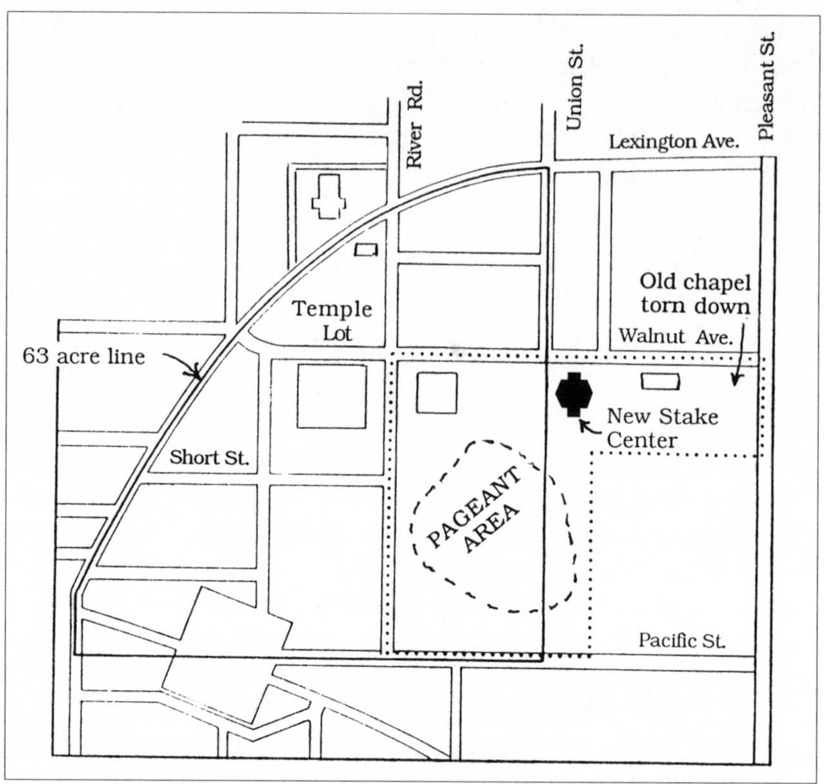

FIG. 29 | *An LDS Stake Center replaces the old chapel as the church gradually focuses on building more westward on the property. The outdoor pageant is introduced on the "meadow."*

location is just east of Partridge's original purchase. Despite the error, members likely see all LDS-owned land as sacred.

By the late 1970s, the church had also established a live pageant to dramatize Jackson County events of the 1830s, one of several that the church organizes across the country ("Drama beneath the Stars" 1991). The central theme of the play was the Missouri expulsion of the Latter Day Saints, so not all the locals in Independence viewed it favorably. This outdoor play, replete with three hundred actors, galloping horses, frontier wagons, and traditional dress, took place annually on the land of the "meadow" to the south of the Visitor's Center until 1996 (see Figure 29). After nearly twenty years of "A Frontier Story—1833," the Independence pageant was put on indefinite hold. The exact reason is not known, but evidence points toward political correctness. An *Independence Examiner* article stated that the church was developing a new script featuring more of a "general demonstration of the people and events that came through Independence," one that would "involve the community more" (Adkins 1997). Clearly, some non-Saints were put off by a play that vividly represented the burning of homes by Missourians in the 1830s. "It was too real," explained one elderly missionary at the LDS Visitor's Center. At present, Independence still has no LDS pageant.

Sacred Space Enlarged: Adam-ondi-Ahman

Throughout the twentieth century, the LDS Church gradually gave more emphasis to areas of northwestern Missouri, in addition to Independence. Far West, Liberty, and Richmond, Missouri, are important in this regard, but now unpopulated Adam-ondi-Ahman in Daviess County has become a focus, a site notably linked to millennial happenings. Not much has been constructed here, but in verbal stance and land acquisition the area has become quietly important.

Alvin Dyer, apostle Bruce R. McConkie, and former Mormon President Joseph Fielding Smith, were all major contributors to the emphasis of additional sacred sites in Missouri in the 1950 to 1970 period. McConkie's *Mormon Doctrine* (1966), which discussed a variety of themes relating to northwestern Missouri, including an emphasis on Adam-ondi-Ahman, as earlier discussed, was perhaps the most important single work. Though scriptural and historical references were quoted, all of these authors were frequently innovative and provided seeds for a renewed interest in Missouri sites, especially to the north of Jackson County.

In these writings and locally, Adam-ondi-Ahman often surpasses even Independence in premillennial significance. The church purchased part of the site in the 1930s, and in December 1966 another 140 acres were added (Dyer 1976:16). Most of the valley acreage is currently farmed, and additional parcels in the area have been purchased since. The site is believed to be the place where Adam and his family dwelt after he and Eve were cast out of Eden—today's Jackson County (Holland 1976:23). It is the place where Adam will eventually come again "in power and glory, revisiting the scenes of his earthly pilgrimage" (Dyer 1976:185). The idea of this as a "post-garden" site is entrenched in the local LDS psyche even more than is the idea of Jackson County as the original Eden.

According to Dyer (1973:433; 1976:186) and McConkie (1966:493, 500), a semiprivate "great council" will someday be held "in the valley" of Adam-ondi-Ahman where Adam and other resurrected beings will return authority to Jesus Christ in preparation for His official Second Coming at Independence. Here is another parallel to dispensational premillennialism with a private and local advent before a public and glorious one. No rapture is evident, however, and as always the Mormon view is place specific. McConkie (1966:20, 34) was sure that Adam-ondi-Ahman covered a large region since scriptures varyingly refer to its "land," its "valley," and its "mountains." Joseph Fielding Smith also emphasized a larger area and wrote how postdiluvian place-names obviously had to be transferred from central North America to Southwest Asia. The names of the Euphrates, Tigris, and other places were originally given to rivers and landforms in northwestern Missouri and then naturally applied to sites in the Middle East sometime after Noah came to rest upon Ararat (Smith 1979:2:95). Brigham Young University scholar Hugh Nibley wrote that early writings discussing the Americas as Zion seem "anachronistic," but such is the way God connects millennial future with biblical past (Nibley 1977:82), and LDS tradition makes northwestern Missouri the true Old World. "The great city New Jerusalem will be in the place where Eden was," wrote Joseph Fielding Smith (1979:4:24; see also Holland 1976:23), but heavenly millennial events must occur *first* in the rural hills of Daviess County where Adam dwelt.

Given new emphasis by LDS writers in the twentieth century as a place preparatory to the establishment of the New Jerusalem, today the location of Adam-ondi-Ahman seems more fixed than the site of the future New Jerusalem. One Ricks College professor maintained a detailed Web page on writings regarding Adam-ondi-Ahman (Satterfield 2001a). Not surprisingly, he maintained no Web page regarding the New Jerusalem or Jackson County. General authority Graham W. Doxey in the *Encyclopedia of Mormonism* even downplayed the importance of Jackson County with regard to its being the location of the Garden of Eden. He said that many had heard Joseph Smith tell them so, but "neither Biblical record nor secular history and archeological research identify the dimension and location of the Garden in terms of the present-day surface of the earth" (Doxey 1992a:533–34). On the other hand, revelations in the *Doctrine and Covenants* do mention the specific importance of Adam-ondi-Ahman.

Although scripture justifies the sacredness of the place, a major reason for the LDS emphasis on Adam-ondi-Ahman could be the increased competition among Latter Day Saint factions around the Temple Lot in

Independence. As various groups clamor for visibility there, the LDS Church has given emphasis to other sacred sites in western Missouri.

Known for its thick and thorny vegetation, the Adam-ondi-Ahman area has been cleaned up over the past decade. Many members view the sprucing as preparation for prophesied events yet to occur. One LDS missionary told me he had heard that the church was growing trees and other vegetation in the form of an outdoor meeting place. Informal discussions with prominent leaders in the LDS Topeka and Kirtland stakes (that is, in Kansas and Ohio) reveal a popular, but unverified, notion that in Adam-ondi-Ahman cisterns have been constructed to supply large amounts of water, perhaps for millions of future visitors. The implication is that the church is preparing for a very large meeting. Who might attend is a matter of debate. Some members believe that the meeting will involve only heavenly messengers, and thus no earthly soul will be aware of the "council"—sort of the opposite of rapture. In typical Mormon humor, one member commented that this might be a good scenario since then no one would have to "set up chairs!" By contrast, others believe that since the meeting has to do with the LDS Church, logically, church members would have to be involved; presumably, both earthly and heavenly visitors would be instructed to attend. In another of Dyer's works (1973:433–34), he claimed that many LDS leaders "now living" (six of the present LDS first presidency and apostles as of 2004) would participate in this grand meeting but that neither the world at large nor the church at large would know about it. On the other hand, another member expressed a view that coverage of the meeting would be like a current priesthood meeting, broadcast around the world by the church's satellite system, as are LDS General Conferences and other church programs. Such views imply a meeting before the development of the millennial city.

A more extreme belief is that of author Duane Crowther (1989), who claimed that more than one hundred million people will be in attendance at Adam-ondi-Ahman (currently, just over five million people live in all of Missouri). He asserted that the meeting will occur *after* the New Jerusalem has been built in Independence, after many of the Lamanites come to the New Jerusalem, and after Jesus Christ has made his appearance at the temple there. Daybell's (2000:158–63) postapocalyptic view reflects many of Crowther's ideas, and his description of Adam-ondi-Ahman is the most vivid of any author. His novel, oriented toward LDS teens, describes about a million people and resurrected beings attending the grand council. Residents from the already constructed New Jerusalem arrive by solar bus to the "acoustically perfect" valley. They are seated up front since the eyes and ears of mortals do not work as well as those of the other heavenly beings present (159–60). All the prophets symbolically hand earthly dispensational authority back to Christ, who magnanimously accepts—in a pre–Second Coming appearance. The meeting is handled in typical LDS manner—Adam presides, Seth conducts, and Noah and Abraham give the opening and closing prayers (160–61).

Another extreme view is that held by a little-known break-off group who keep Adam-ondi-Ahman central to their beliefs. For them, the valley is the precursor to the building of the Holy City. People are already receiving "keys" from Adam while gradually filtering in and out of the site, thus no physical gathering or meeting is taking place there, yet an overall gathering is being accomplished—and no chairs will have to be set up! ("Shulemna Gathering" 1998).

Pattonsburg Dam

A proposed flooding of the Adam-ondi-Ahman site in the early to mid-1960s may have been one impetus for the resurgence of LDS interest in this and other non-Independence sacred sites in Missouri. The U.S. Army Corps of Engineers announced a master plan for flood control in the Grand River basin that became public law in 1965 (Dyer 1976:206–9; U.S. Army Engineer Division 1991:37). Located at Pattonsburg, the largest of seven dams proposed would have flooded all of the valley of Adam-ondi-Ahman (U.S. Dept. of Health, Education, and Welfare 1963). Alvin Dyer, then president of the Central States Mission, expressed concern to engineers involved, and the plan for the Pattonsburg Dam was revised. The proposed dam site was relocated one mile upstream, so the sacred valley was spared (Dyer 1976:206–9).

Dyer soon came to view the planned dam as a possible asset for the church. Tourists to the reservoir might want to visit a proposed information center at Adam-ondi-Ahman. The dam itself was millennial technology; it would provide providential power to northwestern Missouri (Dyer 1976:207–9), but it was never built. Recreational speculation resulted a moot issue, since federal funding for large agricultural flood-control programs was decreasing about this time (Wolfender 1992), and reports questioned the economic feasibility and generating capacity of this particular dam (U.S. House 1965:xvii, xix–xx, xxii–xxiii, xxxi, 430–33). The new reservoir would have also required that Interstate 35 be raised to a higher level. A 1973 study called the Grand River proposals economically unjustified and the projects were placed on indefinite hold (U.S. Army Engineer Division, 1991:37, 38). As a result, Adam-ondi-Ahman has been left in relative isolation. Among Mormons familiar with the history, the prevalent view today is that God saved the site from destruction. In this view, the whole process of reduced interest in grand dam projects in the United States has divine origin and as a result saved an important millennial place.

Despite the local aura of Daviess County among devout Latter-day Saints, the official LDS attitude toward Adam-ondi-Ahman today is permeated with official church silence. Members view Adam-ondi-Ahman as important, but the site itself is given little fanfare. In fact, the area's importance is restrained considering the limited physical access to the site so far. In a map packet given to tour-takers in 1990, one local LDS leader wrote, "onsite study at Adam-ondi-Ahman is not permitted. Permission should not be asked for. The grounds at Adam-ondi-Ahman are sacred, and all individuals must stay on the historical point of interest provided at Tower Hill" (Jenkins 1990).

Some members say that the church does not allow people to roam freely at Adam-ondi-Ahman for practical reasons of safety and insurance. "If the valley there is really so sacred," asked one member rhetorically, "would the church be farming it?" The interesting question of farming as divinely condoned activity aside—perhaps representing an urban-suburban view—the member suggested that the church did not like the insurance problems presented by curious people who might injure themselves while wandering around on the property, much of which is steeply sloped.

Far West and Liberty, Missouri, have also been discussed as part of a greater LDS sacred area. Liberty Jail, in Clay County, is an important site because Joseph Smith was imprisoned there. It was there he wrote a number of his most often quoted revelations. During the 1960s, the church bought the house that had been built over the original site ("Postcard" 1990), tore it down, painstakingly re-created the jail on the original stone floor, and constructed a visitor's center around it, but no biblical imagery has ever been applied to Liberty.

McConkie's interpretation of scripture suggested that Far West is located within the sacred sphere around Adam-ondi-Ahman rather than Independence (McConkie 1966:20). In this view, the tables have turned from early church history when Far West was the dominant site and Adam-ondi-Ahman the peripheral one. One belief, heard on occasion, is that Far West was the site where Cain killed Abel (Romig 1991). This idea is not scriptural—as Latter-day scriptures go—but neither is that of Jackson County as the Garden of Eden. Church leaders themselves would likely say the belief is born more of oral tradition than revelation. The idea is consistent, however, with the LDS tendency to validate sites of church history by applying biblical or *Book of Mormon* relevance to them.

In LDS lore, other sites not in Missouri have also borrowed sanctity from events in the remote past. Joseph Smith Jr. found gold plates in the Hill Cumorah near Palmyra, New York. These had been deposited there hundreds of years ago by the angel Moroni until their location was revealed to Smith and they were translated into the *Book of Mormon*. Decades after Joseph Smith, Brigham Young wrought another place legitimization, this time in southern Utah. Members had wanted to move the location of the St. George temple (the first LDS Temple built in Utah) from a desolate swampy locale, but Young would not hear of it. According to lore, he said the Nephites had dedicated the spot in *Book of Mormon* times and that since they could not build it, the modern Saints would ("Temples of the Church" 2003). This scriptural validation of sacred places is part of an important process of the LDS "recapitulation" of Old World sites onto New World land discussed by Shipps (1985:54–58), but the process began earlier than Shipps identified and has been maintained into the present with the construction or reconstruction of new temples on sacred historical sites.

The Paradox of Temple Location

The LDS Church has always been extremely proud of its special structures called temples. These buildings play a different role than the regular church meetinghouse, a role that stems largely from the evolution of Joseph Smith's theology during the Nauvoo period of the early church. In these edifices, faithful Mormons do work that has special significance. Within temples, eternal marriage and family "sealing" ceremonies cement a belief in genealogical relationships that can continue after death. Ordinances also are performed there for deceased persons who, it is believed, may have never associated with the LDS Church in life but who have the opportunity to accept the church's teachings and ordinances in the hereafter.

Since the late 1800s, it has been church policy to build temples close to clusters of the membership. In the nineteenth century, temples were all located in Utah, where the majority of LDS people lived.[3] In the early 1900s, temples were added in Alberta, Arizona, and Hawaii to reflect large memberships in those areas as well. By the mid-1960s, the church had added temples in several foreign countries and two in California.[4] As the year 2000 passed, the times were seen as millennial, and new temple locations have been announced at an unprecedented rate; however, the precise year 2000 has not been mentioned as a particular instigator of the chiliasm (Hinkley 1999b). Since 1998, from the High Plains eastward the church has announced twenty-one new temples, most of them of smaller size (Hinkley 1998). In the West, fifteen new temples have been announced, including in Alaska, Hawaii, and Canada's westernmost provinces. As of mid-2001, the number of temples built or announced all over the globe was 125 (see "Family Forever" 2003; "Temples of the Church" 2003). With a few exceptions, these have been located in important metropolitan suburbs.

The longstanding belief in Independence as a paramount sacred site has created a paradox in this persistent plan for temple placement, and on official church lists it is commonly placed in a "historical" or "special" category ("Temples of the Lord" 1993). Kansas City has become an important center of Mormon populace in the Midwest, yet it has no temple. The LDS Church commonly builds temples to service large urban regions, but it seems reluctant to do so in Kansas City, possibly for fear of millennial misinterpretation or speculation by the membership. Here, prophecy has destined the eventual construction of the millennial temple of all temples, but the announcement of even a regular LDS temple might foster a chiliastic response among the membership. At the very least, a normal operating temple, say on the meadow south of the Visitor's Center, would have to be accompanied by several official caveats.

Current temple-goers in the Kansas City area must travel either to Omaha, St. Louis, or Nauvoo, the closest locations of newer temples ("Mormon Church Plans" 1990; "Temples of the Church" 2003). The St. Louis temple, the first in Missouri, is presumably far enough away from Jackson County to avoid undue millennial alarm, though the location strategy is reminiscent of how the LDS Church first positioned buildings on land farther away from the Temple Lot on Walnut Street in Independence. One can view the St. Louis, Missouri, location as a type of renewal of sacred territory commencing from the eastern part of the state (Baugh 2001:55). In terms of both land acquisition and placement of sacred structures, the LDS presence anew in Missouri has been tentative, peripheral, and incremental.

I was informed by an influential LDS member in eastern Kansas that one vocal church leader who oversaw the Kansas City region had encouraged members to prepare and continue to grow so that the church might place a temple there for their use, as had been done in other metropolitan areas. Reportedly, that leader was quietly removed from his position to maintain the church's taciturn attitude toward Jackson County. Though an unsubstantiated rumor, it supports the premise of paradox. Even more recently, I was told that in a local priesthood meeting it was said that if the church gained fifty thousand members in the Kansas City area, a temple would be built. No other urban area east of the Rocky Mountains with or without a temple has this many members, so why should Kansas City? More than eleven thousand members resided in the Kansas City region as of 2001, and the church sees Jackson County's identity as distinct.

A rough comparison of the density of church membership and the placement of temples can be made using numbers of Mormon congregations in eleven large midwestern cities (Table 1).[5] If each city's 1997 metropolitan population is divided by the number of congregations listed for each city, the resulting figure is urban population per LDS congregation. The lower the number, the higher the Mormon density. LDS congregations (wards) rarely exceed six hundred people, so an average number of four hundred per congregation is used here to estimate LDS populations for each city.

Kansas City was no denser in LDS congregations than many cities of the central United States and denser than some that already have temples. Naturally, Mormon density in metropolitan areas is greater in the west and

Table 1. Mormon Density of Congregations for Selected Midwestern American Cities

Rank	City	Population[a]	Number of Congregations/ Population[b]	Population per LDS Congregation
1	Denver[c]	2,318,355	100 (40,000)	23,183
2	Wichita	530,508	13 (5,200)	40,808
3	Des Moines	429,717	10 (4,000)	42,971
4	Omaha[c]	687,454	14 (5,600)	49,103
5	Dallas/Fort Worth[c]	4,683,013	89 (35,600)	52,618
6	Oklahoma City[c]	1,030,504	17 (6,800)	60,617
7	Kansas City	1,709,273	27 (11,000)	63,306
8	Tulsa	764,396	12 (4,800)	63,700
9	Indianapolis	1,503,468	18 (7,200)	83,526
10	St. Louis[c]	2,557,806	26 (10,400)	98,377
11	Minneapolis/St.Paul[c]	2,792,137	26 (10,400)	107,390

[a] According to MSA 1997 census

[b] These numbers are approximate

[c] Mormon temple in service or planned

lessens toward the east. The high density apparent in Denver is expected since the city is the closest in the sample to Utah. Beyond this, Wichita, Des Moines, and Omaha's positions are unexpected, having greater density of Mormon population. Omaha, however, is unique, containing important sites of the nineteenth-century Mormon trek westward, and a temple has been built in Winter Quarters, emphasizing the sacredness of the historical site. Built partially in recognition of the Mormon exodus, in a sense this represents a recapitulation of a recapitulation.

Though fairly well populated with Latter-day Saints, Des Moines and Wichita simply do not have the weight of membership to yet qualify for temples. Out of the eleven cities examined, Kansas City ranked seventh and is more densely LDS than either St. Louis or Minneapolis–St. Paul, both of which have temples. Oklahoma City, of approximately the same LDS congregation density as Kansas City, merited a normal operating temple as well, while Kansas City has none.

The LDS Church examines statistics other than metropolitan density of membership when locating a temple.[6] After placement, a temple becomes a central node for a region. Yet if the construction of a temple "is the ultimate mark of maturity of an area pertaining to the establishment of the gospel," as Thomas S. Monson of the LDS First Presidency has said (Robertson 1988:49), then Kansas City is as worthy as any other city on the list. Besides its own LDS population, it would serve stakes in Topeka, Wichita, Joplin, St. Joseph, Columbia, and Springfield.

One prominent LDS analogy of temple placement accounts for the lack of plans for Kansas City. The source is the prophet Isaiah (33:20, 54:2), who reported that the tent of "Zion" (that is, the church eventually centered in Jackson County) would be surrounded by "stakes," the name given to administrative groupings of ten or so Mormon congregations. A temple is the grandest development of any grouping of stakes; a sign of maximum spiritual maturity. Figuratively, the tent is unobtrusively laid flat until the final supporting pole is placed in the center and raised up ("Temple to Bring" 1992:7). That final central support will be complete only with the finishing touches on the New Jerusalem and its magnificent temple. With new temples built for historical sites in Nauvoo, Palmyra, and Winter Quarters amidst the many others in metropolitan areas, many LDS members envision the tent as nearly raised, and Gordon B. Hinkley's reference to these new temples' "crowning blessings" provides a similar analogy (Hinkley 1998). This view is that the church is avoiding Kansas City for temple placement until the time is right.

LDS Acquisitions into the 1990s

After the modest LDS construction in Independence through the early 1980s, the church again returned to a more reserved attitude toward the New Jerusalem. This official stance of silence has become even more pronounced at the turn of the millennium. Even though the church has continued to purchase agricultural and urban land in the Kansas City region and members continue to speculate on millennial events, leadership reservation has had the effect of pushing the Second Coming further off into the future.

Members and outsiders alike have shown interest in the church's purchase of large acreage in Jackson County and surrounding areas. Though the church seems to brush off the significance of the purchases, saying they are for investment or welfare purposes (and some of them are), the lands acquired are sizable and make observers wonder if millennial plans are indeed brewing somewhere in the LDS Church Administration Building in Salt Lake City. The church retains the purchases made in the early 1900s, the more recent purchases of the historic sites of Far West and Adam-ondi-Ahman, and the important lots comprising Liberty Jail. Even more impressive are almost 14,500 acres of new lands in Jackson and Clay Counties (Figures 30 and 31).

More than 4,700 acres in the floodplain and adjacent bluffs north of the Missouri River in Clay County were purchased around 1980 (Figure 30; "Nichols Co. Land Sale" 1990). One might question the wisdom of any plan to build the City of Zion in a floodplain, but the southern portion of these lands is leased to local non-LDS farmers, and the church has developed a portion of this land into an industrial park and has sold off lots (Allen 1992). Just south of Birmingham on Highway 210, the Grainger Company, a commercial and industrial equipment supplier, operates a large distribution center in this area on land purchased from the LDS Church in 1981 (Bracco 1992). The bluff area farther north is used mainly for cattle grazing but also has some historical significance since the home of Joel Turnham, a lawyer friendly to the original Saints, still stands there.

An LDS bishop's storehouse has also been constructed on this floodplain property, just east of Birmingham. This storehouse supplies food and household goods to needy LDS members in a four-state region covering most of Kansas, Missouri, Nebraska, and Iowa. A large tractor trailer stands ready to provide sustenance for victims of unforeseen regional disasters. For several years, this storehouse has been the national producer of gelatin for the church welfare program (Rudd 1995:239). A Mormon bishop's storehouse,

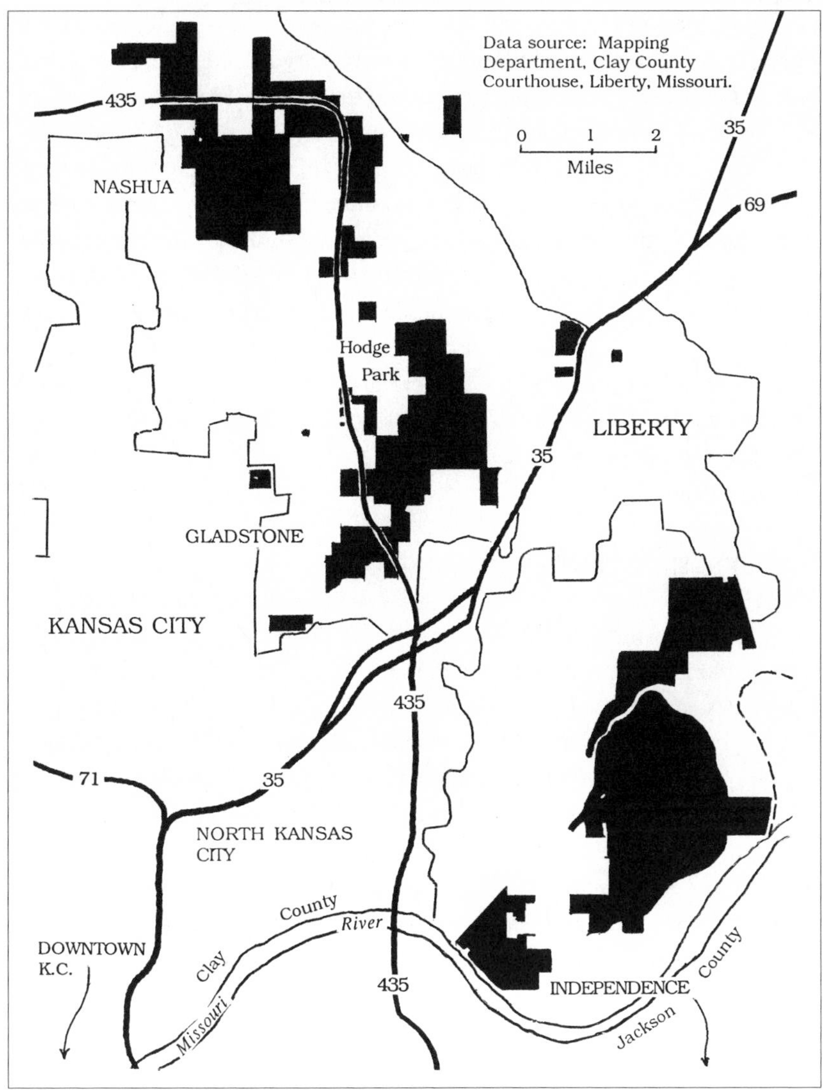

FIG. 30 | *LDS landholdings in Clay County, 1992. Data from Mapping Department, Clay County Courthouse, Liberty, Missouri.*

like a Mormon temple, is a common LDS regional element. Though in a central position for the church's local welfare program, unlike a temple, the storehouse in the Jackson County area carries little specific millennial clout.

About 5,550 acres of new land were purchased in central western Clay County from Curry Investment Company in 1981 (Faser 1992). These lands are located between the built-up areas of Liberty and Gladstone, roughly along Interstate 435, north of Kansas City (Figure 30). These lands, on rolling hills with cattle grazing and mixed crop and livestock farms, are not currently being developed.

Two tracts of land have been purchased in Lee's Summit, Missouri, in Jackson County, southeast of Kansas City. One, bought in the early to mid-1980s (Kemp 1992), consists of approximately 1,100 acres arranged in a narrow band between Lake Jacomo and Highway 470 (Figure 31). In February 1990, the LDS Church purchased another large chunk of land, this time southeast of Kansas City also in Lee's Summit. Acquired were 3,265 acres of farmland from the J. C. Nichols Company, a major Kansas City developer from as early as the 1920s (again see Figure 31; Kemp 1992; "J. C. Nichols Reports" 1990).

Significance of the Purchases

LDS land investment in the Kansas City area may be an indication of millennial planning, but this is difficult to prove since church leaders and employees are reluctant to discuss the purchases. Obviously, the LDS Church has made a habit of buying land in the greater Kansas City region, but one wary employee of Investment Property Corporation (one of several LDS Church corporations)[7] would not say whether the church was investing more in the Kansas City area than in, say, St. Louis or Denver (Faser 1992). In most cases, the church seems more interested in purchasing large acreage of rural land farmed to provide food for the church's welfare program, or leased for long-term investment, but speculative suburban purchases of the type seen here are generally avoided (Swiatek 1993). One church employee in charge of farm management reported that the property in Lee's Summit was bought for eventual transformation into residential or commercial use for a profit. The pattern is not the norm for LDS purchases, especially in the Middle West (Lamoreaux 1992). Another employee for Investment Properties Corporation said that the land was under the planning label of "special purpose" and was currently being farmed. None of the church employees wanted to speculate on what the church might do with the land, which is normal business practice, especially in the LDS realm (Kemp 1992; "Nichols Co. Land Sale" 1990).

The largest tract of land the church owns in an area that could be perceived as within the greater Kansas City hinterland was purchased in

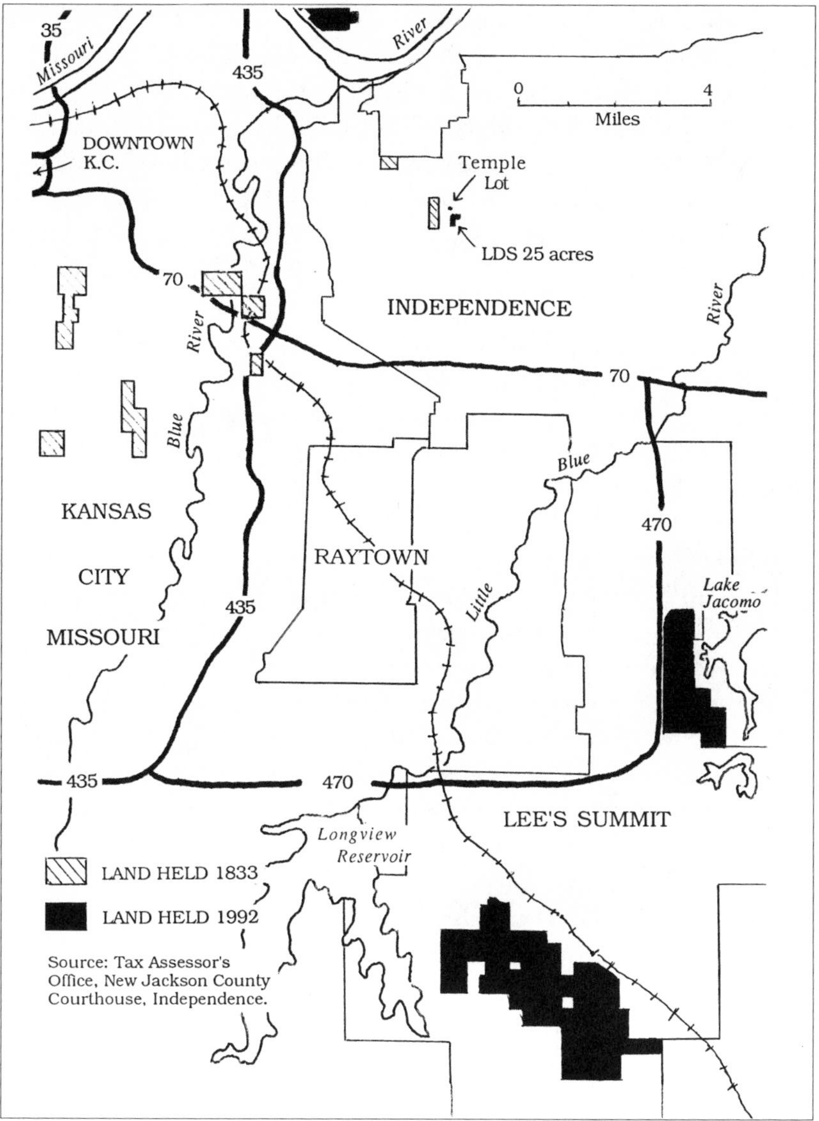

FIG. 31 | *LDS landholdings in Jackson County, 1992. Data from Tax Assessor's Office, New Jackson County Courthouse, Independence, Missouri.*

1989. It consists of five largely contiguous ranches of about seventy thousand total acres in Osage County in northeastern Oklahoma ("Church Considers" 1989; Lamoreaux 1992). A smaller farm was also purchased in the Kansas Flint Hills near the Oklahoma border but was later sold. If the prominence of the Native American within Mormon ideology is taken into account, one could read all kinds of millenarian theology into a northeastern Oklahoma setting, as several of the smaller break-off groups have. Nevertheless, I was told that these lands were bought for purely agricultural, not historical or religious, reasons (Lamoreaux 1992). Although the LDS Church might well be buying land according to regular business norms, and despite the taciturnity, leaders still might somehow see Oklahoma within a potentially greater New Jerusalem "Lamanite region," or as a beginning for large land acquisition. The employees of church corporations that I spoke with, however, certainly did not outwardly hold any millennial viewpoint; in fact, they went to lengths to emphasize that land acquired was for agricultural or economic purposes, not religious ones. When pressed to comment on, or connect their activities with religious or millennial themes, they were reluctant.

Individual LDS members have seen such land acquisition in ultramillenarian terms. One Web site dedicated to lampooning Latter-day Saint practices asked if the church might be preparing for a "rapid development in the Jackson County area in preparation for the Second Coming" and provided a message board for individual responses. Some contributors called the church's real estate department and received responses similar to those reported above. One anonymous author claimed that "the Mormon Church owns farmland in practically every county in every major midwestern and southern state" and that "in the Missouri/Iowa/Nebraska area they own an enormous amount." Furthermore, the claim was made that the church takes advantage of floods, buying abandoned land with "billions of dollars of tithing money" in order to be able to someday provide "at least 80 acres for every active Mormon family in North America" ("What Preparations" 2000–2001). The eighty-acre figure has no historical basis. The original Saints in the 1830s were normally allotted fifteen to twenty acres, even before the plats for the city of Zion were proposed where acreage would have been a tenth of this. This Web poster's assumption was that *all* Latter-day Saints will one day return to the center of the United States, a notion not often heard in the earlier discussions by church leadership. In fantastical calculations, if five hundred thousand active LDS families exist in North America, it would signify forty million acres of land needed for such settlement—about three and a half Missouris!

That the church owns land in practically every midwestern or southern county is surely an exaggeration, though land for meetinghouses is being purchased across the country with continued membership growth, particularly in suburban settings. The norm is not purchases of farmland, but this skeptical author was sure of "some looney return to a modernized version of the old united orders by Mormons in a time of crisis, for full tithe payers only. Don't kid yourself, they have their plans and whether grounded in reality or some fantasy, they are probably going to do something with all this land in the Mid-West some day" ("What Preparations" 2000–2001). This particular writer's circumstances are unknown, but it seems even the so-called Jack-Mormons of questionable faith may be so steeped in tradition as to believe that the church is planning something big.

Church Lands and Eschatology

The modern LDS trend to purchase territory brings to consideration some traditional Second Coming paradoxes. The prospect of large amounts of recently acquired land in Jackson County has caused changes in millennial discussion by some LDS members. One elderly missionary at the Independence Visitor's Center told me on two separate occasions that the construction of the RLDS Temple near the Temple Lot and across from the LDS Visitor's Center provides too much religious competition. He thought that the LDS Church might therefore build its temple of the New Jerusalem elsewhere, perhaps on one of the newly acquired properties. He even offered a *Doctrine and Covenants* revelation of Joseph Smith as scriptural basis for a different location:

> Verily, verily, I say unto you, that when I give a commandment to any of the sons of men to do a work unto my name, and those sons of men go with all their might and with all they have to perform that work, and cease not their diligence, and their enemies come upon them and hinder them from performing that work, behold, it behooveth me *to require that work no more* at the hands of those sons of men, but to accept of their offerings.
>
> Therefore, for this cause have I accepted the offerings of those whom I commanded to build up a city and a house unto my name, in Jackson county, Missouri, and were hindered by their enemies, saith the Lord your God. (*Doctrine* 1981:124:49, 51; italics added)

The passage above was written in 1841 in Nauvoo, two years after the early Saints had vacated Missouri. In the 1950s, the phrase "to require that work no more" was interpreted by Joseph Fielding Smith to mean *when* rather than *where*, since Joseph Smith Jr. had repeatedly written that the Lord would not remove Zion "out of her place" (*Doctrine* 1981: 90:37, 97:19, 101:17). "Others," said Joseph Fielding Smith, "have tried to convince themselves that the original plan has been changed, [but] we have not been released from this responsibility, nor shall we be" (Smith 1956:3:78). A cautious 2001 article on Missouri history in the *Ensign* basically reiterated Joseph Fielding Smith's view while not overtly stating that the Saints are planning to return en-masse to Jackson County at any future time (Baugh 2001, 48, 54).

The alternate notion that God may not only alter the time frame for the New Jerusalem but also the location (within reason) may be gaining popularity. At one time more strictly interpreted, "not removing Zion out of her place" might now be construed by some as a different location for the temple within, or near to, Jackson County.

Graham W. Doxey, an LDS general authority during the 1980s, supported this view (perhaps inadvertently) in the *Encyclopedia of Mormonism*. Under the heading "New Jerusalem," Doxey wrote that in 1831 it was prophesied that the "city of Zion and its temple would be built in Independence, Missouri," but when talking of events yet to come he only stated that "there is to be a 'center place' for the New Jerusalem located in the Western Hemisphere" (Doxey 1992b:1009–10). This image presents a clear dilemma for regular temple placement in Jackson County and the surrounding region of western Missouri. Any normally operating temple placed in the region would have to be announced with a clear caveat that it is not *the* millenarian New Jerusalem structure, because if the building is to be placed on land other than the sixty-three-acre plot, the seeds of dissent and schism could be sown. Conversely, if a regular smaller sized operating temple were to be placed in the "meadow" area or nearby, some Saints may not see it as being millennial *enough*.

Believers in chiliastic "rapture" outside the LDS realm may not understand the LDS view of eschatology, a principle tenet of Underwood's thesis that the original Saints were basically premillennial. If the earlier belief in a massive destruction of America prevails, why would the church buy land that might eventually be given to it anyway? Still, the early instructions to the Saints were to purchase Jackson County. The LDS Church has a strong belief in learning through experience, trial, and error. Possessing and preparing property certainly provides such learning, though the stewardship of lands in question would today be more authoritarian in direction, led from the top down, rather than from individual or familial decision, as was more the case in 1831 in Independence. The Jeffersonian urge to obtain property, to the extent of identifying sacred space, apparently remains strong in the LDS Church, but such is not a regular feature of dispensational premillennial, postmillennial, or amillennial Christian groups. With a greater religious and economic LDS presence developing in Jackson County, the pre–New Jerusalem destruction view may be sliding out of favor. Premillennialist belief is still held by Mormons, but the patient words of the leadership encourage improving lives spiritually and temporally. Members sometimes tend to more speculation and see the Second Coming just around the corner, while the leadership says little about it.

Recent official church teachings have even indicated that the American system of government will survive *because of* the stability of the LDS Church. A rhetorical question-and-answer session written by the apostle Mark E. Peterson taught against the prevalent idea that America would be destroyed. A "cleansing" was certain, but "if the United States were to be completely destroyed, what effect would that have on other nations? The conclusion is quite clear: Both the nation and the Church must be preserved to carry out the purposes of the Lord. Therefore, the cleansing of America is the act of a loving Father, and we can be assured that he will preserve both his kingdom and the Constitution during those times" (*Great Prologue* 1976:19).

The leadership rarely discusses what this cleansing might consist of and how it might affect the urban area of Kansas City. As places, Kansas City and the New Jerusalem have traditionally been mutually exclusive in LDS talk, and if the "gentile" urban region is no longer designated for divine wrath, the LDS Church may feel somewhat conflicted about methods for establishing the New Jerusalem today. It must be pointed out that, similar to teachings in the 1800s when the goal of the New Jerusalem was presented as a carrot urging members along righteous paths, on occasion the future city is still used instructively to instill good behavior. One lecturer at Brigham Young University coaxed students not to delay their spiritual development. He said, "Let's make certain the road we travel both collectively and individually leads forward to the New Jerusalem, and not back to Athens, or to Rome" (Millet 1996:14). Whereas those ancient cities are often seen as repositories of iniquity as much as of cultural enlightenment, the church in parallel feeling today may see itself as a quiet displacer of present urban interests in Missouri, the restorer of a decadent urban region. This is especially true in light of the church's ever-greater influence in American society. The new land purchases may be seen as a sprout that will grow into a fruitful tree. With its wealth and influence, this LDS tree could gradually overshadow local gentile interests eventually to dominate in the form of a heavenly city. The emphasis here should be given on the word *gradual*. In such a way, the LDS Church sees inevitable future transformation of the center place, but perhaps not with the Temple Lot right at ground zero in the development. The gradual transformation idea is similar to the RLDS idea of "social Zion" prominent around the turn of the twentieth century.

Utah as Zion, and Then . . .

Generally, when millennial themes surface in conference talks, by LDS leaders, if place is mentioned it is usually the gathering center of Utah. For example, LeGrand Richards, an apostle known for his lengthy extemporaneous discussions of scripture, gave one 1967 General Conference talk that detailed the LDS belief in two future millennial world centers as interpreted from Isaiah 2:3. He discusses the subject for at least five paragraphs but not once mentions Missouri. He mentions Utah as a "great gathering place . . . where Israel would be gathered here in these valleys of the mountains and I think that the temple on this block is the very house of the God of Jacob that Isaiah was privileged to see" (Richards 1967:25). A return to Missouri is not exempted, but Utah has become the LDS core, and such wording is common. Any Old Testament scripture mentioning mountains is usually interpreted in LDS talk as prophetically aligned with Utah ranges.

In the 1970s the church gave more emphasis to the wider view of gathering, especially since it was now gaining substantial membership in foreign countries. "Every nation is the gathering place for its own people" taught President Harold B. Lee (*My Kingdom* 1979:160), emphasizing that people should build up the church wherever they happened to live. Some members, however, still took gathering to New Jerusalem seriously. The islands of the Pacific Ocean are an interesting example. At the turn of the twentieth century, the church had much success among the Hawaiians and some had ironically gathered to the valleys of Utah (Stegner 1981: 136–41). At least one hundred LDS Western Samoans and some Tongans suddenly arrived in Independence in the early 1970s ready to help build the New Jerusalem. The church advised them to return to their countries, but many Polynesians remain in the vicinity.[2] The LDS Church's official position, however, is best stated in a 1979 church history manual used for Sunday school courses:

> Zion cannot be fully realized until the central city, the New Jerusalem, has been built and the glory of the Lord rests upon it. However, in terms of possessing the keys, authority, and power to transform the hearts of those willing to receive and, also, of extending and expanding this work over the earth, Zion is on the earth now, for the church is Zion. Speaking of the task before the church, [President] Spencer W. Kimball has stated: "As we speak of Zion, we think of the world, since this now has become a world-wide church." (*My Kingdom* 1979:163)

Missouri is not mentioned, and even the appearance of "a central city" or "New Jerusalem" is increasingly rare in LDS talk. Recently, church leaders have continued to support the idea of "each nation its own gathering place" as the church has continued to grow. LDS apostle Boyd K. Packer (1992) taught that individuals or groups who might in deceit encourage members "to gather to colonies or cults" should be avoided. Packer said that such were teaching that LDS authorities do not recognize millennial signs. Packer vigorously retorted that "the Brethren, by virtue of traveling constantly everywhere on the earth, certainly know what is going on, and by virtue of prophetic insight are able to read the signs of the times." Independence was not mentioned, but Packer said "if there is to be any gathering, it will be announced by those regularly ordained and known by the church to have authority" (Packer 1992:73). Historically, Utah itself has been a gathering place of the Saints, so Packer was referring to any newly announced move.

That Utah has been an important center of gathering in the American West is apparent whether one has a religious view of it or not. Bruce Satterfield, a Ricks College religion instructor, laid out many scriptural references to gathering, backed up by quotations from LDS Church leaders. In more than ten pages of discussion on gathering, Missouri is only mentioned twice, both times in historical, not future, context. Zion is treated as developing in the West, in the United States, or throughout the Americas in general (Satterfield 2001b). It has been difficult for any Latter-day Saint leader to mention Missouri and the New Jerusalem within two sentences of each other.

Since the slightly more millenarian 1960s, very little has been published by LDS members or officials on millennial beliefs. In 1976, Allen and Leonard said Joseph F. Smith's purchase of the meadow plot in 1904 simply represented a "continued interest" of the church in Missouri, a muted view of millenarian themes but typical of the LDS approach (Allen and Leonard 1976:445).

Membership, Leadership, and Technology

The church has always taken an amazingly proactive view of technology, so its application to teaching and spreading Mormon thought has direct implications for church growth and church gathering. As satellite, CD-ROM, and Internet technology have swept over America, the Church of Jesus Christ of Latter-day Saints has always remained in the lead, if not the cutting edge. Who maintains technological control in LDS chiliastic outcomes, especially in the area of communications, is particularly fascinating. In the early 1990s, one Web site entitled "The New Jerusalem" was constructed by missionaries of the distant LDS Korea Pusan Mission, and showed a gleaming ethereal collage of current LDS temple spires with a millennial quotation captioned from Revelation 21 ("New Jerusalem" 1999). Perhaps as a result of some of these locally driven views, the church asserted more control over its corner of the Internet. As of 2001, all local congregations, stakes, and missions of the LDS Church were counseled to cease publishing local Web sites. The Independence Second Ward, however, saw fit to maintain its Ward Calendar and Missouri Church History tour on the Web for a couple of years, but it, too, finally closed (see Independence Second Ward 2001). As of 2003, the renewed establishment of local unit Web sites was again allowed, now under stricter guidelines, reinforcing the top-down structure of church authority. The purpose was to reinforce corporal church policy, but a side effect was to quiet local millenarian speculation.

Most LDS membership views of the New Jerusalem can only be culled as an insider asking opinions during informal discussion. If one does not ask, little will be heard in the ordinary LDS ward on the subject. Nevertheless, the following views were unsolicited. Such opinions are very personal and rarely published. The view discussed earlier of the LDS member perceiving the Independence Visitor's Center's columns and how that structure might be converted into a temple is one example of individual millenarian expression from the mid-1990s. Another member shared with me a dream experienced around 1990 of having to bicycle with family members from Arizona to Jackson County. Apparently, the idea of a return with moderated technology had leaked through the decades of LDS millenarian psyche. Another example was that of an elderly LDS upholsterer in the Kirtland stake chosen in 2002 to recondition furniture for the newer and smaller Columbus Temple. Proud of his ability to serve, he expressed his desire for a greater contribution at the "Jackson County job."

There are a couple of exceptions to the normally private interpretations of contemporary LDS New Jerusalem belief. One is a rather apocalyptic audiocassette series by Duane Crowther. Another is the view of Chad Daybell in his teen novel *Escape to Zion*. Though informed by scripture and prophetic pronouncement, both authors' views represent individual interpretations and are more imaginative than any LDS general authority is likely to pronounce.

An Apocalyptic Product

Crowther's views are extreme and rather sensationalized and not necessarily shared by the general membership. Though he quotes numerous versus of scripture, he seems simply to be trying to sell millennial goods. Crowther said that the "destruction" of Jackson County, Missouri, took place during the violence of the Civil War, and thus this predicted phase has already passed. Though hinted at in the 1860s, this is an idea not seen anywhere else. Lund (1971:90), however, thought that the Saints may have been originally expelled from Missouri because to live there during the Civil War would have been unbearable and counterproductive to the great plan of central Mormon gathering.

Using varied interpretations of scripture, Crowther outlines his views. In a future scenario of warfare and desolation, he said transportation systems will break down and American "cities, strongholds, and chariots" will be destroyed in a period of "anarchy" after a "Third World War." Though the church at the time will be "the only people not at war," a "cleansing" may also take place within it, and when it arrives in Jackson County, "even apostles and prophets may fall" (Crowther 1989).

Crowther spoke further of desolated Missouri and of the return to the New Jerusalem of the anciently scattered ten tribes of Israel. These people will outnumber members of the church, he argued, and "as people gather in to the New Jerusalem, the church will expand into nearby areas and . . . those that gather in will be able to find shelter in nearby cities which . . . have been left uninhabited." He associated the present location of nuclear arms in western Missouri (probably meaning the missile silos at Whiteman Air Force Base) with a future post–nuclear war era that would "cause cities to be abandoned because of radiation or other type of contamination." How the Saints and tribes of Israel will withstand the radiation, Crowther did not explain. He was sure, however, that the core area of the New Jerusalem would become too densely populated for some, who would make their way to settle in Israel, which presumably would be less populated. At this time the headquarters of the Savior would "alternate between the New and Old Jerusalems," following the dual millennial capitals view taken from Isaiah, though that scripture is usually interpreted as meaning the two cities will have different functions (Crowther 1989).

Emma's Errand

More recently, Chad Daybell authored a commercially published novel aimed at LDS teens, particularly girls. *Escape to Zion*, published in 2000, is the most imaginative view of a postapocalyptic New Jerusalem found anywhere at any time and can be seen as the epitome of how members more well-read in the canon envision future scenarios. Daybell gives credit to the ideas of many church presidents and apostles and recommends Lund (1971, especially pages 224–25) but borrows heavily from Crowther as well. Though written for a youthful audience, the book is vivid and unsettling. Third in a trilogy, this is a first-person account of a young married Utah woman sent by the Lord on "errands" through time. After experiencing adventures in 1860s Salt Lake City in Brigham Young's time and in 1940s New York, Emma finds herself on a journey to the future, about a decade after World War III. The time is between 2025 and 2030. The time travel element of the novels adds an odd sense of science fiction with a contemporary acceptance of relativity theory within the scope of premillenarian expectation (Daybell 2000:125). Jules Verne could not have thought up this story, and neither could any LDS member before about 1970.

At the beginning of the story, Emma awakes at a future Salt Lake City abandoned by the Saints, except those staying behind to protect various temples. The idea of few Saints remaining in the West has not been the standard teaching by LDS leaders. Accounts say the church will be reheadquartered, but, with the exception of Card (1989), who portrays the Salt Lake Temple as flooded in several feet of postglacial warming lake water, most ideas center around the continued importance of Salt Lake for the LDS populace (Lund 1971:104–5). In any case, Emma finds the Salt Lake and Provo Temples surrounded by electric fences—well fortified against ill-meaning gangsters and hooligans—and Salt Lake City has become a "false-site" of gathering for those not valiant enough to go to Missouri (Daybell 2000:17, 56). In the Wasatch Valley, postapocalypse hailstorms have wiped out crops, floods have changed land-use patterns, and earthquakes have remodeled the landscape (16, 55, 104).

As many prophets have indicated, Daybell likewise sees a return to Missouri with a minimum of technological aid. LDS tent cities are established all across the United States in protection from wandering bands of evildoers who have lost all moral sense. When the time is right, the Lord's chosen are informed by short-wave radio that the New Jerusalem is to be developed (55–56). The Lord could make the trip easy if he wanted to, but the journey is considered a purifying "test of faith," and the Saints return in wagons, often made from the parts of old cars and trucks (46, 59, 142). Some even return by the traditional, honored handcart (145). In an odd tip of the hat to modern society, however, the main characters are swept across the Great Plains in a handy Nissan sedan—apparently preserved just for their use, even though earthquakes have destroyed much of the Interstate system (103–4).

The Saints arrive in Missouri to find nothing and nobody (142). Apparently, Kansas City will not exist after World War III, and Lund's comments that destruction and collapse could "easily be the result of widespread war and mobocracy" are taken seriously (Lund 1971:111). Subsequently, the New Jerusalem is built up at Independence seemingly by magic. Millions of Saints eventually settle there, as have tribes from the 'North Countries' and many other worthy immigrants (Daybell 2000:11, 135–36), which is a change from earlier projections. In 1873, Orson Pratt wrote that "thousands and tens of thousands" would return to Missouri, while nine years later Joseph F. Smith thought that "two or three hundred thousand" Saints would "wend their way" back to Jackson County, ten times Pratt's number. Smith's projections were more clairvoyant, but even he probably could not have envisioned a metropolitan Salt Lake region of more than 1.2 million or a Kansas City metro area of 1.7 (Lund 1971:109, 111). Daybell's "millions" in Zion handily fit present urban suburban populations.

Descriptions of the outskirts with addresses such as 23,300 East reveal a town of heavenly Salt Lake–like order, approximately fifty by fifty miles square if one considers an average block to be about one-tenth of a mile (Daybell 2000:117). Average home lots, however, are much larger, so Daybell probably has an even bigger place in mind—one of his characters even expresses that the city might stretch "halfway across Kansas"! (105, 117). Eastern suburbs are where most of the Anglo Saints have settled, while newer Lamanite and "North Tribes" arrivals move into the newer western parts of the city (122). Current Kansas City suburb names like Overland Park, Raytown, Shawnee, or Lee's Summit are chiliastically obliterated, and cardinal directions from the central New Jerusalem are commonly used (143). Besides three historical references to Kansas City and one reference to Independence, the only other town name mentioned is Liberty—perhaps rightly so, since none remains through the rest of the United States.

Transport, communications, education, and employment are sufficiently spectacular for a millenarian scenario. The "reverent aura" throughout the city is contrasted with the efficiency of a solar-powered light-rail system, solar-powered buses described as "glorious," and, blessedly, little traffic (117–18). The New Jerusalem contains the only fully operative TV station in the world, and the *Deseret News* is the only regularly published paper (9, 19). The only things left of Kansas City are a peripheral steel mill, its power grid—made to operate again by the Saints—and a few older apartment buildings used by some of the new immigrants (25, 142). Why not just use the larger abandoned homes in the area?

In this New Jerusalem there is no one "best job." A vivid description is given of the Law of Consecration and its operations. Attending to the welfare of the Saints is the bishop who now has no other job, and the dispersal of goods in the New Jerusalem is done through utopian ideal (126–27). In one case an empty-nester couple reasonably trades homes with another family that has had more children (132–34), but the assumption is that the nonnuclear family might still be the norm under chiliastic circumstances. Given the Mormon emphasis on cementing genealogical relationships, wouldn't large communal family apartment complexes be a more expected occurrence in the LDS utopia? Daybell tries to present a practical and useful city of Zion, but he has plenty of difficulty reconciling his exposure to modern technology with the desire to portray the humble roots of the Saints. Most of the membership must return in a low-tech way to build up a hi-tech lifestyle, and the irony is often apparent. The schools depicted are a further example. Schooling is mostly vocational and practical, and in the New Jerusalem there is room for neither professional students nor left-wing social dialectic (140–41).

Following such practical thought, agriculture–more specifically, gardening—is a main occupation. Families have large backyards where fruits and vegetables are grown (117). New Jerusalem farmers finally gain the respect they never had in the contemporary urban scene. They are not considered bumpkins; rather they are among the most valued contributors to millenarian society. In the New Jerusalem, soil is abundantly richer and crop production well increased, though neither specific agricultural methods nor pollutants are discussed. Daybell emphasizes horticulture several times, while commercial grain does not seem a major part of the future city (23, 141). This Fruit and Vegetable Zion makes one wonder if people got sick of all that grain used up from LDS food storage after World War III.

Approaching the Second Coming, recreation and leisure are yet important. People still dress in colorful outfits, so the New Jerusalem is not about stifling creativity (139). Mormons have always emphasized modesty but not plainness. Softball is played, but—alas, BY's Cougars!—with brutality and competition removed from play (127). Holidays are toned down with the religious aspects paramount: the commerciality of Santa Claus and the Easter Bunny has ceased to influence credit-mad buyers, and Halloween, the "dark holiday," is gone (150–51). Most disturbing is the popularity of the group Oz3g, which stands for the third generation of Osmonds, who regain airtime with a new version of "Puppy Love," an excruciating idea (133).

Daybell's city shows variety and imagination. It is full of fountains, plazas, towers, and acoustically perfect settings (119–20, 156). The LDS Family History Center is twenty-five stories tall, and one supposes it must be if the records of the granite vault up Little Cottonwood Canyon have been transferred. The centerpiece of architecture, of course, is the New Jerusalem temple, and Daybell's interpretation is the most vivid since that of Porter and Ruf in the 1960s. The temple is a complex of twenty-four buildings placed in a circular pattern, built by angels and men together. The buildings are connected by walkways with ceiling gardens and towers—the Conference Center in Salt Lake City having become the architectural prototype (121–22). Huge eastern doors await the Savior's "official" Second Coming, but this temple is already seen as his "de facto" residence. Within the temple is a room with all the records from the arrival of the north tribes and a twenty-thousand-seat chapel with a great arched ceiling—also an architectural tribute to the Salt Lake Conference Center theme (156).

The twenty-four structures are each the size of the Provo Temple, and each with a supporting arch rising into the sky with glass between, forming a vast ribbed dome, from the center of which projects a 1,500 foot spire—which the 1,815-foot Canadian National Tower in Toronto would still best.

New Jerusalem architecture is not dowdy by any stretch of the imagination, but neither is it impossible, at least in Daybell's view. The architecture, however, is not without irony. He combines the lowly and blocky style set by the LDS Conference Center with the flying spires of the Washington, D.C., or San Diego temples. The most intriguing part of the scene is not what is described but what is not. The two-and-one-half acre Temple Lot is swallowed up by the immensity of the structure—and not mentioned. How the RLDS Auditorium and Temple were felled is not described.

Daybell's is a thoroughly developed LDS vernacular view. Though he gives credit to many prophets, apostles, and prominent LDS writers, no one since the early 1970s has given such an extensive explanation of the possible vista. That the scene presented is written for teens makes it all the more intriguing—though a novel, this is the audience most likely to be influenced.

Diminished Talk

No doubt millennial LDS thinkers are prone to search the daily news for apocalyptic meaning. In fact, church members are taught to look for signs, though specific individual world events are rarely identified as millennial by the LDS leadership (see Lund 1971:119–20). For example, in 1966, the apostle Marion G. Romney hoped that church members would be familiar with the predictions of the coming events, including "the building of the New Jerusalem," but utterance of the phrase has been rare, and Romney said little more on the subject (Romney 1966:51–52). In western Missouri, however, members have accepted with mild millennial expectation headlines such as "Two Arrested in Protest at Whiteman Missile Silo" (Scharnhorst 1992) or "New Noise Plagues Wolf Creek" (nuclear power plant) (Rosenberg 1992), but the scholar has little evidence of contemporary LDS views on the New Jerusalem besides the official land purchases and the rather limited development near the Temple Lot. Even September 11, 2001, was given no particular millennial significance. The LDS leadership expressed tender sympathy and even caution, but members were left to their own interpretations. The LDS search for the millennium and the New Jerusalem has become a very personalized affair.

Talk on the New Jerusalem today can be heard more among the general LDS membership than in leadership directives, but even membership talk has diminished over the past decade. General millennial discussion can be found throughout the church in America but is more prevalent in the Kansas City area, where members are more familiar with local church history. The impression is that the membership sees millennial events as being more imminent than does the leadership, which is the opposite of the situation in the nineteenth century. The membership wants millennial events to unfold presently, while the leadership's attitude is to wait until the proper time.

In official LDS activities, the New Jerusalem is conspicuous by the lack of reference to it. A 1977 General Conference speech given by Spencer W. Kimball, reprinted in 1984, defines Zion as the work that the membership undertakes. The speech does not refer to Missouri (Kimball 1984). Ezra Taft Benson, president of the LDS Church from 1985 to 1994 and former U.S. secretary of agriculture under Dwight Eisenhower, continued the tradition of taciturnity, but with some millennial hints. He declared the church was still under a condemnation for not paying proper heed to the scriptures, particularly the *Book of Mormon* (Benson 1986a:78, 1986b:4–5). In 1989, Benson said, "My dear brothers and sisters we must prepare to redeem Zion. It was essentially the sin of pride that kept us from establishing Zion in the days of the prophet Joseph Smith. Pride is the great stumbling block to Zion. . . . We must cleanse the inner vessel by conquering pride" (Benson 1989:7). In the past, the phrase "redeeming Zion" indicated a return to Missouri; Benson's implication is that the weight of disobedience still thwarts a return. Not mentioning Missouri, he promised members that the Second Coming will come and that all the Lord's words will be fulfilled. Benson's attitude is representative of a leadership that wishes to urge members to good living without undue consternation regarding geographic upheaval.

Entering the new century, the largest symbol that the LDS Church has established seems the antithesis to any projected Missouri development, though Daybell's novel used it as a model. Announced in 1998, the new Conference Center in Salt Lake City was ready in 2000 for seating of some twenty-one thousand people compared to the Tabernacle's humble six thousand (Hinkley 1999c). This monumental structure, replete with roof garden, roof fountain, and the latest in multimedia technology, supplants the historic tabernacle for biannual official conferences broadcast worldwide by satellite. The completion of the new building was celebrated in October 2000. Millennial overtones were evident but subdued. In prayer, President Gordon B. Hinkley dedicated the structure as the "gathering place of Thy people" (Hinkley 2000:70). Indeed, it is the largest gathering place ever built for any of the Saints, anywhere, at any time. The sacred "Hosanna

Shout," usually reserved only for the dedication of temples and not normally viewed by the public, was broadcast across public satellite, television, and radio frequencies (Hinkley 2000:69–70). The atmosphere was solemn and emotional as many saw this unique ritual for the first time.

In his dedicatory address, President Hinkley quoted Isaiah (2:2–3), viewing the Conference Center as the culmination of the Old Testament words, saying, "the mountain of the Lord's house shall be established in the tops of the mountains . . . and all nations shall flow unto it." He also repeated the Zion vs. Jerusalem geographic dichotomy, stating that the prophecy not only applied to the Salt Lake Temple "but also to this magnificent hall. For it is from this pulpit that the law of God shall go forth, together with the word and testimony of the Lord" (Hinkley 2000:69). Where this places the Missouri New Jerusalem in LDS millenarian eschatology is unclear, but in a rare statement of definition it marks Salt Lake City as ultimately matching Jackson County in millennial importance. The question is, does this weaken Missouri any in importance to the LDS Church as a future millennial headquarters? The faith of most of the Saints to return to Missouri has weakened since the 1870s.

Loren C. Dunn, a previous LDS area president for the region, was quoted in the *Kansas City Star* as saying that "the day will come when there will be a temple." As to the time and exact location, he said only that "all of this is in the hands of the Lord" ("Sacred Ground" 1990). At one special meeting, the president of the LDS mission based in Independence spoke on the subject of the "Gathering of Israel" (Holmes 1990). Many scriptures were read, but the phrase "New Jerusalem" was not mentioned once. Another special regional meeting held at the Independence Stake Center had a typical theme of "Strengthening Families" (1990) and was designed to attract nonmembers with a number of popular Mormon sports figures. Again, no emphasis was given to Independence as a sacred site. Even more telling was the official Independence Regional Conference held in May 1991, in downtown Kansas City. Two members of the church's twelve apostles and two from its Quorum of the Seventy spoke. Besides mentioning the historical significance of the area, nothing of the New Jerusalem was mentioned.

What about millennial talk in other areas of historical importance to the church? The Nauvoo temple has now been rebuilt, and along with the Salt Lake Temple Gordon B. Hinkley has symbolically referred to them as great bookends, facing each other and encompassing the great pioneer history of the church (Hinkley 2002:6). The view looks more to the past than to the future, but is appropriate, even though it skims over the importance of Missouri. One might also look to Kirtland for utterances, since parts of the LDS Kirtland Village have recently been reconstructed similar to the missionary/tourist appeal developed in Nauvoo. At the Kirtland Stake Conference held at the Packard Music Hall in Warren, Ohio, on April 13, 2003, Karl Anderson, a former stake president and apologetic author on Kirtland history, quoted *Doctrine and Covenants* 124:83, which discusses Kirtland being "built up" in the future. Not many prophecies in scripture, he stated, discuss places to be built up, but Kirtland is one of them. The New Jerusalem was implied but not mentioned overtly. Likewise, stake president Walter Selden, in closing remarks at the same meeting, discussed how members might work harder to build up the Kirtland stake since it was the first stake of the church and should thus be more progressive. He said members should seek after things that are sacred and prepare for the Savior's return. "I trust he will do what he said he would do—and forgive me of my sins," said an emotional Selden. Neither the New Jerusalem nor Jackson County was mentioned.

One exception to the official quiet on the subject of the millenarian New Jerusalem was found in a New Testament student study guide for the LDS Church's seminary program of religious education for teenage youth. A diagram labeled "Future Jerusalems" shows a distinction between the city that the Saints will eventually build in Missouri and the New Jerusalem that John speaks of in Revelation 21, which is called "a holy city that descends to unite with a celestial earth" (*New Testament Study Guide* 1999:152). A one-inch square map of Missouri is presented with a stylized temple labeled "Independence, Missouri," yet the book states that the New Jerusalem "coming down" out of heaven spoken of in Revelation 3 and 21 "is not the same city that is to be built on the American continent as part of the last days and the Second Coming of Christ" (178). Instead, a union of heaven and earth in a postmillennial celestialized state is referenced. Thus the church has taught millenarian themes to youth, again emphasizing duty, but generally avoids them in public discourse.

The church continues to increase its landholdings quietly, not only in the Jackson County area but also around Adam-ondi-Ahman and in Far West. The LDS presence also grows in the surrounding region. Suburban Johnson County, Kansas, one of the most affluent counties in the United States, had many new congregations established in the 1990s. Despite church growth, the Kansas City area remains a paradox of the LDS realm. Some might say that hesitation is bred of uncertainty, but the LDS Church does not want to cause undue millenarian speculation and unrest among the members. Also, partly because of the LDS Church's attention to worldwide growth, partly because it feels it has to wait for further divine instruction, partly because of a stigma of unworthiness, and partly because competition for land at the Temple Lot causes difficulty in explanation and thus sanctification, church officials generally remain silent on the matter of New Jerusalem.

The Community of Christ

Ideological Transition

> The time has come for a start to be made toward building my temple in the Center Place. It shall stand on a portion of the plot of ground set apart for this purpose many years ago by my servant Joseph Smith, Jr.
>
> —Revelation reported by W. Wallace Smith, *The Book of Doctrine and Covenants*

BEFORE WORLD WAR II, RLDS MEMBERS WERE A FAIRLY CONSERVATIVE GROUP. MOST MEMBERS BELIEVED IN A LITERAL SECOND COMING OF JESUS CHRIST AND IN THE ESTABLISHMENT OF A PEACEFUL millennium, but their perspective of the "Center Place of Zion" was quite different from LDS leanings. The RLDS leadership maintained a practical ideal of social Zion that implied gradual maturity (Edwards 1951:295). Similar to other midwestern churches, the organization has been democratic and has maintained a conciliatory stance toward its numerous neighbors, quite a different situation from the LDS Church isolated in the West. The LDS Church has been able to develop a successful concentrated hierarchical organization, while the RLDS Church has had to temper fundamentalist tones within a body of unlike people within the sea of America. With about a quarter of a million members (about thirty thousand in the Independence area), the church has traditionally straddled a line between liberal Protestantism and orthodox Mormonism.

Toward the end of the 20th century, the RLDS realm has undergone a cascade of change and the millennial views of Zion held by many RLDS members have increasingly diverged from the liberal stance of the leadership. The dissent became particularly acrimonious in the 1980s, stemming from the church's decision in 1984 to allow women ordination to the RLDS priesthood. Though the church has grown steadily, it has encountered fundamentalist divisions that have taken more than 10 percent of its membership. Thus, much of the RLDS Church's recent activity in the environs of the Temple Lot has revolved around gaining greater regional acceptance and retaining its membership. It is a precarious balance.

In the midst of these changes, and in part as a result of them, the RLDS Church has built a temple in the center place—one that, according to their interpretation, is the result of the original prophecy of Joseph Smith Jr. As the latest symbol of change, the church has also officially adopted a new name—the Community of Christ.

The Social Zion of Frederick M. Smith

At the death of Joseph Smith III, his son, Frederick Madison Smith, was already in control of the RLDS Church. F. M. Smith assumed the office of president in 1915 and remained the head of the church until his death in 1946. He projected Independence to be the center of a future Zion that would be built by faithful RLDS Saints according to "old time prophesies" mixed with his own blend of "social welfare" goals focused on the Independence community.

"Onward to Zion" was a motto favored by F. M. Smith, but his model of ideal community was not overly chiliastic. He held an urban-oriented social gospel view and advocated the development of Zion through a variety of social programs that were influenced by his advanced training in sociology and psychology (Hunt 1982, vol. 1). During his tenure, construction on The Auditorium was begun, continued care for the aged was stressed, the church's publishing concern was expanded, and missionary work was upgraded. It must be remembered that the RLDS Church is a separate church in the Latter Day Saint group with no clerical, organizational, or ecumenical affiliation with the LDS Church. All activities of the RLDS Church are undertaken in the context of a distinct religious tradition stemming from Joseph Smith Jr. but in open view of many other Protestant and Catholic congregations. Thus the church has forged a more open, democratic, and moderate path to appease possible critics, who surround the RLDS Church on all sides. This was the largest Latter Day Saint experience among people not of the western tradition. The gradual social orientation has been a catalyst that has ever more quickly moved the

FIG. 32 | *Architectural Rendering of the Auditorium.*

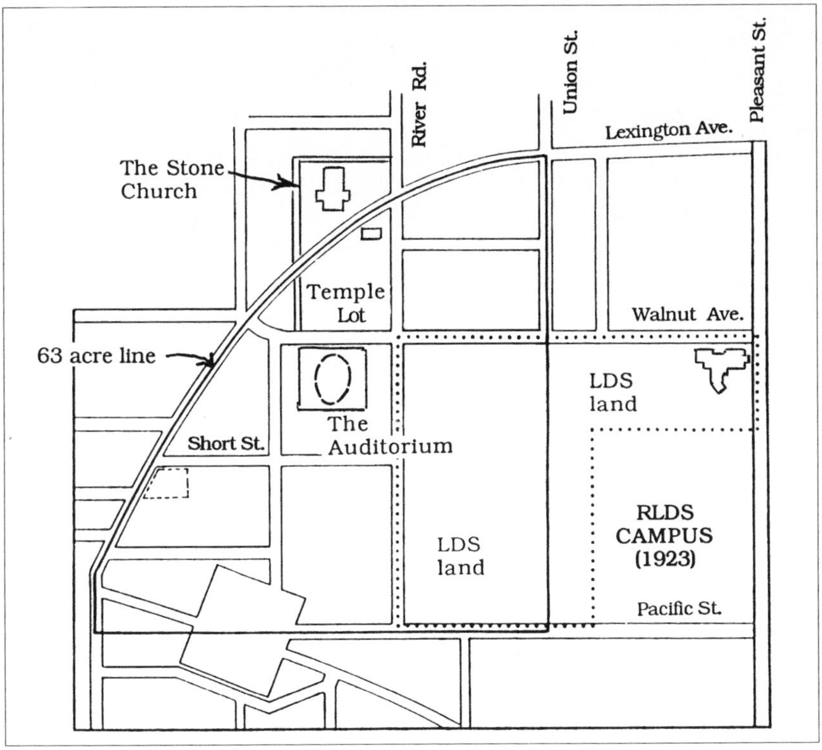

FIG. 33 | *The RLDS auditorium design as proposed in the 1920s. Reprinted by permission of Kansas City Public Library.*

RLDS Church in an anti-traditional direction of seeking an improved position within the general cultural milieu.

The Auditorium

In such an environment, the development of a sophisticated, social-welfare Zion was more important to F. M. Smith than were millennial themes. In 1928, observing Jackson County's dense population and fine transportation system, he argued that the RLDS Church should take advantage of the economic opportunities of the location (Ruoff 1981:24). Smith proposed several new ideas. He instituted a number of education, health, and welfare programs, and his centerpiece, proposed in 1920, was to be a huge conference center and church headquarters, an immense magnet for the gathering Saints. It was designed as a five-story pseudo-Roman square with pronounced pilasters on the facade, topped with a broad copper dome (Figure 32; "Architect's Study" 1933; see also *Results of County Planning* 1933:14). When finished, the building's conference chamber would seat seven thousand people, one thousand more than the LDS Tabernacle in Salt Lake City. The placement of the RLDS Auditorium was as impressive as its size. Five separate sites were considered, but the building was finally located "on original temple ground" (Wilcox 1979:540–45). Its location on Walnut Street was the former site of Columbian School, where Harry Truman had attended several grades from elementary through middle school. More important, like the Stone Church built forty years before, it was oriented in an obvious symbolic position facing northward—toward the Temple Lot (Figure 33).

The Auditorium was begun in 1926, and the outer shell and basement chamber were finished before the Great Depression stopped construction. Work on the building would not resume for almost thirty years ("Auditorium" 1926; "Auditorium Building" 1926). At this time the church suffered "severe financial difficulties," and an accrued debt of nearly two million dollars was not paid off until 1944 (Davis 1989:580; *Book of Doctrine* 1989: 136; Wilcox 1979:544–45). The Auditorium required substantial sacrifice, and F. M. Smith saw it as a great "ideal of Zion brought into realization" (Ruoff 1981:158).

Gathering amidst Depression

From the beginning of his leadership, F. M. Smith promoted gathering the Saints to the center place of Independence and to "regions round about."

On occasion he waxed millennial in hoping to someday see "the glittering towers of Zion" (Ruoff 1981:223), but his pragmatic social view of gathering was usually presented minus millennial trappings, an approach similar to that of his father, Joseph Smith III. The Saints were admonished to gather to Zion but with great preparation and "good judgment" in order to fit comfortably into the existing social and economic surroundings (Carmichael 1925:1200; Ruoff 1981:20–21, 24). Surely the stigma of the 1830s expulsion of the Saints from Jackson County and then from Missouri altogether has lent sensitivity to RLDS gathering—perhaps itself a reason for increased liberal change in the church's worldview.

Smith's strongest talk of gathering to Zion was during the Great Depression when few Saints had the means to migrate. The situation has some similarity to 1850s LDS talk when millennial themes were used to give people hope for a better day. Though he always urged caution and preparedness, Smith stated that gathering to Zion would even help to alleviate economic woes and would prevent another depression (Ruoff 1981: 132). The years were difficult, but he was also anxious for more Saints to be influential in city politics and to promote "socially meliorative legislation" (Hunt 1982:1:156). Smith was pleased that "thousands were thinking and talking of coming to Zion," but during the depression most stayed put in Illinois and Iowa. As a result, the growth the RLDS Church attained was greater in peripheral regions than at the center place, contributing to the rather unconcentrated pattern of general church membership today (Ruoff 1981:23, 130–31; Hunt 1982:1:160–61, 197–98).

The RLDS membership became increasingly sparse, somewhat like a spider that has a small body but long thin legs (Gaustad and Barlow 2001:237). At the end of World War II, only about 10 percent of church population was located in Jackson County (Ruoff 1981:232–33; Hunt 1982:1:156, 162). Thus the RLDS Church has also had to deal with the difficulties of serving members scattered across the United States, a situation quite different from that of the LDS Church in the West, where cultural dominance of the central body of Mormon population was the norm. This further increased a tendency to appeal to the diverse needs of the RLDS congregations that became part of distinct Reorganized Latter Day Saint traditions.

Although the principle of gathering was still endorsed at the end of the war, Smith's caution increased to the point of trepidation. It was almost as if he feared an increased burden on the church by its own members (Ruoff 1981:101–2, 112–13, 185–89). He also had to worry more about how the local non-RLDS population would react to a steady influx of members. He said that many had come "uncalculatingly and unthoughtedly" and again emphasized preparation prior to gathering (Ruoff 1981:99–100). The idea of repeating 1830s events was not tolerable.

The RLDS Redemption of Zion

The RLDS version of "redemption of Zion" seems less of an event than in the LDS realm. The Utah church traditionally has held that the redemption of Zion meant an intervention by God to put divine geography straight. After mass repentance, God would first have to forgive the sinfulness of the church, after which a great portion of the people and the church headquarters would move to Jackson County. There the New Jerusalem and temple would be built and the area readied for Christ's eventual return.

For the RLDS Church, already headquartered in Independence, the "redemption of Zion" involved no mass movement of people—it was a gradual trickle. The New Jerusalem would not miraculously appear but instead would mature and be beautified incrementally through the economic and social efforts of individual "stewards" (Ruoff 1981:60–61, 113, 135). Such development, according to F. M. Smith, would culminate in the building of a temple, which would "symbolize the social work of the church" and, ultimately, would herald the return of Christ (Ruoff 1981:96–97).

Officially, however, the church began to shy away from references to the Second Coming—they seemed token offerings to a hopeful membership. The official RLDS view of Zion was as social experiment, and it increasingly had a nonmillennial, even secular, feel to it. It was an incremental and less utopian approach, in sharp contrast with the LDS interpretation of the Missouri Zion as a millennial event. The LDS Church is a practical organization, but future events are seen as mapped out in Heaven and ready to take place on earth when the time is right. F. M. Smith saw the future waters of the RLDS Church as uncharted. "No man living can sit down now and work out all the details of the untried experiment we must make" (Ruoff 1981:138). Later, Wallace B. Smith would make similar remarks, indicative of the fence straddling that a historically prophetic church has to balance with its voting membership. No LDS leader has ever said that the future path of the church was unclear.

Clearly, Smith's view of Zion was not as literal as that either of the LDS Church or of the general RLDS membership. For example, he mentioned that although many Saints believed that "the God of the Universe

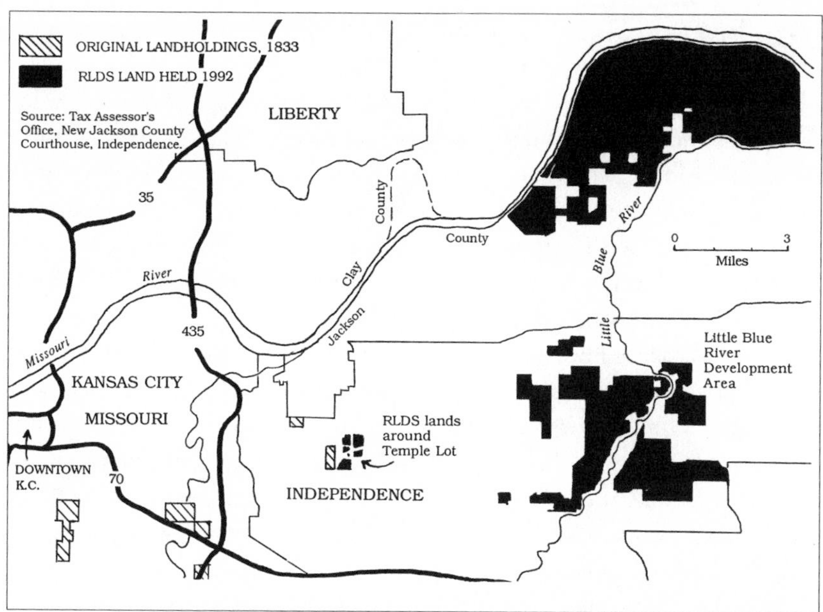

FIG. 34 | *RLDS landholdings in Jackson County, 1992. Data from Tax Assessor's Office, New Jackson County Courthouse, Independence, Missouri.*

might send down the city of Zion, fully panoplied and ready for their occupancy," this would not be the case. Though such an event could be supported by quoting the book of Revelation, Smith said that, "Christ would come to his own" only when the proper social conditions have been developed at the earthly, visible Zion (Ruoff 1981:104–5). The implication is for a social collective self-actualization and not necessarily a tangible millennial return. Thus, even from the depression era, a course was set for a less literal and less millennial RLDS interpretation of unfolding events.

F. M. Smith said that "Zionic Redemption" meant that the Saints should either purchase land or convert the existing landowners (Hunt 1982: 1:157, 159; *Book of Doctrine* 1989:136:3c). Since conversion of the old Missourians was unlikely, the church followed the former path and gradually purchased over nine thousand acres of land in Jackson County through the 1940s. These lands, apparently obtained to provide future Zionic space and investment, were located east of Independence in far northern Jackson County between the Missouri and the Little Blue Rivers (Figure 34). How these lands were later dispensed with, as will be seen, was to become a real question for leadership and membership alike.

The Millennial Membership

Upon scrutiny, the views of Frederick M. Smith are surprisingly distinct from those of the millennial-minded RLDS membership. Later, the thinly dispersed, and therefore more isolated, church membership—represented by voting delegates to General Conferences—would also contribute to change. The leadership maintained the social Zion stance, and a semisecular attitude toward human welfare became more official. The members, however, did not commonly echo Smith's ideas.

The Order of Enoch was established at Lamoni, Iowa, in 1870 to provide land at equitable prices for gathering Saints. The order was operated by millennial-minded members and was so successful that it eventually lured the RLDS leadership to reside in Iowa. As more members relocated to Independence, the order began to shift its acquisitive interests to Jackson County, again in advance of the leadership. In 1910, for example, the order purchased eighty acres of land in south Independence ("History of the Enoch Hill Church" 1956:981), and by 1914 many Saints had purchased lots and named the neighborhood Enoch's Hill, in the hope that future residents would become as Enoch's people of old, "who, according to Latter Day Saint scripture, were so righteous that they were taken up into Heaven" ("Local Historians' Reports" 1991:3; "History of the Enoch Hill Church" 1956:981). In this case the congregation may have seen themselves in a future union with Enoch, which, having been taken up, would once again descend to earth "out of heaven from God," as described by Joseph Smith and implied from Revelation (21:10–12; see also the Book of Moses [7:63] in *Pearl* 1981). By 1917, development at "Enoch's Hill" was brisk, though "good lots" were still available (RLDS 1976:7:154).

An Order of Enoch separate from the Lamoni organization was established in Independence in 1915 (RLDS 1976:7:74), and, from this time forward, interest waned in Lamoni as an RLDS growth pole. In 1921, the order bought additional acreage in southeastern Independence (RLDS 1976:7:480). The Enoch Hill congregation became a vibrant center of Independence RLDS activity that rivaled the central Stone Church congregation, located just north of the Temple Lot. Most of the early Enoch Hill Saints were "those urged to come Zionward" who had bought lots from the Order of Enoch in the spirit of Joseph Smith's early law of consecration ("Local Historians' Reports" 1991:1; Ruoff 1981:60–61). All this Zionic activity dated from around 1910, but it was not until 1920 that Independence was officially declared the city of Zion by the RLDS leadership and the headquarters of the church moved from Lamoni (Davis 1989: 579, 605). As early as 1925, a special program for gathering Saints was established with the cooperation of the church's presiding bishopric, but this development, too, seems to have had its impetus in the millennial sentiment among the membership of local congregations, not in prophetic directives from Frederick Madison Smith.

Another example of the millennial spirit of land acquisition was the purchase in 1923 of the parcel of land known as "the Campus," near the Temple Lot (see Figure 33). Spurred by earlier LDS purchases and development, the RLDS Church set itself on buying additional lands offered for sale by the wealthy Swope family. The price of the Campus parcel was set at fifty thousand dollars, but the church had no difficulty raffling off squares of the property to the membership in order to raise the necessary down payment (Wilcox 1979:472). In purchasing land, the goals of the membership seemed consistently millennial. In general, the Saints were anxious to "redeem Zion" and looked forward to one day being "Temple Builders" ("Beautiful Enoch Hill Church" 1951:514–15; "Local Historians' Reports" 1991:1–2), but the leadership was always more business and welfare oriented. No doubt at the time of the purchase of the Campus a duality of RLDS opinion existed regarding the use of the parcel. Today the parklike setting of the campus is used for RV parking and other outdoor gatherings.

Signs of the Times

Through the mid-1900s, RLDS members commonly referred to Independence with the biblical appellation of Mt. Zion (Smith 1945:169). Members were striving to build up the New Jerusalem to prepare for the "personal and visible" return of Jesus Christ, and scriptures regarding millennial events were seen as "about to be fulfilled" (Edwards 1951:292, 349). An editorial in the official RLDS magazine, the *Saints' Herald*, called a 1914 Colorado labor dispute a sign of the times and declared that millennial predictions were coming true. The editor thought that unrest in the nation was mounting and that mobs of Saints would soon rush to independence in order to escape calamity ("Another Criticism" 1914: 465). Jackson County voted itself as a dry county later in 1914, another perceived sign of the approaching redemption of Zion ("Notes and Comments" 1914: 804). The "signs" seem to have been local manifestations of a Europe boiling over.

During the 1930s, the economy prevented many Saints from moving to Independence, but millennial feeling remained intense. World War II seems to have had a varied effect on apocalyptic interpretations, however, and the culmination of Hiroshima caused at least one RLDS religious scholar to wonder about the possible destruction of the Jackson County area. Placing Zion in a precarious position, he wrote, "What happened in Japan may happen in Kansas City, or in any other city, if and when changing world events put such devastating agencies into the hands of a hostile people who have the air power to deliver them" (Smith 1945: 236–37). Obviously, the RLDS membership could not favor the idea of a total destruction of the Kansas City region before the establishment of the New Jerusalem as the LDS Church could in the West. Familiarity breeds pragmatism and caution, and the warning does not seem overly millennial.

RLDS Sacred Space

Substantial details were given in the early years on the scale and nomenclature of the RLDS Zion. The RLDS hierarchy recognized "Independence" as the "center place of Zion," and both of these terms became the operative descriptions for the place. The alternate phrases "New Jerusalem" and "Jackson County" were rarely employed, perhaps because they continued to be used with feeling by the LDS Church in Utah. Likewise, the RLDS population never adopted or used the term "Mormon" to describe themselves and have always strongly resisted the name "Missouri Mormons."

F. M. Smith gave several specific details of what the important areas "round about" the center place might be, but he was not geographically consistent. In 1923, he admonished that "every acre that lies from fifty miles north of Lamoni clear to Independence" should be purchased (Ruoff 1981:147). Purchasing every acre in a dominantly non-RLDS region makes Smith's words seem spoken in a brief moment of impracticality. Though the RLDS Church did not place as strong an emphasis on some of the earlier gathering sites of the Saints, like Adam-ondi-Ahman and Far West (Ruoff 1981:183–84), the old headquarters at Lamoni was clearly still part of Zion. The city was referenced frequently in the writings of RLDS Church leaders and presidents.

Gradually Lamoni's intensity as a hub of Zion lessened as descriptions focused on an area radiating instead from Independence. On the eve of World War II, F. M. Smith described Zion's periphery in the form of an elongated diamond with Independence at the center. Lamoni marked the north-

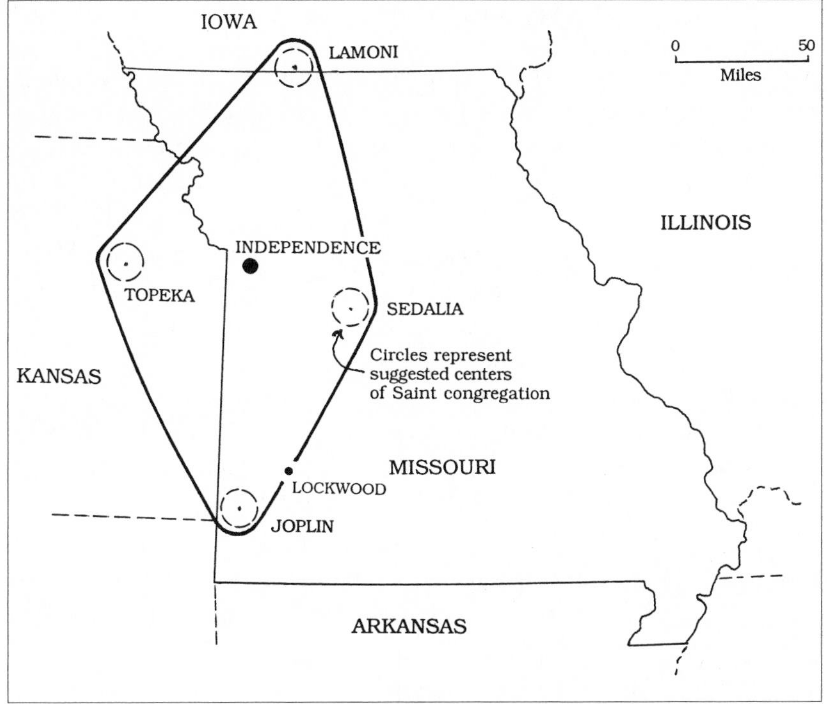

FIG. 35 | *F. M. Smith's diamond of "regions round about" Independence.*

ern point while Topeka, Kansas, and Sedalia, Missouri, marked the western and eastern limits. Joplin, Missouri, was the southern point (Figure 35). Smith said that the organization of church groups "should be proscribed" within this region (Ruoff 1981:230), yet the design is too geometric to have been carefully thought out: most millennial descriptions of Zion fade southward. More often than not, the closer to the Christian/Pentecostal influences in the Ozarks, the less sacred the Latter Day Saint space, though this may be the reason several break-off groups of Saints in smaller numbers have organized here (see Gaustad and Barlow 2001:368–69). Even contradicting his own limits, Smith later advised Saints settling at Lockwood, Missouri, that they were not within the environs of Zion (see Figure 35; Ruoff 1981:205). Many RLDS congregations were established within this region by the World War II years, but after the death of F. M. Smith, the RLDS Church diminished emphasis on gathering and has held no official stance delineating any magnet region. No outer towns have designated Zion's periphery since.

Postwar Years in Zion

In 1946, Israel Alexander Smith, younger brother of Frederick Madison, became president of the RLDS Church. During Israel Smith's presidency (1946–58), the church's presence in Independence continued to develop along the incremental lines of F. M. Smith's social Zion. Israel Smith oversaw the construction of a new nursing home, additions to the Independence Sanitarium and Hospital, and an expansion of Graceland College in Lamoni (Davis 1989:590). For many years, the sanitarium itself had been seen as a sacred resort whose construction had been commanded by God and as complementary to the RLDS Church's Temple in Kirtland. The RLDS apostle Joseph Luff originally viewed the structure as a place where Saints gathering from Lamoni to Independence could seek aid and rest (Luff 1910). In 1956, work on the Auditorium was resumed, but Israel Smith died in an auto accident before its completion in 1961 (Davis 1989:590–91).

Many in the RLDS membership may not like the comparison, but the history of the construction of the Auditorium is strikingly reminiscent of the Utah LDS Church's extended efforts to complete the Salt Lake Temple between the 1850s and the 1890s. Both represent a group's maximum physical expression of faith. While the Auditorium is a gathering and office structure in function, unlike the Salt Lake Temple, its core is a twentieth-century version of the Mormon Tabernacle, traditionally the major meetinghouse of the Utah Saints, even down to having a visual focus of a prominent organ and a two-tiered oval conference chamber where church conferences are held. The Auditorium was supposed to be F. M. Smith's ultimate symbol for the development of the RLDS Zion in Independence. With the possible exception of the Truman Library, it was the most prominent structure in the city from 1930 until 1991 when the new RLDS spiral Temple was built.

The Progressive RLDS Church

RLDS Church membership in the United States is widespread but thin. Members are relatively isolated and separated from the core and headquarters of the church, a concentration only mildly evident on a national map of churches per county, an overall geography that has remained basically unchanged since 1890 (Gaustad and Barlow 2001:237–38). By contrast, the LDS Church has done all it can to centralize its far-flung membership to Salt

Lake City by connecting as many local chapels as it can to church headquarters by satellite, computer, and now the Internet. The sparse geographic nature of the RLDS membership has sped change in church policy, most of which takes place during the church's democratic General Conferences. In fact, the RLDS tradition of having a General Conference once every two years instead of every six months or yearly, as in most of the other Latter Day Saint churches, seems to have been instituted as a mechanism for bridling momentous change. If that is the case, the mechanism has not worked, making one wonder what the RLDS Church would look like today if its General Conferences had been held at six months intervals.

By reported revelations as well as by conference vote, the church has adopted increasingly liberal stances. By the 1980s, drastic shifts were appearing in church policy, perhaps as a result of the general incompatibility of some Latter Day Saint doctrines with those of the surrounding non–Latter Day Saint peoples. One important change has been the de-emphasis of sections of the *Doctrine and Covenants* that discuss polygamy, baptisms for the dead, and eternal marriage. Except for polygamy, these teachings are still major tenets in the Utah church. The RLDS Church has never endorsed these principles, and the sections were moved to the back of the RLDS *Doctrine and Covenants* by vote of the 1970 conference and dropped altogether by vote of the 1990 conference (*Book of Doctrine* 1989:appendices; RLDS 1990:359; "Saints from Many Lands" 1990:27–28).

Some RLDS members wish to loosen ties to the *Book of Mormon* as well, in order to be more fully accepted by other denominations. A recent RLDS pamphlet on the church's faith and beliefs makes this evident. It says, "The Bible is the central book of scripture for the church. The Book of Mormon and the Doctrine and Covenants are additional witnesses of God's love and Christ's ministry" (*Faith and Beliefs* n.d.). This wording is quite different from the LDS view, which often places the *Book of Mormon* in a doctrinally superior position. The RLDS view reflects a more conciliatory approach in a relatively diverse Protestant religious landscape (Sopher 1967:84; Gaustad and Barlow 2001:368–69).

As of 1978, W. Wallace Smith, who replaced Israel Smith as church leader in 1958, became prophet emeritus. Though Frederick Madison Smith had previously taken control of the RLDS Church before his father Joseph III had passed away, this action became a bone of contention for fundamentalist members who could not understand the "retirement" of a prophet of God. Smith appointed his son, Wallace B. (Bunnell) Smith to succeed him as prophet and president of the church. Wallace B. Smith proved a dynamic leader with controversy following his every step. He countered increasing dissension in the church with administrative verve, supporting change that some saw as ultimately Zionic but others viewed as a godless liberal drift.

The most divisive RLDS change under the new leadership was an affirmative vote by church delegates in 1984 to accept a revelation of Wallace B. Smith calling for the ordination of women to the RLDS priesthood (*Book of Doctrine* 1989:156:9; RLDS 1984:330–34). This move instigated dissent never faced before. Many took the changes in stride, faithfully believing that a new kind of Zionic presence was coming about in Independence, but others felt the latest moves clashed with tradition. These latter fundamentalists eschewed the liberal divergence of the RLDS Church. They usually called their congregations "Restoration Branches" and added an entirely different retro-view to the Latter Day Saint mix of attitudes toward Zion.

An example of debate between mainstream and fundamentalist RLDS beliefs revolves around the use of church lands and resources in Jackson County. The RLDS Church holds a total of about 12,500 acres in Missouri, Iowa, and Kansas ("Church Contracts for Plan" 1989:30). About 9,000 are in Jackson County. The church purchased most of these lands in the 1930s but announced in the early 1990s plans for the development of what appeared to be an ordinary suburban community in eastern Jackson County on about 2,700 acres—but according to Zionic ideals (see Figure 34; "Church Contracts for Plan" 1989:29–30; McGuire 1991). In the development process, much of the land would be either leased or sold. The plan, overseen by private developers, was along a stretch of the edge of the Little Blue River floodplain.

These real estate plans have been one cause for contention among the fundamentalist RLDS groups, who have viewed RLDS proposals for the land as less than millennial. Another thorn appeared in 1995 when the RLDS Church–controlled Community Water Company announced the sale of its water plant and water rights in the Atherton bottoms area of northeastern Jackson County to Kansas City for $3 million. This time, fundamentalist church members were not the only people alarmed by church decision. Officials from Independence, Blue Springs, and Lee's Summit expressed frustration and surprise, as they feared the hegemony of Kansas City into Independence affairs. While expressing concern for the "stewardship of the land and what is under the land," the board chairman of Community Water still saw Kansas City's offer as the soundest business decision ("Eastern Jackson County" 1995). For the mainstream RLDS Church, such decisions are viewed as conventional business practice. Fundamentalists, however, see the RLDS Church as gaining profit from sacred lands that should be reserved for millennial purposes. Twelve years after the sales plans were originally announced, however, the church had yet to sell the land (R. Price 2001c). Since the concern is of break-off fundamentalist RLDS groups, this story is revisited in the next chapter.

An RLDS Temple at the Center Place

Since the mid-1960s, the RLDS Church has supported the concept of a new temple to be built close to the traditional Temple Lot. In the view of faithful RLDS adherents, this temple combines the best of the New Jerusalem tradition with modern tendencies of the church to halt internal dissent rooted in the 1984 decision to allow women in the priesthood. Another reason for the temple was to make a favorable impression on other American denominations. The RLDS Temple is the most visible landscape element of doctrinal change in the church.

In an attempt to refocus RLDS attention on Independence as the center place, W. Wallace Smith began to hint of new construction in Zion in 1966 when he wrote that "Zionic procedures should be applied more fully than hitherto," so that the purposes of the Lord could "be achieved more fully even now" (*Book of Doctrine* 1989:148:9a). The RLDS Church at a General Conference accepted the following writing of W. W. Smith two years later. It was the first time an RLDS prophet had spoken of a temple in a document presented as revelation:

> The time has come for a start to be made toward building my temple in the Center Place. It shall stand on a portion of the plot of ground set apart for this purpose many years ago by my servant Joseph Smith, Jr. The shape and character of the building is to conform to ministries which will be carried out within its walls. These functions I will reveal through my servant the prophet and his counselors from time to time as need for more specific direction arises. (*Book of Doctrine* 1989:149:6a)

The paragraph is instructive of the evolving RLDS perception of sacred space on at least two major points. First, this document seems to be a default admission that since the RLDS Church could not obtain the original dedication spot from the Church of Christ (Temple Lot), divine injunction now permitted its construction on RLDS land nearby. The RLDS Church had earlier failed to acquire Joseph Smith's Temple Lot through legal means, so the temple instead would "stand on a portion of the plot" of sixty-three acres that Edward Partridge had purchased for the early church (Howard 1987). Second, that "the shape and character of the building" would conform "to the ministries . . . within its walls," indicated that Joseph Smith's earlier experiments with multiple structures at the site were no longer in force. Any direct reference to the early plans was decidedly avoided. The phrase also showed a rejection of the Nauvoo temple practices inherited by the LDS Church and taken west.

Further instruction about the temple was presented to the church in 1968 only four days after the document above. This revelatory addendum distinguished the proposed RLDS Temple from rival LDS "Mormon" temples by emphasizing that its full and complete use was yet to be revealed but that there was no provision for secret ordinances, now or ever. The edifice would, however, provide instructional opportunities that would necessarily be restricted to particular priesthood offices (*Book of Doctrine* 1989:149A:6). Another revelation, written in 1972, demonstrated that it was up to the RLDS Church to decide the exact location (not decided at the time) and even the purpose of the temple (*Book of Doctrine* 1989:150:8). Apparently, such matters would not all be revealed through an RLDS prophet; rather, the leadership and membership should decide together.

Seashells and Temples

RLDS preparation for a temple in Independence culminated through the 1980s. Wallace B. Smith's controversial revelation of 1984 mentioned that the planning for the temple should "continue at an accelerated rate" since there was "great need of the spiritual awakening" that would take place "within its walls" (*Book of Doctrine* 1989:156:3). Purposes of the proposed structure were defined as the amplification of RLDS priesthood; the pursuit of peace; the reconciliation and healing of the spirit; the strengthening of faith for witnessing, fostering wholeness of body, mind, and spirit; and the healing and redeeming agent as inspired by the life of Christ. The structure was to be "an ensign to the world of the breadth and depth of the devotion of the Saints" (*Book of Doctrine* 1989:156:4–5, 6).

The emphasis on reconciliation, healing, and wholeness is notable. In light of the fundamentalist backlash that the RLDS Church was beginning to endure, the words are apropos. At its inception, the temple idea was more to ameliorate divisiveness than to welcome back Jesus Christ. Wallace B. Smith even admitted, "We are not building our temple as a means of signaling the Second Coming" (Howe 1990:E1). Though the temple may help "to prepare worshipers for Christ's return," the church has stressed that the main purpose of the structure is to encourage peace and to foster an attitude of wholeness (Spillman 1990:14). "Indeed . . . the church no longer carries the same burden of expectations regarding the immediacy of the millennial reign" that the early church had (Temple Project Committee 1987:7). Some mainstream RLDS members still retain millennial ideals, but others began to reject millennialist talk altogether. The temple plan seemed to represent a path of compromise between fundamentalism and a certain extreme of Protestant liberalism.

At the time of the 1986 conference, internal division was mounting. Through revelation, Wallace B. Smith pleaded with members to stay true to the faith, pointing out how some had been "fearful and reluctant to trust in the instructions" given. As a consequence, it was written, "some had faltered" (*Book of Doctrine* 1989:157:13a). In 1987, a $60 million RLDS fundraising campaign was begun for the temple (Potter 1988), $35 million of which was to be spent on parking redesign, landscaping, and the temple itself, and the other $25 million to be used for a temple endowment fund to provide needy members with opportunities to visit Independence and to finance studies of peace and instruction. RLDS members were encouraged to pledge donations to the RLDS Church Temple Fund; assuming an active church population of 225,000, the amount needed per church member came, at least, to a hefty $267.[1] Considering the substantial splintering within the church, the donation per capita was even higher.

A revelation reported at the 1988 conference stated that the temple should be prepared even at great sacrifice "as a shining symbol of my love and my desires" (*Book of Doctrine* 1989:157:8–9). Costs rose after the early projections, but the church reported that by April 1991, 72 percent of the funds necessary had been received and 38 percent had been expended ("Temple Fund Progress" 1991:4).

The first architectural rendering of the RLDS Temple was presented to the public in September 1988.[2] The structure was to be a 340-foot-tall logarithmic spiral, an image taken from spiral forms found in nature, such as "the nautilus seashell, the DNA molecule, and the cosmic spirals of the galaxies" (Figure 36; Potter 1988:A1; "Temple Design Announced" 1988). In this quasi-scientific mode, Wallace B. Smith called the design "a

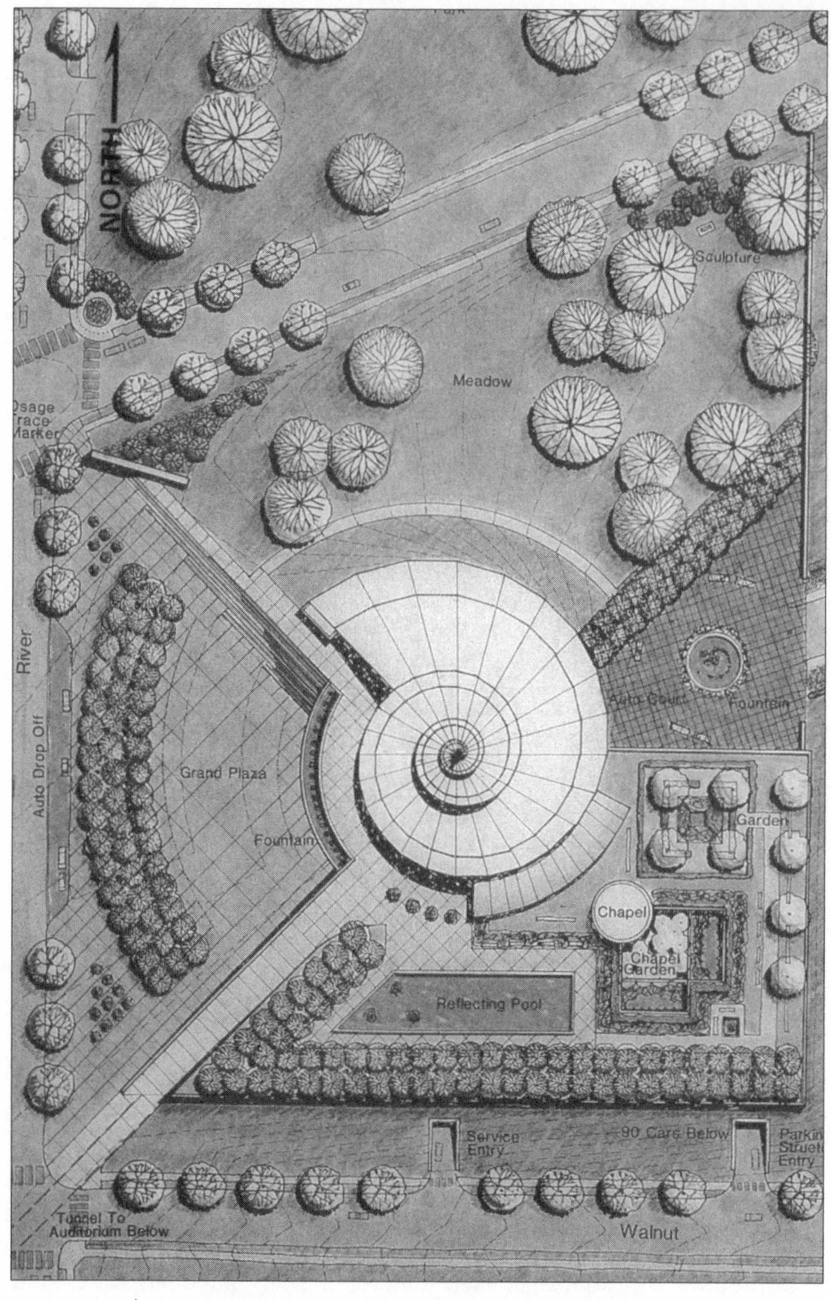

FIG. 36 | *The RLDS Temple as a nautilus. Reprinted, by permission, from "Temple Design Announced" (1988).*

✯ FIG. 37 | *The RLDS temple, announced September 1988. Reprinted, with permission, from* The Temple: Ensign of Peace *(1990).*

timeless expression of God's creative energy" (Figure 37; Potter 1988:A1). Built to exceed by 25 percent Independence zoning requirements for earthquake stress, the temple was to stand through "the centuries," verbally equaling Brigham Young's declaration over one hundred years earlier that the LDS Salt Lake Temple would stand "through the millennium" ("Temple Sanctuary Construction" 1990:26; "Temple Stone to Be Granite" 1990:30).

With the increasingly progressive stance of the RLDS Church, however, new symbolism for the temple was evident. The seashell spiral not only has been a traditional symbol of cycles in nature and the eternities,[3] but also a strong feminine emblem. In Africa and the ancient Mediterranean, worship of the Magda Mater among early Romans was common;

her importance may have later been retained in the Virgin Mary (Jordan 1996:83). Seashells have long stood as tokens of this ancient earth goddess who often represented death. The shapes of the spiral conch and the cowrie, in particular, resemble female reproductive organs and have been used for centuries in paintings, at gravesites, and in other religious decoration to symbolize the "rebirth of the dead" (Jordan 1982:21–25).

Consciously or not, such symbolism fits the evolving RLDS scene. With the RLDS Church now offering the traditionally male roles of the priesthood to women, the seashell analogy is meaningful. Even Wallace B. Smith emphasized such a connection with words given at the groundbreaking ceremony for the temple in April 1990. After discussing the logarithmic spiral form found in "so many seashells and of the myriad other examples . . . in nature," Smith invoked the feminine, saying, "I was prompted recently to think again of the spiral as I held one of my granddaughters in my arms. As I looked at the soft golden down on her head, I noticed once more the spiral in the crown of her hair. She was so beautiful and perfect—I felt a joy I could hardly contain" (Smith 1990:7).

Since Wallace B. Smith has only daughters, some members speculated that he was anticipating a future nomination of a daughter or granddaughter to the role of prophet. Such an event would have been the epitome of liberal trends but did not occur—at least not yet. In other RLDS literature, the gender issue has arisen as well. A rhetorical question was raised as to whether the significance of the new temple should emphasize the authority of individuals, following the "male pattern," or the more social situations of "typically female" interactions (Brown 1990a:8). The rhetorical answer delicately danced around the issue, saying that the RLDS Temple should be used in a "social rather than a private way" (Brown 1990a:8; Mische 1990:14–15). That the church would build a "temple at the same time that the ministerial roles of priesthood have been opened to women" is not a coincidence but rather a natural step for some RLDS believers (Brown 1990a:10).

The increase in politically correct discussions on gender included perceptions of deity, which caused much discussion—and backlash. As the RLDS Church decided to change its name, it adopted one particular hymn, "Bring Many Names," in which the nature of God is referred to in a variety of symbolic ways, such as "Strong Mother God" and "Old Aching God." The hymn has been referred to as "all inclusive" and reinforces the church's openness to gender issues, brushing God's feminine traits.

Joseph Smith Jr.'s original account stated that God *the father* and Jesus Christ originally appeared to Joseph Smith in bodily form, so this

Fig. 38 | *The shell as a new symbol for the RLDS Church:* a, b, *stylized nautilus symbols;* c, *jewelry as advertised in the Herald House catalog. Illustrations courtesy of Herald House Publishing and the Community of Christ.*

expression is quite untraditional. Accordingly, fundamentalist RLDS members have decried the trend—and the hymn—and have rejected its symbolism (R. Price 2001a:4). At the very least, its use shows an alignment with more liberal Protestantism, as the hymn is used by and has been the subject of sermons in the United Methodist Church, Unitarian-Universalist Congregations, and the United Church of Christ (for examples, see McIntyre 2001; Hoyt 2000; Baer 1998).

With the church's publishing house selling an assortment of chambered nautilus jewelry and loyal RLDS women wearing seashell print dresses

(Monsees 1990:5), it seems the RLDS Church with its new temple has created a powerful new symbol (Figure 38; *Temple Endowment Fund* 1992; *World Conference* 1992; "Herald House Inventory" 1990–91:back page). Only time will tell in what direction this imagery will take the church.

The Temple Journey

The appearance, imagery, and feel of the RLDS temple have been carefully created to avoid comparison with LDS temples. Conversely, the LDS Church does not like to refer to the new RLDS structure as a temple at all, preferring "headquarters buildings" instead (Baugh 2001:47). Whereas LDS temples, with their rites and ordinances, can be viewed as descending in function from the 1840s Nauvoo temple, the RLDS temple is not grounded in that heritage. It carries a "separate meaning" (Howard 1991:10). In historical comparison, the new RLDS temple has some similarity to the prototype 1830s Kirtland temple, which was not used for specific ordinances or rites. Mormon temples emphasize priesthood rites for the dead, which both men and women perform, with an emphasis on tying together past generations into one huge family unit. Through a process of interviews and the issue of an official "recommend," adult LDS members in active church standing are permitted entry to one of many temples as an ultimate step in spiritual growth; others cannot enter. In contrast, the RLDS Church will not "restrict access and participation [to] those lacking proper credentials or worthiness." Since everyone can freely enter the RLDS temple, it has been labeled as not only "sacred space" but also publicly "usable space" ("Temple Rises" 1991:19).

One RLDS author wrote "surely the [RLDS] Temple should be the one place open to all people so they can come deliberately into the presence of divinity" (Brown 1990a:8). In the LDS temple endowment, after one has to prove him- or herself worthy of entry he or she undergoes a symbolic progression from the presence of God in the Garden of Eden, out into the bleak world, and finally into the presence of God once again. The RLDS temple endowment, on the other hand, is to be more of an inner experience of divine grace than an outward ritual. In the RLDS temple, however, divinity is not seen as literally as in LDS idiom. Whereas LDS members often speak of Christ actually coming and inspecting Mormon temples, the RLDS temple helps members come to grips with a more abstract "Christ that lives within us" (Higdon 1991:16).

In the new experience of temple building, as with the historical treatment of other themes such as polygamy, the RLDS Church continually disassociates itself from its larger Utah cousin. Inside the RLDS temple in Independence, events can be compared only loosely with those of LDS temples. A "worshipers path" representing the walk through life prepares the visitor for the divine and is somewhat reminiscent of the life stages symbolized in Japanese gardens (*Temple: Dedicated* n.d.). The path begins at the immense foyer of the complex and contains artwork that, among other things, commemorates Joseph Smith's vision in upstate New York; so church history has not been entirely abandoned (Tyree 1991:6). The dimly lit path is followed along a semicircle that displays a cross as well as an inspirational sculpture and fountain.[4] The path brightens as the visitor ascends one complete story until the curving ramp finally meets the main sanctuary, seating 1,800 (*Temple: Dedicated* n.d.). Here the gaze is drawn into the disappearing shadows of the impressive overhead spiral, "which may remind us of our belief in revelation and the prophetic function" (Tyree 1991:6). Just as one in the LDS temple journey finally ends up back in the celestial presence of God, the RLDS journey likewise brings the pedestrian to a culmination, albeit a strikingly organic one. Arriving at the womblike main sanctuary is like entering a giant nautilus; looking up into the two-hundred-foot spiral is at once dizzying and awe inspiring (see McGuire 1992). After the worship service, the path leads the visitor to an exit decorated with a stained-glass window portraying a field ready to harvest, which conveys the importance of RLDS missionary work. Out of doors, a large map on the floor of the cement plaza meets the traveler on the temple's west side, adjacent the Temple Lot (Tyree 1991:10). The map invites members to take the message of peace throughout the globe no matter how divided the RLDS Church at Independence becomes ("A People Who Seek Peace" 1992). Each day of the year, a prayer of peace is offered in the temple, and most focus on individual countries ("Daily Prayer" 2003). For example, on July 4, 2001, the prayer for peace was for the United States.

New Meanings for the Temple Lot

Though the RLDS temple structure is a rounded spiral in shape, its ornate main courtyard still faces the land of the original Temple Lot. The plaza of the "new" temple grounds thus pays symbolic homage to the earlier lot, as

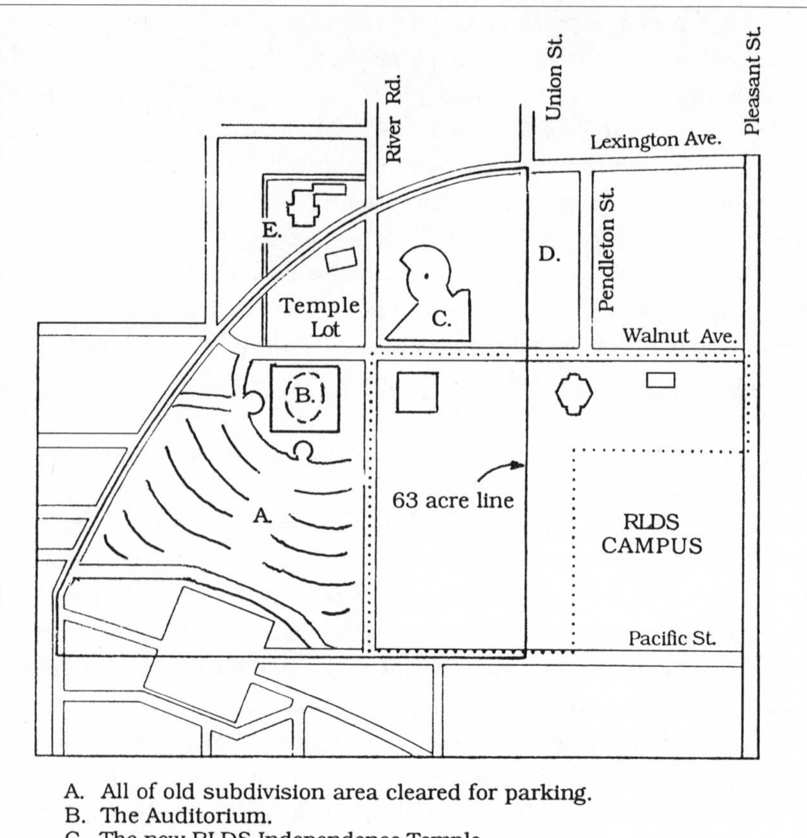

FIG. 39 | *The RLDS realm, 2000.*

do both the Auditorium and the old Stone Church. Since the original Temple Lot could not be obtained, the church maintains that the Lord has shifted sacred space slightly eastward and that this temple is the culmination of revelatory events from the time of Joseph Smith, but this amazing structure carries little millennial meaning. The traditional Temple Lot remains historically sacred, but little more. The position of the RLDS Church toward the Temple Lot is, therefore, rather ambiguous. On the one hand, the new RLDS Independence temple location replaces the old Temple Lot. On the other hand, the Temple Lot is surrounded by RLDS

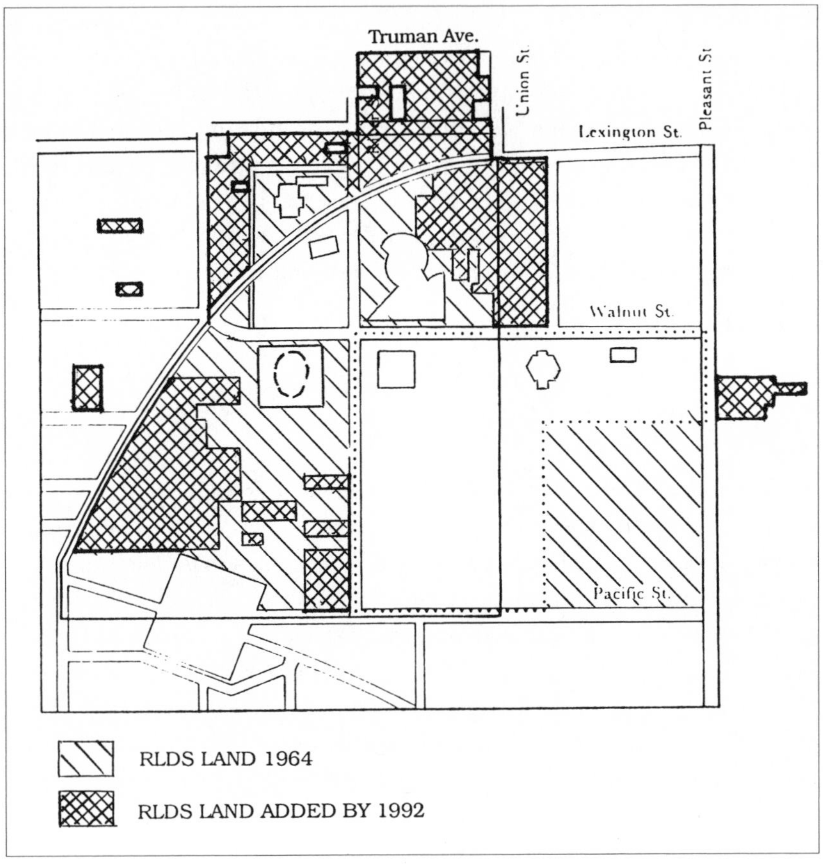

FIG. 40 | *RLDS landholding increases in the Temple Lot vicinity, 1964–92. Data from Tax Assessor's Office, Jackson County Courthouse, Dyer (1976), and Jenkins (1990).*

land, the Church of Christ headquarters is surrounded on three sides by RLDS structures, and the Temple Lot appears ever more besieged (Figure 39). The RLDS presence completely upstages the tiny Temple Lot Church. Notably, this is also the only place in the world where the LDS Church is visibly less dominant than the RLDS Church, for even in Kirtland the LDS presence is growing with the Nauvoo-like development of Kirtland Village.

In the new RLDS view of the Temple Lot area, dominance indeed seems to be a major goal. Since the announcement of the Independence temple, the church has steadily purchased lots around the central sacred zone. It now owns a nearly contiguous two-block tract directly north of the new temple site and some lots to the northwest and east.[5] These land-holdings represent a substantial increase from 1930 and show that the church has put considerable effort into consolidating territory from a number of private owners (Figure 40). A few of these lots have been cleared. The church may be aiming to increase the grassy open setting found in the vicinity of the traditional Temple Lot. While rejecting doctrinal origins, the RLDS Church is intensifying its landscape influence surrounding the Temple Lot.

A Whirlwind of Change

In many of the latest RLDS writings, members as well as leaders have expressed mixed reactions to the sweeping change around Zion (Brock 1990:10). Alterations inside the RLDS Church have paralleled the pace of certain evolving American cultural values and even global political transformation, and the change is alternately viewed as instigated by God or as out of control. The new temple is the most visible element of this change, and even President Wallace B. Smith expressed uncertainty about the church's direction when he said that the temple "has a life of its own and a future we cannot fully predict" (Smith 1990:7).

One prominent church editor, Richard A. Brown, wrote a comparison of past and present RLDS temple beliefs that shows just how radical doctrinal changes have been in recent decades. He stated that his childhood view during the late 1950s was based on a literal return of Jesus Christ to an RLDS temple that would be located on the traditional Temple Lot. As a child, he had been taught that the heathen nations would recognize, finally, that the RLDS Church should rightfully be put in charge of everything because "we possessed the one true and now restored faith" with the priesthood power and authority lacking in all other churches (Brown 1991:50–51). In forty years Brown's beliefs changed radically. He wrote that he had since accepted the possibility of a "cosmic presence" of Christ in the new temple. Regarding previous millennial beliefs, he wrote, "I no longer look for the Second Coming in such a narrow, literal way. My beliefs changed, partly because I have since rejected that apocalyptic and millennialist panorama. It conflicts with too many basic scientific realities" (51). His thought was that the temple would stand merely as a figurative, even secular, spiritual center for a Zion encompassing all the globe, a belief that is becoming increasingly common (Smith 1992a:11). Brown's new way of thought perfectly summarizes the extremes of a continuum across which the RLDS Church has traveled and the stark dichotomy that now exists between itself and all other Latter Day Saint churches. The question raised is "How does a church transform its basic worldview from firmly millenarian to largely secular?" If there is an answer, it must be "With much dissent." In the temple school's curriculum, many classes are offered on Christ, peace, and administration, but the closest one to a millennial theme is entitled "HI 201: Latter Twentieth Century: The Church and Challenge" ("Latter Twentieth Century" 1998).

This is a challenge to Underwood's thesis that the Latter Day Saints are, overall, premillennial in chiliastic approach. The western LDS Church is still premillennial, if subdued about the imminence of such events. Some of the smaller groups have tended to become more millennial with the passing of time. The RLDS Church overall is no longer overtly millenarian, though many members still are and complain the church has joined a liberal ecumenical Protestant bandwagon. Yet historically, it still straddles a great fence and is having trouble advertising the extremes of a "mainstream Christian belief . . . with a unique history."

Many RLDS adherents have not abandoned millennial stances, and the contrast between the viewpoints of, say, the 1950s with the 1990s is startling. As a result of such change, and out of necessity, the word *paradigm* has become important on the RLDS scene (Young 1990). Total doctrinal overhaul is mollified and justified through the positive connotations of a quasi-scientific word. Moreover, the RLDS transformation is ongoing, and its liberal stance becomes more pronounced with every new conference resolution (Wenske 1990a). For example, at the 1992 General Conference, an investigation was endorsed to study whether the church should continue to rebaptize members who had previously been members of other churches (RLDS 1992:324–25); a radical departure for a Latter Day Saint church. Many members no longer saw the need for literalist millenarian precepts such as Joseph Smith as original prophet, ongoing revelation, or the *Book of Mormon* as scripture. Fundamentalists, however, view these as steps along a trail of wickedness leading to complete apostasy of the original RLDS organization.

The tradition of a descendant of Joseph Smith Jr. as prophet of the RLDS Church has also ceased. Wallace B. Smith retired in 1996, and at his suggestion, W. Grant McMurray, a non-Smith, was approved as church president. Since Wallace B. Smith had only daughters, speculation had been that the successor might be female. The church did, however, call two female apostles in 1998 (Gray 1995; McCleary 1998). The church has stated that having a Smith as president was a wonderful tradition but was not doctrine, and President McMurray, in true nonmillenarian direction, resists being called a prophet. For the fundamentalist RLDS member, the change to a nonlineal descendant as president was an additional straw added to the camel's back (Launius 1996:1–2).

The New Name: Millenarian vs. Secular

In 1992, another resolution recommended changing the church's name (RLDS 1992:328). Several names had been discussed, but through the mid-1990s the name World Church had become prominent. In 1999, this name appeared at least forty times on the official RLDS Web site (RLDS 1999). On April 7, 2000, out of 2,540 General Conference church delegates, 78 percent approved a name change from the Reorganized Church of Jesus Christ of Latter Day Saints to Community of Christ (Naylor 2000). The change was made official exactly one year later with the introduction of new signage and a new Web site (McFarland 2001).

The name change has caused some soul searching, not to mention what might happen among membership represented by the 561 delegates—22 percent—who voted not to adopt the new name. For members, a certain relief has arrived, which hopefully will give a reprieve from having to clarify "who they are not" in comparison with the LDS Church. One supporter complained that she always had to explain the name "Reorganized," which admittedly covers a convoluted doctrinal history, and begged the question of whether the church from 1830 to 1860 was either unorganized or disorganized. According to church leaders, the new name is more representative of the church's new direction and global orientation, since the name Reorganized Church of Jesus Christ of Latter Day Saints was extremely difficult to translate in many languages, much less to understand (Curtright 2001).

Though many have an emotional connection to the RLDS name, members are attracted to the idea that the new name emphasizes a group of Christians, an important concept, as some have claimed the western Mormons are not ("Sharing Our New Name" 2001). Though the new name aids in avoiding difficult explanation, this seems to many RLDS members a whitewash of a very complex church history whose identity and distinction cannot, ultimately, be so easily simplified. This is most glaringly true when considering the Independence temple, whose meaning as a sacred place for the CoC (the new acronym) has become less millennial and more vague. Former RLDS church historian Richard Howard made this pointedly evident in a church document openly investigating the boundaries that cannot be ignored in the adoption of the new name—boundaries between mainline Christianity, Mormonism, and Zionic principles (Howard 2001).

The CoC's position at a crossroads was shown in "Prayer for a New Name," a telling poem published on the church Web site. The poem reveals the CoC's position as perfect reflection of doctrine, history, and geography intersecting in one church. The first part of the poem calls on deity in a rather distant way, then reviews early church history:

> "You, who are nameless, have named us and called us your own.
> We have heard you in the rustling leaves of a grove,
> the trek of rumbling oxcart,
> sweeping skirts on a frozen river,
> martyr's blood, the tears of widows.

The poem continues with the theme of the renaming of the RLDS Church:

> We have heard your voice in swirling temple stones
> and calls to transformation, calls to journey forward,
> building on what has been, while straining for what's to be.
> Always moving, always calling.
> Many names, but the same call.
> We hear you this morning blessing us with a new, yet old name—
> a name to which we have *always* responded,
> the name of your Son, Jesus.

Then the poem treads into quasi-millennial territory, which is very strange considering liberal secular trends. The author quotes Revelation 3:12:

> *"I will make you a pillar in the temple of my God;*
> *you will never go out of it.*
> *I will write on you the name of my God,*
> *and the name of the city of my God,*
> *the new Jerusalem that comes down from my God out of heaven,*
> *and my own new name."*
>
> (Belrose 2001:21)

The temple must be interpreted as the RLDS temple, yet what of the New Jerusalem? If the RLDS Church is abandoning millennial themes to bridge the gap to other Protestant churches, what becomes of the millennial city in the poem? The "appearance" of the "new Jerusalem" may simply be seen as the social establishment of peace and joy among community members. If this is so, then developing the city of God is a gradual process, perhaps in the same gradual Zionic sense of social planning that the church had been encouraging over the past one hundred years. On the other hand, the invocation of Revelation provides an imminent millennial twist or a retroactive appeal to a millenarian state that happens to be a remarkable justification for renaming the church. In this case, however, perhaps the millenarian emphasis should not be overstated. Most likely, the wording is simply symbolic of the ideological boundaries of the CoC, similar to other nonmillennial approaches of liberal Protestantism. Only millenarians read such words literally, so the CoC and the LDS approaches are bifurcating across an ever-widening ideological gulf, where the two remain friendly in historical perspective but can never come to terms on doctrine or geography. With regard to Independence, the CoC faces a paradox perhaps of greater magnitude than the LDS Church. It has strengthened its presence around the core of the sixty-three-acre parcel while speeding away from the original premillennial significance of the land as fast as it can.

The sales of varied church properties, such as RLDS Herald House (the church's traditional press), Independence Sanitarium, and the old RLDS Crossroads shelter, besides the lands and water rights mentioned earlier, mark a new era where the church sells real estate to focus on its central building campaign (Graceland 1997a; Haight 1999; Cramer 1999). Such a loosening of traditional standards seems typical of the doctrinal shift to the left and is alarming to the remaining fundamentalist and premillenarian members who see the RLDS Church as divesting itself of the Zion it long struggled to build.

Most CoC members view the changes as spiritual—within the norm of democratic church procedure. Brown wrote that the church had "benefited" from its "uncertain path." In his view, "the church for the sake of Christ has lost its life in order to find it" (Brown 1990b: 13, 16). Distinct histories and stories are in the balance, but the change is overwhelming and the gap between millenarian breakaway fundamentalist RLDS and the new nonmillennial CoC is as wide as the traditional gap between RLDS and the western LDS Church. With such a gulf of separation, the CoC/ fundamentalist rift will never be mended and is another Latter Day Saint paradox at the center place.

A note on the views of fundamentalist Christians toward these traditions should be made as well. The Latter Day Saint movement has an approach to Christianity that includes elements foreign especially to most Protestants (extra scripture, revelation, prophets, twelve apostles, angelic visits, etc.). Many fundamentalist Christian groups specifically preach to "save the works obsessed" Latter Day Saints who are seen as led by "false prophets" who teach "false doctrines." In a way, it is ironic and, in another, expected, that the efforts to make the RLDS Church more "progressive" do not meet with their approval. It is ironic because the CoC aspires to become a liberal Protestant organization in many ways, and it is expected because outsiders will never see the church as traditional Christianity. One such organization, called "Refiner's Fire Ministries" published a Web page "alert": "They began on April 6, 1830, by rejecting the Christian Church. Beginning April 6, 2001, they want to appear as one. Don't be fooled. They're still Latter Day Saints" (Refiner's Fire Ministries 2001).

Many letters from RLDS members to the *Saints' Herald* have openly debated the change in church direction.[6] Though the church seems to have had little problem raising money for the structure, some RLDS members did not fully back the idea of the new temple, the most visible landscape marker of change. Members familiar with church history are fully aware that this version has no similarity to Joseph Smith Jr.'s early plans. Smith's view of the New Jerusalem in Missouri was as millennial utopia, and his temple plans evolved into a complex of several separate buildings of different general and priesthood functions. The early temple was to prepare the gathering Saints for the Second Coming of Christ at the optimal central settlement location in the United States between Anglo and Native, and it was the first proposal for a temple of any kind. Subsequent temple proposals by different Latter Day Saint churches are outgrowths of this initial step, but officially the RLDS temple is nonmillenarian and nearly nonutopian. Though some CoC members believe one large structure in many ways fits the needs of contemporary Latter Day Saints better than the original proposal of many small ones (Romig 1990), one RLDS woman in the early 1990s told me that the church was "grasping at straws with this temple." Indeed, many have seen it as too wild a structure for God's humble people. Many who have rejected CoC ways see the new temple as one more step toward the desacralization of traditional sacred space (Smith 1992a:11).

Contrasting with the official view of secular peace and reconciliation, discussion on Graceland College's Internet bulletin board revealed desire among some RLDS members to fit the temple into millennial expectations.

At best, the impressive spiral was seen as an architectural wonder whose functions parallel the original Kirtland temple as a "house of learning" where basic ordinances such as "washing of feet" would be performed. At worst it was seen as a structure without a purpose, some believing that the Lord would one day reveal a use for the building (Graceland 1997a, 1997b). If fundamentalist-minded members do not come around to the vague, internal, and symbolic style of nonmillenarian Protestantism, the temple will never carry any meaning for them. "Millenarian-literalist" and "nonmillenarian-secular" are views in opposition with no point of reference for easy mutual understanding.

One prominent RLDS scholar, Roger Launius, expressed near alarm that the new temple, "a symbol of the Reorganization's roots in Mormonism[,] . . . will be built by and for the people who have rid the church of whatever few reasons it ever had to build a temple" (Launius 1996:50–51). The new spiral is sometimes graphically, and ominously, referred to as the "tip of the iceberg" (Brown 1990b:16). Still, the debate is typical of the openness and diversity of RLDS liberal thought; myriad ideas are freely expressed, and pluralism of thought, for better or worse, is the norm (Tyree 1990).

During the April 1992 RLDS General Conference, one tour guide for the new temple expressed his feeling that it represented Zion being built and how workers of all types toiled in unity to complete the great spiral structure. The imagery was ironic since that same day the church had approved an "inspired document" from Wallace B. Smith that dwelt on the problems of "divisions, separations, reductions in participation, and limited resources" that had "jeopardized the vigor of . . . the church" (Smith 1992:319).[7] Other descriptives such as "setbacks," "discouragement," "anguish," and "uncertainties" were scattered throughout the document. The gloomiest revelation ever received by an RLDS prophet, the document shows the increasing pressures of dissent and its effect on the church. Since 1992 the CoC has not so much sought "reconciliation" as it has a doctrinal freeway toward liberal transformation.

Desanctifying Space

The RLDS Church in the twentieth century has reversed direction from a millenarian and literal theology toward a more diverse nonmillennial doctrinal atmosphere. This movement has been influenced by democratic church tendencies, ecumenical pressures, the tradition of higher education among the leadership, and the ever widening geographical base of the membership. The fundamentalist backlash has only served to increase the liberalization of the church. The result has been a more diffuse and decidedly less Latter Day Saint orientation. Architecturally, the new temple is a marvel and widely admired, so much so that talk has ceased of the "regions round about," highly pondered as gathering sites by Joseph Smith III and Frederick M. Smith. No current RLDS issues revolve around gathering anywhere, much less to areas once seen as important "safety valves" to church population in Independence. The Reorganized Saints never emphasized Adam-ondi-Ahman, doctrine perceived as developing after Joseph Smith Jr. had "fallen" as a prophet. Far West is only mentioned in historical retrospect as a previous headquarters of the early church. A few Missouri and Kansas congregations are sometimes mentioned, but except for the continued prominence of Graceland College, even Lamoni, Iowa, once the center of the RLDS Zion, is much diminished in emphasis.

Kenneth Foote (1997, 179) has discussed how the sanctification of space involves "a ritual process in which sacred sites are delimited and consecrated." While other Latter Day Saint groups have had difficulty sanctifying space in Independence, in many ways the nonmillennialization of the Temple Lot area is the opposite. The CoC is desanctifying space, perhaps because, consciously or unconsciously, it feels the history of the Saints, especially Missouri history, is too difficult to reconcile with modern culture trends. Thus a change has transpired either to a more acceptable liberal religious organization or something completely different—a result vaguely Latter Day Saint but too disjointed to be mainstream Protestant. Yet the new seashell symbolism is unprecedented in the church's history. The form of the temple, with all its organic feel and cues of gender equality, adds a new dimension and new strength to the CoC. With fundamentalists gone, perhaps the church can forge a new and distinct direction. If one looks beyond the substantial dissent, the church has created for itself novel and powerful meanings for the twenty-first century. But these are far from traditional Latter Day Saint symbolism.

Narrow Views of Zion and Anti-Zion Space

> We find that the revelation refers to a certain spot. It does not say a great plot, a great portion of land, or large amount of land, but it refers to a spot, indicating . . . that it would be a very small place, and not a great tract of land as some have intimated it would.
>
> —Clarence Wheaton, Temple Lot apostle

The more prominent stories of the LDS and RLDS Zions at Independence have been told. Equally significant are the views of the smaller Latter Day Saint groups. These range from the Church of Christ (Temple Lot), which holds land of sacred importance in Independence, to groups ranging from a few hundred to only a few members and even one-person publishing concerns. Since this chapter discusses important new traditions developing among the Latter Day Saints, break-off groups of the RLDS Church are also examined.

The common thread that ties the groups in this chapter together is that of Latter Day Saint denominational underdog. Many of these smaller groups and churches feel bullied or overshadowed by the LDS Church and the CoC. The resulting views, though more limited in numbers of adherents, often approach oppression or paranoia. Some views go to extremes of apocalyptic negativism. Images of cleansing, purging, and destruction are more common to the smaller groups. In these scenarios, the "rich and corrupt" churches now at center stage will ultimately be destroyed. Many groups believe that a purge will eventually free historically sacred lands for pure and proper millennial inheritors.

The Temple Lot Church and Its Temple

The membership of the Church of Christ (Temple Lot) at the turn of the century was small, but it soon surged. In 1916, a decision was made that those who could demonstrate baptism with the early Saints could be accepted into the Church of Christ without rebaptism (Flint 1953: 134–35). The key was the definition of "early Saints," which was very loosely interpreted as the Church of Christ grew from two hundred members in 1915 to over four thousand in 1926. Many of the transferals lived in the Great Lakes states. Demonstrated in this growth were two schismatic trends. First, the Saints showed a vernacular desire to be as much a part of the Temple Lot territory as possible—it was a millenarian opportunity. Second, they came because of an early distrust of leftist authority and decision-making power of the RLDS organization, which was more peripheral to the Temple Lot (137–39). The exodus was a reflection on Frederick M. Smith's social policies and perhaps the questioned task of building the auditorium—a monumental structure *not on the Temple Lot*. The schism was as great in effect, proportionately, as the recent one in the RLDS realm. The effects on the little Church of Christ were at once wondrous and wrenching.

New growth, members' dreams, and revelations all combined to herald millenarian events at the Temple Lot during the 1920s. An example is a dream shared by one of the older members of the Church of Christ. In it was described a hewn dead tree, with new green sprouts emerging from an exposed stump at the Temple Lot. Symbolically the dead tree represented the RLDS Church and the new sprouts were the transferals of RLDS members to the Temple Lot group (Flint 1953:131, 139). Such living tree examples abound in the Latter Day Saint traditions, and this one presaged a fantastic growth from an interrupted beginning. The fantastic growth never occurred, though fantastic schism did. No "grafting" imagery was used, and the accuracy of vision could be questioned as the dead trunk could infer that the Church of Christ had its origin directly in the RLDS Church, which was not so. Nevertheless, the growth spurred the Temple Lot Church to publish a series of tracts in 1922 that exhibited premillennial expectation. Of these, three carried titles with millenarian themes: "The City of Zion," "The Building of the Temple," and "The Gospel and the Millennium of Christ" (137).

In February 1927, one of the Temple Lot Church's apostles, an RLDS transfer named Otto Fetting, living in Port Huron, Michigan, began to report chiliastic messages. Purportedly, he had received them from the resurrected John the Baptist, who Joseph Smith originally claimed had appeared to him and restored the Aaronic priesthood in 1829. John the Baptist is important doctrinally as the one who, teaching in the wilderness, prepared the way for the teachings of Jesus Christ (Evans 2001b). Thus John the Baptist was a logical choice as a messenger of a restored gospel, though in LDS eschatology, he lacked the higher priesthood.

The prevalent theme of these messages was a call for construction of the prophesied temple (see *Word of the Lord* 1988). Fetting's second message, written in 1927, was particularly prophetic and included a vision of people building that sacred structure. Fetting was shown the Temple Lot as if elevated and at the center of the troubled Americas, if not the world. He said he was taken "to the northeast corner of the Temple Lot and . . . [saw] men coming with their tools, going to the middle of the Temple Lot, laying their tools down. Some put on masons' clothes; others carpenters' aprons; but all were solemn and quiet and slowly they started to work on the Temple. . . . The work started very slowly but it began to grow. . . . To the west, the east, the north and the south, in the sky stood the figures in large letters, '1929'" (*Word of the Lord* 1988:2:4–5, 7).

The content is typical of the narrow spatial view maintained by the Temple Lot Church, where all things millennial would start at the important sacred spot and expand to cover an entire region. By the fifth message (*Word of the Lord* 1988:5) details of the temple's architecture were becoming clear. The main element was a patterning after the ancient temple of Solomon, even down to its exact measurements (Flint 1953:141; Smith 1930:173). As with the Old Testament design, the inside of the temple was to include an "outer court" that would seat 3,500 people (*Word of the Lord* 1988:5:8; Billeter 1946:135) and a holier inner court for sacred prayer and worship ("Plans of the Temple" 1930:170–71). Furthermore, since it reportedly took workers seven years to complete the temple of Solomon, the Saints of the Church of Christ (Temple Lot) were to construct their millennial edifice in the same amount of time (Smith 1930:174).

Adjustment, Precision, and Justification

The messages to Fetting from John the Baptist often used Old Testament scripture and imagery, which was unlike messages given for the more incremental, multiple usage structures of Joseph Smith Jr. The temple was described as a millennial center, "the seat of the government of God on earth, from which the law of the Lord shall go forth to all nations" (*Word of the Lord* 1988:8:5). The temple would be a "haven of rest" to the Saints, a spiritual school of knowledge. As described in Isaiah (4:5), a glorious "cloud" would rest upon the temple there, but only when the Saints were gathered within (*Word of the Lord* 1988:5:8, 12).

By November 1928, Fetting was told by John the Baptist to hire an architect to draft plans for the building (*Word of the Lord* 1988:8:4, 9:3). Soon after the first revelations were dictated, stakes were placed to mark the excavation, but a concern existed that the placement was incorrect, and the tenth message directed the stakes be reset ten feet farther westward on the Temple Lot, so the structure would "stand upon the place that has been pointed out by the Finger of God," presumably to Joseph Smith in 1831 (*Word of the Lord* 1988:10:2). Such a revision might have had the effect of solidifying support by implying the Lord was closely guiding the whole process.

The effects of nature were even considered in the messages. The tenth message called for the specific strengthening east to west of the porch cornice since "storms shall come from the southwest" (*Word of the Lord* 1988:10:5). On a number of occasions it was mentioned that the temple should be fireproof inside and out since "the world shall be cleansed by fire, by storms and by tempest. Satan shall destroy all he can by his power" (8:10; see also 10:5).

Ground was broken for the temple on April 6, 1929, just one year before the centennial of Joseph Smith's organization of the early church and according to the date seen in vision by Fetting two years earlier. In the course of excavation two marked stones were found. One was inscribed "1831" with what appear to be letters, their meaning uncertain. The other stone bore the inscription "SECT 1831." It has always been assumed by the Church of Christ that these were stones laid by Joseph Smith at the time of the original dedication of the Temple Lot and that their unearthing was divine intervention. This showed the precision of God's message through John the Baptist and showed the beginning of a new, though smaller, tradition of Latter Day Saint revelatory experience. Other Latter Day Saint churches have dismissed the stones as "planted."

Fetting's twelfth message carried seeds of dissent. It admonished rebaptism of the membership of the entire Church of Christ, ostensibly a protest against Temple Lot Church doctrine that members previously baptized into other Latter Day Saint groups could "transfer" without being redipped. Most Temple Lot members chafed at Fetting's new directive and the Church of Christ rejected rebaptism in the fall of 1929. Otto Fetting and another apostle named Walter Gates, however, began rebaptizing members and established their own church, so the first major Temple Lot Church schism occurred about the same time as the stock market's Black Friday (Bronson n.d.: 6; Flint 1953:142; Billeter 1946:145–46).

It was relatively easy to say that Fetting had fallen away, such was believed about Joseph Smith from about 1838 onward. Still, through about 1932 the Temple Lot Church remained enthusiastic about the idea of Fetting's temple and even hired an architect to elaborate on his descriptions. A number of detailed renderings were completed. Though the internal layout and functions of the building had been Hebrew inspired, the outward architecture was more rooted in nineteenth-century America; the design was Greek Revival. The structure would have eight columns around the porch, narrow windows, and parallel pilasters surrounding the building (Figure 41; Wilkinson 1930:167–68). The temple would completely dominate the Church of Christ's two-and-one-half-acre site, taking up about one-fourth of it (Figure 42).

After the departure of Fetting, however, and without adequate funds to even start the structure, excavation work halted. In 1936, through conference vote, the Church of Christ (Temple Lot) rejected all of Fetting's revelations (Flint 1953:143), and in the fall of 1943, with all financial hopes dashed, the official temple program was terminated (Billeter 1946: 146). For sixteen years the excavation site remained open to the elements and became an eyesore that the Church of Christ finally filled in 1946 (Wheaton 1972:9–10).[1]

Whereas much of the Latter Day Saint millenarian urge has been based on hardship and adversity, much of the millenarian Temple Lot speculation took place during the amazing ascendancy of the stock market through 1928 and most of 1929. The rise and fall of the Church of Christ's temple plan coincides well with this spectacular economic wave. Ground was broken for the temple by the Church of Christ near the peak of average stock prices. Schism was concurrent with the crash, and relations between Fetting backers and the main body of the Church of Christ deteriorated from that time.

Despite its official rejection of Fetting's revelations in 1936, the Church of Christ (Temple Lot) has maintained a belief in the building of the temple. The group owning the Temple Lot has remained dedicated to the Greek Revival design, contracted post Fetting in 1930, as the inspired manifestation of God's will (see Figure 41 and Figure 42). The sacred area

Fig. 41 | *The proposed temple of the Church of Christ (Temple Lot), based on Fetting's description. Reprinted, with permission, from the cover of* Zion's Advocate *7, no. 17 (1930).*

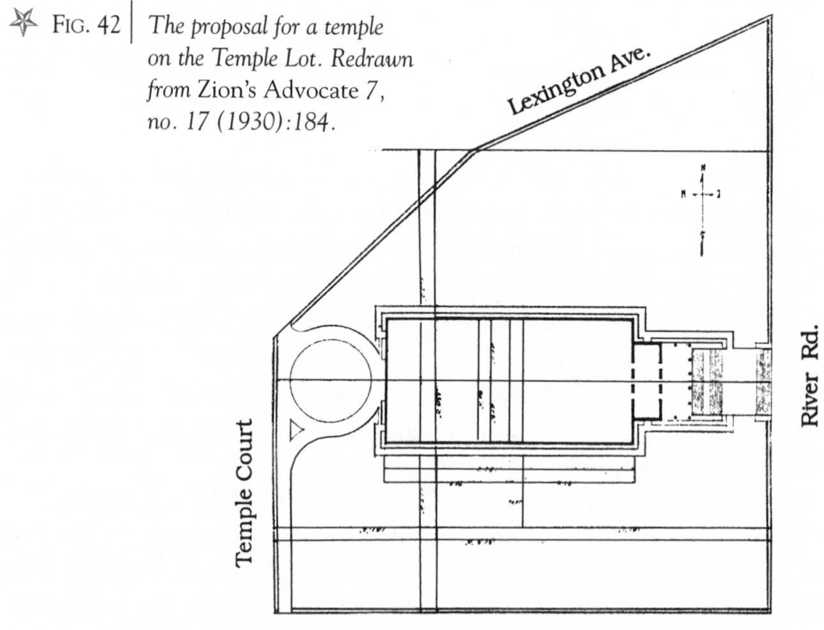

Fig. 42 | *The proposal for a temple on the Temple Lot. Redrawn from* Zion's Advocate *7, no. 17 (1930):184.*

for the temple, however, was never seen to be anything more than the two-and-one-half-acre Temple Lot. Throughout the years, the spatial (and doctrinal) view of the Temple Lot Church has been quite limited spatially; the sacred spot for the temple is to be nothing more than their two and one-half acres (Smith 1973:3). No spiritual or millennial importance is given to the sixty-three acres that Edward Partridge once purchased; this larger tract of land, now shared by the RLDS and LDS Churches, was simply a required purchase in order to obtain the smaller spot of dedication. The Temple Lot was basically a formation from the subdivisions of the 1850s, but Church of Christ members give no significance to the carving and purchase of the artificial lots. Elder Clarence L. Wheaton, an influential apostle in the Temple Lot Church, summarized the diminutive view in 1928. Wheaton said, "We find that [Joseph Smith Jr.'s] revelation refers to a certain spot. It does not say a great plot, a great portion of land, or large amount of land, but it refers to a spot, indicating by that it would be a very small place, and not a great tract of land as some have intimated it would. . . . Joseph Smith laid a cornerstone at the northeast corner of the contemplated temple. It does not say he dedicated 63 acres of land for the temple" (Wheaton 1928:4–5).

Elder Wheaton made a map of the area around the Temple Lot that reflected his attitude toward the other groups. RLDS lands were colored purple "as in the royal monarchy of Reorganized territory" (a reference to the RLDS tradition of a blood descendant of Joseph Smith as church president/prophet). LDS landholdings in the vicinity were red, colored for the "great blotch of apostasy of the brethren of the West" ("apostasy" likely a reference to polygamy; Wheaton 1928:6). The smaller Temple Lot parcel was colored green, as in evergreen and everlasting. Wheaton noted that red (LDS) could be turned easily to purple (RLDS), an indication that he feared RLDS more than LDS hegemony, but that all these colors could readily be turned to green if the different groups accepted the true way (Wheaton 1928:6). Sooner or later, Wheaton was sure that the other groups were bound to come over to the Temple Lot Church's point of view.

Fettingites

At least six churches today derive from Fetting's 1929 split from the Church of Christ (see appendix 4). Most carry on that body's basic organization but continue acceptance of Otto Fetting's thirty messages from John the Baptist as scripture. Some of these groups have since accepted additional divine messages. Among most of these groups the belief in the sacred spot for the temple has been carried on, so naturally a certain amount of friction has developed between the Temple Lot Church and its factions.

Fetting left the Temple Lot Church in 1929, taking 1,400 members, or approximately one-third of the Temple Lot Church's adherents (Melton 1989:580). After the divisive twelfth message on rebaptism, subsequent messages naturally assured the validity of the split. The thirteenth message read that only one "Church of Christ" existed, obviously led by Fetting, and that if the Temple Lot Church did not heed the messages, God would raise up another people to build the temple (*Word of the Lord* 1988:13:4, 6–7), an idea which is a common thread in most Temple Lot Church break-off groups who have headquartered themselves at some distance from the Temple Lot. Only days before Black Friday, a message to Fetting said "you have borne witness to the Church of Christ, now you must bear witness to others that Christ's coming is near" (16:1). The schism coincided perfectly with the stock market crash, and Fetting's followers surely took the change in economic climate as an apocalyptic sign. Message 18, received on January 6, 1930, was given "in time of trouble," in a "dark" period of "selfishness" (18:1). The message foresaw labor unrest, financial inequality, hunger, and the strife of the Great Depression. Massive population migrations were foreseen, and the destruction of (presumably American) cities was foretold along with raging war (18:11–12).

Otto Fetting became wary in his new position as an outsider to the Temple Lot. The break with the Temple Lot Church put the Fetting group in a precarious position, one that all Temple Lot factions today face, with or without new divine messages. Fetting wrote that only people who were holy could enter the temple and that the Lord's people were not yet holy and could not enter the temple even if it were constructed (*Word of the Lord* 1988:28:5, 30:2). It is curious that Fetting claimed further instructions regarding the temple, but he did not reveal specifics. Messages were reported but often no written text was given, and time after time Fetting was commanded to "withhold" already revealed information regarding the temple (15:2; 16:5; 17). Such an approach may have attracted members from the Temple Lot Church. If Fetting could not belong to the church that held the sacred plot of land, he could at least appear to have divine inside information regarding the Temple Lot. Thus, Fetting rejected the Temple Lot Church's version of temple plans, fearing that "temples will be built that God has not commanded to build," and the unrepentant will "go to destruction" (20:9). The Temple Lot Church became "the enemy," having "rejected the message" of rebaptism and true temple building (15:1, 16:6). It should not be forgotten that two separate but similar temple ideologies emerged between 1927 and the mid-1930s; the undefined one envisioned by Fetting and the other one drafted (and begun with excavation) by the Temple Lot Church.

Fetting's messages became increasingly apocalyptic in the 1930s as political tensions grew in Europe. In September 1932, four months before his death, he envisioned a war between England and Germany. According to Fetting, postwar devastation in Europe would herald the Second Coming. While Fetting envisioned the European calamities to be, he saw Christ appear "in the Heavens going west" and wrote, "He continued west, and in the far off west [as seen from either Europe or Fetting's home of Michigan] I could see the Temple, its walls and dome glittering in the distance, and there was wonderful peace" (29:26). So, Fetting's temple was to have a dome! It was the only outward architectural clue Fetting ever gave.

Fetting died early in 1933, but his "rebaptism" group has continued, with its headquarters in Independence just two miles southeast from the Temple Lot.[2] This Church of Christ is often called the Fetting/Bronson church, after Fetting and his successor. A major rationale for the Fetting/Bronson church is the message John the Baptist gave through Fetting, commanding realignment for the site of temple construction ten feet farther west. As a result, the engraved marker stones (now held by the Temple Lot Church) were discovered, tangible proof of the validity of Fetting's thirty messages. This discovery of artifacts through divine correction is the revelatory glue binding all the Fettingite churches, the word *churches* stated in the plural, as further schism was afoot (see appendix 4). The Fetting/Bronson group, however, follows only Fetting's messages and is sometimes referred to as the "thirty message" group (Bronson n.d.:6; Smith 2001a). They feel they are the only Latter Day Saint church established according to the divine pattern and the only group that can build the temple at the Temple Lot ("Articles of Faith and Practice" n.d.). Temple construction is to take place in the "not too far distant" future, a favored phrase of these millenarian groups (Shields 1990:132–33, 135). Population estimates for the Fetting/Bronson church hover around two thousand members, but unlike many other Restorationist groups they publish little, have no Web page, and remain out of the limelight.

Fetting's group subsequently endured at least three divisions, one of them of equal importance to Fetting's earlier dissent (see appendix 4). For most of these factions, comprising something less than twenty thousand total people, Otto Fetting has become a prophet of even greater importance than Joseph Smith, since, in their view, Joseph Smith's later revelations were flawed and not of divine origin (Melton 1986:85–86; Sorgen 1992). An event encouraging further splintering took place in 1937 when a member, Wilhelm (William) August Draves, began receiving more messages from John the Baptist. One peripheral group of Fetting congregations in the Deep South promptly rejected Draves's messages and split off to form a new group based in Morton, Mississippi. Like all groups derived from the Temple Lot Church, the Mississippians believed "a temple will someday be built in Independence" (Shields 1990:135), but they rejected both the Temple Lot Church and the original Fetting church. This early Mississippi break-off is obscure. It is unknown if it still exists. The Draves group, however, is a major contributor to Latter Day Saint Independence lore and receives further treatment below.

The Fetting church split again in 1956 over which day should be celebrated as the Sabbath. Fetting protégé T. S. Bronson received a revelation changing the holy day to Saturday. Most of his followers agreed, but a minority vowed to stay with Fetting Sunday worship and this latter group of perhaps three hundred split away and is now based in Lee's Summit, Missouri, east of Independence (Melton 1989:580).

Begging for the Temple Lot: Draves's Followers

Wilhelm Draves's group, begun in Nucla, Colorado, in 1937, has become the largest of any of the Temple Lot factions. Draves, a leader of the local Fettingite church in Nucla, claimed to receive the continuation of Fetting's visits from John the Baptist. At the outset, most members of Fetting's church accepted these revelations, but then the organization divided between the Fettingite groups of Draves and of Bronson. The Bronsonites remained dedicated to Fetting's messages and no more.

Draves moved his group back to Independence and named his church the Church of Christ Established Anew in 1929, in accordance with the date Fetting saw in vision (*Word of the Lord* 1988:30:6), also the time Fetting broke with the Temple Lot Church. By 1944, Draves had lost a court case for the land and buildings of the Fetting/Bronson church on Gudgill Street in Independence and began to strengthen his new organization otherwise (Shields 1990:144).

Between 1937 and his death in 1994, Draves claimed to have received eighty-nine personal visits from John the Baptist. These messages, often millenarian, have produced a new, if small, Latter Day Saint tradition, with its own new published book of scripture called *Word of the Lord* (1988). For believers, the messages from John the Baptist tend to overshadow even the *Book of Mormon* (which Fettingite groups usually call the "Record of the Nephites") and reveal the often-uncertain view of a group chosen to build on the small Temple Lot while not possessing it. The Temple Lot, certainly, will eventually be theirs.

The messages Draves wrote during the division from the Fetting Church of Christ (1937–40) were often vague, and referred to the future establishment of a peaceful Zion and an inevitable millennium (*Word of the Lord* 1988:36:3, 37:5, 41:13, 43:6–8, 44:1, 49:2). Considering the rapid evolution and division of these churches, the lack of specificity on Draves's part regarding the status of temple building is not surprising, despite Otto Fetting's concrete beginning. The few early instructions given to Draves regarding the temple only stated that it would be built by many clean Saints raised up in "preparation for the Bridegroom," who was Christ (36:7, 38:14, 43:27, 48:16, 21).

With the start of World War II in 1939, Draves temporarily became ultra-apocalyptic. Like Fetting, Draves saw the war culminating in the Second Coming of Christ. This event was, of course, to be at the temple on the Temple Lot in Independence. Draves ultimately saw

> the Temple in the distance and we floated gently towards it. As we neared, I read the words over the door, "THE TEMPLE OF THE LORD."
>
> We stopped at the door of the Temple and it seemed I was lifted so I could see in every direction and many Saints were marching toward the Temple, while hosts were coming from the seashores. Their eyes were focused on the Temple and the cloud that rested upon it. I looked until the people approached the Temple grounds, then the messenger took me home. (*Word of the Lord* 1988:45:39, 42)

During the wartime years, millennial, and thus temple, anticipation in these churches was high. In a vision reported in late 1942, Draves saw himself in the basement of the future temple with about five hundred other Saints. In vision of a millennial bomb shelter, the Savior himself appeared and passed the emblems of the sacrament (Draves 1971:56).

When World War II ended, temple talk abated, but sometimes temple expectations were exhibited through others besides Draves. In 1955, apostle J. W. Savage reported that through the "tongue and interpretation" of a local sister, two years were given to prepare "to start digging for the Temple" (Savage 1955). The year 1957 passed, however, with no significant temple activity reported by any Temple Lot splinter group, though the "day of worship" schism occurred that split the Fetting/Bronson group. Through the prosperous 1950s, though Draves gave nineteen messages, the temple was not mentioned once, very different compared to the times of optimistic temple preparation seen when Fetting's original messages began in 1927. A strange new directive, however, appeared in 1964. Possibly frustrated by the Temple Lot's continued possession of the sacred spot, Draves's eightieth message called for Saints to "fear not and worry not about the Temple of the Lord, for the Lord can choose the place, the time to build, and direct in His work when He desires His Temple to be built. But with all let there be churches and buildings dedicated to the Lord's Work everywhere—in the name of the Church of Christ with the Elijah Message" (*Word of the Lord* 1988:80:10).

Once again, seeds of dissent were sown, since the message not only implied that the temple could be built anywhere the Lord desired, but also directed a change in the name of the church. It was to be called the Church of Christ with the Elijah Message, a name indicating the prominence of John the Baptist's ongoing communications to Draves as well as a strengthened missionary work in the church. The new name eliminated the phrase "established anew in 1929." For a time, Draves and his more staunch supporters appeared to be taking the "greater Zion view," advocating that if the unrighteous possessors of the Temple Lot would not surrender sacred territory, then the Lord might point out a new spot somewhere else in Independence or Jackson County. Savage, long a backer of Draves, seemingly advocated this view. He mentioned the "spot" pointed out by the Lord, but, using an image from the Old Testament, he placed it in a much broader region of the sacred Missouri River watershed:

> The city and temple shall be in North America. This we have established—but where? Psalms 46 tells of a great river—the Father of Waters—the streams whereof shall make glad the city of

God. One of the streams is the Missouri River, which joined by the Kaw, Blue, Little Blue flow past the city of Independence, Missouri, a very noted city in very deed, in the history of the west, in the history of the Restoration and of the world. It is destined to be even greater as the temple of the Lord is built on the spot pointed out by the Lord 126 years ago and again in 1929. (Savage 1972:119)

Exhibiting an unorthodox view, the message extended Independence's greatness as a city established by gentiles straight through to New Jerusalem establishment. Such blending of profane with future sacred is unusual in most talk of the Saints.

Draves's eightieth message of 1964 also directed that a headquarters building for the church be constructed, but this was not cause for contention since it was no temple. That building has since been built, just over two miles northeast of the Temple Lot.[3] Uncertainty lingered in the church until March 30, 1965, when another message affirmed the new church name, called for dissenters to "be removed," and did nothing to correct the view of a temple dislocated from the Temple Lot (*Word of the Lord* 1988:81:5, 8, 21). Seven of the church's apostles and three bishops revolted, denying the divinity of Draves's message and taking him to court for impeding the editor of the church's publication the *Voice of Peace* ("Church Dispute Leads to Suit" 1965). The court ordered Draves to relinquish hold on the *Voice of Peace* and to place authority back in the hands of the church's board of publications ("Divine Message" 1965). Despite the legal triumph of those who opposed the messages, Draves called new apostles and bishops, and most members followed his church now with "the Elijah Message." By 1966, Draves wrote that the church should be called by the more conglomerated name of the Church of Christ with the Elijah Message Established Anew in 1929, which merged all of the former titles (*Word of the Lord* 1988:83:11). This was a compromise that eased tensions somewhat and brought some members back, but overall substantial dissent in Draves's group had been sown.

Draves's group had also established an agricultural cooperative near Holden, Johnson County, Missouri (Shields 1990:175). Two people involved in the court case, Howard Leighton-Floyd (a former apostle) and H. Harris Burt (a former bishop) formed their own church in Holden apart from Draves's group. Leighton-Floyd, though, later left this group, returning to the Temple Lot Church since he always believed in the sacred spot, which Draves's latest messages apparently repudiated (Shields 1990: 296–97).

Leighton-Floyd, ever the wanderer, later returned to Draves's group (Draves 1994). The Holden group, led by H. H. Burt, now consists of only about thirty-five Saints.

The 1960s were wrenching years of uncertainty and change for Draves's group. The eightieth message had almost split the church, but its call for a new headquarters building was a positive sign of growth. In the late 1960s, Draves, perhaps affected by the rampant unrest of the times, again became intensely apocalyptic. The feeling was maintained during the 1970s but is reflected more in the writings of the church's official publication, the *Voice of Peace*, rather than in the messages.

The eighty-sixth message of 1968 foretold millennial events in substantial detail. Now the messages approached the apocalyptic fervor of Bible Belt fundamentalist Christians as documented by Boyer (1992). Specific dates were even given, again forcing a precarious path on the Elijah Message church. "A peaceful solution and condition for the Colored people" was to be in effect by 1980, and "many great powers" would change, fail, or end by 1989 (*Word of the Lord* 1988:86:14–15, 32). In the summer of 1989, two of the messages mentioned "great shaping" and the "closing conditions" that would soon take place, and Zion, meaning the Americas, would shortly be cleansed (Board of Publication 1989a:9, 1989b:6). Undoubtedly, the momentous Velvet Revolution in Eastern Europe and the subsequent fall of the Soviet Union were seen as the precise fulfillment of these messages.

It was not until 1985 that Draves finally and firmly reversed the "open" temple policy of 1964. He reiterated the old refrain that "Zion shall not be moved from her place, nor the Temple from the spot pointed out by the hand and voice of God," a similar wording to Joseph Smith's earlier revelation in the *Doctrine and Covenants* (*Word of the Lord* 1988:102:20; see also *Doctrine* 1981:90:37, 97:19, 101:17). Since it was also believed that the battle of Armageddon would commence the millennium during the "late 90s" (*Word of the Lord* 1988:86:34), the Church of Christ with the Elijah Message was obliged for a time to accept that the temple on the Temple Lot had to be built before the year 2000 (Sorgen 1992). Predictably, the year 2000 passed with no change in hands of the Temple Lot.

In 1989, Draves reported that John the Baptist was definitely not pleased with temples built "which the Lord has not commanded," a clear reference to the recently announced spiral structure of the RLDS Church. The 104th message stated that such false "works will crumble and fall" (Board of Publication 1989a:13). In the message, the Temple Lot Church was approached in a notably forward, even desperate tone, and by the

106th message, in the providential time of late November 1989, John the Baptist appealed directly to Temple Lot leaders and members. The Temple Lot group was blessed because "they have preserved and kept Sacred the Holy Spot," but that they should now arise above their "blindness" and "bring to pass God's Great Plan" (Board of Publication 1989c:3–4). The Temple Lot people were told to "accept the baptism" of the Elijah Message church to prepare for the beginning of the temple (12–13). Meanwhile, the Elijah Message church was commanded once again to choose an architect to bring forth the plans for the temple, the Temple Lot group being further commanded to relinquish the lot or "have their houses laid waste" and their "ruins" cleansed (14, 17). Through obedience, they would still be the Lord's people because of their protection of the Temple Lot through the decades. Hence, possession is still nine-tenths of the law, but possession without authority only leads to lenient treatment at apocalyptic commencement.

The Elijah Message Church was instructed to send the entirety of the 106th message to the Temple Lot Church. By all indications the inspired begging was ignored, and the Elijah people were probably brimming with millennial ecstasy when the Temple Lot Church building burned down, just one month later, on January 1, 1990. With no apparent results on the horizon, the 111th message contained another divine plea. In it the Lord was "grieved" because "the churches" had not heeded the "Plan of God" (Board of Publication 1991:3). In the voice of deity, it was pleaded, "Where is the House built unto me? You live in your sealed houses—with sealed set minds—established in your own man made and evil doctrines" (Board of Publication 1991:4). This pre-Armageddon plea, whose urgency was certainly prodded by the Persian Gulf War, was subsequently published as a religious advertisement in the *Independence Examiner* on June 13, 1992 (p. 8). Everyone else ignored it.

Divine Trespassers

On the afternoon of January 11, 1992, the apostles and bishops of the Elijah Message church, at least nineteen men, gathered boldly at the Temple Lot to offer prayer to "petition God to begin building the Temple" ("Quorum Insights" 1992:54). Everyone present was given the opportunity to pray at the lot. Such reunions at the lot to pray, beg, or envision the future are popular. The leader of one obscure splinter announced in 1982 that anyone interested should meet him "any day at 1:00 p.m. S. E. of the

Temple Lot" (Shields 1990:213). Another Elijah Message church member admitted to the author that he moved as close to the Temple Lot as he could, saying "I go to the Temple Lot often," stopping by "several times a week." He said, "I find my prayers are answered immediately there" (Smith 2001b). Trespassing is a common experience at the Temple Lot—Elijah Message members and others viewing it as a place where one "can spend time with God" and pray when the worries of the world stack up. "It is land which has been pointed out by God and angels on several occasions" (Smith 2001b).

During one of these prayer circles on the Temple Lot, one Elijah Message member expressed the common disdain members have toward the RLDS temple, which was referred to as a "big corkscrew." The visitor described an overcast night with low misty clouds with thousands of bats circling the floodlit building. With Stokerian slant, it was clear the Elijah Message group has imprinted on the Temple Lot itself, not relating well to the new RLDS/CoC interpretation of the site. At best the view of this Dravesite toward the RLDS temple was "pretty creepy" (Evans 2001c). Created was a unique gothic view of profane space.

The tone of Draves's last nine messages was decidedly mild. Amidst more dissent in the church, the last millennial reference was in 1993 when the church was told that "far more than ten-thousand times ten-thousand are waiting at the gates to enter and be part of the Kingdom and Zion of God." The church was still advised to take its messages to "those who have long represented Christ" (Draves 1993), but Wilhelm Draves passed away in 1994, opening the door for new schism.

After Draves's death, at least two Elijah Message members claimed to receive messages from John the Baptist. One was the wife of one of the church's apostles (Smith 2001a). The second, one Jared Smith, claims to have received ten additional messages from John the Baptist, which have not been accepted by the main Elijah Message church (Smith 2001a; "Ten Messages" 2002). Smith, a former street person who admits having problems with depression and schizophrenia, said that John the Baptist laid his hands upon him and accepted him as mouth when Smith "came to the temple lot before sunrise and kneeled in faith and silence" ("Ten messages" 2002). Smith's messages call the Elijah Message church as well as to the Church of Christ Temple Lot to prepare and build a temple, but there is no sign that the main body of the twelve apostles of the Elijah Message church, or anybody else, have taken the new messages seriously. They do, however, reinforce that when a charismatic leader dies without establishing a successor, or if John the Baptist does not tell who he is going to visit next, the path lay open for anyone to become mouth (Miller 1991). The ten messages also reinforce the trend of begging for the Temple Lot, but possession precludes any Fettingite church from getting close to getting the land needed to bring about their "fullness" of Zion.

In conversions, the Church of Christ with the Elijah Message has been the most successful of all the Temple Lot splinter groups, with a membership of at least twelve thousand and perhaps as many as twenty-five thousand with active missionary work being focused on Latin American and sub-Saharan Africa (Sorgen 1992). The church's continued growth may ride on how well it interprets its own prophecies, which are studiously examined by the members—providing no new messages cause dissent. It could either continue to beg for the Temple Lot or reveal messages that would place the temple elsewhere. With the former tactic, the church may risk convert attrition; with the latter, it risks fragmentation. Success may also ride on whom the church sees as the successor of the voice of John the Baptist. Members believe he may already have returned to visit with someone else, but that person may be too scared yet to reveal it (Evans 2001a).

Imminent Apocalypse: The Temple Lot Church Today

After the above examinations of the views of many of the Temple Lot break-off groups, some questions become obvious. What is the reaction of the Temple Lot Church to the approaches of other Temple Lot–oriented groups? What do its members think about others marching on to the Temple Lot to have meetings and prayer? At this juncture, it is appropriate to return to the group in possession of the Temple Lot and study their own position toward the little parcel that so many hold dear.

The Temple Lot Church has largely ignored overtures from other groups who have coveted their property, but in the late 1990s the church has been defensive as people have sent mailings asserting that the Temple Lot Church will either sell its property or unite with another group, accusations the church fervently denies ("Temple Lot Property" 1994; "Statement of Reaffirmation" 1997). The church has rejected revelations from other churches regarding its proper authority or who should possess the lot (Brickhouse 1998). Despite the tensions, the Temple Lot Church recognizes that many see the site as sacred and they tolerate a great amount of intrusion onto their land. No fence encloses the two-and-one-half-acre lot. A Temple Lot apostle summed up the approach:

> the call to Zion whispers in the hearts of many. I have personally heard many who visited the Temple Lot visitor's center say: We gathered to Zion "recently" . . . "a few years ago," etc. There are frequent visits to the dedicated site for individual and collective prayer, and oft-times the removal of shoes in the belief that they are on sacred ground. Some of our elders have initiated or responded to requests by those outside the Church of Christ for meetings in which to pray collectively and discuss the prospects for a gathering of the saints of God, to find where there are mutual concerns for Zion. I appreciate and applaud such efforts. (Sheldon 1998:195)

Though the tone is ecumenical, the Temple Lot Church sees itself at the center of any New Jerusalem development. No attempts are made to interfere with people roaming the lot, but visitors are often invited to enter the building for a message. I was once invited off the lot shortly after lawn fertilizer had been spread; the Church of Christ authority was concerned the fertilizer would be tracked to other places where it could make people ill. Certainly the Church of Christ is sensitive about the ground it holds sacred. This view is exhibited in July Fourth celebrations, when the LDS Church offered to let the city use the "meadow" pageant area behind the Visitor's Center for fireworks. Some members within the Temple Lot Church worried that the crush of people attending would overrun the Temple Lot. Alvin Harris, a trustee for the church, appeared before the Independence City Council pleading they would move the celebration from the location, saying he feared "the damage and litter will desecrate the Temple Lot" (Hite 2000). The fireworks, also sponsored by the RLDS Church, went off in the meadow without alteration.

When compared especially to some of the Utah church's beliefs, the Temple Lot Church stance (in both land held and temple belief) is diminutive. This is not a pejorative statement; it is psychological fact. The reference in Isaiah (2:2) that "the mountain of the Lord's house shall be established in the top of the mountains" is interpreted literally by the LDS Church to signify the construction of the Salt Lake Temple nestled in the Wasatch Range, but also symbolically as the "Hill of the Lord" meaning any temple, anywhere (Faust 2001). By contrast, the Temple Lot Church view of this scripture is less literal, more restrictive, and more midwestern in topographical interpretation. Temple Lot apostle and spokesman William Sheldon explained: "The term mountain, manifestly refers to the place of His government, and being 'in the top of the mountains,' would be in the midst of other governments, evidently of the world. It is not unreasonable to presume it refers specifically to the place of the central government of all the United States governments—the state of Missouri!" (Sheldon 1974:5).

The limited eschatological nature of the Church of Christ was observed when Sheldon also wrote that Zion "is not a present reality," yet "the nucleus of the Kingdom" had been established (Sheldon 1974:1, 3–4). That nucleus is the Temple Lot Church on the Temple Lot proper. It does not have the least reference either to the greater sixty-three-acre purchase of Edward Partridge or to those who now occupy that greater tract. This viewpoint becomes increasingly evident in light of Sheldon's remark that "the center place of Zion has not become filled with the Saints of God," supposedly meaning Saints of the Temple Lot variety (Sheldon 1990c:107). Though many Latter Day Saint groups are now present in the area, the Temple Lot Church does not view as chosen the RLDS, LDS, or other Temple Lot break-offs. It remains fiercely loyal to the revered two-and-one-half-acre parcel.

On January 1, 1990, the historic building of the Church of Christ at the Temple Lot burned beyond repair, in circumstances similar to the burning of the original church cabin in 1898 (Blakeman and Potter 1990). "We believe this to have been motivated by our enemy, the Devil," wrote Sheldon (1990a:18; see also Jensen 1992:60–61), but Roland Sarratt, another Temple Lot apostle, agonizingly wondered if the burning may have been the result of warnings of the Lord gone unheeded (Sarratt 1990a:18). In December 1990, the church's elderly general bishopric member C. LeRoy Wheaton told the author that some in the church, himself included, thought the Lord had withheld protection from the building because the Temple Lot Church had not worked hard enough to establish the temple as had once been directed.

Furthermore, the idea of a premillennial purge of the area seems to be a common belief in the church, where such is rarely spoken of today in the LDS Church and never in the CoC. William Sheldon mentioned that he was sure that fire, or some other destruction, would further cleanse Independence someday, clearing it for millennial development. Such a purge would remove even "our little building," said Sheldon (1990f). Though the future New Jerusalem to be established will no doubt provide "chambers" of safety and a "hiding place," or harbor, for the Saints (McIndoo 1997:159), the stigma of being the "small guy" whose buildings keep burning may cause some paranoia among the membership. It is popular for Temple Lot members to believe that the other Latter Day Saint churches are waiting for the Church of Christ membership to "just die off," leaving their land to one of the larger groups (Sheldon 1990f). After the building burned, one Temple Lot member claimed that the church would rebuild "despite efforts from the two bigger churches" (Moser 1990:34). What those efforts were the writer did not say, but the LDS Church and the CoC are nevertheless indirectly accused of imperialist attitudes, and the Temple Lot Church chafes at being referred to as merely a temporary "custodian" of the lot (Sheldon 1999:36), a view held by many outside the church (Warren [1985?]: last page).

In their view, the Temple Lot is exclusively the stewardship of the small church, including any activities for the building of the temple and subsequent rise of the New Jerusalem. "Think what might otherwise have been built had they (the LDS or RLDS) returned first" (Seibel 1997:74). In conversation with the author, Sheldon was adamant that continued gathering will take place around the real Temple Lot and (pointing to the adjacent RLDS temple construction) "not over there" (Sheldon 1990f). In *Zion's Advocate*, the church's monthly periodical, one lady shared a story that an RLDS woman had told her. While admiring the spiral RLDS temple with a young niece, the lady reported that the girl pointed to the Temple Lot adjacent to the RLDS structure and said, "That's where Jesus is going to come" ("East Local News" 1997:10). For the Temple Lot group, their position truly found confirmation "out of the mouths of babes." By contrast, most LDS children know little about the Temple Lot.

In April 1999, yet another crazed man entered Church of Christ meetings, waved around a compressed-air gun, and beat churchgoers with what was described as a "tree switch" (Campbell 1999). As the possessor of the Temple Lot, the church seems in a precarious position. Besides the possible escalation of fire insurance rates, one wonders who might try to influence or cleanse, through words or deeds, the land of this beleaguered little church. For the increasing spiritual pressure and millenarian burden placed on this small piece of land, the Temple Lot Church carries on with commendable composure.

When discussion on the future of the Temple Lot proceeded after the headquarters building burned, one of the options was to "demolish the current structure and begin to plan and build the Temple itself," but this thirteen-word proposal was the only serious temple talk at the time ("Temple Lot Building Proposal" 1990:32). The plans for the new Temple

Lot building were viewed as being provided by God and as a structure to be used "for church business . . . not necessarily appropriate" for a temple ("Temple Lot Local Gives Thanks" 1990:164; Sarratt 1990b:105). Perhaps because revelation had not been newly received, temple construction was not anticipated, but when a temple was to be built, readers were assured, it would be according to the Temple Lot's contracted temple drawings of 1930 and not to the imaginative but vague ideas of Fetting or his followers (Sheldon 1990e:171).

The early Fetting experience in some ways inhibited the Temple Lot Church's ambition. His messages of hope ultimately became a factional crisis. The Church of Christ cannot afford another fragmentation, and therefore the church talks millenarian yet is hesitant to specify details regarding temple building. "A spirit of doubt concerning the temple" has affected the membership (Sheldon 1990c:108), and the temple goal has been on the back burner for more than six decades. For a time the Temple Lot of the Second Coming was the "Temple Lot of hesitation," but a renewed millennial tone has emerged in the late 1990s.

Native Americans

With the construction of their new church building, a regeneration of zeal toward Zion and the millennium took place, despite the problem of temple building (Sheldon 1990c:107; Sheldon 1990e:171; Sheldon 1992; McIndoo 1992; Jordan 1992). The Temple Lot Church still believes in gathering the true Saints, and the church will view any future growth as "the gathering" in progress (Sheldon 1992:80). Sheldon saw that influx starting when the Temple Lot Church grew as a result of the influx of RLDS membership during the 1920s (Sheldon 1974:10). In the Temple Lot view, however, the gathering will also be made up of large numbers of Native Americans who are seen as major builders of the New Jerusalem (Sheldon 1990e:171; *Did You Know?* n.d.; McIndoo 1992:77–78). Such a view is opposite what the LDS Church has usually said about the important but lessened part the Native American will play, but it is consistent with the meager resources of the Temple Lot Church. In fact, three of the church's apostles currently live in Phoenix, Arizona—seen as the Native American outreach center for the church.

Lately, the church has amplified into myth a story that, even before the time of Joseph Smith, Native Americans were once called by the "Great Spirit" to gather at the Temple Lot. They were commanded to go into their own particular lands—each later to bring a stone to pile at the site seen as the "hub of the wheel" and a place where someday a "Lodge would be built in honor of their Great Spirit" (Seibel 1997:75). The source of the story is "clouded in the wisps of time," but no matter; it has become important lore for the Temple Lot people and is the strongest pre-Columbian (but postbiblical and post–*Book of Mormon*) sacred place justification by any Latter Day Saint group (Brantner 1999:127).

Another oft-told story talks of the visit of one Native American to the Church of Christ's Navajo Fair in Arizona. The visitor viewed a painting of Jesus with hands extended toward a group of Navajo people. It was captioned indicating that the Navajos would help build the city of New Jerusalem, "as many as would come." The Navajo related how he had once visited the Temple Lot, where he saw a "shaft of light coming out of heaven." As he prayed there he saw the Temple Lot differently. It was swept clean, with all buildings gone. The Navajo said then that the Savior appeared, "turned and pointed and said that He had to cleanse it" (Temple 2000:73).

In the church's General Conference proceedings of 1998, apostle Marvin E. Ely received inspiration that six people were to be called to fill vacancies in the twelve apostles when only five were needed. Ely was questioned on his math, but the seventy-seven-year-old leader reiterated the same six names. Uncertainty became a painful miracle when Ely died of a heart attack the same day, opening up the sixth position. Two of the six new apostles were Native Americans, called from among the church's small Mexican membership in the Yucatán. In one fell swoop, prophesy was certified, the church's quorum of twelve apostles was filled for the first time in decades, and two of those new members were Native Americans (McIndoo 1998:107). Subsequently, these apostles from far-flung Yucatán were ordained and more articles have appeared in *Zion's Advocate* on church work in Mexico, Honduras, and Guatemala.

At the New Millennium

A greater emphasis on the theme of temple building appeared with the approach of the millennium. *Zion's Advocate* articles displayed temple talk more often as a result of the combination of the appearance of the RLDS temple across the street, the approach of the millennium, and perhaps even quasi-millennial announcements by the LDS Church, such as that to rebuild the temple in Nauvoo, Illinois. Sheldon appeared more frustrated

FIG. 43 | *The new Temple Lot building, built in 1991. Reprinted, with permission, from the cover of* Zion's Advocate *67 (1990).*

that perhaps people had become so "stung with false revelation in the past" that they had concluded that a temple was not needed. He sharply criticized those who believed that "we do not need a temple now, for we need only to consecrate our lives . . . as temples for God" (Sheldon 1997: 21–23). His tone has been desperate as he pronounced that the idea of building Zion and the New Jerusalem was often taken more seriously by believers outside the church than by members within (Sheldon 1998:195). Despite Sheldon's criticisms, the church has yet to agree on any specific fund-raising plan for a temple. It must be reiterated that the Temple Lot Church has no first presidency made up of a prophet and two counselors, as in the larger churches; decisions are made in the Quorum of the Twelve. The small church's democratic voting procedure mixed with this diffuseness of leadership weakens the possibility of authoritative revelation on mundane subjects, much less millenarian ones. Pronouncements must come in particular charismatic ambiance to be accepted by a majority.

In 1997, millennial Temple Lot Church writer Harvey Seibel discussed the place of the New Jerusalem, emphasizing again that Native American influence would be necessary to build it (Seibel 1997). Though Seibel is not a church authority, his writings appear in a prominent position in the church and seem generally accepted by the leadership and membership alike, as they hold some of that dramatic charisma that feels authoritative. That same summer, Sheldon said the Lord would come to a "literal temple" in the New Jerusalem (Vogle 1997:129), and Elder Andrew Brantner wrote a most urgent plea for the people to gather to Zion without delay

(Brantner 1999). The article heralded the release of two new postcard photos of the Temple Lot from the air. One showed the open lot in comparison to surrounding RLDS and LDS buildings. The other, in quite millennial fashion, showed a bird's-eye view of expectant Temple Lot members standing on the lot outlining the form of the proposed temple structure as drawn up decades before (Brantner 1999:130–31).

Considering the visitors that the RLDS temple, auditorium, and LDS Visitor's Center attract, and a new plaque posted on the south side of the prominent Temple Lot by the Missouri Mormon History Foundation, the Temple Lot Church today is more visible than ever (Figure 43; Sarratt 1992; Walking Trail Dedication 2000; Harlacher 2000:11). Official church talk waxes more millennial with every church conference. Temple Lot writers have even called Harry Truman, of Independence, the "President from Zion" and a part of God's millennial plan, since he so forcefully recognized Israel's independence in 1948, heralding the latter-day scheme in the Old World (Gordon 1999). To local Saints this is a providential sign. It is no mystery why Truman should hail from Independence.

The church's April 2000 conference report was more millenarian than usual, with accounts of a variety of Temple Lot–oriented visions and dreams by church members. An apocalyptic cleansing of the Temple Lot seemed the fervor of the conference. Many Native American–centered stories were told imagining the Savior purging the lot. Also given were accounts of visions and dreams of destruction, including one discussing the eventual appearance of a "bright red ring" that would enlarge "the borders of Zion by judgment," which would be "poured out on the city of Independence." At these events, two different scenarios for the Saints were given. In one there would be "a canopy of safety" for the Saints while the destruction takes place. "The Saints are told not to look at the destruction." This apocalyptic protective cover is referred to as "Zion" and reinforces the theme that those protected would be gathered at a fairly small space. The other account was a dream where "Saints will gather at the Temple Lot." An apostle [presumably of the Church of Christ] will tell members to "go home and rest and then come back, but tell no one," while the destruction around Independence is imminent. The report finishes, expressing that the main theme of the coming 2001 conference would be to "PREPARE" (Temple 2000:73, 74).

Later in the year, William Sheldon said that the Saints would be protected during the cleansing of Independence in the last days just as Noah and company were protected in the ark. The modern-day "Zion," the New Jerusalem, would be the spiritual ark for the Saints (Sheldon 2000:179). One wonders if Sheldon had seen the movie *Deep Impact,* where the "ark of protection" was based on Kansas City's incomparable underground caverns, but he does not mention the ark as a real place or shelter—his reference is specific to the divine shelter provided at the Temple Lot itself. Sheldon distinguishes between a nearer New Jerusalem to be "built following great tribulation" in Independence and the postmillennial New Jerusalem written of in Revelation that shall "come down from heaven" and not be built "with men's hands" (Sheldon 2000:179).

Shy in temple pronouncements after the Fetting debacle, the Temple Lot leadership has gradually become more outspoken, in part because of the writings and pronouncements of those outsiders who have claimed and wish to possess the lot. Much more apocalyptic in stance toward the millennium than the CoC or the LDS Church, the Temple Lot Church believes that a purging will yet take place (Sheldon 1990e:170), the Saints will yet gather, Zion will yet flourish, and the members of the Church of Christ will humbly build a temple. This sacred structure will be made, with the help of Native Americans, according to established specifications, to "honor their God" just as Solomon's people did (Sheldon 1990d:124).

The year 2000 saw a great boom of millenarian talk and apocalyptic expectation. Though the Church of Christ apostles are not date setters, a tendency to do so is increasing in the church's official outlet, *Zion's Advocate*. Most apocalyptic events, wrote Seibel, should happen by 2007 (Seibel 1992:12). In mid-2001 Seibel wrote that 2002 would be the end of six thousand years of history and that "the opening of the 6th Seal and the day of the Lord" would likely occur "sometime in the Spring" (Seibel 2001:83). The tragedy of September 11, 2001, came a tad early, but leaders still saw imminent apocalypse. America was considered "caught up in prophecy," and writers addressed how the land of the United States should be "possessed," which was "through righteousness." That the land itself is given such concrete attention is unique to the Latter Day Saint experience (McGhee 2001; McIndoo 2001). Seibel wrote that the "millennial reign of Christ with his Saints," referred to as the "time of blessedness spoken of by Daniel," might occur around 2005, after the Battle of Armageddon (Seibel 2001:83, 87). Surely, the escalation of violence in Israel and Iraq through 2003 is seen as Armageddon itself, if not its commencement, but Seibel says that before any of these events occur, the Church of Christ will build its temple and New Jerusalem. According to Seibel's own predictions, however, the time is already up, and new dates are likely to be set.

The belief is that the Lord will come to reign, all through the instrumentality of this little "remnant" of the original church. Nothing will be accomplished if the Temple Lot members are not obedient, a view shared with the LDS Church. Members of the Temple Lot Church are sometimes chided for their unbelief in building Zion or a temple. The Temple Lot leadership in many ways seems more millennial in its stances than the membership, which is different from the Mormons. Members of the LDS Church sometimes wax millennial while the leadership is silent. The reason for the position of the Church of Christ is unclear, but it might be a feeling of discomfort at the past abortive attempt at building a temple combined with the church's small size and limited influence in view of the more impressive construction projects seen in the larger churches. Whatever the leadership/membership ratio of millennial emphasis, the group arguably presents the most imminently millenarian approach to Joseph Smith's New Jerusalem of any of the groups, down to nearly setting dates. Admittedly, its daughter church, the Church of Christ with the Elijah Message Established Anew in 1929, has been nearly as apocalyptic. Though the LDS Church is geographically and historically more composed and complete in its millenarian approach, the Church of Christ maintains much more millenarian fervor as a proportion of talks and articles presented. How the church reacts to world events in the next few years, however, could set a very different millenarian stage. If events do not transpire soon, the Temple Lot Church may be forced to backtrack, increasing its cautious nature toward the temple. The majority of the lot remains open lawn, and despite possible backtracking, it would not be unexpected to hear "revelations" received by Temple Lot apostles announcing a sacred structure or some sort of "Temple Fund drive" very soon (Sheldon 1990b:105).

Other Groups

A number of other groups related to the Temple Lot Church or to one of its factions also exist on the religious stage of Independence. Some of these consist of only a family or even a single person, but others claim several hundred adherents. They range widely over the spectrum of Latter Day Saint beliefs. Some have totally dropped Joseph Smith, the *Book of Mormon,* and sacred space talk relating to Missouri from their doctrines (Warren 1999), but most retain Saintisms, especially some feeling of Independence as sacred, or at least a belief in some form of temple.

Retreating from Zion

One split from the Temple Lot Church was made by Thomas Nerren and E. E. Long from a small congregation in Denver, Colorado. Nerren's group followed Otto Fetting's messages but remained independent of Fetting's church. Oddly, the Denver congregation remained loyal to the Temple Lot organization while it supported the Fetting revelations of the temple. When the Temple Lot Church rejected Fetting's messages in 1936, Nerren's group split. From this point on, the Nerren group saw general leadership of the Temple Lot Church as fallen, as was the case with most of the groups who followed Fetting. Fetting's original instructions called for the building of the temple within seven years, in likeness of the construction of the biblical temple of Solomon. Nerren proclaimed the Temple Lot Church out of order and out of favor with God since he had given them "seven years . . . and the work was to start in 1929. That time ended in 1936. I stated plainly in the first message to you; that if they did not build the temple, I would raise up a people that would build it" (Shields 1990:137). Presumably, "I" in this message represents deity, and the people to be "raised up" would be Nerren's group. Since the Temple Lot Church had "gone astray," rejecting Fetting's messages, at precisely the seven-year interval, the temple plans drawn up by the Temple Lot group were seen by Nerren as defective. Since the Temple Lot's own architect admitted he could have designed a "very different building" from Fetting's description, the resultant plans were likely "not after the pattern" originally intended by God (Long 1938:8–9).

Nerren also began to receive revelations from a busy John the Baptist, and a revelation to this group in 1940 directed the church to move to Halley's Bluff near Schell City, Missouri, in northeastern Vernon County. Apparently, a modest temple was built there, but it burned down sometime during the 1950s (Shields 1990:138, 194). The name of the church, the Church of Jesus Christ at Zion's Retreat, indicates the evolution of this group's attitude. Since the Temple Lot would never be legally obtained, the Lord had established a "Temple Retreat" seventy miles south of Independence.

By the early 1970s, the evolution of the retreat attitude was apparent when a majority of this group began to follow beliefs of Christian white supremacy. Out of the earlier Zion's Retreat group, a dominant survivalist-type church split off (Jenista 1977). This group calls itself the Church of Israel. They have since regressed from Latter Day Saint attitudes by dropping the *Book of Mormon* and Joseph Smith from their beliefs. They do not believe in a temple but call their own large two-story headquarters a "Palace of Christ." Many apocalyptic cues and particular words and phrases of this group still carry the feel of Latter Day Saintism (Gayman 1989).

The smaller, nonsurvivalist segment of the Zion's Retreat group still see the Schell City, Missouri, area as a sacred place. This group had retained a majority of the land in a legal battle with the Church of Israel. A union with Leighton-Floyd/Burt Dravesite group from Holden, Missouri, was apparently attempted around 1975. During these negotiations much revelation and prediction took place. The group believed that the Lord had "set aside" Halley's Bluff as an "isolated place" when the more prominent (for this group) Temple Lot Church went astray. It was to be a land for the gathering, and though the Zion's Retreat people had diminished greatly, the Lord's children from the different factions would still gather there "to go forth." It was predicted that the Lord's church would be established anew at this "holy place" (Corbin 1974, 1975).

Hebrew Mormons

An intriguing sprout related to Draves's organization was started by an Ohioan named David L. Roberts. In 1967, one year after his baptism into the Draves "Elijah Message" church, Roberts said the Angel Nephi (a *Book of Mormon* prophet) visited him. After briefly associating with the Strangites in Wisconsin, he was commanded in 1974 by the prophet Elijah to return to Independence to "rededicate" the Temple Lot. This he did, and he moved his small group (consisting mainly of his family) to Independence in 1977 (Shields 1990:177; Melton 1989:592).[4] He and his wife have published profusely and call their organization the True Church of Jesus Christ Restored. Roberts claims he is a successor to James Jesse Strang and is the one chosen to build the temple "in the land of Zion in the Center Place" (Shields 1990:178). Roberts apparently had misgivings about the possibility of obtaining the Temple Lot, however, and later told the *Independence Examiner* that the location for the temple had "not been disclosed yet" (Brockmeyer 1977:6B). It is interesting that in one of Roberts's tracts, his temple for Zion is actually the Nauvoo, Illinois, temple of the early Saints (Roberts 1977). This imagery is conspicuous as a doctrinal twist not seen elsewhere. The RLDS and Temple Lot Churches have never upheld the Nauvoo temple as a model for the center place since they view Joseph Smith as having been long fallen by the Nauvoo period of the 1840s. The groups that still revere the Nauvoo era are the LDS Church, the Strangites, the Pennsylvania Bickertonites, and the Cutlerites. Roberts's claim as the successor to Strang may help link the image of the Nauvoo temple to Independence, but his pamphlets, crudely thrown together, give the impression more of charlatan than of serious sect leader. Through 2000, nothing has been gleaned of Roberts or his work.

The Cutlerites

The Cutlerite branch is a sect apart from other Latter Day Saint churches, since it is not a recent splinter; rather, it dates from the early factions of the Nauvoo era. Alpheus Cutler was a mason for the Nauvoo temple (see appendix 2) and preserved in his group the importance of temple rites. Thus, apart from the LDS Church, the Cutlerites are the only group to hold private temple ceremonies dating from the Nauvoo period.

The temple ceremony of the Church of Jesus Christ (Cutlerite) is held in the second story of their church building in Independence and is not open to public scrutiny. The Cutlerite building is located about five blocks directly south of the RLDS temple at 807 S. Cottage St. It was constructed in 1928 when the group moved to Independence from Minnesota (Shields 1990:62).

The Cutlerites believe in private temple rites, and they believe a temple of the Second Coming will eventually be built in Independence. In a pamphlet written by Rupert J. Fletcher, leader of the Church of Jesus Christ during the 1960s, a troubled view of Zion was expressed. He wrote: "I had prayed much in times past to know how Zion would be brought about, for I saw all around me the disunion among the believers in the Restoration Movement. Now this was the exact opposite of the zionic plan held forth in the scriptures, for the plan to build Zion is based on complete unity among its members" (Fletcher 1965).

Fletcher's outward view is different from that of many other groups who see themselves as chosen and the others as mistaken. Many see God someday miraculously liberating the sacred lands for their particular group, while those of incorrect doctrine will somehow be swept away. In contrast, the Cutlerite group, which has dwindled in size to about thirty members or less (Shields 1990:62; Adherents 2003), ostensibly views a unity among Latter Day Saint groups as necessary for God to recognized "His people." Examined more closely, however, the view of a Latter Day Saint ecumenical movement covers ulterior motives. Other small groups have, at times, used similar words of working together. Fetting and Draves, for example, spoke on various occasions of the churches "flowing together" (*Word of the Lord* 1988:13:3–4, 84:10, 88:29, 102:52). At one point Draves even called members of the Cutlerite church to callings within his own organization. No evidence exists, however, that any Cutlerite came into Draves's group. Views of Latter Day Saint ecumenicalism are reviewed in more detail in chapter 10, but the view has usually been one of "let's all work together, just so long as it is clear that our church is the one in control."

Some of the smaller churches of Saints do not have much hope of gaining hoards of converts from outside the Latter Day Saint family, but they do aspire to attract great numbers from their sister organizations, as the Temple Lot Church did from the RLDS Church in the 1920s. Fletcher, for example, assured his readers that God would "unite His church" and establish Zion in Independence by raising up an important prophet in the future, just as He had used Joseph Smith Jr. in the last century (Fletcher 1965). His call to work together is tempered because the prophet to be raised up would undoubtedly be a Cutlerite.

The Bickertonites: Zion in General

Another group originating with the schism after the death of Joseph Smith Jr. was based in churches established by Sidney Rigdon in Pittsburgh and later in Philadelphia after Smith's death. After Rigdon's splinter failed, William Bickerton organized another group in the Pittsburgh area. This group became known as the Church of Jesus Christ or, to avoid confusion, the Bickertonites. This organization often refers to itself as simply "the Church" and is headquartered in Monongahela, Pennsylvania, with its World Conference Center located in Greensburg, Pennsylvania, twenty miles to the northeast. The eastern flavor of the church can be seen in glancing at the names of its apostles. Seven of the twelve are of Italian ancestry, an eye-raising composition for a Latter Day Saint church (Church of Jesus Christ 2003).

Similar to other Latter Day Saint churches, the Church of Jesus Christ gives particular emphasis to reclaiming the Native Americans as "descendants of Joseph, one of the Tribes of Israel," but has had some of its greatest missionary success in northwest Africa (Church of Jesus Christ 2003). The church today believes in the concept of an American New Jerusalem (Lawson 2001b), but since the Missouri experiment failed, it does not "believe in Independence or some other site" for Zion. "The Church has not taken an official position on where [the New Jerusalem] may be" (Lawson 2001a), and leaders admit that members may contemplate its location, "but God will let us know in His time" (Lawson 2001b). Apparently, the church's historical and geographic separation from the Independence experience has produced less definition for millenarian location. About six thousand adherents follow the teachings of the Bickertonites today. It is the largest Latter Day Saint church headquartered east of the Mississippi River.

A Purge from Within? The RLDS Splinters

Another Latter Day Saint tradition, or perhaps several, is coming about out of the reorganization movement. Many of the fundamentalist RLDS congregations call themselves Restoration Branches. These congregations are certain God will eventually put the RLDS Church on a true path by replacing the current prophet and apostles with new ones who will do God's will *within* the current structure of the RLDS Church. The best source for fundamentalist RLDS news is the magazine *Vision*, produced by Price Publishing. *Vision* is a veritable cornucopia of news of Restoration Branch and RLDS splinter activity. Apart from the Restoration Branches, at least twelve other new churches have splintered from the RLDS Church, a few of which are discussed below (Price 1999; see appendix 3). Some of these indeed have chosen prophets and apostles, rejecting the RLDS Church and establishing completely new organizations. All complain that the liberal tendencies of the RLDS Church/CoC are not inspired. Each believes the center place in Independence is to someday be properly cleansed and occupied by them: God's true people.

The Rightful Owners of the RLDS Church

Division began in the early 1970s when President W. Wallace Smith instituted more liberal programs moving the RLDS Church closer to mainstream Protestantism. Fundamentalist discontent surged late in that decade and exploded in 1984 when Wallace B. Smith (son of W. Wallace Smith) received a revelation to permit the ordination of women to the RLDS priesthood, something unheard of in any Latter Day Saint Church up to this time. Since 1984, between thirty and fifty thousand fundamentalist members (from 10 to 20 percent or more of the total reorganization membership) have to varied degrees split from the church ("News Briefs"

1992:6; Lancaster 2001; Stack 2002). Since the division is so recent, tensions among the RLDS groups run much hotter than, for comparison, tensions among the Temple Lot Church splinters.

Most of the dissenting congregations claim that the hierarchy of the main RLDS Church leaders are acting without God's direction or approval. The authority of the central church is, therefore, dead (R. Price 1990c:29). In the view of Richard Price, the founder of the prolific Price Publishing House, arguably the backbone of the RLDS fundamentalist movement, President Wallace B. Smith became not merely a fallen prophet (Kirksey and Price 1989:10; R. Price 1990a:14), but variously a New Ager ("Wallace B. Smith Aids" 1992:25), an anti-American Marxist (P. Price 1992:26–28, 44; "RLDS Leaders Promote" 1992), and even an outright Satanic leader ("Wallace B. Smith Aids" 1992:26–27).

The Restoration Branches see every move by the RLDS leadership as divisive and decadent. For example, discussion of a merger between the RLDS Church–owned Independence Regional Health Center and a local Catholic hospital was viewed askance by fundamentalists who had seen the "Sanitarium" as a sacred part of Zion (P. Price 1990b:22; "Two Hospitals" 1990). The subsequent sale of the hospital was proof to fundamentalists that the RLDS hierarchy was not inspired by God. Likewise, RLDS involvement in activities sponsored by the National Council of Churches (though it is not officially a member) are seen as treasonous ("Secret Money Payments" 1991:19–21). At one point, a historic RLDS-owned cemetery in Nauvoo, where Edward Partridge and other prominent early church leaders are buried, was traded to the LDS Church for land south of the Auditorium. According to the fundamentalists, the RLDS Church abandoned a valuable and sacred historical site just "to make a parking lot" (P. Price 1989:11).

The biggest RLDS thorn in the side of the Restoration Branches concerns lands in eastern Independence that the "liberal faction" plans to develop and sell or lease for commercial purposes. Fundamentalists quote original verses from the *Doctrine and Covenants* emphasizing the sanctity of land purchases. These lands were purchased in the early 1900s when the RLDS Church was still seen as committed to a Zionic ideal, and though these are not the same "inheritances" owned by the early church, the Restoration Branches treat them with equal importance. The fundamentalist view is that the RLDS "liberal hierarchy" is condemned for dispensing with them for profit in such a cavalier manner (Price and Price 1991:16–17;

"Hierarchy to Sell Water Rights" 1995). The fundamentalists were piqued enough to consider a class-action lawsuit to regain the territories. It is seen that such a suit, yet to be filed, would start the process of a return of the RLDS Church to "its Restoration distinctives," according to Price Publishing (Price and Price 1991:17).

Many members of the Restoration Branches insist that their names not be removed from church records, since they believe they will someday regain their rightful control of the RLDS Church ("Church of Christ, Restored" 1990:22; R. Price 1991b:18). Consequently, the fundamentalists believe that, just as the early church was "reorganized" due to the Lord's displeasure with the Nauvoo experiment, another "reorganization" must soon take place since the "liberal faction" has departed from God's true ways once again (D. Price 1990:9). This position, however, requires much patience and faith that things will eventually turn the fundamentalists' way. Though the "cleansing from within" stance is still popular, more and more RLDS dissidents cannot wait and are joining full-fledged break-off churches.

Gathering the Fundamentalists

The emerging Restoration Branches geography matches that of the RLDS Church in general. Where RLDS congregations are organized, dissent has been present. Because more RLDS members live in Missouri, the fundamentalist movement has taken the firmest hold there, though with no distinct regional tone. For example, the historic Enoch Hill congregation, a few blocks south of the Auditorium, has become a major site of fundamentalist RLDS dissent. In 1981, before the "women in the priesthood" controversy, millennially oriented Enoch Hill members issued a call to gather the Saints to Independence. A few resettled from as far away as Oregon at this time (Kluth 1992). The once thriving congregation became increasingly divided through the 1980s, even to the point of having separate liberal and fundamentalist worship services. According to Pamela Price (1990a:24–25), the RLDS leadership finally stopped the fundamentalist services completely, and since that time only about 50 RLDS members attend the Enoch Hill building, a handful of the 1,200 members during the 1970s. The remainder now meets elsewhere, but the implication is that some RLDS congregations went through a greater upheaval than indicated by the "mere" 10 to 20 percent membership loss often reported. During the 1990 RLDS Church World Conference at the Auditorium, hundreds of dissenters held an "alternate" reunion at William Chrisman High School ("Restoration Gospel Series" 1990:23). Many of these have since organized into a separate church.

The theme of gathering to Zion has sometimes been subdued among the RLDS dissenter groups, but it has maintained its momentum, if not increased it, up to the turn of the millennium. Throughout the first half of the century, as elsewhere discussed, RLDS and Temple Lot members gathered to Independence from a variety of far-flung reaches. Members of distant LDS and Temple Lot congregations trickled to Jackson County from the 1950s to the 1970s. Often these were retirees who were finally free to move to Zion. RLDS dissenters have continued to come to the vicinity through the 1990s, some because they lost their meetinghouses in legal battles with the RLDS Church and saw no better alternative ("Gathering" 1999; Warner 1996). Thus the dissent against RLDS liberalization tendencies has itself caused migration to Missouri and an increase in New Jerusalem diversity hitherto unseen.

The need to gather to Zion has caused some speculation as to how many people can physically come to the Independence area. An Internet discussion board sponsored by the Restoration Branches revealed a wide range of opinion regarding Zion's capacity. One person said he could not see 250,000 people coming to Zion, a large number apparently pulled out of the blue (millennial LDS Church members would find such a number on the low side). Another responded, using the same number, asking if that many *would be worthy* to come to Zion, whenever the time. Another wrote that she had recently come to Zion from Florida and believed that "250,000 could not fit in Independence . . . but they can fit in Jackson County and surrounding areas." Conversely, another finally wrote, "I don't know how many will gather, but why wouldn't 250,000 people be able to gather to Independence and even more. It's a big place and there is still land vacant" ("Gathering" 1999). The urge to gather is strong, but many are at a loss to define Zion's capacity. What is obvious is that the RLDS fundamentalists are devout millenarians, whereas the mainstream CoC is no longer chiliastically disposed.

Those who gather often have a hard time balancing their dreams of a millennial utopia with what they see around Independence. One person wrote of community projects being supported by taxes, with the result that "our poor old Zion looks like a dump" (Graceland 1998). Naturally, millennialists of RLDS ilk seek for Zion and the New Jerusalem to be built around cooperative stewardships where groups of Saints work together driven by revelation. In this scene, welfare and building projects undertaken with taxpayer support cannot build Zion, for they would be "the works of men." Another writer, perhaps tempering her disappointment with the local scenery, wrote, "Before we gathered we knew that Zion was not yet established. Therefore we did not expect to walk into a Zionic community when we came" (Warner 1996). Some do not see Zion at all yet, while others have to accept that Zion is somehow gradually being developed. One wrote that to meet millennial expectations, many in the area will have to move out, "especially all the meth labs and gangs" ("Gathering" 1999). Millennialist RLDS and Restoration Branches members talk of building Zion and gradually producing a landscape worthy of Christ's return, whereas LDS and Temple Lot groups are more apt to bring out apocalyptic destruction as necessary before the real building takes place.

The Fundamentalist Temple Lot

The views of Zion, Independence, and the temple to be are radically different for the Restoration Branches than for the main RLDS Church body. Most fundamentalists maintain the doctrine of one small temple on the Temple Lot according to the original Kirtland-like plans. No other Latter Day Saint group goes this far back in history for a temple model (see fig. 7). For them, the completed small temple will signal the return of Jesus Christ and the onset of the millennium. To them, the present RLDS spiral is a hoax, more like a Buddhist structure or the Tower of Babel; a temple built of desperation, not inspiration (Kirksey and Price 1989:7). It is believed that the current RLDS leadership has rejected Joseph Smith's early plan, building in the wrong place (Figure 44; Price and Price 1982:87–101; see also "Fundamentalists Want" 1990). The bitterness of fundamentalists was seen in 1990 when a sign proclaiming the RLDS temple a farce was hung on a temporary fence surrounding the construction site ("Hierarchy's New Age Temple" 1990:43). It read, "This is a false temple design. God's true design was given to the RLDS church in 1833." These words echoed those the Prices wrote in 1982 that "it would be a tragedy to build the Temple in a place which is contrary to the instructions of the Lord—instructions He has already given concerning His own House" (Price and Price 1982:100). Now that the "tragedy" is complete, and with the liberalization of the CoC, the Restoration Branches are even more committed to saving the best and the most devout for whenever God might reconstruct the future RLDS Church from the inside out.

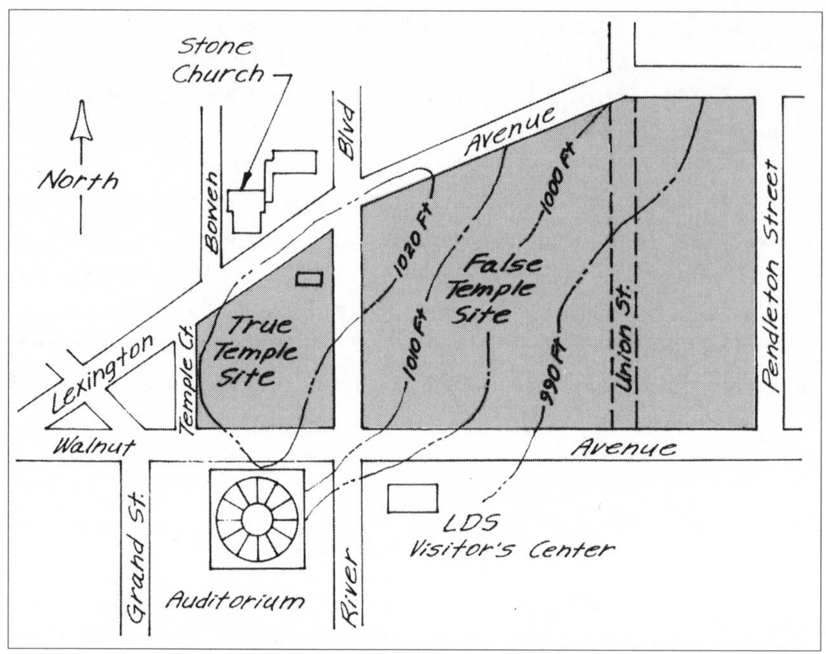

FIG. 44 | *The false temple site according to RLDS fundamentalists. Map reprinted, by permission, from Price and Price (1982:93). © 1982 by Richard and Pamela Price.*

Since other Latter Day Saint groups have taken the most sacred tracts of land in Independence, RLDS splinters have established themselves close to the Temple Lot where they can. One RLDS splinter group, known simply as the Church of Jesus Christ Zion's Branch, purchased one of the older and more modest Protestant church buildings on Pleasant Street just north of LDS property and east of the new RLDS temple (see Figure 45; "Zion's Branch" 1999). Just around the corner, on the north side of Maple, stood an older bungalow-style home with a hand-painted sign saying "School of the Saints." Apparently, a disgruntled RLDS couple has started teaching Latter Day Saint doctrine, home style, a block and a half from the Temple Lot. Another break-off RLDS group, called the Remnant Church of Jesus Christ of Latter Day Saints, has made a bold move by taking control of the old William Chrisman High School just north of the RLDS temple. This group is treated below.

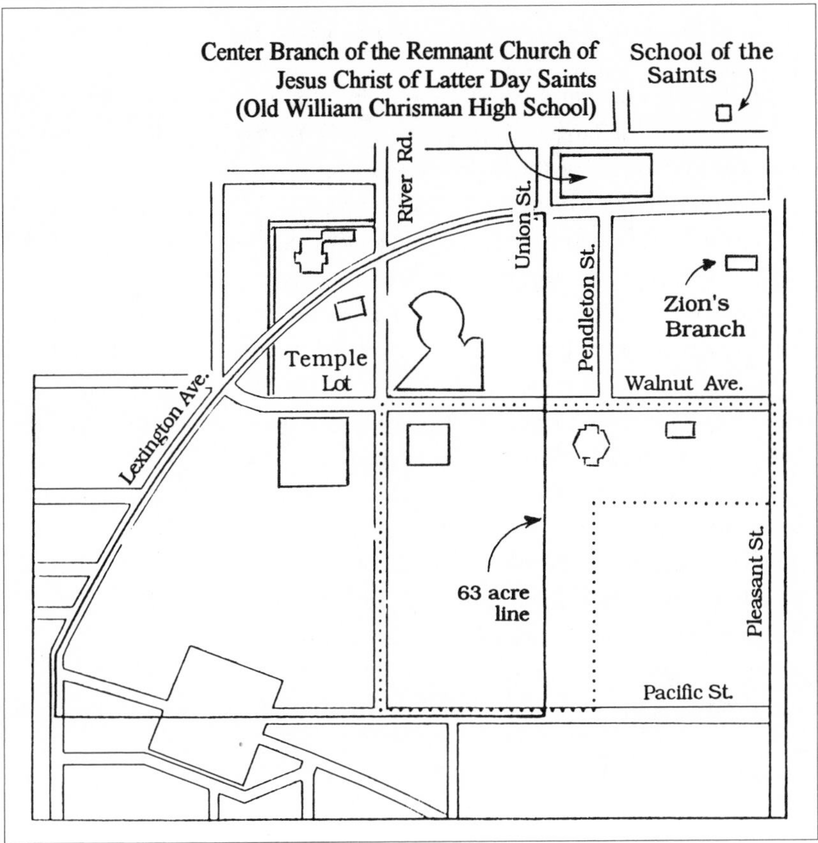

FIG. 45 | *RLDS splinter activity near the Temple Lot.*

One fundamentalist-oriented RLDS message board on the Internet even naively asked if Restorationists "needed the Mormon [LDS] property in Independence . . . located next to the CoC Auditorium?" ("Ron's RLDS" 2001a). This is the only reference the author has found anywhere discussing the possibility of the takeover of LDS land by any group, much less one of RLDS splinter ilk. It was questioned whether there was "ever, or is there now, an active project of trying to obtain the land?" ("Ron's RLDS" 2001a). What actions such a project might entail is not certain, but the LDS Church takes its landholdings seriously, and if the RLDS Church cannot get the land, no small Restoration Branch will be able to either.

Shadows over Zion and Other Views

At the time of the expulsion of the original Saints from Jackson County, Joseph Smith Jr. defiantly spoke of Zion not being "moved out of her place" and said that one day the Saints would return again and build up her "waste places" (*Book of Doctrine* 1989:98:4g). Used as historic rationale, the Restoration Branches, through the unscriptural direction of the liberal RLDS leadership, prophesy a vacating of the church, literally making Independence a "waste place." The city is thus cast under the shadow of the Lord's disfavor and will remain in a "dark and cloudy night" until faithful Saints can vote errant leaders out of office or successfully sue for the church's name and properties (Figure 46). Perhaps divine intervention may also bring the RLDS Church back in line (R. Price 1986:1, 31).

The Prices hope that the church can be saved from the inside out, but in practice this has proven difficult since the RLDS Church has continually locked the Restorationists out of churches, dispossessed them of their buildings, and largely prevented their influence in RLDS World Conferences. The fundamentalists claim that this is odd behavior for a liberal organization, and thus they claim the RLDS hierarchy must have ulterior motives. The fundamentalists have their work cut out for them and they know it. The preparation for the Second Coming of Christ to Independence, in the view of Richard Price, "will take a number of years at the very least" (R. Price 1986:12–13).

✯ Fig. 46 | Shadows over Zion *illustrates negative or hesitant attitudes toward the Temple Lot or toward central Independence. Reprinted, by permission, from Willey (1990:30). © by Price Publishing Co.*

For the fundamentalists, the hollowing of the RLDS Church is somewhat reminiscent of the Palestinian reference to the establishment of the State of Israel as "the disaster." The loss, however, is backed by historical reference and is seen as fulfillment of prophecy, just as the LDS Church maintains a belief in a general apostasy, which occurred after the death of Jesus' original twelve apostles. The belief is that because of wickedness at the time of their deaths, God's authority and true church disappeared from the earth until it was established through Joseph Smith Jr. The early RLDS rationale was that Joseph Smith became fallen and the church had to be reorganized through the 1850s after his death—a time sometimes referred to as "a dark and cloudy day." The new rationale is that the present apostasy of the RLDS Church can be referred to as a "dark and cloudy night," where the only surviving priesthood authority is at the local level, because the RLDS Prophet and apostles have strayed (Whately 2000:3). If the RLDS Church was reorganized once, however, God can reorganize it again. Continuous authority is not a needed tenet, as with the LDS organization.

The Name Change

When the RLDS Church officially changed its name to the Community of Christ in 2001, the Restoration Branches fundamentalists saw it as the epitome of ecumenical liberalization in the main body of the church, but they were not necessarily surprised. Though some saw it as the CoC's way of "wiping out the name of the true church" in order to "liquidate the properties of the Saints," they were not too upset (Ron's RLDS 2001b). In fact, many fundamentalists saw the name change as a divinely inspired way that congregations could hold on to historic and doctrinal roots, through the continued use of the sacred RLDS name. As the name Community of Christ is put up on new churches and Web sites, the fundamentalists are enthusiastic about the opportunity to continue using the original RLDS name even though the CoC holds rights to it (R. Price 2001a, 2001b).

Sprouting on the fundamentalist landscape are such names as the "Original Reorganized Church of Jesus Christ of Latter Day Saints" or "Orthodox Reorganized Church of Jesus Christ of Latter Day Saints." Since the CoC has ceased using the RLDS name, the fundamentalists play word games to appear as the main church body—not considering themselves new churches. Whether they can legally append new prefixes to the RLDS name is yet to be seen—still, a variety of combinations are appearing (see R. Price 2001b). Some of the signs are difficult to decipher because more than a decade of change and dissent is indicated in wordings like "Central Florida Restoration Branch Proclaiming the Original Doctrines of the REORGANIZED CHURCH OF JESUS CHRIST OF LATTER DAY SAINTS." On the sign, the last nine words appear in caps.

Much difficulty exists in the fundamentalist approach. As the CoC/RLDS Church becomes nonmillennial, attempting to breach the gap toward a secular Protestant church, fundamentalist members do not want to remove their membership, believing that God will eventually open the way for them to take control. Yet the CoC is increasingly a different kind of church from what the fundamentalists wish to be associated with. They meet in different buildings and have different organizations, different doctrines, and, now, different names. The name change itself is a major reason to separate from the original church. How the fundamentalist RLDS can continue to retain their membership in the CoC is increasingly in doubt, unless dissent is ignored and the names of the dissenters are kept on record in order to bolster official CoC membership numbers.

Priesthood Justifications: New Restoration Churches

It must be remembered that most RLDS splinter congregations follow no central authority and variations in doctrine and temple belief have appeared, notwithstanding Richard Price's attempts to unify the fundamentalist cause from within the RLDS ranks. Since about 1990, change has occurred rapidly, and the RLDS splintering is an ongoing process whose outcome is uncertain. What is certain is that at least twelve completely new churches have been born out of RLDS dissent, most having a few hundred members at best (Shields 1990:208–13, 289; R. Price 1990b: 20, 1991a:18, 1999:10). Three of the most visible new churches, claiming to completely replace the CoC/RLDS organization, are discussed below (see appendix 3).

Some fundamentalists feel that the CoC/RLDS Church is in decay but not yet completely deceased; therefore, they are hesitant to sever ties, wishing to work from within the existing RLDS organization. Many new RLDS break-off churches have thus separated gradually. Other fundamentalists are convinced that the church is beyond deliverance and have sought revelation elsewhere, finally choosing completely new presidents and apostles. They organize through fascinating justifications of RLDS history. Most of the new churches have tried to return to the original principles of authority or establishment of the RLDS Church to justify their existence. Essentially, this entails reorganizations of reorganizations of churches, but, to avoid redundancy, RLDS dissenters often favor the word *restored* in their title, such as the Restoration Church of Jesus Christ of Latter Day Saints; the Church of Christ, Restored; or the Church of Jesus Christ of Restoration Latter Day Saints. Almost unconsciously, repetitive apostasy has become a tenet. If apostasy from the original 1830s Saints could lead to the RLDS Church by 1860, then new reorganizations are still possible. This is different from LDS history, which overall has seen less total dissent, perhaps by claiming complete continuity and authority since Joseph Smith Jr. with leadership always falling to the senior member of the quorum of the twelve apostles. No other Latter Day Saint church passes on authority in this manner. The RLDS Church had a logical method of succession, with a literal descendant of Joseph Smith Jr. traditionally being president, but that legacy was abandoned in 1996—further rationale for dissent—and justification of a new prophet, through bloodlines or otherwise, is the trend in some of the new churches. The tendency to organize new churches out of the independent Restoration Branches is growing.

The Restoration Church of Jesus Christ of Latter Day Saints

One such group organized from RLDS dissent in peripheral Maine was eventually named the Restoration Church of Jesus Christ of Latter Day Saints. This new church chose apostles, claimed revelation, and reorganized separate from the RLDS Church ("Abramson-Page Movement's History" 1991:17; R. Price 1991a:18). Before organization was complete, former RLDS minister M. Norman Page gave a few revelations that are still accepted by the Restoration Church. The main doctrinal slant in separating was that if the First Presidency and the Apostles become incapacitated, spiritually or otherwise, the lower group of the Seventy could claim all authority (Restoration Church 2001). A later splinter from this group naming itself the Church of Jesus Christ the Lamb of God left the Restoration Church without property or building ("Abramson-Page Movement Divides" 1992), yet the latter group developed a unique doctrinal anchor in the person of Marcus Juby, a Native American. Juby was chosen as prophet, as were twelve apostles. Thus was formed a separate organization from the RLDS Church and from the Restoration Branches. The new church was seen as the true RLDS successor and focused on the fulfillment of *Book of Mormon* prophecies regarding Native Americans becoming important builders of Zion. Juby received at least thirty-six revelations between 1991 and 2001 (many were accepted retroactively), mostly urging caution in gathering to and building Zion as well as emphasizing the importance of paying off the church's new building in Independence, which was finally accomplished in 2001 (Restoration Church 2001: Messages 16, 28). The church has over seven hundred members (Madison 2001).

This church's stance regarding the location of Zion has been vague; one revelation declared, "At this very moment, arrangements are being made to establish, in full measure, the City of Zion." The literalist millenarian reader is let down one sentence later when informed that the "call has been issued . . . and the gathering in heaven has begun" (Restoration Church 2001: Message 25). How physical the gathering and establishment of the New Jerusalem will be is vague at best, and one church authority admitted that the "question of a Temple is not a burning issue with us. However, we do believe that at some future time the Temple . . . will be built on the Temple Lot in the location (more or less) envisioned by the Hedrickites." Without access to that historically sacred land, it is difficult to identify which sacred space, but they "do not presume that [the temple] includes the ecumenical meeting center erected by the Community of Christ" (Madison 2001). About the best Juby's revelations promise is that "Zion will yet be established" (Restoration Church 2001: Message 32).

The Church of Christ, Restored

Another new church organized from individuals disgruntled with RLDS directions during the 1980s was incorporated in 1983 by Robert Buller in Lawton, Michigan. It was called the Church of Christ, Restored. Four years later, one Theron Campbell received a revelation that "only after reorganization of my church can My Spirit be poured out upon My people." The church chose Apostles (later renamed elders) independent of the RLDS organization, in a strict attempt to follow the same model used in the original reorganization in 1853 (Church of Christ, Restored 2002).

Mirroring that time when the fledgling RLDS organization awaited Joseph Smith III, this church likewise has yet to choose a prophet. In a fascinating reflection of history, however, it is arguably the most active church in the Association for the Unity of Restoration Saints, chaired by Joseph F. Smith, a great grandson of Joseph Smith Jr., not to be confused with the earlier LDS president with the same name (Association for the

Unity of Restoration Saints 2003; J. F. Smith 2001a). Whether this group can again claim a literal descendant as prophet is yet to be seen, and Smith himself says some do favor the idea, but the directive "must come from the Lord" (J. F. Smith 2001b). One fascinating indication, however, is that as members of Joseph F. Smith's organization, the church's apostles agreed to be called by the lesser title of "elder" publicly (Virgil 2001). The doctrinal backtracking was a further sign of deference in accepting Joseph F. Smith's bloodline authority (or someone's authority somehow). It would therefore be up to a prophet and not the general church body to choose twelve Apostles.

Most of the four hundred members of the Church of Christ, Restored, reside in a peripheral geography to Zion in Michigan, part of a Great Lakes slant of Restoration churches, but there is one congregation in Missouri and one in Nebraska. The church claims to have no headquarters "in a physical sense," but that "in a spiritual sense" the church "is headquartered in the Quorum of Elders," at least until a prophet is proclaimed (Virgil 2001). Most members derive from earlier RLDS congregations (Church of Christ, Restored 2002).

The Remnant Church of Jesus Christ of Latter Day Saints

One of the newest groups making an important connection with historic sacred territory was formed out of a regular gathering of the priesthood (males only) of the Restoration Branches. This periodic meeting was called simply the Elder's Conference but evolved into a more organized form, changing its name to the Conference of Restoration Elders, or CRE (R. Price 1996). In late 1997, the chairman of this group, David Bowerman, proposed to organize a new church led by twelve high priests in a council (R. Price 1998). This group was organized in mid-1999 as an RLDS modeled restructuring in order to give the Restoration Branches movement an umbrella for indefinite operation, but many fundamentalists did not accept Bowerman's move (R. Price 1998:14, 1999:8).

The group at first claimed not to be a replacement for the RLDS Church (R. Price 2000a). At the beginning, no prophet was selected and the twelve leaders were called high priests (in Latter Day Saint doctrine, literally the higher priesthood office). Just as Juby's group had organized a church with the rationale of finding authority from a grouping of local RLDS Seventies, and as the Church of Christ, Restored, had concentrated on authority to organize from the elders, Bowerman saw the high priests as the body to take on RLDS Church authority. It later developed a full-fledged First Presidency and Quorum of Twelve Apostles. This church, as with those above, became a separate entity among RLDS splinters and claims to be the true successor of the RLDS Church. The name chosen was the Remnant Church of Jesus Christ of Latter Day Saints (R. Price 1999:8). The name comes from a statement from Joseph Smith III, who described Saints not following Brigham Young westward as a "remnant scattered abroad, who remained true to the principle first given as the gospel of Christ" (Stack 2002).

The Remnant Church reports steady growth. For their April 2000 General Conference the church reported 410 people "registered to conduct the business of the conference," while one year later 459 were reported "with an estimated 600 in attendance at some of the services" (R. Price 2000a; Remnant Church 2001b). An article from the *Salt Lake Tribune* in April 2002 reported over 1,000 members (Stack 2002), and in 2003, a member of the church's First Presidency reported 1,200 (Bowerman 2003a). The church claims eighteen branches, mostly clustered in a generally north-south axis peripheral to the Ozarks from western Missouri through the Rogers area of Arkansas on into Oklahoma's Little Dixie (Figure 47). Independence may be the hub of the bustle of millennial belief activity, but this Ozark transition area is home to several groups of Latter Day Saint dissent. Exactly what traditional regional qualities (rural poverty, political conservatism, isolation, Scots-Irish ethnicity) contribute to a tendency of Latter Day Saintness here is uncertain, but the southern regionality is more evident among smaller break-off groups and is opposed to a traditional Strangite, Church of Christ (Temple Lot), and RLDS pattern oriented toward the Great Lakes. Apart from Ozark character, however, Oklahoma's Native American makeup might partially explain the pattern. Readers of the promise in the *Book of Mormon* that the Lamanites will help build the New Jerusalem certainly cannot ignore the meaning of Oklahoma, and some groups have focused proselytizing there. In any event, the geographies of these different break-offs represents the regional sectionalism of RLDS culture.

Access to the Center

The Remnant Church is calmly considering many "endeavors to gather people to the Center Place of Zion and prepare them for the day of my coming" (Larson 2003). This endeavor has made a particularly strong

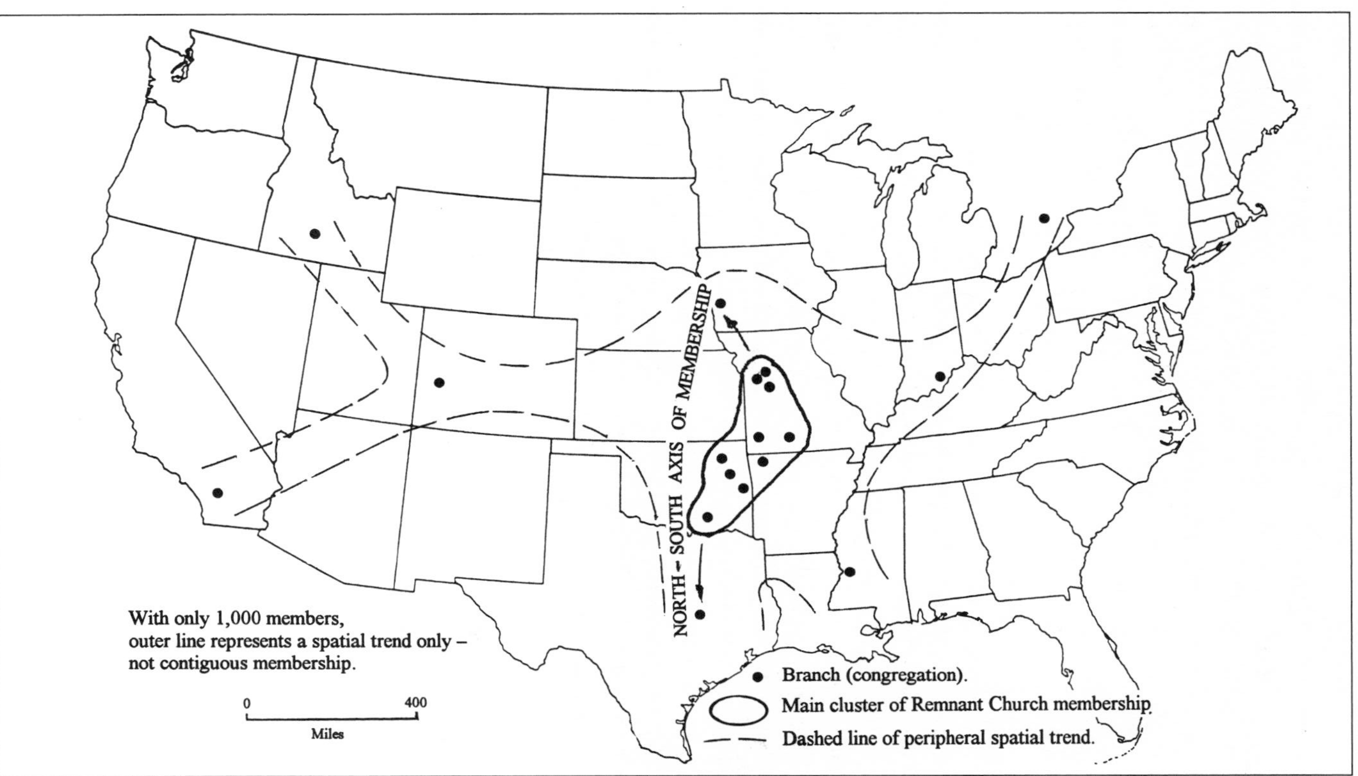

FIG. 47 | *Branches of the Remnant Church of Jesus Christ of Latter Day Saints.*

statement on space close to the Temple Lot. The church gained visibility in Independence when it successfully took control of the Restoration Center Place Branch, which met in the old William Chrisman High School building just north of Lexington Street across from the RLDS temple parking lot at 709 W. Maple. Originally built in 1929, a wealthy Restoration Branch member from Texas purchased the stately rectangular school in the late 1980s, and many fundamentalist members of the RLDS Enoch Hill congregation mentioned previously made the Center Branch their church (see fig. 45). Restorationists meeting in this building had set themselves apart in a Salvation Army–role near the Temple Lot, establishing a meal and clothing program for the needy and homeless, and opened a school and a cannery ("Center Branch Ministers to Needy" 1992; Mason 1992; Gibson 1999). A main challenge has been the cost of upkeep on the large building. In the late 1990s, however, this centrally located group became more actively involved with the CRE, which later sprouted the Remnant organization (Kluth 1992; R. Price 2000b).

In April 2001, the Remnant Church sustained as prophet for the new church Frederick N. Larsen, a great-great-grandson of Joseph Smith Jr. Larsen broke with the RLDS Church in 1984 and is the grandson of Frederick M. Smith, president of the RLDS Church from 1914 to World War II (Stack 2002). Though a move hinted at by other organizations, this is the first of the RLDS break-offs to resume the heritage of literal descendant leadership.

In one *Vision* article, a photograph portrayed the old high school building standing "boldly close to the Hierarchy's New Age Temple," but with the Remnant Church takeover, Price's Restorationist goal to have this visible building adjacent to the Temple Lot was dashed (Mason 1992). As headquarters for the Remnant Church, the former school has been handsomely decorated with large white letters prominently visible from the south (Kluth 1992; Remnant Church 2001a). The Remnant Church thus keeps the other core churches on their toes around the Temple Lot. Notably, the Remnant Church's headquarters address was changed from the Maple Street location to 700 W. Lexington, which generally faces the Temple Lot. The pull of the Temple Lot in this case is apparent, and a member of the church's First Presidency even referred to the location as "strategic" in both a present and historical sense due to its proximity to Partridge's greater parcel (Bowerman 2003b). Significantly, he did not mention the smaller two and a half acre Temple Lot, but emphasized only the larger parcel which enhances their headquarters location. One man reported that upon attending the Center Branch for the first time at the old school "the Spirit spoke to me and said that we were to attend Center Branch and fight for the building." His wife received the same revelation a week after ("Gathering" 1999). The site is practically guaranteed a future position of prominence, if not sanctity, and the new Remnant Church has an excellent gallery seat on the revered sixty-three-acre parcel (see Figure 45). Up to this point the members of the Remnant Church seem to see their headquarters as on the periphery of the sacred. The question, then, is whether this territory can be adopted into territory already seen as sacred for a century. If the mother RLDS/CoC organization can alter what land is traditionally seen as sacred, a smaller church can probably do it as well, though attempts to declare 700 W. Lexington as a new Temple Lot will, as always, meet with some dissent. The old school location, as independent Restoration Branch, or as headquarters of the Remnant church, is the newest attempt by a Latter Day Saint group to monopolize on location close to the Temple Lot. It undoubtedly will not be the last, but with a descendant of Joseph Smith Jr. at the helm, the Remnant Church is bound to make its mark.

Unlike the three new church examples above, most of the Restoration Branch congregations wish to save the existing RLDS Church from within, but their members do not suppose to know from where God will gather a new prophet and apostles. This fact in itself indicates that over the long run the scales may tip toward the establishment of new RLDS-rooted churches instead of RLDS fundamentalist organizations operating from within the current Community of Christ entity. The new churches have not met with the approval of Price, but they have succeeded in attracting several thousand adherents. Ostensibly out of frustration with the RLDS Church and the intense competition for sanctified land around the Temple Lot, some believers have even abandoned the common Latter Day Saint ideals of building up a material New Jerusalem as well. One Restoration Branch member, a county employee in Independence, confided in me that she thought Richard Price was nobly trying to put the church in order, but that her group believed that no temple structure would be built before Christ's Second Coming. Rather, He would suddenly come to Independence in the "temple of his own body." Her group views the return as imminent. When asked whether Jesus was expected to come in days, years, or decades, her reply of "seconds" was startling.

Core vs. Periphery of the New Zions

Among Latter Day Saint groups centered on Independence, schism has occurred in the core as well as at the periphery. In almost every case of splintering within the Temple Lot family of churches, innovation has occurred at the periphery of the sacred center. After establishing a divine message on the periphery, new churches invariably moved back to Missouri, usually as close to the Temple Lot as possible (Figure 48). John the Baptist made most of his visits to Otto Fetting in Port Huron, Michigan. Likewise, W. A. Draves resided in remote Nucla, Colorado, when he claimed the resumption of angelic messages started with Fetting. One group began in Mississippi and remained there. Nerren's group was first based in Denver, Colorado, far from any substantial influence of the main Temple Lot body. David Roberts's odd blend of beliefs originated in Columbus, Ohio. It can be theorized that the process of sanctification for such a complex sacred place as Independence is easier to engineer from a peripheral location where semicharismatic leaders convince a few local members of the importance of a division through some doctrinally supported stance. When these groups move back to the sacred core, they often become ripe for further division.

The model of peripheral innovation fits the Temple Lot groups well, though subsequent innovation among them has occurred in the Independence area with the emergence of altered doctrines in the new churches. Some of these, like the Leighton-Floyd (Holden, Missouri), and the non–Saturday Sabbath Fetting (Lee's Summit, Missouri) groups have moved outward but are still well within Jackson County influence. It appears that, for the most part, the innovation in the periphery has slowed as the Temple Lot Church and some of its relatives have solidified their doctrinal stances and stabilized their membership.

Faction alterations occur rapidly and recent innovations have been tumultuous. Though some of the RLDS splinters have originated in the extreme peripheries of Washington, Michigan, or Maine, with members subsequently moving to Independence, until now most RLDS division has been restricted to the area around Jackson County. Whether or not the Restoration Branches movement solidifies or splinters, the CoC seems on course to lose its dominant position at the core to fundamentalism. An inventory of CoC, Restoration Branch, Restoration Church, and a few other break-off congregations reveals a pattern quite different from the Temple Lot group's *peripheral* historical geography. Though it should be

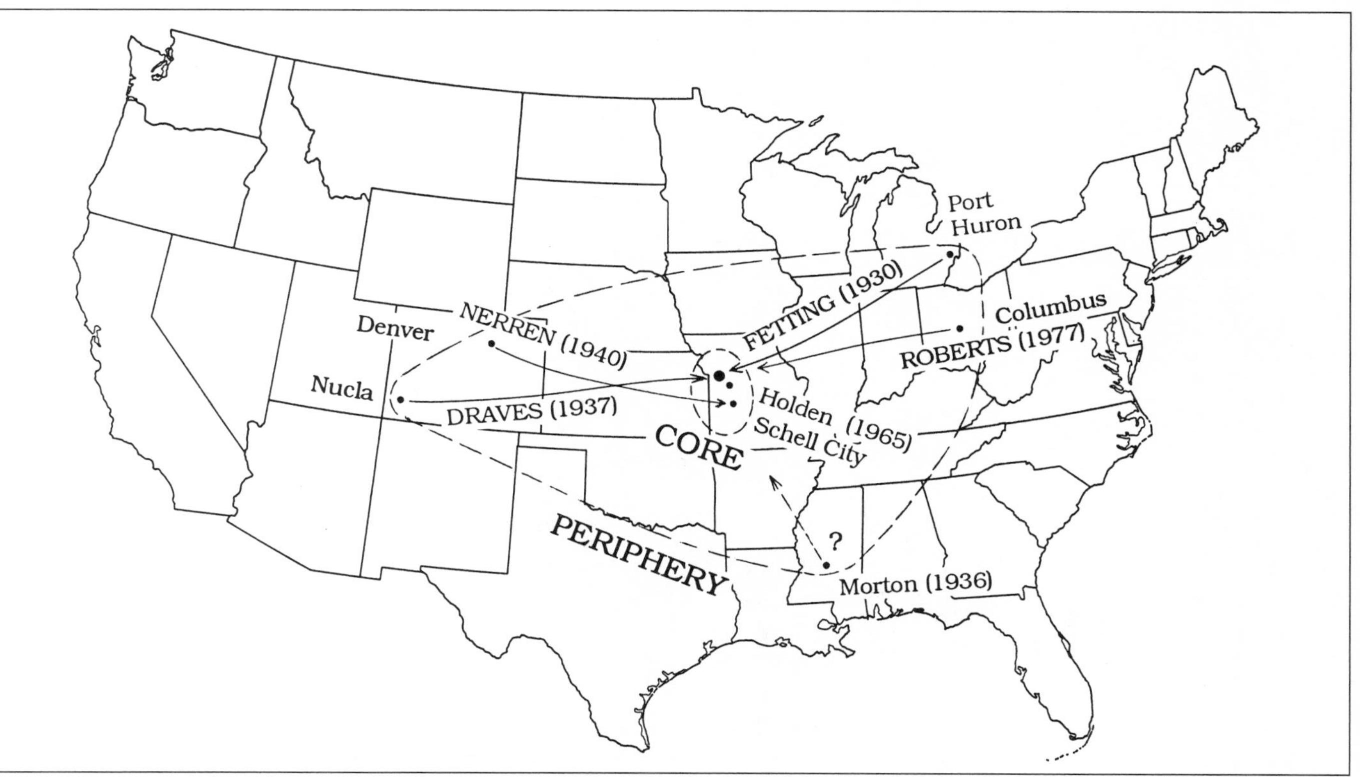

FIG. 48 | *Peripheral innovation of the Temple Lot Church family.*

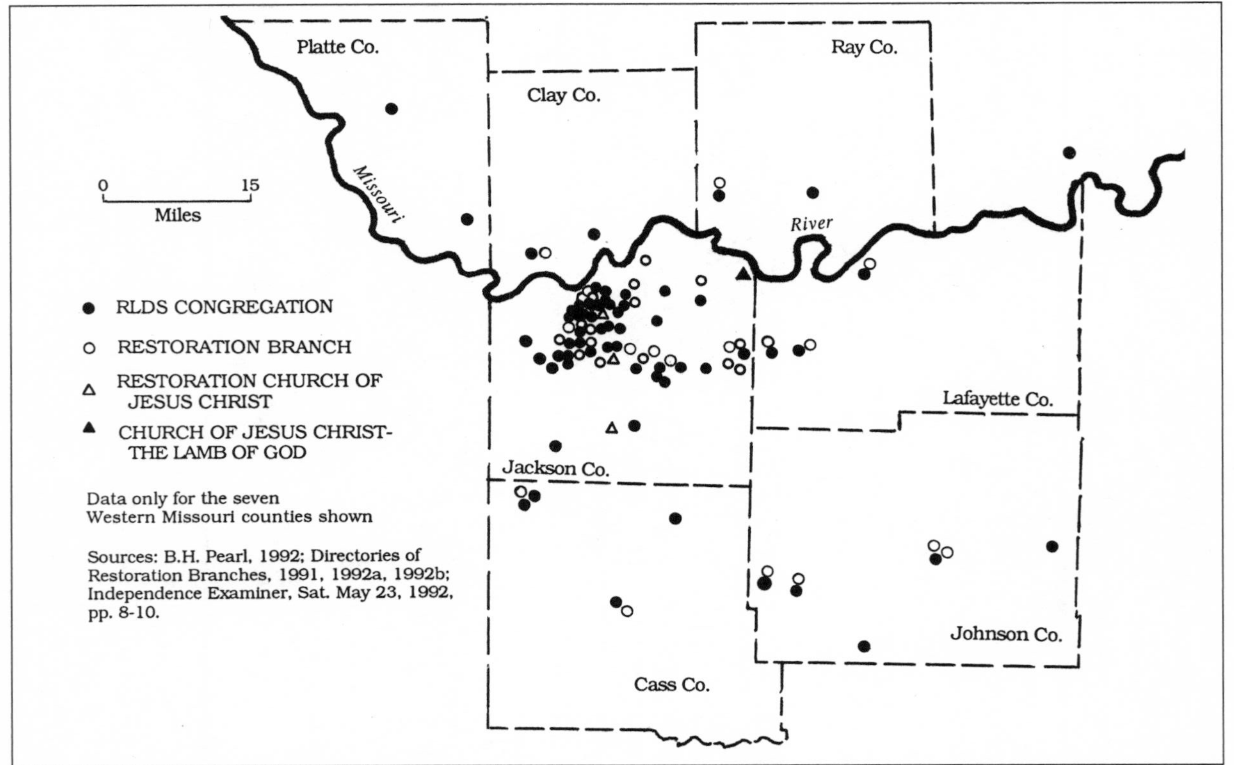

FIG. 49 | *The rise of the Restoration Branches. Data from Pearl (1992), Directories of Restoration Branches (1991, 1992a, 1992b), and* Independence Examiner, *May 23, 1992, pp. 8–10.*

recognized that RLDS dissent has occurred throughout the United States, the pattern is notably *central*, with Independence a major hub of innovation (Figure 49).

Overcast Missouri

The shadows over Zion that the Restoration fundamentalists see become even more ominous with some of the smaller groups. Though some Saints are working to unify different groups ("Association News" 1999), individuals with extreme beliefs about the area may feel dwarfed or constricted by the dominant groups there. For these, the ground in Independence has become temporarily cursed. A purging must therefore take place, and those who would pervert doctrine will be destroyed. Smaller groups, therefore, have notably more apocalyptic themes than the larger, more established churches. Their interpretations of space are physically more limited, thus they revert to change and cleansing originating solely through the hand of God. The theme of the destruction of the wicked, common in the Bible as well as in the *Book of Mormon*, has been applied to any and all groups that are viewed as incorrect or inflexible. The sacred site to be cleansed is always the same: that hillcrest in Independence where the Church of Christ (Temple Lot), the RLDS, and LDS Churches reside.

The main groups, such as the LDS Church, also use the theme of a purge, but it appears incessantly when small groups or individuals feel locked out of the sacred picture. At the extreme of limited access increasing apocalyptic belief, many individuals have taken it upon themselves to preach and publish regarding the Lord's will toward Zion, without attempting to attract adherents or even establish a church. They will often mail their messages to members of the major groups of Saints or place them in prominent places near the Temple Lot (on car windshields, for instance). Raymond E. Wood of Warrensburg, Missouri, wrote one such pamphlet, placed on the author's windshield, around the spring of 1990. It repeatedly discusses a "scourge of the Lord," which will involve "whirlwinds," "plagues," "vengeance," and "devouring fire." According to Wood, the Latter Day Saint groups are worse off now than in the early 1800s, because after having known the original and correct way of the Lord, they have departed from it "like a dog turned to his own vomit" (Wood [1989/90?]:1).

Many aspects of anti-Zion space have already been discussed. The idea goes back as far as the late 1890s, when a man who claimed that the temple site needed to be cleansed burned the Temple Lot Church's first edifice. Another man, ninety-two years later, again claimed to be instructed by God regarding the Temple Lot. He said that a cleansing would take place after an invasion of the United States by Russians who would be using chemical weapons (Blakeman and Potter 1990). This man had openly discussed his troubled ideas with the leaders of the Temple Lot Church, but he was not taken seriously. He succeeded in destroying the building but not in cleansing the site, which the Temple Lot Church, of course, still possesses. It is unknown whether the man, who ironically was named Jordan Smith, actually thought the Russians had invaded the country, but he claimed to have received three dreams of instruction from God (Carroll 1991). The result of the latest fire introduces further irony. Burning is often mentioned in the scriptures as a method of purging evil, but the disturbed arsonist of 1990 was unable to foretell the practical results of his action—namely, that the benefits of modern insurance combined with millennial fervor assured the Temple Lot Church an improved situation post supposed purge. The little church emerged from the fire with better facilities and a more determined attitude. How closely insurance companies are looking at the risks associated with the small church, however, is unknown.

Another small fundamentalist group in Lamoni, Iowa, has taken to a primitive sort of life. They have renounced the use of modern technology and make stone houses with thatched roofs without the use of electric tools (Wenske 1990b). The group's leader, a former RLDS member named Ron Livingston, apparently teaches that the closer one lives to the land, the closer one lives to Christ. If purgings-to-be disrupt high-level infrastructure, then his low-level-technology Amish-like membership might thus be protected at the time of the Second Coming.

In 1990, many in the Livingston group believed that soon "the Soviet Union would unleash" a new weapon. It would consist of multiple "exciter beams" that cause destruction when crossed over a target. This weapon would, possibly at the time of the RLDS World Conference of that year, cause a terrible annihilation (Wenske 1990b:A6). Ground zero, so to speak, was to be Independence, but Livingston has had to alter his chronology several times when predicted desolation did not come to pass. The commune, of course, would be protected, even though Lamoni itself would be "snuffed out" (presumably as a bastion of RLDS apostasy). How the group has fared in light of the collapse of the Soviet Union is uncertain, but it is apparent that many groups sustain their apocalyptic creeds according to the ebb and flow of world events.

A group headed by Jeffrey Lundgren developed another apocalyptic recipe turned tragedy. From 1984 to 1988 in Kirtland, Ohio, Lundgren taught that he himself was a prophet who would lead his people into the wilderness to find the "sword of Laban" (a tool of significance described at the beginning of the *Book of Mormon*). The group was also taught that they were to receive further sacred writings (Stephens 1990a). He told his group that a cleansing needed to take place in order to prepare the group for greater events and, to emphasize his point, he brutally shot a family of five who were beginning to stray from his group. The group then retired to the West Virginia wilderness to engage in military maneuvers preparatory to the taking of the RLDS-owned Kirtland temple by force (Stephens 1990b). Apparently, RLDS members in Kirtland were quite nervous about the teachings of Lundgren. He had acquired a cache of weapons and taught that once the group had gained control of the Kirtland temple, everyone on earth would be destroyed except his little group. After this millennial catastrophe, Zion could be established ("Ex-Cult Member Felt No Remorse" 1990).

Many of Lundgren's followers had been confused RLDS fundamentalists who viewed the Kirtland temple as the church's premier sacred historical structure, perhaps as opposed to the new RLDS temple in Missouri. Lundgren's view of the Kirtland temple as an important site for the commencement of the millennium was undoubtedly attractive to a band distraught over the directions of the RLDS Church (Buzbee and Stephens 1990). Though Kirtland is the only other site in church history where today main groups (LDS, CoC, Restoration Branches, and, at times, the Church of Jesus Christ-Bickertonites) vie for influence, it is understandable that it became easy for the group to see Independence as a rejected site and to view Kirtland with a new importance.

After the training in West Virginia, the group moved to Independence, Missouri, an odd move since action at Kirtland was to precipitate the apocalypse. Lundgren, a former RLDS member who became increasingly deranged and driven for power, was originally from Independence, however. He probably sought further financial support there, having local relatives and acquaintances. He also aimed to bolster his church by attracting other errant RLDS fundamentalists, available there in abundance. In any case, his group fell apart, witnesses fled to the police, and Lundgren and his immediate family fled to California. He was caught, tried, and sentenced to death in Ohio.

Another odd group, one almost unclassifiable, is a group called Israel's Gathering located in Buckner, Missouri, but originating, in the traditional peripheral fashion, in Oklahoma with the teachings of William Dollins. Within this organization lies a more secret core organization called Ephraim's Camp, whose purpose is to assist in the gathering to Zion of the lost tribes of Israel from "the North Countries." Ephraim's Camp receives visits from deceased Saints, the ancient American prophets Nephi (from the *Book of Mormon*) and Epheneal (not in the *Book of Mormon*), and other notables, such as the deceased black scientist George Washington Carver and a devil presence named "Dagnab"! (Price and Price 1994:20). The group has published a book of scripture called *Ephraim's Camp Record* (Dollins 1993) and claims to be the "nucleus through which Zion can and will be redeemed." It reportedly holds meetings in a pyramid-shaped building called a "tabernacle" or "tribal building" that represents the "architectural culture learned by the Children of Israel while in bondage in Egypt" (Price and Price 1994:19). How many members some of these groups have are unknown, but this one probably numbers in the tens.

Unceasing competition for the temple spot in Independence has had a variety of effects upon groups and individuals. Some have seen it necessary to beg for the Temple Lot, even using revelation resorting to outright demand. Others see Independence in a storm of dissent, Zion in spiritual shadow. Still others, tired of waiting, have sought out retreats, or replacement Zions.

For some, religious frustration in Independence is intense enough to require the belief in the area's complete destruction. Commensurate with this destruction have been the Russians, nuclear arms, laser beams, chemical warfare, and, undoubtedly in recent years, Saddam Hussein, war in the former Yugoslavia, the Palestinian-Israeli issue, Osama bin Laden's terrorists, and a variety of hurricanes and earthquakes. As current events unfold, be assured that every sort of twist imaginable will be used to maintain Independence as a sacred millennial place.

Independence Classified
World Precedents

> Human action is conditioned not by reality, but what is assumed to be reality.
>
> —Walter M. Kollmorgen

As a place where many religious views coexist in competition, Independence, Missouri, is not typically American. Different Native American groups see certain mountains in the southwest as sacred in varied ways, some of these attitudes spilling into popular culture (Blake 1997), but postcolonial sacred sites in North America tend to be rather one dimensional—those seeing them usually share a common viewpoint (Foote 1997:265–66). In earlier times, entire civilizations shared myriad religious and community perceptions (Wheatley 1971), but such traditional, multidimensional, sacred space is generally rare in the development of young North America, especially on the frontier. Whether a local Marian shrine on a hillside in Pittsburgh or a more institutional site such as the mother church of the Christian Scientists in Boston, landscapes of the sacred proliferate in the United States at varied scales of sanctity, but not generally with the intensity of devotion seen in other nonindustrialized places around the globe or in long-lived traditional sites.

Relatively few places in North America have developed to the point where the sacred is contested in multiple viewpoints. Most religious schism in the United States has been along ideological, doctrinal, or social lines and has not focused on the importance of place. Admittedly, the American historical setting is unique—it is thinner historically and less populous than other parts of the world. The beginnings of the American New Jerusalem were on the infant frontier. One could argue that a central location seen by relatively few as sacred is not comparable to Old World examples.

Besides, in the United States a distinct administrative, business, and legal climate influences cultural choice at all levels. Nevertheless, Independence, not popularly recognized as a premier religious site in America, has developed an impressive layering of competing interpretations and has managed to do so in a surprisingly short period, even in the midst of a very modern economic and political milieu. In grappling with the morphology of sacred regions, comparisons are in order with sacred places of more remote origin. These are mostly, but not exclusively, found in Asia.

Guiding Principles

Four basic principles rule sacred space: validation, delimitation and form, politicization, and conflict mitigation. Not all four apply to every sacred place, but all can. Validation involves the reason or rationale behind the sanctity of a place. Once established, sacred space is delimited by the imposition of paths, rites, behavioral demands, or taboos. The space can become politicized as state, local, or other authorities attempt to control it while not treading overmuch its sacred nature. The mixing of the sacred with the political usually results in a delicate dance of activities. When different religions overlap belief over the same site, conflict over sacred space can produce landscapes of jumbled symbols. Without explanation or some sort of key these are difficult to interpret.

In lesser or greater degrees, all the stages above apply to Independence, Missouri, but just as useful have been Foote's stages of sanctification, designation, rectification, and obliteration in his examination of the memorializing of sites of violence and tragedy (see Table 2). This frame-

Table 2. Steps to Place Sanctity Compared with Foote's Stages of Memorialization

Traditional Steps to Place Sanctity Long Term (centuries or millennia)	Foote's Stages of Memorialization Short Term (decades to a few centuries)
1. Validation	1. Delayed sanctification
2. Delimitation and form	2. Designation
3. Politicization	3. Rectification
4. Conflict mitigation	4. Obliteration

work applies to shorter-lived sites mainly in areas of postcolonial settlement, while those laid out in the above paragraph apply to sites sacred for hundreds or thousands of years. His frame is narrower than that for long-lived sacred sites, but Foote's stages often apply so well to Independence that they cannot be dismissed (Foote 1997:8–27). The implication is that two sets of theories of sacred space should be applied considering the brevity or longevity of the development of place sanctity.

For example, Foote's stages of sanctification and designation are similar to validation and delimitation here, but their meanings are somewhat inversed. Long-lived sacred places (Jerusalem, Mecca, Varanasi) draw on a convoluted mix of history and myth to validate the place, in a timeless realm where fact becomes clouded and fable emerges. "Validation stories" of ancient sites become ingrained over long periods of time. Social and cultural practices eventually define the sacred through acts and rituals. By contrast, in the shorter term, Foote's category of sanctification arguably defines a more local and legal generation of place. Newer sites are less shrouded by legend and tend to be firmer in specific facts of memorializing (like Gettysburg or Independence Hall in Philadelphia). In this shorter perspective, particular sites are designated, by official ceremony, act, or pronouncement, perhaps after decades of first becoming sacrosanct, where fable has yet to develop as a part of the sanctity of place. Conversely, designation is an act long lost or obscured in the world's oldest sacred places. Perhaps designation never happened and sanctity has evolved over centuries through a variety of complex events evolving at the site.

For such as Jerusalem or Cordoba, the third and fourth stages of politicization and conflict mitigation are more salient, so the four main stages of the construction of sacred places are discussed below with deference to insights added by Foote's classification. Foote's stages of rectification and obliteration, however, are applied more to places of tragedy and doubt and might be steps more applicable to short-term explanations of place aura. Accordingly, they are discussed last, but they have great significance to perceptions of Independence. It is a sacred place developed over a relatively short duration and thus exhibits many stages similar to Foote's, yet it also has quickly forged elements of sacred places much longer lived. Independence retains elements of both categories, perhaps because typically American processes of intense millenarian schism have been focused on one particular site (whether lot, town, or county). The convergence of such processes on special places, however, is *not* typical of the broader American Protestant scene.

Validation of Timeless Places

Places such as the Egyptian Pyramids or Cambodia's Ankor Wat stay alive in modern minds, though the cultures that produced them have been gone for centuries. To a great degree this is simply because monumental architecture has endured on the land. Writers, yearning for the wonders of the past, sometimes interpret such monuments anew or project the structures into some alternative future. Past and future become blurred, and the observer can become disoriented with regard to place in time. Validation of places of great religious sentiment can give the effect of transcending time.

In the harsh landscape of the Australian Aborigine, every hill, rock, and tree is associated with a mythical event or ancestor. Here past and present exist simultaneously (Strehlow 1947). In *The Fountains of Paradise* (1979), Arthur C. Clarke honors some of the more amazing sites of his adopted home, Sri Lanka, by extending their past religious and political glories two hundred years into the future. Clarke transforms one of the sites, Adam's Peak, known for its large footprint attributed to the Buddha himself, into the only place on earth where an orbital space tower might be constructed. Through Adam's Peak, Sri Lanka is made a port for the entire solar system. Here, the religious admittedly overlaps with the popular, secular, and technological, but the importance of the site rises beyond the merely now. Popular presentation aside, such is the nature of the most enduring of sacred places. A place's versatility of perception bodes well for its future.

The architectural layering of a particular site can also indicate a place's ability to reach through time. The Great Mosque in Cordoba, Spain, is, from the outside, a large but drab structure (Michener 1968: 204–5). Upon entering, however, the mind boggles at the vast expanse of colorful Moorish columns, which represent eternity (Calvert and Gallichan 1907:Plates 61–71). The reason for the site proper has been lost since antiquity, but during Roman times, a pagan temple to Janus was first constructed here and later razed to make way for a Visigothic Christian Church. It was presumably destroyed when the Moors conquered Spain and the Great Mosque was built over the site. Later, in a frail attempt to top Islam with Christianity, a Catholic cathedral was constructed by clearing some of the columns from the central area of the mosque (Michener 1968:209). That the Great Mosque reflects the overlay of different political influences is clear; once a certain threshold of sanctity is reached, the aura of a site seems maintained more or less in perpetuity.

The Temple Lot in Independence, whose sanctity dates from an 1831 prayer and pronouncement in a small stand of trees, has little deep history. The site at the time was on the border between Anglo settlement and Native American resettlement in the Kansas Territories. Apparently, an old Native American trail had passed nearby, and a few myths have evolved justifying its importance in pre-Columbian times, but there is no pre-colonial significance to the site known among the general public. Joseph Smith Jr. pointed to it and it was done. Independence has, however, rapidly developed a competition of viewpoints over a relatively short period, partly due to the application of biblical imagery to western Missouri and partly due to the multiple views promoted through schism among the Latter Day Saint churches. The aura of the Temple Lot is not broadly based through American culture, but it is on its way.

Mecca, the most sacred place for Muslims, is associated with the place where Abraham and Ismail originally built the Kaba cube, on which is mounted a sacred black stone, representing Allah's covenant with Ismail and, subsequently, with the Muslim community. After prayer, the black stone is usually touched and kissed (Burton 1964:168–69). The Kaba had previously been the place where traders on the Arabian caravan trail established a center to worship multiple deities (Esposito 1991:5–8, 16, 22, 92). There is a less steeped parallel in the several cornerstones discovered on the Temple Lot during excavations by the Church of Christ (Temple Lot). These, on display, validate the sanctity of the site. All Latter Day Saint groups, however, do not accept them as authentic, nor are they treated with the same emotional fervor as the Kaba's black stone. Perhaps one day they shall, though no particular biblical imagery has been applied to the cornerstones themselves.

At the center of Lamaist Buddhism in Lhasa, Tibet, the eternal is portrayed in the Potala Palace, with its many gold-plated mausoleums. The meaning, however, is lost on most Westerners. Tibetan Buddhists believe that their living leader, the Dalai Lama, is a reincarnation of the noblest of gods, perhaps the Buddha himself. The mausoleums contain the remains of former Dalai Lamas, and thus Potala becomes much more than merely the gargantuan traditional home of the Lamaist leader (Chapman 1938: 68–69). Rather, it is the eternal residence of the Tibetan Buddhist deity, serving on earth, body by body, searching for eternal release. At the nearby Jo-Khang temple even mice go undisturbed, since they may be the incarnations of former temple guardians (155). In Lhasa, eternity is portrayed from the greatest to the smallest.

Though Missouri in general is sometimes associated with expulsion and persecution (especially by the western LDS Church), there are no symbols near the Temple Lot directly associated with death or the afterlife, besides the occasional Community of Christ cross. The Independence sites seem much more attuned to collective belief and identity, whereas Old World sacred sites often exhibit traits much more accommodating to individual credence. Latter Day Saints in their New Jerusalem, however, see the eternal nature of the site connecting it across a mythical span from biblical beginnings to apocalyptic endings. Especially for Utah Mormons, Jackson County is believed to be the site of the Garden of Eden. After expulsion, moreover, Adam's family then inhabited western Missouri, which is thus the location of prediluvian biblical events. The other groups of Saints generally do not apply biblical significance to the sites, but they still have applied a complex ordering of historical justifications and possible apocalyptic events to the Temple Lot and vicinity. Virtually all groups of Saints believe that the Kansas City area (along with apocalyptic Jerusalem) will be a site for the return of Jesus Christ, where a millennial city will be built.

Consequently, for most believers, modern Independence is a place of temporal betweenness. Though, for some, apocalyptic events are imminent, believers dwell in a time between historic local biblical events and future millennial ones, where the focus is usually on the importance of the Americas as God's chosen land through divine restoration. The impressive sprawl of suburban Kansas City is largely unimportant in the millennial view; it is seen as in a temporary and relatively iniquitous state. It is an amazing achievement that in less than two hundred years Independence has gained so much depth and aura among Latter Day Saint groups, while it took Cordoba, Adam's Peak, and Lhasa at least a thousand. Independence does not have their depth, but it has audacity. In America, however, traditions of land ownership, Manifest Destiny, and economic enterprise reduce the tendency to apply sacred meaning to specific sites. Independence as sacred, however, was unique, its growth paralleling the ubiquitous American tradition for churches to endlessly splinter. In its own manner, and under these conditions, North America apparently does have (or did exhibit) limited mechanisms to quickly fashion sacred place. Such places are so enshrouded in the depth of historical and religious meaning that they acquire an otherworldly permanence. Cycles of discovery and rediscovery are set in motion and people become caught up in preserving the essence and power of place. Fundamentalist trending groups in Independence struggle to maintain what they view as the original purpose and meaning of the site. Depending on interpretations of Smith's original pronouncements, different groups of Saints approach the demarcation of place in different ways. Though perhaps less pronounced than in eastern sacred sites, behaviors are gradually being established appropriate to sites of more long-lived spiritual authority, yet within the unique modern political and economic American environment.

Delimitation and Form

Sacred places are delimited as otherworldly in a variety of ways. Nonbelievers may not be permitted entry. Proscriptions on behavior usually apply. Rituals, such as prostration and prayer with specific movements or orientations may be suggested or required to help eternally connect the believer with the place. Sacred places commonly portray unique spatial structure. The internal geography varies, but two characteristics common to almost all sites are paramount: the tendency to form an earthly realm modeled after that of the Heavens and the proclivity to organize sacred space into ever holier concentric rings. The division between the sacred and the profane must be shown. Stones or monuments may mark the sacred, or a number of circumambulation, or walking, paths can surround a sacred center. Sacred space is a balance between the maintenance and stability of the core contrasted to less sacred peripheral influences.

Imprinting Heaven and the Centrality of Being

The religious scholar Mircea Eliade has noted that areas perceived as sacred "manifest a wholly different order" from profane locations (Eliade 1959: 11). Like the *New Yorker* cartoon showing a sign along a road to the Rocky Mountains stating "Entering God's Country, Next Secular Area 450 Miles" (*New Yorker* 1992), those seeing the sacredness of a city or patch of land view something otherworldly, not just grass, bushes, telephone poles, and buildings. The French sociologist Jean Baudrillard saw this character during a visit to Salt Lake City. He wrote that it "has the transparency and supernatural, otherworldly cleanness of a thing from outer space. A symmetrical, luminous, overpowering abstraction" (Baudrillard 1989:2). The sacred in the environs of Independence carries multiple forms. Not just one otherworldly perception exists, but many different (though related) views are in competition for the same site. Believers likewise credit many places as copies of heaven both in their minds and on the landscape. Of a necessity, one's personal interpretation is that which pleases deity. Such places are commonly seen as cosmic centers of creation or of culmination; perceptions that are often archaic and based in ancient myth (Tuan 1977: 85–100). Some of the following examples no longer exist—but others persist. Otherworldliness is intensified when competing views develop among believers, whether through schism, splintering, or overlap, and the same sacred place is viewed in varied ways.

The Mayans oriented their temples according to the "axes of the universe" and the traveling sun arc on the day the rainy season began. Their ceremonial pyramids were likewise oriented to the solar path. Reflecting the surrounding Central American volcanic environment, the cordilleras were seen as mythical mountains of creation (Wolf 1959:83). The Mayans lived in a trembling, unstable world of fickle gods and labored to keep them "in their heaven" through appeasing sacrifices (Wolf 1959:1–3, 79).

Patterns in Navajo life also tie directly to a heavenly pattern. Their perception is centered among four sacred mountains in the southwestern United States symbolizing the points from which the gods undertook creation. Outside the circle delimited by these peaks, the realm of Navajo existence ceases to have true meaning (Johnson 1988:41–42). Even the traditional Navajo house, the hogan, is an architectural representation of the circle of the peaks, a sacred space in microcosm, with the individual at its hearth (Johnson 1988:40–41). Those seeking a link to the original creation and to heaven sometimes make pilgrimages to the sacred mountains close by.

Only a three-hour drive from the geographic center on the conterminous United States, the Latter Day Saint acceptance of Independence is otherworldly. The central location is a varied cultural anchor: at the center one finds an origin, at the center one finds balance and stability, at the center one finds God. For Latter Day Saints, a central location signifies more than pastoral or moral life, rather, an antediluvian biblical site projected into millennial dress. While the center of North America is sacrosanct, the coasts are antichthones and signify a profane, even wicked, life. The Missouri-Kansas Border is also the median between early urban settlement meeting more remote pastoral and frontier values westward. For the western Mormons, sanctity is also applied to remote Utah in isolation, a place of important preparation.

To Tibetans, many Himalayan Mountains are sacred as the dwellings of pre-Buddhist gods (Bernbaum 1988). Some of the most sacred mountains there are purely mythical. Mount Shambhala, for instance, is believed to be a place of peace and stability where the faithful Buddhist, as a reward, may be born in future lives. One of the most important mythical mountains for Buddhists is Mount Meru, which is supposed to be the "gravitational center of the world," the place where cardinal directions intersect ("This Land of Snow Ridges" 1988:7). To Buddhists it is not important if these are real peaks or symbolic ones. Oddly enough, the famed Mount Everest is apparently seen by most Tibetans as possessed of a worldly deity and is, therefore, "not important for enlightenment" (1988:6). Since many who try to ascend die, it is a logical local assessment.

Latter Day Saint groups commonly use references from Isaiah referring to "Mount Zion" (8:18) or the "mountain of the Lord's House" (2:2) as meaning Independence. To them, the mountain is a metaphor of great spirituality, the place of the temple of God, and the site of the Second Coming. For Utah Mormons, of course, Isaiah's usage is doubly symbolic; it can mean the Wasatch and the Salt Lake Temple or any of over one hundred operating temples as symbols of a heightened spiritual state gradually surrounding the final American temple to be placed in the center place of Missouri.

Just as mountains are preeminent sacred centers in Tibet and the Western United States, India's sacred counterpart is its rivers. In northern India, the city of Varanasi lies in the ancient culture core in the Ganges River Plain. Here, Hindus focus devotion on Shiva, the god of creation and destruction, and the Ganges River is believed a strand of Shiva's hair fallen to the land (Rau 1986:251; Eck 1982:30–31). Birth and death are symbolized as the Hindu faithful adorn phallic statues with flowers and feel compelled to purify themselves through immersion in the untreated water. While the river is sacred in the extreme, only one of its banks falls into the realm of the holy. One hopes to die on the west bank, in Varanasi, but the east bank is profane space; if a person dies there, his or her next incarnation is said to be an ass (Eck 1982:11–12, 352).

For most Jews, Israel is sacred historical territory, and Jews, Christians, and Muslims alike hold the city Jerusalem in the highest esteem (Wilken 1986:301). Since the establishment of Israel in 1948, many Jews view the political developments there as a sign of God's loyalty to His chosen people (Houston 1978:232; Judge 1983). For religious Jews, this is the homeland and most sacred place, where God's people await redemption. Nearly every town has scriptural-historical significance (Bar-Gal 1984). The fundamentalist Jewish sect Gush Emunim, who have taken the lead in establishing Jewish settlements in the controversial West Bank, characteristically choose places associated with ancient scripture as premier sites, thus linking heaven with earth. Hebron, a Gush Emunim center, is prominent as the traditional site of the burial of Abraham. Another settlement has been made on a newer site named Shilo, known as the place of the first tabernacle set up by Joshua ("This Is Our Land" 1992). In the West Bank, where rabbis commonly refuse to distinguish earthly sites from scriptural ones, the ultimate nightmare of the Gush Emunim is the "land for peace" process in which Israel turns over sacred land to Palestinian control (Wilken 1986:304).

Latter Day Saints often apply the qualities of heaven on earth and sacred center to Independence. When Independence was originally platted it was at the western edge of European settlement in America. Joseph Smith wrote that the New Jerusalem should be established in Jackson County between the Natives and the non-Mormons in the center of America. He also taught that Independence was the site of the original paradise, as well as the place of millennial activities yet to be. Similar to the custom of traditional sacred places, the New Jerusalem was viewed as a universal beginning and ending place, to be established at the geographical center of North America, though the meaning is lost on most of the citizens of Missouri today. Though the RLDS Church in Independence may have pulled away from this interpretation, it is clear that many characteristics possessed by the world's most prominent sacred places have a solid beginning at Missouri's New Jerusalem.

Rings of Sacredness

Sacred places of renown also commonly divide territory into concentric rings from the sacred to the profane. Tuan's (1975:153–55) treatment of space in the American home provides a good conceptual metaphor. American homes commonly maintain a range and intensity of space that can be considered sacred. In most, a communal more secular area is used to entertain guests. This living room is, in fact, primarily for guests; often children are not allowed to play there, where the best, but stuffiest, furniture is carefully arranged. Normally a space for guests, strangers enter directly through a front door; friends use the back. A separate and more remotely located family room reveals a more comfortable, well-worn place of gathering. Eating places in the home may also be divided between the more ceremonial and the more familiar. The bedroom is the inner sanctum of privacy and intimacy, a place of recovery and renewal, a place we go, as Tuan observes, "when we can no longer maintain a brave front before the world" (1975:154).

The world's most sacred places maintain regions of familiarity and ritual not unlike those of the home. The city of Varanasi contains at least

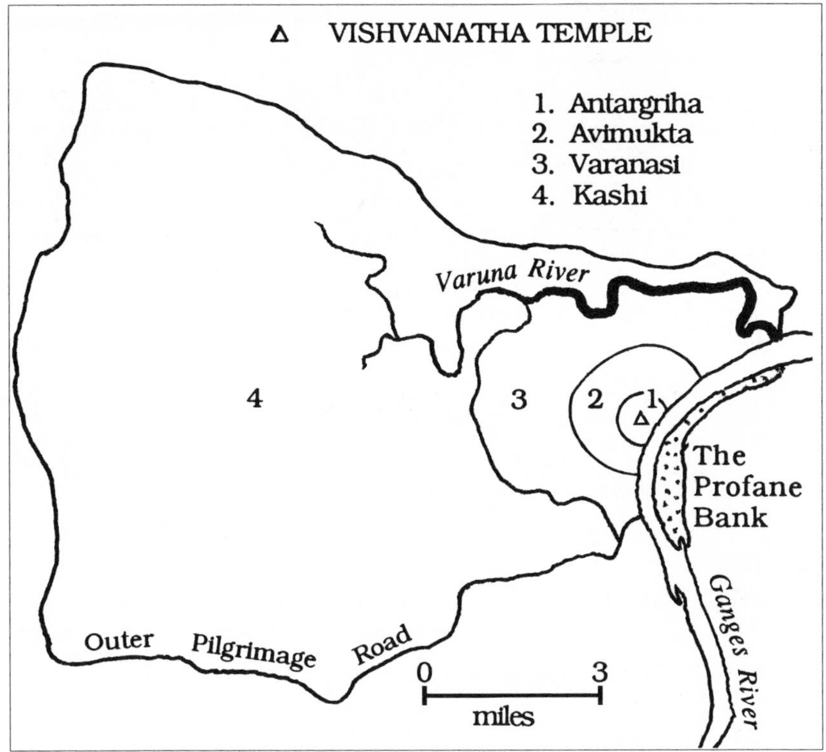

FIG. 50 | *Sacred rings around Banaras.*

four distinct rings of intensity that are progressively "charged with power" (see Figure 50; Eck 1982:350; Rau 1986:224). Specific pilgrimage routes delimit each (Eck 1982:350–57). The outermost region of approximately nine by eleven miles is called Kashi—known for its ability to liberate faithful Hindus from the cycle of incarnations upon death (28–29). The next concentric region inward is called Varanasi, named for the tributary of the Ganges forming its northern border. Then follows the zone of Avimukta, seemingly a transition region between Varanasi and the core. The inner sanctum of Antargriha, about three-quarters by three-quarters of a mile in size, revolves around the Vishvanatha Temple. This is considered the most holy edifice in the city and, within it, the phallic symbol (a linga) of the god Shiva is the center of clamorous Hindu attention (121–23). The Ganges River truncates the sacred zones and the east bank is not considered sacred.

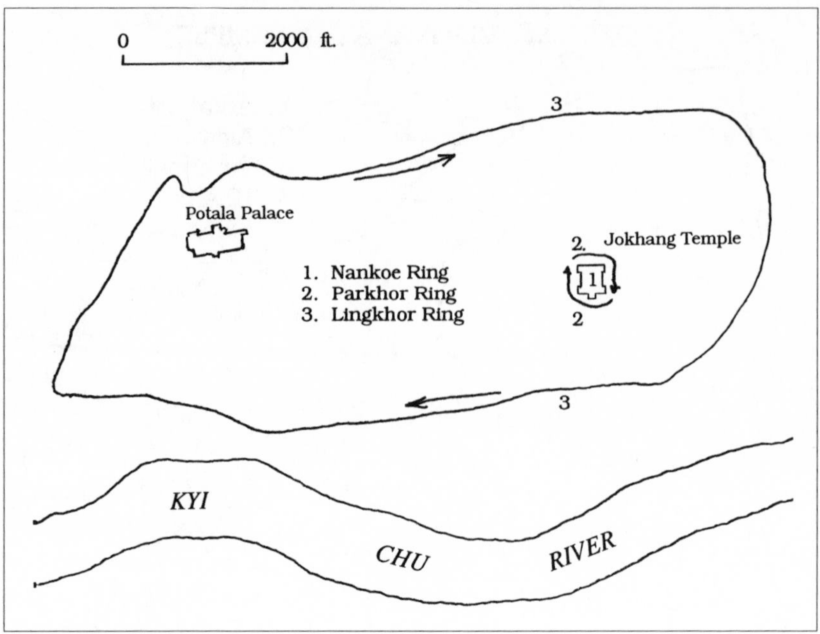

FIG. 51 | *Circumambulation rings around Lhasa.*

Like Varanasi in the Hindu realm, Lhasa, Tibet, is a most sacred Buddhist center. Pilgrims' circumambulations encircle it, too, denoting increasing intensity of sacred space (Figure 51). Within Tibet's most sacred temple, the Jokhang, worshipers traditionally circled the statue of the Buddha clockwise (Harrer 1984:156). This innermost path is called Nankoe (David-Neel 1927:269). Around the Jokhang Temple, a greater circumambulation (the Parkhor ring) takes place. Pilgrims along this route also move clockwise, "some by the length and some by the breadth of their bodies," many frequently prostrating themselves on the ground in a complex ritual (Harrer 1984:155). Farther out runs the Lingkhor Road, a four-mile circuit around the whole of Lhasa, which the faithful walk daily (Chapman 1938:160–67). This path circumscribes a sacred area containing the Jokhang Temple as well as the Dalai Lama's Potala Palace. Along the Lingkhor path, special temples and shrines of the Buddha can be visited. Here also live the lower classes responsible for removing corpses and refuse from the city. Leather workers, whose trade involves killing animals, are likewise outcast and live on the Lingkhor ring. Along the Lingkhor, profane periphery and sacred center mix.

James Duncan's work (1990) on the Kandyan Kingdom of central Sri Lanka described a similar profane to sacred spatial hierarchy. Foreign embassies from Colombo had to travel about sixty miles to reach Kandy from the coast. They were received in an incremental manner, continuously halted by messengers of the king along the route. The trip sometimes took months. The slowness of the procession was painful for the impatient Westerners, who had little inkling that they were symbolically entering heaven (Duncan 1990:140, 145–51).

Upon arrival, the procession had to stay at a rest house outside Kandy, often for several days. When the king finally received the pilgrims, an interminable night march began. A combination of seven thorn hedge and rampart gates were ceremoniously passed, marking entry into the city. After delay for a meal, the procession resumed at midnight, symbolically about to enter Mount Meru, the abode of Sakra, the king of the gods. A moat was crossed, steps negotiated, and more gateways passed. Entering the huge audience hall, the leaders of the group still had to ascend another flight of stairs and pass through seven white curtains before viewing the king. Even then, while slowly advancing, the British ambassador had to advance and prostrate himself three separate times. Discussion through at least two interpreters then took place, in an extraordinarily circuitous ritual. It apparently took twenty to thirty minutes to answer a simple question, preventing complex issues from being taken up before the king. The procession into Mount Meru was not complete until about six o'clock in the morning. The symbolic encounter, not counting the days of travel and the days in wait outside the city, took approximately eleven hours for a simple greeting and presentation of gifts, but this was the requirement to enter heaven and converse with God.

A tendency to order space in a symbolic spatial hierarchy is found in Jewish tradition as well. In a study of the ancient Jewish sect of the Mishnah Qorashim, Bokser identified no less than eleven degrees of place holiness (1985:289–90). These ranged from the Land of Israel at the most general extent to the most Holy City of Jerusalem next, down to the inner sanctuary of the Jewish high priest in the temple Mount, known as the Holy of Holies.

For the Muslim, Mecca is seen as holy from both near and afar. Muslims pray, prostrate if possible, facing Mecca, and the devout are also required to visit that city on a spiritual pilgrimage (the Hajj) at least once in his or her lifetime. The Muslim community, regardless of location, is unified spiritually and geographically. On approach to the city, whether by road or by air, the pilgrim shouts, "Oh, Lord, I am here." In preparation, men are required to wear white clothing symbolizing purification. During the Hajj in Mecca a variety of redemption, devotion, and commemoration rituals are undertaken. At the black cube structure of the Kaba, many pilgrims circle seven times counterclockwise (Esposito 1991: 92–93).

Mormon space in Salt Lake City is also hierarchical but is distinct from the more mythical space of multifaceted Independence. The LDS Church owns most of Salt Lake City's center, whereas it is only one of many players in Independence. The symbolic, geographic, and survey core for the entire Mormon realm is the Salt Lake Temple, though most believe that focus will someday shift to Independence. Until then, the Salt Lake Temple is "the mountain of the Lord's house," spiritually taller than any physical peak in the Rockies. Within the temple, the faithful Mormon passes, room by room, through levels of spiritual growth until arriving at the ultimate goal: the central Celestial Room where the devout symbolically encounter the presence of God. Here heaven is exposed to, and only to, the faithful. Non-Mormons and even less active LDS cannot enter. The Salt Lake Temple is located within a two-block section of LDS-owned museums, auditoriums, and church offices. Today, a wall surrounds one block of what is known as Temple Square, but it is not an absolute boundary. In the time of Brigham Young a wall surrounded the entire city center, including Young's home and farm (Young 1970:1–5; Morgan 1973: Plate 6). Today, the new Church Conference Center on the site of the old LDS gymnasium is now complete and can be considered conceptually included within Temple Square. Also in the area, more church offices and a high-rise building owned by the church are dominant (the ZCMI department store used to be owned by the church), but these have become intermixed with other offices, stores, residences, and hotels. Immediately outside Temple Square some mixing of the sacred with the profane appears, but church influence is expanding. Beyond, a more profane business environment prevails such as at the Olympic influenced Gateway Mall, but these are heavily influenced with sites of LDS interest. On a regional scale, the Mormon realm is usually divided according to Meinig's (1965) model of its urban core, the Utah domain, and a peripheral sphere of LDS influence.

For the many Latter Day Saint groups who hold Independence in reverence, the sacred core is also obvious—the two-and-one-half-acre Temple Lot, owned by the Church of Christ—but there is no LDS temple here to mark that sacred importance. It is seen by the LDS Church as a future center and is left up to the substantial imagination of the individual members to interpret the meaning of the site. Most Latter Day Saint groups believe that Christ's eventual return here will establish heaven, of sorts, on earth, in concert with millenarian activities at the Jerusalem of old. The small Temple Lot Church sees this sacred spot, and only this, as sacred. Other groups vary in their interpretations of the core's size and location, and the historical dominance of the Temple Lot has recently been disputed. The CoC/RLDS Church has given up attempts to possess the lot, saying that the site for the temple now lies across the street.

Most groups, however, still hold the central site sacred and look forward to the day when they might possess it. Around the Temple Lot are about sixty acres of secondary sacred space, with ownership divided about evenly between the CoC/RLDS and LDS Churches. The LDS Church in particular tends to view all of the greater sixty-three acres as sacred, and not only the smaller Temple Lot, and has recently given (consciously or unconsciously is unknown) greater emphasis on its own landholdings in Independence even at the expense of the Temple Lot. Since the RLDS Church could not obtain the lot, peripheral land in the immediate vicinity became important. One RLDS member claimed her grandfather was inspired to stop farming and travel 50 miles to Independence to buy land just north of the Temple Lot where the Stone Church would stand (Brown 2001). Through the 1990s, in an apparent attempt to consolidate a sacred ring around Temple Lots, old and new, the RLDS Church bought a majority of residential lots immediately to the north and northwest.

Away from church-owned property at the core, greater Independence is often viewed as at least somewhat sacred; most RLDS and Temple Lot break-off groups located in the city, eye the Temple Lot as their own. At times they have designated other spots as sacred—or the possibility of other spots, but this always results in schism. The LDS Church is more prone to speak of the centrality of the larger area of Jackson County, while both the LDS Church and the CoC also view sites farther away in Clay and Caldwell Counties with awe. Since the early church sent missionaries to teach the Native Americans in Kansas Territory, the LDS Church has usually included eastern Kansas within the New Jerusalem zone. In Daviess County, some seventy miles north of Independence, only the LDS Church now venerates land. The point is that a hierarchy in the sacred space surrounding Independence exists, but interpretations of it are multiple and divided among the various groups.

The Sacred Core

Revered space is commonly hierarchical in organization, ordered from the most profane to the most sacred. The core is sacred space at its most extreme, the highest representation of the otherworldly. Here are exhibited unique traits ranging from the intangible of a notably changed or charged environment to varied rituals and prohibitions on space. Peripheral Kansas City and its suburbs are usually considered profane. In Independence, the grassy Temple Lot is spiritual ground zero. Believers treat it not with the complex rituals seen in a Varanasi or a Mecca, but they often try to live close by. The area there is mostly open, and believers sometimes stroll on the grass as if the divine location helps them to face difficult decisions. People walk on the lot, around it, and pray at it, or contemplate the future while gazing hopefully at the sacred structure of their choice. No walls, fences, or prohibitions of any type yet bar entry. Anyone, Latter Day Saint or not, may stroll on the site, and the Temple Lot Church is tolerant of a fair amount of intrusion on their land. In deference to possession, some will ask for permission first, sometimes not, in rejection of the small church's authority. As the years pass, and with increasing numbers of Latter Day Saint splinter churches, activity around the Temple Lot will become more complex. What regulations may need enforcement is difficult to tell, but an increase of requests for activities of different groups there will increase the Temple Lot Church's role as manager of sacred space.

Just as the grandeur of the built environment of any sacred place cannot adequately express the full sentiments believers encounter, some places achieve the connection between material and spiritual more intensely and thoroughly than others. At the sacred center of Buddhism, the Jokhang Temple in Lhasa, Tibet, one senses a mystical, dark feel of almost primeval earthiness (David-Neel 1927:280; Chapman 1938:153–55; Harrer 1984: 156–59). Here the statue of the Buddha reminds of the eternal nature of Lhasa as home of Lamaist Buddhism in general and of the Dalai Lama as the incarnation of the Buddha in particular. Mecca, with multiple sites for prayer and multiple circuits to Allah, also expresses sanctity to an emotional degree.

The depth of belief at the Temple Lot is visibly expressed in the architecture around the periphery of the lot itself. At Lhasa, Mecca and the Temple Lot perceptions only partly visible are represented. All are the tips of symbolic icebergs. Though people come to pray at the lot, visitors are usually respectably behaved; but each has his or her own vision of a New Jerusalem yet to be established. Mecca and Lhasa have more ability to incite emotional response reflected in public action among devotees. With longevity Independence will yet as well, if not prohibited by secular authority.

Prohibitive and Divided Cores

Restrictive sanctions apply to many sacred cores, especially the more ancient ones. These restrictions attempt to keep out the profane and to lessen conflict among the different believers. At many sites, absolute prohibitions are enforced. In Varanasi, at the central temple of Vishvanatha, only Hindus are allowed to worship (Eck 1982:121). At Kandy, Sri Lanka, very few were privileged to enter the sacred center of the city; as earlier described, the trip to the center by outsiders was arduous.

Sometimes the sacred core is ultra prohibitive. Even the ancient Israelites, God's chosen people, were not allowed to view the sacrosanct container of commandments, the Ark of the Covenant. In addition, the ancient Jews maintained innumerable regulations on sacred space. The temple of Herod was sacred, for example, and non-Jews were not allowed entry. The temple's most revered spot, the Holy of Holies, was open only to the Jewish High Priest (Bokser, 1985:287, 290).

Today, in an attitude of better safe than sorry, most Jewish religious authorities prohibit entry to the ancient Temple Mount because it is not known exactly where the Holy of Holies was located (Wigoder 1989: 696; Glasse 1989:102). The prohibition was fortunate, since two Muslim mosques now cover the site: Al-Aqsa and the central Qubbat Al-Sakhra (known in English as the Dome of the Rock) (Glasse 1989:208). Israeli police usually keep Jews and others from entry to the Temple Mount, the third most important site to believers of Islam (Wigoder 1989:696). When Israeli Prime Minister Ariel Sharon arrogantly toured the Temple Mount in September 2000, a renewed intifada followed that continues to this day.

At times, sacred prohibitions encompass larger areas. All of Mecca and Medina, the two holiest cities of the Islamic world, are off-limits to non-Muslims. For the pilgrims themselves, certain denials are required. During the Hajj, sexual activity and hunting are not permitted. For the visit to the Kaba in the Grand Mosque, males often shave their heads. Jewelry and perfume are prohibited as ungodly distractions (Esposito 1991:92).

Concerning prohibition, Independence is yet in its youth. Prohibition has not affected its landscape, though members of some of the groups obviously feel uncomfortable traversing the land of other groups. The small

Church of Christ (Temple Lot) sometimes appears wary, but is yet tolerant of others' beliefs and intrusions onto the lot. At times, emotional or unstable individuals have caused havoc there. If disturbances become common or conflict between two or more of the groups perchance escalates, restrictive boundaries may yet appear on the landscape. It is conceivable that at some future point the Church of Christ might construct a fence around the lot, particularly if it ever decides to construct a temple. Other Latter Day Saint groups, particularly those derived from the Temple Lot Church, would see this as a desecration.

Influences on Core and Periphery

Sacred space is seldom static. A sacred core may be the origin of all change as spiritual innovations ripple away from a disturbed or inventive center. Furthermore, the sacred core is not always maintained; the center can shift through time. Sacred sites in the Latter Day Saint realm have shifted from New York state to Kirtland, Ohio, to western Missouri, to Nauvoo, Illinois, and then finally to Salt Lake City with westward movement.

In some cases, a sacred space, or some part of it, changes in intensity over time. In the past, Jerusalem was much more important to the Muslim world than it is today. This site, where Mohammed had his night vision, formed the original prayer orientation for Muslims (Glasse 1989:102). The direction has since changed to Mecca. Likewise, Varanasi's core has changed over the centuries, shifting a mile or so to the south, but, considering the city's age, the change is minimal.

In its early years, the Latter Day Saint New Jerusalem also went through a slight shift in location. Most Latter Day Saints in the original settlement of the 1830s lived in what is now Kansas City, Missouri, and if the original missionaries had not been prohibited from preaching to the Indians in the Kansas Territory, the New Jerusalem site might have been established some twenty-five miles farther west.

Some sites experience change forced from their periphery more than from the core. Since the early 1800s the LDS Church has gradually given more importance to Missouri from periphery to center by institutional choice. The RLDS/CoC organization has experienced peripheral influence in a different way, with more of its grassroots membership spread throughout the United States than in the center place. Though ultimate splintering was at the core, splintering was reinforced by the diffuse peripheral membership. Even the Temple Lot Church, headquartered at the spiritual core, has perhaps hesitated to build a temple partly because of the range of emotions that break-off churches have toward the lot. Hierarchical church directives or perception of the believers, therefore, are not the only regulators of change. Change can also be the result of secular control applied from without the sacred space. If evolutionary, so be it, but if change or control originates outside of the sacrosanct region, at best the result will be tension.

The State and the Secular

All sacred places today are bounded within modern states, and usually secularly regulated. In normal state function, sacred places can be exposed to the high drama of national politics. In such instances, the ironies of otherworldly belief can clash with the perceived needs of political control and civil service. In the necessities of law enforcement, social welfare, utility provision, or tourism, sacred places offer special challenges.

Stability of Sacred Space

For example, in Varanasi, the provision of health care becomes difficult when Hindus often will not leave sacred areas to attend to their needs in health facilities nearby. For the devotee, medical service lies emphatically outside sacred territory and the risk of losing the eternities is greater than the risk of dying from mere mortal infirmity. Also, how does society in general maintain the societal survival norm when there is temptation to commit suicide to achieve a greater goal? This has, on occasion, been a problem in Varanasi (Eck 1982:126), but it was also recently observed in the American scene when the Heaven's Gate group committed mass suicide just north of San Diego in the belief that they were "leaving their earthly containers" to board a UFO traveling behind the passing Hale-Bopp comet (Kenworthy and Schwartz 1997).

State control of sacrosanct places is problematic. In Jerusalem even the repair of mundane utilities can present a religious dilemma. Imagine only being able to fix a telephone line if you are of a particular religious persuasion. In the fall of 1996, ostensibly for tourism and historical appreciation, the Israeli government briefly opened a tunnel under the ancient Temple Mount table (Goodheart 1996). Jews were nervous, but Muslims were aghast; such an act defiled the sacred space of the two Muslim mosques on the Mount by tunneling under it.

The Military and the Sacred

If sacred space does not conform to secular or national models of behavior, the state may intervene. Such events usually cause high tensions, and sometimes carnage, yet they are part of the overall synthesis of place identity. Two prominent examples are the Sikhs of the Punjab and Chinese-influenced Tibet.

The center of the Sikh religion focuses on the Golden Temple in Amritsar, India. The site has often exuded a religio-military air (Stevens 1984a). The Golden Temple complex is the most sacred center of Sikhdom, and Sikhs of all classes go there for enlightenment and renewal. Though the Harmandir Sahib, the innermost and most sacred building of the complex, is open to all, some Sikhs have grown fearsome of visiting, because

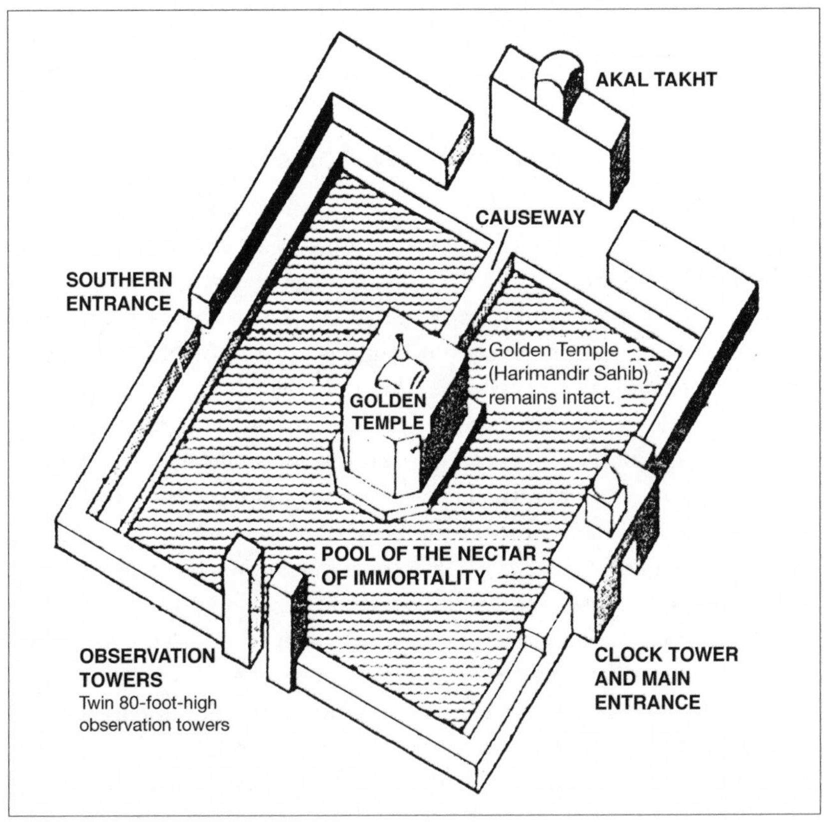

FIG. 52 | *The Golden Temple complex of the Sikhs in Amritsar, India. Reprinted, by permission, from Stevens (1984c).*

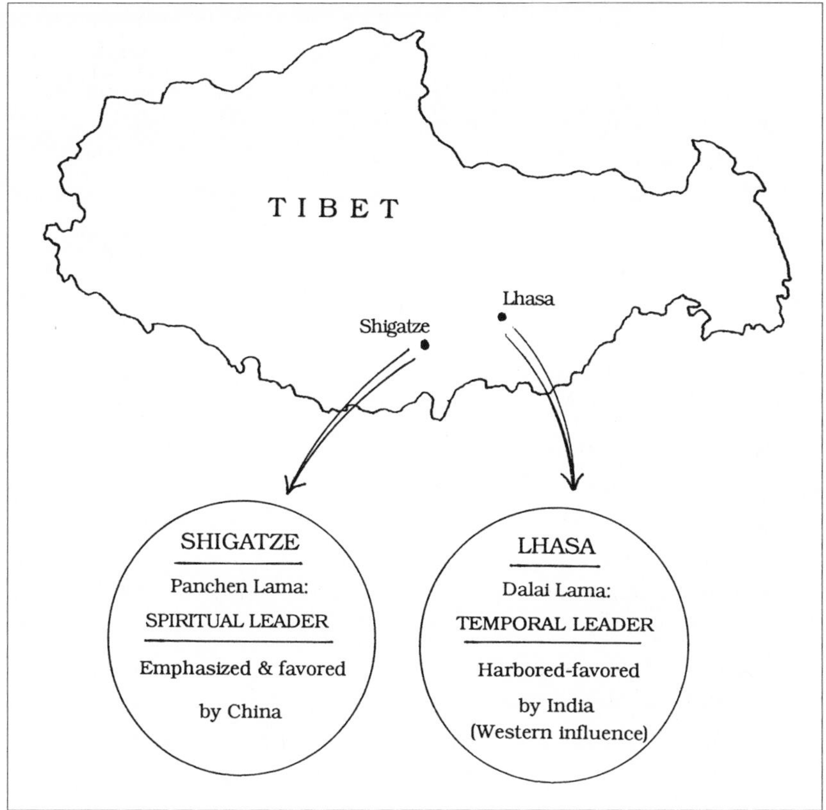

FIG. 53 | *The dual sacred centers of Tibet.*

of the occasional violence there between religious and secular forces (McGill 1984; Surjeet 1988:459). Historically speaking, the Golden Temple is a relatively recent sacred place (built in 1577), yet it has only become more well known internationally since about 1980, when militant Sikhs began to fear consumption by Indian federal politics and Hindu society (Kapur 1986:226–28; Cole and Sambhi 1990:58). Since this time the Golden Temple has become a recurring focus of militant Sikhs who call for a separate Sikh state to be called Khalistan, the establishment of which God purportedly approves.

Skirmishes at the Golden Temple in Amritsar have been between militant Sikhs and the Indian Police, but the strife is complex. A military theme has been present in the teachings of many Sikh gurus for hundreds of years. Sikh extremists are few in number; yet, during the 1980s they used the Golden Temple complex as a fortress, barricading themselves inside, even in the central sacred structure of the Harmandir Sahib (Figure 52). Until Indian intervention, the temple was used as a hideout, an armory, a communications center, and the focus of Sikh religious legitimacy (Stevens 1984a, 1984c).

The first Indian raid on the Golden Temple in 1984 killed several hundred Sikhs, and one would think that use of the Golden Temple as a sacred harbor for militants would not be repeated, but religious convictions die hard (Stevens 1984b). In 1986, police again routed Sikh militants hiding in the Golden Temple (Tenorio 1986). In 1988, a similar situation ended with more militants surrendering from the temple complex, this time without bloodshed ("Sikh Extremists Surrender" 1988), so evidently, the Golden Temple was believed to offer divine protection even after several routings. For separatist Sikhs, the occupation of sacred space has been congruent with divine approval of militant action. The Indian government plainly recognized the potential for religious conflict and by 1991 had torn down both residential and commercial buildings for a distance of thirty meters all around the Golden Temple complex, making room for further military action if necessary (again see Figure 52; Crossette 1990a). Here secular authority mirrored sacred space by clearing a profane periphery.

Most Sikhs are law-abiding citizens frustrated by extremist antics. Their view of the Golden Temple is often now one of fear; Sikh militants often kill Sikh moderates if they are not supportive enough of separatism and thus supposed religious goals. Many have been shot while entering or leaving the Golden Temple (Kapur 1986:227). Extremists have also attacked local Hindus and Muslims, whose view of the temple is, understandably, often negative. Here is an example of religious innovation taking place at the core, continually shaped from outside by the secular Indian government. The heritage of validation is deep, so some see sacred space as self-authoritative, transcending local law and causing tension with secular authority.

This is a major difference with the traditional American scene, where a greater ingrained respect for local authority usually keeps action to a minimum. Whereas in Palestine, Arabs may simply possess a site by throwing rocks at Israeli police, believers in Independence are satisfied to obey authority and wait for the Temple Lot to be turned over in the future through extrasecular means. God will either have to work through current legal/political channels to reduce tension or obliterate contemporary systems altogether. What event might occur to give the impression that the current system has been removed and that groups could somehow stake a claim at the Temple Lot would have to be nothing short of total catastrophe—which is exactly what some Latter Day Saint groups think will happen. Still, even in the apocalyptic scenario, many separate groups would vie for control of the Independence core.

Another extrapoliticized example of the contest for and control of a sacred core is seen in Tibet. Traditionally, the Dalai Lama in Lhasa has been the theocratic leader of Tibetan Buddhism. His authority has, however, sometimes been equaled by the Panchen Lama, another important spiritual leader based for centuries in the town of Shigatze, some 150 miles west of Lhasa (Figure 53; David-Neel 1927:274–75). In 1950, the Chinese first invaded Tibet and courted the favor of the Panchen Lama (Karan 1976:15), even offering him the throne of the departed Dalai Lama. Reportedly, he declined the offer, but not until he had gone to Lhasa to sit briefly on the throne (Chapman 1938:138–41). Two political opponents, the Chinese and the traditional Tibetan, thus assert separate ideologies through two distinct Tibetan sacred places (Figure 53).

Today, the Dalai sits in self-imposed exile in India, while the Chinese continue to court Tibetans who favor the Panchen Lama. With the death of the Panchen Lama in 1989, the Chinese saw their chance to intervene in Tibetan culture (Kristof 1990). Tibetan monks with the aid of the self-exiled Dalai Lama chose a successor, but the child, seen as the most recent incarnation of the Panchen Lama, quickly disappeared (Tyler 1995; Farley 1995). The Chinese then chose their own Panchen Lama and kept him sequestered at Beijing (Chu 1999). The aim of the Chinese was to gain influence over Tibet by shaping spiritual events, but most Tibetans do not accept the Chinese selection.

Likewise, the development of Independence as a sacred space has combined innovation from both core and periphery, with some competition from political authority. In the 1830s, Joseph Smith and others of the original church leadership generally directed the establishment of the New Jerusalem from Kirtland, Ohio, some eight hundred miles distant, as members strived to sort out problems locally. Today, the LDS Church still observes Independence from the periphery (of Utah) and acts on its own portion of sacred space as it cautiously sees fit. The Temple Lot family of churches has traditionally splintered first on the periphery, establishing new churches in Colorado or Michigan, for example. These new splinters have then commonly returned to Missouri, which they see as the rightful place for a headquarters. Such has sometimes been the case with new break-off RLDS groups from a thinly spread church populace, but much of the turbulence at Independence proper has been from fundamentalist members avoiding reformation—from within the church itself. For these, change is prominent at the core. The New Jerusalem, as a total concept, is widely varied in its core-periphery relations.

Secular authority has influenced development in Independence, though most churches there would not admit or recognize it. The Temple Lot Church was told by the city of Independence to fill in the eyesore of foundation dug in the early 1930s when no financial means existed to build a temple. The city of Independence instigated LDS construction activity on its land near the Temple Lot on two separate occasions. After the city wished to obtain LDS land for construction of a high school in the 1950s, the church built a new mission home, donating money to the city for a facility elsewhere. When the city thought of obtaining the meadow area around 1970 for a public park, the church responded by building the LDS Visitor's Center. In American sacred places, community government is arguably a powerful landscape force. Sacred land and, to a lesser degree, sacred structures often are secondary to community, utility, traffic, or other public needs. Even the impressive RLDS temple spire ended up slightly truncated with an obtrusive red light at the top due to Federal Aviation Administration regulations.

Contested Space

Where secular authority overlaps sacred space, tensions rise, but the question is if results tend to unify or divide views on site sanctity. As seen, it is common for groups to develop an "intense degree of union" with a place through the use of "common languages, symbols, and experiences" (Relph 1976:57). The imposition of secular authority often intensifies that union, but people wanting peaceful resolution may be persecuted by the devout, and the view toward sacred space may be lessened or altered. Furthermore, when more than one religious interpretation is overlaid on a site, each perception rubs up against another's concept, making attempts at sanctification problematic. Overlap any interest by civil or municipal authority and a reaction is guaranteed. Independence is a place of multiple identities, which so far are reluctantly shared. Tension and violence have yet been minimal, but when pushed such can last a very long time—even centuries.

Multifarious Sacred Places

The region of Kosovo in Yugoslavia serves to introduce the theme of differing views toward a single place or site. Today, Kosovo is a dominantly Albanian population with a minority of Serbs. Today, French, American, British, Italian, and German NATO troops control the region. Some six hundred years ago, Kosovo was the site of a major Serbian defeat by the Ottoman Empire in 1389. The battle site, which took place near the modern capital of Pristina, now stands as the historical center of Serb nationalism. Orthodox Serbian churches are spread across the region and, though a minority, Serbs see Kosovo as a sacred homeland. Until recently, Serbs maintained complete control over the province, while the population was mainly Muslim Albanian. The two viewpoints (ethnic home majority vs. sacred political homeland for the minority) are mutually exclusive and virtually irreconcilable (Talbott 1992). Warfare in 1999 filled Kosovo with retribution and massacres.

Multiple interpretations of sacred space are also evident in Duncan's description of the Kandyan kingdom of Sri Lanka. Generally, Kandyan kings had constructed a city on the Sakran model of making a Heaven on earth (Duncan 1990:38). The architecture of Kandy was full of symbols replete with celestial meanings. The landscape, however, was not heaven for all. Some of Kandy's kings built paradise at the expense of the people; cruel labor was often the cost. Therefore, the masses were not generally in tune with the symbols of the Sakran landscape, which instead came to symbolize the tyranny of the king (1990:171–78). At other times, some of the Kandyan kings followed a different model of landscape formation, referred to as the Asokan model, which stressed more attention to works completed to enhance the social welfare of the people: monasteries, schools, and public works (1990:38).

In a broad sense, one can identify both Sakran and Asokan mentalities in the history of Independence, Missouri. Heavenly, Sakran Independence might be seen as the reflection of biblical places on the landscape and the millennial-apocalyptic interpretation of various sites in northwestern Missouri. The Sakran views are mostly those of the LDS Church and its membership, but without the servitude lifestyles of the Kandyan realm. Of course, this is not Salt Lake City, the traditional center of LDS activity. There, one could identify both types of sacred vista. The Asokan alternative is exemplified by the traditional RLDS Zionic social experiment. This view, prominent since depression times, has centered on urban welfare, care for the aged, and the establishment of a well-respected hospital. Since the 1980s, however, these roles have reversed to some degree. The LDS Church, while not changing any doctrine, has lessened New Jerusalem talk, increasing its presence with the construction of a central welfare storehouse, two museums, and its normal assemblage of functional stake and ward buildings. The RLDS Church, in contrast, has undertaken elaborate beautification schemes in Independence, which have culminated in a startlingly Sakran-like, though reactionary, temple. Critics have attacked the expensive new temple as an effort by the church to distract attention away from major church schism. This is simply another way of saying that the gulf between the LDS Church and the CoC is vast, as is the divide between the CoC and its break-off fundamentalists.

Jumbled Indian history often enables Jains, Buddhists, Hindus, and Muslims to view the same places with vastly different interpretations (van der Veer 1988:12). Varanasi is the most sacred of Hindu centers, but the city is also sacred to Jains as the birthplace of two of their Tirthankaras (prophet-teachers), and to Buddhists as the site of the first sermon of the Buddha. Today, nearly 25 percent of Varanasi is Muslim (Rau 1986: 228, 232; Kumar 1989). During Muslim domination, the original Hindu temple of Vishvanatha was transformed into Aurangzeb's mosque. In the late 1700s a new temple of Vishvanatha was constructed immediately adjacent to the mosque (Eck 1982:120–29). Today, each shrine is off-limits to the other group, and Hindu-Muslim tension at this site often runs high.

Secular Control of Conflicted Space

Ayodhya, India, is a glaring example of conflicted place maintained by secular authority. How involved secular authority may become in the formation of Missouri's New Jerusalem is yet to be seen. Ayodhya, recognized as the birthplace of the Hindu god Rama, has only become a major center of Hindu attention since British occupation in the mid-1800s, and especially since Indian independence in 1947. The city is also sacred to Jains as the birthplace of their founder and to Buddhists as the ancient town of Saket, where Buddha meditated (van der Veer 1988:1–2). Though few Muslims now live in Ayodhya, some believe it to be the site of Noah's tomb (1988:2). Conflict in Ayodhya is focused on the Babri Mosque, built in the 1600s on Rama's tomb, during the peak of Muslim influence on the subcontinent. Hindu fundamentalists have avidly campaigned throughout India to have the mosque destroyed. According to Hindus, the mosque should be replaced with Ram Janmabhumi, a temple dedicated to the god Rama and his wife, Sita (Crossette 1990b). Muslims, of course, are incensed at the movement and consider extreme the Hindu application of "epic fantasy" to literal place (Goldman 1986:471; Hazarika 1991). After Indian independence, Hindus entered the mosque and placed statues of Rama and Sita (Bakker 1991:97). Riots erupted between Muslims and Hindus, and Indian police forces intervened, closing the mosque. The policing of Ayodhya's sacred space has lasted for over thirty years.

The mosque was briefly opened in the mid-1980s and tensions in Ayodhya heightened (Bakker 1991:98). Hindu fundamentalism was on the rise, possibly as a reaction to Sikh separatism farther west (Gargan 1991). Fundamentalists successfully organized themselves, establishing the Baratiya Janata Party (BJP), which supported the establishment of a Hindu state and backed the construction of Ran Janmabhumi (Weinraub 1991). More radical followers of the BJP carry swords and at times have adorned the Babri Masjid with Hindu nationalist saffron-colored flags. As tension increased, the structure was finally closed to all, and the Indian government built a formidable barricade of iron pipe topped with barbed wire surveyed by closed-circuit television, as the BJP had threatened to tear down the mosque (Hazarika 1991).

Muslim-Hindu violence spread across India over the issue of Ran Janmabhumi, and in 1990 the BJP declared that on October 31 they would march to take the mosque. Police cordoned off the whole town of Ayodhya, but thousands of Hindus marched toward the mosque and at least fifty people were killed (Crossette 1990c, 1990d). The rapidly growing BJP was an important part of Prime Minister V. P. Singh's coalition government, but after the Ayodhya incident, support was withdrawn, and Singh's government collapsed (Tefft 1990; Crossette 1990e). The Ayodhya conflict caused the fall of the Indian government in late 1990.

Hindu fervor came to a boil in December 1992. Fundamentalists rushed the Ayodhya mosque and destroyed it using pipes, rocks, clubs, and bare hands (Gargan 1992a, 1992b). Chaotic crowd mentality followed; innocent bystanders were beaten without reason. Hundreds more were killed as riots ensued across the subcontinent, including in Pakistan and Bangladesh, where violence was conversely directed against Hindu temples ("Thirty Hindu Temples Attacked" 1992). The country's Muslims again were incensed as Hindus were allowed to build a makeshift structure to

Rama inside the ruins of the Babri Mosque constructed of "consecrated bricks" contributed from all over India (Bakker 1991:98–99). Just how widespread was the fundamentalist Hindu support? A mural painting of Rama's temple was observed at the southern tip of India, in Trivandrum, more than 1,400 miles from Ayodhya (Crossette 1990f).

Since the mid-1990s, the BJP has won national elections twice, showing the party's increasing popularity. The formation of shaky coalition governments, however, has caused a backing away from controversial religious platforms, yet the Hindu plan for a temple to Rama proceeds, and much of its artwork has already been crafted. The various layers of influence in the making and transformation of Ayodhya's sacred space are certain.

Overlapping Superlatives

The best-known place of multiple religious interpretations in the world is Jerusalem. Today, Jews and Palestinian Arabs are the two major components of the greater Jerusalem metropolitan area (Cohen 1976), but the old city of Jerusalem better represents the problem of different viewpoints and has been traditionally divided on an ethno-religious basis (Figure 54). Today, the old city consists of a Muslim quarter, a Jewish quarter, a Christian quarter, and an Armenian quarter (Ericksen 1980:115–16). For Christians, Old Jerusalem is the site of much of the sacred teaching of Christ, where miracles were performed, Herod's temple cleansed, and where Jesus was tried and crucified. Christians, however, are not unified in their sanctification of the old city.

For Jews, the site of the sacred Temple Mount of Solomon, at the heart of Old Jerusalem, is revered. Many Jews believe that, one day, the ancient Ark of the Covenant will be found and a new temple constructed on the mount, a belief also strong among Christians. Jews themselves, however, are divided when it comes to things religious. European, American, Middle Eastern, Sephardic, Orthodox, Ultra-Orthodox, and nonreligious Jews in Israel all have separate agendas (Judge 1983:496–97,509–10).

Flipping the coin, Muslims believe that Mohammed was taken on his night journey through the seven heavens directly from the Temple Mount. In subsequent centuries, two mosques were built on the mount and adorn it to this day. The smaller, known as the Dome of the Rock, is thought by many to overlay the original site of the Jewish Holy of Holies. From its square base to octagonal walls and circular dome, the whole structure is an architectural representation of Mohammed's celestial visitation

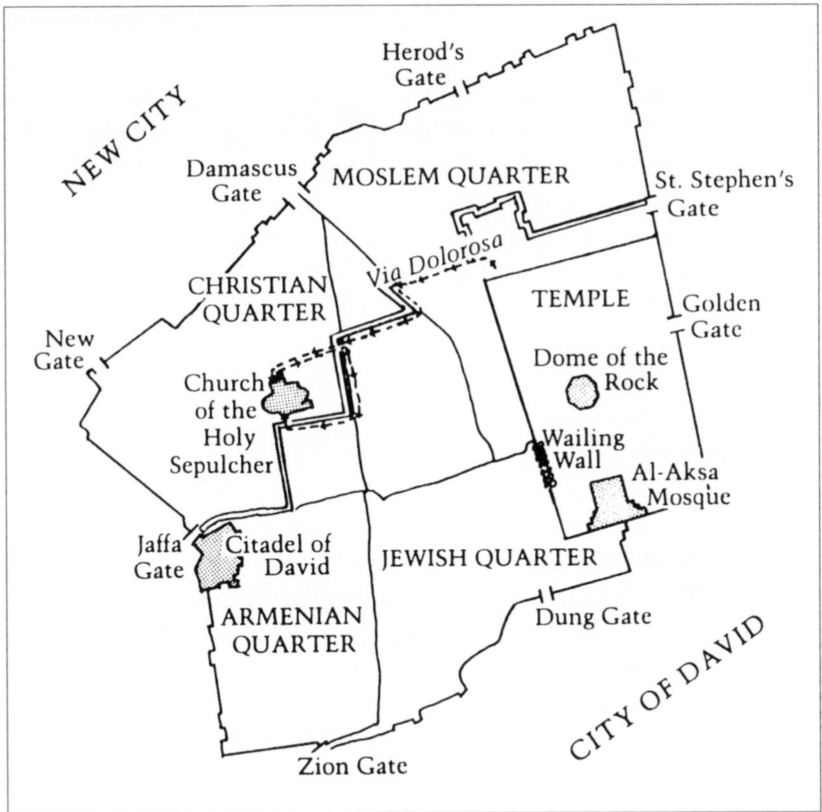

FIG. 54 | *The Old City of Jerusalem. Reprinted, by permission, from Ericksen (1980:116).*

(Glasse 1989:102, 301). A Muslim council currently administers the Temple Mount, though it has been occupied by Israel since 1967 (Wigoder 1989:697). As mentioned earlier, most Jews will not enter the mount because of the uncertainty of the location of the original Jewish Holy of Holies. Muslims normally forbid Jews entry anyway. The most orthodox of Jews, however, congregate frequently outside the southwest Wailing Wall of the Temple Mount to pray, an act that was impossible before the 1967 Six Day War, when Jordan administered the old city (Map 38).

As the newspapers daily show, violence is ever present throughout Israel. It is uncertain whether the Palestinians will gain a completely sovereign state, but whatever the scenario, Jerusalem, tucked between Israel and the West Bank may likely be a focal point of explosive trauma (Cohen

1976:287). On the other hand, violence has sometimes been directed away from the city just *because* of its sacred nature. In 1991, when Iraq's Saddam Hussein bombed Israel in the Persian Gulf War, the inaccuracy of his scud missiles steered him well clear of Jerusalem. If he could have pinpointed the Knesset, it would have been another matter.

Brutal violence has been commonplace in Israel over the past few decades. Palestinian extremists have begun to assassinate fellow Palestinians accused of collaborating with the Israeli government. Infighting among Jewish groups with highly varied visions of God's Israel is common as well. Orthodox Jews in the city often block roads in attempts to keep the less devout from attending movie theaters or even from driving their cars on the Sabbath. The Orthodox group expanded their territory and sphere of influence substantially over the past thirty years, especially into the disputed West Bank (Shilhav 1983).

Differences of opinion among Jewish and Palestinian groups in Israel provide a parallel to Independence, Missouri, where opinions among incipient but diverging Latter Day Saint churches likewise complicate the character of sacred place. Perhaps the situation at Independence can best be compared to that of the Christian Quarter of the old city where a multitude of Christian churches—Greek Orthodox, Roman Catholic, Armenian Orthodox, Russian Orthodox, Arab Christian, Coptic, and various Protestant groups—all vie for prominence (Judge 1983:493). Merely trying to take a quiet walk or to rest on a bench can be problematic in the Christian Quarter unless you pertain to the proper religion for the neighborhood or bench (ABC News 1996). As a traditional site of Christ's crucifixion, resurrection, and burial, the area is held sacred by various schisms of one religion.

Within the Christian Quarter, perhaps the most applicable place to compare to the Temple Lot is the Church of the Holy Sepulchre, which only occupies a couple of acres of land. Here Roman Catholics, Greek Orthodox, Armenians, Syrians, and Copts all hold spiritual claim to one structure where many believe that Jesus was entombed. Ethiopian Copts have occupied the roof of the structure since the mid-1800s. Others claim specific authority over doors, benches, and walls ("Old City Jerusalem" 1996).

Sacred places of such intense multiple interpretations are rare, especially in North America. Most of the examples discussed above have only two main parties in conflict, though other groups may see a site as sacred. In Amritsar the groups in conflict are the Sikhs and the Indian government; in Varanasi and Ayodhya they are Hindus and Muslims; in Jerusalem they are Jews, Arabs, and Christians (and multitudes of divisions among them). Is the theme of violence applicable in Independence, Missouri, too?

Future Superlative

At the Temple Lot religious fervor has not yet extended to the dissection of individual buildings, but imagine with the current splinters and attitudes of nearly twenty-five different Latter Day Saint churches in the area, what will be the pattern in a hundred years, or a thousand (assuming that one of the churches does not sooner turn out correct in its millenarian projections). Three of these hold lands of historic and sacred importance: the Temple Lot, the LDS Church, and the RLDS Church. One RLDS break-off, the Remnant LDS Church, has sought greater proximity to sacred space, and others are bound to do so as well. With time, space now seen as peripheral may rise in sanctity.

The potential for stress between the Church of Christ Temple Lot and its daughter church, the Church of Christ with the Elijah Message, is present. The latter group essentially demands that sacred territory be handed over. Violence in Independence has been a minor concern thus far, but it can be envisioned with the Temple Lot Church having been burned twice by zealots in only 130 years of history. Might some future groups attempt to settle on the Temple Lot beyond the ability of civil authority to remove them? That does not seem likely, as even the millenarian Latter Day Saints are accustomed to obeying the law and the outcome of the courts, but imagine what might have happened by now if the law had not harbored the Temple Lot Church.

Relations between the RLDS and LDS Churches have been tense in the past. They are fairly amicable now, though doctrinally disparate. In the past, when the RLDS and Temple Lot Churches were in a conflict over land, the matter was taken to the courts and the decision accepted mutually, abating former tensions. On the other hand, if the RLDS Church had won the Temple Lot case, it would now possess the most sacred spot, and it might have constructed a very different temple—*on the Temple Lot*. If possessing the Temple Lot would have increased millenarian fervor, curtailing liberal-secular trends and therefore decreasing dissent, we will never know, but if the same seashell temple design were to have been placed on the *Temple Lot* under RLDS auspices, eventual fundamentalist clashes would have been even more pronounced, which is difficult to fathom, since the contemporary relationship between the RLDS Church and its schism congregations is full of invective. The tension leads to two outcomes, either schism or violence. Near the Temple Lot, schism is now the most common solution to dissent.

Also to be considered are relations with non–Latter Day Saint Missourians. Saint-Missourian violence broke out once when protection of civil liberties was less instilled in the land, and Harry Truman, an Independence native, insisted in the early 1970s that animosity still existed between Missourians and Latter Day Saints. "The old Independence families won't have anything to do with Mormons," said Truman (Miller 1973: 450). Even though Lilburn Boggs's extermination order was officially rescinded in 1976, some of these doubts about the Latter Day Saints are bound to persevere. Such were exhibited even in the late 1990s when complaints were aired over the LDS Church's "Frontier Story" pageant, which described the expulsion of the Saints from Jackson County. Modern Missourians become nervous when their ancestors are portrayed as barbarians.

Rectification and Obliteration Applied

This leads discussion to the treatment of Foote's stages of rectification and obliteration. Foote wrote, "Rectification is the process by which a tragedy site is put right and used again" (1993:23). The original Saints were expelled first from Jackson County and then from the entire state of Missouri. Beyond 1838, the Saints had to reconcile the stigma of accepting Jackson County as ultimately the most sacred place imaginable with the fact that violent means had been used to expel them from their millenarian homeland. Certainly, the return of each individual and each group involved are attempts at rectification. In the cases of the Church of Christ (Temple Lot) and the RLDS Church, rectification caused hesitation of at least thirty years in returning and then hesitation in church doctrines of gathering, though individuals came anyway, acting apart from the suggestions of church leadership. The LDS Church did not headquarter a mission in Jackson County until 1900—over sixty years of delay. Granted it faced its own problems in the West, but it did not buy land in Independence until 1904. It did not build a structure there until 1914 and still has no temple there, though the Kansas City area could certainly use a conventional one, even if of the newer smaller size. The LDS Church *has* placed a temple in Missouri—a temple was dedicated as the church's fiftieth in St. Louis in 1997—more than two hundred miles east of Independence. It is located almost as far away from the old sacred, though conflicted New Jerusalem site as one can get yet still within Missouri. Rectification has been an achingly slow process compounded by the complexities of schism.

Obliteration has also played a part in Independence. In order to get along with the old Missouri folk, the Latter Day Saint groups have often had to downplay their historical losses. The fact that the LDS Church canceled its well-known pageant on the meadow for 1997 is evidence that Missourians still rankled when faced with the bare facts of violence enacted against the early Latter Day Saints, even nearly thirty years after Missouri officially rescinded the extermination order. Certainly, the Missourians in the 1830s obliterated what they saw as a strange scourge on the land, and subsequently the lands of the Saints were taken by force. Only one diminutive marker denotes the several thousand acres the Saints once legally held in western Kansas City, Missouri, now some of the town's most valued real estate. Saints and Missourians both have come a long way in terms of mutual respect, but there remains a certain pall over the losses, issues that were even taken to President Martin Van Buren and Congress in 1839 without any resulting aid.

This almost tangible veil is exhibited in Mormon views of Independence as less sacred than other sites of Palmyra, Kirtland, or Salt Lake City, despite its supreme millenarian destiny (Jackson and Henrie 1983). Losses less than a decade later in Nauvoo also contributed to such views, though it seems the LDS Church in particular has started to clear the historic cobwebs with the amazing reconstruction of the historic Nauvoo temple. Some have argued that the Jackson County area is less sacred for the LDS realm than other historic sites and therefore not as worthy of study. Nothing could be further from the truth, as the Independence scene represents a fascinating bipolarity of religious psyche. For the LDS Church, the Missouri obliteration is being rectified step by step and from the periphery toward the center.

The RLDS Church has gradually responded to the obliteration as well. It has tried to rectify early losses by continually treading a road more in tune with, or even beyond, mainstream American Protestant attitudes of the East. It is trying to appear more Protestant and liberal even than most of Missouri, perhaps in an unconscious attempt to reach beyond the old purge. In its remaking, the CoC/RLDS institution has distanced itself from several early Latter Day Saint traditions—and the resulting schism has been remarkable. Perhaps the smaller Church of Christ (Temple Lot) family of churches has simply found cultural refuge from the bitter earlier times simply in their smaller numbers. They remain millenarian and apocalyptic.

For them safety comes in obscurity, and sacredness arises from one point—the Temple Lot.

For their part, the millenarian viewpoint does substantial obliterating as well. The Latter Day Saint Churches tend to not accept modern Kansas City and Independence infrastructure and development as worthy of consideration in the millenarian scheme of things. Apocalyptic imagery is even used to imagine the end of 1.8 million basically iniquitous people in the metropolitan area. The pure New Jerusalem is not Kansas City as now constituted, and the current legal, civic, and utility infrastructure will cease to be. Community networks now influential across the country are expurgated from the millennial scenarios of most of the Latter Day Saint groups. One interesting aside is that the headquarters offices for the Church of the Nazarene are located on the Paseo in Kansas City—such is never mentioned in Latter Day Saint talk. There is some question, then, about how these and other groups will be included in the New Jerusalem. In the imagery of the subjective future city, such have little or no place.

The same can be said for Kansas City business names of renown. Will Yellow Freight, headquartered in Kansas City, somehow still supply goods and services to the purified city? Will church interests eventually take control of local factories like the Claycomo Ford plant or the Fairfax General Motors plant? Occasionally, inquiring Saints ponder the current landscape, but most seem to think all current gentile interests will disappear. Two of the nation's premier greeting and gift companies, Hallmark Cards and Russell Stover Candies, are headquartered in Kansas City. What is a New Jerusalem without the legendary chocolates and greeting cards? The pastoral and family value–oriented Hallmark "Hall of Fame" ideal surely fits well with the New Jerusalem, but the native businesses of Kansas City are not mentioned in the Latter Day Saint vision of the future metropolis, if metropolis is not too euphemistic a description. Everything depends on the timing of apocalypse and views on that occurrence are far from firm.

Nonrational Landscapes

Though relatively recent in formation, Independence is one of the most multifaceted of religious places. Neither fence nor wall separate the Latter Day Saint churches there, but vast doctrinal divides exist between the groups, and what constitutes the sacred and the profane is highly varied.

Ideological walls as thick as the real ones separating some Catholic and Protestant neighborhoods in Northern Ireland divide the different Latter Day Saint doctrines. All believe Joseph Smith, in different degrees, was a prophet, most adhere to the *Book of Mormon*, and most agree that Independence is a place of special millennial significance. Beyond these basic beliefs, the LDS splinters diverge. No one can say if violence will ever be a major part of the Latter Day Saint factional scene in Independence, but the aged Asian examples show the tendency.

In these places, a duality or multiplicity of belief often leads to the creation of ironic landscape images, particularly for the outsider, but sometimes for the believer as well. For example, at Ayodhya, between 1948 and 1992, one found a Muslim mosque with Hindu statues inside surrounded with outward fortifications that resembled a prison. It was a religious structure that no one was allowed to enter. At Varanasi, it seems strange that keeping Muslim and Hindu symbols from coming in contact with each other has become a traditional celebration. With the fall of the USSR, at Red Square in Moscow the previously sacred tomb of Lenin suddenly became an object of scorn in the early 1990s. Of course, the landscape interpretations surrounding these sites become clearer when the nature of Muslim-Hindu relations or the history of the communist Soviet Union are learned.

A Muslim mosque with a Catholic church in its center in Cordoba, neighborhoods walled and sealed off from other neighborhoods in Belfast, and Orthodox Jews fervently praying at an old, crumbling wall in Old Jerusalem are seemingly absurd images until one understands the chronology of events behind their formation. One particularly striking image is that of heavily armed Indian soldiers walking respectfully barefoot in the Sikh's Golden Temple while policing and cleaning up after the 1984 raid that killed hundreds. It is a scene where conflict, hatred, and respect are all set on symbolically thin ice.

Such amazingly complex images represent the strange impositions, overlays, and balances of history that make sacred places what they are. Independence is different from these examples, perhaps in that its sacred landscape is still youthful. Like Ayodhya, Varanasi, Cordoba, and Jerusalem, images are jumbled among the different Latter Day Saint groups who all see themselves as having the primary mission in establishing Zion—somehow.

The small Church of Christ at the Temple Lot possesses the most sacred piece of territory in Latter Day Saint Independence, the original spot Joseph Smith dedicated for a temple. Except for a modest church, the triangular plot remains expectantly vacant. Much exists there in the minds of those who believe in the New Jerusalem, however. Around the Temple Lot, the architecture of the Latter Day Saint churches is of a variety of styles and scales. The RLDS Church has erected a fragile-looking but provocative spire at a time when many members are unsure of the church's direction. It stands in great contrast to the mammoth RLDS auditorium, which seems to be an earthy outgrowth somehow of Jackson County's geology. The LDS Church has usually constructed buildings in Independence only when its lands were threatened by the city's development plans. This bigger church has had trouble incorporating this important sideshow site into its successful presence, not only through the collective perception of the membership in the United States but also worldwide. The LDS Church waits for future inspiration while continuing to purchase lands throughout the surrounding area. Other smaller groups carry their own unique images of the area, though these are not generally evident immediately around the Temple Lot. Like the sacred places of Asia, the landscape of Independence is incongruous to the outsider without a "Urim and Thummim" of interpretation.

Traditional archaic examples of sacred spaces reach back to the very origins of history, where legend and fact are indistinguishable. Some of the interpretations of the New Jerusalem in Independence are similarly archaic in that place belief is derived from biblical and *Book of Mormon* imagery. This place is unique, however, because it has developed in the period of modern American industrialization. Independence represents a place where American political, legal, and economic development has been congruent with the evolution of a chiliastic sacred site. No rival to Independence, Missouri, can be found in North America. In fact, it may have no rival in the entire developed world.

In a Coming Day

Amelioration and Pseudo-Ecumenicalism

Israel, Israel God is speaking.
Hear your great Deliverer's voice!
Now a glorious morn is breaking
For the people of his choice.
Come to Zion,
Come to Zion,
And within her walls rejoice.

—"Israel, Israel God Is Calling,"
LDS hymn

A summary of the doctrinally as well as geographically varied Latter Day Saint viewpoints toward Independence concludes this book. Differing perceptions of the scale of sacred space there are intricately tied to the historical interpretations of early church doctrine and history. In analyzing doctrinal change, both the LDS and RLDS Churches push for or accept change in millenarian belief, and thus are both relatively progressive, but their resulting attitudes toward Independence are very dissimilar. Others, like the Temple Lot Churches or the RLDS Restoration Branch break-offs are more conservative or fundamentalist. Though the millenarian reactions of smaller groups might be similar, their attitudes toward sacred space are not. Amelioration of conflict and the ecology of religious space in Independence are critical topics. Scenarios for the future Latter Day Saint landscape are entertained.

Varieties of Perceptual Scale

Perceptions on the dimensions of sacred space in and around Independence vary considerably. Areas viewed as sacred by the Church of Christ Temple Lot, the RLDS Church, and the LDS Church are contrasted and mapped here. The views of other groups are also discussed, but most derive from the ideas of the main three. Two different sources of information were used to define sacred space regions. First, place-names and historical sites of the original church in the 1830s were evaluated as to their degree of importance to the three groups today. For example, Adam-ondi-Ahman was an important site for the original church and remains so for the LDS Church, but the modern adherents of the RLDS and Temple Lot Churches, and their break-offs, rarely mention it. The modern literature of the LDS Church emphasizes Jackson County more than does the RLDS Church, which more commonly uses the names Independence or Zion. Second, geographical data were collected, including landholdings and the locations of congregations, giving evidence of church influence in a particular area. The traits of nomenclature, landholdings, and meetinghouse sites combine to provide unique views on the sacred core and periphery for the three groups. The interpretation is admittedly subjective, but the purpose is to portray spatial variation in Latter Day Saint millenarian belief toward Independence.

Throughout the following discussion, Meinig's (1965) "core, domain, and sphere" model is loosely used, but these terms are applicable to Independence only in a general sense. Meinig's usage indicated actual concentrations of church members and therefore religious influence. His classification was not a reflection of perceptual region. Sacred space surrounding the New Jerusalem transcends mere measurement of physical properties and approaches the mythical, especially to believers. For example, in the LDS realm, if places are important in the minds of the believers, they are included within areas denoted as sacred, whether church members reside there or not.

Independence itself, specifically the Temple Lot, is the center of the *core* for all groups, not just one. The Temple Lot is the sacred core for more than twenty-five religious groups, though many of these churches are few in number. Schismatic activity in Latter Day Saint churches has generally been as diverse and colorful as with other Protestant divergences, but here each church still sees the original spot as sacred.

Beyond the core, more problematic is Meinig's term *domain*, which implied one dominant group through an area. None of the Latter Day Saint groups makes up a majority of the population anywhere in western Missouri or eastern Kansas, though the CoC and LDS influence in the Independence area is substantial in community and civic affairs. Here different perceptual areas overlap among the groups, and the label "zone of influence" is used instead of Meinig's "domain." Zone of influence reflects the perceptual emphasis of a particular church—in other words, the immediate region seen as the most important in historical as well as millenarian events. Historical sites, sacred sites, church landholdings, and of the locations of congregations have been mapped as the main elements of this geography.

Meinig's term *sphere* is likewise not appropriate for present purposes, but place-names such as Independence, Jackson County, Ray, Clay, or Caldwell Counties indicate areas of graded spatial importance to different groups and thus carry strong historical and spiritual meaning. These places comprise outer, often rural, peripheries of sacredness, where little direct church influence is usually evident.

The LDS Church's total view of sacred space in Missouri is broad, both geographically and doctrinally. Though at times reluctant to take a strong spatial or development stance on the New Jerusalem topic, the LDS Church helps to maintain the sacred core and has established an influential presence there. It operates the Visitor's Center immediately diagonal from the Temple Lot and holds several acres used for tourist, missionary, congregational, and other community activities. Away from the center, the zone of influence for the church is spread more widely than that of the traditional RLDS Church. Both churches have experienced immense change in recent years but in vastly different ways: the RLDS Church because of rapid liberalization and the LDS Church because of rapid growth. The LDS Church has congregations dotted throughout the Kansas City area and owns much acreage in Jackson and Clay Counties (Figure 55). Liberty Jail is close to LDS lands in Clay County and is such a popular and emotional site for LDS visitors that it, too, must be included within the area of influence. In addition, members of the LDS Church give somewhat more historical and tourist emphasis than the other groups of Saints to the lands that the early church owned in the Kansas City, Missouri, area. Other groups may see such places as profane space within Kansas City, but since the term Jackson County is so dominant in LDS usage, the Kansas City, Missouri, area must be included.

It must be remembered, however, that until 1835 Jackson County included the present counties of Cass and Bates, though no contemporary Latter Day Saint group discusses them much or realizes their historical

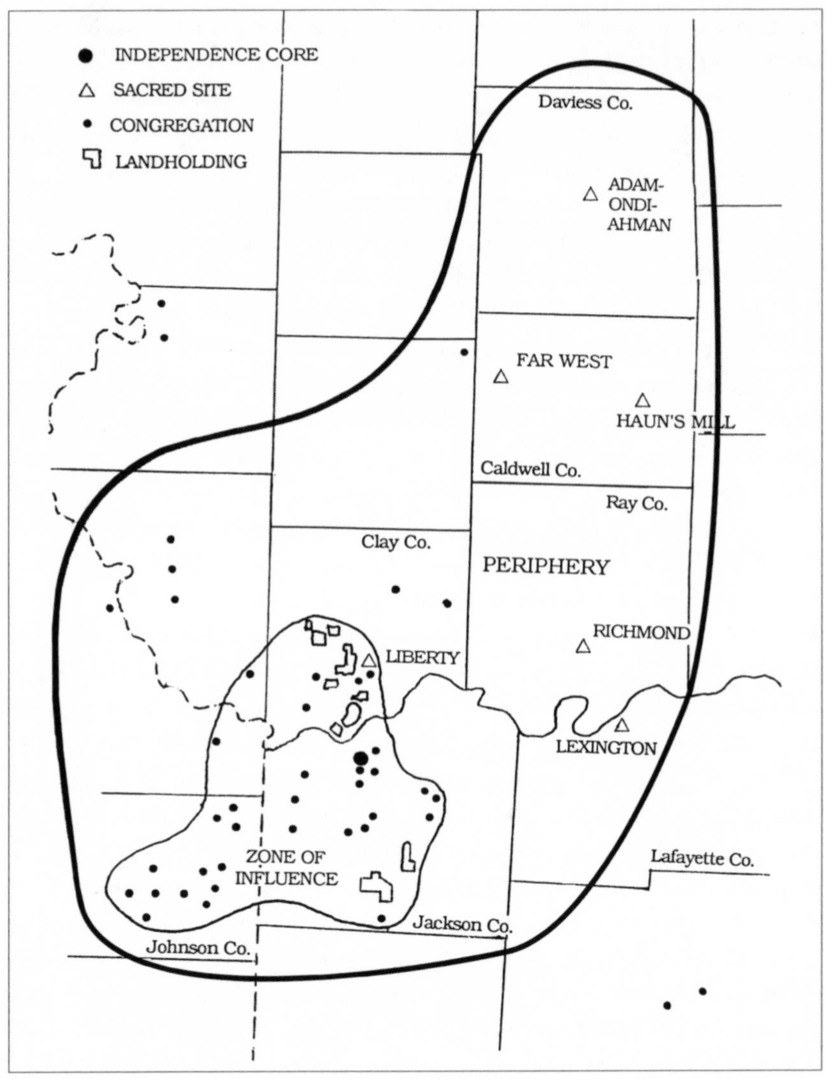

FIG. 55 | *Sacred space of the LDS Church.*

importance. In terms of political boundaries, then, Latter Day Saint memory is generally as short as that of most other Americans, who usually project current boundaries into the past, as if they had always existed that way. In reality the past is truly a foreign land quite independent of the vernacular present (Lowenthal 1985). Furthermore, the early Saints held the Kansas Indian Territory in high esteem as a Lamanite center to which the

American *Book of Mormon* gospel would eventually return. Thus the areas of influence of the original Saints compared to modern Latter-day Saints do not coincide. Area perceived as generally sacred originally started at Independence, widening to the west and south (compare Figures 11 and 55). Though the modern area of LDS influence also extends into a portion of Johnson County, Kansas, because of the cluster of LDS congregations there, the early Saints saw all of the Kansas Territory as providential. Kansas thus has been reduced in sanctity over time.

The LDS Church has also given biblical meaning to various American sites, particularly those in western Missouri. Traditionally, Jackson County has been seen as the original prediluvian site of the Garden of Eden. It is believed that Noah's ark left first from somewhere in the Americas and came to rest on Ararat or elsewhere in the "Old World" after floodwaters resided. Adam-ondi-Ahman in Daviess County is seen as the place where Adam dwelt after expulsion from the garden. Far West has been mentioned as the site where Cain slew Abel. These sites become important both in biblical-historical terms as well as future millenarian ones, establishing a religious continuity of place between past and future. The continuity was not definite, however, as form altered through chronology.

The peripheral zone of sacredness for the LDS Church extends farther than that of the CoC, which does not apply biblical importance to Missouri sites ("Adam-ondi-Ahman" 1979). Both churches are similar in their reverence for Caldwell County, though Daviess County is added to the LDS periphery, but the CoC does not hold it in esteem, because the place is seen as a concoction of Joseph Smith Jr.'s ample imagination. The LDS Church emphasizes other places of historical importance that the CoC or Restoration Branches may also. At Richmond, Missouri, Pioneer Cemetery is leased by the LDS Church and kept spotless, and LDS and Restoration Branch members also visit the Richmond city cemetery. Here the gravestone of David Whitmer, an early witness to Joseph Smith's gold plates, is revered. Just to the south lies Lexington, Missouri, where in 1852 a steamship carrying LDS immigrants on their way to Utah exploded, killing at least eighty Saints (Haight 1992). The church has recently given more emphasis to this site, and it is included in the LDS periphery.

The focus of CoC (RLDS) sacred space used to be the Temple Lot itself, but since the construction of the new temple, the precise core is vague. The three main CoC buildings face the Temple Lot, so CoC sacred space begins either at the Temple Lot itself or in the form of a broken donut, surrounding three sides the Temple Lot they do not own but have historically coveted. In an attempt to create a new central spot for the RLDS Church, the new spiral temple has not been entirely successful, since it contrasts with past doctrine regarding the temple and temple placement.

The domain of CoC sacred space coincides with the area where most members live, an east-west oblong centered on Independence itself. Included in this area of influence are the central clustering of congregations and what landholdings remain to the church in eastern Independence (Figure 56). Lamoni, Iowa, with CoC-owned Graceland College, was once contiguous with RLDS sacred space, but today it could be considered an outlying portion of the CoC area of influence disconnected from the center place. As defined by earlier church presidents, millennial space for gathering the Reorganized Saints once stretched northward into Iowa, westward into Kansas, and took up half of Missouri, but with the doctrinal drift, CoC perceptions of sacred space are shrinking or dissolving rather suddenly as the church distances itself from traditional Latter Day Saint beliefs.

The CoC periphery yet encompasses many congregations spread throughout the Kansas City metropolitan area and extends northward through Clay and Caldwell Counties. There, RLDS tradition gives emphasis to Far West as an early church headquarters (Figure 56). The site of Haun's Mill Massacre, also in Caldwell County, is kept cleanly groomed by the CoC. It is also included in the periphery, but how long the CoC will retain even this area as sacred is uncertain. Today, with its nonmillennial direction, it is easy to see a CoC perception of little sacred space at all beyond the area near the Temple Lot. The church continues to buy old residential lots nearby, even while planning to sell church lands elsewhere in the county. Ironically, the sacred periphery for the Community of Christ is rapidly contracting, in large part because the RLDS Church traditionally has had a thinly spread membership across the United States. The CoC de-emphasis of peripheral sacred space in western Missouri has come about as a combination of the influence of peripheral diffuse church membership (as represented in delegates to General Conferences) with diverging liberal leadership trends. Fundamentalists blame church leadership for the liberalization, but change is just as much a result of the church's thin geographic expression nationally.

The daughter Restoration Branches—many of which still consider themselves RLDS—continue in millenarian and fundamentalist directions, in complete doctrinal extreme to the CoC. They see sacred space in the widest view of Figure 56, but their perception has no shrinking or dissolution—only apostasy and pollution. Also, the Restoration Branches and

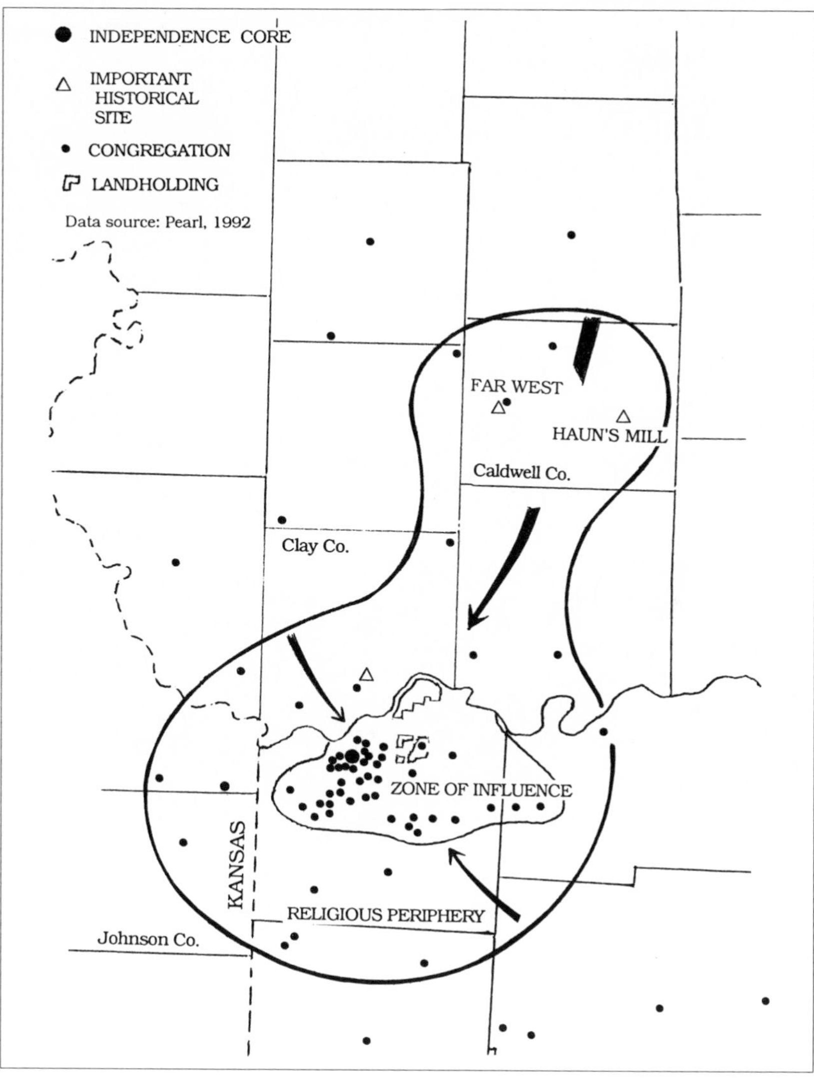

FIG. 56 | *Contraction of RLDS sacred space. Data from Pearl (1992).*

Temple Lot break-offs all have congregations focused more to the east and southeast of Independence and Jackson County—extending through the neighboring suburban fringe of Lafayette, Johnson, and Cass Counties. This direction has only been salient since about the 1980s, as RLDS splintering has surged. A region of dissent can be generally envisioned in this area, from where groups still covet the Temple Lot, but cannot possess it

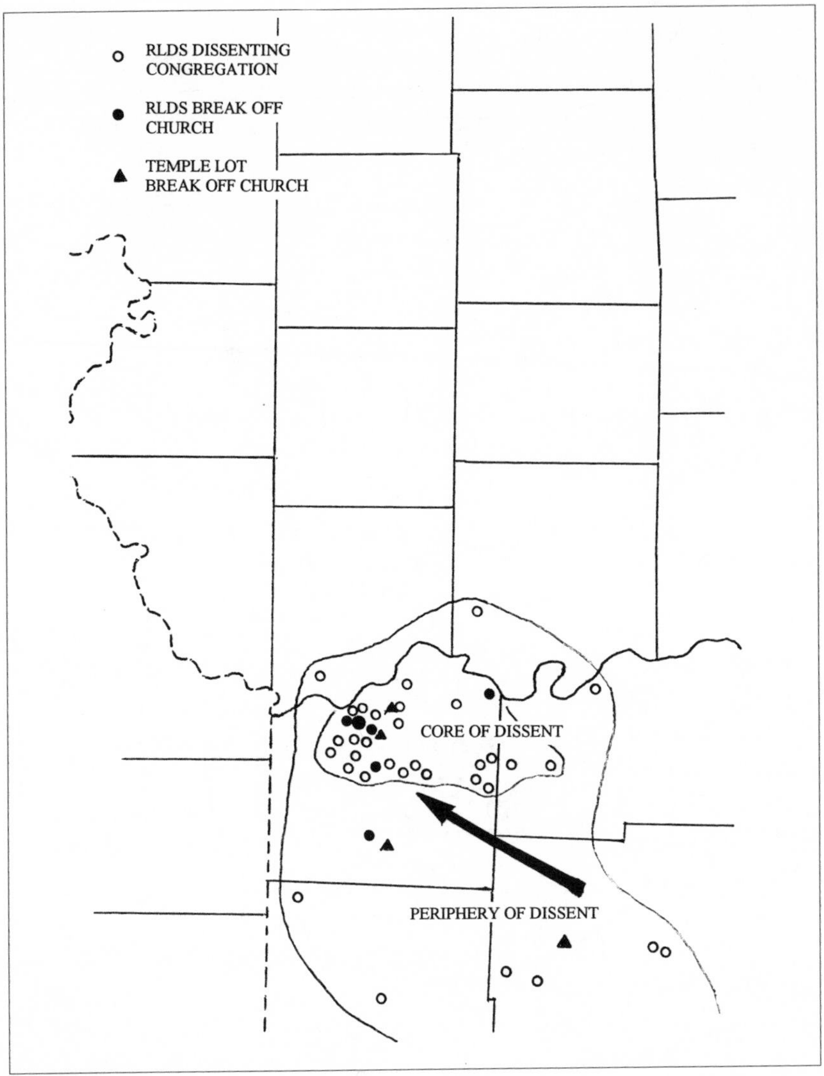

FIG. 57 | *Retaking Zion, the region of dissent.*

(Figure 57). This is displaced Zion, and, in the collective, these groups desire to retake the Temple Lot in a northward chiliastic thrust. The Restoration Branches, now tending to use the original RLDS acronym somewhere in their names, seek to supplant the CoC as its true members. These congregations show signs of both congealing into larger groups around Independence as well as further splintering. One of those factions, the Remnant Church of Jesus Christ of Latter Day Saints, has acquired the property of the old William Chrisman High School just northeast of the Temple Lot, and with a leader who is a direct descendant of Joseph Smith Jr. the group promises to remain a visible element in landscapes of the sacred at the center place.

As discussed in the previous chapter, the Church of Christ, Temple Lot, is diminutive in its view of sacred space in Independence. The Temple Lot itself is so obviously sacred that members figuratively cannot see the forest for the trees. All focus on sacred space is at the Temple Lot, and members believe in the return of Jesus Christ to a temple to be built here someday. The only other building the Church of Christ owns in the area is located on Holke Road in eastern Independence, not quite five miles from the Temple Lot. Though the church attributes no sacred significance to lands outside of the Temple Lot, it is generally believed that someday a large gathering will take place and that the city of the New Jerusalem will extend some ways away from the lot, but perhaps not quite the distance that some LDS members might envision (Sheldon 1990f). Therefore, the core of sacred land for the Church of Christ is the Temple Lot itself, with a periphery extending no further than a rather arbitrary five miles from this central point (Figure 58). The church's population is small and it only holds a few acres in Independence; the church has no discernable area of influence, but, nearing 2000, and with increasing missionary work in the southwest and Mexico, the Temple Lot group seems poised with a new millennial enthusiasm.

The splinter groups from the Temple Lot Church usually have similar diminutive concepts of sacred space. The Church of Christ with the Elijah Message, for example, also reveres the Temple Lot as the most important place in Independence, yearns to possess it, and has begged for it, but its view of sacred space gives more emphasis to the periphery. Revelations of the church have stated that the Lord might build his temple wherever and whenever He sees fit. In general, the groups that cannot acquire the land imbued with millenarian meaning develop a variety of apocalyptic responses that range from "shadows over Zion," where the center place will eventually and gradually need to be spiritually renewed, to "total purging" that will enable groups to take their rightful central place(s) on the Temple Lot.

Imagined together, the sacred domains and peripheries of the Temple Lot, RLDS, and LDS Churches plainly portray varied spatial expressions of the sacred in western Missouri. The original Saints in Missouri passed down

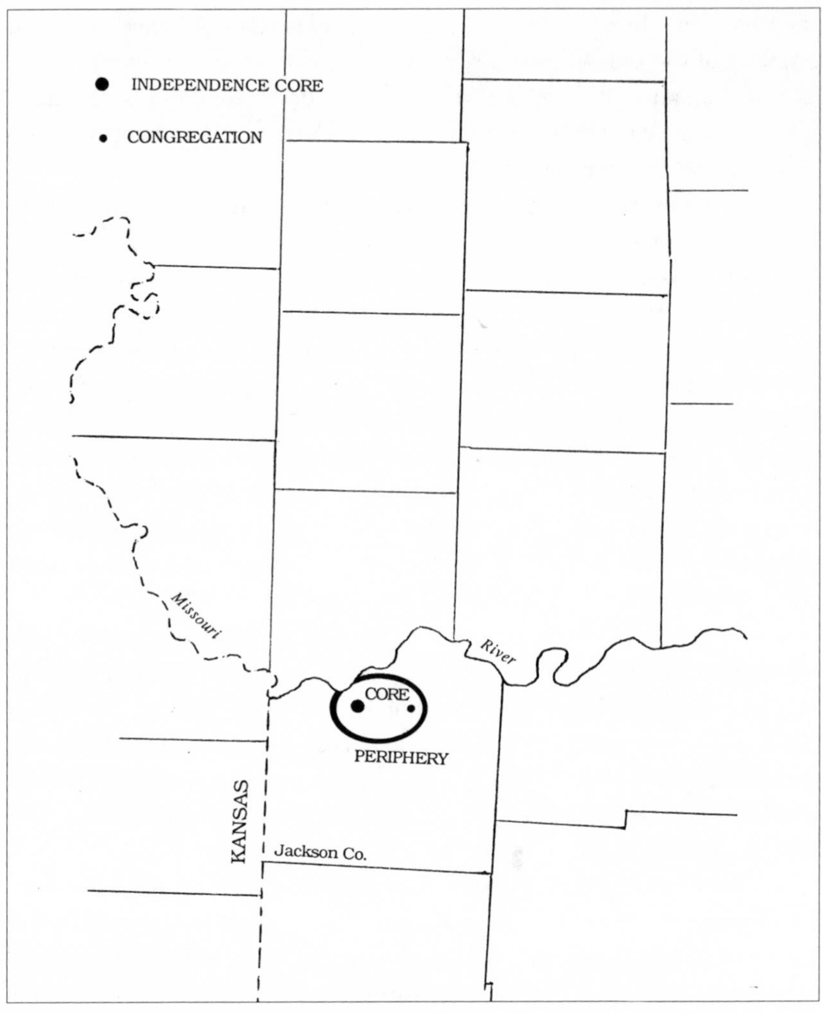

✯ FIG. 58 | *Sacred space of the Temple Lot Church.*

views that have diverged since, and we arrive at the different views expressed today. The early experience of the Saints in Missouri was molded by conflict born of mutually exclusive pastoral and political views of the Latter Day Saint and the Missourian. Today tension exists among competing groups of Latter Day Saints, but also somewhat yet between the Saints and the Old Guard Missouri Christian Protestants, who fail to see distinctions among the Saints today. Spatial elements from the early period have been retained but with differing degrees of doctrinal interpretation.

Whereas farming was the mainstay of the original Saints, views of sacred space today are molded in the environment of a much more complex urban-industrial society. The Latter Day Saint churches today have to deal with greater and lesser immersion into mainstream American society. For our purposes, it is assumed that the bigger the organization, the more thorough its immersion into broader America culturally, but when the CoC and the LDS Churches are compared, it is almost painfully evident that the two approach mainstream in very different ways. Historically the LDS Church, now large and increasingly influential, approaches acceptance from the cautious vantage point of traditional rejection or exclusion from mainstream America, while the CoC has a tradition of being nominally part of the Protestant culture mix of the Midwest. The CoC has chosen a path that has altered its ideologies, while the LDS Church uses advanced communications, widespread missionary efforts, and organizational flexibility to maintain strength without fundamental change in doctrine. Both have diminished their millennial attitudes but from opposite directions.

Compared to the original 1830s Saints, the Temple Lot Church's view has contracted over time. Today it sees sacred space totally contained within Independence, yet it holds the most apocalyptic view of premillennial events. It must remain apocalyptic to maintain hope of a New Jerusalem superceding the more dominant churches in the vicinity. The CoC traditionally has seen a large area as sacred, but the area of influence is centered on Independence and is rapidly diminishing with the onset of the leftward paradigm. The LDS Church views the largest area as sacred. For the Utah group, however, this sacred space is a paradox, an uncomfortable historical fact in light of Salt Lake City as its operational center, and the dominance of the RLDS Church in Independence.

Varieties of Doctrinal Scale

Grant Underwood (1993) asked, "Is Mormon eschatology millenarian?" For most Mormons the answer has been a solid affirmation since the very beginning, so one of the main questions this book asks is "What are the differences in Latter Day Saint millenarian eschatology from group to group, and how is such maintained geographically?" To a great degree, attitude variation in landscape sanctity is a reflection of respective doctrines. Spatial perceptions are governed by the emphasis on different parts of Latter Day Saint history—say from 1820, when Joseph Smith received the

First Vision, to 1844, when he was killed. Doctrinal selectivity occurs, consciously or unconsciously, heightening distinctions between groups. Their histories emphasize selected critical points of doctrine, which lends each church self-authenticity. Therefore, the spatial and the doctrinal within each group intertwine.

The LDS Church has been the most historically encompassing of the groups, with the possible exception of the RLDS Restoration Branches. The LDS view can be labeled historically inclusive, since it accepts all church chronology as important, though the church *does* emphasize details that cast it in a positive light. From Joseph Smith Jr.'s youth, at the very least, through 1844 in Nauvoo and beyond (even including the period of polygamy), the LDS Church accepts each stage of doctrinal development as legitimate, inspired by revelation, and relevant to the present. All the years of early church history are seen as prophetic and inspired, so the LDS Church maintains many historical sites throughout the United States, seeing them all as valid to the growth of God's kingdom. Likewise, Missouri church history is a subset of the national church history with each historical event accepted as valid, thus a greater area of Missouri is viewed as sacred. Today the LDS Church's development of historical sites, temples at historical sites, and general global temple placement are all seen as logical progressions working toward a culmination.

The CoC (RLDS Church) is more choosy on what was revelation and what was not among Joseph Smith's pronouncements. In the traditional RLDS realm, it is generally accepted that he was a fallen prophet by the Nauvoo period. In this view, Joseph lost proper channels of communication with God and instead followed his own vivid imagination in Nauvoo. Joseph was left without the benefit of divine prompting, thus the church had to be reorganized to distinguish itself, legitimizing its separation, doctrinally as well as spatially, from the Utah Mormons. The doctrines of eternal marriage and baptisms for the dead, so important in the continuity of the Utah church, became iffy at best for the RLDS Church and have been removed from their *Doctrine and Covenants* (*Book of Doctrine* 1989:appendices). A further example is that in the Nauvoo period a history of the church was compiled with the approval of Joseph Smith with previously unknown or little-publicized details elaborated. In it, Adam-ondi-Ahman is mentioned with more fervor. The LDS Church has accepted this interpretation as a doctrinally valid building of religious concept (*Doctrine and Covenants* 1981:116), but the RLDS Church view was more limited because by this time Joseph Smith was already seen as fallen. This apparently meant his vivid imagination had more control than divine prompting. The traditional RLDS Church would ask why this information on Adam-ondi-Ahman was not brought out more fully earlier.

Liberalization through the 1990s has centered the RLDS interpretation of sacred space near the Temple Lot. The church has explained Joseph Smith's original plan for twenty-four temples as adequate for the 1830s but not for the present. Today, God has provided for the construction of a larger temple structure in accordance with the needs of a larger church population in these more symbolic times. The church operates within urban postindustrial society in the midst of a diverse American Protestantism tinged with New Age philosophy. Naturally, the functions of the new Independence temple are unrelated to, and disconnected from, Nauvoo-era developments, which are extended to the present in modern LDS temples. The CoC views the functions of its modern Independence temple as more related to the Kirtland temple, built at an earlier time when Smith's temple concepts were less—in the CoC view—convoluted. With the new structure, the CoC has instituted new symbolisms of peace and gender equality. The Independence temple, in particular, exhibits a theology that is distinctly feminine.

The CoC mode of interpretation might be labeled historically exclusive, and the view acts to severely limit sacred space. Spatially and doctrinally, the church has traditionally walked a fine line between the larger and the smaller Latter Day Saint churches as well as between Protestantism and Latter Day Saintism. As a result there is a great diversity within the CoC along a continuum from millenarian fundamentalist to liberal secular; and this gulf of extremes is ever widening. As more fundamental RLDS believers break away from the main church, the difficulty of walking that line is becoming more apparent. As the CoC has rapidly changed, abandoning earlier doctrinal roots, its sacred space is contracting to match. Some wonder whether the CoC might even abandon altogether the distinctive beliefs in Joseph Smith Jr. as prophet of a restored church of Jesus Christ or in the *Book of Mormon*. The break-off Restoration Branches do not want to change at all; rather they prefer an ideological return to the basics of early church history, hoping to retain the RLDS name and heritage. Their growth and splintering is the beginning of a new Latter Day Saint realm whose path is now being blazed and whose sacred space is broad if somewhat disjointed.

Historically and spatially, the Temple Lot Church truncates itself considerably more than even the RLDS Church. Its view of history and doctrine is specifically exclusive. The view of Joseph Smith is that he fell from prophet status shortly after the Saints moved into Independence in 1831. He dedicated the spot for the temple of the New Jerusalem, but soon thereafter his human failings cut short his prophetic calling (Flint 1953: 62–68). No greater area for Zion than the Temple Lot was ever indicated by God; the sixty-three-acre tract became only a tract of purchase; and no importance was ever attributed to Far West, Adam-ondi-Ahman, or Nauvoo. The original church's landholdings in Kansas City are not emphasized. Undoubtedly, the church might discuss them more if it had had the means to buy them when it returned to Jackson County in 1867. The Temple Lot Church sees itself as the true remnant of the original church that was left to return to Independence. It hopes to save the Temple Lot after much religious flailing by the larger, errant Latter Day Saint groups, after an apocalyptic purge cleanses the land. Perhaps in part because of the pressure of its break-offs and, in part, the surrounding large churches, it has intermittently become very millenarian, at times even proposing specific years for apocalyptic events.

Doctrinal innovations present in both the RLDS and LDS Churches are absent in the organization of the Temple Lot Church. Here, Joseph Smith was the first prophet and none was needed after he established the church—therefore, at the head of the Temple Lot Church are twelve apostles but no prophet. For them, the later addition of a First Presidency in both the RLDS and LDS Churches (the leadership unit of a prophet with two counselors making a leadership of fifteen instead of twelve) was also seen as doctrinally unfounded.

The daughter splinters of the Temple Lot Church are variously more missionary oriented or more reserved, but most of these maintain similar views toward the doctrine of sacred space. Ultimately a failed effort, only one of the Temple Lot break-offs, the Nerren group in Vernon County, Missouri, was bold enough to attempt a building of a temple, but in southwestern Missouri, not near the sacred Temple Lot. The Temple Lot Churches either beg for the Temple Lot or simply wait for it to fall into their hands through divine intervention. The Elijah Message church is normally adamant in its quest to regain the Temple Lot somehow with God's help, but the possibility of temple construction elsewhere in the area has also surfaced. These groups use to their chiliastic advantage a new Latter Day Saint tradition of apocalyptic messages given either to Otto Fetting starting in 1927 or later through Wilhelm Draves until his death in 1994. These churches believe they are in a superior position doctrinally (especially in the case of the Church of Christ with the Elijah Message), since the messages given are from John the Baptist and are not mere revelation but rather a direct personal connection with the heavens, such as Joseph Smith Jr. originally claimed. These messages to Draves indicated that millennial preparations should be taking place immediately, before the year 2000, but with his death the benefit of direct angelic communication has been postponed. The group awaits a new scribe for John the Baptist. Several have received messages that have not been accepted by the main body of the church, so whatever authoritative benefit this new tradition justifies, it is inherently fragile and sown with dissent. At times it has driven itself into an ultra-millenarian, almost "Millerite" dilemma, like the main Temple Lot body, but no messages accepted by the Elijah Message church have been received since 1994. For this group, change is inevitable.

The *Book of Mormon* portrays the Lamanite Native Americans as important to the establishment of the New Jerusalem—another twist that is fascinating in the variety of interpretation among the different groups. LDS and RLDS Churches have always claimed that the Native Americans were essential in various ways to the building of Zion and to the future development of the New Jerusalem. This has often meant proselytizing in the southwestern United States and elsewhere in the Americas, but the most pressing spatial implication for the central United States may be the proximity of Independence, Missouri, to Oklahoma, where more Native Americans live on nonreservation land than in any other state. The LDS Church has bought several thousand acres in the northeastern part of that state. Some of the new RLDS break-off churches have developed notable concentrations of members in northeastern Oklahoma, and one of them has made a Native American its prophet. The millennial future of Oklahoma is unknown, but it seems its importance in the Latter Day Saint realm is bound to grow.

If one looks at the national view from centralized Independence considering all history and all millenarian posturing compounded, a compelling image appears. Millenarian geography takes on a westward widening sweep in national form consisting of two axes, with the center place in the middle. One axis extends eastward away from Missouri in a narrowing band. This is the historical axis containing most aspects of early church history, but it is also the formative area for the RLDS, Church of Christ, Fettingite groups, and other newer fundamentalist RLDS dissenters. The arc of this region extends from Maine and Vermont through upstate New York, Pennsylvania, Ohio, Michigan, Wisconsin, Illinois, and Iowa. It widens slightly as it approaches Missouri, but oddly, Indiana is an exception, almost devoid of notable Latter Day Saint history. Apart from the LDS influence directly westward, the other is the millenarian axis and is a more imaginary fanning out to the Southwest. It includes break-off groups in Oklahoma and Texas, but, more important, it carries the millenarian weight of Native Americans in Oklahoma, Texas, New Mexico, and Arizona, perceptually broadening through Mexico farther southward. The Lamanites, who will have a major hand in the building of the New Jerusalem in one way or another, originate here, so the southwest is an expectant and chiliastic region. In each axis one can imagine a large arrow pointing to the center place, and Independence is centrally balanced between historical events and millenarian future.

Amelioration of Tension

The sum of the diversity of Latter Day Saint experience around Independence is the possibility for tension, and where tension increases, the possibility for conflict is also present. The mechanisms that groups use for ameliorating tension in sacred space are important in any analysis. For comparative purposes, some of the same Asian places used in chapter 9 are occasionally revisited for comparison.

In multifaceted sacred places, religious tension is lessened through mechanisms ranging from a stance of ignoring another's views to the extreme of physical restriction on sacred space. Depending on the cultural makeup of the place, a variety of social and economic functions can sustain a community despite group tensions. Whether through civil action, legal threat, cultural routine, or transreligious festival, a sort of religious ecology is often evident in Independence—a delicate balance of interacting cultural systems.

Ignoring the Other Saints

One basic mechanism for lessening tensions in Independence is simple avoidance or nonrecognition of others groups. All churches in the Latter Day Saint family do this to some degree, and it usually pertains more to doctrinal perception than to interpersonal or group relations. On the surface the churches may use their common religious history to maintain cordial relations, while individual and collective perceptions emphasize distinctiveness. Therefore one is outwardly (and genuinely) friendly but inwardly aloof. For example, LDS members living in Independence or visiting the site do not readily recognize the RLDS Church in their concepts of future outcomes. The mental landscape is all LDS, and in talk of the Second Coming or future temple, non-LDS structures are conspicuously absent. The rest of Kansas City is largely ignored, so not only does religious competition disappear, but conflict with the secular landscape is eliminated as well. Daybell's (2000) vivid novel treats the future establishment of a glorious LDS New Jerusalem, mentioning Kansas City only three times, and then only in historical perspective.

The fact that the Temple Lot itself is owned by a separate little church comes as a surprise to LDS members who visit the lot, because the smaller church is not usually discussed in historical or doctrinal manuals of the church. One common perception is that the small church is a caretaker of the Temple Lot, which will someday be taken over by the LDS Church, whether through purchase or calamity. One unverified rumor was that at every LDS General Conference a seat was reserved for the president of the Temple Lot Church, an idea reflecting LDS ignorance since the Church of Christ has twelve apostles but no president or prophet, as have the LDS Church or the CoC. The closest that the Church of Christ comes to a president is William Sheldon, the church's "General Church Representative." The millenarian view is that the Temple Lot Church is ultimately subservient to the LDS organization, but some believe that the Utah church may ultimately choose another spot for an eventual New Jerusalem temple.

Among many LDS members, it is thought that territory owned by the RLDS Church at the sacred core of Independence will somehow eventually fall into the hands of the LDS Church. One unlikely rumor is that the LDS Church lent money to the RLDS Church for the construction of the RLDS Independence temple during the 1980s, thus putting the RLDS organization in spiritual as well as financial debt to the LDS Church. More specifically, some believe that RLDS lands, possibly the Auditorium itself, were used as collateral for securing such loans. The vernacular LDS hope centers on talk that the RLDS Church might eventually default on the loan, causing lands to somehow revert to the LDS Church.

The huge RLDS Auditorium is usually inconspicuous in LDS talk, but its functional and architectural similarity to the Mormon Tabernacle (or, now, to the LDS Conference Center) on Temple Square has prompted some to wonder if, when acquired, it may be transformed into an important gathering center for premillennial Mormons, just as it is now for the nonmillennial Community of Christ membership. The new RLDS Independence Temple also presents a problem, perhaps a more difficult one. Situated directly across Walnut Street from the LDS Visitor's Center, it is too striking to ignore yet too unconventional to include in most LDS perceptions. It seems the structure, at the very least, has made LDS members suddenly and uneasily aware of the existence of the CoC as an organization that will not just somehow fade away. Ironically, however, LDS talk in the Independence area brims millenarian as it views RLDS dissent. The view is that perhaps the CoC will keep breaking up and ultimately blow away. What most LDS members do not see is the breadth, if not the depth, of the liberal reformation remaking the RLDS organization.

Often, LDS members describe the new spiral temple disparagingly as a tower of Babel or an upside-down ice-cream cone. Since the traditional LDS meaning of a temple is set in stone, members are uncertain of the significance of the new RLDS structure, and any discussion of it is commonly couched in terms of their own LDS temple experience. Questions of LDS orientation are expected. Is the temple open to anyone? (LDS temples are not). What kinds of ceremonies are performed in it? (The reference is to ordinances for the living and dead, such as baptisms performed in LDS temples). Is Christ expected to come there? (According to many LDS authorities Christ visits most LDS temples, at least to accept their dedications). Some LDS members have no desire to go near the CoC Temple, but naturally others are intrigued and want to explore. When considering chiliastic scenarios, however, most LDS members expunge the reformist RLDS spiral from the landscape.

As an example, Daybell's (2000) imaginative future LDS New Jerusalem completely erases the RLDS Church from the land. There is no RLDS Auditorium or Temple and these structures would be very difficult to miss, even if in apocalyptic ruin. No RLDS presence whatsoever remains. When reporting on millennial events to occur at the great council at Adam-ondi-Ahman, Daybell has Emma appearing with Joseph Smith Jr. In reality, after the murder of her husband, Emma and Brigham Young did not see eye to eye, and she stayed behind with her son Joseph Smith III, who later became first prophet of the RLDS Church. Daybell has Emma and Brigham, now in resurrected form, with all disagreements patched up (Daybell 2000:162). Not surprisingly, Joseph Smith III was not among the heavenly beings mentioned. Oddly, the Temple Lot, so revered now by everybody, is not mentioned in Daybell's chiliastic tour de force. In a future LDS New Jerusalem, apparently the drama becomes too large to consider one small plot of land.

The same expurgation is basically true for the Temple Lot groups and the Restoration Branches. They all have their own views of chiliasm and the city of the New Jerusalem, none of which include the views or buildings of other groups. Ecumenical directions among the groups of Saints are rare. In discussion with the author, apostle Sheldon of the Temple Lot Church wagged his finger toward the RLDS Temple. "That is not the spot," he emphatically stated. Despite perceptions that the LDS and RLDS Churches might be waiting for the Temple Lot Church to simply die out and relinquish its land, the Temple Lot group sees itself as the sole inheritor of New Jerusalem rights. The New Jerusalem will eventually stretch out from the Temple Lot, and none of the buildings of the other groups are present in the vision. Or, better stated, LDS, CoC, and Temple Lot break-off groups' buildings will be obliterated during the apocalypse. The Temple Lot proper, however, will be preserved.

The more liberal members of the Community of Christ are the only Saints who sometimes view themselves not as the sole benefactors of the Independence sacred site, but rather as participants in a general religious experience. Their leftward leaning quasi-secular view allows them this luxury. One RLDS female priest compared the RLDS Church to the LDS. She said, "The Mormon Church is a big church, a rich church. We see ourselves as the little church. We hope all Saints can share this place together." She was obviously concerned by inter-Saint tensions, but her view did not include the Temple Lot Church. If the quarter-million-member RLDS Church is the little church, then what is the two-thousand-member Temple Lot Church? It would be nothing if it did not hold the key portion of sacred space, but the CoC does not need the Temple Lot *now* (so they imply), and it has traditionally been common for members to compare themselves only to the LDS realm. Break-off groups from the Temple Lot Church that have grown larger than itself are unknown organizations to most LDS and RLDS members. Some LDS members, who believe their church to be the only true one, are shocked to find out the number of Latter Day Saint groups.

Occasionally, the factions of Saints have divided in terms of stratification, from bigger to smaller, richer to poorer, greater to lesser, and also in perceptions of better to worse. This approach is common in religious studies and among some sociologists (Stark and Bainbridge 1985). Such views in isolation should not be given credence. Aspects of stratification among Latter Day Saint groups already have been demonstrated in this chapter, but their religious bases reach deep into the human psyche—too deep, it seems, to be explained simply in socioeconomic terms.

Alternative Sacred Places

Alternative sacred spaces sometimes provide a temporary antidote to conflict. Jews and Muslims at Jerusalem have restrictions on the Temple Mount, and since devout Jews do not allow themselves within that sacred area (and are not normally allowed within), many are satisfied to stand at the Wailing Wall of the ancient temple and recite prayers. Artificial sacred sites are sometimes formed when the real ones are inaccessible.

At Independence, such space alterations are beginning to appear. Members of the Church of Christ with the Elijah Message pondered building *the* temple on some site other than the Temple Lot. Varied interpretation of revelations to Joseph Smith Jr. have caused LDS members and authorities alike to occasionally speculate if the Lord might shift the establishment of the New Jerusalem to some other place nearby. Most members do not seem to favor that idea. When the traditional Temple Lot could not be acquired after multiple court battles, the RLDS Church finally chose an alternate, less sacred, site right next to the old authentic one. As time passes, especially as the turn of twenty-first century approaches, more shifting of sacred space can be expected in Independence.

Latter Day Saints of various stripes like to walk, ponder, and pray at the Temple Lot, and generally the Church of Christ has been tolerant, even encouraging of such activity. The Temple Lot Church was also burned down twice in the twentieth century. As the Church of Christ becomes more besieged with zealous people seeking solace there, what if it were to build a fence around the lot? Other groups with spiritual investment in the site who are accustomed to gathering and praying on the lot would surely make their grievances known. The possibility of such a move cannot be ignored and would drastically alter relationships around Independence. Would such a move tip a perceptual balance? The outcome cannot be certain, but bordering sidewalks along Walnut and River Streets would undoubtedly take on new meaning.

Litigation and Zoning

Contention is ingeniously mitigated in a variety of ways beyond the pronouncement of alternate sacred places. Independence city laws and zoning regulations generally have served to keep control over sacred landscape. Such demanded that an unsightly sacred hole dug into the Temple Lot for the foundations of a temple that was never built be filled in the 1940s. At times, however, the city has inadvertently been a religious instigator. When it sought LDS land in the 1950s for a new high school and in the 1960s for park development it inadvertently prompted the respective construction of the LDS Mission Home and LDS Visitors Center.

In Independence, typical American processes of politics and litigation have dissipated religious tension. Instead of resorting to war or violence, the RLDS Church chose to take the smaller Church of Christ to court to resolve the dispute over the Temple Lot in the 1890s. The acceptance by both sides of court authority was perhaps a more important sign than the outcome of the case. Whatever the religious affiliation, the American mindset often seems predisposed to higher legal authority and respects its ultimate decision, even at times in apparent contradiction to what believers see as God's will. If the legal outcome is not to one group's liking the tendency is still to appeal and, finally, to be resigned. "In God we trust" means that divine will is exhibited in civil, legal, or political outcomes. This is one aspect of this American sacred space that is quite distinct from Asian examples.

Contrast the Temple Lot case with that of the Ram Janmabhumi Temple in Ayodhya, which was supposed to have been taken up by Indian courts (Gargan 1991). In religiously charged India, however, the people have taken control. Hindu fundamentalists destroyed most of the Muslim Babri Masjid, and a popular movement is gradually constructing a temple to Rama on the same spot. Any move usually takes place outside the law and affects tens of millions of emotional people. The police intervene when they can, but secular authority seems fleeting when compared to eternal sanctity of place. The possibility for civil disturbance is tremendous, and once violence starts, the police often stand aside, taking up positions once the trouble subsides. Independence may have such a capacity for turbulence, but its religious texture does not yet supercede civil authority.

Independence as Religious Ecumene

In Banaras, India, the minority Muslims often loudly celebrate special holidays by parading miniature mosques called Tazias through the narrow streets of the city. Police are stationed between the Muslim procession and the Hindu temple to ensure that the two structures do not make contact. To do so could be disastrous, but all jointly, and in the mood of celebration, form a human buffer zone between opposing religious ideals. It is even claimed that Banarasness prevails over local religious differences, that the place itself blurs religious distinctions (1989:158–61, 165–66). In this scenario, tension is accepted as tradition.

Perhaps Independence could become like Banaras in that Independence-ness would prevail over RLDS-ness or Temple Lot-ness. An example of this for a time was the Independence pageant, which the LDS Church sponsored for almost three decades. The play was successful in bringing together different Latter Day Saint groups around Independence, overshadowing doctrinal differences—for three or four hours anyway. The pageant, however, rubbed the Missourian Protestants the wrong way.

Relations between the RLDS and LDS Churches in the late 1800s were rather bitter, but tensions have cooled. Today, through great doctrinal and ideological rifts, RLDS and LDS Church leaders make token efforts to visit one another in order to preserve a common heritage. As early as 1934, the Mormon Tabernacle Choir sang at the incomplete RLDS auditorium, where RLDS president Frederick M. Smith and LDS president Heber J. Grant entered the chamber together in symbolic historical unity ("Mormon Choir's Visit" 1992). In July 1992, the choir returned to the auditorium after a fifty-eight-year absence (Cantrell 1992). Again, token meetings took place between church leaders; the choir even toured the new RLDS temple (Romig 1992; Avant 1992a, 1992b).

Some of the more liberal thinking Saints (think Community of Christ) see a day when all four corners of River and Walnut Streets in Independence will have their own versions of a temple, and the organs of all four structures will play in unity together. The Saints are mutually cordial and the image is impressive, but such an ecumenical activity would be a token gesture. Despite some notable efforts at unifying the various groups, it is doubtful that traditional modes of belief will slip away so easily.

One honorable example, however, is the efforts of the Missouri Mormon Frontier Foundation (MMFF), a nonsectarian, nonprofit organization established in the early 1990s. Its most prominent contribution was that of the establishment of a walking trail in central Independence that marks historic church sites from downtown to the Temple Lot. Thirteen sites are memorialized with plaques designed by CoC artist Henry Inouye (Missouri Mormon Frontier 2003; Walking Trail Virtual Tour 2000). For example, the bronze plaque placed at the south side of the Temple Lot portrays Joseph Smith preaching to eleven men. Its inscription reads, "The Mormon Prophet

Joseph Smith and Mormon leaders dedicated this area for construction of a Temple, 3 August 1831. A Temple complex was envisioned as the center of a city to be called Zion." The walking tour seeks to unite in a purely historical context. Highly impartial, the tour only gives emphasis to Mormon history through 1838 at the latest. It has been hailed by most Latter Day Saint groups as a "positive step" in interfaith relations (Harlacher 2000:11).

There are, however, some interesting cues of bias on the tour and the MMFF Web site. Everything regarding church history is called Mormon, indicating either that the LDS Church has a dominant influence over the MMFF or that all groups have no complaint referring to the early Saints as Mormons, an idea that the LDS Church would not oppose since this nomenclature reinforces continuity between the original Saints and their church today. Though half of the fifteen officials and board members are LDS, the president is a Restoration Branch member, the vice president is a CoC historian along with one other board member, and other members are AME Methodist (an African American), a Unitarian, and a Catholic (Missouri Mormon Frontier 2003; Romig 2001).

Ron Romig, the vice president of the MMFF, wrote that it has been particularly difficult to get participation from the Church of Christ (Temple Lot), with the Temple Lot Church historian Roland Sarratt coming to about every third meeting. The MMFF did get the Temple Lot Church's permission for placement of the plaque, "though it is in the city right-of-way." Romig reported that the Temple Lot Church has "warmed up to the idea" of the MMFF but that communication with the smaller groups has not been easy (Romig 2001). It may not help relations with the Temple Lot Church that one of the MMFF virtual Web site photos of the Temple Lot looks eastward toward the CoC temple, ignoring the small Church of Christ and giving the impression that the spiral is located on the Temple Lot or that the CoC is the dominant church on the Temple Lot.

Another organization emphasizing ecumenical melding is the Association for the Unity of Restoration Saints. Most members of the association belong to a variety of Restoration Branches, but churches such as the Church of Christ (Temple Lot), the Church of Christ, Restored, and the Restoration Church of Jesus Christ of Latter Day Saints regularly participate. The interesting angle of this organization for restoration unity is that Joseph F. Smith, a great grandson of Joseph Smith Jr. and a member of the Church of Christ (Temple Lot), leads it (he is not to be confused with Joseph F. Smith, president of the LDS Church from 1901 to 1918).

Teaching that "within the heart of every Latterday [*sic*] Saint there must live the hope of the gathering and the establishment of the city of Zion, the New Jerusalem that has been promised" the group hopes unity among the Saints will "push forward the cause of Zion" ("Association News" 1999, 2000). One wonders if Smith's lineage might be used as a doctrinal basis for a new church, for this is how Latter Day Saint groups think. It would be the second church in the area to have a Smith at the helm. True ecumenicalism is rare, since it requires a diluting of doctrine, which most individuals cannot tolerate. Since 1995, association meetings have been held in Missouri, Illinois, Michigan, and Kirtland, Ohio.

One article appearing in the LDS *Ensign* in 1993 was one of the most impartial seen anywhere ("Bridge Building" 1993:76). The article, rare for an LDS publication, briefly discusses the histories of the RLDS and Temple Lot Churches and even has quotations from prominent RLDS and Temple Lot members regarding "friendly interaction" and "amiable feelings" among the groups. The writer, however, only mentions the RLDS center east of the Temple Lot as its "large world headquarters" and does not utter the word "temple" anywhere. A photo caption in a separate article in the same *Ensign* likewise referred to the RLDS Independence temple only as the "headquarters buildings of the Community of Christ" (Baugh 2001:47), which is not incorrect, but it is not quite forthcoming either. Nevertheless, a real ecumenical sense pervades this unusual piece. The different groups are mentioned as "growing toward a common purpose despite their theological differences." One RLDS member said, "Our common enemy is not other churches, it is Satan and the world" (1993:76). Most LDS readers, however, undoubtedly understand the common purpose mentioned to be the LDS way of baptism, missionary work, temple work, and Apostolic authority and receipt of the prophetic mantle by seniority.

It is true that most church members are very cordial and friendly toward each other, but the commonality mentioned is mostly historical, because the different churches are diverging at various rates of speed. Though attempts at the establishment of common ground are laudable, the differences among today's Latter Day Saint churches are not simply doctrinally divided; they reside at different extremes of millenarian eschatology temporally and geographically. At one extreme, the trend in the CoC is toward liberalization into a nonchiliastic, nonmillenarian church. It feels it must adopt this ideology to gain greater acceptance in the world. The LDS Church remains millenarian, but it is softening its tone to enhance broader appeal. Apocalyptic scenarios have not disappeared by any means in the

LDS realm, but they are discussed less by membership and leadership alike. Church of Christ (Temple Lot) groups as well as many Restoration Branches of the RLDS realm are all notably more apocalyptic and often are ultra millenarian, at least up to a point where the extremism of revelation causes schism. The gulf between even the Church of Christ (Temple Lot) and the Church of Christ with the Elijah Message is broad and unbridgeable considering the belief of continued angelic messages held by the latter. The smallest groups are the least ecumenical, perhaps because of millenarian defensiveness, or perhaps because they "require a high level of commitment and participation within the group to continue to exist" (Romig 2001). The tendency is that they shut themselves off from the rest of the world and other churches, reinforcing varieties of apocalyptic belief. Certainly the groups that are talking to each other are less apocalyptic. One wonders if the Church of Christ (Temple Lot), traditionally more apocalyptic, might become less so as it interacts with surrounding churches and visitors. Such a shift, however, is not yet apparent.

Doctrinally, then, common history is the strongest cord binding the Latter Day Saint churches. Otherwise, they see themselves as chosen and therefore quite distinct from their neighbors. For example, Church of Christ (Temple Lot) postcards with aerial views emphasize only the Temple Lot; other surrounding structures are truncated—though mentioned on the reverse. Another aerial photo of Independence in an LDS *Ensign* article looked eastward emphasizing LDS Church properties and downtown (Baugh 2001:47). Both large RLDS structures are seen in the periphery of the photo, but, surprisingly, only a small portion of the southeast corner of the sacred Temple Lot appears! The LDS Church has a long tradition of not overemphasizing the Temple Lot itself, since it does not wish to bring undo recognition to what is basically seen as a historical faction, an unfortunate twist of history.

Chronological Alternation

Independence has developed its own unique form of religious ecology. Plotted on a graph, the construction of religious structures by all Latter Day Saint groups at or near the Temple Lot takes on an interesting pattern. Evident is a revolving chronological tendency for groups to take center stage at different times (Figure 59).

In 1867, the Temple Lot Church arrived in Independence and soon thereafter began purchasing lots. RLDS membership, however, was also

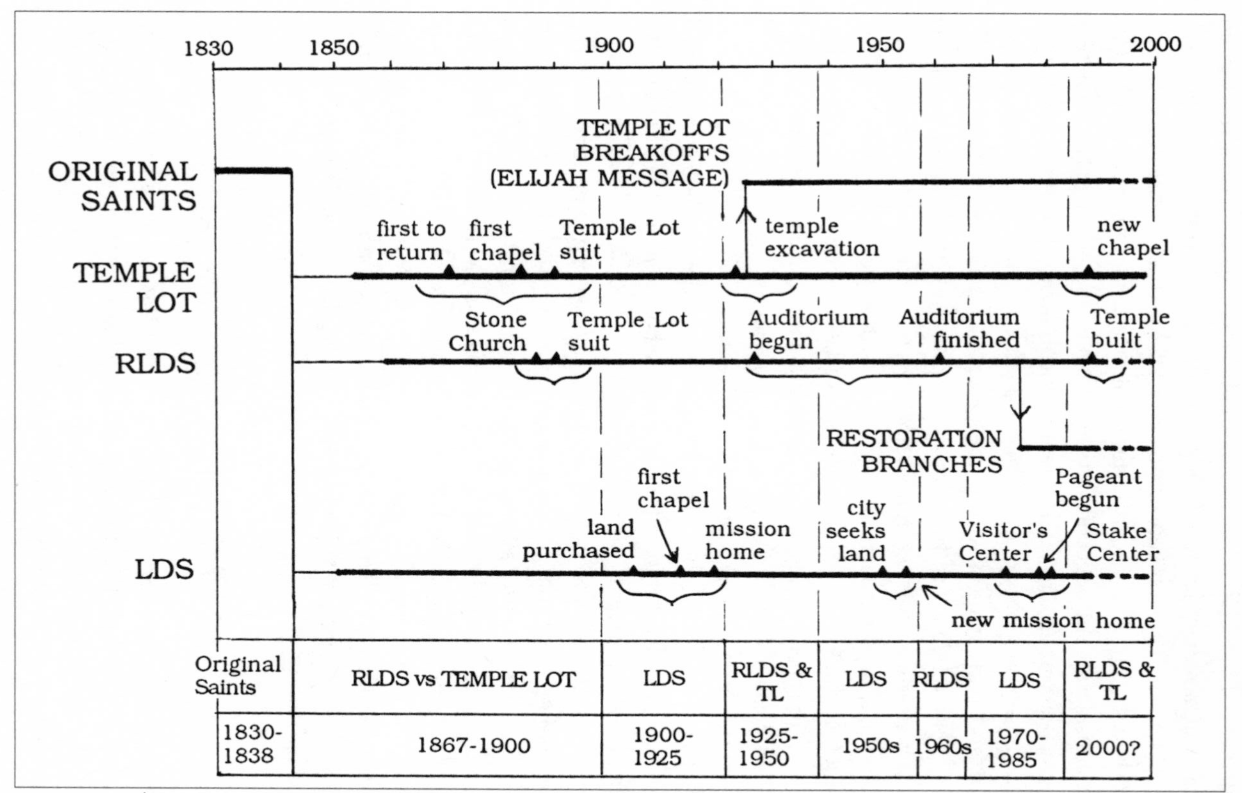

FIG. 59 | *Chronology of Temple Lot activity.*

burgeoning and by 1888 construction on the Stone Church had begun. Friction between these two groups over the sacred Temple Lot increased to the point of litigation. The period from 1867 to about 1900 was the first phase of factional interest in Independence and marked a continuing tendency of the RLDS and Temple Lot Churches, which side by side have shared Independence history and membership, to simultaneously also share the spotlight of New Jerusalem development.

Though the RLDS and Temple Lot Churches continued to grow at the turn of the century—the Temple Lot Church at the expense of the RLDS Church—it was the LDS Church that took center stage from just after 1900 to about 1925. In 1906, land was first purchased in Independence, and in 1914 the first LDS building, a large meetinghouse, was dedicated. A mission home was added on to it in 1920.

The period from approximately 1925 until the early 1960s is more difficult to interpret. It was a time of a mixture of influence, yet somehow orchestrated so that no churches' toes would be stepped on. The large RLDS auditorium was begun in 1926 but halted by the depression in the early 1930s. During this same period, the Church of Christ was going through an ultra-millenarian phase. According to the instructions of apostle Otto Fetting, the construction of a temple on the Temple Lot was begun. From 1929 through World War II, the Temple Lot Church divided and redivided, producing several independent churches. The Temple Lot splintering stabilized by the end of the war. At this time the RLDS Church made preparations to finish the Auditorium, which was finally dedicated in 1962, after a lapse of thirty years. History reveals a sensitive landscape interplay between RLDS and Temple Lot Churches.

Notwithstanding the RLDS push to finish the Auditorium, the LDS Church was the only group to build a new structure in the vicinity of the Temple Lot during the 1950s. This development, however, was inadvertently instigated by the city of Independence. When the city sought church land to build a new high school, the church demurred and soon thereafter began construction of a new mission home to forestall further city action. Apparently, a similar situation occurred in the late 1960s when the city considered an appropriation of church land for park development. The church responded with the construction of the LDS Visitor's Center at the site and later used the rest of the land for its yearly pageant and new Stake Center meetinghouse. In the vicinity, the 1970s and early 1980s were overwhelmingly LDS years.

In 1984 the spotlight quickly changed again as turbulence erupted in the RLDS Church with the announcement that women could be ordained to the priesthood. Fundamentalist members objected and RLDS congregations began to splinter. In 1988, the RLDS Church announced plans to build its Independence Temple, dedicated to "peace" and "reconciliation of the spirit," an understandable goal considering the dissent. Into the 1990s hopeful members closely watched the temple rise, while fundamentalists decried its design as absurd. Meanwhile, the LDS Church bought valuable farmland in the Kansas City periphery. With a change of name and further liberalization much in line with general trends in liberal Protestantism, the Community of Christ continues to struggle between leftward direction and fundamentalist history. Today, new RLDS break-off churches are becoming more visible on the scene; to a great degree, circa 2000, activity around Independence has focused on these fundamentalists.

The RLDS Church has been forced to share the marquee of the sacred core in recent years with the Temple Lot Church. The historic headquarters of the Temple Lot group burned on the first day of 1990. Then, as the giant RLDS spiral surged three hundred feet into the air, a modest new Temple Lot building next door defiantly pulled itself up two proud stories. Relations between the two churches, however, are practically nonexistent.

A religious ecology of sorts has developed at Independence similar to India's Banaras, though without the depth that spans centuries. The various groups of Saints have shared Temple Lot surroundings, grudgingly perhaps, but for the most part managing to stay clear of each other's development. The RLDS Church and the Temple Lot Church have managed to share the stage on three different occasions: in the 1890s during the Temple Lot suit, the late 1920s during the temple building enthusiasm of the Temple Lot Church and the beginning of construction of the Auditorium, and again in the early 1990s with the rise of the new RLDS Temple and the new Temple Lot headquarters building. When the LDS Church has added to the Independence landscape, the other two groups have not been in competition. Somehow the RLDS and Temple Lot Church realms are closer in ecology—when they dance, they dance delicately together. With the Remnant Church of Jesus Christ of Latter Day Saints making its headquarters in the old high school northeast of the Temple Lot soon after the construction of the RLDS temple and the new Temple Lot Church headquarters, the religious complexity at the core is entering a new phase.

Future Scenarios

Independence now is home to more Latter Day Saint groups than ever before. Five groups are situated within a few blocks of the Temple Lot. At least four other influential groups exist in Independence, with about twenty smaller ones also operating in the area. What will happen to the mix is unpredictable, but some scenarios may be pondered.

Barring a major catastrophe, or major schism, the Church of Christ is likely to retain control of the Temple Lot for some time. Though it is a small church, it has maintained the same population for several decades. With new missionary efforts in Mexico, and the selection of two Mexican apostles, it is easy to imagine the Temple Lot Church planning the construction of a modest temple soon. Such a pronouncement, however, requires an accepted revelation, and, as has been seen, with revelation comes the increased probability of schism. With schism, the church could lose millennial momentum and could be forced back to a position of millennial maintenance or expectance status quo. That scenario could lead to perpetual attrition. Effective growth has to come from a delicate balance of millennial promise with prophetic prowess. Apocalyptic vision notwithstanding, the possessor of the most sacred spot may also be influenced by interfaith activities and continued exposure to others at spiritual ground zero. Other groups, who claim the lot and try to exert religious hegemony over it, however, continually besiege the Temple Lot Church, mainly through revelatory edicts. This is especially true for the vigorous Elijah Message Church, which desperately seeks divine intervention to regain the Temple Lot before the Second Coming. This event is imminent for the Temple Lot Church in their way and the Elijah Message church in theirs. How forceful the Elijah Message community will become in their quest is unknown, but the members are generally respected people of the community.

What will happen to the CoC/RLDS realm is uncertain, too. Despite extreme liberalization, including the change of its name, the RLDS Church has been adamant in maintaining influence at the sacred core through the construction of its new temple and in the purchase of residential property immediately to the north of the Temple Lot. At the same time, the church has been selling off properties and institutions elsewhere in Independence. Local dissent has been strong and shows no sign of abating. Fundamentalist Restoration Branches and other RLDS break-off churches are growing, particularly in the Jackson County area. Likely the splintering will continue with perhaps a hundred or more RLDS-based churches vying for position. With their own prophets and apostles, many of these splinters from the RLDS institutional 'failure,' however, will likely congeal into fewer churches according to varied doctrinal rationales, such as specific church organization, accepted Prophets or apostles, blood lineage, or the inclusion of Native Americans. Many of the existing RLDS break-offs will disappear. All will likely give importance to the sacred Temple Lot, but when any acts on the millennial urge to build, schism looms, because the closer any one leader gets to God's concrete will toward landscape, the greater the possibility that people will not accept the new vision. People are extremely particular when God's will is pronounced, and tampering with the historic Temple Lot will not be tolerated. Often, new break-offs will be short lived. With one now headquartered in the old William Chrisman School just north of the RLDS temple, with a literal descendant of Joseph Smith at the helm, it is a sign these new churches are already exerting fresh influences on sacred space.

One thing is almost certain: the CoC will not be saved from within, as the RLDS fundamentalists imagine. The liberal alteration is a process too ingrained in much of the modern American experience to reverse. In fact, this millenarian-literalist/liberal-secular division within the Latter Day Saint family of churches indicates a general paradigm split dividing the whole of American society. Some groups will always tend to read events, works, and words more literally and specifically than others who will always see the symbolic and general in all things. Ideologically, the two sides share little; it just so happens that the dualism is clearly portrayed in space that the Latter Day Saints hold dear.

The LDS Church is in a most interesting situation with respect to Jackson County. Will the church actually move its headquarters to Independence one day as generally taught? Though doctrinal stances generally remain pure to history, with increasing visibility, the church has lessened the appearance of being extreme by giving greater emphasis to world and community welfare service, to being Christ-centered, and to strengthening the family. Beliefs regarding Independence have not changed, but have been de-emphasized. The LDS Church still claims a millennial heritage but has a harder time expressing it to an increasingly national and global audience. Church membership is growing in the Kansas City metropolitan region, but little has been said officially about the development of a New Jerusalem or the building of even a regular service temple for the Kansas City area, much less a temple for the Second Coming.

Despite this, the LDS Church has built temples at several historic sites. Among these is the reconstruction of the historic Nauvoo temple in Illinois; one at Palmyra, New York, adjacent to Joseph Smith's sacred grove; and one at Brigham Young's gathering station for the trek west at Winter Quarters, near Omaha. Only Kirtland, Ohio, and western Missouri remain in the raising of the LDS temple tent. With its exclusive holdings of valuable Jackson and Clay County acreage it is difficult to believe that the church is preparing only for the development of shopping malls or residential areas (Heinerman and Shupe 1985). With growth in membership signified by a variety of temples now encircling Independence, the Kansas City area becomes conspicuous for its lack of an LDS temple of any kind. Paramount is a conflict in meaning between the idea of a normal operating temple and a future millennial temple. By what means will the church fill this sacred historical gap? Most members and leaders would say through revelation.

Independence as a sacred core will grow in force. More Saints of different ilk will move to the Kansas City area. It is likely dominant American traditions of legal system and land possession will eventually push many groups of Latter Day Saints to choose various sacred lots and plots in the vicinity of Independence as close to the Temple Lot as possible for their distinct New Jerusalem visions. The origins of the Temple Lot dedication are vague, and the revelation to Joseph Smith Jr. that the temple site was to be a spot of land on a lot "lying westward" from the courthouse certainly leaves room for varied rendition (*Doctrine* 1981:57:3). A little imagination reveals an Independence landscape dotted with individual sacred plots and structures generally radiating away from the Temple Lot, as various groups buy them and develop according to their own interpretations of scripture and church organization. So a question remains as to how sacred the Temple Lot itself will stay over a great period of time.

Among the individual believers, interest in Independence as sacred millennial space has increased over the years, especially within Jackson County, while scholars have neglected it. The variations in Latter Day Saint belief, particularly among smaller groups, have generally been obscure to non–Latter Day Saint scholars. Conversely, most scholars of the Latter Day Saint realm are Latter Day Saints, usually of the LDS or CoC organizations, and they have given less attention to Independence than to other historical sites because of its complex perceptual geography, a jumble of confusing vistas even to the believer. Richard Jackson (1983) confirmed this rather bipolar view in a study of typology of sacred space using places important to western Latter-day Saints. When asked to rate the "future City of Zion," the millennial settlement yet to be, Mormons gave a rating second only to the Salt Lake Temple. At the opposite extreme, present-day Jackson County, Missouri, the perceived place for that "future City of Zion" was rated second lowest, only slightly more sacred than the Lincoln Memorial on the mall (Jackson 1983:102). Believers project sanctity to a millennial place while, ironically, not seeing the views of other believers as sacred, nor accepting the prosaic urban reality of present-day Kansas City as much more than historically significant. There is a perceptual separation between the place of the imagination and the place in reality; thus the same place can be ranked highly sacred in one expectant part of the mind and lower in more mundane modes of thought.

The overlapping of related multifarious beliefs causes caution and hesitancy among the believers. Being persecuted causes hesitancy as well, another reason for the scholarly taciturn attitude, one born out in part by Kenneth Foote in his purview of landscapes of violence and tragedy. Scholarly neglect of Independence is not from a lack of importance or interest. Each Latter Day Saint group has constructed its own geographic vision of New Jerusalem space, and each has taken turns in the historical spotlight. Though token ecumenical activity occurs, factions ideologically distance themselves from each other's New Jerusalems while sharing the same site.

As a new century opens, the next few decades should be exciting ones for western Missouri. In New World contexts, Independence is a highly conflicted sacred place. As the new millennium unfolds, views toward its sacred space will become more plural as Temple Lot, RLDS, and LDS Churches and their break-off groups show more interest in gathering or building in Jackson County and its environs. What *environs* means for each group however, will vary. Different cultural, historical, legal, and civic mechanisms have served to lessen tension among the different groups, but these have not decreased divergence, whose pace appears to be quickening. Many groups will ask for or demand the Temple Lot and try to place themselves near it. Some individuals have attempted to destroy or harm the Temple Lot Church. Unfortunately, such violence could reoccur and may even be likely. Some may plan and build millennial temples peripheral to the Temple Lot. Independence is a peerless laboratory for observing the divergent paths of millenarian Latter Day Saint belief, and New Jerusalem interpretations are becoming ever more disparate.

Appendix I
The Main Splinters of the Early Church

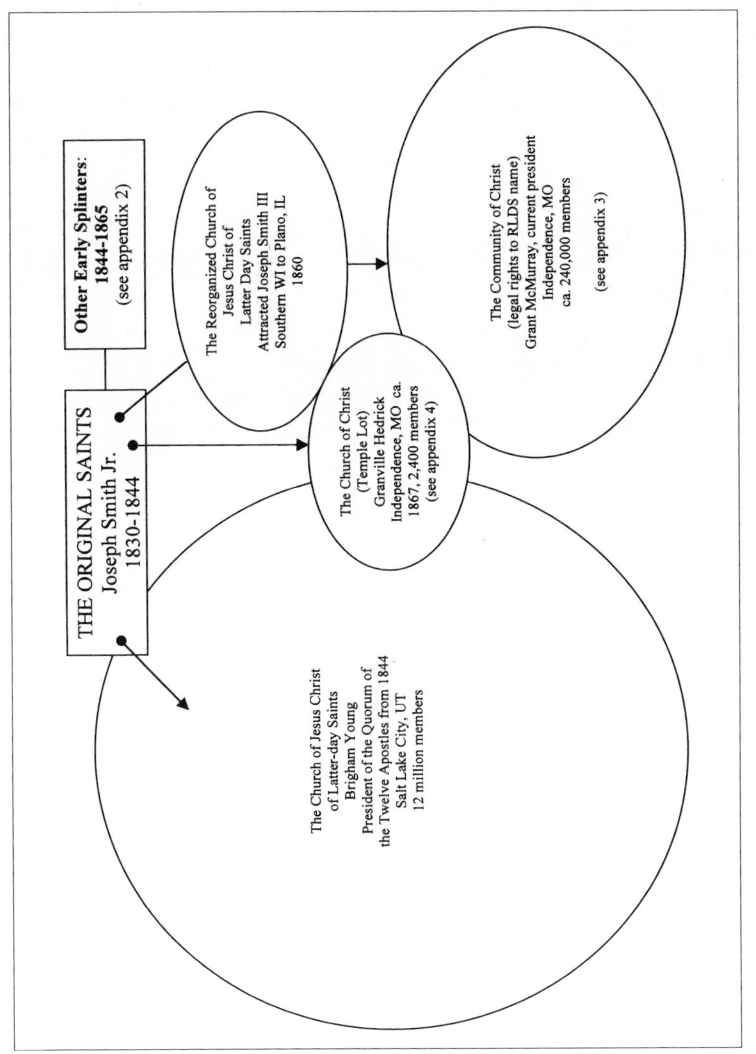

From Chapter 4, A Splintering and a Return. Main Splinters of the Early Church. Circle sizes are generally representative of church size, but are not proportional. Arrow points represent present day.

Appendix 2

Other Early Splinters and Their Descendents

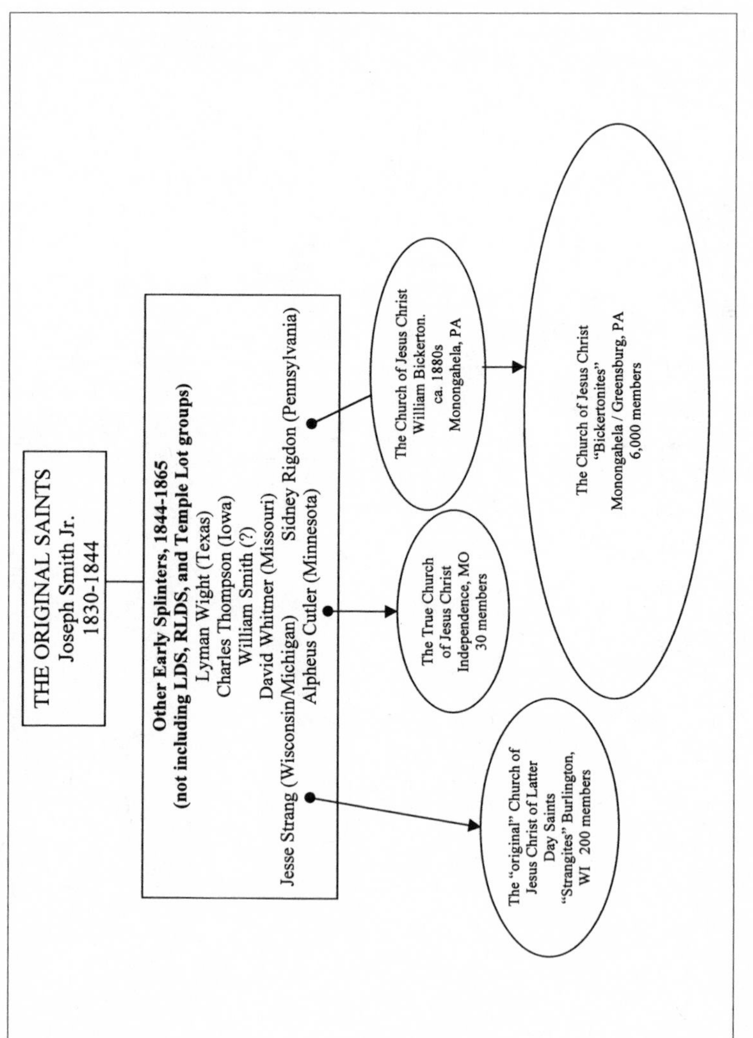

From Chapter 4, A Splintering and a Return. *Other early splinters and their descendents. Circle sizes generally representative of church size, but are not proportional. Arrow points represent present day.*

Appendix 3

Splinters of the Reorganized Church of Jesus Christ of Latter Day Saints

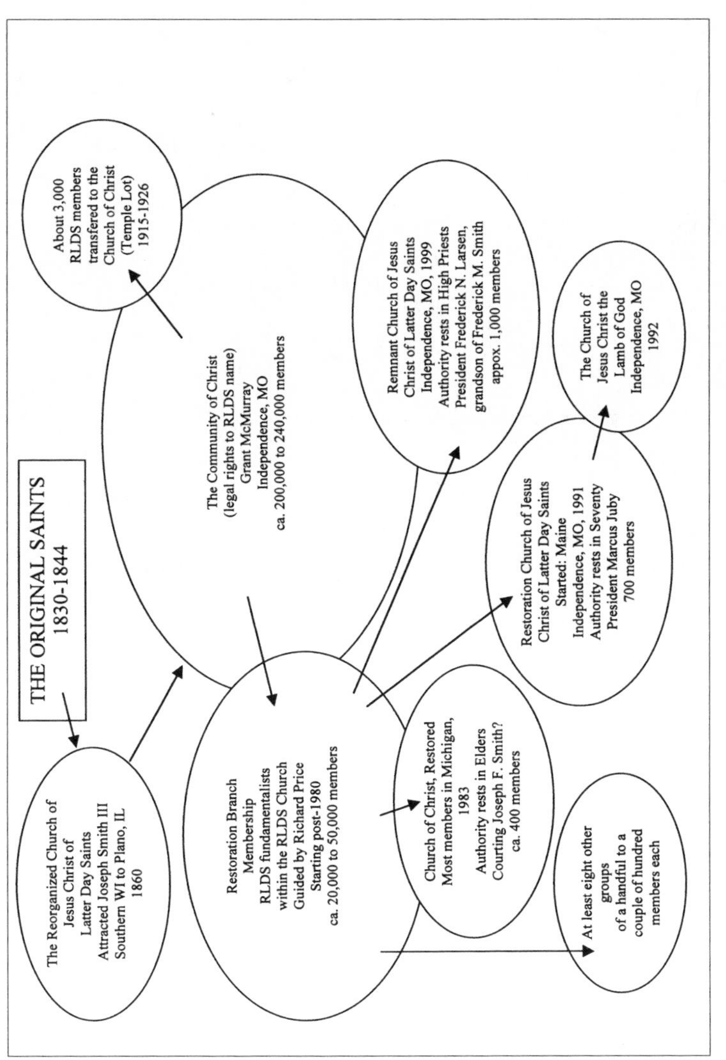

From Chapter 8, Narrow Views of Zion and Anti-Zion Space. Splinters of the Reorganized Church of Jesus Christ of Latter Day Saints. *Circle sizes are generally representative of church size but are not proportional. Arrows represent general time progression.*

Appendix 4

Splinters of the Church of Christ (Temple Lot)

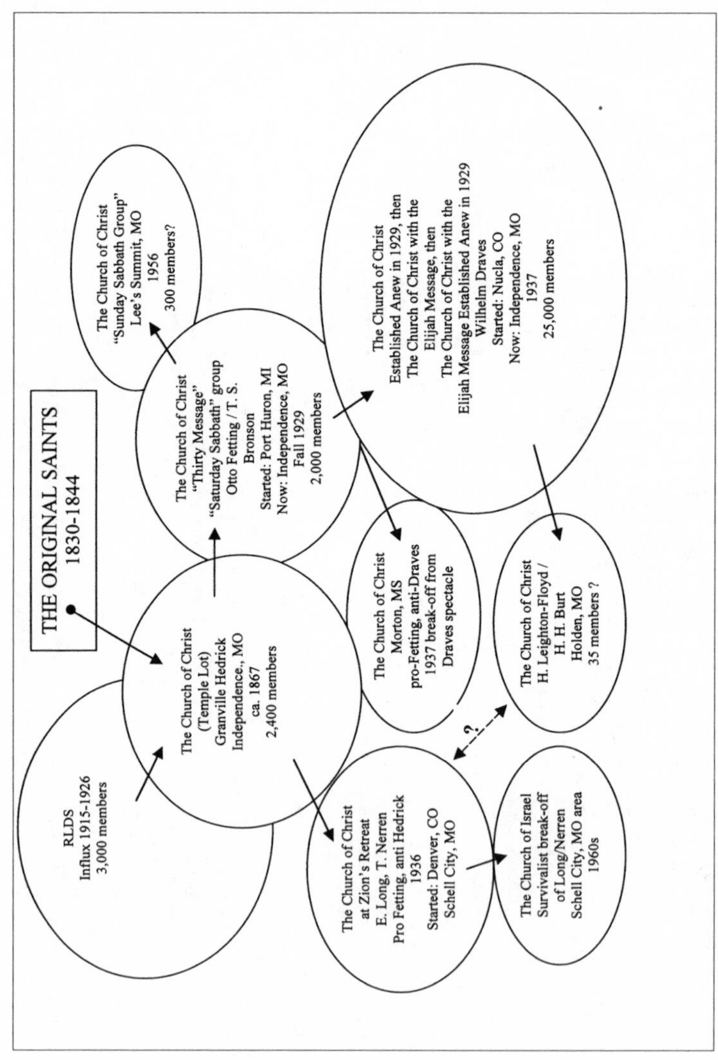

From Chapter 8, Narrow Views of Zion and Anti-Zion Space. Splinters of the Church of Christ (Temple Lot). *Circle sizes are generally representative of church size but are not proportional. Arrows represent general time progression.*

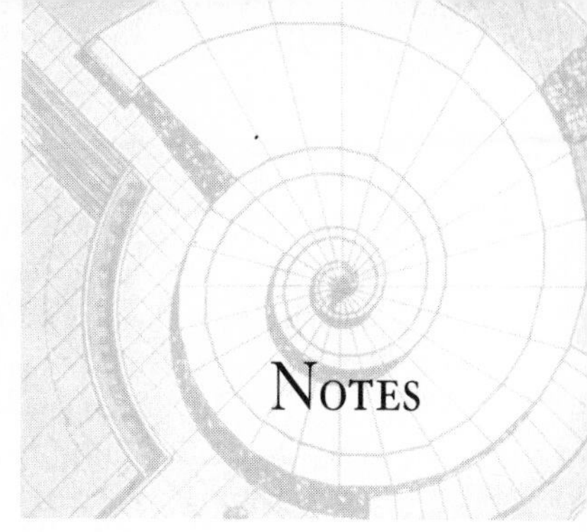

Notes

Preface

1. In the early history of the Saints, the term *Zion* was closely associated with the term *New Jerusalem*, but the meanings were subtly different. *New Jerusalem* usually referred to the actual heavenly city to be built on earth in preparation for the Second Coming of Christ; the term *Zion* was slightly more general in usage, temporally and spatially. *Zion* also referred to the collective influence of individual Saints. Consequently, early Saints in Jackson County were settling in Zion in order to aid in the establishment of the New Jerusalem. Joseph Smith called Zion a "goodly land," and often the Saints culled meaning for it from Old Testament writings; the word is applied to chiliastic Christian events, real or prophesied. On the other hand, the New Jerusalem also signified that heavenly city yet to be constructed, although the phrase "city of Zion" was a common synonym. Alterations in the meanings of these terms among the different Latter Day Saint groups, however, vary through time.
2. It should be noted that many, but not all, of the churches rooted in the teachings of Joseph Smith Jr. still use "Latter Day Saints" in their official names. The RLDS Church is the Reorganized Church of Jesus Christ of Latter Day Saints, with all capital letters, while the Utah church is the Church of Jesus Christ of Latter-day Saints with a hyphen and lowercased *d*. The term *Latter Day Saints*, with all caps, is not intended to favor any particular group; rather, it refers to the original group of members who followed Joseph Smith Jr. and to the body of churches that developed from this beginning. After the death of Smith in 1844, however, a major splintering of the Latter Day Saints took place. Three of these groups are paramount to this study: the Church of Jesus Christ of Latter-day Saints, based in Salt Lake City, Utah; the Reorganized Church of Jesus Christ of Latter Day Saints, headquartered in Independence, Missouri; and the Church of Christ (Temple Lot), also headquartered in Independence, Missouri. The largest group is the Utah church, which claims some twelve million members. This group is referred to herein as LDS, Mormons, or the Utah group. The Reorganized Church of Jesus Christ of Latter Day Saints claims more than

200,000 members, many of whom reside in Missouri (*Temple* 1988, 1990). This group will be called the Reorganized Church or simply the RLDS Church (its members do not favor the Mormon nickname). Officially, the RLDS Church changed its name in 2001 to the Community of Christ (CoC), so in this work I normally use the more recognized RLDS acronym in historical reference, but I also use CoC when referring to contemporary or future trends in the church. The Church of Christ (Temple Lot) has about 2,400 members (Sheldon 1990) and is referred to herein by its full name or as the Temple Lot Church. These three groups are among the oldest splinters of the Latter Day Saint movement and are the ones most prominent in the landscape of Independence today.

Various smaller splinter groups, including derivatives of LDS, RLDS, and Temple Lot are also put under scrutiny. The Temple Lot group of churches does not use the Latter Day Saint name, though they are within the Latter Day Saint family of churches. Some of these are simply smaller churches that have rather conventional Latter Day Saint beliefs, but others vary considerably in doctrine. A few have evolved into authoritarian movements; others, surprisingly, have abandoned beliefs based on Joseph Smith's writings altogether. These more diminutive groups will be referred to by name or, where appropriate, by the name of a particular leader. None of them accept the Mormon nickname; some even refer to *The Book of Mormon* as the *Record of the Nephites*.

Throughout the book, the terms *church* and *group* are used to indicate that several different Latter Day Saint churches exist. The term *splinter* is also used where appropriate. An attempt was made not to use the word *faction* often, as its connotation could seem condescending. It is a harrowing task to define different believers' views without offending. It is not my intention to condescend or slight, and I thank many who have helped me reduce bias in written word.

3. Many sources report general directives of the various churches' leaders through time. These sources can be considered official and are more or less primary. Among them are the words of Joseph Smith and other church leaders as recorded in current LDS (Roberts 1957, 1978) and RLDS (1967) histories. These histories are comparable, up to a point, since both use the original writings of Joseph Smith Jr., with footnotes and commentary according to the subsequent history of each church. Special care has been taken with these, however, in determining when material in them was written. For example, Roberts's *History of the Church* is largely a chronological rendering by Smith of early history, but substantial parts of the history were written in the 1840s and refer to earlier time periods. Thus, chronological events are taken as written, but commentary beyond these is attributed to the later period. Early letters, diaries, and other correspondence were culled from various archives to catch the earliest views of the common members. Early newspapers were also used, including the Latter Day Saint *Evening and Morning Star* of Independence, the later *Messenger and Advocate* out of Kirtland, and the *Times and Seasons* out of Nauvoo.

In dealing with the early history of the Latter Day Saints, the revelations of Joseph Smith are heavily used. Both the LDS and RLDS Churches refer to these writings as the *Doctrine and Covenants*. The dual versions of the early revelations are virtually identical; hence I usually refer to the LDS version (*Doctrine and Covenants* 1981) of the revelations since it is the more easily accessible of the two. The two versions vary considerably in their later additions, however, and the RLDS version (*Book of Doctrine* 1989) is quoted as the need arises. These revelations of Joseph Smith were available and extremely influential to the members of the early church. They vary greatly in length and, as Smith released them, were published in the *Evening and Morning Star* as quickly as possible for immediate use by the Saints. The LDS Church also uses other writings by Smith as scripture. Some of these are compiled in an additional LDS canon called *The Pearl of Great Price* (1981).

Hundreds of conversations and a variety of interviews with leaders and members of the various churches were undertaken, some formal and some informal. In the chapters that follow, when the information from such sources is factual or intellectual in nature, the sources are appropriately referenced. Sometimes, however, I felt that the conversation was treading on sensitive ground or that the informant was revealing private feelings. In such cases, I state the church affiliation of the informant but withhold the name.

Beyond the above primary sources, a variety of other writings have interpreted the attitudes and practices of the various groups in different time periods. Most of these are sympathetic works, but skeptical views are brought to bear when available. Countless books describe LDS doctrine and way of life, but only a few of these treat the New Jerusalem or Zion in detail (Billeter 1946; Porter and Ruf 1960; Doxey 1965; Dyer 1976; Launius 1984; Burton 1985). A variety of older as well as recent LDS church magazines such as the *Improvement Era* and the *Ensign* provide some excellent insights and are often used. These same magazines have reported the talks and actions of the LDS Church's semiannual General Conferences for most of the twentieth century. General Conference talks are a prime source for following the evolving LDS leadership moves and directives.

The RLDS Church also has a variety of useful books and writings. The church's World Conference Bulletin helps to guide the reader through the maze of RLDS resolutions and delegatory procedures. These RLDS conferences take place every two years. The RLDS monthly magazine, *Saint's Herald*, has yielded priceless information, as has the local newspaper, the *Independence Examiner*. The *Kansas City Star* and the now-defunct *Kansas City Times* were also used extensively. Some books treating formative RLDS history are available, such as Launius's *Joseph Smith III: Pragmatic Prophet* (1988), Inez Smith Davis's *The Story of the Church* (1989), and Mary Anderson's *Joseph Smith III and the Restoration* (1952). Various compilations of writings and speeches of past RLDS presidents, such as Ruoff's *The Writings of President Frederick M. Smith, Vol. III, The Zionic Enterprise* (1981), were also valuable.

The recent RLDS Restoration Branches movement, a traditionalist backlash to current RLDS liberal directions, has produced several rich publications, most under the aegis of Price Publishing Company in Independence. These include the magazines *Vision* and *Restoration Voice*. *The Temple of the Lord*, a useful book by Richard and Pamela Price (1982), explains the view of the Restoration Branches toward the sacred Temple Lot site.

Sources of information for the smaller splinter groups are harder to come by. The *Independence Examiner* was often consulted since announcements by smaller groups are often reported there. The Church of Christ (Temple Lot) has published a thin monthly magazine called *Zion's Advocate* during most of this century. B. C. Flint's book, *An Outline History of the Church of Christ (Temple Lot)* is the most substantial history written by that group. Also of great value are the reported revelations of Otto Fetting and William Draves in *The Word of the Lord* (1988). These started factions based on Temple Lot church teachings. Most of the other groups publish some sort of regular newsletter, and I have sought out a variety of booklets, pamphlets, and leaflets. The Shields Collection at the RLDS Archives in Independence is a gold mine of information and has been used extensively.

Throughout this book, an attempt has been made to reflect the development and alteration of attitudes by specific groups at specific times. For example, *A Series of Pamphlets by Orson Pratt*, published in Liverpool, England, in 1851 may reflect and repeat many attitudes of the earliest of the Latter Day Saints, but it is used here primarily as an indicator of the attitudes of the Utah church toward Independence during the 1840s (Pratt 1851). In another case, Joseph Smith stated during the Saint's settlement of Daviess County, Missouri, in 1837 that Jackson County, Missouri, was the actual site of the Garden of Eden. This idea seems to have lain more or less dormant until being gradually revived in the LDS realm during the latter part of the twentieth century (Barrett 1973:373). The approach here is basically chronological, with sources of a particular time normally used to examine perceptions at that time period under scrutiny. Thus, for example, modern-day Mormon doctrinal works are avoided in identifying New Jerusalem attitudes in the 1830s, unless they add historical insight relevant to that period.

Other recent secondary interpretations provide general guides for understanding trends in Latter Day Saint scholarship and act as possible umbrellas for this study. A few scholarly works deal directly with early Latter Day Saint history and community in Independence (de Pillis 1960; Colette 1977; Romig and Siebert 1986, 1988). Other scholarly sources include Shipps's (1985) view of Mormonism as a new "religious tradition," O'Dea's (1957) explanation of Latter Day Saint life as purely Yankee in origin, Kephart's sociological approach (1976:194–242), Campbell's (1988) views that the success of the Mormons was caused by constant exposure to hardship and obstacles, and Bushman's (1984) interpretation of the life of Joseph Smith. Most of these works focus on the Utah branch of Latter Day Saints; not much scholarly work has been done on the Reorganized Church or the other splinter groups beyond Melton's in-depth listing of splinter groups in *The Encyclopedia of American Religions* (1989: 572–92) or his *Biographical Dictionary of American Cult and Sect Leaders* (1986). Scholarly exceptions are Shields's *The Latter Day Saint Churches: An Annotated Bibliography* (1987) and *Divergent Paths of the Restoration* (1990). A couple of books on the Michigan Strangite movement during the mid-1800s are also available (Fitzpatrick 1970; Van Noord 1988).

4. The religious accounts tell of Joseph Smith being shown the location of a stack of bound and sealed gold plates by an angel named Moroni in 1823. They had been inscribed with a type of hieroglyphic and buried in a glacial drumlin near his home, close to the town of Palmyra in the Finger Lakes region of western New York State. A few years after the location of the plates was revealed, Smith was finally allowed to take the plates and transcribe them by the gift and power of God. Joseph Smith said that the plates were written in "Reformed Egyptian" (*Book of Mormon*, Mormon 9:32). Since the account of Smith is that he translated *The Book of Mormon* and did not write it himself, the word translated is used in this study.

2. The Missourians and the Saints

1. Mormon and RLDS scholars have not always seen all Native American groups as being descended from The Book of Mormon Lamanites. In fact, works often restrict the setting of The Book of Mormon to very limited areas (see Sorenson 1985). Despite these quasi-scientific speculations regarding a religious work, it is common to hear the average LDS member refer to any Native American as a "Lamanite."
2. This winter has been documented as one of the most severe in Missouri history. RLDS historian Inez Smith Davis (1989:91–95) has provided a well-researched summary of local conditions. Among other vivid descriptions, she noted that the winter was so harsh that elk disappeared completely from the Missouri and Illinois plains, never to return.
3. Sidney Rigdon was one of the first Latter Day Saint converts from the Kirtland area of Ohio. He was a Baptist minister before joining the Disciples of Christ movement founded by Alexander Campbell. He was an enthusiastic orator whom Joseph Smith quickly began to utilize as spokesman and assistant.
4. Some sources mention the size of the parcel as being 63.27 acres.
5. The existence among the main groups of Saints today of both a Melchizedek and an Aaronic priesthood is found in the declaration of Joseph Smith that heavenly messengers appeared to him and gave authority. John the Baptist conferred upon him the lesser, or Aaronic, priesthood, and later Peter, James, and John conferred upon him the higher, or Melchizedek, priesthood. Joseph Smith indi-

cated that this latter priesthood was the one that disciples had received from Jesus Christ Himself. The main offices in the Melchizedek priesthood were Elder, Seventy, High Priest, and Apostle, all to figure as instrumental in the forming of new Latter Day Saint churches at later times.

6. One has to be careful when looking at reproductions of the original first plat for the city of Zion because there has been a confusing alteration of the temples' locations and their numbering. On some plat reproductions the number 5 temple and its location have been slightly changed, and the original temple location, symbolized by a circle with a cross through it, has been removed. Therefore, one can find the cross mentioned in the plat description but not the circle it denotes. On the altered version, the number 5 has been removed, yet it seems a new circle has been made out of the bowl of the 5. The best comparison can be made at the LDS Visitor's Center in Independence, where both of the plats—correct and altered—are on display.

3. The Displacement of Zion

1. A Kentuckian by birth and education, Alexander Doniphan was a well-known Missouri attorney, soldier, and politician (Allen 1897; Conard 1901, 2:292–95). Besides heading up local militias, he was later called upon to lead a military expedition into Mexico during the 1846–47 war (Conard, 1901, 2:297–303). Despite adverse circumstances, the trek was daring and successful, a major factor in winning the Mexican War. Doniphan was active in local and state politics and education throughout his life. On the coattails of the military successes against Mexico, Doniphan's name was placed alongside that of Zachary Taylor as a good Whig candidate for the vice presidency in 1848, but he preferred to remain in his Richmond, Missouri, law practice (Mering 1967:142–44). Doniphan was nominated by the Whigs for governor in 1852, but he would have nothing to do with the plan. He did run for the senatorial seat in 1854 but was beat by the Democrat, David R. Atchison (Mering 1967:203; Parrish 1961:157–58).

   David Rice Atchison, also raised in Kentucky, was active in Missouri law, militia organizations, and politics (Parrish 1961). He served in the state legislature as a judge in Missouri's northwestern twelfth circuit court and as an influential Missouri senator from 1843 to 1855. In the Senate, Atchison served as president pro tem several times. He actively promoted slavery for the state of Kansas, which was a contrast with his earlier support of the Yankee antislavery Saints. Despite very different political outlooks and a rivalry in state government, Doniphan and Atchison were close friends throughout their lives.

   At the time of the 1838 "Mormon problem," James S. Rollins was a future star on Missouri's political horizon. He was a Whig nominee for governor in 1848, upon the refusal of Doniphan to run, and was a nominee for state senator in 1854. In this election he was uprooted by the more popular Whig, Doniphan, but Atchison won the seat. Rollins remained active in Missouri politics until after the Civil War.

2. Roberts's *History* gives two accounts of Joseph Smith's arrival in Far West, both in Smith's words. The first (Roberts 1978, 2:521) gives the date of arrival as "the latter part of October or first of November" of 1837. The second account (1978, 3:8) gives the date as "the 13th of March" 1838. I assume that Smith wrote the two accounts at different times, confusing the chronology of events. I have chosen to use the latter account, which is more precise and richer in detail.

3. The cornerstones are still visible at the site, the only extant features of Far West today, though local residents have dug up a variety of artifacts.

4. A photocopy in my possession of one version of the Far West plat is quite detailed. Its origin is sketchy, but the plat is similar to others. On the photocopy, the following is printed:

> Description of Far West Plat (copy of a copy of a presumed plat of Far West). This copy was taken by Bertha Booth* of Hamilton, Missouri from a copy made by F. B. Clark, from a visit in the law office of a lawyer named Selby in Gallatin, about 20 years ago (1928–1932). He saw what Selby called a plat of Far West. He wished then to buy the "original," as Selby called it, but Selby would not part with it. After his death, the paper could not be found in his documents, hence it is believed that he might have sold or given it away before his death. The original paper had a drawn plat which Clark did copy.
>
> *Bertha Booth, State Historical Society of Missouri, Columbia, Missouri.

Researchers should consult the State Historical Society of Missouri Archives for the plat. It is interesting that this plat's 121 blocks are numbered in a clockwise spiral from the center temple square. Another plat drafted on sheepskin is numbered row by row according to the layout of standard township sections of the US Public Land Survey (Church Educational System 1989:185). The original numbering system used by the Saints in Far West is uncertain.

5. Subsequently, leaders of the LDS Church have commented on the definition of *Adam-ondi-Ahman*. In the late 1800s, the LDS apostle Orson Pratt said the phrase meant "The Valley of God where Adam dwelt" (Gentry 1986:54 n. 13).

6. For more descriptions from Phelps's 1831 account, see chapter 2.

7. Shot four times in the head and neck, Boggs made an amazing recovery and later moved to California.

8. Joseph Smith Jr.'s bodyguard Orrin Porter Rockwell was tried and acquitted of shooting Boggs. To quote Gayler (1955:10), "No conclusive proof was given that a Mormon or a group of Mormons had been responsible for the assassination

attempt. However, that *some* Mormon fired the shots is within the limit of strict probability."

4. A Splintering and a Return

1. According to Price (1982:41–50), Martin Harris, an important figure in the earlier history of the Saints, was given title to the Temple Lot in the mid-1840s as security for loans made available to the church in order to purchase lands in Jackson County. Harris never lived in Missouri, though, and his deed to the Temple Lot was never recorded. The only evidence for Harris's ownership survives in a document made at Winter Quarters, Nebraska (then Indian Territory), in 1848, which shows that Brigham Young and others knew of Harris's possession of the Lot (Price 1982:44–46). Whatever became of Harris's deed is unknown.

   In the murky cadastral history of the Temple Lot, at least two other deeds also existed. The widow and children of Edward Partridge made a quitclaim deed in 1848, and the lot was sold to a James Pool (or "Poole"), a non–Latter Day Saint, for three hundred dollars (Britton 1922:152; Price 1982:87). Shortly afterward, Pool sold the tract to one John Maxwell. Another deed appeared and was sold by Lemuel I. Edwards to Samuel H. Woodson for the same property. The origin of the Edwards document is unknown, but some speculate this was Harris's deed (Price 1982:87). Another curious deed later appeared, naming three nonexistent children of Oliver Cowdery as heirs to the parcel (Britton 1922:152–53; Reimann 1961:118–22).

2. During the Nauvoo period, Joseph Smith's brother, Hyrum, was another counselor.

3. Joseph Smith Jr.'s wife, Emma, chose not to go west, probably because of a mutual animosity with Brigham Young that developed after her husband's death. She later married businessman Lewis C. Bidamon and both joined the Reorganization movement (Launius 1988:56–57).

4. The name is taken from a prominent city in *The Book of Mormon*.

5. The LDS and RLDS organizations were both interested in the Whitmers. David Whitmer was one of the original three witnesses who reportedly saw an angel and handled the original gold plates from which *The Book of Mormon* was translated. He later helped organize the early church in Manchester, New York, and later, in Missouri, he was instrumental in choosing the twelve Apostles. After the death of Joseph Smith Jr., some of the Whitmers organized a local Latter Day Saint church, which did not last very long. John Whitmer was RLDS church historian for a time and kept in his possession early records of the church. David Whitmer reportedly held an original manuscript of *The Book of Mormon*. Both the LDS and RLDS movements sought these records, and even today different Latter Day Saints respectfully, and somewhat affectionately, refer to Whitmer family members as "Whitmerites."

6. The fuzzy use of the scriptural term *Gentile* with regard to building the New Jerusalem has resulted in a variety of interpretations among the different Latter Day Saint churches over time. In subsequent chapters, the interpretations of this term are scrutinized.
7. By this time, Frederick M. Smith had gone on to receive a Ph.D. in psychology under G. Stanley Hall at Clark University.

5. Views of Jackson County from Utah, 1845–1900

1. The fact that Brigham Young anticipated a move to Jackson County did not mean that work on local structures, such as the Salt Lake Temple, was of a temporary or shabby nature. He had stated that "this temple must stand through the millennium"; its granite walls were built "sixteen feet thick at the foundation, tapering to six feet thick at the top" (Berrett 1977:372). The final capstone of the edifice was placed in April 1892, after forty arduous years of construction (Truman and the Salt Lake Temple 1978). Over one hundred years later, Gordon B. Hinkley would also attribute millennial themes to the new LDS Conference Center (see the chapter 6).
2. Charles L. Walker, an English convert, was a prominent leader of the LDS Church in Utah and one of the principal founders of the southern settlement of St. George, Utah.
3. Under the instruction of Brigham Young, Orson Pratt was the first church leader to openly give a confirmation of, and to publicly talk on, the subject of polygamy.
4. To be changed in a "twinkle of an eye" refers to an immediate resurrection after death, which, according to Mormon tradition, has happened to a few faithful prophets and Saints (meaning church members) throughout history. The doctrine is that most people, however, at the time of death, are confined for an indeterminate time to a "spirit world," which is sort of an afterlife, but pre-resurrection, school.
5. When Brigham Young died in 1877, John Taylor, the senior apostle, became president of the LDS Church. At Taylor's death in 1877, Wilford Woodruff became president.
6. In LDS temples, workers wear special white clothing symbolic of purity and the priesthood. The atmosphere tends to be quiet yet busy, orderly yet reflective. This makes the imagery especially impressive to the Mormon who reads Woodruff's diaries.
7. This was the son of Hyrum Smith, Joseph Smith Jr.'s older brother.
8. In Kirtland, February 1835, at the meetings where the twelve apostles were first chosen in the modern Latter Day Saint experience, Smith said regarding the second coming of Jesus Christ that "fifty-six years should wind up the scene" (Roberts 1978, 2:182). In April 1843, Smith said he was once praying very earnestly about the coming of Jesus Christ; he heard a voice say that if he

lived until he was "eighty-five years old" he would see the "face of the Son of Man" (*Doctrine and Covenants* 1981, 130:14–15). Both cases add up to 1891, but the Latter-day Saint variety of Adventism always took millennial dating with a grain of salt.

6. LDS Views since 1900

1. The story of this rumor was told to me by Dennis Jenkins, the director of the LDS Institute of Religion in the early 1990s at Haskell Indian Junior College in Lawrence, Kansas. Local leaders who had been on the trip refuted the angel's appearance, but the story's origin does seem to have come from an actual incident at the site. Apparently, when the LDS entourage arrived at Adam-ondi-Ahman, a church member was there who was so pleasantly surprised to encounter President McKay that he offered to help clear a path among the ubiquitous thorn brambles down into the valley.
2. This information was provided by Barbara Remlinger, an LDS member from Kansas City who knows many of the LDS Samoans.
3. These Utah temples are at St. George, Logan, Manti, and Salt Lake City.
4. Los Angeles and Oakland were the sites of the earliest California temples. Newer temples along the Pacific coast are at Seattle, Portland, and San Diego. More have been announced for the greater Los Angeles area, Fresno, Sacramento, and San Bernardino.
5. In order to match the 1997 census figures, the numbers of LDS congregations were culled from the meetinghouse locator on the homepage of the Church of Jesus Christ of Latter-day Saints at http://www.lds.org/basicbeliefs/meetinghouse/.
6. Temple sites are chosen by examining a variety of church statistics, including growth of the membership in an area, sufficient tithe payers, quality and number of priesthood leadership, and the structure and size of church "stakes" in a given city and its surrounding region (Hinkley 1999d).
7. The names that I have found church land under are numerous. Historical sites are generally held under the church's entire official name—i.e., The Church of Jesus Christ of Latter-day Saints or with the name shortened to Latter-day Saints. Farm Management Corporation often holds large farms used for the church's welfare program. Investment properties are found under Corporation of the Presiding Bishop, Deseret Title Holding Company, Property Reserve, Inc., or the older Ensign Investments.

7. The Community of Christ

1. This figure excludes more than 25,000 or more of the RLDS population who have declared themselves members of the fundamentalist Restoration Branches group or of other break-off RLDS Churches. These Latter Day Saints do not believe in the temple and other modernist tendencies of the CoC, though they do believe in the RLDS Church itself and do not wish their names removed from church rosters.
2. The original design for the RLDS Temple called for the exterior use of Italian Isola limestone for the walls and copper for the roof, which would have provided a dark green spiral reminiscent of the Auditorium's colors. After these materials failed to meet stress and wear tests, however, they were changed to speckled granite and a stainless steel roof, making for a notable brightening of the structure's exterior appearance.
3. It was only a matter of time before another architectural firm produced a similar spiral form. RLDS adherents found themselves scratching their heads when a plan surfaced in Denver to build an aquarium of nearly identical design (Smith 1992b). Admittedly, the organic spiral symbol works just as well, or better, for an aquarium as it does for a religious structure.
4. The RLDS Church uses the cross in a subdued manner. The LDS Church, however, eschews it as a rather morbid symbol commemorating the death of Christ rather than His life, a symbol that negates the belief that He lives and guides His church. It is also a not so subtle reminder that the LDS tradition has a unique history—one that, despite its squeaky clean image today, in past times was in serious conflict with American values and U.S. governmental control.
5. Lands used for church buildings are usually held under the church's name, but the Central Development Association (CDA), an investment arm of the RLDS Church, purchased most of these lots. The church's lands in eastern Jackson County are held in the name of the CDA or the Presiding Bishopric of RLDS Trustee Appointee Members.
6. For further discussion of the paradigm shift and division in the RLDS Church, see the "Letters" sections for the September, October, November, and December issues of the *Saints' Herald* for 1990, as well as the February 1991 issue. It is notable that negative as well as positive comments are printed. This reflects a church style very different from the LDS Church, which tends to emphasize the positive while curbing criticism.
7. The "inspired document" was approved by a unanimous vote of the 1992 RLDS World Conference as the "mind and will of God" and is added to subsequent editions of the RLDS *Book of Doctrine and Covenants* as section 158.

8. Narrow Views of Zion and Anti-Zion Space

1. An air photograph in Billeter's *The Temple of Promise* (1946:5) clearly shows the scars of the temple excavation at the Temple Lot.
2. The Church of Christ (Fetting/Bronson) has had its headquarters in a plain white church building at 1138 E. Gudgell in Independence since the 1930s.
3. This brown brick A-frame building at 608 Lacy Rd. has been the headquarters for the Church of Christ, with the Elijah Message "Established Anew since 1965." It is well maintained with a paved parking lot and a handsome granite sign.
4. The church headquarters for the True Church of Jesus Christ Restored through the 1970s was a small white house (Roberts called it a parsonage) at 1533 E. Mechanic St., only about three blocks from the Elijah Message church.

Bibliography

Many of the Latter Day Saint materials used in this research were found in two main collections: the CoC/RLDS Library and Archives, located in the new temple and headquarters, in Independence, Missouri, and the LDS Library and Archives in the LDS Church Office Building in Salt Lake City, Utah. Sources on general geography, history, and religion were found principally in the Watson and the Spencer libraries at the University of Kansas in Lawrence. Some of the citations below refer to the Jackson and Clay County courthouses, where church landholdings were researched. Finally, many references were obtained directly from the Latter Day Saint factions or from individual members of the various groups, either from personal interviews or from web site or email correspondence.

The bibliography that follows is organized into six sections to facilitate the reader's search. Since some overlap between subjects exists, a few references are repeated in different sections. The themes are as follows:

1. General Works of Geography and History
2. Missouri History
3. The Early Saints, 1820–44 (also containing general works on Latter Day Saints)
4. The LDS Church
5. The Reorganized Movement
6. The Temple Lot Churches, Restoration Branches, and Other Factions

General Works of Geography and History

ABC News. 1996. Jerusalem Stories. One-hour broadcast featuring Peter Jennings. Aired Dec. 19.

Bakker, Hans. 1991. Ayodhya: A Hindu Jerusalem. An Investigation of "Holy War" as a Religious Idea in the Light of Communal Unrest in India. *Numen: International Review for the History of Religions* 38(1):80–109.

Bar-Gal, Yoram. 1984. The Subjective Significance of the Landscape of Tsfat. *Folklore* 95(2):245–50.

Baudrillard, Jean. 1989. *America*. London: Verso Books.

Bernbaum, Edwin. 1988. Sacred Mountains. *Parabola* 13(4):12–18.

Blake, Kevin S. 1997. The Landscape Symbolism and Identity of a Sacred Southwestern Mountain. Paper presented at the annual meeting of the Association of American Geographers, Thursday, Apr. 3, Fort Worth, Tex.

Bloch, Ruth. 1985. *Visionary Republic: Millennial Themes in American Thought, 1756–1800*. Cambridge: Cambridge Univ. Press.

Bokser, Baruch M. 1985. Approaching Sacred Space. *Harvard Theological Review* 78(3–4):279–99.

Book of Mormon: An Account Written by the Hand of Mormon. 1981 [1830]. Translated by Joseph Smith Jr. Salt Lake City: Church of Jesus Christ of Latter-day Saints.

Boyer, Paul. 1992. *When Time Shall Be No More: Prophecy Belief in Modern American Culture*. Cambridge, Mass.: Belknap Press of Harvard Univ. Press.

Brooke, John L. 1994. *The Refiner's Fire: The Making of Mormon Cosmology, 1644–1844*. Cambridge: Cambridge Univ. Press.

Brown, Ralph H. 1943. *Mirror for Americans: Likeness of the Eastern Seaboard, 1810*. New York: American Geographical Society.

Burton, Sir Richard F. 1964 [1893]. *Personal Narrative of a Pilgrimage to Al-Madinah and Meccah*. Vol. 2. New York: Dover Publications.

Calvert, Albert F., and Walter M. Gallichan. 1907. *Cordova: A City of the Moors*. New York: John Lane Co.

Chapman, F. Spencer. 1938. *Lhasa: The Holy City*. London: Chatto and Windus.

Chu, Henry. 1999. Controversial Chosen One Tours Tibet. *Los Angeles Times*, June 29, 1.

Clarke, Arthur C. 1979. *The Fountains of Paradise*. London: Victor Gollancz Ltd.

Cleveland, Catherine C. 1959 [1916]. *The Great Revival in the West, 1797–1805*. Gloucester, Mass.: Peter Smith.

Cohen, Saul B. 1976. Geopolitical Bases for the Integration of Jerusalem, *Orbis* 20(2):287–313.

Cole, W. Owen, and Piara Singh Sambhi. 1990. *A Popular Dictionary of Sikhism*. Glenn Dale, Md.: Riverdale Co.

Cross, Whitney R. 1950. *The Burned-over District: The Social and Intellectual History of Enthusiastic Religion in Western New York, 1800–1850*. Ithaca, N.Y.: Cornell Univ. Press.

Crossette, Barbara. 1990a. India Uproots Thousands Living Near Sikh Temple. *New York Times*, June 3, p. 19.

———. 1990b. India Ready to Bar Hindu Move Today. *New York Times*, Oct. 30, p. A3.

———. 1990c. Toll in India Clash at Mosque Rises. *New York Times*, Nov. 1, p. A3.

———. 1990d. Hindu Militants Try Again to Storm Mosque. *New York Times*, Nov. 3, p. 3.

———. 1990e. India's Cabinet Falls as Premier Loses Confidence Vote, by 142–346, and Quits. *New York Times*, Nov. 8, p. A3.

———. 1990f. Hindu Rightists Call and Foreboding Is the Answer. *New York Times*, Dec. 1, p. 6.

David-Neel, Alexandra. 1927. *My Journey to Lhasa: The Personal Story of the Only White Woman Who Succeeded in Entering the Forbidden City*. New York: Harper and Brothers Publishers.

Davidson, James West. 1977. *The Logic of Millennial Thought: Eighteenth-Century New England*. New Haven, Conn.: Yale Univ. Press.

Duncan, James S. 1990. *The City as Text: The Politics of Landscape Interpretation in the Kandyan Kingdom*. Cambridge: Cambridge Univ. Press.

Eck, Diana L. 1982. *Banaras, City of Light*. New York: Alfred A. Knopf.

Eliade, Mircea. 1959. *The Sacred and the Profane: The Nature of Religion*. New York: Harcourt, Brace and Co.

Ericksen, E. Gordon. 1980. *The Territorial Experience: Human Ecology as Symbolic Interaction*. Austin: Univ. of Texas Press.

Esposito, John L. 1991. *Islam: The Straight Path*. New York: Oxford Univ. Press.

Farley, Maggie. 1995. China Dubs Rival Tibetan Holy Figure. *Los Angeles Times*, Nov. 29, sec. A, p. 12.

Fletcher, R. Louise. 1977. Shakerland: A Topographic History. *Landscape* 21(3): 36–44.

Foote, Kenneth E. 1997. *Shadowed Ground: America's Landscapes of Violence and Tragedy*. Austin: Univ. of Texas Press.

Gargan, Edward A. 1991. Indian Myth Sharpens Reality of Religious Strife. *New York Times*, Dec. 22.

———. 1992a. Hindu Militants Destroy Mosque, Setting off a New Crisis in India. *New York Times*, Dec. 7, pp. A1, A6.

———. 1992b. At Least 200 Killed in India as Muslim-Hindu Riots Rage. *New York Times*, Dec. 8, pp. A1, A7.

Gaustad, Edwin, and Philip Barlow. 2001. New Historic Atlas of Religion in America. Oxford: Oxford Univ. Press.

Glacken, Clarence J. 1967. *Traces on the Rhodian Shore: Nature and Culture in Western Thought from Ancient Times to the End of the Eighteenth Century*. Berkeley: Univ. of California Press.

Glasse, Cyril. 1989. *The Concise Encyclopedia of Islam.* San Francisco: Harper and Row.

Goldman, Robert R. 1986. A City of the Heart: Epic Mathura and the Indian Imagination. *Journal of the American Oriental Society* 106(3):471–83.

Goodheart, Adam. 1996. Archeology Is Destiny. *New York Times,* Oct. 1, p. 25.

Harrer, Heinrich. 1984. *Return to Tibet.* London: Weidenfeld and Nicolson.

Harvey, David. 1989. *The Condition of Postmodernity.* Cambridge, Mass.: Blackwell.

Hatch, Nathan O. 1977. *The Sacred Cause of Liberty: Republican Thought and the Millennium in Revolutionary New England.* New Haven, Conn.: Yale Univ. Press.

———. 1989. *The Democratization of American Christianity.* New Haven, Conn.: Yale Univ. Press.

Hazarika, Sanjoy. 1991. Shrine Where Hindus Died Reopens in Calm. *New York Times,* Mar. 31, p. 6.

Houston, James M. 1978. The Concepts of "Place" and "Land" in the Judeo-Christian Tradition. In *Humanistic Geography, Prospects and Problems,* ed. David Ley and Marwyn S. Samuels, 224–37. Chicago: Maaroufa Press.

How Hindu an India? 2001. *Economist,* Aug. 16, at http://www.economist.com/world/asia/displayStory.cfm?Story_ID=744990

Hudson, John C. 1988. North American Origins of Middlewestern Frontier Populations. *Annals of the Association of American Geographers* 78(3):395–413.

Hudson, Winthrop S. 1974. A Time of Religious Ferment. In *The Rise of Adventism: Religion and Society in Mid-Nineteenth-Century America,* ed. Edwin S. Gaustad, 1–17. New York: Harper & Row.

Jackson, J. B. 1977 [1951]. Ghosts at the Door. In *Changing Rural Landscapes,* ed. Ervin H. Zube and Margaret J. Zube, 41–52. Amherst: Univ. of Massachusetts Press.

Jackson, Richard H. 1978. Mormon Perception and Settlement. *Annals of the Association of American Geographers* 68(3):317–34.

Jackson, Richard H., and Roger Henrie. 1983. Perception of Sacred Space. *Journal of Cultural Geography* 3(2):94–107.

Jakle, John A. 1977. *Images of the Ohio Valley: A Historical Geography of Travel, 1740–1860.* New York: Oxford Univ. Press.

Jefferson, Thomas. 1964 [1861]. *Notes on the State of Virginia.* New York: Harper Torchbooks, Harper & Row.

Jewish Virtual Library. 2003. A Division of the American–Israeli Cooperative Enterprise, at http://www.us-israel.org/jsource/loc/hoah.html

Johnson, Trebbe. 1988. The Four Sacred Mountains of the Navajos. *Parabola* 13(4):40–47.

Johnston, R. J. 1983. *Philosophy and Human Geography*. London: Edward Arnold.

Jordan, Terry G. 1982. *Texas Graveyards: A Cultural Legacy*. Austin: Univ. of Texas Press.

Jordan, Terry G., and Matti Kaups. 1989. *The American Backwoods Frontier: An Ethnic and Ecological Interpretation*. Baltimore: Johns Hopkins Univ. Press.

Judge, Joseph. 1983. This Year in Jerusalem. *National Geographic Magazine* 163(4): 478–515.

Kapur, Rajiv A. 1986. *Sikh Separatism: The Politics of Faith*. London: Allen and Unwin.

Karan, Pradyumna P. 1976. *The Changing Face of Tibet: The Impact of Chinese Communist Ideology on the Landscape*. Lexington: Univ. Press of Kentucky.

Kay, Jeanne. 1989. Human Dominion over Nature in the Hebrew Bible. *Annals of the Association of American Geographers* 79(2):214–32.

Kenworthy, Tom, and John Schwartz. 1997. On the World Wide Web, Group's Links to This World and Another. *Washington Post*, Mar. 28, p. 17.

Kollmorgen, Walter M. 1969. The Woodsman's Assaults on the Domain of the Cattleman. *Annals of the Association of American Geographers* 59(2):215–39.

Kramer, Frank R. 1964. *Voices in the Valley: Mythmaking and Folk Belief in the Shaping of the Middle West*. Madison: Univ. of Wisconsin Press.

Kristof, Nicholas D. 1990. Lamas Seek Holy Child, but Politics Intrude. *New York Times*, Oct. 1, p. A4.

Kumar, Nita. 1989. Work and Leisure in the Formation of Identity: Muslim Weavers in a Hindu City. In *Culture and Power in Banaras: Community, Performance, and Environment, 1800–1980*, ed. Sandria B. Freitag, 147–70. Berkeley: Univ. of California Press.

Lane, Belden C. 1988. *Landscapes of the Sacred: Geography and Narrative in American Spirituality*. New York: Paulist Press.

Lemon, James T. 1966. The Agricultural Practices of National Groups in Eighteenth-Century Southeastern Pennsylvania. *Geographical Review* 56(4):467–96.

Library of Congress. 1910. *Calendar of the Papers of Martin Van Buren*. Washington, D.C.: Government Printing Office.

Lowenthal, David. 1961. Geography, Experience, and Imagination: Towards a Geographical Epistemology. *Annals of the Association of American Geographers* 51(3):241–60.

———. 1968. The American Scene. *Geographical Review* 58(1):61–88.

———. 1985. *The Past Is a Foreign Country*. Cambridge: Cambridge Univ. Press.

Lowenthal, David, and Martyn J. Bowden, eds. 1976. *Geographies of the Mind: Essays in Historical Geosophy in Honor of John Kirtland Wright*. New York: Oxford Univ. Press.

Manning, Carl. 2000. Garden of Eden, Eden on Earth. *Denver Rocky Mountain News*, Jan. 23.

Marini, Stephen A. 1982. *Radical Sects of Revolutionary New England*. Cambridge, Mass.: Harvard Univ. Press.

Marx, Leo. 1964. *The Machine in the Garden: Technology and the Pastoral Ideal in America*. London: Oxford Univ. Press.

McGill, Douglas C. 1984. Golden Temple in Amritsar, Sikhism's Most Sacred Shrine Cordoned Off. *New York Times*, June 4, p. A6.

McGreevy, Patrick. 1987. Imagining the Future at Niagara Falls. *Annals of the Association of American Geographers* 77(1):48–62.

Meinig, Donald W. 1965. The Mormon Culture Region: Strategies and Patterns in the Geography of the American West, 1847–1964. *Annals of the Association of American Geographers* 55(2):191–220.

———. 1966. Geography of Expansion, 1785–1855. In *Geography of New York State*, ed. John H. Thompson, 140–71. Syracuse, N.Y.: Syracuse Univ. Press.

Merk, Frederick. 1963. *Manifest Destiny and Mission in American History: A Reinterpretation*. New York: Alfred A. Knopf.

Michener, James A. 1968. *Iberia*. Greenwich, Conn.: A Fawcett Crest Book.

Mikesell, Marvin W. 1969. The Deforestation of Mount Lebanon. *Geographical Review* 59(1):1–28.

Miller, Merle. 1973. *Plain Speaking: An Oral Biography of Harry S. Truman*. New York: Berkley Books.

Miller, Perry. 1956. *Errand into the Wilderness*. Cambridge, Mass.: Belknap Press of Harvard Univ.

———. 1965. *Orthodoxy in Massachusetts, 1630–1650*. Gloucester, Mass.: Peter Smith.

Miller, Perry, and Thomas H. Johnson. 1938. *The Puritans*. Vol. 1. New York: Harper Torchbooks, Harper & Row Publishers.

Miller, Timothy. 1991. *When Prophets Die: The Postcharismatic Fate of New Religious Movements*. Albany: State Univ. of New York Press.

Morgan, Dale L. 1973 [1947]. *The Great Salt Lake*. Albuquerque: Univ. of New Mexico Press.

Nash, Gary B. 1979. *The Urban Crucible: The Northern Seaports and the Origins of the American Revolution*. Cambridge, Mass.: Harvard Univ. Press.

Nash, Roderick. 1982 [1967]. *Wilderness and the American Mind*. New Haven, Conn.: Yale Univ. Press.

New Yorker. 1992. Cartoon featured Apr. 6, p. 40.

Norris, Kathleen. 1993. *Dakota: A Spiritual Geography*. Boston: Houghton Mifflin.

Old City Jerusalem. 1996. Map. Washington, D.C.: National Geographic Society.

Porter, Philip W., and Fred E. Lukerman. 1975. The Geography of Utopia. In *Geographies of the Mind: Essays in Historical Geosophy*, ed. David Lowenthal and Martyn J. Bowden, 197–223. New York: Oxford Univ. Press.

Rau, Santha Rama. 1986. Banaras: India's City of Light. *National Geographic Magazine* 169(2):214–51.

Relph, Edward. 1976. *Place and Placelessness*. London: Pion Limited.

Sauer, Carl O. 1963. *Land and Life: A Selection from the Writings of Carl Ortwin Sauer*. Ed. John Leighly. Berkeley: Univ. of California Press.

Shilhav, Yosseph. 1983. Communal Conflict in Jerusalem—The Spread of Ultra-Orthodox Neighborhoods. In *Pluralism and Political Geography: People, Territory, and State*, ed. Nurit Kliot and Stanley Waterman, 100–113. London: Croom Helm.

Shipps, Jan. 1985. *Mormonism: The Story of a New Religious Tradition*. Urbana: Univ. of Illinois Press.

Shortridge, James R. 1984. The Emergence of "Middle West" as an American Regional Label. *Annals of the Association of American Geographers* 74(2):209–20.

———. 1985. The Vernacular Middle West. *Annals of the Association of American Geographers* 75(1):48–57.

Sikh Extremists Surrender. 1988. *Virginia Ledger Star* (Associated Press Article), May 18, p. 5.

Sloan, Irving, ed. 1969. *Martin Van Buren, 1782–1862: Chronology—Documents—Bibliographical Aids*. Dobbs Ferry, N.Y.: Oceana Publications.

Smith, Henry Nash. 1970 [1950]. *Virgin Land: The American West as Symbol and Myth*. Cambridge, Mass.: Harvard Univ. Press.

Sopher, David E. 1967. *Geography of Religions*. Englewood Cliffs, N.J.: Prentice-Hall.

Stark, Rodney, and William Sims Bainbridge. 1985. *The Future of Religion: Secularization, Revival, and Cult Formation*. Berkeley: Univ. of California Press.

Stegner, Wallace. 1981 [1942]. *Mormon Country*. Lincoln: Univ. of Nebraska Press.

Stevens, William K. 1984a. Sikh Temple: Words of Worship, Talk of Warfare. *New York Times*, Feb. 29, p. A2.

———. 1984b. Indians Report Day Long Battle at Sikh Temple. *New York Times*, June 6, pp. A1, A12.

———. 1984c. Aftermath at Golden Temple: Holes and a Hollow Silence. *New York Times*, June 15, pp. A1, A4.

Stilgoe, John R. 1976. The Puritan Landscape: Ideal and Reality. *Landscape* 20(3):3–7.

Strehlow, T. G. H. 1947. *Aranda Traditions*. Melbourne, Australia: Melbourne Univ. Press.

Surjeet, Harkishan Singh. 1988. The Punjab Situation Continues to Defy Solution. In *Political Dynamics and Crisis in Punjab*, ed. Paul Wallace and Surendra Chopra, 451–64. Amritsar, India: Dept. of Political Science, Guru Nanak Dev Univ.

Swedenborg, Emanuel. 1857. *Miscellaneous Theological Works of Emanuel Swedenborg*. New York: Swedenborg Foundation.

Talbott, Strobe. 1992. The Serbian Death Wish. *Time* 139(22):74.

Tefft, Sheila. 1990. Temple Dispute Threatens India's Government, Secular Tradition. *Christian Science Monitor,* Nov. 1, pp. A1–A2.

Thirty Hindu Temples Attacked in Pakistan. 1992. *New York Times*, Dec. 8, p. A7.

This Is Our Land. 1992. *The Glory and the Power: Fundamentalisms Observed*. PBS television series, aired June 22.

This Land of Snow Ridges. 1988. *Parabola* 13(4):4–9.

Tocqueville, Alexis de. 1956 (1835/1840]. *Democracy in America*. New York: A Mentor Book published by New American Library.

Tuan, Yi-Fu. 1975. Place: An Experiential Perspective. *Geographical Review* 65(2): 151–65.

———. 1977. *Space and Place: The Perspective of Experience*. Minneapolis: Univ. of Minnesota Press.

———. 1986. *The Good Life*. Madison: Univ. of Wisconsin Press.

Tuveson, Ernest L. 1949. *Millennium and Utopia: A Study in the Background of the Idea of Progress*. Berkeley: Univ. of California Press.

———. 1968. *Redeemer Nation: The Idea of America's Millennial Role*. Chicago: Univ. of Chicago Press.

Tyler, Patrick. 1995. China Rejects Choice of Boy as Tibet Lama. *New York Times Current Events Edition*, Nov. 13, sec. A, p. 7.

Underwood, Grant. 1993. *The Millenarian World of Early Mormonism*. Urbana: Univ. of Illinois Press.

van der Veer, Peter. 1988. *Gods on Earth: The Management of Religious Experience and Identity in a North Indian Pilgrimage Centre*. London School of Economics Monographs on Social Anthropology, No. 59. London: Athlone Press.

Weber, Eugen. 1999. *Apocalypses: Prophecies, Cults, and Millennial Beliefs through the Ages*. Cambridge, Mass.: Harvard Univ. Press.

Weber, Timothy P. 1983. *Living in the Shadow of the Second Coming: American Premillennialism, 1875–1982*. Grand Rapids, Mich.: Acadamie Books.

Weinraub, Bernard. 1991. Hindu Nationalists' Power Solidifies. *New York Times*, June 17, p. A9.

Wheatley, Paul. 1971. *The Pivot of the Four Quarters: A Preliminary Inquiry into the Origins and Character of the Ancient Chinese City*. Chicago: Aldine.

White, Ronald C., and C. Howard Hopkins. 1976. *The Social Gospel: Religion and Reform in Changing America*. Philadelphia: Temple Univ. Press.

Whittlesey, Derwent. 1929. Sequent Occupance. *Annals of the Association of American Geographers* 19: 162–65.

Wigoder, Geoffrey, ed. 1989. *The Encyclopedia of Judaism*. New York: Macmillan.

Wilken, Robert L. 1986. Early Christian Chiliasm, Jewish Messianism, and the Idea of the Holy Land. *Harvard Theological Review* 79(1–3):298–307.

Wolf, Eric R. 1959. *Sons of the Shaking Earth*. Chicago: Univ. of Chicago Press.

Wood, Joseph S. 1991. "Build, Therefore, Your Own World": The New England Village as Settlement Ideal. *Annals of the Association of American Geographers* 81(1):32–50.

Wright, John K. 1953. The Open Polar Sea. *Geographical Review* 43(3):338–65.

———. 1966. *Human Nature in Geography*. Cambridge, Mass.: Harvard Univ. Press.

Zamora, Lois Parkinson. 1982. The Myth of Apocalypse and the American Literary Imagination. In *The Apocalyptic Vision of America: Interdisciplinary Essays on Myth and Culture*, ed. Lois Parkinson Zamora, 97–138. Bowling Green, Ohio: Bowling Green Univ. Popular Press.

Zelinsky, Wilbur. 1973. *The Cultural Geography of the United States*. Englewood Cliffs, N.J.: Prentice-Hall.

———. 1994. Gathering Places for America's Dead: How Many, Where, and Why? *Professional Geographer* 46(1):29–38.

Missouri History

Allen, D. C. 1897. *A Sketch of the Life and Character of Colonel Alexander W. Doniphan*. Liberty, Mo.: D. C. Allen.

Atkeson, William O. 1918. *History of Bates County, Missouri*. Topeka, Kans.: Historical Publishing Co.

Brown, A. Theodore. 1963. *Frontier Community Kansas City to 1870*. 2 vols. Columbia: Univ. of Missouri Press.

Brown, A. Theodore, and Lyle W. Dorsett. 1978. *K.C.: A History of Kansas City, Missouri*. Boulder, Colo.: Pruett Publishing Co.

Chamber of Commerce of Kansas City, Missouri. 1938. *Where These Rocky Bluffs Meet. Including the Story of the Kansas City Ten-Year Plan*. Kansas City, Mo.: Smith-Grieves Co. Printers.

Conard, Howard L., ed. 1901. *Encyclopedia of the History of Missouri*. 6 vols. New York: Southern History Co.

Conoyer, Daniel J. 1973. Missouri's Little Dixie: A Geographical Delineation. Ph.D. diss. Saint Louis: Saint Louis Univ.

Gerlach, Russell L. 1986. *Settlement Patterns in Missouri: A Study of Population Origins with a Wall Map*. Columbia: Univ. of Missouri Press.

Gregg, Josiah. 1845. *Commerce of the Prairies*. 2 vols. New York: J. and H. G. Langley.

Harris, William W. 1933a. Westport's Founder Himself Termed the First Public Sale of Lots There a "Parody on Booms." *Kansas City Star*, Mar. 12, sec. B, p. 1.

———. 1933b. Westport Won the Santa Fe Trade from Independence. *Kansas City Star*, Mar. 19, sec. C, p. 2.

History of Jackson County, Missouri: A History of the County, Its Cities, Towns, Etc. 1881. Kansas City, Mo.: Birdsall, Williams & Co.

Hudson, David S., ed. 1989. *The Plaza: Kansas City's World-Famous Shopping District*. Prairie Village, Kans.: Harrow Books.

Illustrated Historical Atlas Map of Jackson County, Mo.: Carefully Compiled from Personal Examinations and Surveys. 1976 [1877]. Independence, Mo.: Jackson County Historical Society.

McCurdy, Frances Lea. 1969. *Stump, Bar, and Pulpit: Speechmaking of the Missouri Frontier*. Columbia: Univ. of Missouri Press.

McGlumphy, W. H. S. 1923. *History of Caldwell County*. Topeka, Kans.: Historical Publishing Co.

Mering, John Vollmer. 1967. *The Whig Party in Missouri*. Vol. 41, *University of Missouri Studies*. Columbia: Univ. of Missouri Press.

Miller, Merle. 1973. *Plain Speaking: An Oral Biography of Harry S. Truman*. New York: Berkley Books.

Miller, W. H. 1881. *The History of Kansas City, Together with a Sketch of the Commercial Resources of the Country with Which It Is Surrounded*. Kansas City, Mo.: Birdsall & Miller.

Nagle, Paul C. 1977. *Missouri: A History*. Lawrence: Univ. Press of Kansas.

O'Brien, Pat. 1982. Old Rail Depots in Independence Represent Important Era of History. *Jackson County Historical Society Journal* 24(2):6–8, 11.

Parrish, William E. 1961. *David Rice Atchison of Missouri: Border Politician*. Vol. 34, *University of Missouri Studies*. Columbia: Univ. of Missouri Press.

Platt Book of Jackson County, Missouri: Compiled from County Records and Actual Surveys. 1911. Kansas City, Mo.: Berry Publishing Co.

Political History of Jackson County: Biographical Sketches of Men Who Have Helped to Make It. 1902. Kansas City, Mo.: Marshall & Morrison.

Rafferty, Milton D. 1983. *Missouri: A Geography*. Boulder, Colo.: Westview Press.

Schusky, Ernest L. 1971. The Upper Missouri Indian Agency, 1819–1868. *Missouri Historical Review* 65(3):249–69.

Spalding, C. C. 1858. *Annals of the City of Kansas and the Great Western Plains*. Kansas City, Mo.: Van Horn & Abeel's Printing House.

Western Monitor. 1833. Fayette, Missouri, newspaper. August 2.

Wilcox, Pearl. 1975. *Jackson County Pioneers*. Independence, Mo.: Pearl G. Wilcox.

———. 1979. *Independence and Twentieth Century Pioneers: The Years from 1900 to 1928*. Independence, Mo.: Pearl G. Wilcox.

Writers' Program of the Works Projects Administration in the State of Missouri. 1941. *Missouri: A Guide to the "Show Me" State*. New York: Duell, Sloan and Pearce.

The Early Saints, 1820–44

Allen, James B., and Glenn M. Leonard. 1976. *The Story of the Latter-day Saints*. Salt Lake City: Deseret Book Co.

Anderson, Richard Lloyd. 1971. Jackson County in Early Mormon Descriptions. *Missouri Historical Review* 65(3):270–93.

———. 1974. New Data for Revising the Missouri "Documentary History." *Brigham Young University Studies* 14(4):488–501.

———. 1986. Atchison's Letters and the Causes of Mormon Expulsion from Missouri. *Brigham Young University Studies* 26(3):3–47.

Arrington, Leonard J. 1972. Early Mormon Communitarianism. In *Mormonism and American Culture*, ed. Marvin S. Hill and James B. Allen, 37–58. New York: Harper & Row, Publishers.

———. 1974. *Charles C. Rich, Mormon General and Western Frontiersman*. Vol. 1, *Studies in Mormon History*. Provo, Utah: Brigham Young Univ. Press.

Arrington, Leonard J., Feramorz Y. Fox, and Dean L. May. 1976. *Building the City of God: Community and Cooperation among the Mormons*. Salt Lake City: Deseret Book Co.

Barrett, Ivan J. 1973. *Joseph Smith and the Restoration: A History of the LDS Church to 1846*. Provo, Utah: Young House, Brigham Young Univ. Press.

Berrett, William Edwin. 1977. *The Restored Church*. Salt Lake City: Deseret Book Co.

Book of Doctrine and Covenants: Carefully Selected from the Revelations of God, and Given in Order of Their Dates. 1989. Independence, Mo.: Board of Publication of the Reorganized Church of Jesus Christ of Latter Day Saints, Herald Publishing House.

Book of Mormon: An Account Written by the Hand of Mormon. 1981 [1830]. Trans. Joseph Smith Jr. Salt Lake City: Church of Jesus Christ of Latter-day Saints.

Britton, Rollin J. 1920. *Early Days on Grand River and the Mormon War*. Columbia, Mo.: State Historical Society of Missouri.

———. 1922. Mormon Land Titles: A Story of Jackson County Real Estate. *Annals of Kansas City* 1(3):145–53.

Bush, Lester E., Jr. 1973. Mormonism's Negro Doctrine: An Historical Overview. *Dialogue: A Journal of Mormon Thought* 8(1):11–68.

Bushman, Richard L. 1960. Mormon Persecutions in Missouri, 1833. *Brigham Young University Studies* 3(1):11–20.

———. 1970. The Historians and Mormon Nauvoo. *Dialogue: A Journal of Mormon Thought* 5(1):51–61.

———. 1984. *Joseph Smith and the Beginnings of Mormonism*. Urbana: Univ. of Illinois Press.

Cannon, Donald Q., and Lyndon W. Cook, eds. 1983. *Far West Record: Minutes of the Church of Jesus Christ of Latter-day Saints, 1830–1844*. Salt Lake City: Deseret Book Co.

Church Educational System. 1989. *Church History in the Fullness of Times: The History of the Church of Jesus Christ of Latter-day Saints*. Course manual for Religion, 341–43. Salt Lake City: Church of Jesus Christ of Latter-day Saints.

Colette, D. Brent. 1977. In Search of Zion: A Description of Early Mormon Millennial Utopianism as Revealed through the Life of Edward Partridge. Master's thesis, Dept. of History, Brigham Young Univ.

Corrill, John. 1839. *A Brief History of the Church of Christ of Latter-day Saints (Commonly Called Mormons)*. St. Louis: John Corrill.

Cowdery, Oliver. 1834a. Letter to "Brother John," Jan. 1, from Kirtland, Ohio. Oliver Cowdery Papers from the Henry E. Huntington Library, Independence, Mo., RLDS Archives, Independence Temple, microfilm, p. 14.

———. 1834b. Letter to Samuel Brent of Pontiac, Mich., Jan. 7, from Kirtland, Ohio. Oliver Cowdery Papers from the Henry E. Huntington Library, Independence, Mo., RLDS Archives, Independence Temple, microfilm, p. 18.

———. 1834c. Letter to Lyman Cowdery, Jan. 13, from Kirtland, Ohio. Oliver Cowdery Papers from the Henry E. Huntington Library, Independence, Mo., RLDS Archives, Independence Temple, microfilm, p. 20.

Crawley, Peter, and Richard L. Anderson. 1974. The Political and Social Realities of Zion's Camp. *Brigham Young University Studies* 14(4):406–20.

Cross, Whitney R. 1950. *The Burned-Over District: The Social and Intellectual History of Enthusiastic Religion in Western New York, 1800–1850*. Ithaca, N.Y.: Cornell Univ. Press.

Davis, Inez Smith. 1989 [1934]. *The Story of the Church: A History of the Church of Jesus Christ of Latter Day Saints, and of Its Legal Successor, the Reorganized Church of Jesus Christ of Latter Day Saints*. 13th ed. Independence, Mo.: Herald Publishing House.

de Pillis, Mario Stephen. 1960. The Development of Mormon Communitarianism, 1826–1846. Ph.D. diss. Yale Univ.

Dewey, Richard Lloyd. 1986. *Porter Rockwell: A Biography*. New York: Paramount Books.

Doctrine and Covenants of the Church of Jesus Christ of Latter-day Saints, Containing Revelations Given to Joseph Smith, the Prophet, with Some Additions by His Successors in the Presidency of the Church. 1981. Salt Lake City: Church of Jesus Christ of Latter-day Saints. Divided into sections and verses.

Dyer, Alvin R. 1976 ([1960]. *The Refiner's Fire: The Significance of Events Transpiring in Missouri*. Salt Lake City: Deseret Book Co.

Eakin, O. B., and Joanne Eakin. 1985. *Record of Original Entries to Lands in Jackson County Missouri with Additional Records Relating to First Land Ownership*. Independence, Mo.: O. B. and Joanne C. Eakin.

Flanders, Robert Bruce. 1965. *Nauvoo: Kingdom on the Mississippi*. Urbana: Univ. of Illinois Press.

———. 1970. The Kingdom of God in Illinois: Politics in Utopia. *Dialogue: A Journal of Mormon Thought* 5(1):26–36.

Gayler, George R. 1955. The Attempts of the State of Missouri to Extradite Joseph Smith, 1841–1843. *Northwest Missouri State College Studies* 19(1): 1–18.

———. 1961. The "Expositor" Affair, Prelude to the Downfall of Joseph Smith. *Northwest Missouri State College Studies* 25(1):3–15.

Gentry, Leland H. 1973. Adam-ondi-Ahman: A Brief Historical Survey. *Brigham Young University Studies* 13(4):553–76.

———. 1986. The Land Question at Adam-ondi-Ahman. *Brigham Young University Studies* 26(2):45–56.

Ham, Wayne. 1970. *Publish Glad Tidings: Readings in Early Latter Day Saint Sources*. Independence, Mo.: Herald Publishing House.

Hampshire, Annette P. 1985. *Mormonism in Conflict: The Nauvoo Years*. Vol. 11, *Studies in Religion and Society*. New York: Edwin Mellen Press.

Hansen, Klaus J. 1970. *Quest for Empire: The Political Kingdom of God and the Council of Fifty in Mormon History*. East Lansing: Michigan State Univ. Press.

Harlacher, Larry. 2000. Missouri Mormon Walking Tour Dedicated. *Vision* 35 (Sept.): 9–11.

Harlacher, Nancy. 1989. The Zion Temple [Painting]. *Vision* 1 (summer): cover.

Howe, E. D. 1831. *Painesville (Ohio) Telegraph*, June 14.

Jennings, Warren A. 1971. The First Mormon Mission to the Indians. *Kansas Historical Quarterly* 37(3): 288–99.

Kimball, Stanley B. 1978. Nauvoo West: The Mormons of the Iowa Shore. *Brigham Young University Studies* 18(2):132–42.

Launius, Roger D. 1984. *Zion's Camp: Expedition to Missouri, 1834*. Independence, Mo.: Herald Publishing House.

LeSueur, Stephen C. 1986. "High Treason and Murder": The Examination of Mormon Prisoners at Richmond, Missouri, in Nov., 1838. *Brigham Young University Studies* 26(2):3–30.

———. 1987. *The 1838 Mormon War in Missouri*. Columbia: Univ. of Missouri Press.

Lifchez, Raymond. 1976. Inspired Planning: Mormon and Fourierist Communities in the Nineteenth Century. *Landscape* 20(3):29–35.

Lucas, Robert. 1839. Letter to Martin Van Buren, Apr., 22, from Iowa Territory. Presidential papers microfilm, Martin Van Buren Papers, series 2, reel 21, Government Documents, Univ. of Kansas, Lawrence.

Luce, W. Ray. 1990. Building the Kingdom of God: Mormon Architecture before 1847. *Brigham Young University Studies* 30(2):33–45.

Lyon, T. Edgar. 1972. Independence, Missouri, and the Mormons, 1827–1833. *Brigham Young University Studies* 13(1):10–19.

Matthews, Robert J. 1972. Adam-ondi-Ahman. *Brigham Young University Studies* 13(1):27–35.

McKiernan, F. Mark. 1971. *The Voice of One Crying in the Wilderness: Sidney Rigdon, Religious Reformer, 1793–1876*. Lawrence, Kans.: Coronado Press.

Messenger and Advocate. 1834. Latter Day Saint newspaper published at Kirtland, Ohio, no. 1, Nov.

Missouri Mormon Frontier Foundation. 2003. At "http://www.sunflower.org/~ronromig/mmffhp.htm"

O'Dea, Thomas F. 1957. *The Mormons*. Chicago: Univ. of Chicago Press.

Pearl of Great Price: A Selection from the Revelations, Translations, and Narrations of Joseph Smith, First Prophet, Seer, and Revelator to the Church of Jesus Christ of Latter-day Saints. 1981 [1851]. Salt Lake City: Church of Jesus Christ of Latter-day Saints.

Phelps, William W. 1831. *Ontario (New York) Phoenix*, Sept. 7.

———, ed. 1832a. *Evening and Morning Star (Independence, Mo.)*, July edition.

———, ed. 1832b. *Evening and Morning Star (Independence, Mo.)*, Aug. edition.

———, ed. 1833. *Evening and Morning Star (Independence, Mo.)*, January edition.

Porter, Kenneth W., and Hermann O. Ruf. 1960. *Chosen Missouri and the Question of Zion*. Salt Lake City: Deseret News Press.

Price, Richard, and Pamela Price. 1982. *The Temple of the Lord: The Location and Purposes of the Temple Which Is to Be Built in Independence, Missouri*. Independence, Mo.: Price Publishing Co.

Rigdon, Sidney. 1839. Letter to Martin Van Buren, Nov. 9, from Springfield, Ill. Presidential papers microfilm, Martin Van Buren Papers, series 2, reel 22, Government Documents, Univ. of Kansas, Lawrence.

Roberts, B. H. 1957. *A Comprehensive History of the Church of Jesus Christ of Latter-day Saints*. 6 vols. Provo, Utah: Brigham Young Univ. Press.

———, ed. 1978 [1951]. *History of the Church of Jesus Christ of Latter-day Saints: Period I, History of Joseph Smith the Prophet by Himself*. 7 vols. Salt Lake City: Deseret Book Co.

Romig, Ronald E. 1990. Interview, Dec. 19, Independence, Mo.

———. 1991. Interview, Oct. 3, Independence, Mo.

———. 2001. E-mail, Aug. 16, Independence, Mo.

Romig, Ronald E., and John H. Siebert. 1986. Jackson County, 1831–1833: A Look at the Development of Zion. In *Restoration Studies III: A Collection of Essays about the History, Beliefs, and Practices of the Reorganized Church of Jesus Christ of Latter Day Saints*, ed. Maurice L. Draper, 286–304. Independence, Mo.: Herald Publishing House.

———. 1988. The Genesis of Zion and Kirtland and the Concept of Temples. In *Restoration Studies IV: A Collection of Essays about the History, Beliefs, and Practices of the Reorganized Church of Jesus Christ of Latter Day Saints*, ed. Marjorie B. Troeh, 99–123. Independence, Mo.: Herald Publishing House.

Selections from the Book of Moses. 1981 [1830]. *The Pearl of Great Price*. Salt Lake City: Church of Jesus Christ of Latter-day Saints.

Shipps, Jan. 1985. *Mormonism: The Story of a New Religious Tradition*. Urbana: Univ. of Illinois Press.

Smith, Joseph, Jr. 1832. Letter to Emma Smith, Oct. 13, from New York City, Portfolio 5, Folder 1 (P5, F1), RLDS Archives, Independence Temple, Independence, Mo.

Smith, Joseph Fielding, ed. 1977. *Teachings of the Prophet Joseph Smith, Taken from His Sermons and Writings as They Are Found in the Documentary History and Other Publications of the Church and Written or Published in the Days of the Prophet's Ministry*. Salt Lake City: Deseret Book Co.

Vogel, Dan. 1988. *Religious Seekers and the Advent of Mormonism*. Salt Lake City: Signature Books.

Walking Trail Dedication. 2000. Web page of the Missouri Mormon Frontier Foundation, http://www.sunflower.org/~ronromig/mmwt.htm

Walking Trail Virtual Tour. 2000. Web page of the Missouri Mormon Frontier Foundation, http://www.sunflower.org/~ronromig/mmtour.htm

Wight, Lyman. 1839. Letter to Martin Van Buren, Presidential Papers Microfilm, Martin Van Buren Papers, series 2, reel 22, Government Documents, Univ. of Kansas, Lawrence. Note: In the *Calendar of the Papers of Martin Van Buren*, Wight's name is misspelled as "Wright."

The LDS Church

Adam-ondi-Ahman and Nearby Historic Sites. 1979. Pamphlet. Salt Lake City: Church of Jesus Christ of Latter-day Saints.

Adkins, Jeff. 1997. This Year's Frontier Pageant Is Off. *Independence Examiner*, Apr. 17.

Allen, Jack. 1992. Telephone conversation, Feb. 20, Kansas City, Mo.

Anderson, Vern. 1990. Mormon Churches Revise, Update "Endowment Ritual." *Lawrence Journal-World* (Associated Press article), May 1, p. 5.

Arrington, Leonard J. 1966 [1958]. *Great Basin Kingdom*. Lincoln: A Bison Book, Univ. of Nebraska Press.

Avant, Gerry. 1992a. Tabernacle Choir's Musical Journey. *LDS Church News*, Aug. 8, pp. 3, 10.

———. 1992b. Singers Receive Tributes, Praise. *LDS Church News*, Aug. 8, pp. 8–10.

Banks, Paul N. 1999. Overview of Alternative Space Options for Libraries and Archives. National Archives and Records Administration (NARA) at http://www.nara.gov/arch/techinfo/preserva/conferen/banks.html Website formerly available at this address. Hardcopy of original page in the author's possession.

Baugh, Alexander. 2001. From High Hopes to Despair, Missouri Period: 1831–39. *Ensign* 31(7):44–55.

Benson, Ezra Taft. 1986a. A Sacred Responsibility. *Ensign* 16(5):75–78.

———. 1986b. The Book of Mormon-Keystone of Our Religion. *Ensign* 16(11):2–7.

———. 1989. Beware of Pride. *Ensign* 19(5):2–7.

Berrett, William Edwin. 1977. *The Restored Church*. Salt Lake City: Deseret Book Co.

Billeter, Julius C. 1946. *The Temple of Promise: Jackson County, Missouri*. Independence, Mo.: Press of Zion's Printing and Publishing Co.

Bracco, Dennis. 1992. Telephone conversation, Feb. 20, Chicago.

Bridge Building in Independence. 1993. *Ensign* 23(4):76.

Buchanan, Frederick Stewart, ed. 1988. *A Good Time Coming: Mormon Letters to Scotland*. Salt Lake City: Univ. of Utah Press.

Burton, Alma P. 1985. *Toward the New Jerusalem*. Salt Lake City: Deseret Book Co.

Campbell, Eugene E. 1988. *Establishing Zion: The Mormon Church in the American West, 1847–1869*. Salt Lake City: Signature Books.

Cantrell, Scott. 1992. Choir Delivers Goods, and Good Feelings. *Kansas City Star*, Aug. 1, p. C2.

Card, Orson Scott. 1989. *The Folk of the Fringe*. New York: A Tor Book, Tom Doherty Associates.

Church Considers Purchasing Land. 1989. *Lawrence Journal World*, Aug. 17, p. 6.

Church Educational System. 1979. In *Book of Mormon Student Manual*, 121–22. Salt Lake City: Church of Jesus Christ of Latter-day Saints.

Church History Surrounds Independence Tract Said to Be Worth Million Dollars. 1952. *Kansas City Times*, Oct. 30.

City Is of Great Significance to the Church. 1971. *LDS Church News*, June 5, pp. 3, 5.

Clayton, Corliss. 1993. Making Friends: Julianne Burkhardt of Independence, Missouri. *Friend*, Sept., p. 38.

Crowther, Duane S. 1989. The New Jerusalem and Council at Adam-ondi-Ahman. Audiocassette. Bountiful, Utah: Horizon Publishers.

Daybell, Chad. 2000. *Escape to Zion*. Springville, Utah: Cedar Fort.

Doctrine and Covenants of the Church of Jesus Christ of Latter-day Saints, Containing Revelations Given to Joseph Smith, the Prophet, with Some Additions by His Successors in the Presidency of the Church. 1981. Salt Lake City: Church of Jesus Christ of Latter-day Saints. Divided into sections and verses.

Doxey, Graham W. 1992a. Garden of Eden. In *Encyclopedia of Mormonism*, ed. Daniel H. Ludlow, 2:533–34. New York: Macmillan.

———. 1992b. New Jerusalem. In *Encyclopedia of Mormonism*, ed. Daniel H. Ludlow, 3: 1009–10. New York: Macmillan.

Doxey, Roy W. 1965. *Zion in the Last Days*. Salt Lake City: Olympus Publishing Co.

———. 1973. Zion's Welfare Is My Portion. *Ensign* 3(2):55–58.

Drama beneath the Stars: A Frontier Story, 1833. 1991. Pageant night program. In possession of the author.

Driggs, Howard R. 1920. Rambling around Independence. *Juvenile Instructor of the LDS Church* 55(11):539–42.

Duesterhaus, Mike. 1992. Telephone conversation, Feb. 26, Independence, Mo.

Dyer, Alvin R. 1970. The Process of the Second Coming. *Lectures in Theology—Salt Lake Institute of Religion*. Salt Lake City: LDS Library/Archives, Church Office Building.

———. 1971. Remarks by Elder Alvin R. Dyer, Visitor's Center, Independence, Mo., May 31, LDS Library/Archives, Church Office Building, Salt Lake City.

———. 1973 [1966]. *Who Am I?* Salt Lake City: Deseret Book Co.

———. 1976. *The Refiner's Fire: The Significance of Events Transpiring in Missouri*. Salt Lake City: Deseret Book Co.

Ellsworth, S. George, ed. 1990. *The Journals of Addison Pratt*. Salt Lake City: Univ. of Utah Press.

Family Forever: Temples of the Church of Jesus Christ of Latter-Day Saints. 2003. Private Web page at http://www.familyforever.com/temples/

Faser, Wayne. 1992. Telephone conversation, Feb. 20, Salt Lake City.

Faust, James E. 2001. Who Shall Ascend into the Hill of the Lord? *Ensign* 31(8):2–5.

First Presidency Calls Three New General Authorities. 1991. *Ensign* 21(2):74.

The Great Prologue: A Prophetic History and Destiny of America. 1976. Booklet. Salt Lake City: Deseret Book Co.

Gunnerson, Lee. 1992. Telephone conversation, Feb. 26, Salt Lake City.

Haight, Frank, Jr. 1992. Residents Research Explosion of Saluda. *Independence Examiner*, June 9, p. 3.

Hansen, Klaus J. 1970. *Quest for Empire: The Political Kingdom of God and the Council of Fifty in Mormon History*. East Lansing: Michigan State Univ. Press.

Head of Mormons Is Here: President Smith to Dedicate New Church in Independence. 1914. *Kansas City Star*, Nov. 22, p. 4A.

Heinerman, John, and Anson D. Shupe. 1985. *The Mormon Corporate Empire*. Boston: Beacon Press.

Hinkley, Gordon B. 1998. New Temples to Provide "Crowning Blessings" of the Gospel. *Ensign* 28(5):87–88.

———. 1999a. Thanks to the Lord for His Blessings. *Ensign* 29(5):88–89.

———. 1999b. At the Summit of the Ages. *Ensign* 29(11):72–74.

———. 1999c. Good-bye to This Wonderful Old Tabernacle. *Ensign* 29(11):90–91.

———. 1999d. Welcome to Conference. *Ensign* 29(11):4–6.

———. 2000. This Great Millennial Year. *Ensign* 30(11):67–71.

———. 2002. "O That I Were an Angel, and Could Have the Wish of Mine Heart." *Ensign* 32(11):4–6.

Holland, Jeffrey R. 1976. A Promised Land. *Ensign* 6(6):23–24.

Holmes, Michael B. 1990. The Gathering of Israel. Discourse given Feb. 11 at LDS Topeka Stake Center.

Independence Second Ward. Independence, Missouri, Stake. 2001. Online at http://www.zionslight.com/independence/2/ Website formerly available at this address. Hardcopy of original page in the author's possession.

Jackson County Deed Office. 1924. Deed books on microfilm, no. 459, p. 242, New Jackson County Courthouse, Independence, Mo.

———. 1965. Deed book no. 1812, pp. 522–27, Nov., New Jackson County Courthouse, Independence, Mo.

J. C. Nichols Reports Gains from Land Sale. 1990. *Kansas City Star*, Dec. 20, p. B1.

Jenkins, Dennis. 1990. Maps from LDS Church Historical Sites Tour packet. LDS Institute of Religion, Haskell Junior Indian College, Lawrence, Kans. Complete packet in possession of author.

Journal of Discourses by Brigham Young, His Counsellors, the Twelve Apostles, and Others. 1966 [1854–86]. 26 vols. London: Latter-day Saints' Book Depot.

Kemp, Norm. 1992. Telephone conversation, Jan. 30, Salt Lake City.

Kenney, Scott G. 1983. Wilford Woodruff's Journal, 1833–1898. Typescript. 9 vols. Midvale, Utah: Signature Books.

Kephart, William M. 1976. *Extraordinary Groups: The Sociology of Unconventional Life-Styles*. New York: St. Martin's Press.

Kimball, Spencer W. 1984 [1977]. And the Lord Called His People Zion. *Ensign* 14(8):2–6.

Lamoreaux, Bob. 1992. Telephone conversation, Jan. 30, Salt Lake City.

Larson, A. Karl, and Katherine Miles Larson, eds. 1980. *Diary of Charles Lowell Walker*. 2 vols. Logan: Utah State Univ. Press.

Lee, Harold B. 1968. Remarks at the Groundbreaking Services in Independence, Mo., LDS Library/Archives, Church Office Building, Salt Lake City.

Lee, John Doyle. 1877. *Mormonism Unveiled*. St. Louis, Mo.: D. M. Vandawalker and Co.

The Life and Teachings of Jesus and His Apostles. 1979. Salt Lake City: Church of Jesus Christ of Latter-day Saints.

Lund, Gerald N. 1971. *The Coming of the Lord*. Salt Lake City: Bookcraft.

Matthews, Robert J. 1992. Proclamations of the First Presidency and the Quorum of the Twelve Apostles. In *Encyclopedia of Mormonism*, ed. Daniel H. Ludlow, 3:1151–57. New York: Macmillan.

McConkie, Bruce R. 1966. *Mormon Doctrine*. Salt Lake City Utah: Bookcraft.

Millet, Robert L. 1996. "So Glorious a Record." *Liahona* (Feb.):14.

Mormon Choir's Visit Here Not Its First; Sang in 1934. 1992. *Independence Examiner*, July 2, p. 3.

Mormon Church Is Ready: The $25,000 Independence Structure to Be Dedicated. 1914. *Kansas City Times*, Nov. 21, p. 18.

Mormon Church Plans to Build Temple. 1990. *Kansas City Star*, Dec. 29, p. C2.

Mormon Visitor's Center. 1971. LDS pamphlet. LDS Library/Archives, Church Office Building, Salt Lake City.

Mormons Rebuying Land: Have Added Twenty-five Acres to Their Holdings in Independence. 1904. *Kansas City Star*, Apr. 17, p. 4.

My Kingdom Shall Roll Forth: Readings in Church History. 1979. Salt Lake City: Church of Jesus Christ of Latter-day Saints.

Nebeker, Richard. 1990. Personal communication, December 19.

New Jerusalem. 1999. The New-Jerusalem site for Latter-day Saints and their friends, at http://www.new-jerusalem.com/.

New Testament Student Study Guide. 1999. Church Educational System. Salt Lake City: Church of Jesus Christ of Latter-day Saints.

Nibley, Hugh. 1977. A Strange Thing in the Land: The Return of the Book of Enoch, Part 12. *Ensign* 7(12):78–83.

Nichols Co. Land Sale to Mormons Complete. 1990. *Kansas City Times*, Feb. 21, pp. B1, B3.

O'Dea, Thomas F. 1957. *The Mormons*. Chicago: Univ. of Chicago Press.

Packer, Boyd K. 1992. To Be Learned Is Good If . . . *Ensign* 22(11):71–73.

Pearl of Great Price: A Selection from the Revelations, Translations, and Narrations of Joseph Smith, First Prophet, Seer, and Revelator to the Church of Jesus Christ of Latter-day Saints. 1981 [1851]. Salt Lake City: Church of Jesus Christ of Latter-day Saints.

Peterson, Mark E. 1975. *The Great Prologue*. Salt Lake City: Deseret Book Co.

Porter, Kenneth W., and Hermann O. Ruf. 1960. *Chosen Missouri and the Question of Zion*. Salt Lake City: Deseret News Press.

Postcard from Old Kansas City. 1990. *Kansas City Star*, Mar. 30, p. C11.

Pratt, Orson. 1851. *A Series of Pamphlets by Orson Pratt*. Liverpool: Printed by B. James.

President Kimball Dedicates Orson Hyde Memorial Garden in Jerusalem. 1979. *Ensign* 9(12):67–68.

Pusey, Merle J. 1981. *Builders of the Kingdom*. Provo, Utah: Brigham Young Univ. Press.

Reimann, Paul E. 1961. *The Reorganized Church and the Civil Courts*. Salt Lake City: Utah Printing Co.

———. 1981. A Generous Gift from the First Presidency in 1950 for Education at Independence, Mo., LDS Library/Archives, Church Office Building, Salt Lake City.

Review of *Deep Impact*. 1998. At http://www.cinema1.com/movies98/deepimpact/us2.html Website formerly available at this address. Hardcopy of original page in the author's possession.

Rich, Russell R. 1972. *Ensign to the Nations: A History of the Church from 1846 to the Present*. Provo, Utah: Brigham Young Univ. Publications.

Richards, LeGrand. 1967. General Conference Talk. Official Report of the 137th Annual General Conference of the Church of Jesus Christ of Latter-day Saints, 20–25. Salt Lake City: Church of Jesus Christ of Latter-day Saints.

Rival Prophets Friends: Saints and Mormons Mingled at Church Dedication. 1914. *Kansas City Times*, Nov. 23, p. 5.

Roberts, B. H. 1957. *A Comprehensive History of the Church of Jesus Christ of Latter-day Saints*. 6 vols. Provo, Utah: Brigham Young Univ. Press.

———, ed. 1978 [1951]. *History of the Church of Jesus Christ of Latter-day Saints: Period I, History of Joseph Smith the Prophet by Himself*. 7 vols. Salt Lake City: Deseret Book Co.

Robertson, Richard. 1988. Toronto: A Growing Light in the East. *Ensign* 18(9): 46–49.

Romig, Ronald E. 1990. Interview, Dec. 19, Independence, Mo.

———. 1991. Interview, Oct. 3, Independence, Mo.

———. 1992. Interview, Aug. 21, Independence, Mo.

Romney, Marion G. 1966. *October Conference Report.* Salt Lake City: Church of Jesus Christ of Latter-day Saints.

Rosenberg, Martin. 1992. "New Noise Plagues Wolf Creek." *Kansas City Star,* Mar. 18, pp. B1, B8.

Rudd, Glenn L. 1995. *Pure Religion: The Story of Church Welfare since 1930.* Salt Lake City: Church of Jesus Christ of Latter-day Saints.

Ruf, Hermann O. 1964. *Three Days in the Holy City Zion.* Springfield, Mo.: Hermann O. Ruf.

Satterfield, Bruce. 2001a. Adam-ondi-Ahman. Dept. of Religious Education,

Ricks College, at http://www.ricks.edu/Ricks/employee/SATTERFIELDB/quotes Website formerly available at this address. Hardcopy of original page in the author's possession.

———. 2001b. The Scattering and Gathering of Israel. Dept. of Religious Education, Ricks College, at http://www.ricks.edu/Ricks/employee/SATTERFIELDB/ quotes Website formerly available at this address. Hardcopy of original page in the author's possession.

Scharnhorst, A. 1992. Two Arrested in Protest at Whiteman Missile Silo. *Kansas City Star,* Apr. 18, p. C3.

Selections from the Book of Moses. 1981 [1830]. *The Pearl of Great Price.* Salt Lake City: Church of Jesus Christ of Latter-day Saints.

Shipps, Jan. 1985. *Mormonism: The Story of a New Religious Tradition.* Urbana: Univ. of Illinois Press.

Shulemna Gathering. 1998. At http://eagle-net.org/shulemna/gathering.htm Website formerly available at this address. Hardcopy of original page in the author's possession.

Smith, George A. 1950. *The Journals of George Albert Smith.* 22 vols. Microfilm no. MS8407, LDS Archives, Church Office Building, Salt Lake City.

Smith, Hyrum M., and Janne M. Sjodahl. 1967. *Doctrine and Covenants Commentary.* Salt Lake City: Deseret Book Co.

Smith, Joseph Fielding. 1955. *Doctrines of Salvation.* Vol. 2. Salt Lake City: Bookcraft.

———. 1956. *Doctrines of Salvation.* Vol. 3. Salt Lake City: Bookcraft.

———. 1979 [1957–66]. *Answers to Gospel Questions.* 5 vols. Salt Lake City: Deseret Book Co.

Sorenson, John L. 1985. *An Ancient American Setting for the Book of Mormon.* Provo, Utah: Deseret Book Co. and Foundation for Ancient Research and Mormon Studies.

Stegner, Wallace. 1978. Rocky Mountain Country: New Jerusalem. *Atlantic* 241(4):74–84.

———. 1981 [1942]. *Mormon Country*. Lincoln: Univ. of Nebraska Press.

Strengthening Families: Preparing Children for the Real World. 1990. Flyer for meeting held at the LDS Independence Stake Center, Apr. 29. In possession of the author.

Swiatek, Jeff. 1993. Mormons Till Rich Investment in Indiana. *Indianapolis Star*, Jan. 17, pp. 1, 12.

Talmage, James E. 1925. *A Study of the Articles of Faith*. Salt Lake City: Church of Jesus Christ of Latter-day Saints.

Temple to Bring "Brighter Day" to Florida. 1992. *LDS Church News*, June 27, pp. 3, 7.

Temples of the Church of Jesus Christ of Latter-day Saints. 2003. At http://www.ldschurchtemples.com/

Temples of the Lord. 1993. *Friend* (Jan.):27.

Todd, Jay M. 1968. Four Sustained in New Callings. *Improvement Era* 71(5):8–11.

Top, Brent L. 1989. Legacy of the Mormon Pavilion. *Ensign* 19(10):22–28.

Truman O. Angell and the Salt Lake Temple. 1978. Pamphlet. Salt Lake City: Church of Jesus Christ of Latter-day Saints.

U.S. Army Engineer Division, Missouri River. 1991. *Water Resources Development by the U.S. Army Corps of Engineers in Missouri*. Omaha, Neb.: U.S. Army Corps of Engineers.

U.S. Dept. of Health, Education, and Welfare. 1963. *Water Resources Study, Grand River Basin, Iowa and Missouri*. National Technical Information Service microfilm PB-216 557, Spahr Engineering Library, Univ. of Kansas, Lawrence.

U.S. House. 1965. *Grand River and Tributaries, Missouri and Iowa*. 89th Cong. 1st sess., July 13.

Van Orden, Dell. 1971. Independence Center Dedicated. *LDS Church News*, June 5, pp. 3, 5.

Vogel, Dan. 1988. *Religious Seekers and the Advent of Mormonism*. Salt Lake City: Signature Books.

Whalen, William J. 1964. *The Latter-day Saints in the Modern Day World: An Account of Contemporary Mormonism*. Notre Dame, Ind.: Univ. of Notre Dame Press.

What Preparations Are Really Being Made in Jackson County: Zion? 2000–2001. LDLAMPOON: Latter-day Saints Laughing Together, at http://www.latterdaylampoon.com/foyer/jackson/

Wilson, Keith. 1992. Finally, Choir Will Visit Our City. *Independence Examiner*, July 13, p. 4.

Wolfender, Mike. 1992. Telephone conversation, May 14.

Wolfson, Hannah. 2002. The Temple: A Second Coming in Missouri? *Salt Lake Tribune*, Jan. 26.

Woodward, Donald. 1998. *Use of Underground Facilities to Protect Critical Infrastructures: Summary of a Workshop*. Commission on Engineering and Technical Systems. Ebook of the National Academy Press, at http://books.nap.edu/ books/ 0309062888/html/33.html

Young, S. Dilworth. 1970. *The Beehive House*. Pamphlet. Salt Lake City: Church of Jesus Christ of Latter Day Saints.

The Reorganized Movement

Anderson, Mary Audentia Smith, ed. 1952. *Joseph Smith III and the Restoration*. Independence, Mo.: Herald Publishing House.

Another Criticism. 1914. Editorial. *Saints' Herald* 61(20):465–66.

Architect's Study of Completed Building. 1933. Postcard of RLDS Auditorium. Special Collections, Kansas City Public Library, Kansas City, Mo.

The Auditorium. 1926. *Saints' Herald* 73(39):915.

The Auditorium Building. 1926. *Saints' Herald* 73(39):923–28.

Baer, Reed. 1998. Bring Many Names, Sermon. United Church of Christ, West Barnstable, Mass., Nov. 8. Online at http://www.westparish.org/sermons/ SR981108.html

Beautiful Enoch Hill Church. 1951. *Saints' Herald* 98(22):514–15.

Belrose, Danny. 2001. Prayer for a New Name. *Saints' Herald* 148(3):21.

Book of Doctrine and Covenants: Carefully Selected from the Revelations of God, and Given in Order of Their Dates. 1989. Independence, Mo.: Board of Publication of the Reorganized Church of Jesus Christ of Latter Day Saints, Herald Publishing House. Divided into sections and verses.

Briggs, Jason W. 1854a. *A Word of Consolation to the Scattered Saints*. Pamphlet. RLDS Church Archives, Independence Temple, Independence, Mo.

———. 1854b. The Voice of the Captives Assembled at Zarahemla. Pamphlet. RLDS Church Archives, Independence Temple, Independence, Mo.

Brock, Carolyn. 1990. Expressions of Community Worship. *Saints' Herald* 137(9):5–10.

Brown, Daisy Bowen. 2001. How the Land Was Obtained to Build the Stone Church. *Vision*, no. 36:31.

Brown, Richard A. 1990a. Keys of Temple Endowment. *Saints' Herald* 137(4):7–10.

———. 1990b. Laying the Foundations. *Saints' Herald* 137(11):13–16.

———. 1991. *Temple Foundations: Essays on an Emerging Concept*. Independence, Mo.: Herald Publishing House.

Carmichael, Albert. 1925. The Order of Enoch. *Saints' Herald* 72(45):1200–1203.

Church Contracts for Plan in Little Blue Valley. 1989. *Saints' Herald* 136(11):29–30.

Cramer, Eric. 1999. Herald House Leaving Noland Location. *Independence Examiner*, Feb. 10.

Curtright, Amanda. 2001. Community of Christ: RLDS Prepares for New Name. *Independence Examiner*, Mar. 24.

Daily Prayer for Peace. 2003. Web page for the Community of Christ, at http://cofchrist.org/prayerpeace/

Davis, Inez Smith. 1989 [1934]. *The Story of the Church: A History of the Church of Jesus Christ of Latter Day Saints, and of Its Legal Successor, the Reorganized Church of Jesus Christ of Latter Day Saints* (13th ed.). Independence, Mo.: Herald Publishing House.

Early Minutes of the Reorganization, June 1852–June 1860. 1959. RLDS Church Archives, Independence Temple, Independence, Mo. Typewritten copy.

Eastern Jackson County Officials Express Shock. 1995. *Independence Examiner*, Mar. 28, pp. 1, 12.

Edwards, F. Henry. 1951 [1936]. *Fundamentals: Enduring Convictions of the Restoration*. Independence, Mo.: Herald Publishing House.

Faith and Beliefs. n.d. Pamphlet of the RLDS Church. In possession of the author.

Graceland College. 1997a. Zion and the Sale of San. Mail archives message, May 12, at http://www.graceland.edu/mail-archives/theology-1/0418.html

Website formerly available at this address. Hardcopy of original page in the author's possession.

———. 1997b. Re: Temples. Mail archives message, May 28, at http://www.graceland.edu/mail-archives/theology-1/0639.html, and May 30, at http://www.graceland.edu/mail-archives/theology-1/0698.html Website formerly available at this address. Hardcopy of original page in the author's possession.

Gray, Helen T. 1995. RLDS Head Announces His Successor. *Kansas City Star*, Sept. 20, pp. A1, A9.

Haight, Frank, Jr. 1999. New Complex Dedication Will Be Saturday. *Independence Examiner*, Mar. 29.

Herald House Inventory Reduction Sale. 1990–91. Catalog dated Dec. 26, 1990, through Jan. 31, 1991. Independence, Mo.: Herald Publishing House.

Higdon, William T. 1991. Empowerment for Witness. *Saints' Herald* 138(4):15–17.

History of the Enoch Hill Church. 1956. *Saints' Herald* 103(41):981.

Howard, Richard P. 1970. The Reorganized Church in Illinois, 1852–82: Search for Identity. *Dialogue: A Journal of Mormon Thought* 5(1):62–75.

———. 1987. The Spot for the Temple. *Saints' Herald* 134(6):5–8.

———. 1991. Avoiding the Heresy of "Ahistory." *Saints' Herald* 138(2):9–12.

———. 2001. Boundary Issues and Zion/Community in the Church's Evolving Name. *Saints' Herald* 148(3):11–15.

Howe, Jennifer. 1990. Sacred Ground. *Kansas City Star,* Apr. 5, p. E1.

Hoyt, Ricky. 2000. Bring Many Names. Sermon, Unitarian Universalist Church, La Crescenta, Calif. Online at http://www.revricky.com/sermons/bringmanynames.html

Hunt, Larry E. 1982. *F. M. Smith, Saint as Reformer, 1874–1946.* 2 vols. Independence, Mo.: Herald Publishing House.

Jenkins, Dennis. 1990. Maps from LDS Church Historical Sites Tour packet. LDS Institute of Religion, Haskell Junior Indian College Lawrence, Kans. Packet in possession of author.

Jordan, Terry G. 1982. *Texas Graveyards: A Cultural Legacy.* Austin: Univ. of Texas Press.

———. 1996. *The European Culture Area.* New York: Harper Collins.

Lancaster, Kerry. 2001. Re: What Would It Take? Imagicomm Restoration archives message, Oct. 1, at http://www.imagicomm.com/mailinglists/restoration-1/archives/0319.html Website formerly available at this address. Hardcopy of original page in the author's possession.

Latter Twentieth Century: The Church and Challenge. 1998. RLDS Temple School Curriculum course number HI201. Online at http://www.rlds.org/templeschool/Curriculum/hi201.htm Website formerly available at this address. Hardcopy of original page in the author's possession.

Launius, Roger D. 1988. *Joseph Smith III: Pragmatic Prophet.* Urbana: Univ. of Illinois Press.

———. 1996. The RLDS Church and the Decade of Decision. *Sunstone* 19:45–55.

Local Historians' Reports. 1991. Enoch Hill Congregation, microfiche, RLDS Church Archives, Independence Temple, Independence, Mo.

Luff, Joseph. 1910. The Spiritual Purpose of the Sanitarium. *Saints' Herald* 57 (14):353–56.

McCleary, Frank. 1998. RLDS Women Make Church History. *Independence Examiner,* Mar. 31.

McFarland, Darla. 2001. It's Official: RLDS Name One for the Books. *Independence Examiner,* Apr. 7.

McGuire, Donna. 1991. RLDS Unveils Its Plans for Independence Development. *Kansas City Star,* May 15, pp. C5–C6.

———. 1992. Visitors Get Chance to Admire Temple. *Kansas City Star*, Apr. 4, p. C2.

McIntyre, Dean. 2001. The Faith We Sing Hymn Interpretation "Bring Many Names," No. 2047. Online at http://www.gbod.org/worship/events/faithsing/manynames.html

Mische, Patricia. 1990. Envisioning Peace. *Saints' Herald* 137(4):13–15.

Monsees, Laurie. 1990. Breaking Ground for Peace. *Saints' Herald* 137(6):5–7.

Naylor, Susan. 2000. Community of Christ. RLDS Church press release, at http://RLDS.org/news/nrconfcomofchrist.htm Website formerly available at this address. Hardcopy of original page in the author's possession.

Notes and Comments. 1914. *Saints' Herald* 61(34):804.

A People Who Seek Peace. 1992. RLDS advertisement in the *Independence Examiner*, July 18, p. 8.

Potter, Beverly. 1988. Spire Toward the Sky: Temple Will Realize RLDS Dream. *Kansas City Times*, Sept. 17, p. A1.

Price, Richard. 2001. "Community of Christ" Name Adopted by Revisionists. *Vision*, no. 37:3–5.

Refiner's Fire Ministries. 2001. Online at http://www.help4rlds.com/

Reimann, Paul E. 1961. *The Reorganized Church and the Civil Courts*. Salt Lake City: Utah Printing Co.

Results of County Planning, Jackson County, Missouri. 1933. Kansas City, Mo.: Produced by Holland Engraving.

RLDS. 1967. *The History of the Reorganized Church of Jesus Christ of Latter Day Saints*. 8 vols. Independence, Mo.: Herald House.

———. 1984. *World Conference Program*. Independence, Mo.: RLDS Church.

———. 1990. *World Conference Program*. Independence, Mo.: RLDS Church.

———. 1992. *World Conference Program*. Independence, Mo.: RLDS Church.

———. 1999. Reorganized Church of Jesus Christ of Latter Day Saints Web site, at http://www.rlds.org/

Ruoff, Norman D., ed. 1981. *The Writings of Frederick M. Smith, Vol. III: The Zionic Enterprise*. Independence, Mo.: Herald Publishing House.

Saints from Many Lands Participate in World Conference. 1990. *Saints' Herald* 137(6):25–28.

Sharing Our New Name with Others. 2001. Online at http://cofchrist.org /name /calledbyanewname/sharing.asp

Smith, Elbert A. 1945. *Restoration: A Study in Prophesy*. Independence, Mo.: Herald Publishing House.

Smith, Jan. 1992a. Temple Pleases Many Conferees. *Independence Examiner*, Apr. 7, pp. 1, 11.

———. 1992b. Aquarium Resembles Temple. *Independence Examiner,* Aug. 15, pp. 1, 16.

Smith, Wallace B. 1990. Groundbreaking Remarks. *Saints' Herald* 137(6):7.

———. 1992. Inspired Document. *World Conference Bulletin*, Apr. 6, pp. 318–319.

Spillman, W. B. 1990. Question Time. *Saints' Herald* 137(6):14.

Temple Design Announced. 1988. *Saints' Herald* 135(10). Special Four Page Brochure.

The Temple: Dedicated to the Pursuit of Peace, Reconciliation, and Healing of the Spirit. n.d. Pamphlet. Independence, Mo.: RLDS Church. In possession of the author.

The Temple Endowment Fund: The Forgiving Heart. 1992. Booklet. Independence, Mo.: RLDS Church.

The Temple: Ensign of Peace. 1988. Booklet. Independence, Mo.: Temple Fund, Reorganized Church of Jesus Christ of Latter Day Saints.

The Temple: Ensign of Peace. 1990. Pamphlet. Independence, Mo.: Reorganized Church of Jesus Christ of Latter Day Saints.

The Temple Fund Progress. 1991. *Saints' Herald* 138(4):4.

Temple Project Committee. 1987. Temple Ministries: A Statement of Purpose. *Saints' Herald* 134(4):5–8.

The Temple Rises before Us. 1991. *Saints' Herald* 138(1):18–19.

Temple Sanctuary Construction Well Underway. 1990. *Saints' Herald* 137(11): 25–26.

Temple Stone to Be Granite. 1990. *Saints' Herald* 137(9):30.

Tyree, Alan D. 1990. Story Slanted. *Kansas City Star,* Apr. 12, p. C8.

———. 1991. Temple Art. *Saints' Herald* 138(1):5–6, 10.

Wenske, Paul. 1990a. RLDS Church Shaken by Fundamentalist Dissent. *Kansas City Star,* Mar. 31, pp. A1, A14.

———. 1990b. Iowa Group Waits for Armageddon. *Kansas City Star,* Apr. 9, pp. A1, A6.

Wilcox, Pearl. 1959a. Independence in Retrospect, part VII. *Saints' Herald* 106(42):14–16.

———. 1959b. Independence in Retrospect, part VIII. *Saints' Herald* 106(43): 14–16.

———. 1979. *Independence and Twentieth Century Pioneers: The Years from 1900 to 1928*. Independence, Mo.: Pearl G. Wilcox.

World Conference. 1992. Welcome catalog. Independence, Mo.: Herald Publishing House.

Young, Leonard M. 1990. When the Paradigm Shifts. *Saints' Herald* 137(8): 10–12, 25.

The Temple Lot Churches, Restoration Branches, and Other Factions

Abramson-Page Movement Divides. 1992. *Vision*, no. 10:26.

Abramson-Page Movement's History Outlined by High Priest Assembly. 1991. *Vision*, no. 6:17, 33.

Adherents. 2003. Web page monitoring church membership from varied sources, at http://www.adherents.com

Anderson, C. LeRoy. 1981. *For Christ Will Come Tomorrow: The Saga of the Morrisites*. Logan: Utah State Univ. Press.

Articles of Faith and Practice of the Church of Christ (Fetting/Bronson). n.d. Shields Collection, file B1 F18, RLDS Church Archives, Independence Temple, Independence, Mo.

Association for the Unity of the Restoration Saints. 2003. *Restoration Newsletter*, May, at http://www.hopeofzion.com/unity/ Website formerly available at this address. Hardcopy of original page in the author's possession.

Association News. 1999. Association for the Unity of Restoration Saints, May, at http://www.hopeofzion.com/unity/

———. 2000. Association for the Unity of Restoration Saints, Apr., at http://www.hopeofzion.com/unity/

Billeter, Julius C. 1946. *The Temple of Promise: Jackson County, Missouri*. Independence, Mo.: Press of Zion's Printing and Publishing Co.

Bitton, Davis, ed. 1970. *The Reminiscences and Civil War Letters of Levi Lamoni Wight: Life in a Mormon Splinter Colony on the Texas Frontier*. Salt Lake City: Univ. of Utah Press.

Blakeman, Karen, and Beverly Potter. 1990. Ex-Church Member Dances as Vintage Sanctuary Burns. *Kansas City Times*, Jan. 2, pp. A1, A7.

Board of Publication, The Church of Christ with the Elijah Message. 1989a. *One Hundred Fourth Message*. Independence, Mo.: Church of Jesus Christ with the Elijah Message.

———. 1989b. *One Hundred Fifth Message*. Independence, Mo.: Church of Jesus Christ with the Elijah Message.

———. 1989c. *One Hundred Sixth Message*. Independence, Mo.: Church of Jesus Christ with the Elijah Message.

———. 1991. *One Hundred Eleventh Message*. Independence, Mo.: Church of Jesus Christ with the Elijah Message.

Bowerman, David. W. 2003a. E-mail, Nov. 5, Independence, Mo.

———. 2003b. E-mail, Nov. 6, Independence, Mo.

Brantner, C. Andrew. 1999. The Generation of the Gathering. *Zion's Advocate* 76(8):125–32.

Brickhouse, Smith N. 1998. To the Members of the Church. *Zion's Advocate* 75(7):131.

Brockmeyer, Karen. 1977. Hebrew Mormons "Here to Stay." *Independence Examiner*, Oct. 15, p. 6B.

Bronson, S. T. n.d. *The History and Origin of the Church of Christ (Fetting/Bronson)*. Pamphlet. Shields Collection, file B1 F18, RLDS Archives, Independence Temple, Independence, Mo.

Buzbee, John, and Joe Stephens. 1990. Amid Emotions of Rift, Members Were "Easy Prey." *Kansas City Times*, Jan. 11, pp. A1, A19.

Campbell, Chonda. 1999. Group Attacked in Church. *Independence Examiner*, Apr. 3.

Carroll, Diane. 1991. Church Arsonist Convicted. *Kansas City Star*, Jan. 17, p. C2.

Center Branch Ministers to Needy. 1992. *Vision*, no. 10:19, 26.

Church Dispute Leads to Suit. 1965. *Independence Examiner*, June 8, pp. 1–2.

Church of Christ, Restored. 2002. History of the Church (A Brief Summary). Online at http://www.hopeofzion.com/ccr/history.html

———. 2002. Revelation through Patriarch Theron Campbell. Online at http://www.hopeofzion.com/ccr/campbell.html

Church of Christ, Restored, Is Not Part of Restoration Branches Movement. 1990. *Vision*, no. 4:20, 22.

Church of Jesus Christ. 2003. Official Web site at http://www.the-church.org/

Congregations. 2003. Remnant Church of Jesus Christ of Latter Day Saints, at http://theremnantchurch.com/congregation/congregations.htm

Corbin, Dean. 1974. Revelation Given through Dean Corbin at Schell City, Mo., Oct. 6. Shields Collection, file B1 F19, RLDS Archives, Independence Temple, Independence, Mo.

———. 1975. Revelation Given by Dean Corbin at Schell City, Mo., Jan. 5. Shields Collection, file B1 F19, RLDS Archives, Independence Temple, Independence, Mo.

Dewey, Richard Lloyd. 1986. *Porter Rockwell: A Biography*. New York: Paramount Books.

Did You Know? n.d. Pamphlet. Independence, Mo.: Board of Publications, Church of Christ (Temple Lot).

Directory of Restoration Branches. 1991. *Vision*, no. 7:28–31.

Directory of Restoration Branches. 1992. *Vision*, no. 8:47 and no. 10:31.

A Divine Message Leads to a Suit. 1965. *Kansas City Star*, June 8.

Dollins, Bill J. 1993. *Ephraim's Camp Record*. Independence, Mo.: Bill J. Dollins.

Draves, William A. 1971. A Vision. *Voice of Peace* 27(4):56.

———. 1993. Message 115. At http://www.elijah-message.org/message .20115.html

———. 1994. Message 118. At http://www.elijah-message.org/message.20118.html

East Local News. 1997. *Zion's Advocate* 74(1):9–11.

Evans, Brad. 2001a. E-mail, Sept. 18, Boulder, Co.

———. 2001b. E-mail, Sept. 19, Boulder, Co.

———. 2001c. E-mail, Sept. 20, Boulder, Co.

Ex-Cult Member Felt No Remorse for Months. 1990. *Kansas City Star*, Dec. 18, p. B2.

Faust, James E. 2001. Who Shall Ascend into the Hill of the Lord. *Ensign* 31(8):2–5.

Fitzpatrick, Doyle C. 1970. *The King Strang Story: A Vindication of James J. Strang, Beaver Island Mormon King*. Lansing, Mich.: National Heritage.

Fletcher, Rupert J. 1965. *About Zion*. Pamphlet. Independence, Mo.: Rupert Fletcher. Shields Collection, file B5 F10, RLDS Archives, Independence Temple, Independence, Mo.

Flint, B. C. 1953. *An Outline History of the Church of Christ (Temple Lot)*. 2d ed. Independence, Mo.: Board of Publications, Church of Christ (Temple Lot).

Fundamentalists Want RLDS to Return to Its Roots. 1990. *Olathe Daily News*, July 7, p. 9A.

Gathering. 1999. Topic on Centerplace Web site for Restoration Branches, at http://www.centerplace.org/discus/messages/ Website formerly available at this address. Hardcopy of original page in the author's possession.

Gayman, Dan. 1989. Letter to Mr. John Dawson of Newcastle upon Tyne, England. Shields Collection, file B6 F1, RLDS Archives, Independence Temple, Independence, Mo.

Gibson, Diana. 1999. The Center Branch Building Serves Many Purposes. *Vision*, no. 31:8.

Gordon, Jim. 1999. Harry S. Truman Remembered. *Zion's Advocate* 76(2):15.

Graceland College. 1998. Re:[theology-1]–Re: Zion. Mail archives message, Apr. 18, at http://www.graceland.edu/mail-archives/theology-1/3908.html

Gregory, Thomas J. 1981. Sidney Rigdon: Post Nauvoo. *Brigham Young University Studies* 21(1):51–67.

Hajicek, James D. 2000. The True Faith. At http://www.vorsoft.com/faith/index.html

Harlacher, Larry. 2000. Missouri Mormon Walking Tour Dedicated. *Vision*, no. 35:9–11.

Harlacher, Nancy. 1989. The Zion Temple [Painting]. *Vision* 1 (summer): cover.

The Hierarchy's New Age Temple Draws Interest. 1990. *Vision*, no. 5:43.

Hierarchy to Sell Water Rights to Atherton Lands. 1995. *Vision*, no. 19:7.

Hite, Robert. 2000. Church Members Worry Temple Lot Will Be Trampled. *Independence Examiner*, June 20.

Jenista, Dwain A. 1977. The Church of Christ at Halley's Bluff. Paper for Dr. Timothy Miller, Religious Studies 602, Univ. of Kansas. Shields Collection, file B6 F1, RLDS Archives, Independence Temple, Independence, Mo.

Jensen, Robert H. 1992. Prayer of Dedication. *Zion's Advocate* 69(5):60–61.

Jordan, T. J. 1992 [1950]. The Gathering. *Zion's Advocate* 69(7):94–97.

Kansas City Public Library. 2002. Postcard Web page, at http://www.kclibrary.org/sc/post/nearbycities/nearbycities2.htm

Kirksey, Nathan, and Richard Price. 1989. RLDS Leaders Reject God's Temple Design. *Vision*, no. 1:5–7, 10.

Kluth, Nancy. 1992. Interview, Aug. 21, Independence, Mo.

Lancaster, Kerry. 2001. Re: What Would It Take? Imagicomm Restoration archives message, Oct. 1., at http://www.imagicomm.com/mailinglists/restoration-1/archives/0319.html Website formerly available at this address. Hardcopy of original page in the author's possession.

Larson, Frederick N. 2003. Section R-146. Webpage at http://www.theremnantchurch .com/conference2003/conference/htm

Lawson, Richard W. 2001a. E-mail, July 3, Monongahela, Pa.

———. 2001b. E-mail, July 5, Monongahela, Pa.

Long, E. E. 1938. Let the Truth Be Told. *Arimat* 1(1):6–10. Shields Collection, file B1 F9, RLDS Archives, Independence Temple, Independence, Mo.

Madison, R. Ben. 2001. E-mail, Aug. 20, Independence, Mo.

Mason, Shirley. 1992. Gateway Restoration School. *Vision*, no. 11:22.

McGhee, Mike. 2001. Possess the Land! *Zion's Advocate* 78 (10):187–90.

McIndoo, Don. 1992. Great Views of Things to Come. *Zion's Advocate* 69(6): 76–78.

———. 1997. A Message for Our Special Day. *Zion's Advocate* 74(9):158–60.

———. 1998. Marvin Ellis Ely: An Apostle of Jesus Christ. *Zion's Advocate* 75(5): 105–7.

———. 2001. Caught Up in Prophecy. *Zion's Advocate* 78(10):191–95.

Melton, J. Gordon. 1986. *Biographical Dictionary of American Cult and Sect Leaders*. New York: Garland Publishers.

———. 1989. *The Encyclopedia of American Religions*. 3d ed. Detroit: Gale Research.

Miller, Timothy. 1991. *When Prophets Die: The Postcharismatic Fate of New Religious Movements*. Albany: State Univ. of New York Press.

Moser, Donna. 1990. Letter. *Zion's Advocate* 67(3):34.

News Briefs. 1992. *Vision*, no. 8:6.

Original Church of Jesus Christ of Latter Day Saints. 2001. Web page of the Strangite Mormons, at http://www.Strangite.org/Welcome.htm

Pearl, B. H. 1992. *RLDS Church Jurisdiction Maps for United States*. RLDS Archives, Independence Temple, Independence, Mo.

Plan of the Temple at Voree. 2001. Online at http://www.Strangite.org/Tour.htm

The Plans of the Temple. 1930. *Zion's Advocate* 7(17):170–71.

Price, David. 1990. What's in a Name? *Vision*, no. 4:9, 12.

Price, Pamela. 1989. RLDS Leaders Trade Historic Nauvoo Cemetery for Parking Lot Space. *Vision*, no. 1:11–13.

———. 1990a. Enoch Hill Reflects the Crisis in the Church. *Vision*, no. 4:24–25.

———. 1990b. Sanitarium May Be Merged. *Vision*, no. 4:22.

———. 1992. President Wallace B. Smith Refused to Address Departing Troops. *Vision*, no. 8:26–28, 44.

Price, Richard. 1986. *Restoration Branches Movement, Pamphlet #1—Forming of Restoration Branches*. Independence, Mo.: Price Publishing Co.

———. 1990a. Comments on the Associated Press Article. *Vision*, no. 4:14.

———. 1990b. Church of the Lamb of God Splits Two More Restoration Branches. *Vision*, no. 4:20.

———. 1990c. Hierarchy Speaks Against "Unauthorized" Congregations. *Vision*, no. 4:28–29.

———. 1991a. Abramson-Page Movement Forms a New Church. *Vision*, no. 6:18.

———. 1991b. Restorationists Will Regain Control of the RLDS Church. *Vision*, no. 7:18.

———. 1991c. Interview, Jan. 22.

———. 1996. Elder's Conference Asked to Approve New Program in May. *Vision*, no. 22:22–24.

———. 1998. Chairman Bowerman Unveils Plan to Form "Remnant Church." *Vision*, no. 27:13–14.

———. 1999. High Priests' Group Organizes Twelfth Restoration Church. *Vision*, no. 32:8–10.

———. 2000a. Remnant Church Claims to Be the Successor of the RLDS Church. *Vision*, no. 34:16–18.

———. 2000b. Remnant Church News. *Vision*, no. 35:18.

———. 2001a. "Community of Christ" Name Adopted by Revisionists. *Vision*, no. 37:3–5.

———. 2001b. Hierarchy Threatens Legal Action about RLDS Name. *Vision*, no. 37:5.

———. 2001c. Church Lands to Be Sold to Finance Community of Christ Leaders. *Vision*, no. 37:5.

Price, Richard, and Pamela Price. 1982. *The Temple of the Lord: The Location and Purposes of the Temple Which Is to Be Built in Independence, Missouri*. Independence, Mo.: Price Publishing Co.

———. 1991. Hierarchy Moves to Sell Sacred Lands. *Vision*, no. 7:16–17.

———. 1994. Ephraim's Camp Publishes Book of False Scripture. *Vision*, no. 16: 19–21.

Quorum Insights. 1992. *Voice of Peace* 48(4):53–54.

Remnant Church of Jesus Christ of Latter Day Saints. 2001a. News Briefs. Webpage at http://www.theremnantchurch.com/newsbriefs/newsbriefsfeb2001.htm

———. 2001b. General Conference Over. News Briefs. Webpage at http://www.theremnantchurch.com/newsbriefs/newsbriefsapr2001.htm

Restoration Church. 2001. Web site of the Restoration Church of Jesus Christ of Latter Day Saints, at http://www.restorationchurch.net/

Restoration Gospel Series Conducted during Conference. 1990. *Vision*, no. 3:23.

RLDS. 1992. Advertisement for RLDS congregations, *Independence Examiner*, July 11, p. 9. (See any Saturday religious section of the *Examiner* for RLDS congregation listings.)

RLDS Leaders Promote Marxist Liberation Theology. 1992. *Vision*, no. 8:4–22.

Roberts, David L. 1977 (postmark). The Voice of Eternal Life, #2. Shields Collection, file B8 F15, RLDS Archives, Independence Temple, Independence, Mo.

Ron's RLDS Message Board. 2001a. Message posted Jan. 4, at http://www.voy.com/10454/99.html

———. 2001b. Message posted June 15, at http://www.voy.com/2124/1/3513.html

Sarratt, Roland. 1990a. It's in the Hands of the Lord. *Zion's Advocate* 67(2):17–18.

———. 1990b. The Lord Can Turn a Trial into a Blessing. *Zion's Advocate* 67(8): 104–5.

———. 1992. A Sense of Direction. *Zion's Advocate* 69(5):62.

Savage, J. W. 1955. Letter, Dec. 14. Shields Collection, file B1 F20, RLDS Archives, Independence Temple, Independence, Mo.

———. 1972 [1957]. There Shall Be a Tabernacle. *The Voice of Peace* 27(8):118–20.

Secret Money Payments to the NCC Revealed by Documents from the Auditorium. 1992. *Vision*, no. 7:19–21.

Seibel, Harvey E. 1992. With the Flame of Devouring Fire. *Zion's Advocate* 69(1):12.

———. 1997. The Place of the New Jerusalem: The City of Zion in the Last Days. *Zion's Advocate* 74(5):71–76.

———. 2001. A Voice of Warning (3999 B.C.–1999 A.D.). *Zion's Advocate* 78(5): 83–87.

Sheldon, William A. 1974. *Zion and the Temple of the Lord.* Booklet. Independence, Mo.: Board of Publications, Church of Christ (Temple Lot).

———. 1990a. Special Day for Fasting and Prayer. *Zion's Advocate*, 67(2):18.

———. 1990b. Temple Lot Church to Break Ground. *Zion's Advocate* 67(8):105.

———. 1990c. Zion's Temple, The House of the Lord, Part Two. *Zion's Advocate* 67(8):107–8.

———. 1990d. Zion's Temple, The House of the Lord, Part Three. *Zion's Advocate* 67(9):124–25.

———. 1990e. Zion's Temple, The House of the Lord, Part Five. *Zion's Advocate* 67(12):170–71.

———. 1990f. Interview, Dec. 14, Independence, Mo.

———. 1992. Our Heritage: Historical Presentation for Temple Lot Building Dedication. *Zion's Advocate* 69(6):78–80.

———. 1997. From Babylon to the New Jerusalem with Its Holy Temple in This Generation. *Zion's Advocate* 74(2):19–26.

———. 1998. The Gathering: A Principle of God, Part IV. *Zion's Advocate* 75(10):195–97.

———. 1999. A Synoptic History of the Church of Christ on the Temple Lot Dedicated by Joseph Smith in Independence, Missouri. *Zion's Advocate* 76(3):33–36.

———. 2000. Babylon's Fall and the Way of Escape. *Zion's Advocate* 77 (11):175–80.

Shields, Steven L. 1987. *The Latter Day Saint Churches: An Annotated Bibliography.* New York: Garland Publishers.

———. 1990. *Divergent Paths of the Restoration: A History of the Latter Day Saint Movement.* Los Angeles: Restoration Research.

———. 1991. The Latter Day Saint Movement: A Study in Survival. In *When Prophets Die: The Postcharismatic Fate of New Religious Movements*, ed. Timothy Miller ed. Albany: State Univ. of New York Press.

Shulemna Gathering. 1998. Online at http://eagle-net.org/shulemna/ gathering .htm Website formerly available at this address. Hardcopy of original page in the author's possession.

Smith, Arthur M. 1973. *Temple Lot Deed.* Independence, Mo.: Board of Publication, Church of Christ (Temple Lot).

Smith, Jared. 2001a. E-mail, July 3, Independence, Mo.

———. 2001b. E-mail, July 16, Independence, Mo.

Smith, Joseph F. 2001a. E-mail, Aug. 18, Independence, Mo.

———. 2001b. E-mail, Aug. 19, Independence, Mo.

Smith, Willard J. 1930. The Pattern of Heavenly Things. *Zion's Advocate* 7(17): 172–74.

Sorgen, James F. 1992. Telephone conversation, May 14, Independence, Mo.

Stack, Peggy Fletcher. 2002. Joseph Smith Descendent at Helm of LDS Remnant Church, *Salt Lake Tribune*, Apr. 20, online at http://www.sltrib.com/2002/apr/04202002/saturday/729857.htm

Statement of Reaffirmation. 1997. *Zion's Advocate* 74(9):167–68.

Stephens, Joe. 1990a. Thirteen Charged in "Cleansing" Deaths. *Kansas City Times*, Jan. 6, pp. A1, A14.

———. 1990b. Cult Aimed to Start a Holocaust. *Kansas City Star*, Jan. 7, pp. 1A, 15A.

Temple Lot Building Proposal. 1990. *Zion's Advocate* 67(3):32.

Temple Lot Local Gives Thanks. 1990. *Zion's Advocate* 67(12):164.

The Temple Lot Property. 1994. *Zion's Advocate* 71(5):83.

Temple, Darl. 2000. Conference Report. *Zion's Advocate* 77(5):72–74.

Ten Messages from God, Delivered by the Angel John the Baptist: "The Elijah Message." 2002. Web page of Jared Smith, at http://www.trios.org/fireinzion/tenmessages/index.html Website formerly available at this address. Hardcopy of original page in the author's possession.

Two Hospitals Eye Possible Joint Venture. 1990. *Independence Examiner*, July 26, p. 11.

Van Noord, Roger. 1988. *King of Beaver Island: The Life and Assassination of James Jesse Strang*. Urbana: Univ. of Illinois Press.

Virgil, Doug. 2001. E-mail, Aug. 20, Independence, Mo.

Vogle, Debbie. 1997. Conference Report. *Zion's Advocate* 74(7):127–30.

Walking Trail Dedication. 2000. Web page of the Missouri Mormon Frontier Foundation, at http://www.sunflower.org/~ronromig/mmwt.htm

Wallace B. Smith Aids the Secret Combination. 1992. *Vision*, no. 8:24–43.

Warner, Sharon. 1996. Look for the Beautiful—In Zion! *Vision*, no. 24:25.

Warren, Christopher C. [1985?]. The Word of the Lord: A Short Exegesis of the Harbinger Revelations of the Church of Christ with the Elijah Message. Unpublished paper in file on the Church of Christ with the Elijah Message, RLDS Archives, Independence Temple, Independence, Mo.

———. 1999. Web site of the New Covenant Church of God (NCCG), at http://www.nccg.org/

Wenske, Paul. 1990a. RLDS Church Shaken by Fundamentalist Dissent. *Kansas City Star*, Mar. 31, pp. A1, A14.

———. 1990b. Iowa Group Waits for Armageddon. *Kansas City Star*, Apr. 9, pp. A1, A6.

Whately, Keith A. 2000. Be Patient—All Will Be Well. *Vision*, no. 35:3–4.

Wheaton, Clarence L. 1928. *That Interesting Spot of Land West of the Court House, What and Where Is It?* LDS Library/Archives, Church Office Building, Salt Lake City.

———. 1972. *Historical Facts Concerning the Temple Lot: That Interesting Spot of Land West of the Court House at Independence, Missouri.* Independence, Mo.: Board of Publications, Church of Christ (Temple Lot).

Wilkinson, Norman L. 1930. Description of Church of Christ Temple at Independence, Mo. *Zion's Advocate* 7(17):167–68.

Willey, Jan. 1990. Shadows Over Zion. Illustration. *Vision,* no. 4:30–32.

Wolfson, Hannah. 2002. The Temple: A Second Coming in Missouri? *Salt Lake Tribune,* Jan. 26.

Wood, Raymond E. [1989/90?]. *Prepare Yourselves for the Great Day of the Lord.* Warrensburg, Mo.: n.p. Leaflet in possession of the author.

Word of the Lord, Brought to Mankind by an Angel. 1988 [1929]. Official publication of the Church of Christ with the Elijah Message Established Anew, Independence, Mo.

Zion's Branch. 1999. Web site for the Church of Jesus Christ Zion's Branch, at http://www.zionsbranch.com/

INDEX

Note: Page numbers in bold refer to figures

41 Jackson Co land owned by LDS
58 " " areas of influence
72 NW Missouri counties